Learn to Read in Japanese

A Japanese Reader
Volume II

A Catalogue of 1,208 Target Kanji

An Index to 2,800 Kanji Pronunciations

1,660 Japanese Sentences

2,900 Vocabulary Words and Phrases

and more than 2,000 Mnemonics
to Assist in Learning Vocabulary

by

Roger Lake and Noriko Ura

Learn to Read in Japanese

A Japanese Reader

Volume II

Contents

Introduction

This book is designed for students who are at least somewhat familiar with the 608 kanji that were introduced in *Learn to Read in Japanese, Volume I.* Both books are based on the idea that the most enjoyable and efficient way to learn to read in Japanese is dive in and start reading almost immediately, learning new kanji as you go.

In order to make this approach workable, we introduce new kanji at the beginning of each chapter and then ask you to take a quick pre-test on their pronunciations before you start to read. The practice reading material in each lesson includes **only kanji characters that you know** or are in the process of learning, and we provide **immediate feedback** about your reading accuracy in the form of same-page romaji equivalents and translations.

Like the first book, this volume includes **at least three practice sentences for each new kanji**, totaling about 1660 sentences. We would like to thank the people associated with the Tatoeba.org website, the *Japanese* dictionary app by renzo Inc., the *Japanese for Everyone* textbook, and a number of other Japanese textbooks and websites for making many of these sentences available.

You will discover **a few changes to the format** of this book, compared to Volume I. **First**, we *reduce* the number of kanji that we introduce in each chapter from ten to eight. **Second**, we *group* the new kanji in the Kanji Catalogue by chapter, so that it is easy to study them in groups of eight before starting a new lesson.

Third, in addition to providing *sentence* reading practice, we include more than 2,900 Japanese words and phrases for *vocabulary* reading practice. This vocabulary comes from three sources: the **EXAMPLES** in the Kanji Catalogue, the practice sentences in each chapter, and the optional supplemental reading material available online.

We introduce **600 new kanji** in this book. In addition, the Kanji Catalogue near the back of the book includes all of the kanji that were introduced in the first book, for a **total of 1208**. The inclusion of kanji from the previous book adds considerable bulk to this volume, but we think that students will want to have ready access to information about all of the kanji that they may encounter as they read.

In addition to the vocabulary and the sentences provided in the book, we have identified some **supplemental** Japanese reading material for students to explore as they use these lessons. This material can be found in two online resources: *Satori Reader* and *Read in Slow Japanese.* Please see pages 2-8 and 48-194 for more information.

This supplemental reading material meets the following **criteria**: it includes *romaji or kana equivalents of the kanji*, it includes English *translations*, and it does *not contain furigana*, since furigana can interfere with the acquisition of reading fluency.

In order to ensure that these resources contain only kanji that you know or are learning, **we introduce kanji in this book in the same order that they are introduced in the resources**. As a result, when you have completed Chapter 2 of this book, you will be able to read the first article in *Satori Reader*. When you have completed Chapter 3, you will be able to read the second article, and so on. Likewise, when you have finished Chapter 48 of this book, you will be able to read the first article in *Read in Slow Japanese*. When you have finished Chapter 50, you will be able to read the second article, and so forth.

Understandably, the authors of these resources charge nominal fees for access to their original work. If you are unable to afford those fees, you may consider this supplemental reading practice material *optional*.

However, we hope that you will be able to subscribe to these two resources, at least briefly. You will almost certainly experience a thrill when you find that you are able to read the compelling Japanese text that they provide. You will probably want to save that text and re-read it several times. In addition, during the time that you subscribe, you will have a chance to listen to the audio versions of the articles, and you will be able to read the excellent explanatory material that accompanies them.

How to Use this Book

Both Volume I and Volume II of this book are based on "**Active Recall**" which can be defined as "learning by answering questions" or "flashcard learning." This is the same method that we employ in our free audio lessons, available for download at JapaneseAudioLessons.com.

In the audio lessons, the "questions" are presented in the form of *English* phrases or sentences which students are asked to translate into *Japanese*. In this book, and in the previous volume, the "questions" appear as *Japanese* phrases or sentences which students are asked to read and translate into *English*.

New kanji characters are listed in a "New Kanji" table at the beginning of each of the following chapters, in the order in which they first appear. Using the reference numbers printed *before* the kanji, you can find information about these characters in the Kanji Catalogue near the back of the book. The numbers printed in parentheses *after* each kanji indicate the number of different pronunciations that are associated with that character.

This book is designed to teach new kanji in **five steps**:

Step One. Kanji Catalogue. Before you start a chapter, turn to the Kanji Catalogue and take some time to review the eight new kanji that are listed in the New Kanji table at the beginning of the chapter. Your aim should be to acquire the ability to recognize each kanji and associate it with its pronunciations.

Step Two. Pronunciation Pre-Test. Next turn to the chapter that you are about to start reading and take the "Pronunciation Pre-Test." To do this, look at the New Kanji table and try to voice each of the pronunciations for all eight of the kanji in the table. Use the table at the bottom of the page to check your accuracy. Repeat this test several times until you feel ready to start reading.

Step Three. Vocabulary List with Mnemonics. Next start reading the Vocabulary List, being careful to cover the "answers" on the right side of the page with a piece of paper or your thumb. You will usually have a chance to practice reading each new kanji multiple times in different words. You will also see more than 2,000 **mnemonics** for the words that appear in the Vocabulary Lists.

Don't worry too much about perfection while reading the vocabulary. It's OK to look at the text on the right whenever necessary.

Step Four. Practice Sentences. Next read the Practice Sentences that are provided in each chapter. Again, be sure to cover the text on the right side of the page as you read, but don't hesitate to uncover it if you aren't sure about kanji pronunciations or when you don't know how to translate the Japanese text.

Step Five. Supplemental Reading. We hope that you will take this last step, but it is optional. As mentioned in the Introduction, we have identified some fascinating Japanese language articles online that use *only* the kanji that you have learned up to this point. These articles are available from *Satori Reader* and from *News in Slow Japanese*. Please read the information on pages 2-8 and 48-194 to learn how to obtain them at a reasonable cost.

We sincerely hope that this book will help you to master the basics of reading in Japanese.

Roger Lake

San Jose, California

July 1, 2018

Chapter 1

New Kanji in this Chapter

# 609 至 (2)	# 610 極 (3)	# 611 然 (2)	# 612 到 (1)
# 613 丈 (2)	# 614 夫 (4)	# 615 可 (1)	# 616 能 (1)

Vocabulary List with Mnemonics

from the Kanji Catalogue

至る — itaru = to lead to, to reach, to result in; *this road leads to some Italian ruins*

至急 — shikyuu = immediately, urgently; *the sheep were cute, but I had to go to the bathroom urgently*

至難の — shinan no = extremely difficult; *the sheets that the nanny had torn were extremely difficult to repair*

南極 — nankyoku = the Antarctic or South Pole; *my nanny drank Kyoto Kool-Aid when she went to the Antarctic*

極力 — kyokuryoku = as much as possible, to the best of one's ability; *after drinking Kyoto Kool-Aid, Pope Leo bakes cookies to the best of his ability*

至極 — shigoku = extremely; *the sheep and the goats like Kool-Aid, but it makes them extremely fat*

極める — kiwameru = to attain or master; *the key to war is to have a merciless ruler who can master his soldiers*

極めて — kiwamete = extremely; from kiwameru = to master

全然 — zenzen = not at all in negative sentences, completely in positive sentences; *to sit in one Zen session followed by another Zen session is not at all what I want to do*

自然 — shizen = nature; *both Shinto and Zen favor the preservation of Nature*

当然 — touzen = justly, natural; *if you only dip a toe into Zen, you will justly not achieve enlightenment*

天然 — ten'nen = natural; *ten nen [years] ago, this was all a natural forest*

到着する — touchaku suru = to arrive; *Tony Blair drank champagne and Kool-Aid while he waited for the queen to arrive*

Kanji Pronunciations

# 609 – ita, shi	# 610 – kyoku, goku, kiwa	# 611 – zen, nen	# 612 – tou
# 613 – jou, take	# 614 – otto, fuu, fu, bu	# 615 – ka	# 616 – nou

到来する	tourai suru = to arrive; *I will eat <u>toast</u> and <u>rice</u> after I <u>arrive</u>*
丈夫な	joubu na = healthy, hearty, strong; *<u>Joan</u> of Arc was a <u>boon</u> to the French cause, since she was <u>healthy</u>, <u>hearty</u>, and <u>strong</u>*
大丈夫	daijoubu = all right; *the <u>diet</u> that <u>Job</u> recommended was <u>all right</u>*
丈	take = size, height; *this guy drinks a <u>tall keg</u> every day, which might explain his <u>size</u>*
夫	otto = husband; *<u>Otto</u> Preminger was a good <u>husband</u>*
工夫	kufuu = ingenuity; *it was a <u>cooler</u> full of <u>food</u>, packed with considerable <u>ingenuity</u>*
水夫	suifu = sailor; *<u>sailors</u> like <u>sweet food</u>*
可愛い	kawaii = cute; *some of the <u>cars</u> in <u>Hawaii</u> are <u>cute</u>;* (the "w" is inserted as a bridge to make the pronunciation smoother, compared to saying "ka aii")
可能な	kanou na = possible; *it's <u>possible</u> to cook it with <u>Canola</u> oil*
不可能な	fukanou na = impossible; from fu = negation + kanou = possible
能力	nouryoku = ability, competence, skill; *in <u>Norway</u>, Pope <u>Leo</u> made Kool-Aid, demonstrating his <u>ability</u>, <u>competence</u> and <u>skill</u>*
有能な	yuunou na = able, competent; *<u>you know</u> I'm <u>competent</u>*
性能	seinou = performance, efficiency; *<u>sane old</u> people demonstrate good <u>performance</u> and <u>efficiency</u> on our tests*
能	nou = Noh, old-style Japanese theater

from the Practice Sentences

服用する	fukuyou suru = to take medicine; *eating <u>Fukuoka yogurt</u> is like <u>taking medicine</u>*
可能性	kanousei = a possibility; *it's a <u>possibility</u> to cook with <u>Canola</u> and <u>save</u> money*
からかう	karakau = to ridicule or jeer; *in <u>Caracas</u> the <u>cows</u> are <u>ridiculed</u>*
北極星	hokkyokusei = North Star; *at the <u>hotel</u>, we drank <u>Kyoto Kool</u>-Aid, and then we set <u>sail</u> using the <u>North Star</u> as a reference*
時間内	jikan'nai = on time; from jikan = time + nai = inside or within

Practice Sentences

1. 一日でもこの薬を服用しなければ死に至る。

Ichinichi demo kono kusuri wo fukuyou shinakereba shi ni itaru.
Even one day, if he doesn't take this medicine, it will lead to death.

2. これは極めて珍しい。

Kore wa kiwamete mezurashii.
As for this, it's extremely rare.

3. 彼女が怒るのも当然だ。

Kanojo ga okoru no mo touzen da.
For her to get mad even is natural.

4. 到着は何時ですか。

Touchaku wa nanji desu ka.
What time is the arrival?

5. 彼はとても丈夫だ。

Kare wa totemo joubu da.
He is very strong.

6. 可能性あるかな？

Kanousei aru kana?
Is there a possibility, I wonder?

7. 至極当然のことだ。

Shigoku touzen no koto da.
It's an extremely natural thing.

8. 彼は最後に到着した。

Kare wa saigo ni touchaku shita.
He arrived last.

9. 彼女は夫をからかった。

Kanojo wa otto wo karakatta.
She ridiculed her husband.

10. 見て、あれは北極星だよ。

Mite, are wa hokkyokusei da yo.
Look, that is the North Star, for sure.

11. あなたは有能な方ですね。

Anata wa yuunou na kata desu ne.
You are a competent person, huh.

12. これ、可愛いな。

Kore, kawaii na.
This is cute.

13. 至急お願いします。

Shikyuu onegai shimasu.
Immediately, I beg you.

14. 全然大丈夫だよ。

Zenzen daijoubu da yo.
Everything is OK, for sure.

15. 彼は時間内に到着した。

Kare wa jikan nai ni touchaku shita.
He arrived in time.

16. それはほとんど不可能だ。

Sore wa hotondo fukanou da.
As for that, it's almost impossible.

17. すごく顔色が悪いよ！大丈夫？

Sugoku kao iro ga warui yo! Daijoubu?
Terribly the face color is bad, for sure.
Are you OK?

18. 全然痛くないよ。

Zenzen itakunai yo.
It doesn't hurt at all, for sure.

19. 天然ガスは空気より軽い。

Tennen gasu wa kuuki yori karui.
As for natural gas, compared to air, it's light.

Chapter 2

New Kanji in this Chapter

# 617 才 (1)	# 618 解 (3)	# 619 確 (2)	# 620 卓 (2)
# 621 超 (1)	# 622 頑 (1)	# 623 迷 (3)	# 624 惑 (2)

Vocabulary List with Mnemonics

from the Kanji Catalogue

九十才 — kyuujussai = 90 years old; from kyuujuu = 90 + sai = age; *he lived to an advanced age due to science*

才能 — sainou = talent; *he has a talent for sighing through his nose*

天才 — tensai = genius; *ten scientists said that he is a genius*

理解 — rikai = understanding; *reading the Kaiser's writings, I achieved understanding*

解ける — tokeru = to be solved or untied, intransitive; *the toys that Kennedy kept in his room were tied up in bundles, and they got untied;* cf. 溶ける tokeru = to melt away or dissolve, # 815

解く — toku = to untie, unfasten, solve; *he solved the problem by adding tomato juice to the Kool-Aid*

解決 — kaiketsu = solution, settlement, resolution; *the Kaiser poured ketchup into his soup as he pondered a settlement, solution or resolution of his problem*

読解 — dokkai = reading comprehension; *the dopes who work for the Kaiser have poor reading comprehension*

正確 — seikaku = precise, accurate, exact; *when sane people kaku [write], their writing is accurate and exact*

確かに — tashika ni = for sure, certainly; *if you take a takushii (taxi) and bring a camera to my niece, she will certainly be able to take some photos*

確かめる — tashikameru = to ascertain or confirm; *if you take a takushii (taxi) and bring a camera, you can take photos of the rooster & ascertain its qualities*

食卓 — shokutaku = dining table; *I showed her the Kool-Aid which I made by combining tap water and Kool-Aid powder at the dining table*

卓球 — takkyuu = pingpong; *some tacky youths are playing pingpong*

Kanji Pronunciations

# 617 – sai	# 618 – kai, to, ge	# 619 – tashi, kaku	# 620 – taku, ta
# 621 – chou	# 622 – gan	# 623 – mai, mei, mayo	# 624 – mado, waku

頑張る — ganbaru = to persevere, to do one's best; *when Gandalf is at a bar with his roommates, he does his best to control his drinking*

超人的な — choujinteki na = superhuman; from chou = super; *Margaret Cho did a super job during her performance*; + jin = person + teki = related to

頑丈 — ganjou = sturdy, strong; *Gandalf and Joan of Arc are sturdy and strong*

迷子 — maigo = lost person; *I might go look for that lost person*

迷信 — meishin = superstition; *maybe Shintoism is based on superstition*

迷惑 — meiwaku = trouble, annoyance; *the way that May walks spells trouble*

迷う — mayou = to lose direction, get lost; *I got lost in the mayonnaise factory*

惑わす — madowasu = to delude or seduce; *outside the mado (window) was Superman, trying to delude me*

当惑 — touwaku = embarrassment, bewilderment; *when I accidentally drank Toner during the War on Kool-Aid, it caused me embarrassment*

from the Practice Sentences

木星 — mokusei = Jupiter; *there's more Kool-Aid in the Safeway stores on Jupiter*

惑星 — wakusei = planet; *waffle mix and Kool-Aid packages are sold at all of the Safeway stores on the planet*

正解 — seikai = correct answer; *a sage told the Kaiser the correct answer*

念入りな — nen'iri na = elaborate, meticulous; *my negative nephew irritates people with his elaborate arguments*

信頼 — shinrai = trust, confidence, reliance; *I have confidence in Shinto rice*

from Satori Reader

直行便 — chokoubin = nonstop flight; *I chose corn and beans to eat on the nonstop flight*

英会話 — eikaiwa = English conversation; from eigo = English + kaiwa = conversation

やって行く — yatte iku = to get along, manage; from yaru = to do + iku = to go

どきどき — dokidoki = thump-thump, pitter-patter, to palpitate; from the sound a heart makes when it beats

ものの — monono = but, although; *he plays monotonous notes, but he's considered a musician*

Practice Sentences

1. 彼女は８才だ。

Kanojo wa hassai da.
She is 8 years old.

2. 全て理解していますか。

Subete rikai shite imasu ka.
Are you understanding everything?

3. 私の時計は君のより正確だ。

Watashi no tokei wa kimi no yori seikaku da.
My watch is more accurate than yours.

4. 食卓にたくさんの皿が残っている。

Shokutaku ni takusan no sara ga nokotte iru.
On the dining table, a lot of dishes are remaining.

5. 超疲れた！

Chou tsukareta!
I got super tired!

6. 試験頑張ってね。

Shiken ganbatte ne.
Do your best on the test, huh.

7. 彼女は道に迷った。

Kanojo wa michi ni mayotta.
She lost her way.

8. 彼は才能のある人だ。

Kare wa sainou no aru hito da.
He is a talented person.

9. 木星は大きい惑星ですね。

Mokusei wa ookii wakusei desu ne.
Jupiter is a big planet, huh.

10. 彼は念入りに書類を確かめた。

Kare wa nen'iri ni shorui wo tashikameta.
He checked the documents meticulously.

11. 今人気の「おばあちゃんの食卓」に行ったことがありますか。

Ima ninki no "obaachan no shokutaku" ni itta koto ga arimasu ka.
Have you been to the now-popular "Grandma's Dining Table"?

12. 夢に向かって頑張ってね。

Yume ni mukatte ganbatte ne.
Head toward your dream, and do your best, huh.

13. ピンポン、ピンポン！正解です！

Pinpon, pinpon! Seikai desu.
Ding, ding! It's the correct answer.

14. 今日は超寒い。

Kyou wa chou samui.
Today is super cold.

15. もう誰にも迷惑かけたくない。

Mou dare ni mo meiwaku kaketakunai.
I don't want to cause trouble for anyone anymore.

16. 確かに彼は信頼できます。

Tashika ni kare wa shinrai dekimasu.
Certainly you can rely on him.

17. 彼はテニスも卓球もうまい。

Kare wa tenisu mo takkyuu mo umai.
As for him, tennis also, pingpong also, skillful.

18. 旅先では迷子になりやすい。

Tabisaki de wa maigo ni nariyasui.
At travel destinations, it's easy to become a lost person.

19. 彼って超天才じゃん！

Kare tte chou tensai jan!
As for the one called him, it's a super genius, isn't it! (jan = ja nai)

20. その問題を解くのは難しい。

Sono mondai wo toku no wa muzukashii.
That problem is difficult to solve.

21. 彼は頑丈そうに見える。

Kare wa ganjou sou ni mieru.
It looks like he appears to be strong.

22. ご迷惑でなければ、お願いし
たいのですが。

Gomeiwaku de nakereba, onegaishitai no desu ga.
If it isn't honorable trouble, I would like to humbly request, but...

Supplemental Reading Practice

After you have finished reading Chapter 2 of this book, you may visit *Satori Reader* at SatoriReader.com and read the **two articles for Day 1 in the series "Akiko's Foreign Exchange,"** i.e., the easier and the harder versions. These articles employ only kanji that you have learned, including the 608 taught in Volume 1 of this book. We are not affiliated with *Satori Reader* in any way, but we think that their work is magnificent.

When you read the articles in *Satori Reader*, make sure that "Standard spelling" is selected in the Kanji section and that Furigana are turned off.

You will find that *Satori Reader* is an excellent resource that can help you to learn Japanese. However, if you need to economize, after you complete Days 1 and 2 of the "Akiko" series, which are free of charge, you may choose to sign up for only a one-month subscription at first. During this period, you should be able to save the Japanese text from **"Akiko's Foreign Exchange," Days 1-28**, both the easier and the harder versions, and from **"Kona's Big Adventure," all 45 articles**, for future reference.

Satori Reader does not provide a romaji transcript, but at this point you may no longer need one. (However, if you prefer a romaji transcript, it's easy to create one using Google Translate.) You should save **two versions** of the Japanese text, one for **Reading Practice** and one for **Reference**. For the Reading Practice version, set Kanji to "Standard spelling" and Furigana to "None." For the Reference version, set Kanji to "None." Save the text for each version in separate documents, setting the font size to at least 14.

Next, quickly read through the lessons on the Satori Reader web site, in order to take advantage of the clear explanations provided and hear the pronunciations. As you read, you should **add notes** to the **Reference** versions of the documents that you have saved, to make it easier for you to understand the text when you read it again later.

When you have learned the kanji that you will need for a given article and are ready to start reading in earnest, if your subscription to *Satori Reader* has expired, please print or display both versions of the text for the article and read the **Reading Practice** version. Whenever you need help with the kanji, you can refer to the hiragana equivalents in the **Reference** version. In addition, if you need help with grammar or vocabulary, you can refer to the notes that you have made in the Reference version.

Finally, you may want to create a **merged** document by alternating a line or two of Reference text (e.g., font size 10, color red, containing hiragana, katakana and any explanatory notes that you have written), *after* each line of Reading Practice text (e.g., font size 14, color black, containing Standard spelling). If you use a merged document like this for reading practice, you will find it easier to locate the answers to questions that come up as you read.

To obtain a **discount code** for *Satori Reader,* please visit the "How To Read Japanese" page at JapaneseAudioLessons.com.

Chapter 3

New Kanji in this Chapter

# 625 街 (3)	# 626 灯 (1)	# 627 停 (1)	# 628 駄 (2)
# 629 汗 (2)	# 630 周 (2)	# 631 差 (1)	# 632 慎 (2)

Vocabulary List with Mnemonics

from the Kanji Catalogue

街道	kaidou = highway, path; *the Kaiser built doughnut shops along the highway*
街角	machikado = street corner; *a man is lighting matches behind a car door at the street corner*
街灯	gaitou = street light; *the guide hit his toe on a street light*
電灯	dentou = electric light; *the dentist's toe collided with the electric light*
消灯	shoutou = lights out time; *I was ready to show my toys, but it was lights out time*
バス停	basutei = bus stop; from basu = bus + tei = stop; *the tailor works near the bus stop*
地下街	chikagai = underground shopping mall; *in Chicago, our guide took us to an underground shopping mall*
無駄な	muda na = useless, wasteful; *to move the dam would be wasteful*
下駄	geta = Japanese clogs; *when I went to get apples, I wore my Japanese clogs*
汗をかく	ase wo kaku = to sweat; from ase = sweat; *asses sweat when they work;* + kaku = to draw and other meanings
発汗	hakkan = perspiration; *the hacker ate candy all day and sat in his perspiration*
周り	mawari = surrounding; from mawaru = to turn or spin; *I turned the dial too far on Ma's washing machine and ruined it*
周辺	shuuhen = neighborhood, vicinity; *I throw shoes at the hens in this vicinity*
一周	isshuu = round, tour; from ichi = one + shuu = circumference; *the skaters's shoes were scattered around the circumference of the rink*
時差	jisa = time difference; *the genius saw that the time difference was 13 hours*
時差ボケ	jisaboke = jet lag; *the genius saw that boring Ken was suffering from jet lag*

Kanji Pronunciations

# 625 – kai, machi, gai	# 626 – tou	# 627 – tei	# 628 – ta, da
# 629 – ase, kan	# 630 – mawa, shuu	# 631 – sa	# 632 – shin, tsutsushi

交差点	kousaten = traffic intersection; *they were selling <u>Ko</u>rean <u>sa</u>rdines for <u>ten</u> dollars at the <u>intersection</u>*
差し上げる	sashiageru = to give humbly; *when the <u>sa</u>d <u>sheep</u> <u>ageru</u> (give), they <u>give humbly</u>*
慎重な	shinchou na = careful, prudent; *the <u>Shin</u>to priest did his <u>chore</u>s early, since he is <u>prudent</u>*
慎む	tsutsushimu = to be discreet, to refrain from; *there were t<u>suit</u>s and t<u>suit</u>s and <u>sheet</u>s scattered in the <u>moon</u>light, but I <u>was</u> <u>discreet</u> and didn't tell anyone*

from the Practice Sentences

停電	teiden = power failure; *during the <u>power failure</u>, the <u>tai</u>lor and the <u>den</u>tist started kissing*
行動	koudou = actions; *one of his <u>actions</u> was to make a <u>Ko</u>rean <u>door</u>;* cf. 高度 koudo = advanced level, height, elevation
停車駅	teisha eki = scheduled train stop; from teisha = train stop; *when the <u>ta</u>ser was fired at the <u>Shah</u>, the <u>train</u> stopped; +* eki = station

from Satori Reader

果たして	hatashite = really, ever; from hatasu = to accomplish or realize; *it was <u>hard</u> for the <u>tall</u> <u>supervisor</u> to <u>realize</u> his dream of serving in a submarine*
やばい	yabai = dangerous, risky; *it's <u>dangerous</u> for a <u>yak</u> to ride a <u>bike</u>*

Practice Sentences

1. 街灯がつき始めました。
Gaitou ga tsukihajimemashita.
The street light turned on.

2. バス停で待ってるよ。
Basu tei de matteru yo.
I'll be waiting at the bus stop, for sure.

3. 彼に話しかけても無駄だ。
Kare ni hanishikakete mo muda da.
To him, to address even is a waste. (i.e., it's useless to talk to him)

4. われわれは暑さで汗をかいていた。
Wareware wa atsusa de ase wo kaite ita.
We were sweating due to the heat.

5. 船で世界一周をしてみたい。
Fune de sekai isshuu wo shite mitai.
By boat, I would like to do a once-around of the world and see.

6. 時差ボケで辛い。
Jisa boke de tsurai.
Due to jet lag, painful.

7. そこの街角で事故が起こりました。
Soko no machikado de jiko ga okorimashita.
The accident happened at that street corner.

8. あっ、停電だ。

A, teiden da.
Oh, it's a power failure.

9. 彼は電灯を消し忘れた。

Kare wa dentou wo keshiwasureta.
He forgot to turn off the electric light.

10. 言葉を慎みなさい。

Kotoba wo tsutsushimi nasai.
Be discreet in what you say.

11. 彼は顔の汗をふいた。

Kare wa kao no ase wo fuita.
He wiped the sweat on his face.

12. 無駄にする時間はない。

Muda ni suru jikan wa nai.
As for time to waste, it doesn't exist.

13. 僕は周りを見回した。

Boku wa mawari wo mimawashita.
I looked around at the surroundings.

14. 地下街にたくさんの店がある。

Chikagai ni takusan no mise ga aru.
In the underground shopping mall, there are a lot of stores.

15. 彼は行動が慎重だ。

Kare wa koudou ga shinchou da.
His actions are prudent.

16. 消灯は何時ですか？

Shoutou wa nanji desu ka.
What time is "lights out"?

17. 段差注意。

Dansa chuui.
Step-difference warning (seen on a sign).
(i.e., watch out for the irregular step)

18. なんで汗が目に入ると痛いの？

Nande ase ga me ni hairu to itai no?
Why does it hurt if sweat gets into your eyes?

19. 中山さんの時間を無駄にするな。

Nakayama-san no jikan wo muda ni suru na.
Don't waste Nakayama's time.

20. 次の停車駅はどこですか。

Tsugi no teisha eki wa doko desu ka.
Where is the next train stop?

21. 慎重に運転してください。

Shinchou ni unten shite kudasai.
Please drive prudently.

22. 月は地球の周りを回っている。

Tsuki wa chikyuu no mawari wo mawatte iru.
The moon is revolving around the Earth.

23. ただで差し上げます。

Tada de sashiagemasu.
I will humbly give it free of charge.

Supplemental Reading Practice

After completing Chapter 3 of this book, you should be able to read the articles for Day 2 from "Akiko's Foreign Exchange" in *Satori Reader*.

Chapter 4

New Kanji in this Chapter

# 633 成 (4)	# 634 功 (1)	# 635 継 (2)	# 636 単 (1)
# 637 余 (2)	# 638 陣 (1)	# 639 数 (4)	# 640 感 (1)

Vocabulary List with Mnemonics

from the Kanji Catalogue

成功	seikou = success; *the Safeway corporation is a success*
成る	naru = to consist of; *after something naru (becomes) it consists of whatever it has become*
成り立つ	naritatsu = to consist of, to materialize; *the buildings at Narita that tatsu (stand up) consist of concrete and steel*
成田	Narita = city and airport near Tokyo
継ぐ	tsugu = to succeed to, to inherit; *I had to tsue (sue) my goofy parents in order to be allowed to inherit money from my grandparents*
乗り継ぐ	noritsugu = to connect (to a different flight, train, etc.); *Noriko tsued (sued) the goofballs at the airline when they didn't allow her to connect to a flight*
継ぎ目	tsugime = joint, seam; *the tsuitcase where I keep my guitar caused a mess when its seam split*
単語	tango = word; *when I asked her to dance the tango, she answered with one word*
単位	tan'i = credit (school) or unit; *my school gives credit for tanning classes*
単行本	tankoubon = special book, separate volume; *I sat in a tank of cold water and chewed a bone while I read a special book*
余る	amaru = to be left over, to remain; *Amanda ruined the food that was left over*

Kanji Pronunciations

# 633 – sei, nari, na, jou	# 634 – kou	# 635 – tsu, kei	# 636 – tan
# 637 – ama, yo	# 638 – jin	# 639 – kazo, kazu, suu, zuu	# 640 – kan

余り   amari = surplus, remainder; from amaru = to be be left over

余計   yokei = excessive, all the more; *the yogi kicked his cage excessively*

余分   yobun = surplus, extra; *yogurt and hamburger buns are among the surplus items*

陣地   jinchi = encampment, position; *the gin was cheap in our encampment*

背水の陣   haisui no jin = back to the wall, last stand; *we hiked to the Swiss Alps, took some notes, drank some gin, and made our last stand*

数える   kazoeru = to count; *he counted the number of kazoku [family] members that were erudite*

数   kazu = number; *the number of kazoos determines the number of people who can play in the band*

人数   ninzuu = number of people; *number of nin (people) at the zoo is 50*

数字   suuji = numeral, figure; *I will sue Jesus about the number of apostles*

数学   suugaku = mathematics; *I will sue that gakusei (student) if he keeps talking about mathematics*

感じる   kanjiru = to feel or sense; *I feel or sense the meaning of the kanji found in the ruined castle*

感じ   kanji = impression, perception, feeling; from kanjiru = to feel or sense

感動する   kandou suru = to be moved; *I was moved by her candor*

感心な   kanshin na = impressive, admirable; *the candles' sheen was impressive*

from the Practice Sentences

家業   kagyou = family business; *our family business supplies cabbage for gyoza*

単なる   tan'naru = mere; *in Montana, roosters make up a mere fraction of the animals*

陣痛   jintsuu = labor pains; *the genius tsued (sued) the hospital over her labor pains*

同感する   doukan suru = to have the same opinion or feeling; *the dopes in Canada have the same opinions as the dopes in the U.S.*

科目   kamoku = academic course; *the academic course about camels is the most cool*

目的   mokuteki = purpose, goal; *on mokuyoubi (Thursday), the techie achieved his goal*

達成する   tassei suru = to accomplish; *Tarzan saved money in order to accomplish his goals*

勝ち取る   kachitoru = to win/take; from katsu = to win + toru = to take

見込み   mikomi = prospects; *if you meet that Commie, you will see that he has excellent prospects to rise in the Party*

4-14

from Satori Reader

やった！ — yatta! = hurray!; *the Yankee tax collector said hurray when he finished work*

いよいよ — iyoiyo = more and more, increasingly, at last; *Eeyore and Eeyore's friends started coming around more and more*

分け — wake = placement (in a class); from wakeru = to divide or classify

開始 — kaishi = start, commencement; *the Kaiser's sheep ranch project will have its start next year*

なんとなく — nantonaku = somehow or other, for some reason or another; from nan = something + to = if + naku = adverbial form of nai = not; so this could be understood as, "if something, not" or "maybe yes, maybe no"

はなまる — hanamaru = flower circle = an award given to school children when they do good work, similar to a gold star; from hana = flower + maru = circle

迷わず — mayowazu = mayowazuni = mayowanai de = not getting lost

Practice Sentences

1. 彼女は成功した。
Kanojo wa seikou shita
She succeeded.

2. 彼は家業を継いだ。
Kare wa kagyou wo tsuida.
He inherited the family business.

3. これは単なる夢だよ。
Kore wa tan'naru yume da yo.
This is a mere dream.

4. 余分な金はない。
Yobun na kane wa nai.
There is no extra money.

5. 陣痛が始まりました。
Jintsuu ga hajimarimashita.
The labor pains (related to childbirth) began.

6. お金を数えています。
Okane wo kazoete imasu.
He's counting the money.

7. 全く同感です。
Mattaku doukan desu.
I agree with you completely.

8. 昨日成田に着きました。
Kinou narita ni tsukimashita.
Yesterday, I arrived at Narita.

9. 余計なことはするな。
Yokei na koto wa suru na.
Don't do excessive things. (i.e., it's none of your business)

10. 彼の息子達はどちらとも家業を継ぎたがらない。
Kare no musukotachi wa dochira tomo kagyou wo tsugitagaranai.
Both of his sons appear not to want to take over the family business.

11. この科目は何単位ですか。

Kono kamoku wa nan tan'i desu ka.
As for this course, how many credits is it?

12. 冷たい風が吹くのを感じました。

Tsumetai kaze ga fuku no wo kanjimashita.
I felt the cold wind blowing.

13. 背水の陣だった。

Haisui no jin datta.
It was a last-ditch stand. (haisui no jin = "backs to the water," based on an old Chinese war story)

14. 余り楽しくなかったな。

Amari tanoshikunakatta na.
It wasn't very pleasant.

15. その計画は必ず成功する。

Sono keikaku wa kanarazu seikou suru.
That plan will certainly succeed.

16. 出席する人の数を確かめてください。

Shusseki suru hito no kazu wo tashikamete kudasai.
Please ascertain the number of people who will attend.

17. 私は将来、父の仕事の後を継がなければならないだろう。

Watashi wa shourai, chichi no shigoto no ato wo tsuganakereba naranai darou.
As for me, future, my father's work's afterwards, I will have to succeed, probably. (i.e., I will probably have to take over his business)

18. 単語を2，3個だけ知っている。

Tango wo ni san ko dake shitte iru.
I only know a few words.

19. 彼は目的を達成した。

Kare wa mokuteki wo tassei shita.
He accomplished the purpose.

20. いつもと感じが全然違いますね。

Itsumo to kanji ga zenzen chigaimasu ne.
Her with-always appearance completely changes, huh. (i.e., she looks completely different from her usual appearance)

21. 彼らは陣地を勝ち取った。

Karera wa jinchi wo kachitotta.
They won/took the position (referring to a battlefield position).

22. 数字を一つ選んで。

Suuji wo hitotsu erande.
Choose a number.

23. 成功の見込みはない。

Seikou no mikomi wa nai
Prospects for success don't exist.

Supplemental Reading Practice

After completing Chapter 4 of this book, you should be able to read the articles for Day 3 from "Akiko's Foreign Exchange" in *Satori Reader*.

Chapter 5

New Kanji in this Chapter

# 641 暮 (3)	# 642 限 (2)	# 643 貴 (2)	# 644 揃 (1)
# 645 掃 (2)	# 646 除 (3)	# 647 爪 (2)	# 648 簡 (1)

Vocabulary List with Mnemonics

from the Kanji Catalogue

暮らす — kurasu = to make a living; *I make a living by teaching kurasu (classes)*

暮らし — kurashi = living, life; from kurasu = to make a living

暮れ — kure = year-end, nightfall; *at nightfall, we went to a Kuwaiti restaurant*

お歳暮 — oseibo = year-end gift; *the old sailor got off the boat to give me my year-end gift*

日暮れ — higure = nightfall, dusk; *sometimes I hear the goose outside the restaurant at dusk*

一人暮らし — hitorigurashi = to live alone; from hitori = one person and gurashi = kurashi = life

限界 — genkai = limit; *Genghis flew kites along his borders to mark the limit of his domain*

最低限 — saiteigen = minimum; *the science of tasers under Genghis was at its minimum*

最大限 — saidaigen = maximum; *the science of dikes under Genghis reached its maximum*

限る — kagiru = to be limited to; e.g., ni kagiru = it's limited to; *she can call geese and roosters, but otherwise her skills are limited*

限らない — kagiranai = it isn't limited to, or not necessarily; from kagiru = to be limited to

貴重な — kichou na = valuable, precious; *the kitchen in Margaret Cho's house has a counter made from precious stones*

貴ぶ — toutobu = to value, respect; *Tony Blair offered toasts of booze to people he respected*

Kanji Pronunciations

# 641 – ku, bo, gu	# 642 – gen, kagi	# 643 – ki, touto	# 644 – soro
# 645 – sou, ha	# 646 – jo, nozo, ji	# 647 – tsuma, tsume	# 648 – kan

揃う	sorou = to be complete, to be equal, to be the same, to assemble; *when my family assembles, we are equal, but we feel sorrow that we are poor*
揃える	soroeru = to arrange, prepare, put in order, make uniform; *the sorrowful erudite guy arranges things*
掃除する	souji suru = to clean; *using soap and wearing my jeans, I do cleaning*
掃く	haku = to sweep; *the hackers sweep up after the hackathon*
掃き集める	hakiatsumeru = to sweep up together; from haku = to sweep + atsumeru = to gather
除く	nozoku = to remove; *in the No Parking Zone, a Kool-Aid truck was parked, but a tow truck removed it*
爪	tsume = nail, claw; *I use my nails to open tsumetai (cold) cartons of milk*
爪きり	tsumekiri = nail cutter; *I found a tsumetai (cold) kitty and cut his nails with a nail cutter*
簡単	kantan = simple and easy; *getting a Canadian tan is easy during the summer*

from the Practice Sentences

暮らし向き	kurashimuki = life direction; from kurashi = life + muki = direction
門限	mongen = curfew; *the monks under Genghis had a strict curfew*
送別会	soubetsukai = farewell party; *sober Betsy came to her farewell party*
引っ込める	hikkomeru = to retract claws; from hiku = to pull + komeru = to go into, to be crowded
取り除く	torinozoku = to remove; from toru = to take + nozoku = to remove
掃除機	soujiki = vacuum cleaner; from souji = cleaning + kikai = machine
歩道	hodou = sidewalk; *the homeless doorman slept on the sidewalk*
除雪する	josetsu suru = to remove snow; *Joan of Arc is our settlement's super pioneer, and she is good at removing snow*

Practice Sentences

1. 彼の暮らし向きは良くなった。

Kare no kurashimuki wa yoku natta.
His life-direction became good. (i.e., his living circumstances improved)

2. 門限時間は何時？

Mongen jikan wa nanji?
What time is the curfew?

3. 貴船という所が京都にある。

Kibune to iu tokoro ga kyouto ni aru.
The place called Kibune is in Kyoto.

4. 皆様がお揃いになったので、
   送別会を始めます。

Minasama ga osoroi ni natta node, soubetsukai wo hajimemasu.
Since very honorable everyone honorably assembled, we will start the farewell party.

5. 部屋を掃除しなさい。

Heya wo souji shinasai.
Clean up the room.

6. ねえ、ここにしまってあった
   爪切り知らない？

Nee, koko ni shimatte atta tsumekiri shiranai?
Hey, don't you know the were-at-here-put-away nail clippers? (i.e., don't you know where they are?)

7. 心配しないで。簡単だよ。

Shinpai shinai de. Kantan da yo.
Don't worry. It's simple, for sure.

8. 二人はその日を限りに、二度
   と会わなかった。

Futari wa sono hi wo kagiri ni, nido to awanakatta.
As for the two of them, at that day's limit, they did not meet with two times. (i.e., they didn't meet again after that day)

9. 一人を除いて全員出席した。

Hitori wo nozoite zen'in shusseki shita.
All but one person attended.

10. 全部揃っているようです。

Zenbu sorotte iru you desu.
It looks like everything is assembled. (i.e., we have everything)

11. お歳暮は１２月に贈る贈り物
    ですよ。

Oseibo wa juunigatsu ni okuru okurimono desu yo.
"Oseibo" is an in-December-to-give gift, for sure. (i.e., you give it in December)

12. 猫は爪を引っ込めた。

Neko wa tsume wo hikkometa.
The cat retracted its claws.

13. それほど簡単ではない。

Sore hodo kantan de wa nai.
It isn't that simple.

14. それを取り除きたいのです。

Sore wo torinozokitai no desu.
I want to remove that.

15. 時間ほど貴重な物はない。

Jikan hodo kichou na mono wa nai.
Compared to time, nothing is as precious.

16. 必ずしもお金持ちが幸せとは
    限らない。

Kanarazu shimo okanemochi ga shiawase to wa kagiranai.
Not necessarily, rich people, as for the one called happiness, it isn't limited. (i.e., they aren't necessarily happy)

17. 猫は掃除機が好きじゃない。

Neko wa soujiki ga suki ja nai.
Cats don't like vacuum cleaners.

18. 魚は水の中で暮らす。

Sakana wa mizu no naka de kurasu.
Fish live in water.

19. 夕食には家族全員揃います。

Yuushoku ni wa kazoku zen'in soroimasu.
As for at the evening meal, the family, all members, assembles.

20. 金は鉄よりも貴重だ。

Kin wa tetsu yorimo kichou da.
Gold is more precious than iron.

21. 私は落ち葉を掃き集めた。

Watashi wa ochiba wo hakiatsumeta.
I swept up the fallen leaves.

22. 強い足と長い爪で、リスは簡単に木に登ることができる。

Tsuyoi ashi to nagai tsume de, risu wa kantan ni ki ni noboru koto ga dekiru.
With strong legs and long claws, a squirrel can easily climb trees.

23. 彼らはシャベルで除雪する。

Karera wa shaberu de josetsu suru.
They do snow removal with a shovel.

Chapter 6

New Kanji in this Chapter

# 649 涙 (1)	# 650 煎 (2)	# 651 身 (2)	# 652 己 (2)
# 653 幕 (2)	# 654 流 (3)	# 655 韓 (1)	# 656 費 (2)

Vocabulary List with Mnemonics

from the Kanji Catalogue

涙	namida = tears; *when the Nazis broke her mirror, my daughter shed tears*
煎じる	senjiru = to boil; *the senator's jeep was ruined when the radiator boiled over*
煎る	iru = to roast or toast; *it's easy to ruin breakfast by toasting the bread too much*
身長	shinchou = a person's height; *the Shinto priest and Margaret Cho are the same height*
出身	shusshin = birthplace, hometown, alma mater, alumnus; *at my alma mater, I majored in shoe shining*
身	mi = body, person, e.g., 一人身 hitori mi = one person; *the body is made out of meat*
親身に	shinmi ni = kindly; *the Shinto priest fed me a meal kindly*
身元	mimoto = identity, lineage; *the median age of those motorcars tells you something about their lineage*
己	onore = self; *my self was the honoree at the banquet*
利己的な	rikoteki na = egotistical, self-centered; *that rico (rich, in Spanish) techie seems to be egotistical*
利己主義	rikoshugi = egotism, selfishness; *that person who is rico (rich, in Spanish) and has nice shoes and lots of guitars displays some egotism*
幕	maku = theater curtain, act of a play; *we bought a theater curtain at a mall in Kuwait*
字幕	jimaku = subtitle; *when Jimmy Carter got macular degeneration, he couldn't read subtitles*
流す	nagasu = to flush; *Nagaina sued her husband for flushing her wedding ring*
流れる	nagareru = to flow; *when Nagaina chased the red rooster, it jumped across a ditch which had water flowing through it*

Kanji Pronunciations

# 649 – namida	# 650 – sen, i	# 651 – shin, mi	# 652 – onore, ko
# 653 – maku, baku	# 654 – naga, ru, ryuu	# 655 – kan	# 656 – tsui, hi

流行   ryuukou = vogue, fashion; *reused corn cobs are now in fashion as hair ornaments*

一流の   ichiryuu no = first-rate; *those itchy reusable hats are first-rate*

風流な   fuuryuu na = refined; *sometimes food can be reused and refined into something better*

電流   denryuu = electric current; *when the dentist reused an old drill, he felt some electric current flowing into his hand*

韓国   kankoku = South Korea; from kan = Korea; *there is good candy in Korea;* + koku = country

費やす   tsuiyasu = to spend time or money; *I spend time and money with tsuite (sweet) Yasuko*

費用   hiyou = cost; *healing yogurt has a high cost*

会費   kaihi = membership fee; *the Kaiser heeded advice and paid the membership fee*

from the Practice Sentences

中身   nakami = contents; from naka = inside + mi = body

開きかける   hirakikakeru = to start to open, to be about to open; from hiraku = to open + kakeru = to start to do something; *the car that Kennedy ruined was starting to show its age*

煎茶   sencha = green tea; *the senator's cha (tea) is green tea*

閉じる   tojiru = to close; *I told the genius and Ruth to close the door*

自己   jiko = self; *my jeans and coat are an expression of my self*

自己中心的な   jikochuushinteki na = selfish; from jiko = self + chuushin = center; *I choose to visit that Shinto temple because it's in the center of town;* + teki = related to

信念   shin'nen = belief; *the Shinto that my negative nephew follows promotes strange beliefs*

涙ぐむ   namidagumu = to be moved to tears; from namida = tears + gumu = kumu = to ladle or scoop water; *in that goofy movie, the actors ladled water*

生活費   seikatsu hi = living costs; from seikatsu = livelihood; *my livelihood is to cook safe ton katsu;* + hiyou = cost

from Satori Reader

それぞれ   sorezore = each, respectively, severally; from sore = that + zore = sore = that

少人数   shouninzuu = few people; from shou = few + ninzuu = number of people

プータロー   puutaroo = freeloader, unemployed person, vagrant; *that poor talented rogue is a vagrant*

Practice Sentences

1. 余りのショックに、涙も出な
   ければ声も出なかった。

   Amari no shokku ni, namida mo
   denakereba koe mo denakatta.
   By excessive shock, if tears also do not
   emerge, the voice also did not emerge.
   (i.e., I couldn't cry or speak)

2. このお茶を10分間煎じてくだ
   さい。

   Kono ocha wo juupunkan senjite
   kudasai.
   Please let the tea steep for 10 minutes.

3. 箱の中身は何？

   Hako no nakami wa nani?
   What are the contents of the box?

4. 己を知ること、これほど大切
   なことはない。

   Onore wo shiru koto, kore hodo taisetsu
   na koto wa nai.
   To know one's self: compared to this,
   there is nothing more important.

5. その時、幕は開きかけてい
   た。

   Sono toki, maku wa hirakikakete ita.
   At that time, the curtain was starting to
   open.

6. 彼女は涙を流した。

   Kanojo wa namida wo nagashita.
   As for her, she flushed tears. (i.e., the
   tears flowed)

7. 韓国旅行が三泊四日で三万円
   だって。

   Kankoku ryokou ga sanpaku yokka de
   sanman yen da tte.
   A Korean trip of three nights and four
   days is 30,000 yen, reportedly.

8. 時間を費やしてしまったね。

   Jikan wo tsuiyashite shimatta ne
   You spent time completely, huh. (i.e.,
   you lost time)

9. 煎茶が飲みたい。

   Sencha ga nomitai.
   I want to drink green tea.

10. 身長何センチ？

    Shinchou nan senchi?
    The height, how many centimeters?

11. 流行はすぐ変わります。

    Ryuukou wa sugu kawarimasu.
    Fashions soon change.

12. 彼は自己中心的な人だ。

    Kare wa jikochuushinteki na hito da.
    He's a selfish person.

13. 私は韓国人です。

    Watashi wa kankokujin desu.
    I am a South Korean person.

14. この店は色々な煎茶を売って
    います。

    Kono mise wa iroiro na sencha wo utte
    imasu.
    This store is selling various kinds of
    green tea.

15. 彼は感動して涙ぐんだ。

Kare wa kandou shite namidagunda.
As for him, he was touched and moved to tears.

16. この費用は誰が払うの？

Kono hiyou wa dare ga harau no?
Who will pay this expense?

17. その物語は彼の死で幕を閉じた。

Sono monogatari wa kare no shi de maku wo tojita.
As for that story, with his death, the curtain closed. (i.e., the story ended with his death.)

18. トイレの水を流した。

Toire no mizu wo nagashita.
I flushed the toilet.

19. 私はウエストテキサス大学の出身です。

Watashi wa uesuto tekisasu daigaku no shusshin desu.
I'm an alumnus of West Texas University.

20. 彼女は自己の信念を決して変えようとしなかった。

Kanojo wa jiko no shin'nen wo kesshite kaeyou to shinakatta.
As for her, herself's beliefs she never tried to change. (i.e., she never thought of changing her beliefs)

21. 辛い韓国料理は余り好きじゃない。

Karai kankoku ryouri wa amari suki ja nai.
I don't like spicy Korean food very much.

22. 日本語の映画を見る時は字幕がいります。

Nihongo no eiga wo miru toki wa jimaku ga irimasu.
As for the time when I watch Japanese movies, subtitles are needed

23. 生活費が高くなった。

Seikatsu hi ga takaku natta.
Living costs became higher.

Supplemental Reading Practice

After completing Chapter 6 of this book, you should be able to read the articles for Day 4 from "Akiko's Foreign Exchange" in *Satori Reader*.

Chapter 7

New Kanji in this Chapter

# 657 仲 (2)	# 658 紹 (1)	# 659 介 (1)	# 660 裕 (1)
# 661 福 (1)	# 662 羨 (2)	# 663 希 (1)	# 664 望 (3)

Vocabulary List with Mnemonics

from the Kanji Catalogue

仲 — naka = relationship; *you have underlined relationships with people who are naka (inside) your in-group*

仲良し — nakayoshi = close friend; *my close friend works at the National Cathedral, and he eats yogurt made from sheep milk*

仲介 — chuukai = mediation; *I will choose the Kaiser to do the mediation*

紹介 — shoukai = introduction; *I will introduce a Showman to the Kaiser*

仲介者 — chuukaisha = mediator; *I will choose a kaisha (company) to be the mediator*

裕福な — yuufuku na = rich, in the sense of affluent; *I know a youth in Fukuoka who is rich*

福 — fuku = good luck, fortune; *I had the good luck to visit Fukuoka*

幸福 — koufuku = happiness; *the cola I drank in Fukuoka brought me happiness*

羨望 — senbou = envy; *I feel envy that you have sen (1,000) boats*

羨ましい — urayamashii = envious; *when we learned that the Uranium mine in the yama [mountain] was owned by Shiites, we were envious*

希望 — kibou = hope; *the kindergarten's bowling team had hope of winning*

望み — nozomi = hope, dream, wish; *in the Norwegian zone, they have plenty of meat, and my hope is to visit there*

所望 — shomou = desire, wish, request; *my desire is that you show me your motorcycle*

from the Practice Sentences

以上 — ijou = not less than, now that; *at Easter, Joan of Arc would eat not less than three eggs*

幸運 — kou'un = good luck; *it was good luck that the koala was under the bridge when the train came*

Kanji Pronunciations

# 657 – naka, chuu	# 658 – shou	# 659 – kai	# 660 – yuu
# 661 – fuku	# 662 – sen, uraya	# 663 – ki	# 664 – bou, nozo, mou

優勝	yuushou = victory; *I won a <u>victory</u> at the <u>yucca show</u>*
仲間	nakama = colleague or buddy; *since Ma (Mother) stays inside the house, she's a <u>naka</u> (inside) <u>Ma</u> and a <u>colleague</u>*
上司	joushi = supervisor; *<u>Josephine</u> the <u>Shiite</u> is my <u>supervisor</u>*
余裕	yoyuu = surplus; *we have a <u>surplus</u> of <u>yogurt</u> in the <u>Yukon</u>*
取引	torihiki = business deal; *if you do <u>business deals</u> with birds, you may get a <u>tori</u> (bird) <u>hickey</u>*
機会	kikai = opportunity; *if he gets the <u>opportunity</u>, he will <u>kick</u> you in the <u>eye</u>*; cf. 機械 kikai = machine

Practice Sentences

1. 優勝できたのは、仲間の助けがあったからです。

Yuushou dekita no wa, nakama no tasuke ga atta kara desu.
As for was able to do championship thing, it is because colleagues' support existed.

2. 彼は娘を私に紹介した。

Kare wa musume wo watashi ni shoukai shita.
He introduced me to his daughter.

3. 私は裕福でもなければ有名でもない。

Watashi wa yuufuku de mo nakereba yuumei de mo nai.
I am neither rich nor famous.

4. いい上司で羨ましいです。

Ii joushi de urayamashii desu.
Since you have a good boss, I'm jealous.

5. 彼は海外に行くことを希望している。

Kare wa kaigai ni iku koto wo kibou shite iru.
He is hoping to go abroad.

6. 仲良くしよう。

Nakayoku shiyou.
Let's get along.

7. 自己紹介させて下さい。

Jiko shoukai sasete kudasai.
Please allow me to introduce myself.

8. 僕には車を持つ余裕がない。

Boku ni wa kuruma wo motsu yoyuu ga nai.
As for to me, to have a car surplus doesn't exist. (i.e., I can't afford a car)

9. 彼は望みを捨てた。

Kare wa nozomi wo suteta.
He threw away hope. (i.e., he abandoned all hope)

10. 幸福は買えない。

Koufuku wa kaenai.
You can't buy happiness.

11. 多くの人は上田さんの成功を羨ましがっている。

Ooku no hito wa ueda san no seikou wo urayamashigatte iru.
A lot of people seem to be envying Ueda's success.

12. これ以上希望はしない。

Kore ijou kibou wa shinai.
More than this I do not do hope. (i.e., I don't hope for more than this)

13. 彼女に自己紹介する機会がなかった。

Kanojo ni jiko shoukai suru kikai ga nakatta.
There wasn't an opportunity to introduce myself to her.

14. 裕福になるためには幸運と大変な努力が必要だ。

Yuufuku ni naru tame ni wa kou'un to taihen na doryoku ga hitsuyou da.
As for in order to become wealthy, good luck and extreme effort are necessary.

15. 私は留学した学生たちが羨ましかった。

Watashi wa ryuugaku shita gakuseitachi ga urayamashikatta.
I envied the students who studied abroad.

16. 彼女は希望をすべて無くした。

Kanojo wa kibou wo subete nakushita.
She lost all hope.

17. 仲介者がしっかりしていると取引がスムーズに行く。

Chuukaisha ga shikkari shite iru to torihiki ga sumuuzu ni iku.
If a mediator is doing reliably, a business deal will go smoothly.

Chapter 8

New Kanji in this Chapter

# 665 垢 (2)	# 666 離 (2)	# 667 貯 (2)	# 668 旦 (2)
# 669 那 (1)	# 670 捕 (4)	# 671 浮 (4)	# 672 未 (2)

Vocabulary List with Mnemonics

from the Kanji Catalogue

歯垢	shikou = dental plaque; *this sheep drinks too much cola and suffers from dental plaque*
垢	aka = dirt; *our academy has dirt floors*
離れる	hanareru = to part; *Hannah owned a red rooster, but she had to part from it*
離婚	rikon = divorce; *an incident on a reef in the Congo led to my divorce*
貯金	chokin = savings; *too much household savings is choking the Japanese economy*
貯める	tameru = to save (money); *after buying a tapestry in Mexico, Ruth had to save money again*
一旦	ittan = for a moment, once; *once I got my Italian tan, I was happy*
旦那	danna = husband, master; *my husband was a dancing Nazi*
旦那さん	dannasan = male customer, master; from danna = master
捕る	toru = to catch; *my toes were ruined when I used them to catch a scorpion*
捕まえる	tsukamaeru = to capture, catch or seize; *Tsuperman (Superman) calculated that the massive eruption was dangerous, and he decided to catch the lava*
捕まる	tsukamaru = to be caught; the intransitive form of tsukamaeru = to catch
捕らえる	toraeru = to arrest, capture or understand; *he has studied the Torah and is quite erudite, so we cannot hope to capture him*
浮かぶ	ukabu = to float, intransitive; *at underline{UC} (University of California) they abuse men who are afraid of water by making them float in pools*
浮く	uku = to float, transitive; *in Uruguay the cool people float toy boats*

Kanji Pronunciations

# 665 – kou, aka	# 666 – hana, ri	# 667 – cho, ta	# 668 – tan, dan
# 669 – na	# 670 – to, ho, tsuka, tora	# 671 – u, uwa, fu, uki	# 672 – ima, mi

浮気	uwaki = extramarital affair; *in Uruguay, it's considered wacky to have extramarital affairs*
浮世	ukiyo = floating world, transitory life; *in Uruguay, people live on quiche and yogurt in a floating world*
未だに	imada ni = even now, still, until this very day; *my imaginary daughter and my niece still have not appeared*
未来	mirai = future; *mirrors will be made of ice in the future*
未開	mikai = primitive; *I will meet the Kaiser in a primitive village*
未経験	mikeiken = inexperienced; from mi = yet; *the meeting has yet to start;* + keiken = experience

from the Practice Sentences

名案	meian = good idea; *mailing ants is a good idea*
未婚	mikon = unmarried; from mi = yet; *the meeting has yet to start;* + kekkon = marriage
数日間	suunichikan = a few days; from suu = number + nichi = day + kan = duration
未成年者	miseinensha = a minor; *the meek sailor and his negative nephew live in a shack by themselves, even though they are minors*
人類	jinrui = human race; *the jeans that Louis wears are designed for the human race*

from Satori Reader

正社員	seishain = regular employee, permanent employee; from sei = correct, regular; *Safeway is a regular grocery store;* + shain = employee
しかも	shikamo = moreover, nevertheless, and yet; *the sheep was camouflaged; nevertheless the wolf found it*
その上	sono ue = furthermore, on top of; from sono = that + ue = above
見習う	minarau = to follow another's example; from miru = to watch + narau = to learn
にもかかわらず	ni mo kakawarazu = nevertheless, in spite of, regardless; *the needy moping cabbie carries the warrant to the zoo regardless of whether he is authorized to do so*
地下室	chikashitsu = basement; from chika = underground, e.g., chikatetsu = subway; + shitsu = room
めったに	metta ni = rarely, seldom; *I give Mexican taffy to my niece rarely*
調子	choushi = condition, way, manner, style; *the chores I do for my sheep improve their living condition*

取り掛かる   torikakaru = to begin or set out; from toru = to take + kakaru = to start moving; *after the carpenter calculated the monthly room charges, he decided to start moving*

徒歩   toho = walking, going on foot; *Tolstoy went home walking*

Practice Sentences

1. 垢を落としに風呂に入ろう。

Aka wo otoshi ni furo ni hairou.
I shall enter the bath in order to remove the scale (from my skin).

2. 両親が離婚した。

Ryoushin ga rikon shita.
My parents got divorced.

3. 彼は貯金を増やした。

Kare wa chokin wo fuyashita.
He increased his savings.

4. はい、旦那様。

Hai, danna sama.
Yes, master.

5. 来た者は皆捕まった。

Kita mono wa minna tsukamatta.
As for the people who came, all were caught.

6. 名案が浮かんだ。

Meian ga ukanda.
A good idea floated. (i.e., it occurred to me)

7. まだ未婚です。

Mada mikon desu.
I'm still unmarried.

8. 電車は一旦停車した。

Densha wa ittan teisha shita.
The train stopped for a moment.

9. 耳垢を取って欲しい。

Mimi aka wo totte hoshii.
I want the ear wax taken out of my ears.

10. 数日間、町を離れます。

Suunichikan, machi wo hanaremasu.
I will leave town for a few days.

11. 息子は未だにサンタクロースがいると信じている。

Musuko wa imada ni santakuroosu ga iru to shinjite iru.
My son still believes that Santa Claus exists.

12. 彼は大学へ行くのにお金を貯めている。

Kare wa daigaku e iku noni okane wo tamete iru.
He is saving money in order to attend college.

13. 右手でボールを捕った。

Migi te de booru wo totta.
I caught the ball with my right hand.

14. 彼女の旦那さんは私の友達です。

Kanojo no dannasan wa watashi no tomodachi desu.
Her husband is my friend.

15. 彼は浮気していた。

Kare wa uwaki shite ita.
He was having an affair.

16. 彼女はまだ未成年者だ。

Kanojo wa mada miseinensha da.
She is still a minor.

17. 歯垢を取らなければなりません。

Shikou wo toranakereba narimasen.
We have to remove the dental plaque.

18. 私から手を離せ！

Watashi kara te wo hanase!
Separate your hands from me!

19. 貯金箱の中にはお金が全く残っていなかった。

Chokin bako no naka ni wa okane ga mattaku nokotte inakatta.
There was no money at all remaining inside the savings box.

20. 旦那様をしっかり捕まえていなさい。

Dannasama wo shikkari tsukamaete inasai.
Be holding onto your husband tightly.
(i.e., don't let him get away)

21. 池に落ち葉がたくさん浮かんでいる。

Ike ni ochiba ga takusan ukande iru.
In the pond a lot of fallen leaves are floating.

21. 人類の未来はどうなるのでしょうか。

Jinrui no mirai wa dou naru no deshou ka.
As for the future of the human race, how will it develop, probably?

Supplemental Reading Practice

After completing Chapter 8 of this book, you should be able to read the articles for Days 5, 6 and 7 from "Akiko's Foreign Exchange" in *Satori Reader*.

Chapter 9

New Kanji in this Chapter

# 673 絶 (3)	# 674 対 (2)	# 675 悔 (3)	# 676 宗 (3)
# 677 応 (2)	# 678 仏 (3)	# 679 壇 (1)	# 680 反 (3)

Vocabulary List with Mnemonics

from the Kanji Catalogue

絶対に	zettai ni = absolutely, definitely, by any means; *the zesty tiger that my niece saw definitely had stripes*
絶交する	zekkou suru = to break off (a relationship); *the zesty coder broke off the relationship*
絶望	zetsubou = despair; *the Zen monk took his tsuitcase (suitcase) to the bowling alley out of despair when he couldn't find another place to spend the night*
絶える	taeru = to discontinue or cease; *the tall expert ruined the evidence, forcing the police to discontinue their investigation*
対する	tai suru = to face toward, to confront; *the Thai soldier confronted his enemy*
対して	taishite = against, in contrast to, as opposed to, toward; from tai suru = to confront
対応	taiou = handling, treatment; *I'm tired of the owner's handling of my complaints*
対応する	taiou suru = to address a problem; from taiou = handling
対決する	taiketsu suru = to confront; *the Thai general poured ketchup in his soup as he confronted his subordinates*; cf. 解決 kaiketsu = settlement, resolution, solution
対の	tsui no = a pair; *the tsuit (sweet) Norwegian only owned one pair of gloves*
後悔	koukai = regret; *he poured Coke into his eye, and now he has regrets*
悔い	kui = regret; *he has cool ears, but he felt regret after he had them pierced*
悔やむ	kuyamu = to regret, repent; *I gave Kool-Aid to the yaks to improve their mood, but now I regret doing so*
悔しい	kuyashii = vexing, mortifying; *the cure of the yak was done by Shiites, which was mortifying to the Sunnis*
宗	mune = religion, sect; *in our sect, we welcome moon experts*

Kanji Pronunciations

# 673 – ze, zetsu, ta	# 674 – tai, tsui	# 675 – kai, ku, kuya	# 676 – mune, sou, shuu
# 677 – kota, ou	# 678 – butsu, bu, hotoke	# 679 – dan	# 680 – han, so, tan

宗教   shuukyou = religion; *the shoes I bought in Kyouto are required by my religion*

宗家   souke = head of family, originator; *the sober Kennedy is the head of the family*

応える   kotaeru = to respond or affect; *the co-eds in the tavern were erudite and responded to our questions*

応じる   oujiru = to respond or comply with; *the old genius and his rooster responded to my invitation*

一応   ichiou = more or less, tentatively, for the time being; *I'm itching to live near the ocean for the time being*

仏壇   butsudan = Buddhist altar found in Japanese homes; *the boots that I dance in are stored next to our Buddhist altar*

仏教   bukkyou = Buddhism; *I read a book kyou (today) about Buddhism*

仏   hotoke = Buddha; *the Buddha enjoyed hottokeeki (pancakes)*

壇   dan = stage; *a dancer needs a stage*

反対   hantai = opposition, the reverse; *due to the opposition we face, our hands are tied*

反り返る   sorikaeru = to bend back or warp; *after you bent back my finger I was sorry that I called you erudite*

反物   tanmono = cloth, textile; *the decor in the tanning booth was monotonous until I added some cloth on the walls*

from the Practice Sentences

確実   kakujitsu = guarantee; *Karl the Kool-Aid vendor gave the jittery superstar a guarantee that the Kool-Aid would be delivered*

招待   shoutai = invitation; *show your tie if you want an invitation*

一方   ippou = one side, the other party, on the other hand, meanwhile; from ichi = one + pou = hou = direction or side

本土   hondo = mainland; *Honda keeps its dough (money) on the mainland*

通信   tsuushin = communication; *the tsuitcase (suitcase) the Shinto priest is carrying contains communication equipment*; cf. 通じる tsuujiru = to communicate

反応   han'nou = reaction, response; *Hansel went to Norway in order to get a reaction from Gretel*

内緒   naisho = secret; *the night show is a secret*

お悔み   okuyami = condolences; *in the oaken yacht's meeting room, I offered condolences*

違反   ihan = offense; *eagle handling is an offense*

教壇   kyoudan = podium, platform; *in Kyouto the dancers stood on a platform* from Satori Reader

言い聞かせる   iikikaseru = to tell someone to do something, to warn or persuade; from iu = to speak + kikaseru = to make hear

号泣する   goukyuu suru = to cry aloud, lament; *when the goat saw the smashed cucumber, it cried aloud*

決意する   ketsui suru = to decide; *seeing ketchup in the soup made it easy for me to decide not to eat at that restaurant*

いまだ   imada = as yet, still, not yet finished; *my imaginary daughter hasn't shown up as yet;* also spelled 未だ, # 672

Practice Sentences

1. 絶対に確実だ。
Zettai ni kakujitsu da.
It's absolutely guaranteed.

2. 何も後悔していない。
Nanimo koukai shite inai.
I am not feeling any regret at all.

3. 彼に話をするときは宗教問題には口を出さない方がいい。
Kare ni hanashi wo suru toki wa shuukyou mondai ni wa kuchi wo dasanai hou ga ii.
To him, as for to do talking time, as for to religion problems, it would be better not to talk. (i.e., don't talk about religion)

4. 私は彼の招待に応じた。
Watashi wa kare no shoutai ni oujita.
I responded to his invitation.

5. また一方で、若者たちは仏教を心の支えに必要なものだと考え始めているようだ。
Mata ippou de, wakamonotachi wa bukkyou wo kokoro no sasae ni hitsuyou na mono da to kangae hajimete iru you da.
Again, on the other side, as for young people, on Buddhism, for the heart's support, a necessary thing it is, they are beginning to think, apparently. (i.e., apparently young people are beginning to find Buddhism a vital spiritual support)

6. 掃除の時間に数人の生徒で教壇を動かした。
Souji no jikan ni suunin no seito de kyoudan wo ugokashita.
At cleaning time, by a few students, they moved the podium.

7. 私はその結婚には反対だ。
Watashi wa sono kekkon ni wa hantai da.
I'm against that marriage.

8. 台風で本土との通信が絶えた。
Taifuu de hondo to no tsuushin ga taeta.
By the typhoon, communication with the mainland was cut off.

9. 日本の家に行ったときに仏壇を始めて見ました。

Nihon no ie ni itta toki ni butsudan wo hajimete mimashita.
At the time I went to a Japanese house, I saw a Buddhist altar for the first time.

10. １対２で負けたなんて悔しい。

Ittai ni de maketa nante kuyashii.
By one to two I lost, such a thing, mortifying.

11. どうして彼らはそんな宗教を信じたのだろうか。

Doushite karera wa sonna shuukyou wo shinjita no darou ka.
Why did they believe in such a religion, probably?

12. それは、良い反応です。

Sore wa yoi han'nou desu.
That's a good response.

13. ひな壇にたくさんの人形が並んでいる。

Hinadan ni takusan no ningyou ga narande iru.
On the doll stand, many dolls are lined up.

14. 彼女には絶対に内緒だよ。

Kanojo ni wa zettai ni naisho da yo.
As for to her, it's absolutely a secret, for sure. (i.e., don't tell her)

15. 日本では主な宗教は神道と仏教である。

Nihon de wa omo na shuukyou wa shintou to bukyou de aru.
As for of Japan, major religions are Shinto and Buddhism.

16. お悔み申し上げます。

Okuyami moshiagemasu.
I humbly say humble condolences. (i.e., please accept my deepest sympathy)

17. お年よりへの対応がひどい。

Otoshiyori e no taiou ga hidoi.
The treatment of the elderly is awful.

18. 法律に違反してはいけない。

Houritsu ni ihan shite wa ikenai.
You must not commit an offense against the law. (i.e., you must not break it)

Supplemental Reading Practice

After completing Chapter 9 of this book, you should be able to read the articles for Day 8 from "Akiko's Foreign Exchange" in *Satori Reader*.

Chapter 10

New Kanji in this Chapter

# 681 香 (2)	# 682 非 (1)	# 683 常 (2)	# 684 営 (2)
# 685 漁 (2)	# 686 団 (2)	# 687 布 (2)	# 688 毛 (3)

Vocabulary List with Mnemonics

from the Kanji Catalogue

線香	senkou = incense stick; *the senator traded coal for incense sticks*
香水	kousui = perfume; *coeds in Sweden use perfume*
香り	kaori = fragrance, aroma; *cows in the Orient are associated with certain aromas*
非常	hijou = emergency; *the healers joked during the emergency, and the patient died*
非常な	hijou na = extreme, great; *the healers joked that Nancy Reagan was a great first lady;* cf. 非常に hijou ni = extremely
非難	hinan = criticism, accusation, blame; *when I gave a hearing aide to our nanny, I received criticism, since her hearing is fine*
通常	tsuujou = usual; *the tsuitcase (suitcase) that Joan of Arc carried was full of books, as usual*
常に	tsune ni = always, continually; *our lives will tsoon (soon) end, says my niece, continually*
経営	keiei = management; *Kay ate a lot of fast food while trying to get into management*
営業	eigyou = business; *our business is selling aging gyoza*
営む	itonamu = to run a business; *we run a business selling instruments with eerie tonal qualities to musicians*
漁	ryou = fishing; *Pope Leo likes to go fishing*
漁業	gyogyou = fishing business; *our fishing business sells fish gyoza to gyoza lovers*
団体	dantai = group of people, an organization; *a group of dancing tigers*
団結する	danketsu suru = to unite or consolidate; *I put dandelions and ketchup in my soup in order to unite yellow and red colors*

Kanji Pronunciations

# 681 – kou, kao	# 682 – hi	# 683 – jou, tsune	# 684 – ei, itona
# 685 – ryou, gyo	# 686 – dan, ton	# 687 – nuno, fu	# 688 – mou, ke, ge

布団	futon = floor cushion, or Japanese bedding; _foolish Tony Blair spilled coffee onto his Japanese bedding_
布	nuno = cloth; _to put cloth on your head when you go out is the new normal_
毛布	moufu = blanket; _Moses looks foolish with that blanket over his head_
流布	rufu = circulation, dissemination; _I climb on my roof and foolishly talk to passersby in order to achieve dissemination of my ideas_
毛	ke = hair, fur, wool; _in Kenya, people wear fur_

from the Practice Sentences

常習者	joushuusha = addict; _Joan of Arc sold her shoes and her shawl to help some drug addicts_
漁村	gyouson = fishing village; _the fish gyoza my son bought came from a fishing village_
髪の毛	kaminoke = hair; from kami = hair + the possessive no + ke = fur
石けん	sekken = soap; _Senator Kennedy always washed with soap_
香料	kouryou = fragrance; _the cologne that Pope Leo uses has a nice fragrance_
漁船	gyosen = fishing boat; _before making fish gyoza, the senator catches fish in his fishing boat_
一団	ichidan = group; _itchy Dan belongs to a support group_

Practice Sentences

1. このお茶は香りがいい。
Kono ocha wa kaori ga ii.
This tea smells good.

2. 彼女は私をうそつきだと非難した。
Kanojo wa watashi wo usotsuki da to hinan shita.
As for her, on me, it's a liar, she accused. (i.e., she accused me of being a liar)

3. 彼はヘロインの常習者だ。
Kare wa heroin no joushuusha da.
He is a heroin addict.

4. 靴屋を経営している。
Kutsuya wo keiei shite iru.
I am managing a shoe store.

5. 小さな漁村に住んでいた。
Chiisana gyoson ni sunde ita.
I lived in a small fishing village.

6. 団体旅行は楽しめないんだ。
Dantai ryokou wa tanoshimenain da.
As for group travel, I can't enjoy it.

7. 妹は布を５メートル買った。
Imouto wa nuno wo go metoru katta.
Younger sister bought 5 meters of cloth.

8. スープに髪の毛が入ってます。

Suupu ni kaminoke ga haittemasu.
A hair is being entered in the soup. (i.e., there's a hair in the soup)

9. この石けんには天然香料が入っている。

Kono sekken ni wa ten'nen kouryou ga haitte iru.
To this soap, natural fragrances are being entered. (i.e., it's infused with fragrance)

10. 非常階段はあそこです。

Hijou kaidan wa asoko desu.
The emergency stairs are over there.

11. その島には漁業を営む人たちが住んでいた。

Sono shima ni wa gyogyou wo itonamu hitotachi ga sunde ita.
People who run a fishing industry were living on that island.

12. 朝になると布団を片付ける。

Asa ni naru to futon wo katazukeru.
When morning becomes, we tidy up the futons (Japanese bedding).

13. 私はバラの香りが一番好きだ。

Watashi wa bara no kaori ga ichiban suki da.
I like the scent of roses best.

14. 彼女は非常に忙しい。

Kanojo wa hijou ni isogashii.
She is extremely busy.

15. 彼は営業部の部長です。

Kare wa eigyou bu no buchou desu.
He is the division manager of the business (i.e., sales) division.

16. 毛布をもう一枚欲しいのですが。

Moufu wo mou ichimai hoshii no desu ga.
I would like another blanket, but...

17. 港にたくさんの漁船が浮かんでいる。

Minato ni takusan no gyosen ga ukande iru.
A lot of fishing boats are floating in the harbor.

18. 子供達の一団が遊んでいた。

Kodomotachi no ichidan ga asonde ita.
A group of children was playing.

19. 常に誰かに見られている気がします。

Tsune ni dareka ni mirarete iru ki ga shimasu.
Always I am being watched by someone, I have a feeling.

20. 今夜は寒くなりそうだから、余分に毛布が必要かもしれないね。

Konya wa samuku narisou dakara, yobun ni moufu ga hitsuyou kamoshirenai ne.
Since tonight will reportedly become cold, extra blankets might be necessary, huh.

Chapter 11

New Kanji in this Chapter

# 689 巨 (1)	# 690 輪 (2)	# 691 指 (5)	# 692 廻 (1)
# 693 興 (3)	# 694 深 (3)	# 695 恋 (2)	# 696 職 (2)

Vocabulary List with Mnemonics

from the Kanji Catalogue

巨大 — kyodai = huge; *the Kyoto diet club is huge;* cf. 兄弟 kyoudai = siblings

巨人 — kyojin = a giant; *the Kyoto gingerbread man is a giant*

車輪 — sharin = wheel; *I am sharing a bicycle wheel with my brother*

三輪車 — sanrinsha = tricycle; from san = three + rin = wheel; *Ringo has cool wheels;* + sha = vehicle;

輪 — wa = round shape (ring, circle etc.); *Washington had a round face*

内輪 — uchiwa = family or inner circle; from uchi = inside + wa = circle; *Washington had a round face*

指 — yubi = finger; *after I place this ring on your finger, you will be married*

指輪 — yubiwa = ring; from yubi = finger + wa = circle; *Washington had a round face*

指先 — yubisaki = fingertip; from yubi = finger + saki = end

指差す — yubisasu = to point to (with finger); from yubi = finger + sasu = to point; *Saturn is super, he said, as he pointed at the sky;* cf. 指す sasu = to point

指定席 — shiteiseki = reserved seat; from shitei = designated; *if you repair your sheets with tape, you will be designated a thrifty person;* + seki = seat

指図 — sashizu = direction, command, order; *the order was to recite "sa shi su se so," with the pronunciation of the third character changing to zu*

指す — sasu = to point; *in Saskatchewan the Uber drivers point out the sights;* cf. 指差す yubisasu = to point

輪廻 — rin'ne = samsara, cycle of death and rebirth; *Rene Descartes worried about samsara*

興味 — kyoumi = interest; *I have an interest in Kyouto meat*

Kanji Pronunciations

# 689 – kyo	# 690 – rin, wa	# 691 – yubi, shi, sashi, sa, za	# 692 – ne
# 693 – kyou, kou, oko	# 694 – fuka, buka, shin	# 695 – koi, ren	# 696 – shoku, sho

興す	okosu = to revive, to raise up; _Oklahoma Sue can raise up the dead_
深い	fukai = deep; _the foolish Kaiser jumped into the deep end_
興味深い	kyoumibukai = very interesting; from kyoumi = interest + bukai = fukai = deep
深夜	shinya = dead of night; _the Shinto yak got up in the dead of night_
深刻	shinkoku = serious, grave; _if you see a sheen on your Coke, it's a sign of grave contamination_
恋人	koibito = lover; _the koi (carp) bit off my lover's finger_
恋しい	koishii = longed for, beloved; _the koi [carp] were separated from the Shiites, and they longed for each other_
恋愛	ren'ai = romantic love; _if you are sharing your rent and your ice cream, that's a sign of romantic love_
職	shoku = job; _my job is to shock people_
職業	shokugyou = occupation; _my occupation is to show Kuwaiti people how to make gyoza_

from the Practice Sentences

回りだす	mawaridasu = to begin to turn; from mawaru = to turn + dasu = to emerge
転生	tenshou = reincarnation; _the ten shows that I watched were about reincarnation_
北部	hokubu = northern parts; _my home and my cool boots are in the northern part of the country_
はめる	hameru = to put on, to fit or mold; _I hammered Ruth's ring into shape before I put it on her finger_
天の川	ama no gawa = the Milky Way; from ama = sky + gawa = kawa = river
辞職する	jishoku suru = to resign; _the genius was shocked when he was asked to resign_

from Satori Reader

行事	gyouji = event, function; _we ate gyoza in the Jeep during the event_
ご先祖様	gosenzosama = very honorable ancestor; from go = honorific prefix + senzo = ancestor; _when I sense that I'm in the zone, my ancestors appear to me;_ + sama = honorable suffix
祭る	matsuru = to pray, worship, celebrate; _the mat that Superman put in the room is a good cushion to kneel on when worshipping one's ancestors_
あえて	aete = daring to do something, venturing; _the attitude of entertainers on that television show is one of venturing into risky territory_

あえて言えば
住職

aete ieba = if I had to say; from aete = venturing + ieba = if I say

juushoku = chief priest of a Buddhist temple; *the juke box shocked the chief priest*

Practice Sentences

1. この飛行機は巨大だ。

Kono hikouki wa kyodai da.
This airplane is huge.

2. 車輪が回りだした。

Sharin ga mawaridashita.
The wheel began to turn.

3. 彼女は彼を指差した。

Kanojo wa kare wo yubisashita.
She pointed at him.

4. 輪廻転生は実際にあることで
すか。

Rinne tenshou wa jissai ni aru koto desu ka.
As for samsara reincarnation, is it a truly to-exist thing? (i.e., does it really exist?)

5. これは興味深い。

Kore wa kyoumibukai.
This is deeply interesting.

6. あの人が恋しい。

Ano hito ga koishii.
I miss that person.

7. 彼の職業は医者だ。

Kare no shokugyou wa isha da.
His occupation is medical doctor.

8. 電車の指定席件を買うために
駅で長い間並びますよ。

Densha no shiteiseki ken wo kau tame ni eki de nagai aida narabimasu yo.
In order to buy a train's reserved seat tickets, at the station, for a long time, they line up, for sure.

9. 北部には巨大な山々がある。

Hokubu ni wa kyodai na yamayama ga aru.
As for in the northern part, many huge mountains exist.

10. 息子は早くから政治に興味を
持った。

Musuko wa hayaku kara seiji ni kyoumi wo motta.
The son (i.e., my son) from early (i.e., from an early age) had an interest in politics.

11. 日曜日はたいてい恋人とデー
トをします。

Nichiyoubi wa taitei koibito to deeto wo shimasu.
On Sundays, generally, I do a date with the lover.

12. 彼はメアリーさんの指に指輪
をはめた。

Kare wa mearii san no yubi ni yubiwa wo hameta.
He put the ring on Mary's finger.

13. プールはまん中が一番深いから、気を付けてください。

Puuru wa mannaka ga ichiban fukai kara, ki wo tsukete kudasai.
As for the pool, since the middle is the deepest, please be careful.

14. 社長は辞職します。

Shachou wa jishoku shimasu..
The president will resign.

15. 天の川は巨大である。

Ama no gawa wa kyodai de aru.
The Milky Way is huge.

16. 輪廻転生は信じられなくもない。

Rinne tenshou wa shinjirarenaku mo nai.
As for samsara reincarnation, not to be able to believe even doesn't exist. (i.e., I can't *dis*believe in reincarnation)

17. 私にあれこれ指図するのは、やめてください。

Watashi ni arekore sashizu suru no wa, yamete kudasai.
To me, this and that, as for to give orders, please stop. (i.e., please don't tell me what to do all the time)

18. 東京で働きたいし日本の会社のシステムに興味がある。

Toukyou de hatarakitai shi nihon no kaisha no shisutemu ni kyoumi ga aru.
She would like to labor in Tokyo, and she has an interest in Japanese company's systems.

19. 会議は深夜まで続いた。

Kaigi wa shinya made tsuzuita.
The meeting continued until late at night.

20. 数千人が職を失った。

Suu sen nin ga shoku wo ushinatta.
Thousands of people lost their jobs.

21. 仏教徒は輪廻を信じている。

Bukkyouto wa rinne wo shinjite iru.
Buddhist followers are believing in samsara (the cycle of death & rebirth).

22. 恋愛と結婚は別だ。

Ren'ai to kekkon wa betsu da.
Romantic love and marriage are different.

Supplemental Reading Practice

After completing Chapter 11 of this book, you should be able to read the articles for Day 9 from "Akiko's Foreign Exchange" in *Satori Reader*.

Chapter 12

New Kanji in this Chapter

# 697 伸 (2)	# 698 勧 (2)	# 699 探 (3)	# 700 改 (2)
# 701 関 (3)	# 702 丁 (2)	# 703 寧 (1)	# 704 断 (3)

Vocabulary List with Mnemonics

from the Kanji Catalogue

伸ばす — nobasu, transitive = to grow long, to lengthen, extend, stretch, develop, expand; *since there is no basu (bus), I will extend my stay*

伸びる — nobiru, intransitive = to lengthen or stretch, to be postponed or prolonged; *since there is no biiru (beer), the party will be postponed*

勧告 — kankoku = recommendation, advice; *his recommendation was to drink a can of Coke*; cf. 韓国 kankoku = S. Korea; cf. 広告 koukoku = advertisement

勧める — susumeru = to advise or recommend; *I recommend that Sue attend summer school to get erudite*

探る — saguru = to grope, look for, probe; *the sad guru groped around in his wallet for money*

探す — sagasu = to search or look for; *the sad gasu (gas) station attendant looked for his wallet*

探険 — tanken = exploration, expedition (this can also be spelled 探検 tanken, # 859); *I drove a tank in Kenya during my expedition*

改める — aratameru = to change, renovate, correct; *we are going to renovate a cage for our Arabian tame rooster*

改めて — aratamete = again, anew, another time; *the Arabian tame terriers came again, anew and another time*

関係 — kankei = relationship, connection; *our relationship began in a Canadian cave*

関する — kan suru = to be related to, concerning; *I am related to some Canadians*

関所 — sekisho = checkpoint; *I had a seki (cough) when I went to the show, and they stopped me at a health checkpoint outside the theater*

関わる — kakawaru = to be involved; *if you call a cab, it's warui (bad), since then you will be involved*; cf. かかわらず kakawarazu = regardless

Kanji Pronunciations

# 697 – shin, no	# 698 – kan, susu	# 699 – sagu, saga, tan	# 700 – arata, kai
# 701 – kan, seki, kaka	# 702 – chou, tei	# 703 – nei	# 704 – ta, kotowa, dan

丁目   choume = city block, district of a town; *he chose some men to work in his district*

丁   tei = counter for guns, tools, leaves or cakes of something; *I tape my tools together so that I can use them as counters*

丁寧   teinei = polite, courteous, careful; *be careful not to catch your tail on a nail*

断つ   tatsu = to cut off, discontinue; *when he wants to cut off a conversation, he tatsu (stands up)*

断る   kotowaru = to refuse; *since the koto (Japanese harp) was ruined, he refused to accept it*

中断   chuudan = interruption; *if he chews on the dancer, it will cause an interruption in the show*

from the Practice Sentences

表情   hyoujou = facial expression; *when the Lone Ranger said "Hi-yo Joe," Joe's facial expression brightened*

改正する   kaisei suru = to revise, reform, amend; *following the Kaiser's sage advice, we will reform the laws*

無断で   mudan de = without permission; *don't move the dandelions without permission*

改宗する   kaishuu suru = to convert (to a religion); *the Kaiser will shoot anyone to converts from his religion*

申し出   moushide = a proposal; *he made a proposal that Moses should change the sheets for the debutante*

関心がある   kanshin ga aru = to have an interest or concern; *in Canada, Shinto artifacts are regarded with interest*; cf. 興味がある kyoumi ga aru = to have an interest

しわ   shiwa = wrinkle; *she washed her face every night to prevent wrinkles*

無人島   mujintou = uninhabited island; *I examine the moon, drink gin and stretch my toes on my uninhabited island*

おじぎ   ojigi = a bow (polite gesture); *when he saw the old jeep carrying geese, he bowed to the driver*

from Satori Reader

どうやら   douyara = somehow or other; *if you leave a doughnut in the yard with an apple, somehow or other they will be gone by the next day*

不思議   fushigi = mysterious, strange; *the food that I put out for the sheep and the geese disappeared, which was strange*

起きる   okiru = to occur, to get up, to wake up; *the Okinawa rooster caused the accident to occur*

確実に　kakujitsu ni = certainly; *if you offer cactus plants to that jittery superstar, certainly he will reject them*

非営利　hieiri = nonprofit; *I hear that eighty nonprofit organizations are operating in this town*

英語力　eigoryoku = English ability; from eigo = English + ryoku = power

地元　jimoto = local, hometown; from ji = ground, e.g., jishin = earthquake; + moto = base

とりあえず　toriaezu = for now, for the time being; *the Tories are going to visit the art exhibit at the zoo, for the time being*

そりゃそうだ　soryasou da = sore wa sou da = as for that, it's so = of course it's true

成立　seiritsu = establishment, coming into existence; *the sailor received a written suggestion that he help in the establishment of a center for maritime study*

Practice Sentences

1. 足を伸ばした。
Ashi wo nobashita.
I stretched my legs.

2. 彼は辞職の勧告を受けた。
Kare wa jishoku no kankoku wo uketa.
He received advice to resign.

3. 彼の目は私の顔の表情を探っていた。
Kare no me wa watashi no kao no hyoujou wo sagutte ita.
His eyes were probing my facial expression.

4. 法律が改正された。
Houritsu ga kaisei sareta.
The law was revised.

5. お前には関係はない。
Omae ni wa kankei wa nai.
As for to you, there are no connections. (i.e., it doesn't concern you)

6. お皿を丁寧に洗います。
Osara wo teinei ni araimasu.
I wash the dishes carefully.

7. 彼は無断で仕事を辞めた。
Kare wa mudan de shigoto wo yameta.
He quit work without permission (i.e., without giving notice).

8. 彼女の髪はもとの長さまで伸びた。
Kanojo no kami wa moto no nagasa made nobita.
Her hair lengthened to its original length.

9. 彼は泳ぎに行くことを私達に勧めた。
Kare wa oyogi ni iku koto wo watashitachi ni susumeta.
He suggested that we go swimming.

10. 彼は職を探している。
Kare wa shoku wo sagashite iru.
He is looking for a job.

11. 彼は仏教からキリスト教へ改宗した。

Kare wa bukyou kara kirisuto kyou e kaishuu shita.
He converted from Buddhism to Christianity.

12. その申し出を断った。

Sono moushide wo kotowatta.
I refused that proposal.

13. 政治に関心があるの？

Seiji ni kanshin ga aru no?
Are you interested in politics?

14. 目上の人には、丁寧な言葉を使うものですよ。

Meue no hito ni wa, teinei na kotoba wo tsukau mono desu yo.
As for to superior people, it's to use polite words thing, for sure. (i.e., you should use polite words with superiors)

15. 私はズボンのしわをアイロンで伸ばした。

Watashi wa zubon no shiwa wo airon de nobashita.
I smoothed the wrinkles in my pants with an iron.

16. 私達は彼らとの関係を断っている。

Watashitachi wa karera to no kankei wo tatte iru.
As for us, the relationship with them is being cut (i.e., we've broken off contact). (kotowatte iru, *not* OK; the pronunciation is determined by the context)

17. 彼は医者の勧めでタバコを止めた。

Kare wa isha no susume de tabako wo yameta.
He gave up smoking due to the doctor's advice.

18. 彼は無人島の探険を希望している。

Kare wa mujintou no tanken wo kibou shite iru.
He is hoping to do an exploration of the uninhabited island.

19. 改めて考えると分かんない。

Aratamete kangaeru to wakan'nai.
When I think about it again, I don't understand it.

20. この辺は４丁目だからもう少し先じゃないですか。

Kono hen wa yon choume dakara mou sukoshi saki ja nai desu ka.
Since this area is 4 choume (i.e., the 4th block), isn't it a little further ahead?

21. 私は関わっていない。

Watashi wa kakawatte inai.
I am not involved.

22. その少女は私に丁寧におじぎをした。

Sono shoujo wa watashi ni teinei ni ojigi wo shita.
That little girl bowed to me politely.

Supplemental Reading Practice

After completing Chapter 12 of this book, you should be able to read the articles for Days 10 and 11 from "Akiko's Foreign Exchange" in *Satori Reader*.

Chapter 13

New Kanji in this Chapter

# 705 納 (4)	# 706 得 (3)	# 707 賃 (1)	# 708 税 (1)
# 709 氏 (2)	# 710 慌 (2)	# 711 期 (2)	# 712 素 (3)

Vocabulary List with Mnemonics

from the Kanji Catalogue

納入　nounyuu = payment of taxes, etc, supply (of goods, etc.), delivery; *if there is no nyuusu (news), we have a supply of stories about cats and dogs*

出納　suitou = receipts & dispersements; *we are in the sweet toast business, and these are my receipts and dispersements*

納める　osameru = to pay a bill, to put away (in a closet, etc.), to conclude; *when Osama met Ruth, he was putting away the dishes and paying the bills*

納まる　osamaru = to be settled or solved; *when Osama married Ruth, all of his problems were solved*

納得する　nattoku suru = to acquiesce, agree; *the Nazis were totally cool with the idea and agreed to it*

得る　eru = to get, earn, understand, receive something undesirable (like a punishment); *if you are erudite, you can get, earn and understand things*

得　toku = gain, profit; *it's totally cool that I will make a profit*

得意　tokui = pride, strong point; *my French toast cuisine is my strong point*

家賃　yachin = rent; *here's the rent for the yacht of Mr. Chin*

電車賃　densha chin = train fare; from densha = train + chin = fare; *I hold my fare under my chin while boarding*

税金　zeikin = tax, duty; *the zany king collected taxes*

Kanji Pronunciations

# 705 – nou, tou, osa, na	# 706 – e, u, toku	# 707 – chin	# 708 – zei
# 709 – shi, uji	# 710 – awa, kou	# 711 – ki, go	# 712 – su, so, shirou

中村氏	nakamura shi = Mr. Nakamura; from Nakamura + shi = mister; *the sheep belongs to the mister*
彼氏	kareshi = boyfriend; from kare = he + shi = mister; *the sheep belongs to the mister*
氏名	shimei = full name; *she made up a full name and gave it to the police*
氏	uji = clan; *that uber Jeep belongs to our clan*
慌てる	awateru = to become confused, to panic, to be in a hurry or a frenzy; *awakened by a terrorist, I was in a frenzy*
末期	makki (or matsugo) = the hour of death; *Ma (Mother) praised the king at the hour of his death*; this can also be pronounced "matsugo"; *Matsumoto will go see him at the hour of his death*
時期	jiki = time, season; *I will lend you the Jeep keys at the right season*
期限	kigen = deadline; *the key that Genghis got from the landlord had to be returned by a deadline*
学期	gakki = semester; *the gawky king only attended for one semester*
素晴らしい	subarashii = wonderful, superb; *the sub's Arab captain was a Shiite, and he was wonderful*
素早い	subayai = nimble, speedy; *subatomic particles in yaks eating ice are speedy and nimble*
水素	suiso = hydrogen; *the Swiss and the Soviets agreed that hydrogen could be a good energy source*
要素	youso = component, factor, element; *yogurt was eaten during Soviet times, but it was only one element in the diet*
素人	shirouto = amateur; *using speepdogs and rope to tow the truck was the idea of an amateur*

from the Practice Sentences

最低	saitei = minimum, worst; *the silent table is where there is a minimum of conversation, and it's the worst*
賃金	chingin = wage; *Mr. Chin had gingko trees and paid wages to their caretakers*
国民	kokumin = citizen; from koku = country + min = people
重税	juuzei = heavy taxes; *my jeweler and his zany friends pay heavy taxes*
慌ただしい	awatadashii = hasty; *your decision to awaken me was tadashii (correct) since circumstances made you hasty*
ご笑納ください	goshounou kudasai = please accept; from go = honorable prefix + shonou = to accept; *show no fear and accept the traffic ticket*

期待	kitai = anticipation or hope; *I have <u>anticipation</u> and <u>hope</u> that my <u>kitten's eye</u> will heal*
素数	sosuu = prime number; *the <u>So</u>viet <u>su</u>perintendent was researching <u>prime numbers</u>*
重要な	juuyou na = important; *<u>juice</u> and <u>yogurt</u> are <u>important</u> parts of our diet*
運賃	unchin = fare (transportation); *my <u>Uncle Chin</u> paid my <u>fare</u>*
あり得る	arieru = is possible; (this can also be pronounced ariuru); *that an <u>aristocrat</u> could be <u>erudite</u> is <u>possible</u>*
なし得る	nashieru = to be capable of doing (this can also be pronounced nashiuru); *he started <u>gnashing</u> his teeth when he realized that the <u>erudite</u> guy <u>was capable of doing</u> the work*

from Satori Reader

ナンパする	nanpa suru = to hit on, to pick up a woman on the street; from nanpa = seducer, playboy; *the <u>nanny's Pa</u> is a <u>playboy</u>*
気付く	kizuku = to realize or notice (that this is spelled kiduku when inputting into computers or electronic dictionaries); from ki = spirit + tsuku = to attach
する気はない	suru ki wa nai = I don't have the desire (or intention) to do it; from ki = feeling
気まずい	kimazui = awkward, embarrassing; from ki = feeling + mazui = unappetizing
告白する	kokuhaku suru = to confess, acknowledge; *he <u>confessed</u> that the <u>Coke</u> the <u>hackers</u> were drinking had been stolen*
本音	hon'ne = real intention, what one really thinks; *he has a <u>home</u> in the <u>Netherlands</u>, and his <u>real intention</u> is to return to it*

Practice Sentences

1. 私は彼の説明で納得した。
Watashi wa kare no setsumei de nattoku shita.
I agreed with his explanation.

2. ここでは最低賃金はない。
Koko de wa saitei chingin wa nai.
There is no minimum wage here.

3. 国民は重税に苦しんだ。
Kokumin wa juuzei ni kurushinda.
The citizens suffered by heavy taxation.

4. 彼氏はいますか。
Kareshi wa imasu ka.
Do you have a boyfriend?

5. 私たちは慌ただしい食事を済ませすぐに出発した。
Watashitachi wa awatadashii shokuji wo sumase sugu ni shuppatsu shita.
We finished a hasty meal and left immediately.

6. 二学期は終わった。

Nigakki wa owatta.
The second semester ended.

7. 客からのクレームには、素早く対応しなければならない。

Kyaku kara no kureemu ni wa,
subayaku taiou shinakereba naranai.
As for to from-customer's claims, we
must address them speedily.

8. この紙に住所と氏名を書いてください。

Kono kami ni juusho to shimei wo kaite
kudasai.
Please write the address and full name
on this paper.

9. つまらないものですがご笑納ください。

Tsumaranai mono desu ga goshounou
kudasai.
This is a worthless thing, but please
honorably accept it.

10. 彼は慌てて家を飛び出した。

Kare wa awatete ie wo tobidashita.
He sped out of the house hurriedly.

11. これを期待していたんだ。

Kore wo kitai shite itan da.
I was anticipating this.

12. 料理は得意です。

Ryouri wa tokui desu.
Cooking is my strong point.

13. 教育は重要な要素である。

Kyouiku wa juuyou na youso de aru.
Education is an important component.

14. バスの運賃はいくらですか。

Basu no unchin wa ikura desu ka.
How much is the bus fare?

15. 私たちは税金を納めなければならない。

Watashitachi wa zeikin wo
osamenakereba naranai.
We have to pay taxes.

16. 上田氏が着きましたよ。

Ueda shi ga tsukimashita yo.
Mr. Ueda arrived, for sure.

17. 慌てると無駄になるかもしれない。

Awateru to muda ni naru kamoshirenai.
If you hurry, wasteful will become,
possibly. (i.e., haste makes waste)

18. 冬が近づいてきたので暖かい服を買う時期だ。

Fuyu ga chikazuite kita node atatakai
fuku wo kau jiki da.
Since winter is approaching, it's the
season to buy warm clothing.

19. 僕も素人です。

Boku mo shirouto desu.
I also am an amateur.

13-50

20. それもあり得る。

Sore mo arieru.
That also is possible.

21. 税金をお支払いください。

Zeikin wo oshiharai kudasai.
Please pay the taxes.

Supplemental Reading Practice

After completing Chapter 13 of this book, you should be able to read the articles for Day 12 from "Akiko's Foreign Exchange" in *Satori Reader*.

Chapter 14

New Kanji in this Chapter

# 713 訪 (3)	# 714 加 (2)	# 715 趣 (3)	# 716 湖 (2)
# 717 距 (1)	# 718 環 (1)	# 719 境 (3)	# 720 恵 (3)

Vocabulary List with Mnemonics

from the Kanji Catalogue

訪ねる　　tazuneru = to visit; *I visit the tall zookeeper when he neru (sleeps);* cf.
尋ねる　tazuneru = to ask or inquire

訪問する　houmon suru = to visit; *I visited the doctor to get some hormones*

訪れる　　otozureru = to visit or arrive; *he visited me in order to return the otoscope that I left at the zoo in the cage with the red roosters*

参加　　sanka = participation; *I will participate in drinking Sanka*

加える　　kuwaeru = to add or include; *when they visit Kuwait, erudite people include the library in their itineraries*

趣く　　omomuku = to go or tend toward; *Old Moses attends movies in Kuwait that tend toward comedy*

趣がある　omomuki ga aru = tasteful; *you often chase old mosquitoes in mucky swamps, but the decoration of your home is quite tasteful*

趣味　　shumi = hobby, taste; *he shooed me away because he didn't like my hobby*

湖　　mizuumi = lake; *some of the mizu (water) in the umi (ocean) comes from lakes*

湖水　　kosui = lake water; *I like cold sweet lake water*

距離　　kyori = distance; *the Kyoto soldiers retreated some distance*

環境　　kankyou = environment, surroundings; *if you drop candy wrappers on the street in Kyouto, you will mess up the environment*

境　　sakai = boundary, border; *a policeman will sock you in the eye if you cross the border*

境内　　keidai = the grounds of a temple; *the cave where he died is on the grounds of a temple*

Kanji Pronunciations

# 713 – tazu, hou, otozu	# 714 – ka, kuwa	# 715 – omomu, omomuki, shu	# 716 – mizuumi, ko
# 717 – kyo	# 718 – kan	# 719 – kyou, sakai, kei	# 720 – e, megu, kei

恵む　megumu = to bless, show mercy, give money, bestow a favor, etc.; the _Mexican_ _goose_ in the _movie_ was able to _bestow favors_

知恵　chie = wisdom, intelligence, idea; _if you eat cheese and eggs, you may develop_ _wisdom_

from the Practice Sentences

読書　dokusho = reading; _this document shows signs of extensive reading_

遠距離　enkyori = long distance; _the engineer went to Kyoto to realize his dreams, and he had to travel a long distance_

家庭　katei = home, household; _we have a Catholic tailor in our household_

長距離　chou kyori = long distance; from chou = long; _she chose a long skirt_; + kyori = distance

流れ込む　nagarekomu = to flow into; from nagareru = to flow + komu = to crowd into

歩行　hokou = walking; _the hobo from Colombia is walking down the road_

加速する　kasoku suru = to accelerate; _the car hit a puddle, soaked me and then accelerated_

ぐるっと　gurutto = turning in a circle, going around, encircling; _the guru told me to keep going in a circle_

職場　shokuba = workplace; from shoku = occupation + basho = place

良好　ryoukou = favorable, satisfactory; _Pope Leo says the cold weather is favorable for our hike_

恵まれる　megumareru = to be endowed with; the intransitive form of megumu = to bestow

from Satori Reader

すでに　sude ni = already, too late; _Superman and the dentist's niece already got married_

正直　shoujiki = honesty, integrity; _since I believe in your honesty, I will show you the Jeep keys_

くじける　kujikeru = to lose heart, be dispirited; _the cool jeans that Kennedy ruined were his favorite pants, and he lost heart_

さておき　sateoki = setting aside, leaving to one side; _I'm satisfied with the television station's report on Okinawa, so I'm setting that aside_

母国語　bokokugo = one's native language; from bo = mother, e.g., sobo = grandmother; + koku = country + go = words, e.g., eigo = English

古着　furugi = used clothes; from furui = old + shitagi = underwear

レジ　reji = cash register

申し込む　moushikomu = to apply for; from mousu = to humbly speak + komu = to crowd in

ぴったり　pittari = tightly, exactly, ideally; _the pittance that they're giving you for retiring is exactly what you deserve_

さほど	sahodo = not so, not particularly, not very, not that much; *the <u>satisfaction</u> she gets when I <u>hold the door</u> for her is <u>not that much</u>*
近所	kinjo = neighborhood; *the <u>kindergarten</u> where <u>Joan</u> of Arc worked is in this <u>neighborhood</u>*
発見	hakken = discovery; *the <u>hackers</u> cooperated with <u>Ken</u> and Barbie and made an important <u>discovery</u>*
最高	saikou = the best or highest; *<u>Psycho</u> was <u>the best</u> movie*

Practice Sentences

1. 京都を訪問するべきだよ。
Kyouto wo houmon suru beki da yo.
You should visit Kyoto, for sure.

2. 誰でも参加できる。
Dare demo sanka dekiru.
Anyone can participate.

3. 趣味は読書です。
Shumi wa dokusho desu.
My hobby is reading.

4. この湖はここが一番深い。
Kono mizuumi wa koko ga ichiban fukai.
This lake is deepest here.

5. 遠距離恋愛ってしたことある？
Enkyori ren'ai tte shita koto aru?
Have you ever done the one called "long distance relationship"? (i.e., have you ever had such a relationship?)

6. 子供には幸福な家庭環境が必要だ。
Kodomo ni wa koufuku na katei kankyou ga hitsuyou da.
As for to children, a happy home environment is necessary.

7. 彼はたくさんの知恵をもっている。
Kare wa takusan no chie wo motte iru.
He has a lot of wisdom.

8. 春は冬と夏の間に訪れる。
Haru wa fuyu to natsu no aida ni otozureru.
Spring arrives between winter and summer.

9. スープに塩を加えよう。
Suupu ni shio wo kuwaeyou.
Let's add salt to the soup.

10. 音楽の趣味がいいね。
Ongaku no shumi ga ii ne.
Your taste in music is good, huh.

11. この川はオンタリオ湖に流れ込む。
Kono kawa wa ontario ko ni nagarekomu.
This river flows into Lake Ontario.

12. 長距離の歩行には慣れていない。

Chou kyori no hokou ni wa narete inai.
I am not being accustomed to long distances' walking.

13. 私たちは環境を守るように努力しなければならない。

Watashitachi wa kankyou wo mamoru you ni doryoku shinakereba naranai.
We must make an effort for the sake of protecting the environment.

14. 彼は多くの才能に恵まれている。

Kare wa ooku no sainou ni megumarete iru.
He is endowed by (i.e., with) many talents.

15. 彼らは時々私を訪ねて来た。

Karera wa tokidoki watashi wo tazunete kita.
They visited me occasionally.

16. 車は加速した。

Kuruma wa kasoku shita.
The car accelerated.

17. メキシコの境はどこですか。

Mekishiko no sakai wa doko desu ka.
Where is the Mexican border?

18. この家の趣がいいね。

Kono ie no omomuki ga ii ne.
This house's taste is good, huh.
(suggesting that it is tastefully decorated and gives one a good feeling)

19. 私たちは湖の周りをぐるっと一周歩いてきた。

Watashitachi wa mizuumi no mawari wo gurutto isshuu aruite kita.
We walked one lap all around the lake's circumference and returned.

20. ここからどれくらいの距離ですか。

Koko kara dore kurai no kyori desu ka.
From here, about what distance is it?

21. 恵一さんの職場環境は良好だった。

Keiichi san no shokuba kankyou wa ryoukou datta.
Keiichi's work place environment was favorable.

Supplemental Reading Practice

After completing Chapter 14 of this book, you should be able to read the articles for Days 13, 14 and 15 from "Akiko's Foreign Exchange" in *Satori Reader*.

Chapter 15

New Kanji in this Chapter

# 721 豆 (4)	# 722 腐 (2)	# 723 孤 (1)	# 724 独 (1)
# 725 軍 (1)	# 726 隊 (1)	# 727 奮 (1)	# 728 闘 (2)

Vocabulary List with Mnemonics

from the Kanji Catalogue

豆   mame = bean; *mad men (i.e., people who work on Madison Ave) love beans*

大豆   daizu = soybean; *if an elephant eats too many soybeans, he may die at the zoo*

豆腐   toufu = tofu (bean curd)

腐る   kusaru = to rot, spoil, be corrupted; *I started to eat a cool salad with rhubarb, but it was spoiled*

孤独   kodoku = solitude, isolation; *the co-documentarian lived in solitude and isolation*

独立   dokuritsu = independence; *the document contained written suggestions about how to achieve independence*

独身   dokushin = single, unmarried; *since he consumes a lot of doughnuts and Kool-Aid, that Shinto priest is still unmarried*

軍人   gunjin = soldier; *the soldier keeps a gun in the pocket of his jeans*

海軍   kaigun = navy; *the Kaiser buys guns for his navy*

将軍   shougun = Shogun

軍隊   guntai = army; *the army will need guns to fight the Thai soldiers*

興奮   koufun = excitement; *playing with koalas is fun and leads to excitement*

奮闘   funtou = hard struggle, strenuous effort; *the funny toad made a strenuous effort to catch the fly*

闘う   tatakau = to fight, make war; *the tall taxi driver will kau [buy] a weapon before he fights;* this is more commonly written 戦う tatakau, # 933

from the Practice Sentences

親しい   shitashii = intimate, friendly; *the shita (under)-the-cliff-dwelling Shiites were friendly*

Kanji Pronunciations

# 721 – mame, zu, zuki, tou	# 722 – kusa, fu	# 723 – ko	# 724 – doku
# 725 – gun	# 726 – tai	# 727 – fun	# 728 – tou, tataka

部隊	butai = force, unit, corps; *when the Buddha was tired, a rescue unit came to pick him up*
闘病	toubyou = fighting against an illness; *Tony Blair suffered from B.O. (bacterial overgrowth) and had to fight against his illness*
強力	kyouryoku = powerful; *in Kyouto, Pope Leo made Kool-Aid for his powerful friends*; cf. 協力する kyouryoku suru = to cooperate
むなしい	munashii = empty, fruitless; *under the moon, a Shiite farmer fruitlessly planted seeds*
一生	isshou = a lifetime, all through life; from ichi = one + shou = to live; *I will show my face for as long as I live*
送る	okuru = to spend time, live one's life, send a thing, escort a person; *Oprah's Kool-Aid is rumored to help people live their lives with more zest*

Practice Sentences

1. 帰る途中でお豆腐買ってきてよ。

Kaeru tochuu de otoufu katte kite yo.
To return on the way (i.e., during your return) buy some honorable tofu and come, for sure.

2. 私は親しい友達もなく，孤独な大学時代を過ごした。

Watashi wa shitashii tomodachi mo naku, kodoku na daigaku jidai o sugoshita.
As for me, intimate friends even not existing, I spent a solitary university time.

3. 彼は軍隊に入りたいのだが。

Kare wa guntai ni hairitai no da ga.
He would like to enter the army, but...

4. 大変興奮しました。

Taihen koufun shimashita.
She got very excited.

5. 彼女は病気と闘っている。

Kanojo wa byouki to tatakatte iru.
She is fighting with (i.e., against) a disease.

6. チョコレートはココアの豆から作られる。

Chokoreeto wa kokoa no mame kara tsukurareru.
As for chocolate, it's made from cocoa beans.

7. 父は海軍にいた。

Chichi wa kaigun ni ita.
My father was in the navy.

8. 彼は一生独身で通した。

Kare wa isshou dokushin de tooshita.
He passed through his lifetime as an unmarried person.

9. 彼らはレスキュー部隊が来るまで歌を歌い続けた。

Karera wa resukyuu butai ga kuru made uta wo utaitsuzuketa.
They continued singing songs until the rescue unit came.

10. 牛乳が腐っている。

Gyunyuu ga kusatte iru.
The milk is spoiled.

11. 私の体は興奮で震えた。

Watashi no karada wa koufun de furueta.
My body trembled with excitement.

12. 彼女は孤独な生活を送った。

Kanojo wa kodoku na seikatsu wo okutta.
She lived a solitary life.

13. 豆腐は大豆で作った白くて柔らかい食べ物ですよ。

Toufu wa daizu de tsukutta shirokute yawarakai tabemono desu yo.
Tofu is a from-soybeans-made white and soft food, for sure.

14. その時ほど孤独を感じたことはなかった。

Sono toki hodo kodoku wo kanjita koto wa nakatta.
Compared to that time, I-felt-isolation thing didn't exist. (i.e., at that time, I felt more lonely than at any other time)

15. 日本の軍隊は非常に強力だった。

Nihon no guntai wa hijou ni kyouryoku datta.
Japan's army was extremely powerful.

16. 成功しようと奮闘していて、むなしい気持ちになるときがある。

Seikou shiyou to funtou shite ite, munashii kimochi ni naru koto ga aru.
Doing a difficult struggle to try to succeed, sometimes an empty feeling becomes.

17. 卵は夏には腐りやすい。

Tamago wa natsu ni wa kusari yasui.
Eggs spoil easily in the summer.

18. 長い闘病生活の末、夫は亡くなりました。

Nagai toubyou seikatsu no sue, otto wa nakunarimashita.
The end of a long fight-against-illness life, my husband died.

Chapter 16

New Kanji in this Chapter

# 729 担 (3)	# 730 端 (4)	# 731 固 (2)	# 732 緊 (1)
# 733 愉 (1)	# 734 快 (2)	# 735 札 (3)	# 736 鳩 (1)

Vocabulary List with Mnemonics

from the Kanji Catalogue

担う　　ninau = to carry or bear; *my niece now carries a lot of responsibility*

担当　　tantou = charge (duty); *Tonto is in charge*

担ぐ　　katsugu = to carry on one's shoulder; *the ton katsu (breaded pork) cook bought a goose and carried it on his shoulder*

万端　　bantan = all, everything; *if you ban tanning, then all of the people will leave the beach*

端　　　hashi = end, edge, border; *I marked the edge of the court with hashi (chopsticks)*

端くれ　hashikure = a scrap or piece, an unimportant person; *an unimportant person is smoking hashish and drinking Kool-Aid*

片っ端　katappashi = one side, one edge; *the catapult threw the Padre onto the sheep, which fell over onto one side*

半端　　hanpa = insufficient, incomplete, insincere; *Hansel's Pa was insincere and gave an incomplete explanation about the witch*

頑固な　ganko na = stubborn; *Gandalf has a cold, but he is too stubborn to take medicine*

固定する kotei suru = to rivet, fix, stabilize; *Koreans use tape to stabilize their furniture*

固める　katameru = to harden, solidify, strengthen; *the catapult was described in the meeru (email) as something that would harden our defenses*

固体　　kotai = solid; *the Korean tiger had solid muscles*

緊張　　kinchou = tension, nervousness; *the king chose a psychologist to treat his nervousness*

愉快　　yukai = pleasant, cheerful; *the youthful Kaiser was pleasant and cheerful*

不愉快　fuyukai = unpleasant; *from fu = negation + yukai = pleasant*

Kanji Pronunciations

# 729 – nina, tan, katsu	# 730 – tan, hashi, pashi, pa	# 731 – ko, kata	# 732 – kin
# 733 – yu	# 734 – kokoroyo, kai	# 735 – fuda, sa, satsu	# 736 – hato

快速電車	kaisoku densha = express train; from kaisoku = express; *the Kaiser soaked in the tub on his express train;* + densha = train
全快する	zenkai suru = to recover completely (from illness); *practicing Zen and flying kites allowed me to recover completely*
快い	kokoroyoi = pleasant, comfortable; *because his kokoro (heart) is yoi (good), he is pleasant and comfortable*
値札	nefuda = price tag; *in the Netherlands, my foolish daughter changed the price tags on some merchandise;* cf. 荷札 nifuda = tag, label
千円札	sen'en satsu = 1,000 yen bill; from sen'en = 1,000 yen + satsu = bill; *I paid for a satisfying Superman novel with a 1,000-yen bill*
鳩	hato = pigeon, dove; *the pigeons eat ham and toast*

from the Practice Sentences

負担	futan =responsibility, burden, charge; *the foolish tanning center owner had to take responsibility for causing skin cancer*
断固	danko = resolute; *the dancer who went to Colombia was resolute about winning the dance contest*
札	fuda = label, tag, sign, game card; *my foolish daughter wears a sign on her clothes*
分担する	buntan suru = to share; *Daniel Boone had a tank of gasoline which he shared*
固ゆで	katayude = hard-boiled; from kata = hard; *the catapult was used to harden our defense;* + yuderu = to boil
緊急	kinkyuu = emergency; *the king's cute daughter had a medical emergency*
直前	chokuzen = just before; *he choked the Zen monk just before the funeral*
閉店	heiten = closed store, closing up a store (for the day), going out of business; *I hate it when my tendonitis forces me to close the store early*
中途	chuuto = in the middle, half-way; *as I was chewing my toast, he burst into the middle of my breakfast*

from Satori Reader

準備万端	junbi bantan = every preparation, suggesting that one is completely ready; from junbi = preparation + bantan = all, everything
あっという間に	atto iu mani = in the blink of an eye; *a tow truck driver can take your money in the blink of an eye*
つるむ	tsurumu = to go with a companion, to hang out with; *I left my tsuitcase (suitcase) in my room while I hung out with my friends*

孤軍   kogun = isolated force; *a corrupt goon is using isolated force to extort money from business owners in isolated towns*

孤軍奮闘   kogun funtou = fighting alone; from kogun = isolated force + funtou = hard struggle

荷札   nifuda = tag, label, sign; *while kneeling, my foolish daughter changed the labels on some merchandise*; cf. 値札 nefuda = price tag

Practice Sentences

1. 費用は彼の負担になるだろう。

Hiyou wa kare no futan ni naru darou.
The expense will probably become his responsibility.

2. 旅行の用意は準備万端です。

Ryokou no youi wa junbi bantan desu.
The trip's preparation is preparation everything (i.e., everything is ready).

3. 彼は断固として断った。

Kare wa danko to shite kotowatta.
In the capacity of resolute, he refused (i.e., he refused resolutely).

4. 何をそんなに緊張してんの？

Nani wo sonna ni kinchou shiten no?
On what, so much anxiety are you doing? (i.e., what are you so nervous about?)

5. 彼は愉快なやつだ。

Kare wa yukai na yattsu da.
He's a cheerful fellow.

6. 彼女は店の入り口に閉店の札をかけた。

Kanojo wa mise no iriguchi ni heiten no fuda wo kaketa.
She hung a closed-store sign at the entrance of the store.

7. 鳩は飛んでいった。

Hato wa tonde itta.
The pigeon flew away. (cf. 飛んでいた tonde ita = was flying)

8. タクシー代は君と分担しよう。

Takushii dai wa kimi to buntan shiyou.
I shall share the taxi fare with you.

9. 彼にスピーチを頼んだら、快い返事がもらえた。

Kare ni supiichi wo tanondara, kokoroyoi henji ga moraeta.
When I requested a speech from him, I was able to receive a pleasant reply.

10. 中途半端が一番悪いよ。

Chuuto hanpa ga ichiban warui yo.
As for half-way incomplete (i.e., half measures), they are the worst, for sure.

11. 卵は固ゆでにして下さい。

Tamago wa katayude ni shite kudasai.
Please make the eggs hard-boiled.

12. 試合の直前はいつも緊張する。

Shiai no chokuzen wa itsumo kinchou suru.
As for a game's just-before, I always do anxiety. (i.e., I'm always nervous just before a game)

13. パーティーで愉快に過ごしましたか。

Paatii de yukai ni sugoshimashita ka.
At the party, did you spend (time) cheerfully?

14. この一万円札を見つけた。

Kono ichiman'en satsu wo mitsuketa.
I found this 10,000 yen bill.

15. 鳩山さんは社宅に住んでいるらしい。

Hatoyama san wa shataku ni sunde iru rashii.
It seems that Ms. Hatoyama is living in company housing.

16. 父親は息子の体を担いで部屋から運び出した。

Chichi oya wa musuko no karada wo katsuide heya kara hakobidashita.
The father picked up his son on his shoulder and carried him out of the room.

17. 私は端くれ者だ。

Watashi wa hashikure mono da.
I am an unimportant person.

18. 彼女は頑固です。

Kanojo wa ganko desu.
She is stubborn.

19. 緊急です。

Kinkyuu desu.
It's an emergency.

20. なんて愉快な話でしょう！

Nante yukai na hanashi deshou!
Such a thing, it's probably a cheerful story! (i.e. what a pleasant story)

21. 全部のかばんに荷札をつけなさい。

Zenbu no kaban ni nifuda wo tsukenasai.
Attach labels to all of the bags.

22. 白い鳩が歩道にいます。

Shiroi hato ga hodou ni imasu.
There is a white dove on the sidewalk.

Supplemental Reading Practice

After completing Chapter 16 of this book, you should be able to read the articles for Day 16 from "Akiko's Foreign Exchange" in *Satori Reader*.

Chapter 17

New Kanji in this Chapter

# 737 艦 (1)	# 738 砲 (2)	# 739 現 (2)	# 740 漏 (2)
# 741 根 (2)	# 742 棚 (2)	# 743 餅 (2)	# 744 銭 (2)

Vocabulary List with Mnemonics

from the Kanji Catalogue

軍艦 — gunkan = warship, battleship; *guns from Canada were deployed on a battleship*

鉄砲 — teppou = gun; *in Texas, the police carry guns*

大砲 — taihou = cannon; *I'm tired of holding onto this cannon*

砲火 — houka = gunfire; *homes in California sometimes get damaged by gunfire*

現実 — genjitsu = reality, fact; *Genghis Khan was a jittery superstar, and that's a fact*

現金 — genkin = cash; *Genghis was a king who always paid in cash*

現れる — arawareru = to appear or show up; *the Arab warrior owned some red roosters, and he always showed up to feed them*

漏らす — morasu = to let out, to omit; *Moses was a rascal from Sudan who let out the dogs and omitted feeding them*

漏電 — rouden = electric short circuit; *the robot that assisted the dentist developed a short circuit*

漏水 — rousui = water leak; *our roses smelled sweeter this year, since they benefited from a water leak in the sprinkler system*

屋根 — yane = roof; *yaks in the Netherlands sleep under roofs*

棚 — tana = shelf; *we keep our tangy apples on this shelf*

餅 — mochi = Japanese rice cake; *I want more cheese to eat with my Japanese rice cakes*

煎餅 — senbei = rice cracker; *after the senator bathes, he wants a rice cracker*

小銭 — kozeni = coin, small change; from ko = small + zeni = money; *when Zen monks go out to eat, they need money*

金銭 — kinsen = money; *the king sent me some money*

Kanji Pronunciations

# 737 – kan	# 738 – hou, pou	# 739 – gen, arawa	# 740 – mo, rou
# 741 – ne, kon	# 742 – tana, dana	# 743 – mochi, bei	# 744 – zeni, sen

| 一銭 | issen = 0.01 yen; from i = one + sen = money; *the <u>sen</u>ator needs <u>money</u> for her campaign* |

from the Practice Sentences

実現	jitsugen = implementation, materialization, realization; *in the jiu <u>jitsu</u> tournament, <u>Gen</u>ghis achieved the <u>realization</u> of his dream*
無鉄砲	muteppou = reckless; *influenced by the <u>moo</u>n in <u>Te</u>xas, the <u>po</u>pe became <u>reckless</u>*; cf. 鉄砲 teppou = gun
非現実的	higenjitsuteki = unrealistic; from hi = negative; *the <u>heat</u> has <u>negative</u> effects on me*; + genjitsu = reality + teki = related to
漏れる	moreru = to leak; *after <u>Mo</u>ses bought the <u>red rooster</u>, the barn began <u>to leak</u>*
漏れ	more = a leak; from moreru = to leak
根	ne = root, basis; *in the <u>Ne</u>therlands, the <u>root</u> of our social structure is fraternal love*
金銭面	kinsenmen = money aspect; from kinsen = money + men = mask or face; *the <u>men</u> wore <u>masks</u>*
親子	oyako = parent and child; from oya = parent + ko = child
備える	sonaeru = to be equipped with, to prepare; *when <u>sonar</u> was introduced, <u>eru</u>dite people made sure that warships <u>were equipped</u> with it*
ひび	hibi = crack, fissure; *some <u>Hi</u>malayan <u>bees</u> are living in that <u>crack</u>*
他人	ta'nin = stranger; *I met a <u>stranger</u> in the <u>tanning</u> booth*

from Satori Reader

経理	keiri = management, accounting; *<u>Kay</u> was <u>eating</u> a lot of fast food while she was trying to get into <u>management</u>*
学ぶ	manabu = to study or learn; *the <u>manager</u> of the <u>booze</u> factory was <u>studying</u> at night*
以外	igai = with the exception of; *<u>with the exception of</u> the <u>easy guys</u>, I can't beat anyone at chess*
一気に	ikkini = in one gulp, in one breath; from ichi = one + ki = spirit, air
豆鉄砲	mamedeppou = pea shooter; from mame = bean + deppou = teppou = gun
食らう	kurau = to receive (a blow), to eat or drink; *in <u>Ku</u>wait, <u>Raul</u> Castro <u>ate</u> too much and <u>received</u> a blow as a result*
寄付	kifu = contribution, donation; *I can <u>keep food</u> in the house, thanks to <u>donations</u> from my friends*
作業	sagyou = work, operations, manufacturing; *this <u>sack</u> of <u>gyouza</u> is the result of our <u>work</u>*

バイト	baito = part-time work, an abbreviation of アルバイト arubaito = part-time work
マジ	maji = serious, an abbreviation of 真面目 majime = diligent, serious, earnest
ぼた餅	botamochi = azuki bean mochi; from bota = azuki beans; *that boy has a talent for preparing azuki beans*; + mochi = rice cake
棚からぼた餅だ	tana kara botamichi da = it's azuki bean mochi from the shelf = it's good luck
金銭的	kinsenteki = financially; from kinsen = money + teki = related to

Practice Sentences

1. その軍艦は大砲８門を備えている。
Sono gunkan wa taihou hachi mon wo sonaete iru.
That warship is being equipped (i.e., it is equipped) with 8 cannon.

2. 夢が実現した。
Yume ga jitsugen shita.
The dream came true.

3. 屋根の漏れは大変です。
Yane no more wa taihen desu.
The leak in the roof is terrible.

4. 彼は棚に頭をぶつけた。
Kare wa tana ni atama wo butsuketa.
He hit his head on a shelf.

5. 日本ではお正月にお餅を食べる習慣があります。
Nihon de wa oshougatsu ni omochi wo taberu shuukan ga arimasu.
In Japan, on New Year's, there is a custom to eat honorable mochi.

6. すみませんが小銭がありません。
Sumimasen ga kozeni ga arimasen.
I'm sorry, but I don't have any small money.

7. あいつは無鉄砲な男だ。
Aitsu wa muteppou na otoko da.
That fellow over there is a reckless man.

8. それは大きくて黒いアメリカの軍艦だった。
Sore wa ookikute kuroi amerika no gunkan datta.
It was a big black American warship.

9. それは非現実的だ。
Sore wa higenjitsuteki da.
That is unrealistic.

10. パイプからガスが漏れているようです。
Paipu kara gasu ga morete iru you desu.
Gas seems to be leaking from the pipe.

11. 彼は根はいい人だ。

Kare wa ne wa ii hito da.
As for him, as for the root, it's a good person. (i.e., he's a good person at heart)

12. 本棚から本を1冊取る。

Hondana kara hon wo issatsu toru.
He will take a book from the bookshelf.

13. 私はお茶を飲むときはお煎餅を食べるのが好きです。

Watashi wa ocha wo nomu toki wa osenbei wo taberu no ga suki desu.
As for me, as for when I drink honorable tea, I like to eat rice crackers.

14. 私たちは金銭面で彼を頼りにしている。

Watashitachi wa kinsen men de kare wo tayori ni shite iru.
As for us, of money-aspect, on him we are doing in a reliant way. (i.e., we are relying on him financially)

15. 彼は鉄砲を掃除している。

Kare wa teppou wo souji shite iru.
He is cleaning a gun.

16. 港に軍艦が浮かんでいる。

Minato ni gunkan ga ukande iru.
A warship is floating in the harbor.

17. 彼女は現れなかった。

Kanojo wa arawarenakatta.
She didn't show up.

18. コップにひびが入って中身が漏れている。

Koppu ni hibi ga haitte nakami ga morete iru.
There's a crack in the cup, and the contents are leaking.

19. 彼女は彼の息の根を止めた。

Kanojo wa kare no iki no ne wo tometa.
She stopped his breath's root (i.e., she suffocated him).

20. 棚の一番上にあるものに手が届かない。

Tana no ichiban ue ni aru mono ni te ga todokanai.
The hand does not reach to the things that exist at the very top of the shelf. (i.e., I can't reach them)

21. お餅とお煎餅と、どちらの方が好き？

Omochi to osenbei to, dochira no hou ga suki?
Honorable rice cakes vs. honorable rice crackers, which do you like better?

22. 親子の中でも金銭は他人。

Oyako no naka demo kinsen wa tanin.
Even though in the middle of parent and child, money is a stranger. (i.e., business and family ties don't mix well)

Supplemental Reading Practice

After completing Chapter 17 of this book, you should be able to read the articles for Days 17 and 18 from "Akiko's Foreign Exchange" in *Satori Reader*.

Chapter 18

New Kanji in this Chapter

# 745 舍 (2)	# 746 叫 (2)	# 747 血 (3)	# 748 圧 (1)
# 749 抜 (3)	# 750 焦 (3)	# 751 鳴 (2)	# 752 組 (4)

Vocabulary List with Mnemonics

from the Kanji Catalogue

田舎   inaka = rural area, hometown; *when he was inactive, Karl Marx would go to his hometown*

校舎   kousha = school building; *that Colombian shack used to be a school building*

叫ぶ   sakebu = to shout, yell, scream; *after drinking sake and other booze, he started to scream*

絶叫   zekkyou = a scream or shriek; *I heard a scream from a Zen temple in Kyouto*

血圧   ketsuatsu = blood pressure; *if you put ketchup in the soup at Superman's house, it may raise his blood pressure*

血   chi = blood; *my cholesterol is so high that my blood is like cheese*

気圧   kiatsu = atmospheric pressure; *from ki = air or spirit + atsu = pressure*

圧力   atsuryoku = pressure; *from atsu = pressure; I feel pressure at Superman's house; + ryoku = force*

抜てきする   batteki suru = to select; *some batty techies selected the entertainment for tonight*

抜く   nuku = to extract, omit, outrun or surpass; *if I nuke you, that will extract all of your corks*

抜ける   nukeru = to come out or come off, to fall out, to escape; *the new kettle was ruined when it fell out of the box*

抜きに   nuki ni = without (omitting); *you can't be nuking my niece without permission*

焦る   aseru = to be in a hurry or impatient, to be flustered; *when the asses see the rooster, they get flustered*

焦げる   kogeru = to be scorched or burned; *the Korean guest bumped into the rooster with his cigar, and it got burned*

Kanji Pronunciations

# 745 – ka, sha	# 746 – sake, kyou	# 747 – ketsu, chi, ji	# 748 – atsu
# 749 – ba, batsu, nu	# 750 – ase, ko, shou	# 751 – na, mei	# 752 – so, ku, kumi, gumi

18-67

焦点   shouten = focus or central issue; *I will <u>show</u> <u>ten</u> slides that highlight the <u>central issue</u> or <u>focus</u> of my talk*

鳴る   naru = to chime, ring or sound; *the <u>Na</u>zis came to my <u>room</u> and <u>rang</u> the bell*

鳴く   naku = to chirp, bark or cry (animal sounds); *in <u>Na</u>rnia the <u>Kool</u>-Aid is so tasteless that it makes animals <u>cry</u>*

組む   kumu = to fold arms or legs, to assemble, to make a plan, to partner with; *under a <u>cool</u> moon, we <u>assembled</u>, <u>folded</u> <u>our</u> <u>arms</u> and <u>made</u> <u>a plan</u>*

組   kumi = group, team, school class; *my <u>class</u> drinks <u>Kool</u>-Aid with its <u>meals</u>*

番組   bangumi = TV or radio program; *I saw a <u>TV program</u> about a <u>band</u> that eats <u>gummy</u> snacks*

from the Practice Sentences

放火する   houka suru = to commit arson; *someone <u>committed</u> <u>arson</u> on my <u>home</u> in <u>California</u>*

血圧計   ketsuatsukei = blood pressure monitor; from ketsuatsu = blood pressure + kei = to measure, e.g., tokei = clock

数値   suuchi = numerical value or reading; *<u>Superman</u> <u>cheated</u> by understating the <u>numerical</u> <u>reading</u> on the odometer*

前歯   maeba = front tooth; from mae = front + ha = ba = tooth

輸血   yuketsu = blood transfusion; from yu = to transport, e.g., 輸入 yunyuu = to import; + ketsu = blood, e.g., ketsuatsu = blood pressure

叫び声   sakebigoe = a scream; from sakebu = to scream + koe = goe = voice

高血圧   kouketsuatsu = high blood pressure; from kou = high, e.g., koukou = high school; + ketsuatsu = blood pressure

耳鳴り   miminari = ear ringing; from mimi = ears + naru = to ring

断片   danpen = piece; *the <u>dancer's</u> <u>pen</u> fell and broke into <u>pieces</u>*

組み合わせる   kumiawaseru = to match; from kumu = to partner with + awaseru = to combine or harmonize

育つ   sodatsu = to grow up or be brought up; *I was <u>brought</u> <u>up</u> to put <u>soda</u> in my <u>tsoup</u> (soup)*

守り抜く   mamorinuku = to hold fast or protect to the end; from mamoru = to protect + nuku = to surpass

怒鳴る   donaru = to shout or yell; *<u>Donald</u> Duck came into the <u>room</u> and started <u>yelling</u>*

from Satori Reader

リスニング力   risuningu ryoku = listening ability

英文読解 — eibun dokkai = English reading comprehension; from eigo = English + bun = sentence; *Daniel Boone spoke in complete sentences*; + dokkai = reading comprehension

以来 — irai = since (a point in time); *I've been eating eels with rice since I was a child*

前向き — maemuki = facing forward, positive; from mae = front + muku = to face toward

抜き打ち — nukiuchi = drawing a sword and striking in the same stroke; suddenly, without warning; from nuku = to extract + utsu = to strike

世 — yo = world; *yogis are trying to save the world*

割と — wari to = relatively, comparatively; *the warrior's tone was relatively mild*

冷静 — reisei = calm, composure; *after the boat race, the sailors regained their composure*

土地 — tochi = land, place; *tomatoes are cheap in my homeland*

Practice Sentences

1. 彼は校舎に放火した。
Kare wa kousha ni houka shita.
He did arson to the schoolhouse (i.e., he set it on fire).

2. 彼は叫び始めた。
Kare wa sakebihajimeta.
He began to shout.

3. 血圧計の数値はなんですか。
Ketsuatsu kei no suuchi wa nan desu ka.
What is the blood pressure monitor's reading?

4. 前歯が抜けました。
Maeba ga nukemashita.
The front tooth fell out.

5. 魚が真っ黒に焦げた。
Sakana ga makkuro ni kogeta.
The fish is burnt black.

6. 怒鳴らないで。
Donaranaide.
Don't shout.

7. どんな番組が好きですか。
Donna bangumi ga suki desu ka.
What kind of TV programs do you like?

8. 田舎に住んでいます。
Inaka ni sunde imasu.
I am living in the countryside.

9. 叫び声が聞こえた。
Sakebigoe ga kikoeta.
A scream was audible.

10. 輸血が必要です。
Yuketsu ga hitsuyou desu.
A blood transfusion is necessary.

11. 彼は高血圧だと思います。
Kare wa kouketsuatsu da to omoimasu.
As for him, it's high blood pressure, I think. (i.e., I think he has high blood pressure)

12. 昨日は夕食を抜いた。
Kinou wa yuushoku wo nuita.
Yesterday I skipped dinner.

13. 何をそんなに焦ってるの？
Nani wo sonna ni asetteru no?
On what are you so being so flustered?
(i.e., what is making you so flustered?)

14. 耳鳴りがします。
Miminari ga shimasu.
Ear ringing does (i.e. my ears are ringing).

15. この断片は組み合わせられない。
Kono danpen wa kumiawaserarenai.
This piece is not able to match. (referring to a puzzle)

16. 私は田舎で生まれ育ちました。
Watashi wa inaka de umare sodachimashita.
I was born and brought up in the countryside.

17. 彼女は私が悪いと絶叫した。
Kanojo wa watashi ga warui to zekkyou shita.
She screamed that I am bad.

18. ナイフで切って血が出たんです。
Naifu de kitte chi ga detan desu.
Cutting with a knife, blood emerged.

19. 彼は私に圧力をかけた。
Kare wa watashi ni atsuryoku wo kaketa.
He put pressure on me.

20. 彼は約束を守り抜いた。
Kare wa yakusoku wo mamorinuita.
He held fast to the promise.

21. その花にカメラの焦点を合わせて。
Sono hana ni kamera no shouten wo awasete.
To that flower adjust the camera's focus.

22. 鳥が鳴いた。
Tori ga naita.
The bird sang.

23. 私はテニスで彼女と組んだ。
Watashi wa tenisu de kanojo to kunda.
I partnered with her in tennis.

Supplemental Reading Practice

After completing Chapter 18 of this book, you should be able to read the articles for Day 19 from "Akiko's Foreign Exchange" in *Satori Reader*.

Chapter 19

New Kanji in this Chapter

# 753 織 (3)	# 754 鶏 (2)	# 755 羽 (4)	# 756 演 (1)
# 757 奏 (2)	# 758 描 (3)	# 759 完 (1)	# 760 了 (1)

Vocabulary List with Mnemonics

from the Kanji Catalogue

組織   soshiki = organization; *the people in that <u>organization</u> are <u>so chic</u>*

羽織   haori = short jacket worn over kimono; *she keeps <u>Ha</u>waiian <u>Oreos</u> in the pockets of her <u>short jacket</u>*

織る   oru = to weave; *she <u>weaves</u> cloth in an <u>open room</u>*

鶏   niwatori = chicken; *the <u>niwa</u> (garden) contains a <u>tori</u> (bird) which is a <u>chicken</u>*

鶏肉   keiniku = chicken meat; from kei = chicken; *that <u>chicken</u> was raised in a <u>cage</u>*; + niku = meat

羽   hane = feather, wing; *I saw a bird with <u>feathers</u> at <u>Haneda</u> Airport*

羽毛   umou = down, feathers; *<u>Uru</u>guay has <u>more feathers</u> on its birds, compared to Paraguay*

一羽   ichiwa = one bird; from ichi = one + wa = bird; *that <u>bird</u> ate my <u>waffle</u>*

演奏   ensou = musical performance; *her <u>performance</u> begins at the <u>end</u> of the drum <u>solo</u>*

演じる   enjiru = to perform or act; *an <u>engineer</u> and his <u>rooster</u> will <u>perform</u>*

奏でる   kanaderu = to play a stringed instrument; *a <u>Canadian debutante</u> named <u>Ruth plays a stringed instrument</u>*

描く   egaku (also pronounced kaku) = to draw, paint, depict, describe; this reminds us of 絵 e = picture + gaku = 書く kaku = to write

描写する   byousha suru = to describe; *he <u>described</u> the <u>B.O.</u> (body odor) coming from the <u>shack</u>*

完了する   kanryou suru = to finish; *I <u>finished</u> drinking the soda in the <u>can</u> that Pope <u>Leo</u> gave me*

完全な   kanzen na = perfect, entire; *that <u>Ca</u>nadian <u>Zen</u> monk is nearly <u>perfect</u>*

完成   kansei = completion; *in <u>Ca</u>nada, a new <u>Safeway</u> store is reaching <u>completion</u>*

Kanji Pronunciations

# 753 – ori, o, shiki	# 754 – niwatori, kei	# 755 – hane, ha, wa, u	# 756 – en
# 757 – kana, sou	# 758 – ega, byou, ka	# 759 – kan	# 760 – ryou

終了	shuuryou = ending, termination; *if you shoot Pope Leo, that will cause a termination of our relationship*
了解	ryoukai = agreement, consent, understanding; *Pope Leo and the Kaiser reached an agreement*

from the Practice Sentences

強化する	kyouka suru = to strengthen, fortify; *in Kyouto, calcium tablets are fortified with Vitamin D*; cf. 許可 kyoka = permission, approval
四角	shikaku = square; from shi = four + kaku = corner
任務	ninmu = duty, mission; *the ninja on the moon do their duty*
織物	orimono = textiles; from oru = to weave + mono = things
演説する	enzetsu suru = to make a speech; *I made a speech about an enzyme, but etiquette required me to share credit with Sue*
開演	kaien = start of a performance; *the Kaiser entered just before the start of the performance*
演奏会	ensoukai = concert or recital; from ensou = performance + kai(gi) = meeting
はた	hata = loom; *that Hawaiian guy has a talent for weaving on a loom*

Practice Sentences

1. 私たちは組織を強化しなければならない。

Watashitachi wa soshiki wo kyouka shinakereba naranai.
We must strengthen the organization.

2. 外には鶏が2羽いる。

Soto ni wa niwatori ga niwa iru.
There are two chickens outside.

3. 今演奏しなければならない。

Ima ensou shinakereba naranai.
I have to do a performance now.

4. 四角を描いてくれ。

Shikaku wo kaite kure.
Draw a square for me. (this could also be pronounced egaite kure)

5. 彼は任務を完了した。

Kare wa ninmu wo kanryou shita.
He finished his duty (i.e., mission).

6. あの店にはたくさんの織物が置いてあります。

Ano mise ni wa takusan no orimono ga oite arimasu.
As for to that store over there, a lot of textiles are placed. (i.e., they stock a lot of fabric)

7. 彼は大勢の前で演説した。

Kare wa oozei no mae de enzetsu shita.
He did (i.e., gave) a speech in front of a crowd (of people).

8.鶏に毎日えさをやる。

Niwatori ni mainichi esa wo yaru.
I give food to the chickens every day.

9.鳥が一羽、空高く飛んでいる。

Tori ga ichiwa, sora takaku tonde iru.
A bird is flying high in the sky.

10.会議は終了しました。

Kaigi wa shuuryou shimashita.
The meeting ended.

12.そこで起こったことを正確に描写した。

Soko de okotta koto wo seikaku ni byousha shita.
He accurately described what happened there.

13.ギターを演奏するのは楽しい。

Gitaa wo ensou suru no wa tanoshii.
It's pleasant to play the guitar.

14.その羽まくらは高そうです。

Sono hane makura wa takasou desu.
That feather pillow looks expensive.

15.彼女は彼の笑顔に完全にだまされた。

Kanojo wa kare no egao ni kanzen ni damasareta.
She was completely fooled by his smiling face.

16.開演は何時ですか。

Kaien wa nanji desu ka.
What time is the start of the performance?

17.妹は雪だるまの絵を描いた。

Imouto wa yuki daruma no e wo kaita.
Little sister drew a picture of a snowman. (egaita, also OK)

18.ダチョウは羽はあるが飛べない。

Dachou wa hane wa aru ga tobenai.
An ostrich has wings, but it can't fly.

11.鶏が先か、卵が先か。

Niwatori ga saki ka, tamago ga saki ka.
Which came first, the chicken or the egg?

19.いつ完成したのですか。

Itsu kansei shita no desu ka.
When was it finished?

20.了解です。

Ryoukai desu.
I agree.

21.祖母ははたを織るのが好きだ。

Sobo wa hata wo oru no ga suki da.
My grandmother likes to weave on a loom.

22.演奏会が始まろうとしている。

Ensoukai ga hajimarou to shite iru.
The concert is trying (i.e., about to) start.

Chapter 20

New Kanji in this Chapter

# 761 純 (1)	# 762 格 (3)	# 763 姿 (2)	# 764 派 (2)
# 765 遣 (3)	# 766 浜 (2)	# 767 凧 (1)	# 768 揚 (2)

Vocabulary List with Mnemonics

from the Kanji Catalogue

単純な   tanjun na = simple; *sorting through this tan junk is simple, since most of it is discarded khaki uniforms*

格子   koushi = lattice work or grill; *the coats were decorated with sheepskin strips in a lattice or grill pattern*

格好   kakkou = form, appearance, suitability; *he carved some coral into jewelry that had an attractive appearance*

性格   seikaku = personality, disposition; *when sane people kaku (write), their writing reflects their personalities;* cf. 正確 seikaku = accurate

合格する   goukaku suru = to pass an exam or be accepted to a school; *if she can go to cactus country and interview, she will be accepted to the University of Arizona*

姿   sugata = figure, shape, condition; *the sugar in that tavern is in the shape of cubes*

容姿   youshi = appearance, looks; *the appearance of the yogi's sheep is bad;* cf. 様子 yousu = condition, state

姿勢   shisei = posture, stance; *the sheepdog in the Safeway store adopted a threatening stance*

派遣する   haken suru = to send (a person), to dispatch; *during the harvest, Ken would send Barbie to watch the workers*

派手   hade = showy, gaudy, colorful; *the Hawaiian debutante wore a showy costume*

立派な   rippa na = splendid, impressive; *although there is a rip in your pants, your outfit is splendid*

遣わす   tsukawasu = to dispatch; *when my tsuitcase (suitcase) was taken by the wacky superintendent, I dispatched someone to find it*

Kanji Pronunciations

# 761 – jun	# 762 – kou, ka, kaku	# 763 – sugata, shi	# 764 – ha, pa
# 765 – ken, tsuka, zuka	# 766 – hama, hin	# 767 – tako	# 768 – a, you

気遣う   kizukau = to care for, worry, pay attention (spelled kidukau in electronic dictionaries); *if you wear your <u>ki</u>mono to the <u>zoo</u> and are approached by a <u>cow</u>, <u>pay attention</u>*

海浜   kaihin = seaside; *the <u>Kai</u>ser met some <u>Hin</u>dus at the <u>seaside</u>*

凧   tako = kite; *I eat <u>taco</u>s while flying my <u>kite</u>*

浜辺   hamabe = beach; *the <u>Ha</u>waiian <u>man</u>sion is <u>be</u>st because it's near a <u>beach</u>*

揚げる   ageru = to hoist, to fly a kite, to fry in deep fat; *after I <u>fry</u> food <u>in</u> <u>deep fat</u>, I <u>ageru</u> (raise) it with tongs and put it on a plate*

from the Practice Sentences

価格   kakaku = price, value; *<u>ca</u>bbage, <u>ca</u>ctus and <u>Kool</u>-Aid are sold for a low <u>price</u>*

下着   shitagi = underwear; from shita = below + giru = kiru = to wear clothes

言葉遣い   kotobazukai = speech customs, word use; from kotoba = word + kizukau = to care for

横浜   Yokohama; from yoko = side + hama = beach

揚げ物   agemono = deep-fried food; from ageru = to deep fry + mono = thing

出席者   shusseki sha = attendee; from shusseki suru = to attend + sha = person

純金   junkin = pure gold; from jun = pure; *flowers have especially <u>pure</u> colors in <u>June</u>*; + kin = gold

飛ばす   tobasu = to fly, speed, skip over; *<u>To</u>ny Blair's <u>basu</u> (bus) was <u>speeding</u> down the road*

心遣い   kokorozukai = thoughtfulness, care and consideration; from kokoro = heart + kizukau = to care for

雨上り   ameagari = after the rain; from ame = rain + agaru = to finish; *the balloon will <u>agaru</u> (rise) after we <u>finish</u> adding helium*

うぬぼれる   unuboreru = to be conceited; *after the <u>unu</u>sual <u>bore</u> got a <u>red</u> <u>rooster</u>, he seemed more <u>conceited</u> than usual*

from Satori Reader

ようこそ   youkoso = welcome, nice to see you!; *we <u>welcome</u> guests with <u>yo</u>gurt from <u>Co</u>lombia, which is low in <u>so</u>dium*

話題   wadai = topic, subject; *after the <u>war</u>lord <u>di</u>ed, he was the <u>topic</u> of many conversations*

思考   shikou = thought, consideration; *he puts a lot of <u>thought</u> into protecting his <u>sheep</u> from the <u>cold</u>*

回路   kairo = circuit, cycle, process; *the <u>kite</u> <u>rose</u> and fell in a kind of <u>cycle</u>*

バリバリ   baribari = energetically, actively; *<u>baree</u><u>booru</u> (volleyball) games on <u>Bali</u> are played <u>energetically</u>*

くぐる	kuguru = to go under, pass through; *that cool guru can pass through* concrete *barriers*
来客	raikyaku = visitor or caller; from rai = to come, e.g., rainen = the coming year, + kyaku = customer
キラキラ星	kirakira hoshi = twinkle twinkle star; from kirakira = to glitter, sparkle or twinkle; *the bottle of tequila sparkled*; + hoshi = star
気遣い	kizukai = consideration, concern; from kizukau = to care for, worry, pay attention

Practice Sentences

1. それはとても単純です。

Sore wa totemo tanjun desu.
That's very simple.

2. 価格は重要ではない。

Kakaku wa juuyou de wa nai.
The price isn't important.

3. 彼は下着姿だった。

Kare wa shitagi sugata datta.
He was in underwear condition (i.e., in his underwear).

4. 派手すぎるよ。

Hade sugiru yo.
It's too flashy, for sure.

5. 時と場所に応じて、言葉遣いが変わる。

Toki to basho ni oujite, kotobazukai ga kawaru.
Depending on time and place, the speech style changes.

6. 私は横浜で育った。

Watashi wa yokohama de sodatta.
I grew up in Yokohama.

7. 彼女は凧に糸を付けた。

Kanojo wa tako ni ito wo tsuketa.
She attached a string to the kite.

8. 揚げ物はめったに食べません。

Agemono wa metta ni tabemasen.
I rarely eat deep-fried food.

9. 出席者はそれを純金だと思った。

Shusseki sha wa sore wo junkin da to omotta.
The attendees thought "that is pure gold."

10. 彼女は格好よく見えた。

Kanojo wa kakkou yoku mieta.
She looked good.

11. 彼はまだ姿を見せない。

Kare wa mada sugata wo misenai.
He still doesn't show the shape (i.e., he hasn't appeared yet).

12. 彼は特別な任務でヨーロッパに派遣された。

Kare wa tokubetsu na ninmu de yooroppa ni haken sareta.
He was sent on a special mission to Europe.

13. 日曜日に私たちは浜辺で凧を
飛ばしていた。

Nichiyoubi ni watashitachi wa hamabe
de tako wo tobashite ita.
On Sunday, we were flying a kite at the
beach.

14. おい、天ぷら揚がったから皿
持って来い。

Oi, tenpura agatta kara sara motte koi.
Hey, since the tempura is fried, bring a
plate.

15. 純子さんは性格がいい。

Junko san wa seikaku ga ii.
Junko has a good personality.

16. 彼は自分の容姿にうぬぼれて
いる。

Kare wa jibun no youshi ni unuborete
iru.
He is conceited about his appearance.

17. お心遣いありがとう。

Okokorozukai arigatou.
Thank you for your thoughtfulness.

18. 立派なお宅ですね。

Rippa na otaku desu ne.
It's a splendid honorable home, huh.

19. 一人で、雨上りの浜辺を歩い
てみました。

Hitori de, ameagari no hamabe wo aruite
mimashita.
By myself, I walked and saw the after-
the-rain's seaside.

20. 凧を揚げるのは危険かもしれ
ない。

Tako wo ageru no wa kiken
kamoshirenai.
Flying a kite might be dangerous.

Supplemental Reading Practice

After completing Chapter 20 of this book, you should be able to read the articles for
Day 20 and Day 21, Part 1, from "Akiko's Foreign Exchange" in *Satori Reader*.

Chapter 21

New Kanji in this Chapter

# 769 壮 (1)	# 770 脈 (1)	# 771 美 (4)	# 772 責 (2)
# 773 瞬 (2)	# 774 染 (4)	# 775 胸 (3)	# 776 駆 (2)

Vocabulary List with Mnemonics

from the Kanji Catalogue

壮大な   soudai na = magnificent, imposing; *the Soviet diver was magnificent*

脈   myaku = pulse or vein; *after drinking a lot of Miami Kool-Aid, my pulse was throbbing*

山脈   sanmyaku = mountain range; *Santa appeared in a commercial for Miami Kool-Aid, standing in front of a mountain range*

動脈   doumyaku = artery; *the doorman drank so much Miami Kool-Aid that his arteries hardened*

美しい   utsukushii = beautiful; *I utilize Superman's cushy dressing room to make myself beautiful*

美人   bijin = beautiful woman; *many beach jin (people) are beautiful women*

夏美   Natsumi = a woman's given name; from natsu = summer + mi = beautiful; *mirrors are attractive to beautiful people*

責任   sekinin = responsibility; *I had a seki (cough) when I was near that nin (person), so I have a responsibility for his illness*

責める   semeru = to accuse, reproach, torment; *at the cemetery, Ruth reproached me*

瞬く   matataku = to blink or twinkle; *the master tatami maker drank some Kool-Aid as his eyes twinkled*

瞬く間に   matataku ma ni = in an instant; from matataku = to blink + ma = interval

瞬間   shunkan = moment; *I shun candy because it only provides a moment of satisfaction*

瞬間的に   shunkanteki ni = momentarily; from shunkan = moment + teki = related to

感染   kansen = contagion, infection; *the Canadian senator warned about the risk of contagion from the epidemic disease*

汚染   osen = pollution; *Oprah sensed that pollution was increasing in the environment*

Kanji Pronunciations

# 769 – sou	# 770 – myaku	# 771 – utsuku, bi, mi, o	# 772 – seki, se
# 773 – matata, shun	# 774 – sen, so, ji, shi	# 775 – kyou, mune, muna	# 776 – ka, ku

染まる	somaru = to be dyed or stained, to be influenced, intransitive; *the <u>Somali</u> carpet in the <u>room</u> was <u>dyed</u> black*; cf. 染める someru = to dye, transitive
染みる	shimiru = to pierce or penetrate, to soak in; *the <u>sheep meat</u> <u>ruined</u> the tablecloth when it <u>penetrated</u> it*
染み込む	shimikomu = to soak into or penetrate; from shimiru = to penetrate + komu = to crowd in
胸	mune = chest; *the <u>moon</u> expert puffed out his <u>chest</u>*
度胸	dokyou = courage or audacity; *the <u>doe</u> in <u>Kyouto</u> Station must have had a lot of <u>courage</u> to venture so far*
胸中	kyouchuu = heart, mind or intentions; *in <u>Kyouto</u>, I <u>chewed</u> my food while I asked about her <u>intentions</u>*
胸毛	munage = chest hair; *the <u>moon</u> <u>animals</u> and their <u>guests</u> all had <u>chest</u> <u>hair</u>*
駆ける	kakeru = to run; *I <u>called</u> Kennedy's <u>room</u> to see if he wanted <u>to</u> <u>run</u>*
先駆者	senkusha = originator, pioneer; *the <u>senator</u> lived in a <u>cool</u> <u>shack</u> with some <u>pioneers</u>*

from the Practice Sentences

文脈	bunmyaku = context; *Daniel <u>Boone</u> liked to drink <u>Miami Kool</u>-Aid in the <u>context</u> of kids' parties*
責任感	sekininkan = sense of responsibility; from sekinin = responsibility + kanjiru = to feel
夜空	yozora = night sky; from yoru = night + zora = sora = sky
全速力	zensokuryoku = full speed; from zen = all + soku = fast; *dry ground <u>soaks</u> up the rain <u>fast</u>*; + ryoku = force
正常	seijou = normal; *to tell only <u>safe jokes</u> on government-run TV shows is <u>normal</u>*
染み	shimi = stain; from shimiru = to penetrate
一瞬で	isshun de = in an instant; *the <u>eagle's shunt</u> was only plugged for <u>an instant</u>*
伝染病	densen byou = infectious disease; from densen = infection; *the <u>dentist</u> <u>sensed</u> an <u>infection</u>*; + byou = illness
発生する	hassei suru = to break out, generate, breed, occur; *<u>Hawaii</u> was <u>saved</u> from an epidemic that <u>broke</u> <u>out</u>*
当てる	ateru = to touch (by hand), hit, guess correctly; *a <u>terrible</u> <u>rude</u> person <u>touched</u> me on the subway*
無数	musuu = countless; from mu = negation + suuji = number
いわゆる	iwayuru = what is called, so to speak; *<u>eagles</u> and <u>wasps</u> are <u>united</u> in <u>ruling</u> over their domains in <u>what</u> <u>is</u> <u>called</u> the animal world*

Practice Sentences

1. 壮大な景色ですね。
Soudai na keshiki desu ne.
It's a magnificent view, huh.

2. それは文脈による。
Sore wa bunmyaku ni yoru.
That depends on the context.

3. あなたは大変美しい。
Anata wa taihen utsukushii.
You are extremely beautiful.

4. 彼は責任感が強い。
Kare wa sekininkan ga tsuyoi.
He has a strong sense of responsibility.

5. 夜空には無数の星が瞬いていた。
Yozora ni wa musuu no hoshi ga matataite ita.
In the night sky, countless stars were twinkling.

6. 髪を染めたことある？
Kami wo someta koto aru?
Have you ever dyed your hair?

7. 彼は胸毛が多い。
Kare wa munage ga ooi.
He has a hairy chest.

8. 全速力で駆けた。
Zensokuryoku de kaketa.
She ran at full speed.

9. イギリスで壮大な教会を見ました。
Igirisu de soudai na kyoukai wo mimashita.
I saw magnificent churches in England.

10. あなたの脈は正常です。
Anata no myaku wa seijou desu.
Your pulse is normal.

11. 森の先、美しい湖がある。
Mori no saki, utsukushii mizuumi ga aru.
Beyond the forest, there is a beautiful lake.

12. 自分を責めないで。
Jibun wo semenai de.
Don't reproach yourself.

13. 飛行機は瞬く間に見えなくなった。
Hikouki wa matataku ma ni mienakunatta.
The airplane became unable-to-see in an instant.

14. インクの染みが洗濯しても落ちない。
Inku no shimi ga sentaku shitemo ochinai.
Despite washing, the ink stain doesn't come out.

15. 度胸が足りないぞ。
Dokyou ga tarinai zo.
You are lacking courage.

16. 二階に駆け上がった。
Nikai ni kakeagatta.
I ran up to the second floor.

17. テレビで壮大な結婚式を見ました。

Terebi de soudai na kekkon shiki wo mimashita.
I saw a magnificent wedding on TV.

18. 脈が早いです。

Myaku ga hayai desu.
The pulse is fast.

19. 彼女は大した美人だ。

Kanojo wa taishita bijin da.
She is a great beauty.

20. 責任者は誰ですか。

Sekininsha wa dare desu ka.
Who are the responsible people?

21. 一瞬で終わりだ。

Isshun de owari da.
It's over in an instant.

22. 伝染病が発生した。

Densen byou ga hassei shita.
An infectious disease broke out.

23. 胸に手を当てた。

Mune ni te wo ateta.
He put his hand on his chest (i.e., over his heart).

24. 彼はいわゆる先駆者だ。

Kare wa iwayuru senkusha da.
He is what is called a pioneer.

Chapter 22

New Kanji in this Chapter

# 777 垣 (2)	# 778 巡 (3)	# 779 芝 (1)	# 780 弾 (4)
# 781 詰 (2)	# 782 砂 (4)	# 783 頂 (3)	# 784 徴 (1)

Vocabulary List with Mnemonics

from the Kanji Catalogue

垣根 — kakine = hedge, fence; *my cocky neighbor put up a fence*

垣間見る — kaimamiru = to take a peep at, to catch a glimpse of; *the kind man miru (sees) me when he catches a glimpse of me*

巡る — meguru = to go or come around, to surround; *the men with goo and their rooster keep coming around*

お巡りさん — omawarisan = a policeman; *people in Omaha are wary of policemen*

芝生 — shibafu = lawn; *the Queen of Sheba fooled around on her lawn*

弾く — hiku = to play a piano or guitar; *to play a guitar is to hiku (pull) strings*

弾む — hazumu = to become lively, to accelerate; *at the Hawaian zoo, the movies accelerate when the animals are watching*

弾圧する — danatsu suru = to oppress or suppress; *the dancer I met at Superman's house said that the government had oppressed her*

弾 — tama = bullet; *the tall marathon runner dodged a bullet*

詰める — tsumeru = to stuff, fill or pack into; *on the tsuki (moon), a merry rooster stuffs its mouth*

詰まる — tsumaru = to be packed, to be blocked; *the intransitive form of tsumeru = to stuff*

に詰まる — ni tsumaru = to be at a loss; *my niece had only one tsuitcase (suitcase) when she was marooned, and she was at a loss*

詰問 — kitsumon = cross-examination, close questioning; *the king's tsuitcase (suitcase) contained a Monet painting, and he had to undergo a cross-examination at the border*

砂 — suna = sand; *soon arguments broke out on the sand*

砂利道 — jarimichi = gravel path; *as we drove on it, we realized that the jarring michi (road) was a gravel path*

Kanji Pronunciations

# 777 – kaki, kai	# 778 – jun, megu, mawa	# 779 – shiba		# 780 – hi, dan, hazu, tama
# 781 – tsu, kitsu	# 782 – ja, sha, suna, sa	# 783 – chou, itada, itadaki		# 784 – chou

登頂する	touchou suru = to climb to the summit; *the tortoise choked as it climbed to the summit and let the rabbit go by*
頂	itadaki = peak, summit; *I wore an Italian dark kimono when I climbed to the summit*
頂く	itadaku = to humbly receive, usually spelled いただく; *I will humbly receive Italian dark Kool-Aid*
特徴	tokuchou = characteristic, special feature; *totally cool chores usually include special features, such as opportunities for snacking*

from the Practice Sentences

頂上	choujou = summit; *Margaret Cho told a joke at the summit*
礼儀正しい	reigitadashii = courteous, decorous; from reigi = manners; *during the reign of the guillotine, people had good manners*; + tadashii = correct
飛び越える	tobikoeru = to jump over; from tobu = to fly + koeru = to go across
横になる	yoko ni naru = to lie down; from yoko = side, sideways, horizontal + ni naru = to become
横切る	yokogiru = to cut across; from yoko = side, sideways, horizontal + giru = kiru = to cut
土砂降り	doshaburi = pouring rain; from dosha = earth and sand; *the doughnuts they gave to the Shah were full of earth and sand*; + buru = furu = to precipitate
厚かましい	atsukamashii = impudent, shameless; *at Superman's party, Karl Marx and his Shiite friends were impudent*
にそって	ni sotte = in accordance with, along; *since my niece is a socialist, the television programs she watches are in accordance with her views*
情熱	jounetsu = enthusiasm, passion; *Joan of Arc wanted network superiority for her cell phone, since talking on the phone was her passion*

from Satori Reader

ぜいたく	zeitaku = luxury, extravagance; *my zany friend drinks only tap water and Kool-Aid although otherwise she lives in luxury*
水遊び	mizuasobi = playing in water; from mizu = water + asobu = to play
夕焼け	yuuyake = sunset; from yuugata = evening + yakeru = to be roasted or sunburnt
思わず	omowazu = unintentionally, involuntarily; from omowazu = omowanai de = not thinking
付き合う	tsukiau = to associate with, to keep company; from tsuku = to adhere + au = to come together or match
駆け巡る	kakemeguru = to run about; from kakeru = to run + meguru = to go around
当時	touji = at that time, in those days; *Tony Blair drove a Jeep at that time*

当て付け — atetsuke = insinuation, spiteful remark; *when you told the architect that his tennis racket should have stayed in his tsuitcase (suitcase), that was a spiteful remark*

さっさと — sassa to = immediately, promptly; *in Saskatchewan, I saw a tote bag and purchased it immediately*

かい — kai = is it?, a marker for a yes-no question, sometimes used instead of "desu ka"; *is it that you fly kites?*

リュック — ryukku = an abbreviation of ryukkusakku = rucksack, or backpack

Practice Sentences

1. その家の周りは垣根が巡らされている。
Sono ie no mawari wa kakine ga megurasarete iru.
That house's circumference is being surrounded by a fence.

2. 芝生の上に横になっていた。
Shibafu no ue ni yoko ni natte ita.
He was lying on the lawn.

3. 彼の胸は期待に弾んだ。
Kare no mune wa kitai ni hazunda.
His heart accelerated with expectation.

4. 私は言葉に詰まった。
Watashi wa kotoba ni tsumatta.
As for me, to words I was blocked. (i.e., I was at a loss for words)

5. 目に砂が入った。
Me ni suna ga haitta.
Sand got into my eye.

6. 頂上に登った。
Choujou ni nobotta.
We climbed to the summit.

7. 礼儀正しいのが彼の特徴です。
Reigi tadashii no ga kare no tokuchou desu.
Courteous things (i.e., good manners) are his characteristic.

8. 垣根を飛び越えた。
Kakine wo tobikoeta.
He jumped over the fence.

9. 誰がお巡りさんを呼んだの？
Dare ga omawarisan wo yonda no?
Who called the policeman?

10. 急いで芝生を横切った。
Isoide shibafu wo yokogitta.
Hurriedly, she cut across the lawn.

11. 趣味はギターを弾くことです。
Shumi wa gitaa wo hiku koto desu.
My hobby is to play the guitar.

12. 電車の乗客が多いときは詰めて座ったほうがいい。
Densha no joukyaku ga ooi toki wa tsumete suwatta hou ga ii.
As for the time when a train's passengers are numerous, to stuff and sit is better. (i.e., it's better to sit close together)

13. 今日は一日中、土砂降りだ
    ったなあ。

Kyou wa ichinichi juu, doshaburi datta
naa.
Today, all day, it was a pouring rain.

14. 頂上からの景色は最高だ。

Choujou kara no keshiki wa saikou da.
The view from the summit is the best.

15. 彼の性格の特徴は厚かまし
    いことだ。

Kare no seikaku no tokuchou wa
atsukamashii koto da.
His personality's characteristic is
impudence.

16. 地球を一周巡りまわった。

Chikyuu wo isshuu megurimawatta.
I went around the world one time.

17. 芝生に入ってはいけない。

Shibafu ni haitte wa ikenai.
You must not enter the lawn.

18. 弾圧された人々は自由を願
    った。

Dan'atsu sareta hitobito wa jiyuu wo
negatta.
The were-being-oppressed people prayed
for freedom.

19. どうかしたのと彼女は詰問
    した。

Douka shita no to kanojo wa kitsumon
shita.
"Is something wrong?," she demanded.

20. この砂利道にそって進んで
    ください。

Kono jarimichi ni sotte susunde kudasai.
To this gravel path, in accordance with,
please advance.

21. 山の頂はたくさんの雪が残
    っている。

Yama no itadaki wa takusan no yuki ga
nokotte iru.
A lot of snow is remaining at the mountain
peaks. (*not* OK to pronounce this "yama
no chou," in this context)

22. 彼女の特徴の一つはいつも
    情熱があることだ。

Kanojo no tokuchou no hitotsu wa, itsumo
jounetsu ga aru koto da.
One of her characteristics is that there is
always enthusiasm.

23. 彼女の性格の悪い面を垣間
    見た。

Kanojo no seikaku no warui men wo
kaimamita.
I got a glimpse into the bad aspect of her
character.

Supplemental Reading Practice

After completing Chapter 22 of this book, you should be able to read the articles from
Day 21, Part 2, and Day 22, Part 1, in "Akiko's Foreign Exchange" in *Satori Reader*.

Chapter 23

New Kanji in this Chapter

# 785 雑 (3)	# 786 誌 (1)	# 787 相 (3)	# 788 炎 (2)
# 789 算 (3)	# 790 談 (1)	# 791 額 (2)	# 792 嘆 (2)

Vocabulary List with Mnemonics

from the Kanji Catalogue

雑誌   zasshi = magazine; _Zachory Taylor liked sheep and subscribed to magazines about them_

首相   shushou = prime minister; _I met the prime minister at a shoe show_; cf. 総理 souri = prime minister

相談   soudan = consultation, advice; _I drank soda with a dancer while we engaged in consultation_

相手   aite = opponent or partner; _I drink iced tea and play tennis with my partner_

火炎   kaen = fire; _let's call the engineers to put out the fire_

炎   hono'o = blaze, flame; _there was a flame burning at my home in northern Oregon_

計算   keisan = calculation; _I did a calculation of the number of caissons that were rolling along_

算数   sansuu = arithmetic; _Santa sued his dwarves due to their poor arithmetic_

暗算   anzan = mental calculation; _when Queen Anne visited Zanzibar, she did a mental calculation of the number of Queen Anne chairs there_

金額   kingaku = a sum of money; _the king accumulated a sum of money_

額   hitai = forehead; _he tied a bandana around his forehead_

嘆く   nageku = to lament, grieve; _I nag my guests to drink Kool-Aid and grieve when they refuse_

感嘆する   kantan suru = to admire or be astonished at; _I admire Canadian tanks_; cf. 簡単 kantan = easy

Kanji Pronunciations

# 785 – zatsu, zou, za	# 786 – shi	# 787 – shou, sou, ai	# 788 – en, hono'o
# 789 – san, zan, soro	# 790 – dan	# 791 – gaku, hitai	# 792 – nage, tan

23-86

from the Practice Sentences

炎上する — enjou suru = to blaze up, burn; *the French king encouraged Joan of Arc to fight against the English, but in the end she got burned*;
cf. 援助する enjo suru = to support

雑用 — zatsuyou = chores; *Zach's tsuitcase (suitcase) contained a yoke that he used for his chores with oxen*

速度 — sokudo = speed; *the Soviets used Kool-Aid and doughnuts to entice their athletes to greater speed*

見当する — kentou suru = to analyze, scrutinize; *Barbie will analyze and scrutinize Ken's toes*

雑音 — zatsuon = noise; *Zach's tsuitcase (suitcase) was lost for only a short time, since he made noise until he got it back*

国会 — kokkai = Diet (legislative body); *some members of the Diet have cockeyed ideas*

解散する — kaisan suru = to break up or dismiss (a meeting, etc.); *the Kaiser and Santa dismissed the meeting*

古本 — furuhon = second-hand book; from furui = old + hon = book

倍額 — baigaku = double the amount; *he will buy the gakusei (student) some bait, but he wants double the amount in return if the student catches a fish*

何気ない — nanigenai = casual, nonchalant; *I will ask him in a casual nonchalant way nani (what) he gets from the refrigerator at night*

不安 — fuan = insecurity, anxiety, uneasiness; *my foolish aunt suffers from anxiety*

あおり — aori = a gust of wind; *the owl that was perched on a reed was knocked over by a gust of wind*

あおりたてる — aoritateru = to flap strongly or stir up fiercely; *the owl on the reed tateru (stands) and flaps his wings strongly*

from Satori Reader

特有 — tokuyuu = characteristic (of), peculiar (to); *it's totally cool that the Yukon has so many characteristic features*

とにかく — tonikaku = anyhow, in any case; *I didn't win the Tony Award, but I will kaku [write] a book, in any case*

ドキッと — dokitto = feeling a shock, startling; *the dozing king hurt his toe when he was feeling a shock from an earthquake*

雑談 — zatsudan = idle chat; from zatsu = assorted; *Zach's tsuitcase (suitcase) was lost among assorted other suitcases*; + dan = talk, e.g.., soudan = consultation

Practice Sentences

1. 母は雑誌を読んでいる。

Haha wa zasshi wo yonde iru.
My mother is reading a magazine.

2. 家が炎上していた。

Ie ga enjou shite ita.
The house was on fire.

3. 彼は計算が得意だ。

Kare wa keisan ga tokui da.
Calculations are his strong point.

4. 額に手を当てた。

Hitai ni te wo ateta.
He put his hand to his forehead.

5. その景色の美しさに感嘆した。

Sono keshiki no utsukushisa ni kantan shita.
We were astonished by the beauty of that view.

6. 部長に相談してみたらどうでしょうか。

Bucho ni soudan shite mitara dou deshou ka.
If you consult with the division manager, how would that be, probably?

7. すぐに雑用を終えた。

Sugu ni zatsuyou wo oeta.
He soon finished the chores.

8. これは学生相手の店です。

Kore wa gakusei aite no mise desu.
This is a store that caters to students.

9. 光の速度を計算した。

Hikari no sokudo wo keisan shita.
He calculated the speed of light.

10. 留学にかかる金額の見当をつけて、お金を持っていく。

Ryuugaku ni kakaru kingaku no kentou wo tsukete, okane wo motte iku.
I will analyze the to-spend sum for foreign travel, and take the money with me.

11. 炎を小さくしてください。

Hono'o wo chiisaku shite kudasai.
Please make the flame small.

12. 過去のことで嘆いても何の役にもたたないよ。

Kako no koto de nageitemo nan no yaku ni mo tatanai yo.
Even if you lament about past things, it doesn't even do any good, for sure.

13. 相談に来てください。

Soudan ni kite kudasai.
Please come for the purpose of consultation (i.e., come and talk to me).

14. 雑音で何も聞こえません。

Zatsuon de nanimo kikoemasen.
I can't hear anything due to the noise.

15. 首相は国会を解散した。

Shushou wa kokkai wo kaisan shita.
The prime minister dissolved the Diet.

16. 余り暗算ができない。

Amari anzan ga dekinai.
I can hardly do mental arithmetic.

17. その古本に倍額を払った。

Sono furuhon ni baigaku wo haratta.
I paid double the price for that secondhand book.

18. 何気なくその雑誌を見た。

Nanigenaku sono zasshi wo mita.
I looked at that magazine casually.

19. 身の不安を嘆いた。

Mi no fuan wo nageita.
He lamented his person's insecurity (i.e., his hard fate).

20. 僕には相談相手がない。

Boku ni wa soudan aite ga nai.
As for to me, a consultation partner doesn't exist (i.e., I have no advisor).

21. 風が炎をあおりたてた。

Kaze ga hono'o wo aori tateta.
The wind fanned the flames

22. お店で雑誌を1冊買った。

Omise de zasshi wo issatsu katta.
I bought one magazine at an honorable store.

Supplemental Reading Practice

After completing Chapter 23 of this book, you should be able to read the articles from Day 22, Part 2, in "Akiko's Foreign Exchange" in *Satori Reader*.

Chapter 24

New Kanji in this Chapter

# 793 敗 (3)	# 794 喉 (2)	# 795 鼻 (2)	# 796 邪 (2)
# 797 浸 (3)	# 798 爽 (1)	# 799 垂 (2)	# 800 睡 (1)

Vocabulary List with Mnemonics

from the Kanji Catalogue

敗れる — yabureru = to lose or be defeated; *the Yankees drank booze and danced with red roosters, and the battle was lost*; cf. 破れる yabureru = to be torn or broken

失敗する — shippai suru = to fail or make a mistake; *when I shipped the pies, I made a mistake*

喉 — nodo = throat; *I have no dough (money) to buy medicine for my throat*

鼻 — hana = nose; *the Hawaiian nanny has a tiny nose*

耳鼻科 — jibika = ear, nose & throat specialty; *put on your jeans, grab some beer, get in the car, and let's go see the ear, nose & throat specialist*

風邪 — kaze = upper respiratory infection; *if you stand in the kaze (wind), you might get an upper respiratory infection*

無邪気 — mujaki = innocence; *that movie shows Jackie Kennedy's innocence*

浸かる — tsukaru = to be soaked in; *I lent my tsuit (suit) to Karl Marx, and he ruined it when he got soaked in water*

浸水する — shinsui suru = to be flooded; *a Shinto shrine in Sweden was flooded*

浸す — hitasu = to soak, dip, drench or dunk; *the hero sitting in a tavern was Superman, and he soaked his bread in olive oil*

爽快 — soukai = refreshing, exhilarating; *the soap that the Kaiser gave me has a refreshing smell*

垂直 — suichoku = vertical, perpendicular; *the swing choked me when its vertical rope got caught on my scarf*

垂れる — tareru = to hang, droop, dangle, sag, lower, drip, ooze; *after the talented red roosters ran through the swamp, their feathers were drooping*

睡眠 — suimin = sleep; *Swedish people are mean when they don't get enough sleep*

Kanji Pronunciations

# 793 – hai, yabu, pai	# 794 – kou, nodo	# 795 – hana, bi	# 796 – ze, ja
# 797 – shin, tsu, hita	# 798 – sou	# 799 – sui, ta	# 800 – sui

from the Practice Sentences

鼻水   hanamizu = nasal mucous; from hana = nose + mizu = water

湯船   yubune = bathtub; from yu = hot water + bune = fune = boat

一睡   issui = a wink (of sleep); *at Easter, the Swedish pastor doesn't get a wink of sleep*

垂れ下がる   taresagaru = to hang; from tareru = to hang + sagaru = to hang down

安易   an'i = easygoing, lightly, easily; *Little Orphan Annie was an easygoing girl*

鼻血   hanaji = nosebleed; from hana = nose + ji = chi = blood

ひと泳ぎ   hito'oyogi = a swim; from hitotsu = one + oyogu = to swim

クタクタ   kutakuta = exhausted; *after looking at cool tapestries all day and then drinking Kool-Aid in a tavern, I was exhausted*

from Satori Reader

気を取り直す   ki wo torinaosu = to completely rethink, to pull one's self together; from ki = spirit + toru = to take + naosu = to correct or repair

やっちまう   yatchimau = yatte shimau = to do completely, implying making a mistake

すら   sura = even, if just, as long as (a variation of sae, implying that's all one needs); *Superman will buy a ranch, as long as he can get some cattle*

会計   kaikei = accounting; *the accounting department keeps track of the Kaiser's cake and other food expenses*

やらかす   yarakasu = to perpetrate or to be guilty of; *if the yak or the ram kicked the candle over in Superman's tent, they may be guilty of causing the fire*

使いこなす   tsukaikonasu = to handle (men), to master (a tool or a language); from tsukau = to use + konasu = to be good at; *Conan O'Brien's supervisor is good at comedy*

気づかれ   kizukare = mental fatigue, worry; from ki = spirit + tsukare = fatigue; spelled kidukare in electronic dictionaries

なんか   nanka = something like, somehow, things like; from nani = thing + ka = question marker

ためる   tameru = to accumulate, to amass, to store; *the talented Mexicans had a room where they accumulated corn*

重なる   kasanaru = to be piled up, to happen at the same time, to accumulate; *the film Casablanca caused some nasty rumors to pile up about Humphrey Bogart and Ingrid Bergman*

寝ようっと   neyou tto = I shall sleep!, from neyou = I shall sleep + tto = a suffix used for emphasis

朝一   asaichi = first thing in the morning; from asa = morning + ichi = number one

鼻歌　　　　　　hanauta = humming; from hana = nose + uta = song

Practice Sentences

1. 仕事で失敗しました。
Shigoto de shippai shimashita.
I made a mistake at work.

2. 喉が痛くて、鼻水もでます。
Nodo ga itakute, hanamizu mo demasu.
I have a sore throat, and also nose water emerges (i.e., I have a runny nose).

3. 風邪は伝染する。
Kaze wa densen suru.
Colds are contagious.

4. 湯船に浸かりました。
Yubune ni tsukarimashita.
I soaked in the bathtub.

5. 気分爽快だよ。
Kibun soukai da yo.
It's feeling-refreshed, for sure. (i.e., I feel refreshed)

6. 鼻水が垂れているよ。
Hanamizu ga tarete iru yo.
Nose water is dripping, for sure (i.e., my nose is running).

7. 一睡もしなかった。
Issui mo shinakatta.
I didn't even sleep a wink.

8. 喉が乾いてたまらない。
Nodo ga kawaite tamaranai.
The throat is dry (i.e., I'm thirsty), and it's intolerable.

9. わが国の選手はとうとう敗れてしまった。
Wagakuni no senshu wa toutou yaburete shimatta.
Our country's athletes finally lost completely.

10. 鼻が詰まった。
Hana ga tsumatta.
My nose stuffed up.

11. 風邪が直らない。
Kaze ga naoranai.
The cold (upper respiratory infection) doesn't get better.

12. 船が浸水しはじめた。
Fune ga shinsui shihajimeta.
The boat began to flood.

13. カーテンが垂れ下がっている。
Kaaten ga taresagatte iru.
The curtain is hanging.

14. 山のすがすがしい空気に触れると気分も爽快です。
Yama no sugasugashii kuuki ni fureru to kibun mo soukai desu.
When I experience the mountain's refreshing air, the feeling also is refreshing.

15. 睡眠をとった方がいい。

Suimin wo totta hou ga ii.
It would be better to get some sleep.

16. パンを喉に詰まらせた。

Pan wo nodo ni tsumaraseta.
On bread, I made my throat block (i.e., I got a piece of bread stuck in my throat). (this is the causative tense of tsumaru = to be packed or blocked)

17. 安易な考えで仕事を始めると、失敗する。

An'i na kangae de shigoto wo hajimeru to, shippai suru.
If one starts work with easygoing thinking, one will fail.

18. 鼻血出てるよ。

Hanaji deteru yo.
Nose blood is emerging, for sure (i.e., my nose is bleeding).

19. 無邪気なふりをした。

Mujaki na furi wo shita.
She did innocent pretense (i.e., she pretended to be innocent).

20. 紙の上に垂直線を何本か引いた。

Kami no ue ni suichoku sen wo nanbon ka hiita.
He drew a few vertical lines on the paper. (引く hiku = to draw a line, among other meanings)

21. 布を水に浸した。

Nuno wo mizu ni hitashita.
I soaked the cloth in water.

22. プールでひと泳ぎした後、気分が爽快した。

Puuru de hito'oyogi shita ato, kibun ga soukai shita.
After a swim in the pool, the feeling did refreshing. (i.e., I felt refreshed)

23. 体は睡眠不足でクタクタだった。

Karada wa suimin busoku de kutakuta datta.
From lack of sleep, the body was exhausted.

Supplemental Reading Practice

After completing Chapter 24 of this book, you should be able to read the articles from Days 23 and 24 in "Akiko's Foreign Exchange" in *Satori Reader*.

Chapter 25

New Kanji in this Chapter

# 801 移 (2)	# 802 避 (2)	# 803 暇 (2)	# 804 諦 (1)
# 805 浪 (1)	# 806 没 (2)	# 807 悶 (2)	# 808 術 (2)

Vocabulary List with Mnemonics

from the Kanji Catalogue

移る — utsuru = to move (one's lodging), to change or be infected with; *utilizing Superman, Ruth moved to a new home*

移動する — idou suru = to move (an object); *both an eagle and a doe can move a leaf*

避ける — sakeru = to avoid; *there was sake in the room, but I avoided drinking it*

避難 — hinan = refuge, shelter; *the Himalayan nanny found refuge in Europe*

回避 — kaihi = evasion, avoidance; *the Kaiser heeded his generals' advice and followed a strategy of avoidance*

暇 — hima = free time; *while my wounds were healing on Mars, I had a lot of free time*

休暇 — kyuuka = holiday, day off; *I rented a cute car to use during my holiday*

諦める — akirameru = to give up or abandon hope; *Achilles' ramen was ruined because he gave up on it*

浪費 — rouhi = waste, extravagance; *building another road through the Himalayas is an extravagance*

浪人 — rounin = wandering samurai without a master, a person waiting for another chance to take a university exam; *a roaming nin (person) is like a wandering samurai*

没頭 — bottou = immersing (oneself); *I have bony toes, and I like the feeling of immersing them in hot water*

没する — bossuru = to sink, go down, to set, to pass away, to die, to disappear; *the boat carrying Superman and his rooster sank and disappeared*

日没 — nichibotsu = sunset; *Nietzsche took his friends out in boats to see the sunset*

悶える — modaeru = to be in agony, to worry; *Moses and his dad are erudite, and they tend to worry*

悶々 — monmon = worry, agony, worrying endlessly; *I moan and moan due to worry*

Kanji Pronunciations

# 801 – utsu, i	# 802 – sa, hi	# 803 – hima, ka	# 804 – akira
# 805 – rou	# 806 – bo, botsu	# 807 – moda, mon	# 808 – sube, jutsu

手術 — shujutsu = surgery; *your shoe juts out, suggesting that you have a bunion requiring surgery*

美術 — bijutsu = visual art; *Being juts out into the world through the visual arts*

from the Practice Sentences

美術館 — bijutsukan = museum; from bijutsu = visual arts + kan = large building

避難所 — hinanjo = shelter place; from hinan = taking refuge + jo = place

習得する — shuutoku suru = to master a subject or skill; *his shooting is totally cool, since he has mastered that skill*

放浪する — hourou suru = to wander; *the hobo on the road is wandering*

苦しむ — kurushimu = to suffer, to be worried; from kurushii = hard, painful; *when Madam Curie rushed the Shiites, she sustained a painful injury*

苦しみ — kurushimi = suffering, pain, hardship; from kurushimu = to suffer

from Satori Reader

ぐっすり — gussuri = sound asleep; *after the goofy supervisor retired, he spent his days sound asleep*

点数 — tensuu = score, marks, points; *when we play tennis, Superman keeps score*

一安心 — hitoanshin = a feeling of relief; from hitotsu = one + anshin = relief

息 — iki = breath; *your breath smells icky*

見つけ出す — mitsukedasu = to discover, to locate; from mitsukeru = to discover + dasu = to put out

のしかかる — noshikakaru = to lean on, to weigh on; *in Norway, sheep meat kakaru (costs) more if the butcher leans on the meat while weighing it*

夢中 — muchuu = daze, trance, engrossment; from mu = dream; *I had a dream about the moon; + chuu = middle*

押し切る — oshikiru = to overcome resistance; from osu = to push + kiru = to cut

そっちのけ — sotchinoke = to ignore one thing for another; *the soda is cheap and they have no ketchup, so I ignore the ketchup and drink the soda*

人生 — jinsei = human life; *my human life is to drink gin behind the Safeway store*

ムカムカ — mukamuka = feeling sick or nauseous; *watching movies in the car with a Moonie named Karl made me feel nauseous*

ため息 — tameiki = a sigh; *the tall Mexican released his iki (breath) suddenly, and the result was a sigh*

Practice Sentences

1. 新しい話題に移った。

Atarashii wadai ni utsutta.
They moved to a new topic.

2. 雨を避けるために避難所を探した。

Ame wo sakeru tame ni hinanjo wo sagashita.
In order to avoid the rain, he looked for a shelter place.

3. バーバラさんは毎日暇だからテレビを見ています。

Baabara san wa mainichi hima dakara terebi o mite imasu.
Barbara, every day, because there is free time, is watching TV.

4. 外国語の習得は難しいが、諦めないで続けたいと思う。

Gaikokugo no shuutoku wa muzukashii ga, akiramenai de tsuzuketai to omou.
As for foreign languages' mastery, difficult, but not giving up, I want to continue, I think.

5. 時間と金を浪費するな。

Jikan to kane wo rouhi suru na.
Don't waste your time and money

6. 日没は七時半です。

Nichibotsu wa shichijihan desu.
Sunset is at 7:30.

7. 苦しみ悶えている。

Kurushimi modaete iru.
Suffering, he is in agony.

8. 手術が必要ですか。

Shujutsu ga hitsuyou desu ka.
Is surgery necessary?

9. その事故を避けるのは不可能だった。

Sono jiko o sakeru no wa fukanou datta.
As for to avoid that accident, it was impossible.

10. 来月の休暇はどこに行きますか。

Raigetsu no kyuuka wa doko ni ikimasu ka.
As for next month's vacation, where will you go?

11. 難しいからといって、諦めてはいけない。

Muzukashii kara to itte, akiramete wa ikenai.
Since they say "because difficult," you must not give up.

12. また今年も浪人してしまった。

Mata kotoshi mo rounin shite shimatta.
Again this year also, he completely became a person waiting for another chance (i.e., he failed the entrance exam).

13. 勉強に没頭している。

Benkyou ni bottou shite iru.
She is immersed in studying.

14. 悶々としてしまった。

Monmon to shite shimatta.
In the capacity of agony, I did complete-ly (i.e., I got agonized completely). (to shite = as, or in the capacity of)

15. 美術館に行った。

Bijutsukan ni itta.
I went to a museum.

16. 机を右に移動させた。

Tsukue wo migi ni idou saseta.
I made the desk move to the right.

17. 人を避けるためにハンドルを
きった。

Hito wo sakeru tame ni handoru wo kitta.
I turned the steering wheel to avoid a person. (kiru = to turn a vehicle, among other meanings)

18. 来週の金曜日、暇ですか。

Raishuu no kinyoobi, hima desu ka.
Next week's Friday, is it free time?

19. 諦めるにしろ、一度はやって
みるべきだ。

Akirameru ni shiro, ichido wa yatte miru beki da.
Even if you give up, you should try once. (ni shiro = even though)

20. 彼は全国を放浪した。

Kare wa zenkoku wo hourou shita.
He wandered on all countries. (this could also mean "all over Japan")

21. 月が没した。

Tsuki ga bosshita.
The moon went down.

22. 痛みで悶えて苦しんでいる。

Itami de modaete kurushinde iru.
Due to pain, he is in agony and suffering.

23. 事務所が6階に移った。

Jimusho ga rokkai ni utsutta.
The office moved to the 6th floor.

24. 二年前、胃の手術を受けた。

Ni nen mae, i no shujutsu wo uketa.
I received a stomach operation 2 years ago.

Supplemental Reading Practice

After completing Chapter 25 of this book, you should be able to read the articles from Days 25, 26, 27 and 28 in "Akiko's Foreign Exchange" in *Satori Reader*.

Note: since additional articles in the Akiko series were not complete at the time that this portion of this book was written, in the next chapter we will be introducing new kanji that are found in the "Kona's Big Adventure" series.

Chapter 26

New Kanji in this Chapter

# 809 居 (2)	# 810 求 (2)	# 811 健 (2)	# 812 冒 (2)
# 813 論 (1)	# 814 氷 (3)	# 815 溶 (2)	# 816 岩 (2)

Vocabulary List with Mnemonics

from the Kanji Catalogue

住居 　 juukyo = dwelling; *the jeweler lived in Kyoto, in a dwelling*

居間 　 ima = living room; *ima (now) I'm in the living room*

要求 　 youkyuu = a request or demand; *yogurt and cucumbers are among our requests*

求める 　 motomeru = to ask, request or buy; *the motormen made it a rule to ask passengers for payment*

求む 　 motomu = to seek or demand; *the motor-mouthed movie star demanded higher wages*

健やか 　 sukoyaka = vigorous, healthy, sound; *the super coder, who had a yacht and a car, was vigorous and healthy*

冒険 　 bouken = adventure, risk; *the boyish Kennedy liked adventure*

冒す 　 okasu = to brave or risk, to face or venture; *occasionally Superman risks injury*

口論 　 kouron = argument, quarrel; *in Korea, Ronald Reagan got into a quarrel*

氷 　 koori = ice; *in Corinth people put ice in their drinks*

氷る 　 kooru = to freeze; *when it's cold, the room freezes*

氷山 　 hyouzan = iceberg; from hyou = ice; *the Lone Ranger said "Hi-yo" when he saw ice;* + zan = san = mountain

溶岩 　 yougan = lava; *a yogi told Gandalf to watch out for hot lava*

溶ける 　 tokeru = to melt or dissolve, intransitive; *the butter in the toy kettle in my room melted*

溶かす 　 tokasu = to melt or dissolve, transitive; *I use a torch to light a candle in Sudan in order to melt wax*

岩 　 iwa = rock; *the eastern wall is made from rock*

Kanji Pronunciations

# 809 – kyo, i	# 810 – kyuu, moto	# 811 – ken, suko	# 812 – oka, bou
# 813 – ron	# 814 – koori, koo, hyou	# 815 – you, to	# 816 – iwa, gan

from the Practice Sentences

居眠り — inemuri = a catnap; *it's <u>ine</u>vitable that <u>Muriel</u> will take a <u>catnap</u> during the meeting*

求職 — kyuushoku = looking for work; *the <u>Cu</u>ban got a <u>shock</u> when he was <u>looking for work</u>*

論議 — rongi = discussion; *<u>Ron</u>ald Reagan brought his <u>guitar</u> to the <u>discussion</u>*

別居 — bekkyo = separation of family members; *since I've taken up <u>begging</u> in <u>Kyoto</u>, I've become <u>separated from</u> <u>my family</u>*

理論 — riron = theory; *the <u>reason</u> that <u>Ron</u>ald Reagan believed in his economic <u>theory</u> is that he thought it would allow rich people to pay fewer taxes*

難解 — nankai = difficult to understand; *the <u>nan</u>ny and the <u>Kai</u>ser are <u>difficult to understand</u> when they speak in German*

氷点下 — hyoutenka = below freezing; from hyou = ice + ten = point + ka = below

居心地 — igokochi = feeling in a particular ambience; from i = dwelling; *<u>eels</u> have gotten into this <u>dwelling</u>*; + gokoro = kokoro = heart; + chi = ground or soil

世論 — yoron = public opinion; *<u>you</u>'re w<u>ron</u>g, since <u>public opinion</u> contradicts you*

溶け込む — tokekomu = to blend in or adjust; from tokeru = to melt or dissolve + komu = to crowd in

固体 — kotai = solid; *<u>Col</u>ombian <u>ti</u>gers have <u>solid</u> muscles*

Practice Sentences

1. 居眠りをした。
Inemuri wo shita.
I nodded off (i.e., I fell asleep briefly).

2. 彼女は求職中です。
Kanojo wa kyuushoku chuu desu.
She is in the process of looking for a job.

3. 彼は冒険が好きです。
Kare wa bouken ga suki desu.
He likes adventure.

4. 論議を終えましょう。
Rongi wo oemashou.
Let's finish the discussion.

5. 氷が溶けている。
Koori ga tokete iru.
The ice is melting.

6. 岩の上に立っていました。
Iwa no ue ni tatte imashita.
I was standing on a rock.

7. 助けを求めた。
Tasuke wo motometa.
I asked for help.

8. 妻と別居している。
Tsuma to bekkyo shite iru.
He is separated from his wife.

9. 危険を冒したくない。

Kiken wo okashitakunai.
I don't want to risk danger.

10. その理論は難解だ。

Sono riron wa nankai da.
That theory is hard to understand.

11. 今日も氷点下です。

Kyou mo hyoutenka desu.
Today also it's below freezing.

12. その火山は溶岩を流しだした。

Sono kazan wa yougan wo nagashidashita.
The volcano poured out lava.

13. ここは居心地が悪い。

Koko wa igokochi ga warui.
As for here, the feeling in the ambience is bad (i.e., uncomfortable).

14. 金を要求した。

Kane wo youkyuu shita.
He demanded money.

15. 彼女は健やかに育った。

Kanojo wa sukoyaka ni sodatta.
She grew up in good health.

16. 世論は非常に重要である。

Yoron wa hijou ni juuyou de aru.
Public opinion is extremely important.

17. 空が海と一つに溶け込むように見えた。

Sora ga umi to hitotsu ni tokekomu you ni mieta.
The sky seemed to blend as one with the ocean.

18. 水は氷ると固体になる。

Mizu wa kooru to kotai ni naru.
When water freezes, it becomes solid.

19. この岩は動物の形をしている。

Kono iwa wa doubutsu no katachi wo shite iru.
This rock is doing the shape of an animal (i.e., it resembles one).

20. 新しい冒険を始めた。

Atarashii bouken wo hajimeta.
I started a new adventure.

Chapter 27

New Kanji in this Chapter

# 817 嫌 (4)	# 818 匹 (4)	# 819 泥 (2)	# 820 棒 (1)
# 821 追 (2)	# 822 照 (3)	# 823 振 (3)	# 824 似 (3)

Vocabulary List with Mnemonics

from the Kanji Catalogue

機嫌 kigen = mood, feeling; *the quiche that Genghis ate put him in a good mood*

嫌な iya na = unpleasant, disgusting; *that eerie yacht is disgusting*

嫌い kirai = to hate; *I hate it when kings rise up from the grave*

嫌悪 ken'o = hatred, disgust; *Ken owes Barbie an apology for the hatred he expressed*

二匹 nihiki = two small animals or bolts of cloth; *that small animal gave me a hickey*

泥棒 dorobou = thief; *Dorothy's boyfriend is a thief*

泥水 deisui = muddy water, red-light district; *my date was sweet, but he took me to the red-light district*

棒 bou = a stick; *I made a boat out of sticks*

相棒 aibou = a buddy or partner; *Ike is boring, but he's my buddy*; cf. 相手 aite = partner

追求する tsuikyuu suru = to pursue a goal, to chase; *he's pursuing a dream of a tsuit (sweet) cucumber farm*

追う ou = to chase; *Ahab chased the whale across the ocean*

追いかける oikakeru = to pursue or chase after; from ou = to chase + kakeru = to run

照らす terasu = to illuminate or light; *the terrarium looks super when I illuminate it*

照る teru = to shine; *the television in my room shines all night*

照れる tereru = to be shy or feel embarrassment; *I feel embarrassed about eating that tender red rooster*

日照り hideri = dry weather, drought; *the Himalayan dairy farm was stricken by drought*

Kanji Pronunciations

# 817 – gen, iya, kira, ken	# 818 – hiki, piki, biki, hi	# 819 – doro, dei	# 820 – bou
# 821 – tsui, o	# 822 – te, shou, de	# 823 – shin, fu, furi	# 824 – ni, ne, ji

対照的に	taishouteki ni = diametrically opposite; *the tiger showed the techie a diametrically opposite way of solving the problem*
振り返る	furikaeru = to turn the head, look back, think back; *Lot's wife was furious and wanted to kaeru (return), and she looked back at Sodom*
振り向く	furimuku = to turn around; *I was furious when I had to move the Kool-Aid packages in the display and decided to turn around and talk to the manager*
手を振る	te wo furu = to wave or shake the hand; from te = hand + furu = to wave; *he waved foolishly at the rooster*
銀行振込み	ginkou furikomi = bank transfer; from ginkou = bank + furikomu = to transfer; *the furious Communist transferred the Party's money to his own account*
振動数	shindousuu = frequency; *the Shinto doorman was sued with frequency*
似ている	nite iru = to resemble; from niru = to resemble; *Nietsche and Rousseau resembled each other*
真似	mane = imitation, mimicry; *the man from the Netherlands is selling imitation goods*
類似の	ruiji no = similar to; *Luigi is similar to Mario*
類似品	ruijihin = imitation, or similar article; from ruiji = similar + hin = merchandise

from the Practice Sentences

似合う	niau = to suit or become (as in clothing); *the needlework that the owl is wearing suits it*
泥	doro = mud; *the dopy robot got stuck in the mud*
照会先	shoukaisaki = reference; from shoukai = inquiry, reference; *I showed the Kaiser my references*; + saki = previous; cf. 紹介 shoukai = introduction
振り	furi = pretense or appearance; *the wolf in a furry costume has the appearance or pretense of being a sheep*
振る舞い	furumai = behavior; *the food was ruined by Michael Jackson's behavior*
見事	migoto = wonderful; *the mediator's goal was to tone down the rhetoric, and he did a wonderful job*
寝返える	negaeru = to betray; *the negative erudite guy betrayed us*
実験	jikken = experiment; *the genius and Ken conducted an experiment*

from Satori Reader

同居人	doukyonin = roommate; from dou = the same, e.g., 同情 doujou = sympathy; + kyo = to reside, e.g., juukyo = dwelling; + nin = person
デカイ	dekai = huge; *the deck on the Kaiser's yacht is huge*

言い遅れる　ii okureru = to say something late; from iu = to speak + okureru = to be delayed

反論　hanron = objection, rebuttal; *since Hansel thought that I was wrong, he raised on objection*

そっくり　sokkuri = just like, entirely; *the Soviet curry was identical to the Pakistani curry*

名付ける　nazukeru = to name or christen; from namae = name + tsukeru = to attach

由来　yurai = origin, source, reason, destiny; *the union is right to say that the origin of the problem lies in miscommunication*

何しろ　nani shiro = at any rate, anyhow; from nani = what + ni shiro = even though; *his knee was shiro [white] even though he had spent hours in the tanning booth*

何度か　nandoka = several times, once or twice; from nando = how many times + ka (ka adds the meaning "some" when it follows a question word, e.g., nanika = something, dokoka = somewhere)

引っかく　hikkaku = to scratch or claw; *that hideous cactus plant scratched me*

Practice Sentences

1. 彼は機嫌が悪い。
Kare wa kigen ga warui.
He is in a bad mood.

2. 犬が一匹欲しい。
Inu ga ippiki hoshii.
I want a dog.

3. 泥棒を追いかけた。
Dorobou wo oikaketa.
I chased a thief.

4. 照れていた。
Terete ita.
I was embarrassed.

5. 首を横に振った。
Kubi wo yoko ni futta.
She shook the neck to the side (i.e., she shook her head).

6. 本当によく似合う。
Honto ni yoku niau.
It really suits you well.

7. 嫌なら結構です。
Iya nara kekkou desu.
In case you don't like it, it's fine.

8. 今朝、りすを二匹見かけた。
Kesa risu wo nihiki mikaketa.
I sighted two squirrels this morning.

9. 泥だらけだった。
Doro darake datta.
It was covered with mud.

10. 棒を投げて犬に取って来させています。
Boo wo nagete inu ni totte kosasete imasu.
Throwing the stick, he is making the dog take it and come.

11. 照会先を３件ください。
Shoukaisaki wo sanken kudasai.
Please give us three references.

12. 寝た振りをしても、すぐわかるよ。

Neta furi wo shitemo, sugu wakaru yo.
Are sleeping pretense, even though you do, I soon understand, for sure. (i.e., I see that you are pretending to sleep)

13. 流行を追うな。

Ryuukou wo ou na.
Don't follow the fashion.

14. バカな真似はよせ。

Baka na mane wa yose.
As for the foolish imitation, stop it. (from よす yosu = to cease or desist) (i.e., don't act like a fool)

15. 卵は嫌いです。

Tamago wa kirai desu.
I dislike eggs.

16. 彼の振る舞いは見事だった。

Kare no furumai wa migoto datta.
His behavior was wonderful.

17. 池に大きな魚が三匹泳いでいる。

Ike ni ookina sakana ga sanbiki oyoide iru.
There are three large fish swimming in the pond.

18. 泥棒はその窓を割った。

Dorobou wa sono mado wo watta.
The thief broke that window.

19. あいつ、さっきまでおれの相棒だったのに、もう寝返った。

Aitsu, sakki made ore no aibou datta noni, mou negaetta.
That fellow over there, until previously he was my partner even though, already he betrayed me.

20. 人間は幸福を追求し続けています。

Ningen wa koufuku wo tsuikyuu shi tsuzukete imasu.
Humans are continuing to seek happiness.

21. 時々自分の過去を振り返る。

Tokidoki jibun no kako wo furikaeru.
Sometimes I look back on my past.

22. その二つの実験は類似の結果を出した。

Sono futatsu no jikken wa ruiji no kekka wo dashita.
Those two experiments yielded similar results.

23. 日照りは９月まで続いた。

Hideri wa kugatsu made tsuzuita.
The drought lasted until September.

Supplemental Reading Practice

After completing Chapter 27 of this book, you should be able to read the "Introductions" and "Food Lover" articles from the "Kona's Big Adventure" series in *Satori Reader*.

Chapter 28

New Kanji in this Chapter

# 825 釘 (1)	# 826 騒 (2)	# 827 尻 (1)	# 828 呆 (4)
# 829 褒 (2)	# 830 飼 (3)	# 831 康 (1)	# 832 骨 (3)

Vocabulary List with Mnemonics

from the Kanji Catalogue

釘	kugi = nail or peg; *I used <u>nail</u>s to build a shed for my <u>cool geese</u>*
釘付けになる	kugizuke ni naru = to be unable to take one's eyes from; from kugi = nail + tsuku = to adhere + ni naru = to become
騒ぐ	sawagu = to make noise, to make a fuss; *when he <u>saw</u> the <u>wagon</u> carrying his <u>goose</u>, he <u>made a fuss</u>*
騒々しい	souzoushii = noisy; *a <u>solo</u> (isolated) <u>zou</u> (elephant) was living with some <u>Shiite</u>s, and it was very <u>noisy</u>*
お尻	oshiri = buttocks; *the <u>o</u> (honorable) <u>sheep</u> had a <u>reason</u> to put their <u>buttocks</u> under a lean-to*
呆れる	akireru = to be disgusted or astonished; *<u>Achilles</u> ate the <u>red rooster</u>s, and I was <u>astounded</u>*
呆気	akke = dumbfounded, taken aback; *the <u>ad</u> for <u>Kennedy</u>'s campaign <u>dumbfounded</u> me*
呆け	boke = fool; *riding in a <u>boat</u> while drinking from a <u>keg</u> makes you look like a <u>fool</u>*
褒める	homeru = to praise, admire or speak well of; *we all <u>praise Homer</u>*
褒美	houbi = reward; *the <u>hostess</u> found some <u>beer</u> and earned a <u>reward</u>*
飼主	kainushi = shepherd, pet owner; *the <u>Kaiser</u>'s <u>new sheepherder</u> is a <u>pet owner</u>*
飼う	kau = to keep a pet or raise live-stock; *if you <u>kau</u> (buy) a pet, you have to <u>keep</u> it*
飼い犬	kai'inu = pet dog (this can also be spelled 飼犬); from kau = to keep a pet + inu = dog

Kanji Pronunciations

# 825 – kugi	# 826 – sawa, sou	# 827 – shiri	# 828 – aki, bo, ho, a
# 829 – ho, hou	# 830 – kai, shi, ka	# 831 – kou	# 832 – ko, kotsu, hone

飼育 — shi'iku = breeding, raising, rearing; *sometimes our sheep suffer from ear cooties while we are breeding them*

飼育員 — shi'ikuin = a caretaker at a zoo or aquarium; from shi'iku = to raise an animal + in = member

健康 — kenkou = health; *Ken's colds got better when his health improved*

骨 — hone = bone; *I research bone diseases with the help of my home network*

from the Practice Sentences

打ち込む — uchikomu = to drive in (a nail, etc.), to hit (a ball, etc.); from utsu = to hit + komu = to crowd in

騒音 — sou'on = noise; *the Soviet owner of that car said that it makes very little noise*

ぶつ — butsu = to hit (a person); *my father hit me after I ruined his boots*

無責任さ — musekininsa = irresponsibility; from mu = negation + sekinin = responsibility + sa = a suffix that makes a noun from another word

正直さ — shoujikisa = honesty; from shoujiki = honest; *he showed me his Jeep keys and said that I could use them, so he must think that I'm honest;* + sa = a suffix that makes a noun from an adjective

from Satori Reader

おもちゃ箱 — omochabako = toybox; from omocha = toy; *I omou (think) that I will charge the toy;* + bako = hako = box

振り回す — furimawasu = to swing, to wave about; from furu = to shake or wave + mawasu = to turn

血が騒ぐ — chi ga sawagu = to get excited; from chi = blood + sawagu = to make a fuss

何だか — nandaka = a little, somewhat, somehow; *when the nanny took Darwin for a ride in the car, they fooled around a little*

ムズムズ — muzumuzu = to feel itchy, to be impatient or eager to do something; *while at the museum, you want to visit the zoo; why are you so impatient?*

走り回る — hashirimawaru = to run around; from hashiru = to run + mawaru = to turn

一回転 — ikkai ten = one revolution or rotation; from ichi = one + kai = time + ten = to roll, e.g., jitensha = bicycle

Practice Sentences

1. 木に釘を打ち込んだ。

Ki ni kugi wo uchikonda.
He drove a nail into the wood.

2. 騒音に慣れている。

Sou'on ni narete iru.
I'm used to the noise.

3. 彼女は尻が重い。

Kanojo wa shiri ga omoi.
Her buttocks are heavy (i.e., she's slow).

4. 私は呆気にとられた。

Watashi wa akke ni torareta.
I was dumbfounded.

5. 彼女は彼の正直さを褒めた。

Kanojo wa kare no shoujikisa wo hometa.
She praised his honesty.

6. 犬を飼ってもいい？

Inu wo katte mo ii?
Can I have a dog?

7. 祖父は非常に健康だ。

Sofu wa hijou ni kenkou da.
My grandfather is extremely healthy.

8. 犬に骨をやった。

Inu ni hone wo yatta.
I gave the dog a bone.

9. ハンマーと釘を持ってきてちょうだい。

Hanmaa to kugi wo motte kite choudai.
Please bring a hammer and nail.

10. ここで騒がないで下さい。

Koko de sawaganai de kudasai.
Please don't make noise here.

11. 飼っている猫の名前は何？

Katte iru neko no namae wa nani?
What's the name of the cat you keep?

12. やめなさい、お尻をぶちますよ。

Yamenasai, oshiri wo buchimasu yo.
Stop it. I will hit your bottom, for sure (i.e., I'll spank you).

13. 犬の飼主は首を捕まえた。

Inu no kainushi wa kubi wo tsukamaeta.
The dog's owner grabbed its neck.

14. 彼女の無責任さには呆れてしまう。

Kanojo no musekininsa ni wa akirete shimau.
I am completely astonished at her lack of responsibility.

15. 新聞にその映画は褒められた。

Shinbun ni sono eiga wa homerareta.
By the newspaper, that movie was praised.

16. タバコを吸うにしても、健康やマナーを考えるべきだ。

Tabako o suu ni shitemo, kenkou ya manaa o kangaeru beki da.
You smoke tobacco, even so, you should think about manners, health, etc.

17. この魚は骨が多くて取るのが大変だ。

Kono sakana wa hone ga ookute toru no ga taihen da.
As for this fish, bones are numerous, and to remove them is terrible (i.e., difficult).

18. 彼の目は彼女に釘付けになった。

Kare no me wa kanojo ni kugizuke ni natta.
His eyes became fixed on her.

19. 日本は非常に騒がしい国だ。

Nihon wa hijou ni sawagashii kuni da.
Japan is an extremely noisy country.

20. 彼のお尻は大きいが気にして
いない。

Kare no oshiri wa ookii ga ki ni shite inai.
He has a big bottom, but he doesn't care.

21. そんな易しい計算もできない
なんて、本当に呆れる。

Sonna yasashii keisan mo dekinai nante, honto ni akireru.
Since he cannot even do that kind of easy calculation, such a thing, I get astounded.

22. はい、ご褒美。

Hai, gohoubi.
Yes, honorable reward (i.e., here's your reward).

23. 健康のために、もう少しやせ
ることにしました。

Kenkoo no tame ni, moo sukoshi yaseru koto ni shimashita.
For the sake of health, I decided to thin down a little more.

24. 骨がたくさんある魚は嫌い
だ。

Hone ga takusan aru sakana wa kirai da.
I dislike fish with a lot of bones.

Supplemental Reading Practice

After completing Chapter 28 of this book, you should be able to read the "Tingling with Excitement" article from the "Kona's Big Adventure" series in *Satori Reader*.

Chapter 29

New Kanji in this Chapter

# 833 皮 (3)	# 834 隠 (2)	# 835 沈 (2)	# 836 黙 (2)
# 837 破 (3)	# 838 殺 (3)	# 839 影 (2)	# 840 響 (2)

Vocabulary List with Mnemonics

from the Kanji Catalogue

皮   kawa = skin, peel; *the car wash only cleans the outer skin of my car*

皮肉   hiniku = sarcasm, cynicism, irony; *when I hear you say that the niku (meat) I cooked was great, I detect a hint of sarcasm*

毛皮   kegawa = fur; *the Kennedys started a gas war, and the fur began to fly*

隠す   kakusu = to hide or cover up, transitive; *Karl the Kool-Aid vendor's supervisor told him to hide the evidence from the police*

隠れる   kakureru = to conceal oneself or disappear; *Karl the Kool-Aid vendor bought some red roosters, and then he disappeared*

隠元豆   ingenmame = green bean, string bean; *it's ingenious the way some mame (beans) conceal their beans in pods, and we call those string beans*

沈黙   chinmoku = silence; *after I hit him on the chin on mokuyoubi (Thursday), I've heard nothing but silence from him*

沈める   shizumeru = to sink or submerge, transitive; *the sheep from the zoo in Mexico ruined the boat and sank it*

沈む   shizumu = to set (sun or moon), to sink, to feel depressed; *the sheep from the zoo watched the moon as it set*

黙る   damaru = to keep silent; *when my dad was marooned, he kept silent for a year*

読破する   dokuha suru = to finish reading a book; *the documentary was about a Harvard man who had just finished reading a book*

破る   yaburu = to break, tear or violate; *my yak skin boots were ruined when I broke their clasps*

殺人   satsujin = murder; *the satisfying Superman novel described how some stained jeans helped to solve the murder*

殺す   korosu = to kill; *the corporation's robots attacked Superman and tried to kill him*

Kanji Pronunciations

# 833 – kawa, gawa, hi	# 834 – kaku, in	# 835 – shizu, chin	# 836 – dama, moku
# 837 – ha, yabu, pa	# 838 – satsu, sa, koro	# 839 – ei, kage	# 840 – hibi, kyou

殺到する	sattou suru = to rush at or surge; *the sad-looking toads rushed into the pond*
影	kage = shadow, silhouette; *the carving of a gecko cast a shadow on the ground*
響く	hibiku = to resound, to be heard far away; *I get the heebie jeebies in Kuwait when I heard mortar fire resounding*
響き	hibiki = echo, repercussion, sound; from hibiku = to resound
影響	eikyou = influence, effect; *the ancient temples in Kyouto have an influence on the entire country*

from the Practice Sentences

影響力	eikyouryoku = influence, clout; from eikyou = influence + ryoku = force
自殺	jisatsu = suicide; from ji = self + satsujin = murder
破片	hahen = fragment; *the hacker's henchmen broke my monitor into fragments*

from Satori Reader

おそろい	osoroi = matching, going together; *when the old soldier sang duets with Roy Rogers, they wore matching outfits*
チビ	chibi = small child, runt, dwarf; *the dwarf likes cheap beer*
去勢	kyosei = castration; *in Kyoto the sailor was sentenced to castration*
高熱	kounetsu = high fever; from kou = high, e.g., koukou = high school; + netsu = fever

Practice Sentences

1. 鳥の皮は食べません。

Tori no kawa wa tabemasen.
I don't eat chicken skin.

2. 何か隠してるの？

Nanika kakushiteru no?
Are you hiding something?

3. 語れないことについては、沈黙するほかない。

Katarenai koto ni tsuite wa, chinmoku suru hokanai.
Regarding things of which one cannot speak, one can only be silent.

4. 彼は約束を破った。

Kare wa yakusoku wo yabutta.
He broke the promise.

5. 殺すしかない。

Korosu shika nai.
There is no choice but to kill.

6. 私には影響力がない。

Watashi ni wa eikyouryoku ga nai.
As for to me, influence doesn't exist (i.e., I have no clout).

7. 毛皮のコートが特売中です。

Kegawa no kooto ga tokubai chuu desu.
The fur coats are during a special sale (i.e., they're on sale).

8. 月は雲に顔を隠した。

Tsuki wa kumo ni kao wo kakushita.
The moon hid its face in the clouds.

9. 一日中ずっと心が沈んでいた。

Ichinichijuu zutto kokoro ga shizunde ita.
All day, all the way through, the heart was sinking (i.e., I was feeling depressed).

10. 彼から大きな影響を受けた。

Kare kara ookina eikyou wo uketa.
I received a large influence from him (i.e, he influenced me a lot).

11. 本を読破した。

Hon wo dokuha shita.
I finished reading the book.

12. 父は自殺をした。

Chichi wa jisatsu wo shita.
My father committed suicide.

13. 目的も無しに話すよりは、黙っている方がましだ。

Mokuteki mo nashi ni hanasu yori wa damatte iru hou ga mashi da.
Compared to talking without even a purpose, it's better to keep silent. (mashi = better, similar to いい ii)

14. あの木の後ろで影の動きを見た。

Ano ki no ushiro de kage no ugoki wo mita.
I saw the movement of a shadow behind that tree over there.

15. 皮肉だな。

Hiniku da na.
It's ironic.

16. 机の下に隠れた。

Tsukue no shita ni kakureta.
I hid under the desk.

17. 寝不足の影響が出始めた。

Nebusoku no eikyou ga dehajimeta.
The influence of lack of sleep began to emerge.

18. 月が沈んだ。

Tsuki ga shizunda.
The moon set (i.e., it went down).

19. 黙っていなさい。

Damatte inasai.
Be quiet.

20. 割れた皿の破片を集めた。

Wareta sara no hahen wo atsumeta.
I gathered the fragments of the broken dish.

21. 大勢の人が出口へ殺到した。

Oozei no hito ga deguchi e sattou shita.
Many people rushed to the exits.

22. その建物は長い影を作った。

Sono tatemono wa nagai kage wo tsukutta.
That building created a long shadow.

Supplemental Reading Practice

After completing Chapter 29 of this book, you should be able to read the "Runt" and "The Shelter" articles from the "Kona's Big Adventure" series in *Satori Reader*.

Chapter 30

New Kanji in this Chapter

# 841 添 (3)	# 842 延 (2)	# 843 餌 (2)	# 844 視 (1)
# 845 肩 (2)	# 846 撫 (2)	# 847 精 (2)	# 848 杯 (4)

Vocabulary List with Mnemonics

from the Kanji Catalogue

添える   soeru = to attach to, to garnish a dish, to help or support; *in the Soviet Union, erudite people supported the less educated ones*

付き添う   tsukisou = to accompany, chaperone, take care of; from tsuku = to attach + soeru = to support

力添え   chikarazoe = assistance, support; from chikara = force + zoeru = soeru = to support

添加物   tenkabutsu = an additive (e.g., to food); from tenka = addition; *ten Canadians built an addition to the house*; + butsu = thing

延期   enki = postponement; *if you encourage kicking, there will be a postponement of the match*

引き延ばす   hikinobasu = to delay; *the Himalayan king had no basu (bus), so he delayed his trip*

餌   esa = animal food or bait; *the Eskimos use sardines as animal food*

餌食   ejiki = prey or victim; *the entertainer who was carrying large Jeep keys was a victim of a lightning strike*

無視する   mushi suru = to disregard or ignore; *I heard a mushy story about a person who disregarded warnings*

視力   shiryoku = eyesight; from shi = to see; *sheep can see well*; + ryoku = power

肩   kata = shoulder; *that kata [person] hurt her shoulder*

撫でる   naderu = to rub or stroke; *Ralph Nader likes to stroke the heads of children*

愛撫   aibu = a caress; *I put ice in her booze, and she gave me a caress*

一杯   ippai = one cup, glass, spoon or bowl, or full of; *after you eat that pie, I will give you one glass of milk*

Kanji Pronunciations

# 841 – ten, so, zo	# 842 – en, no	# 843 – e, esa	# 844 – shi
# 845 – kata, ken	# 846 – na, bu	# 847 – sei, shou	# 848 – hai, bai, pai, sakazuki

精一杯	sei'ippai = the best of one's ability, with all one's might; from sei = energy, vitality; *a sage has a lot of vitality*; + ippai = full of
精神	seishin = mind, soul, spirit; *if you say Shinto prayers, you can improve your mind, soul and spirit*
精神的な	seishinteki na = spiritual, mental; from seishin = mind or spirit + teki = related to
精進料理	shoujin ryouri = vegetarian cuisine, as eaten by Buddhist monks; from shoujin = concentration, devotion; *near the shore a genius sits in meditation, showing his concentration and devotion*; + ryouri = cuisine
杯をする	sakazuki wo suru = to share a cup of sake; *after I play sakkaa (soccer) with the zoo keeper, we share a cup of sake*

from the Practice Sentences

乾杯	kanpai = cheers!; *let's eat some Canadian pie, have a drink, and say cheers!*
よだれ	yodare = saliva, drool; *Yoda turned red when I mentioned his drooling*
いじめ	ijime = bullying, teasing; *those ingenious men are guilty of bullying*

from Satori Reader

ボソッと	bosotto = absent-mindedly, vacantly, idly; *the bored soldiers cut their toenails and stared absent-mindedly*
寄り添う	yorisou = to cuddle together; from yoru = to drop in or go closer + soueru = to attach
やってくる	yatte kuru = to turn up, come along; from yaru = to do + kuru = to come
コツコツ	kotsukotsu = tapping, clicking, steadily; *they were making coats and coats steadily, and their needles were clicking*
足音	ashioto = footsteps; from ashi = foot + oto = sound
生き延びる	ikinobiru = to survive or live long; from ikiru = to live + nobiru = to extend
そっと	sotto = softly, gently, quietly; this reminds us of sotto voce (Italian), referring to soft music
持ち上げる	mochiageru = to elevate, raise up, flatter; from motsu = to hold + ageru = to raise
ブルブル	buruburu = to shiver with cold or fear; *my boots were ruined, and soon I was shivering*
震える	furueru = to tremble; *his food ruined, the erudite man trembled as the winter approached*
あったかい	attakai = warm, mild, genial; variant of atatakai = warm
ゴロゴロ	gorogoro = purring, grumbling, thundering, rumbling; *the goat rode in a cart that rumbled down the road*
鳴らす	narasu = to ring or sound; the transitive form of naru = to ring or sound

Practice Sentences

1. ご期待に添えかねます。

Gokitai ni soekanemasu.
To the honorable expectations we are unable to support. (i.e., we can't meet your expectations; kaneru = unable to do)

2. 手紙の返事を引き延ばした。

Tegami no henji wo hikinobashita.
He delayed the answer to the letter.

3. 犬に餌をやりましたか。

Inu ni esa wo yarimashita ka.
Did you feed the dog?

4. 赤信号を無視して走りましたね。

Akashingou wo mushi shite hashirimashita ne.
You disregarded the red light and ran, huh. (i.e., you ran the red light)

5. 肩こりがとれないと毎日辛いですよね。

Katakori ga torenai to mainichi tsurai desu yo ne.
If you cannot remove shoulder pain, every day it's bitter, for sure, huh.

6. 猫は撫でられて嬉しそう。

Neko wa naderarete ureshisou.
When the cat gets petted, it seems pleased.

7. この旅館では精進料理が食べられます。

Kono ryokan de wa shoujinryouri ga taberaremasu.
As for at this Japanese inn, one can eat Buddhist-style vegetarian cuisine.

8. 一杯いかがですか。

Ippai ikaga desu ka.
How about one drink?

9. 赤ちゃんを易しく愛撫した。

Akachan wo yasashiku aibu shita.
She caressed the baby tenderly.

10. お力添えをお願いいたします。

Ochikarazoe wo onegai itashimasu.
I humbly beg your honorable assistance.

11. 運動会が雨で延期になった。

Undoukai ga ame de enki ni natta.
The sports tournament was delayed due to rain.

12. 犬が餌を見てよだれを流した。

Inu ga esa wo mite yodare wo nagashita.
The dog saw the dogfood and drooled.

13. この問題は無視できない。

Kono mondai wa mushi dekinai.
I can't ignore this problem.

14. 肩までの長さでカットしてください。

Kata made no nagasa de katto shite kudasai.
Please cut it shoulder-length.

15. 母は息子の頭を撫でた。

Haha wa musuko no atama wo nadeta.
The mother stroked her son's head.

16. 精神的な強さを試された。

Seishinteki na tsuyosa wo tamesareta.
My spriritual strength was tested.

17. 乾杯しましょう。

Kanpai shimashou.
Let's drink a toast.

18. ごめんなさい、付き添えない の。

Gomen nasai, tsukisoenai no.
I'm sorry. I can't accompany you.

19. 出発を延期する。

Shuppatsu wo enki suru.
I will postpone the departure.

20. 彼はいじめの餌食になった。

Kare wa ijime no ejiki ni natta.
He became a victim of bullying.

21. 最近視力が落ちてきた。

Saikin shiryoku ga ochite kita.
Recently the eyesight is failing.

22. どうしても右肩が上がらない んです。

Doushitemo migi kata ga agaranain desu.
No matter what, the right shoulder (i.e., arm) will not rise.

23. 精一杯努力しよう。

Sei'ippai doryoku shiyou.
Let's do effort with all our might.

Supplemental Reading Practice

After completing Chapter 30 of this book, you should be able to read the "Dark Night" and "Visitors" articles from the "Kona's Big Adventure" series in *Satori Reader*.

Chapter 31

New Kanji in this Chapter

# 849 兆 (2)	# 850 逃 (3)	# 851 悲 (2)	# 852 揺 (2)
# 853 器 (2)	# 854 奇 (1)	# 855 椅 (1)	# 856 妙 (2)

Vocabulary List with Mnemonics

from the Kanji Catalogue

兆し — kizashi = sign, omen; *when she kissed Zach's sheep, it moved, which was a sign that it was still alive*

前兆 — zenchou = premonition, omen; *the Zen temple assigned me the chore of sweeping, and I had a premonition that my broom would break*

一兆円 — itchouen = 1 trillion yen; from ichi = one + chou = trillion; *Margaret Cho earned a trillion yen last year*; + en = yen

逃げる — nigeru = to escape or run away; *the Nigerian rooster ran away*

逃亡 — toubou = escape, flight; *he used a toy boat for his escape*

逃れる — nogareru = to escape; *since he had no gas, he had to walk to town, and while he was gone, his red rooster escaped*

逃す — nogasu = to let go, to allow to escape; *because he had no gas, the policeman allowed the speeder to escape*

悲しい — kanashii = sad; *Canadian Shiites are sad in the winter*

悲鳴 — himei = scream, shriek, cry of distress; *he majored in psychology, but I hear his screams every night*

揺れる — yureru = to sway, shake or rock; *the European restaurant was ruined when it shook during an earthquake*; cf. 震える furu'eru = to tremble, # 265

動揺 — douyou = uneasiness, agitation; *the doorman ate the yogurt with uneasiness*

器 — utsuwa = container or receptacle, ability; *we utilize the supermarket's water to fill our containers*

食器 — shokki = tableware; *this tableware was shocking the child who inserted it into an electric outlet*

奇妙な — kimyou na = strange; *Kim Jong Un thought that the yogurt looked strange*; cf. 妙な myou na = strange, odd, unique

Kanji Pronunciations

# 849 – kiza, chou	# 850 – ni, tou, noga	# 851 – hi, kana	# 852 – yu, you
# 853 – utsuwa, ki	# 854 – ki	# 855 – i	# 856 – tae, myou

好奇心 — koukishin = curiosity; *I plan to wear a <u>coat</u> over my <u>kimono</u> when I visit the <u>Shinto</u> shrine, but I feel <u>curiosity</u> about what other people will wear*

椅子 — isu = chair; *on <u>Easter</u> the <u>superintendent</u> will sit in a fancy <u>chair</u>*

妙なる — taenaru = exquisite; *the <u>tapestries</u> and <u>etchings</u> in the <u>nanny</u>'s <u>room</u> were <u>exquisite</u>*

妙な — myou na = strange, odd, unique; *it's <u>me, oh</u> Lord, cried the <u>nanny</u>, when she saw the <u>strange</u> light*; cf. 奇妙な kimyou na= strange

from the Practice Sentences

悲鳴をあげる — himei wo ageru = to scream; from himei = scream + ageru = to raise up

ブランコ — buranko = swing; *the <u>swing</u> was painted <u>blanco</u> (white, in Spanish)*

思い出 — omoide = memory; from omou = to think + deru = to go out

心地 — kokochi = feeling, sensation, mood; *when I drink <u>cocoa</u> and eat <u>chee</u>se, I get a good <u>feeling</u>*

回復 — kaifuku = recovery; *touching the <u>Kaiser</u>'s <u>fuku</u> [clothing] hastened her <u>recovery</u> from her illness*

不器用な — bukiyou na = clumsy; *I'm <u>clumsy</u>, and when I was <u>booking</u> the <u>yoga</u> class, I dropped the phone twice*

奇数 — kisuu = odd number; *I can only <u>kiss</u> yo<u>u</u> on <u>odd</u>-<u>numbered</u> days*

調べ — shirabe = tune, tone, writing style; *the <u>sheep</u> and the <u>rabbits</u> <u>enjoy</u> that <u>tune</u>*

目覚める — mezameru = to wake up; an abbreviation of me ga sameru = to wake up

近づける — chikazukeru = to draw something near, to introduce a person to another; from chikai = close + tsukeru = to attach

from Satori Reader

おとなしい — otonashii = obedient, docile, quiet; *the <u>otola</u>ryngologist was <u>gnashing</u> his teeth, but he was <u>quiet</u>, <u>docile</u> and <u>obedient</u>*

引き取る — hikitoru = to take back, take over, claim, take charge of; from hiku = to pull + toru = to take

言い返す — iikaesu = to talk or answer back, to say repeatedly; from iu = to speak + kaesu = to return something

引っ張り出す — hipparidasu = to take out, drag out; from hipparu = to pull + dasu = to take out

飛びつく — tobitsuku = to jump at; from tobu = to fly + tsuku = to adhere

ほっとする — hotto suru = to feel relief, to relax; *when I put a <u>hot</u> <u>towel</u> on my face, I <u>feel</u> <u>relief</u> and <u>relax</u>*

張る — haru = to stretch, spread, become tense, be expensive; *the <u>Hawaiian</u> <u>rule</u>r <u>stretched</u> a rope across his throne room*

張り上げる　hariageru = to raise (one's voice); from haru = to stretch + ageru = to raise

プラスチック　purasuchikku = plastic

Practice Sentences

1. あの雲は雨の前兆だ。
Ano kumo wa ame no zenchou da.
That cloud over there is a portent of rain.

2. 泥棒が逃げた。
Dorobou ga nigeta.
The thief ran away.

3. 彼女は怖くて悲鳴をあげた。
Kanojo wa kowakute himei wo ageta.
She was frightened and screamed.

4. ブランコが揺れている。
Buranko ga yurete iru.
The swing is swinging.

5. お皿を食器棚に戻してくださいませんか。
Osara wo shokkidana ni modoshite kudasaimasen ka.
Will you not return the dishes to the cupboard and give?

6. 隣から奇妙な声がする。
Tonari kara kimyou na koe ga suru.
From next door, a strange voice does (i.e., I hear it).

7. 名前を呼ばれるまでその椅子に掛けていてください。
Namae o yobareru made sono isu ni kakete ite kudasai.
Until the name is called, please be sitting on that chair.

8. 1兆円は約90億ドルです。
Itchouen wa yaku kyuujuu oku doru desu.
One trillion yen is about nine billion dollars.

9. ソビエトへ逃亡した。
Sobieto e toubou shita.
He escaped (i.e., defected) to the Soviet Union.

10. 悲しい思い出は忘れたい。
Kanashii omoide wa wasuretai.
I want to forget sad memories.

11. 地震で家が大きく揺れた。
Jishin de ie ga ookiku yureta.
By the earthquake, the house shook a lot.

12. その器は古い物です。
Sono utsuwa wa furui mono desu.
That container is an old thing.

13. 彼女はとても好奇心が強い。
Kanojo wa totemo koukishin ga tsuyoi.
As for her, exceedingly, curiosity is strong (i.e., she has strong curiosity).

14. 妙な話を聞いた。
Myou na hanashi wo kiita.
I heard a strange story.

15. この椅子は座り心地が悪い。

Kono isu wa suwari kokochi ga warui.
As for this chair, the sitting comfort is
bad (i.e., it's uncomfortable).

16. 経済の回復の兆しが見えてき
た。

Keizai no kaifuku no kizashi ga miete
kita.
The signs of the economy's recovery are
visible and coming.

17. 危険から逃れた。

Kiken kara nogareta.
He escaped from danger.

18. 誰にも私の気持ちを分かって
もらえないのが悲しい。

Darenimo watashi no kimochi o wakatte
moraenai no ga kanashii.
To nobody, my feelings will understand
and I cannot receive thing, sad.

19. 彼はその知らせに動揺した。

Kare wa sono shirase ni douyou shita.
He was agitated by that news.

20. 私は不器用です。

Watashi wa bukiyou desu.
I'm clumsy.

21. ３と５は奇数である。

San to go wa kisuu de aru.
3 and 5 are odd numbers.

22. 妙なる調べに目覚めた。

Taenaru shirabe ni mezameta.
I woke up to an exquisite melody.

23. 椅子をもっと机に近づけなさ
い。

Isu wo motto tsukue ni chikazukenasai.
Move the chair closer to the desk.

Supplemental Reading Practice

After completing Chapter 31 of this book, you should be able to read the "Picked"
and "A Goodbye and a Hello" articles from the "Kona's Big Adventure" series in *Satori
Reader*.

Chapter 32

New Kanji in this Chapter

# 857 比 (2)	# 858 鮮 (2)	# 859 検 (1)	# 860 査 (1)
# 861 膝 (1)	# 862 我 (3)	# 863 腹 (5)	# 864 寂 (2)

Vocabulary List with Mnemonics

from the Kanji Catalogue

対比する — taihi suru = to compare, contrast; *the Thai hero compared his options*

比べる — kuraberu = to compare; *the kuuraa (air-conditioner) looks better on the roof, compared to installing it on the ground*

新鮮な — shinsen na = fresh; *the Shinto shrine sent me some fresh fruit*

鮮明な — senmei na = bright, clear, vivid; *the senator's maid wore a bright colored dress*

鮮やかな — azayaka na = colorful, bright, vivid, impressive, beautiful; *the art that I saw in Zach's yacht and car was vivid and beautiful*

検査 — kensa = investigation, examination; *Ken saw to it that Barbie received a careful examination*

探検 — tanken = exploration, expedition; *the tan that Ken acquired during his expedition with Barbie is impressive (see alternative spelling below)*

探険 — tanken = exploration, expedition (see alternative spelling above); cf. 点検 tenken = inspection

調査 — chousa = investigation, survey, analysis; *we chose Samsung to conduct the investigation*

巡査 — junsa = patrolman; *the junior salaryman flagged down a patrolman*

膝 — hiza = knee, lap; *he's a little drunk and has fallen onto his knees*

我が国 — wagakuni = one's country; from waga = I, my; *I will pay for the water and gas*; + kuni = country

我がままな — wagamama na = selfish, spoiled; from waga = I, my; *I will pay for the water and gas*; + mama = as is, as you are; *Mama says you are all right as you are*

我 — ware = self; *Washington rested in this house, which belongs to my self*

我々 — wareware = we; from ware = self

Kanji Pronunciations

# 857 – hi, kura	# 858 – sen, aza	# 859 – ken	# 860 – sa
# 861 – hiza	# 862 – wa, ware, ga	# 863 – fuku, puku, naka, hara, para	# 864 – jaku, sabi

我ら	warera = we; from ware = self + ra = plural, e.g., kore = that, korera = those
腹痛	fukutsuu = stomachache; from fuku = stomach; *in Fukuoka, some people suffer from stomach problems*; + tsuu = pain, e.g. zutsuu = headache
空腹	kuufuku = hunger; from kuu = empty; *the Kool-Aid pitcher is empty*; + fuku = stomach
お腹	onaka = honorable stomach; *my old nasty cat was suffering from honorable stomach problems*
腹	hara = stomach, abdomen; *a Hawaiian rascal stabbed me in the stomach*
静寂	seijaku = silence, stillness; *in the Safeway store, Jack Nicholson assumed a stony silence*
寂しい	sabishii = lonely; *after the salaryman's favorite beerhall was closed by the Shiites, he was lonely*

from the Practice Sentences

代表する	daihyou suru = to represent; *a diet of healing yogurt represents a different approach to weight loss*
一人ぼっち	hitoribotchi = solitude, loneliness; from hitori = one person + botchi = loneliness; *he played bocce ball to escape his loneliness*
訪れ	otozure = arrival; from otozureru = to visit or arrive
片膝	katahiza = one knee; from katahou = one side + hiza = knee
点検	tenken = inspection; *ten Kennedys conducted the inspection*; cf. 探険 tanken (or 探検 tanken) = expedition
隣同士	tonari doushi = nextdoor neighbor; from tonari = neighbor + doushi = colleague, peer; *the dozing sheepdog belongs to my colleague*
ペコペコ	pekopeko = very hungry, starving; *all I've had for nourishment is pekoe tea, pekoe tea, and I'm starving*
昨年	sakunen = last year; from saku = previous, e.g., sakuban = last night; + nen = year; cf. 去年 kyonen = last year

from Satori Reader

通す	toosu = to lead (into a house), to show in, to force or let through, to penetrate, to proceed logically; the transitive form of tooru = to pass through
便器	benki = toilet bowl, urinal, bedpan; from benri = convenient + ki = container; *I keep quiche in a container*
つるつる	tsurutsuru = smooth, slippery; *the tsuitcase (suitcase) in the room has a smooth exterior*
に加えて	ni kuwaete = in addition; from kuwaeru = to add or include

流し台 — nagashidai = a sink; from nagasu = to flush + dai = platform

ウトウト — uto'uto = dozing; *riding in an Uber car on a toll road, I started dozing*

おやつ — oyatsu = between-meal snack; *we had some o (honorable) yak tsoup (soup) as a snack*

ジューシー — juushii = juicy

とろける — torokeru = to melt, to be charmed; *while riding on the toll road, Kennedy ruined his suit when some ice cream melted on it*

生まれて始めて — umaretehajimete = for the first time in one's life; from umareru = to be born + hajimeru = to begin

無我夢中 — mugamuchuu = losing oneself in, being absorbed; from mu = negation; + ga = self; *my self has the gift of gab*; + mu = dream; *I dream about the moon*; + chuu = inside

Practice Sentences

1. あの人と比べないで下さい。
Ano hito to kurabenai de kudasai.
Please don't compare me to that person.

2. このお魚はとても新鮮です。
Kono osakana wa totemo shinsen desu.
This honorable fish is very fresh.

3. 明日は胃の検査をします。
Ashita wa i no kensa o shimasu.
Tomorrow I will do a stomach exam.

4. 彼女は転んで膝を痛めた。
Kanojo wa koronde hiza wo itameta.
She fell over and hurt her knee.

5. 我々は日本を代表する選手だ。
Wareware wa nihon wo daihyou suru senshu da.
We are athletes who represent Japan.

6. お腹がペコペコだった。
Onaka ga pekopeko datta.
I was really hungry.

7. 私は一人ぼっちで寂しい。
Watashi wa hitoribotchi de sabishii.
Since I am alone, I'm lonely.

8. 昨年に比べて今年は春の訪れが遅かった。
Sakunen ni kurabete kotoshi wa haru no otozure ga osokatta.
Compared to last year, as for this year, spring's arrival was late.

9. 写真ほど鮮明な物はない。
Shashin hodo senmei na mono wa nai.
Compared to photographs, nothing is more vivid.

10. 彼はアフリカへ探検旅行に行くのが好きだ。
Kare wa afurika e tanken ryokou ni iku no ga suki da.
He likes to go on adventure trips to Africa.

11. この事件は調査中です。

Kono jiken wa chousa chuu desu.
This incident is under investigation.

12. 片膝を立てた。

Katahiza wo tateta.
He put up one knee. (i.e., he sat with one knee raised)

13. 我が国の法律に違反した。

Wagakuni no houritsu ni ihan shita.
He broke the laws of our country.

14. ひどい腹痛がした。

Hidoi fukutsuu ga shita.
I had an awful stomach ache.

15. 山の中は静寂だった。

Yama no naka wa seijaku datta.
It was silent in the mountains.

16. 日本はアメリカに比べるとまだ夏休みは短いです。

Nihon wa amerika ni kuraberu to mada natsuyasumi wa mijikai desu.
As for Japan, if you compare to the U.S., summer vacations are still short.

17. 鮮やかな赤い花が庭に咲いている。

Azayaka na akai hana ga niwa ni saite iru.
Bright red flowers are blossoming in the garden.

18. その車は点検してもらう必要がある。

Sono kuruma wa tenken shite morau hitsuyou ga aru.
It's necessary that that car be checked and I receive.

19. すぐに巡査がきた。

Sugu ni junsa ga kita.
A patrolman came right away.

20. 膝をついて掃除をします。

Hiza wo tsuite souji wo shimasu.
Kneeling, I clean.

21. 我らは隣同士だ。

Warera wa tonari doushi da.
We are next-door neighbors.

22. 腹が立つときは、10まで数えなさい。

Hara ga tatsu toki wa, juu made kazoenasai.
At get-angry times, count to ten.

23. 誰も会いに来てくれないので寂しい。

Daremo ai ni kite kurenai node sabishii.
Because nobody, for the purpose of meeting, doesn't come and give, lonely.

Supplemental Reading Practice

After completing Chapter 32 of this book, you should be able to read the "A New Home" and "Naptime and Snacks" articles from the "Kona's Big Adventure" series in *Satori Reader*.

Chapter 33

New Kanji in this Chapter

# 865 敷 (2)	# 866 丸 (2)	# 867 局 (1)	# 868 突 (3)
# 869 恐 (2)	# 870 永 (2)	# 871 戸 (4)	# 872 句 (1)

Vocabulary List with Mnemonics

from the Kanji Catalogue

敷く — shiku = to lay out, spread or enact; *the sheep food and the Kool-Aid packages have been laid out in the pantry*

座敷 — zashiki = Japanese-style room with tatami flooring; *Zach found the missing shift key in the tatami room*

屋敷 — yashiki = estate, mansion, residence; *the yakuza (gangster) pressed the shift key when he wrote emails in his mansion, so that they would appear in capital letters*

丸 — maru = circle, a whole; *I was marooned on an island shaped like a circle*

丸い — marui = round; from maru = circle

弾丸 — dangan = bullet; *the dancer and Gandalf were struck by bullets*

結局 — kekkyoku = after all; *the Kennedys joined the Kyoto Kool-Aid club after all*

突然の — totsuzen no = abrupt or sudden; *the total time that Superman spent at the Zen center was less than a minute, and his departure was quite sudden*

突入する — totsunyuu suru = to enter or rush into; *the total time that Superman spent in nyuu yooku (New York) after rushing into the city was one day*

突き当たり — tsukiatari = dead end; *on the tsuki (moon), the Atari office is located at a dead end*

恐れる — osoreru = to be afraid or apprehensive; *the old soldier looked at the red rooster and was afraid*

恐れ — osore = fear; from osoreru = to fear

恐ろしい — osoroshii = frightening, terrible; *the old soldier rose from his seat and gave the Shiite general a terrible look*

永遠 — eien = eternity; *when I fly on ANA (All Nippon Airways), it seems to take an eternity to get to Japan*

永眠 — eimin = death; from eien = eternity + suimin = sleep; *after eating some sweet mints, I fell asleep*

Kanji Pronunciations

# 865 – shiki, shi	# 866 – gan, maru	# 867 – kyoku	# 868 – totsu, tsu, to
# 869 – oso, kyou	# 870 – ei, naga	# 871 – to, do, ko, be	# 872 – ku

永久   eikyuu = eternity, forever; *aging Cubans seem to live for an eternity*

戸   to = door; *I caught my toe in the door*

戸棚   todana = cupboard; from to = door + dana = tana = shelf

一戸   ikko = one house or household; from ichi = one + ko = house; *the corporal bought a house*

文句   monku = complaint, phrase, words; *the monk had a complaint*

句読点   kutouten = punctuation marks; *kooky Tolstoy tended to use too many punctuation marks*

from the Practice Sentences

難局   nankyoku = a difficult situation; *that nanny wants to join the Kyoto Kool-Aid club, but she's involved in a difficult situation and may not be accepted*

直面する   chokumen suru = to face or be involved with, to confront with; *if you choke those Ku Klux Klan men, they will confront you*

恐れ入ります   osoreirimasu = I'm overwhelmed, i.e., I'm sorry; from osore = fear + irimasu = to enter

段階   dankai = stage of development or step; *the dancer worked for the Kaiser at a certain stage of her development*

句   ku = phrase or haiku; some *phrases found in haiku are cool*

薬局   yakkyoku = pharmacy; *the yakuza came to the Kyoto Kool-Aid club thinking that it was a pharmacy*

一発   ippatsu = one blow, shot, attempt; from ichi = one + patsu = departure, e.g., shuppatsu = departure

from Satori Reader

ウロウロ   uro'uro = loitering, restlessly; *the urologist was loitering restlessly around the clinic*

飛び乗る   tobinoru = to jump onto a moving object; from tobu = to fly + noru = to board a vehicle

モミモミ   momimomi = massage; *he adds more meat to my food if I give him a massage*

フワフワ   fuwafuwa = fluffy, floating, frivolously, spongy, soft; from fluffy

足す   tasu = to take care of business, to add numbers, to add something; *after putting on a tan suit, I took care of my business*

見合わせる   miawaseru = to exchange glances, to postpone, to refrain from doing something; from miru = to look + awaseru = to put together, to harmonize

Practice Sentences

1. テーブルクロスを敷いてください。
Teeburu kurosu wo shiite kudasai.
Please spread the tablecloth (i.e., put it on the table).

2. 地球は丸い。
Chikyuu wa marui.
The earth is round.

3. 我々は難局に直面している。
Wareware wa nankyoku ni chokumen shite iru.
We are confronted with a difficult situation.

4. その物語は突然終わりになった。
Sono monogatari wa totsuzen owari ni natta.
That story suddenly came to an end.

5. お忙しいところ恐れ入ります。
Oisogashii tokoro osoreirimasu.
An honorably busy moment, I'm overwhelmed. (i.e., I'm sorry to bother you when you're busy)

6. 君を永遠に愛します。
Kimi wo eien ni ai shimasu.
I will love you forever.

7. ケーキがそこの戸棚に入っていますよ。
Keeki ga soko no todana ni haitte imasu yo.
The cake is being entered in that cupboard, for sure. (i.e., it's there)

8. 文句を言わずに食べた。
Monku wo iwazuni tabeta.
I ate without saying complaints.

9. この座敷は広くて立派ですね。
Kono zashiki wa hirokute rippa desu ne.
This tatami room is spacious and splendid, huh.

10. 丸1ヶ月、銀座のホテルに泊まった。
Maru ikkagetsu, ginza no hoteru ni tomatta.
I stayed at a Ginza hotel for a whole month.

11. 結局何もなかった。
Kekkyoku nanimo nakatta.
After all, it was nothing.

12. 新しい段階に突入している。
Atarashii dankai ni totsunyuu shite iru.
We are entering into a new phase.

13. 恐ろしい事故を見ました。
Osoroshii jiko wo mimashita.
I saw a frightening accident.

14. 主人は永眠しました。
Shujin wa eimin shimashita.
My husband did eternal sleep (i.e., he died).

15. 戸を開けっ放しにするな。

To wo akeppanashi ni suru na.
Don't decide to leave the door open.
(i.e., don't leave it open; -ppanashi after
a verb stem = an action or its result
continues)

16. 辞書でその句を調べなさい。

Jisho de sono ku wo shirabenasai.
Look up that phrase in the dictionary.

17. 田舎の屋敷に住んでいる。

Inaka no yashiki ni sunde iru.
He lives in a country estate.

18. 一発の弾丸で殺された。

Ippatsu no dangan de korosareta.
He was killed by a single bullet.

19. ここから一番近い薬局はどこ
ですか。

Koko kara ichiban chikai yakkyoku wa
doko desu ka.
From here, where is the closest
pharmacy?

20. 突き当たりを右に曲がる。

Tsukiatari o migi ni magaru.
At the T-intersection, you turn right.

21. 台風が来る恐れがあります。

Taifuu ga kuru osore ga arimasu.
Fear exists that a typhoon will come.

22. 永久にアフリカを去った。

Eikyuu ni afurika wo satta.
He left Africa forever.

23. 家がこの辺に五戸ある。

Ie ga kono hen ni goko aru.
In this area, there are five households.

24. この作文は句読点が多い。

Kono sakubun wa kutouten ga ooi.
This composition contains a lot of
punctuation marks.

Supplemental Reading Practice

After completing Chapter 33 of this book, you should be able to read the "Together but Alone" and "Good Morning!" articles from the "Kona's Big Adventure" series in *Satori Reader*.

Chapter 34

New Kanji in this Chapter

# 873 敬 (2)	# 874 警 (1)	# 875 戒 (2)	# 876 畳 (3)
# 877 津 (3)	# 878 波 (4)	# 879 隙 (1)	# 880 官 (1)

Vocabulary List with Mnemonics

from the Kanji Catalogue

敬う — uyamau = to respect or venerate; *in Uruguay, the yama [mountain] owls respect and venerate their leader*

敬語 — keigo = honorific language; *on Cape Cod, the golfers use honorific language*

警戒 — keikai = vigilance, watch; *when the cane came flying at the Kaiser, he showed vigilance and ducked*

警戒する — keikai suru = to be cautious or watch out; from keikai = vigilance

戒める — imashimeru = to admonish, warn, prohibit, be cautious; *I imagine that there are sheep in the Mexican ruins, but I warn you not to visit them*

畳む — tatamu = to fold; *the tall talented movie star is folding origami*

畳 — tatami = tatami mat; from tatamu = to fold

六畳 — rokujou = six tatami mats; from roku = six + jou = counter for tatami mats; *Joan of Arc sat on a tatami mat*

津々 — shinshin = flowing, everlasting; *the Shinto priest used shingles to protect his shrine from flowing rain water*

興味津々 — kyoumi shinshin = very interesting; from kyoumi = interest + shinshin = flowing; cf. 興味深い kyoumibukai = very interesting

津波 — tsunami = tidal wave

波止場 — hatoba = pier, wharf; *in Hawaii people eat toast at bars near the piers*

音波 — onpa = sound wave; *my only parent is studying sound waves*

突破する — toppa suru = to break through; *the Tory party broke through the opposition*

隙 — suki = gap, opening, carelessness, inattentiveness; *there is a gap in the wall at the sukiyaki restaurant*

Kanji Pronunciations

# 873 – kei, uyama	# 874 – kei	# 875 – kai, imashi	# 876 – tatami, tata, jou
# 877 – shin, tsu, zu	# 878 – wa, nami, ha, pa	# 879 – suki	# 880 – kan

隙間	sukima = gap, hole; from suki = gap + ma = between
警官	keikan = policeman; *I always give cake and candy to that policeman*
仕官	shikan = military officer; *the Shiite Canadian became a military officer*

from the Practice Sentences

のぞく
nozoku = to peek or snoop, often spelled 覗く; *while parked in a No Parking Zone in Kuwait, I peeked into my lunch sack*; cf. 除く nozoku = to remove

につながる
ni tsunagaru = to be connected to; *my niece spent the tsunami on the garage roof, and this experience is connected to her fear of the ocean*

隙間風
sukimakaze = a draft (air current); from suki = gap + ma = between + kaze = wind

警告
keikoku = warning, caution; *consuming too much cake or Coke will result in a warning*

四畳半
yojouhan = 4 ½ tatami mats; from yo = four + jou = counter for tatami mats; *Joan of Arc sat on tatami mats*; + han = half

引き起こす
hikiokosu = to cause or trigger; from hiku = to pull + okosu = to cause, or to wake someone up

すり
suri = pickpocket; *surely we can eliminate pickpockets*

from Satori Reader

全開
zenkai = opening fully, full throttle; from zenbu = everything + kai = open; *the Kaiser opened a new museum*

広がる
hirogaru = to spread out, to extend; from hiroi = spacious

戸惑う
tomadou = to be bewildered or perplexed; *when someone threw tomatoes at my door, I was bewildered*

一歩
ippo = one step, level, stage; a small degree or amount; from ichi = one + po = to walk, e.g., sanpo = walk

体勢
taisei = stance, posture; *the Thai sailor assumed a defensive stance*

きょろきょろ
kyorokyoro = looking around restlessly; *the Kyoto rogues looked around restlessly*

Practice Sentences

1. 親を敬うのは当然だ。

Oya wo uyamau no wa touzen da.
It's natural to respect one's parents.

2. 彼がやることに警戒した方が
   いいですよ。

Kare ga yaru koto ni keikai shita hou ga ii desu yo.
It's better to watch out for what he will do (i.e., it's best to keep an eye on him).

3. 畳に座っていたので足が痛い。

Tatami ni suwatte ita node ashi ga itai.
Because I was sitting on the tatami mat, my legs hurt.

4. ドアの隙間からのぞいた。

Doa no sukima kara nozoita.
I peeked from the gap in the door.

5. 津波で家が流されました。

Tsunami de ie ga nagasaremashita.
Due to the tsunami, the house was flushed away.

6. 彼は警官を見て逃げた。

Kare wa keikan wo mite nigeta.
He saw the policeman and ran away.

7. 先祖を敬うべきだ。

Senzo wo uyamau beki da.
We should venerate our ancestors.

8. 子供を戒めた。

Kodomo wo imashimeta.
I admonished the child.

9. 着物を畳んでください。

Kimono wo tatande kudasai.
Please fold the kimono.

10. 興味津々に絵を見ていた。

Kyoumi shinshin ni e wo mite ita.
With flowing interest (i.e., intensely interested), I was looking at the painting.

11. たくさんのボートが波止場につながれていた。

Takusan no booto ga hatoba ni tsunagarete ita.
A lot of boats were attached to the pier.

12. 隙間風が吹いてとても寒い。

Sukimakaze ga fuite totemo samui.
A draft blows, and it's very cold.

13. 警官は少年からナイフを取りあげた。

Keikan wa shounen kara naifu wo toriageta.
The policeman took the knife away from the boy.

14. 目上の人に敬語を使わない若者が多い。

Meue no hito ni keigo wo tsukawanai wakamono ga ooi.
Young people who do not use polite language with superiors are numerous.

15. 医者の警告でタバコを辞めた。

Isha no keikoku de tabako wo yameta.
Due to the doctor's warning, I stopped tobacco.

16. 四畳半の部屋に住んでいました。

Yojouhan no heya ni sunde imashita.
I was living in a room the size of 4 ½ tatami mats.

17. その地震で大きな津波を引き
起こした。

Sono jishin de ookina tsunami wo
hikiokoshita.
Due to that earthquake, it caused a large
tsunami.

18. 逃げる隙がなかった。

Nigeru suki ga nakatta.
There was no escape opening.

19. 彼は海軍士官の任務を受け
た。

Kare wa kaigun shikan no ninmu wo
uketa.
He received a naval officer's duty (i.e., a
commission as a naval officer).

20. すりには警戒しろよ。

Suri ni wa keikai shiro yo.
Watch out for pickpockets, for sure.

Supplemental Reading Practice

After completing Chapter 34 of this book, you should be able to read the "A Beckoning New World" article from the "Kona's Big Adventure" series in *Satori Reader*.

Chapter 35

New Kanji in this Chapter

# 881 敵 (2)	# 882 辿 (1)	# 883 及 (2)	# 884 腰 (3)
# 885 平 (4)	# 886 観 (2)	# 887 裏 (2)	# 888 原 (3)

Vocabulary List with Mnemonics

from the Kanji Catalogue

敵	teki = enemy, opponent; *that <u>techie</u> is my <u>enemy</u>*
敵	kataki = enemy, rival; *that <u>cat</u>apult is the <u>key</u> to defeating our <u>enemies</u>*
素敵な	suteki na = great, wonderful; *<u>Super</u>man and the <u>techies</u> make a <u>wonderful</u> team*
辿る	tadoru = to follow or trace; *that <u>tan doe</u> on the <u>roof followed</u> me here*
辿り着く	tadoritsuku = to find one's way to a place at last, to struggle on; from tadoru = to trace or follow + tsuku = to arrive
普及する	fukyuu suru = to become popular or widespread; *<u>food fads in Cu</u>ba are <u>widespread</u>*
及ぶ	oyobu = to reach or extend to; *an insect that <u>oyogu</u> (swims) in a <u>boot</u> full of water can <u>reach</u> the other side*
及び	oyobi = and, in addition; *the shells that I can <u>oyobu</u> (reach) on the <u>beach</u> will be added to my collection, <u>in addition</u> to what I already have*
腰	koshi = low back, waist, hip; *a <u>co</u>bra bit the <u>Shi</u>ite on his <u>low back</u>*
腰痛	youtsuu = low back pain; *carrying too much <u>yogurt</u> in my <u>tsui</u>tcase (suitcase) caused my <u>low back pain</u>*
平和	heiwa = peace, tranquility; *after the <u>hatred of war</u>, it's wonderful to have <u>peace</u>*
平気な	heiki na = unconcerned, nonchalant, calmness; *the <u>hated King</u> is <u>nonchalant</u>*
平らな	taira na = flat, level; *a <u>tiger</u> can outrun a <u>rat</u> on <u>level</u> ground*
平屋	hiraya = one-story house; *I keep my <u>Hi</u>malayan <u>rams</u> and <u>yaks</u> in a <u>one-story house</u>*
観光	kankou = sightseeing; *I went <u>sightseeing</u> to see <u>canned corn</u>*

Kanji Pronunciations

# 881 – teki, kataki	# 882 – tado	# 883 – kyuu, oyo	# 884 – koshi, goshi, you
# 885 – byou, hira, hei, tai	# 886 – kan, mi	# 887 – ura, ri	# 888 – gen, hara, bara

楽観 — rakkan = optimism; *the rabbi faced his cancer with optimism*

花を観る — hana wo miru = to view flowers (this can also be spelled 花を見る)

裏 — ura = back, rear, hidden aspect; *the uber ram lives in the back*

裏切る — uragiru = to betray or deceive; from ura = back + giru = kiru = to cut

表裏 — hyouri = two sides, inside and out; *the Lone Ranger said "Hi-yo" at the rear of the house and again at the front, so he said it on two sides*

野原 — nohara = field; *there is no harassment allowed in my fields*

海原 — unabara = ocean; *the Unabomber played ball with some rascals near the ocean*

from the Practice Sentences

天下 — tenka = realm, world, nation; from ten = heaven + ka = below

秋葉原 — Akihabara = area near Akihabara Station in Tokyo; from aki = autumn + ha = leaves + bara = hara = field

国境 — kokkyou = border; *there is no border between Kobe and Kyouto, since Osaka lies between them;* cf. 境 sakai = boundary, border

かがめる — kagameru = to bend or stoop; *Karl Marx and Gandalf went to Mexico to see some ruins and had to stoop to get through the doorways*

たたく — tataku = to beat or strike; *when the tall taxi driver ran out of Kool-Aid, he began to beat his head against his car*

平たくする — hirataku suru = to make flat; *the hero ran over the taxi driver's Kool-Aid cup and made it flat*

祖国 — sokoku = native country; from so = ancestor, e.g., 祖父 sofu = grandfather + koku = country

原料 — genryou = raw materials; *Genghis Khan and Pope Leo started a company to harvest raw materials*

楽観的 — rakkanteki = optimistic; from rakkan = optimism + teki = related to

from Satori Reader

必死 — hisshi = frantic, desperate, inevitable death; from hitsuyou = necessary + shinu = to die

寝心地 — negokochi = sleep comfort; from neru = to sleep + gokochi = kokochi = feeling or mood

目に入る — me ni hairu = to catch sight of; from me = eye + hairu = to enter

降り注ぐ — furisosogu = to rain incessantly, to pour down (can also be used for sunlight); from furu = to precipitate + sosogu = to pour

ほかほか — hokahoka = steaming hot, very warm; *I hope the candle makes the pot steaming hot, since that will allow us to cook our food*

窓辺	madobe = the window place, next to the window; from mado = window + be = place; *a beggar is standing in that place*
離れ離れ	hanarebanare = scattered, apart; from hanareru = to part
おまけに	omake ni = besides, on top of that; *on top of that, in Omaha Kennedy met my niece*
目玉	medama = eyeball; from me = eye + dama = tama = ball
見開く	mihiraku = to open one's eyes wide; from miru = to look + hiraku = to open
及び腰	oyobigoshi = bent back, timidity; from oyobu = to reach or extend + goshi = koshi = low back
すり寄る	suriyoru = to draw close, to cuddle with; *Superman reads in the yoru (night), cuddled with Lois Lane*

Practice Sentences

1. 彼は天下に敵なしだ。

Kare wa tenka ni teki nashi da.
As for him, in the realm, he is without rival.

2. 森の中の小道を辿っていくと
美しい湖に出る。

Mori no naka no komichi wo tadotte iku to utsukushii mizu'umi ni deru.
If you follow the path through the woods, you will come out to a beautiful lake.

3. 忙しいんだからその会議に出
席するには及ばないだろう。

Isogashiin dakara sono kaigi ni shusseki suru ni wa oyobanai darou.
Since we are busy, to that meeting, as for to attend, it doesn't reach, probably. (i.e., probably we don't have to attend)

4. 昨日、重い荷物を運んだので
腰が痛いんです。

Kinou, omoi nimotsu wo hakonda node, koshi ga itain desu.
Yesterday, since I carried heavy luggage, the low back hurts.

5. 何を言われても私は平気だ。

Nani wo iwarete mo watashi wa heiki da.
What they say on me, even though, as for me, it's calmness. (i.e., whatever they say, I'm calm)

6. 観光で日本に来ました。

Kankou de nihon ni kimashita.
I came to Japan for sightseeing.

7. 彼の言葉には表裏がない。

Kare no kotoba ni wa hyouri ga nai.
As for to his words, there are no "two sides." (i.e., he is sincere in what he says)

8. テレビを買いたいので秋葉原
へ行きます。

Terebi wo kaitai node akihabara e ikimasu.
Because I want to buy a TV, I'm going to Akihabara.

9. 地球は平らだと信じられていた。

Chikyuu wa taira da to shinjirarete ita.
As for the earth, it was flat, it was being believed. (i.e., people thought it was flat)

10. 素敵な日ですね。

Suteki na hi desu ne.
It's a wonderful day, huh.

11. その険しい道を行く以外に、国境へ辿り着く方法はない。

Sono kewashii michi wo iku igai ni, kokkyou e tadoritsuku houhou wa nai.
Except to go on that steep path, to-the-border-to-finally-arrive methods don't exist. (i.e., that path is the only way to the border)

12. お礼には及びません。

Orei ni wa oyobimasen.
As for to gratitude, it doesn't reach. (i.e., it's nothing, or don't mention it)

13. 腰痛持ちです。

Youtsuu mochi desu.
It's to-have back pain (i.e., I have back pain).

14. 花を観るのは楽しいです。

Hana wo miru no wa tanoshii desu.
It's pleasant to view blossoms.

15. 紙の表と裏を間違えないように確かめてください。

Kami no omote to ura wo machigaenai you ni tashikamete kudasai.
On the paper's front side and back side so as not to mistake, please check. (i.e., be sure to use the correct side)

16. 原田ですが、田中さんをお願いします。

Harada desu ga, Tanaka san wo onegaishimasu.
This is Harada, but I beg Mr. Tanaka. (i.e., may I speak to him?)

17. 敵に向かって進んだ。

Teki ni mukatte susunda.
They advanced toward the enemy.

18. 夜1時に家に辿り着いた。

Yoru ichiji ni ie ni tadoritsuita.
At 1:00 at night I finally reached home.

19. 英語は全国に普及した。

Eigo wa zenkoku ni fukyuu shita.
English spread all over the country.

20. 彼女は腰をかがめた。

Kanojo wa koshi wo kagameta.
She bent the back (i.e., she stooped over).

21. ハンバーグの肉をたたいて平たくした。

Hanbaagu no niku wo tataite hirataku shita.
She hit the hamburger meat and made it flat. (from tataku = to hit)

22. 彼は祖国を裏切った。

Kare wa sokoku wo uragitta.
He betrayed his native country.

23. 我が社は原料を輸入して製品を輸出している。

Wagasha wa genryou wo yunyuu shite seihin wo yushutsu shite iru.
As for our company, we import raw materials, and we are exporting finished goods.

24. 三木さんって楽観的だと思う。

Miki san tte rakkanteki da to omou.
I think that Miki is optimistic.

Supplemental Reading Practice

After completing Chapter 35 of this book, you should be able to read the "Part of the Family" article from the "Kona's Big Adventure" series in *Satori Reader*.

Chapter 36

New Kanji in this Chapter

# 889 畑 (2)	# 890 頬 (2)	# 891 陽 (1)	# 892 折 (3)
# 893 覆 (4)	# 894 逆 (2)	# 895 鹿 (3)	# 896 察 (1)

Vocabulary List with Mnemonics

from the Kanji Catalogue

畑   hatake = field for cultivation or field of expertise; *in Hawaii, a tall Kennedy farms a field*

田畑   tahata = field (crops); *Tarzan paid the harbor tax for the crops from his field*

頬   hoo = cheek; *a hornet stung my cheek*

頬   hoho = cheek; *Santa says Ho Ho when you pinch his cheek*

頬張る   hoobaru = to stuff one's cheeks or fill one's mouth with food; *the hobo came into the barroom and stuffed his cheeks with food*

太陽   taiyou = the sun; *when I'm tired of yodeling, I lie in the sun*

陽性の   yousei no = cheerful, positive; *the yodeling sailor is cheerful and positive*

陽気な   youki na = merry, happy-go-lucky; *the yodeling king is merry*

骨折する   kossetsu suru = to break a bone; *a corporation settled with Superman after he broke a bone when he slipped on a wet floor*

折る   oru = to break or fold, transitive; *Oprah ruined the photo when she folded it*

折れる   oreru = to break, intransitive; *in Oregon, a rooster broke a gate*

折り   ori = occasion, opportunity, time; *orientation week is an occasion to learn*

折り紙   origami = Japanese paper folding; *from oru = to break or fold + gami = kami = paper*

時折   tokiori = once in a while; *from toki = time + ori = occasion*

覆う   oou = to cover, conceal, wrap, disguise; *I covered my the oak furniture*

覆面   fukumen = mask; *the Fukuoka men were wearing masks*

転覆する   tenpuku suru = to capsize or overturn; *after ten days of puking from seasickness, his boat capsized, and he drowned*

Kanji Pronunciations

# 889 – hatake, hata	# 890 – hoo, hoho	# 891 – you	# 892 – setsu, o, ori
# 893 – oo, fuku, puku, kutsugae	# 894 – saka, gyaku	# 895 – shika, jika, ka	# 896 – satsu

覆す = kutsugaesu = to overturn or overthrow; *when a king cut Superman's guy's suit, Superman tried to overthrow him*

逆らう = sakarau = to oppose or disobey; *at the sakka (soccer) game, the rowdy fans disobeyed the security staff*

逆さまの = sakasama no = reverse, upside-down, topsy-turvy; *at the sakka (soccer) game, Samantha stood on her head and watched the game upside-down*

逆 = gyaku = contrary, opposite, antithetical; *the geeky yakuza (gangster) has a contrary temperament*

逆説 = gyakusetsu = paradox; *the geeky yakuza (gangster) settled on a soup with a bittersweet flavor, which sounds like a paradox (i.e., bitter and sweet)*

鹿 = shika = deer; *the sheep in California are friendly with the deer*

警察 = keisatsu = police; *the guy wearing a cape while reading a satisfying Superman novel works for the police*

観察 = kansatsu = observation; *the Canadian guy who writes satisfying Superman novels made an interesting observation*

from the Practice Sentences

良質 = ryoushitsu = fine quality; *Pope Leo uses sheets of fine quality*

作物 = sakumotsu = crops; from saku = to produce; *I produce things and keep them in a sack;* + motsu = mono = thing

産出する = sanshutsu suru = to yield or produce; *Santa shoots off fireworks when the elves produce lots of toys*

地面 = jimen = ground; *the G-men (government employees) lay down on the ground*

入り込む = hairikomu = to come into or go into; from hairu = to enter + komu = to crowd in

反逆 = hangyaku = rebellion, treason, betrayal; *the hanged yakuza was guilty of treason*

少数 = shousuu = a few; *I showed the supervisor a few of my drawings*

うっすら = ussura = slightly, faintly, dimly; *the usurper ate the ramen which was only slightly spoiled*

逆転 = gyakuten = reversal, sudden change; *the geeky yakuza playing tennis made a sudden change in his strategy*

形勢 = keisei = situation, condition; *the cake that we bought at Safeway was in good condition*

現場 = genba = actual spot, scene, site, location; *Genghis was shot in this bar, so this is the scene of the crime*

from Satori Reader

日向 = hinata = sunny place, in the sun; *the excessive heat at the national talent show was due to the fact that they held it in the sun*

日向ぼっこ	hinata bokko = basking in the sun; from hinata = in the sun + bokko = basking; *I was basking in the sun with some bowlers from Korea*
日課	nikka = daily lesson or routine; from nichi = day + ka = lesson; *I studied the lesson in the car*
目当て	meate = prospect, aim, goal, intention; *the men bought a tent with the aim of using it for a fishing trip*
親子	oyako = parent and child; from oya = parent + ko = child
同時に	douji ni = at the same time; from dou = the same; *the doughnuts are the same at both shops*; + jikan = time
パキっ	paki = twig-snapping sound; *when I was packing my suitcase, I heard some twig-snapping sounds*
気配	kehai = indication, sign, presence; *Kennedy hired a man to establish a presence on the property, as a sign that it was occupied*
らんらん	ranran = blazing, fiery, glaring; *he ran and ranted in the blazing sun*
逆立てる	sakadateru = to stand on end or bristle (referring to hair); from sakarau = to oppose or disobey + dateru = tateru = to stand up
じっと	jitto = fixedly, intently, motionlessly; *the genius toasted us with a fixed stare*
見上げる	miageru = to look up, raise one's eyes; from miru = to look + ageru = to raise
食べごろ	tabegoro = good for eating, in season; from taberu = to eat + goro = approximate time

Practice Sentences

1. この畑では良質の作物を産出している。

Kono hatake de wa ryoushitsu no sakumotsu wo sanshutsu shite iru.
As for of these fields, they are producing fine-quality crops.

2. 涙が頬に流れた。

Namida ga hoho ni nagareta.
Tears flowed on his cheeks.

3. 太陽は地球の約百万倍の大きさです。

Taiyou wa chikyuu no yaku hyaku man bai no ookisa desu.
As for the sun, it's the earth's approximately one million times's size.

4. 花を折っちゃだめよ。

Hana wo otcha dame yo.
As for to pick the flowers, bad for sure.
(otcha = otte wa)

5. 地面は雪で覆われている。

Jimen wa yuki de oowarete iru.
The ground is being covered with snow.

6. 彼に逆らうな。

Kare ni sakarau na.
Don't oppose him.

548854858588

7. 森に鹿がたくさんいるよ。

Mori ni shika ga takusan iru yo.
There are a lot of deer in the woods, for sure.

8. 警察から妙な情報が入り込んだ。

Keisatsu kara myou na jouhou ga hairikonda.
From the police, strange information came in.

9. 田畑の中にたくさんの道路が次々とできてしまった。

Tahata no naka ni takusan no dooro ga tsugitsugi to dekite shimatta.
In the middle of the fields (of crops) a lot of roads, one after the other, were completely accomplished.

10. そんなにご飯を頬張るな。

Sonna ni gohan wo hoobaru na.
Don't stuff your mouth with food so much.

11. 陽子さんはお酒を飲まなかった。

Youko san wa osake wo nomanakatta.
Yoko didn't drink honorable sake.

12. スキーで足を骨折した。

Sukii de ashi wo kossetsu shita.
From skiing, I fractured the leg.

13. 船は海の真ん中で転覆した。

Fune wa umi no man'naka de tenpuku shita.
The boat capsized in the middle of the ocean.

14. 彼は反逆者だ。

Kare wa hangyakusha da.
He's a rebel.

15. その鹿はライオンの餌食になった。

Sono shika wa raion no ejiki ni natta.
That deer became a lion's victim.

16. 趣味は人間観察です。

Shumi wa ningen kansatsu desu.
The hobby is human observation (i.e., I like to watch people).

17. 少数の人しか畑では働いていない。

Shousuu no hito shika hatake de wa hataraite inai.
Only a few people are working in the fields.

18. 彼女の頬はうっすら赤くなっていた。

Kanojo no hoho wa ussura akaku natte ita.
Her cheeks were becoming slightly red (i.e., flushed).

19. 恵子さんはいつも陽気だ。

Keiko san wa itsumo youki da.
Keiko is always cheerful.

20. 台風で庭の木が折れてしまった。

Taifuu de niwa no ki ga orete shimatta.
By the typhoon, the garden's tree got broken completely.

21. 彼はパーテイーに覆面をして出かけた。

Kare wa paatii ni fukumen wo shite dekaketa.
He left to the party wearing a mask.

22. 形勢は逆転した。

Keisei wa gyakuten shita.
The situation is reversed.

23. 鹿は急いで逃げていった。

Shika wa isoide nigete itta.
The deer hurriedly ran away and went.

24. やっと警察が事故現場に着いた。

Yatto keisatsu ga jiko genba ni tsuita.
The police finally arrived at the scene of the accident.

Supplemental Reading Practice

After completing Chapter 36 of this book, you should be able to read the "The Observer," "An Unexpected Guest" and "Lily" articles from the "Kona's Big Adventure" series in *Satori Reader*.

Chapter 37

New Kanji in this Chapter

# 897 宇 (1)	# 898 宙 (1)	# 899 柵 (1)	# 900 汁 (3)
# 901 犯 (2)	# 902 厳 (3)	# 903 湧 (1)	# 904 徐 (1)

Vocabulary List with Mnemonics

from the Kanji Catalogue

宇宙 — uchuu = universe, cosmos, space; *in Uruguay we chew our meals inside to keep space aliens from stealing our food*

宙返り — chuugaeri = somersault; *I choose Gandalf and Eric for the somersault competition*

宙に浮く — chuu ni uku = to float in air; from chuu = space; *chew your food carefully when you are on a space ship*; + uku = to float

柵 — saku = fence; *I keep my fence posts in a sack*

鉄柵 — tessaku = iron fence; from tetsu = iron + saku = fence

汁 — shiru = soup; *I drank soup with a Shinto ruler*

鼻汁 — hanajiru = nasal discharge; from hana = nose + jiru = shiru = soup, or liquid

肉汁 — nikujuu = gravy; from niku = meat + juu, which reminds us of juice

果汁 — kajuu = fruit juice; from ka = fruit; *I carved up the fruit*; + juu, which reminds us of juice

犯す — okasu = to violate; *occasionally Superman violates the speed limit*

犯人 — han'nin = criminal, culprit; *a criminal is only half a nin (person)*

厳格な — genkaku na = stern, strict; *Genghis called the Kool-Aid ban excessively strict*

厳しい — kibishii = stern, rigid, strict; *if you kibbitz (chat) with Shiites, you will find that they are strict*

湧く — waku = to gush out, well up, appear; *water and Kool-Aid gushed out of the broken pitcher*

徐々に — jojo ni = gradually, step by step; *Joan of Arc joked that she could approach the stake so gradually that she would never get there*

徐行する — jokou suru = to slow down; *Joan of Arc's commute slowed down after Labor Day*

Kanji Pronunciations

# 897 – u	# 898 – chuu	# 899 – saku	# 900 – juu, shiru, jiru
# 901 – han, oka	# 902 – gen, kibi, gon	# 903 – wa	# 904 – jo

from the Practice Sentences

無限の — mugen no = eternal, infinite, endless; from mu = negation + genkai = limit

レモン汁 — remon jiru = lemon juice; from lemon + jiru = shiru = soup

宇宙人 — uchuujin = space alien; from uchuu = space + jin = person

宇宙飛行士 — uchuuhikoushi = astronaut; from uchuu = space + hikouki = airplane + shi = man

飛び降りる — tobioriru = to jump down; from tobu = to jump or fly + oriru = to exit a vehicle

仕切る — shikiru = to divide or partition; from shiyou = means or method + kiru = to cut

しつける — shitsukeru = to train or to teach manners; *I'm going to train you how to wash and iron the sheets that are kept in that room*

世の中 — yo no naka = the world, society, life; from yo = world; *yogis take care of the world*; + the possessive no + naka = inside

新たな — arata na = fresh, new; *the Arabesque tapestry was fresh and new*

from Satori Reader

舞う — mau = to dance; *Mao Tse Tung liked to dance*

軽々 — karugaru = lightly, easily, carelessly; from karui = light + garui = karui = light

ふわり — fuwari = softly, gently, lightly; *the food that the warrior ate was prepared gently*

舞い降りる — maioriru = to swoop down on, to alight; from mau = to dance + oriru = to get down from a vehicle

一口 — hitokuchi = a mouthful; from hitotsu = one + kuchi = mouth

かじる — kajiru = to chew or bite; *Karl Marx had his jeans ruined when a dog chewed them*

はじける — hajikeru = to burst open; *Hansel jeered when Ken ruined the watermelon by dropping it, causing it to burst open*

はじけ飛ぶ — hajiketobu = to pop out, fly off, burst open; from hajikeru = to burst open + tobu = to fly

ぼやく — boyaku = grumble or complain; *my boy adopted a cool dog, but I complained*

人聞き — hitogiki = reputation, respectability; from hito = person + giku = kiku = to hear

人聞き悪い — hitogiki warui = disgraceful, disreputable; from hitogiki = reputation + warui = bad

むっと — mutto = sullenly, angrily; *the Moonies were told to leave the airport, and they did so sullenly*

野生 — yasei = wild (referring to plants or animals); *the yak felt safe back in the wild*

笑い出す — waraidasu = to burst into laughter; from warau = to laugh + dasu = to put out

自然界 — shizenkai = nature, the natural world; from shizen = nature + kai = world, e.g., sekai = the world

幸せ者 — shiawase mono = fortunate person, lucky fellow; from shiawase = happiness + mono = person

Practice Sentences

1. 宇宙は無限だ。
Uchuu wa mugen da.
The universe is infinite.

2. 少年は素早く柵を飛び越えた。
Shounen wa subayaku saku wo tobikoeta.
The boy nimbly jumped over the fence.

3. 紅茶にレモン汁を入れた方が好き。
Koucha ni remon jiru wo ireta hou ga suki.
I prefer to put lemon juice in black tea.

4. 犯人は背が高いようだ。
Hannin wa se ga takai you da.
As for the criminal, he is tall, it appears.

5. 北海道の冬は厳しかった。
Hokkaidou no fuyu wa kibishikatta.
Hokkaido's winter was severe.

6. 宇宙人っていると思う？
Uchuujin tte iru to omou?
Do you think that space aliens exist?

7. 英語の勉強に興味が湧いてきた。
Eigo no benkyou ni kyoumi ga waite kita.
To English study, the interest welled up and came. (i.e., I started to get interested in studying English)

8. 電車は徐々にスピードを上げてきた。
Densha wa jojo ni supiido wo agete kita.
The train began to gradually increase speed.

9. 二人の子供たちが柵の上から飛び降りた。
Futari no kodomotachi ga saku no ue kara tobiorita.
Two children jumped down from the top of a fence.

10. 毎日果汁を飲む。
Mainichi kajuu wo nomu.
I drink fruit juice every day.

11. 犯人は手袋をしていたようだ。
Hannin wa tebukuro wo shite ita you da.
As for the criminal, he was wearing gloves, it appears.

12. 天然のお湯が湧きでている。
Ten'nen no oyu ga wakidete iru.
Natural hot water is welling up and emerging.

13. 車を運転する人が徐々に増え
ている。

Kuruma wo unten suru hito ga jojo ni
fuete iru.
People who drive cars are gradually
increasing.

14. 本田さんは宙返りをした。

Honda san wa chuugaeri wo shita.
Mr. Honda turned a somersault.

15. 庭は柵で小道と仕切られてい
る。

Niwa wa saku de komichi to shikirarete
iru.
The garden is partitioned from the path
by a fence.

16. 彼は子供をしつけるのに厳格
だった。

Kare wa kodomo wo shitsukeru noni
genkaku datta.
As for him, for the purpose of training
children, he was strict.

17. 母はみそ汁の作り方を教えて
くれた。

Haha wa miso shiru no tsukurikata wo
oshiete kureta.
Mother taught me how to make miso
soup.

18. 法を犯した。

Hou wo okashita.
He violated the law.

19. 宇宙飛行士になりたい。

Uchuuhikoushi ni naritai.
I want to become an astronaut.

20. 厳しい世の中だな。

Kibishii yo no naka da na.
It's a tough world (or society), huh.

21. 彼らに新たな希望が湧いた。

Karera ni arata na kibou ga waita.
To them, fresh hope welled up.

22. この道は徐々に狭くなってい
る。

Kono michi wa jojo ni semaku natte iru.
This street is gradually getting narrow.

Supplemental Reading Practice

After completing Chapter 37 of this book, you should be able to read the "A Mystery Solved" and "A Lucky Fellow" articles from the "Kona's Big Adventure" series in *Satori Reader*.

Chapter 38

New Kanji in this Chapter

# 905 想 (3)	# 906 象 (2)	# 907 像 (1)	# 908 亀 (3)
# 909 草 (4)	# 910 斜 (2)	# 911 崖 (2)	# 912 翼 (2)

Vocabulary List with Mnemonics

from the Kanji Catalogue

想像   souzou = imagination; *most people who lived in the Soviet zone could get rich only in their imaginations*

想う   omou = to imagine or contemplate; *this is similar to* 思う omou = to feel or think

愛想がいい   aiso ga ii = sociable; from aiso = amiability; *when Ike was sober, his amiability increased;* + ii = good

象   zou = elephant; *elephants thrive in tropical zones*

対象   taishou = an object; *the tigers living by the shore were the objects of the hunt*

仏像   butsuzou = image or statue of Buddha; from butsu = Buddha + zou = image; *I saw an image representing the signs of the Zodiak*

亀   kame = turtle, tortoise; *the turtle is a friend of the camel*

草   kusa = grass; *the cool saxophone players played on the grass*

草原   sougen = grasslands, prairie, meadow; *when he was sober, Genghis would ride on the prairie*

斜めの   naname no = diagonal, oblique; *Nancy's nanny messed up by allowing her to draw diagonal lines on the wall*

斜面   shamen = slope, slanting surface; *the Shah's men ran up the slope*

崖   gake = precipice, cliff; *gallant Ken leaped from the cliff to rescue Barbie*

断崖   dangai = precipice, cliff; *the dancing guy fell off a cliff*

翼   tsubasa = wing; *when I took my tsuitcase (suitcase) to Barcelona's sandy beaches, I saw some birds with powerful wings*

右翼   uyoku = right wing (politics); *the Uber driver drove yoku (well) and favored right-wing politics*

Kanji Pronunciations

# 905 – so, sou, omo	# 906 – zou, shou	# 907 – zou	# 908 – kame, game, ki
# 909 – kusa, gusa, sou, zou	# 910 – nana, sha	# 911 – gake, gai	# 912 – tsubasa, yoku

38-146

左翼	sayoku = left wing (politics); *the saxophone player guy played yoku (well) and favored left-wing politics*

from the Practice Sentences

理想	risou = ideal; *the reason I'm playing this soul music is that it is ideal for me*
肖像画	shouzouga = portrait; *I showed Zooey my gallstones when she painted my portrait*
実物	jitsubutsu = real thing or person; from jitsu = real + butsu = tangible thing
草花	kusabana = flowering plants, flower; from kusa = grass + bana = hana = flowers
連想する	rensou suru = to associate or be reminded of; *collecting rent from the soldier reminded me of my military service*
急斜面	kyuushamen = steep slope; *in Cuba, the Shah's men climbed a steep slope*
てっぺん	teppen = top, summit; *I carried a Teddy bear and a pen to the summit*
象徴	shouchou = symbol; *the shore was choked with plastic waste, a symbol of consumerism*
解き放つ	tokihanatsu = to release; from toku = to undo or solve + hanatsu = to release; *Hannah's tsuitcase (suitcase) was released by Customs;* cf. 放す hanasu = to release
超常	choujou = paranormality, anomalous phenomena; *Margaret Cho told jokes about paranormal phenomena*
現象	genshou = phenomenon; *Genghis said that the shore was a natural phenomenon*
転落する	tenraku suru = to fall or decline; *tennis and racketball are declining in popularity*

from Satori Reader

よぎる	yogiru = to go by, to cross; *the yogi and his rooster went by my house*
しがみつく	shigamitsuku = to cling; *the sheep that the gambler meets tsuku (adhere) to him and cling to him tenaciously*
恐る恐る	osoru osoru = timidly; *the old soldier stayed in his room timidly*
迷い	mayoi = doubt, indecision, hesitation; from mayou = to lose direction
走り抜く	hashirinuku = to run through, to outrun; from hashiru = to run + nuku = to extract, omit, outrun or surpass
ふもと	fumoto = foot of a mountain, base; from fu, which reminds us of "foot" + moto = base
頭	tou = head, counter for large animals; *Tony Blair has a big head*
合流	gouryuu = confluence (of rivers), merge (of traffic); from gou = to come together, e.g., tsugou = circumstances, + ryuu = to flow, e.g., denryuu = electric current
一向に	ikkou ni = completely, not at all (in negative sentences); *this Eastern cold front nearly froze my plants and was completely and not at all what I wanted*

角　　　　　tsuno = antler, horn; *I keep a tsuitcase (suitcase) full of notes about antlers*

ほほ笑む　　hohoemu = to smile; *Santa said ho ho after the excellent movie and he smiled*

葉っぱ　　　happa = leaf; from ha = leaf; *the Hawaiian padre studied leaves*

張り付く　　haritsuku = to cling to; *Prince Harry tsuku (adheres), in fact clings, to his values*

振り落とす　furiotosu = to throw or shake off; from furikaeru = to look back + otosu = to drop

Practice Sentences

1. 彼は私の理想の人よ。

Kare wa watashi no risou no hito yo.
He is my ideal person, for sure.

2. 象は鼻が長い。

Zou wa hana ga nagai.
Elephants have long trunks.

3. その肖像画は実物そっくりだ。

Sono shouzouga wa jitsubutsu sokkuri da.
That portrait is real-thing identical. (i.e., it resembles the person exactly)

4. 亀には歯がありません。

Kame ni wa ha ga arimasen.
As for to turtles, there are no teeth.

5. この絵は草花を連想させる。

Kono e wa kusabana o rensou saseru.
This picture makes me associate on (or reminds me of) flowering plants.

6. 私達は急斜面をジグザグに登っていった。

Watashitachi wa kyuushamen wo ziguzagu ni nobotte itta.
We climbed the steep slope in zigzag fashion and went.

7. その鳥は翼が折れていた。

Sono tori wa tsubasa ga orete ita.
As for that bird, its wing was broken.

8. 彼女は誰にでも愛想がいい。

Kanojo wa dare ni demo aiso ga ii.
As for her, to anyone, the sociability is good. (i.e., she's friendly to all)

9. 鳩は平和の象徴である。

Hato wa heiwa no shouchou de aru.
Doves are a symbol of peace.

10. うちで小さい亀を飼っています。

Uchi de chiisai kame wo katte imasu.
I am keeping a small turtle at home.

11. 想像力を解き放って考えてください。

Souzou ryoku wo tokihanatte kangaete kudasai.
Please release the imagination force and think. (i.e., be creative)

12. 野生の動物たちが草原を走り
回っていた。

Yasei no doubutsutachi ga sougen wo hashirimawatte ita.
Wild animals were running around the meadow.

13. 彼は帽子を斜めにかぶってい
る。

Kare wa boushi wo naname ni kabutte iru.
He is wearing his hat askew.

14. 「その崖には近づかないで」
と彼女が叫んだ。

"Sono gake ni wa chikazukanai de" to kanojo ga sakenda.
"As for to that cliff, do not approach," she shouted.

15. その時に左翼に走った。

Sono toki ni sayoku ni hashitta.
At that time, he ran to the left wing. (i.e., he became leftist in his political thinking)

16. 田村さんは超常現象に興味が
ある。

Tamura san wa choujou genshou ni kyoumi ga aru.
Ms. Tamura is interested in paranormal phenomena.

17. 浜辺に亀を見に行きました。

Hamabe ni kame wo mi ni ikimashita.
We sent to the beach to see turtles.

18. 草の上に横になった。

Kusa no ue ni yoko ni natta.
He lay down on the grass.

19. 彼女はご機嫌斜めだ。

Kanojo wa gokigen naname da.
She is in an oblique (i.e., bad) honorable mood.

20. バスが崖から転落した。

Basu ga gake kara tenraku shita.
The bus fell off the cliff.

21. 人間に翼があったらいいの
に。

Ningen ni tsubasa ga attara ii noni.
If, to humans, wings existed, good, if only. (i.e., if only humans had wings)

22. 月での生活を想像してみた。

Tsuki de no seikatsu wo souzou shite mita.
I tried to imagine life on the moon.

23. 崖のてっぺんまで登ていっ
た。

Gake no teppen made nobotte itta.
I climbed to the top of the cliff and went.

Supplemental Reading Practice

After completing Chapter 38 of this book, you should be able to read the "A Rare Opportunity," "Into the Wild!" and "Foothills" articles from the "Kona's Big Adventure" series in *Satori Reader*.

Chapter 39

New Kanji in this Chapter

#913 旋 (1)	#914 脅 (3)	#915 威 (1)	#916 権 (2)
#917 兵 (2)	#918 衛 (1)	#919 庫 (2)	#920 防 (2)

Vocabulary List with Mnemonics

from the Kanji Catalogue

旋回	senkai = rotation, turning; *the sensational kite was turning in the air*
旋律	senritsu = melody; *the senator's staff was given a written suggestion to play a happy melody whenever the senator entered a room*
脅す	odosu = to threaten; *the odor Superman smelled was threatening*
脅かす	odokasu = to startle or threaten; *the odor that Karl Marx and Superman smelled startled and threatened them*
脅かす	obiyakasu = to menace or threaten; *the oily beast approached the yak, which assumed that it was an enemy and turned to threaten it*
脅威	kyou'i = a threat, peril, menace; *some Kyouto eagles are a menace*
権威	ken'i = authority; *some Kennedys in the East, e.g., Boston, had a lot of authority*
威厳	igen = dignity; *it was easy for Genghis to behave with dignity*
威張る	ibaru = to look down on, to brag; *the Eagles fans in the bar were rude and bragged about their team's victory*
権利	kenri = right, privilege; *the Kennedys read the Constitution, and they know their rights*
権現	gongen = an incarnation of Buddha, an avatar; *Gonzalez thinks Genghis Khan was an incarnation of Buddha*
兵隊	heitai = soldier; *when he first became a soldier, he was hazed and tied to a chair*
兵庫県	hyougo ken = Hyogo prefecture; *the Lone Ranger said "Hi-yo" when he saw the gold in Hyogo prefecture*
衛生	eisei = hygiene, sanitation; *honest Abe went to Safeway for his hygiene products;* cf. 衛星 eisei = satellite
衛星	eisei = satellite; *eight sailors watched the satellite;* cf. 衛生 eisei = sanitation

Kanji Pronunciations

#913 – sen	#914 – odo, kyou, obiya	#915 – i	#916 – gon, ken
#917 – hei, hyou	#918 – ei	#919 – ko, go	#920 – fuse, bou

防衛   bouei = defense; *Tarzan boasts about the apes that provide defense at his jungle hideout*

車庫   shako = garage; *a shack near the coast served as the garage for my car*

金庫   kinko = safe; *the king keeps his coat in a safe*

防ぐ   fusegu = to prevent or defend; *I filled the fuse with metallic goo to prevent another blackout*

予防   yobou = prevention; *I eat yogurt for my bones as a strategy for prevention of osteoporosis*

消防士   shouboushi = firefighter; from shoubou = firefighting; *he showed me the bonus that he got for firefighting*; + shi = man

from the Practice Sentences

兵力   heiryoku = military force; from heitai = soldier + ryoku = force

投入する   tounyuu suru = to throw into, invest, insert; *Tony Blair went to Nyuuyooku (New York) and threw himself into his work*

上空   joukuu = the sky, upper air; from jou = up or above, e.g., jouzu = skillful; + kuu = sky, e.g., kuuki = air

有する   yuu suru = to own or be endowed with; *I own land in the Yukon*

タカ   taka = hawk; *Tarzan visited California to see the hawks*

市民権   shiminken = citizenship; from shimin = citizen + kenri = right or privilege

兵士   heishi = soldier; *he hated sheep farming, so he became a soldier*; cf. 兵隊 heitai = soldier

防水   bousui = waterproofing; *my boat from Sweden has good waterproofing*

衛生的な   eiseiteki na = sanitary, hygienic; from eisei = sanitation + teki = related to

Practice Sentences

1. 飛行機は東へ旋回した。

Hikouki wa higashi e senkai shita.
The airplane turned east.

2. 病気は人類にとって脅威である。

Byouki wa jinrui ni totte kyou'i de aru.
Disease, from the point of view of human race, is a threat.

3. お前にそれを言う権利はない。

Omae ni sore wo iu kenri wa nai.
To you, to say that, rights don't exist.
(i.e., you have no right to say it)

4. 敵は新兵力を投入した。

Teki wa shin heiryoku o tounyuu shita.
The enemy threw a fresh military force (into the battle).

5. その衛星は地球を十周した。

Sono eisei wa chikyuu wo juushuu shita.
That satellite did ten revolutions around the earth.

6. 金庫に金を入れてきた。

Kinko ni kane wo irete kita.
I put the money in a safe and came.

7. 青木さんは消防士です。

Aoki san wa shouboushi desu.
Mr. Aoki is a firefighter.

8. ヘリコプターが上空を旋回して いるようだ。

Herikoputaa ga joukuu o senkai shite iru you da.
The helicopter seems to be circling on (i.e., in) the sky.

9. 彼の言ったことは脅かしにほ かならない。

Kare no itta koto wa odokashi ni hoka naranai.
As for his said thing (i.e., what he said), it's nothing but a threat.

10. 少年にとって父親は権威だっ た。

Shounen ni totte chichi oya wa ken'i datta.
As far as the boy was concerned, his father was the authority.

11. 兵庫県 の小さい町で生まれ ました。

Hyougo ken no chiisai machi de umaremashita.
I was born in a small town in Hyogo prefecture.

12. 我々は自己防衛の権利を有す る。

Wareware wa jiko bouei no kenri o yuu suru.
We are endowed with the right to self-defense.

13. タカは空を旋回した。

Taka wa sora wo senkai shita.
The hawk circled on (i.e., in) the sky.

14. やくざはその男を脅かした。

Yakuza wa sono otoko wo odokashita.
Yakuza threatened that man.

15. あの人、余り威張るから好き になれない。

Ano hito, amari ibaru kara suki ni narenai.
That person, since he boasts too much, liking cannot become (i.e., I can't like him).

16. 米国の市民権を得た。

Beikoku no shiminken o eta.
I acquired American citizenship.

17. 多くの兵士がここで殺され た。

Ooku no heishi ga koko de korosareta.
A lot of soldiers were killed here.

18. それは予防できない病気だ。

Sore wa yobou dekinai byouki da.
That is an unpreventable illness.

19. アフリカではどの国が一番衛生的で安全ですか？

Afurika de wa dono kuni ga ichiban eiseiteki de anzen desu ka.
As for of Africa, which country is the most sanitary and safe?

20. 車は車庫に止めてあります。

Kuruma wa shako ni tomete arimasu.
The car is parked in the garage.

21. この時計は防水です。

Kono tokei wa bousui desu.
This watch is waterproof.

Chapter 40

New Kanji in this Chapter

# 921 牙 (3)	# 922 雅 (2)	# 923 狩 (3)	# 924 飢 (2)
# 925 傾 (2)	# 926 退 (3)	# 927 屈 (2)	# 928 懐 (3)

Vocabulary List with Mnemonics

from the Kanji Catalogue

象牙	zouge = ivory; from zou = elephant + ge = tusk; *my guest wore a necklace of tusks*
牙	kiba = fang, tusk; *the king of Baghdad wore a necklace of tusks*
優雅な	yuuga na = elegant; *the youthful gambler wore elegant clothes*
温雅	onga = graceful, affable; *the owner of that gas station is affable*
雅びた	miyabita = gracious, elegant, refined; *the mirror that the yakuza gave to beefy Tarzan was elegant*
狩る	karu = to hunt (animals), to gather (flowers, mushrooms, fruit); *the carpenter in that room enjoys hunting and gathering mushrooms*
狩り	kari = hunting, gathering; from karu = to hunt
キノコ狩り	kinokogari = mushroom gathering; from ki no ko = mushroom; *a mushroom is a ki no (tree's) ko (child); + gari = kari = gathering*
飢える	ueru = to starve, to be thirsty or hungry; *I'm starving, thanks to Ueitoresu (waitress) Ruth's slow service*
飢え死に	uejini = death from starvation; from ueru = to starve + jinu = shinu = to die
傾く	katamuku = to tilt or incline, to go down; *the catamaran hit a patch of muck and inclined onto its side*
傾斜する	keisha suru = to tilt or slant; *the cake they served the Shah was tilting to one side*
退屈	taikutsu = boredom; *since these Thai kutsu (shoes) are all the same, they are contributing to my boredom*
退職	taishoku = retirement from office, resignation; *the Thai people were shocked by the prime minister's resignation*
退く	shirizoku = to retreat; *the sheep were reading the signs of the Zodiac and drinking Kool-Aid when they had to retreat from the wolf*

Kanji Pronunciations

# 921 – ge, kiba, ga	# 922 – ga, miya	# 923 – ga, ka, shu	# 924 – ki, u
# 925 – katamu, kei	# 926 – no, shirizo, tai	# 927 – ku, kutsu	# 928 – futokoro, kai, natsu

立ち退く	tachinoku = to evacuate, vacate; *we were attaching a nose to our cool snowman when we were told to evacuate the snowfield*
屈服する	kuppuku suru = to surrender; *the cooped-up ukulele players were forced to surrender*
理屈	rikutsu = argument, theory, pretext; *I returned those kutsu (shoes) on the pretext that they were too big for me*
懐かしい	natsukashii = nostalgic, evocative of times past; *I think of the natsu (summer) when I was cashing in my stocks, and I feel nostalgic*
懐	futokoro = bosom, heart; *I sleep on a futon in my Corolla, and that's where my heart is*
懐が広い	futokoro ga hiroi = is kind-hearted; from futokoro = heart + hiroi = spacious
懐中電灯	kaichuu dentou = flashlight; from kaichuu = pocket; *the Kaiser chooses to keep his hands in his pockets*; + dentou = electric light

from the Practice Sentences

むき出す	mukidasu = to show or bare (the teeth); *after swimming in the mucky pool, Dad threatened to sue the swim club and bared his teeth to show that he was serious*
エステ	esute = aesthetic
至福	shifuku = supreme bliss; *when I was reunited with my sheepdog in Fukuoka, it was a moment of supreme bliss*
ひととき	hitotoki = for a moment, for a while; from hitotsu = one + toki = time
かっとなる	katto naru = to fly into a rage; *when he was caught on the toll road without any coins, he flew into a rage*
立ち退き	tachinoki = eviction; from tachinoku = to evacuate
ついに	tsui ni = finally, in the end; *my tsuit (sweet) niece showed up in the end*
傾向	keikou = tendency, inclination, trend; *when cake is kept cold, it has a tendency to last longer*

from Satori Reader

まさに	masa ni = exactly, naturally, certainly, on the verge; *after she massaged my knee, which she did exactly as expected, she was on the verge of massaging my foot*
ひんやり	hinyari = cool, chilly; *the Hindu's yard was really chilly*
せいせい	seisei = feeling refreshed or relieved; *after the sailors saved me, I felt relieved*
ぎょっと	gyotto = being startled; *I was startled when the gyoza fell onto my toe*
弱肉強食	jakuniku kyoushoku = survival of the fittest; literally, "the weak are meat that the strong eat"; from jaku = weak; Jack Nicholson's tennis game is weak; + niku = meat; + kyou = strong; *a strong man lives in Kyouto*; + shokuji = meal

付け加える	tsukekuwaeru = to add one thing to another; from tsukeru = to attach + kuwaeru = to add or include
そろそろ	sorosoro = before long, slowly, quietly, gradually; the Soviet robot moved slowly
見張り	mihari = guard, lookout, watch-keeping; from miru = to look + haru = to pull or extend, e.g., hipparu = to pull
心地よさ	kokochiyosa = comfort; from kokoro = heart + chi = ground + yoi = good + sa = a suffix that converts an adjective to a noun; cf. kokochiyoi = comfortable, pleasant

Practice Sentences

1. ライオンはさらに牙をむき出した。

Raion wa sara ni kiba o mukidashita.
The lion bared its fangs even more.

2. 洋子さんは優雅な動きでダンスを踊った。

Youko san wa yuuga na ugoki de dansu wo odotta.
Yoko danced a dance with elegant movements.

3. 野田さんは森へ狩りに行きました。

Noda san wa mori e kari ni ikimashita.
Mr. Noda went to the woods for the purpose of hunting.

4. 子供達は愛情に飢えていた。

Kodomotachi wa aijou ni uete ita.
The children were starving for love.

5. 先日の地震で家が傾いて、住むことができません。

Senjitsu no jishin de ie ga katamuite, sumu koto ga dekimasen.
Due to the other day's earthquake, the house slants, and I cannot reside. (i.e., I can't live in it)

6. 立ち退きの報告を受けた。

Tachinoki no houkoku wo uketa.
I received eviction information (i.e., an eviction notice).

7. 敵はついに屈服した。

Teki wa tsui ni kuppuku shita.
At last, the enemy surrendered.

8. 上着のポケットから懐中電灯を取り出した。

Uwagi no poketto kara kaichuudentou wo toridashita.
He took a flashlight out of his coat pocket.

9. この美術館には象牙で作られた美術品がたくさんあります。

Kono bijutsukan ni wa zouge de tsukurareta bijutsuhin ga takusan arimasu.
In this museum, there are a lot of works of art made from ivory.

10. エステサロンで優雅な至福の
ひとときを過ごしてみません
か？

Esute saron de yuuga na shifuku no
hitotoki o sugoshite mimasen ka?
Won't you spend an elegant blissful short
time at an aesthetic salon and see?

11. ここでは鹿を狩ってはいけま
せん。

Koko de wa shika wo katte wa ikemasen.
You may not hunt deer here.

12. あの動物たちは飢えているよ
うだ。

Ano doubutsutachi wa uete iru you da.
Those animals appear to be starving.

13. 父はたまにかっとなる傾向が
ある。

Chichi wa tama ni katto naru keikou ga
aru.
My father occasionally has a tendency to
fly into a rage.

14. 何もすることがなくて退屈で
す。

Nani mo suru koto ga nakute, taikutsu
desu.
Since to do nothing doesn't exist (i.e.,
there's nothing to do), it's boring.

15. 木原さんは懐が広い。

Kihara san wa futokoro ga hiroi.
As for Ms. Kihara, her heart is spacious.
(i.e., she is kind-hearted)

16. その犬の牙が怖い。

Sono inu no kiba ga kowai.
As for that dog's fangs, they are
frightening.

17. 小野さんは温雅な人だ。

Ono san wa onga na hito da.
Ms. Ono is an affable person.

18. 今日は家族でキノコ狩りに出
かけるでしょう。

Kyou wa kazoku de kinokogari ni
dekakeru deshou.
Today, of the family (i.e., with the
family), we will probably depart for the
sake of mushroom gathering.

19. 毎年何百万という人が飢えで
亡くなっている。

Maitoshi nan byaku man to iu hito ga ue
de nakunatte iru.
Every year millions to-call people (i.e.,
what is called millions of people) are
dying of starvation.

20. このビルは少し左に傾いてい
る。

Kono biru wa sukoshi hidari ni katamuite
iru.
This building is tilting a little to the left.

21. 父は６５歳で退職した。

Chichi wa rokujuu go sai de taishoku
shita.
My father retired at the age of 65.

22. 彼の説明は全く理屈に合わない。

Kare no setsumei wa mattaku rikutsu ni awanai.
His explanation doesn't fit the theory at all. (i.e., it isn't reasonable)

23. 子供の頃の思い出が懐かしい。

Kodomo no koro no omoide ga natsukashii.
The child's approximate time's memories are nostalgic. (i.e., I feel nostalgic about my childhood memories)

Supplemental Reading Practice

After completing Chapter 40 of this book, you should be able to read the "Hawk," "The Law of the Jungle," "Catch as Catch Can" and "Reflection" articles from the "Kona's Big Adventure" series in *Satori Reader*.

Chapter 41

New Kanji in this Chapter

# 929 群 (3)	# 930 衆 (1)	# 931 積 (3)	# 932 射 (2)
# 933 戦 (3)	# 934 聴 (1)	# 935 競 (4)	# 936 争 (2)

Vocabulary List with Mnemonics

from the Kanji Catalogue

群れ — mure = herd, crowd, group; *I saw a movie about red roosters that lived in a group*

群集 — gunshuu = a group of living things (including people), a crowd or community; *I keep a gun in my shoe in case a group of living things attacks me*

群衆 — gunshuu = a group of people, a crowd or mob; *I keep a gun in my shoe in case a crowd of people attacks me*

群がる — muragaru = to flock or throng; *the mural that the gambler ruined depicted people flocking to a supermarket opening*

積む — tsumu = to heap up, accumulate, load (transitive); *people heap up tsuitcases (suitcases) on the moon because they rarely get a chance to return to earth*

積もる — tsumoru = to pile up (intransitive); *the tsuitcases (suitcases) in the moron's room are piling up*

面積 — menseki = area; *the mentor of the selfish king owned a large area of land near the castle*

積極 — sekkyoku = positive, progressive; *he sells Kyoto Kool-Aid in a positive and progressive way*

反射 — hansha = reflection; *the reflection showed Hansel holding a sharp sword*

注射 — chuusha = injection; *during the injection, I chewed shark cartilage*

射る — iru = to hit or shoot (an arrow); *it was easy to ruin the balloon by shooting it*

戦 — ikusa = battle; *I carry ear cooties in a sack when I go into battle and scatter them on my enemies*

戦う — tatakau = to fight; *the tall taxi driver will kau (buy) a gun before he fights*

聴衆 — choushuu = audience; *Margaret Cho threw her shoes at the audience*

Kanji Pronunciations

# 929 – mu, mura, gun	# 930 – shuu	# 931 – seki, se, tsu	# 932 – sha, i
# 933 – sen, ikusa, tataka	# 934 – chou	# 935 – kiso, se, kei, kyou	# 936 – araso, sou

聴解力	choukairyoku = listening comprehension; from choukai = listening comprehension; *after glaucoma choked my eyes, I had to work on my listening comprehension;* + ryoku = force, power
競う	kisou = to compete with; *the king's soldiers competed with one another*
競争	kyousou = competition; *in Kyouto, soldiers engage in competition*
競り	seri = auction; *I sold my Segway and my wedding ring at auction*
戦争	sensou = war; *my sensory organs were overwhelmed by the chaos of war*
争う	arasou = to fight, dispute or compete; *Arafat sold his yacht after competing in the boat race*

from the Practice Sentences

運動神経	undoushinkei = reflexes, motor nerves; from undou = exercise, movement; + shinkei = nerves, sensitivity; *shingles is a case of illness in which a nerve is inflamed*
抜群	batsugun = outstanding, fabulous; *a bat suit plus a toy gun add up to a fabulous Halloween outfit*
市長	shichou = mayor; from shi = city + chou = chief
大衆	taishuu = general public; *the general public is tired of shooting incidents*
着	chaku = arrival, order of arrival (in a race); *at the end of the race, the athletes are given either champagne or Kool-Aid, depending on their order of arrival*
公衆	koushuu = the public; *I got cold shoes while waiting for that public phone*
行い	okonai = act, behavior; from okonau = to conduct or perform; *I'm going to Oklahoma now to perform in a play*
積極的に	sekkyokuteki ni = aggressively, positively; from sekkyoku = positive, aggressive + teki = related to
的	mato = target, center of attention; *after I stepped on Ma's toes, I was the center of attention*
決勝戦	kesshousen = final game in a tournament; *Kennedy showed some senators the tournament's final game from his luxury box*
言い争う	ii'arasou = to quarrel or dispute; *on Easter, Arafat sold his share in his yacht after he quarreled with the other owners*
祖国	sokoku = native country; from so = ancestral, e.g., 祖母 sobo = grandmother; + koku = country
行動	koudou = action, behavior; *the Korean doorman's behavior was impeccable*
口調	kuchou = tone of voice, verbal expression; from kuchi = mouth + choushi = condition
現場	genba = site, location; from genjitsu = reality + basho = place, location

Practice Sentences

1. 彼は運動神経が抜群だ。

Kare wa undou shinkei ga batsugun da.
As for him, the reflexes are outstanding.

2. 市長は大衆を前に演説をした。

Shichou wa taishuu o mae ni enzetsu o shita.
The mayor made a speech in front of the general public.

3. トラックに荷物を積んだ。

Torakku ni nimotsu wo tsunda.
I loaded the luggage into the truck.

4. 予防注射をしておきましょう。

Yobou chuusha wo shite okimashou.
Let's do a prevention injection in advance.

5. 戦争が突然始まった。

Sensou ga totsuzen hajimatta.
The war suddenly began.

6. 聴衆は主に学生であった。

Choushuu wa omo ni gakusei de atta.
The audience was mainly students.

7. 彼は競争で5着になった。

Kare wa kyousou de go chaku ni natta.
He received 5th place in the competition.

8. 空高く飛んでいる鳥の群れを見ました。

Sora takaku tonde iru tori no mure o mimashita.
I saw a flock of birds flying high in the sky.

9. 公衆電話はあの角にあります。

Koushuu denwa wa ano kado ni arimasu.
There is a public phone on that corner.

10. 彼は良い行いを積極的にしている。

Kare wa yoi okonai o sekkyokuteki ni shite iru.
He is doing good deeds positively (i.e., assertively or actively).

11. その行動は的を射ている。

Sono koudou wa mato wo ite iru.
Those actions are hitting the target. (i.e., they are on target)

12. わが国の選手は決勝戦でとうとう敗れてしまった。

Wagakuni no senshu wa kesshousen de toutou yaburete shimatta.
As for our country's athlete, at the final round, at last, she lost completely.

13. 彼は聴衆に静かな口調で演説した。

Kare wa choushuu ni shizuka na kuchou de enzetsu shita.
He addressed the audience in a soft tone of voice.

14. 群衆が現場に群がった。

Gunshuu ga genba ni muragatta.
A crowd flocked to the site.

15. 私たちは競争を恐れません。

Watashitachi wa kyousou wo osoremasen.
We are not afraid of competition.

16. カナダはアメリカより面積が広い。

Kanada wa amerika yori menseki ga hiroi.
Compared to the U.S., Canada's area is more spacious.

17. 月の光が湖に反射していた。

Tsuki no hikari ga mizu'umi ni hansha shite ita.
The moon's light was reflecting on the lake.

18. 彼らは祖国を守るために戦った。

Karera wa sokoku wo mamoru tame ni takakatta.
They fought in order to protect their native country.

19. 夕べのピアノリサイタルには大勢の聴衆客でいっぱいだった。

Yuube no piano risaitaru ni wa oozei no choushuu kyaku de ippai datta.
Since there was a crowd of audience guests at the piano recital last night, it was full.

20. 二つのチームは決勝戦で競った。

Futatsu no chiimu wa kesshousen de kisotta.
The two teams competed in the final match.

21. その姉妹はいつも言い争ってばかりいる。

Sono shimai wa itsumo ii'arasotte bakari iru.
Those sisters are always only quarrelling.

22. 戦争は２年続いた。

Sensou wa ninen tsuzuita.
The war lasted two years.

Chapter 42

New Kanji in this Chapter

# 937 眩 (2)	# 938 峰 (3)	# 939 富 (3)	# 940 協 (1)
# 941 襲 (2)	# 942 油 (2)	# 943 禁 (1)	# 944 吠 (2)

Vocabulary List with Mnemonics

from the Kanji Catalogue

眩しい — mabushii = dazzling, blinding; *after drinking Massachusetts booze with some Shiites, I went out into the dazzling sun*

眩む — kuramu = to be blinded or dazzled; *the curator of the moon rocks was dazzled by the amount of money that he was offered for them*

峰 — mine = mountain peak; *there are some minerals near the mountain peak*

名峰 — meihou = famous mountain; *the maid had a home on a famous mountain*

連峰 — renpou = mountain range; *I will rent a pony and explore that mountain range*

富む — tomu = to get rich, to abound with; *Tony Blair's mood improved when he got rich*

富 — tomi = wealth; from tomu = to get rich

富士山 — fujisan = Mt. Fuji

協力する — kyouryoku suru = to cooperate; *when I do Kyouto ryokou [travel] to a cool temple, I need cooperation from a taxi driver*

協同 — kyoudou = cooperation; *in Kyouto, dough (money) can buy cooperation*

襲う — osou = to attack; *the old soldier wanted to attack*

油断 — yudan = negligence, inattentiveness; *the youthful dancer was charged with negligence*

石油 — sekiyu = petroleum; *the selfish king visited the Yukon to look for petroleum*

油 — abura = oil; *they poured sacred oil on a Buddha statue*

禁じる — kinjiru = to prohibit; *after the time when the king's Jeep was ruined, he prohibited everyone from using it*

禁物 — kinmotsu = a forbidden thing; from kinjiru = to prohibit + motsu = thing

吠える — hoeru = to bark, howl, roar, cry; *that hostess is erudite, but her dog barks too much*

Kanji Pronunciations

# 937 – kura, mabu	# 938 – hou, pou, mine	# 939 – fu, to, tomi	# 940 – kyou
# 941 – oso, shuu	# 942 – abura, yu	# 943 – kin	# 944 – ho, bo

遠吠え	tooboe = howling; from tooi = far + boeru = hoeru = to bark

from the Practice Sentences

アンケート	ankeeto = questionnaire; from the French enquete; *she made an anklet out of the questionnaire*
真っ昼間	mappiruma = broad daylight; from ma = genuine, e.g., makoto = sincerity; + piru = hiru = noon; + ma = duration, e.g., mamonaku = before long
得体の知れない	etai no shirenai = questionable, untrustworthy, enigmatic, suspicious; from etai = nature or character; *the expert tilesetter has a unique character*; + the possessive no + shirenai = cannot know
やつら	yatsura = the plural of yatsu = he, that guy; *that yacht club supervisor is a regular guy*
オオカミ	ookami = wolf; *the old can of meat was eaten by wolves*
そびえる	sobieru = to tower over; *the sobieto (Soviet) ruins towered over us*
飲食	inshoku = drinking and eating; *she was in shock when she saw how much drinking and eating was going on*
逃げ去る	nigesaru = to take flight or disappear; from nigeru = to escape or run away + saru = to leave
積み込む	tsumikomu = to load (goods, etc.), to put on board; from tsumu = to heap up or load + komu = to crowd in

from Satori Reader

夕日	yuuhi = evening sun, setting sun; from yuugata = evening + hi = sun
ヤギ	yagi = goat; *yaks and geese get along with goats*
交差	kousa = crossing, intersection; *commuting salarymen wait at intersections*
肉食	nikushoku = meat-eating, carnivorous; from niku = meat + shokuji = meal
草食	soushoku = plant-eating, herbivorous; from sougen = grasslands + shokuji = meal
集団	shuudan = group; *the shooter turned out to be a dancer from our group*
交代	koutai = alternation, shift; *since we only have one coat and tie, my brother and I wear them in shifts*
乗り切る	norikiru = to get through (adversity), to overcome; from noru = to ride a vehicle + kiru = to cut
小鹿	kojika = fawn; from ko = child + jika = shika = deer
生える	haeru = to grow or sprout; *Hansel is an erudite farmer who knows how to make things grow*

突く　　tsuku = to stab, poke, strike, attack; *I used my <u>tsu</u>itcase (suitcase) full of <u>Kool</u>-Aid to <u>strike</u> at the muggers*

Practice Sentences

1. 太陽が眩しいのでサングラスをかける。

Taiyou ga mabushii node sangurasu wo kakeru.
Since the sun is dazzling, I will wear sunglasses.

2. 富士山は日本一の名峰です。

Fujisan wa nihon ichi no meihou desu.
Mt. Fuji is Japan number-one famous mountain.

3. アンケート調査にご協力をお願いします。

Ankeeto chousa ni gokyouryoku wo onegaishimasu.
To the questionnaire investigation, honorable cooperation I beg you. (i.e., please fill out the survey)

4. ３人組が真っ昼間その銀行を襲った。

San nin gumi ga mappiruma sono ginkou wo osotta.
A three-person gang, in broad daylight, attacked (i.e., robbed) that bank.

5. 油断は禁物。

Yudan wa kinmotsu.
Inattentiveness is forbidden. (i.e., be on guard)

6. 彼はアイディアに富んでいる。

Kare wa aidia ni tonde iru.
He abounds with ideas.

7. 突然犬が吠え出した。

Totsuzen inu ga hoedashita.
Suddenly the dog began to bark.

8. 彼は金に目が眩んで結婚した。

Kare wa kane ni me ga kurande kekkon shita.
As for him, to money, eyes being dazzled, he married. (i.e., he married for money)

9. 長野県には北アルプスと言われる連峰がある。

Nagano ken ni wa kita arupusu to iwareru renpou ga aru.
In Nagano prefecture, the "Northern Alps" called mountain range exists.

10. 健康の方が富より大事だ。

Kenkou no hou ga tomi yori daiji da.
Health, compared to wealth, is more important.

11. 家族の協力を抜きに私の成功はなかった。

Kazoku no kyouryoku wo nuki ni watashi no seikou wa nakatta.
On the family's cooperation, without, as for my success, it didn't exist. (i.e., I couldn't have succeeded without my family's help)

12. 何か得体の知れないやつらに
襲われた。

Nanika etai no shirenai yatsura ni
osowareta.
We were attacked by something-
character-unknowable guys (i.e., by a
mysterious or suspicious group).

13. フライパンに油を少し入れ、
卵を二個焼きます。

Furaipan ni abura wo sukoshi ire, tamago
wo niko yakimasu.
To the frying pan, I will insert a little oil,
and I will fry two eggs.

14. あのう、ここは駐車禁止にな
っていますから。

Anou, koko wa chuusha kinshi ni natte
imasu kara.
Say, because, as for here, it is becoming
parking prohibited. (i.e., don't park here)

15. ヘッドライトが眩しくて一瞬
目が眩んだ。

Heddoraito ga mabushikute isshun me ga
kuranda.
The headlights dazzling, and for a moment
the eyes (i.e., my eyes) were blinded.

16. オオカミは月に向かって遠吠
えしていた。

Ookami wa tsuki ni mukatte tooboe shite
ita.
The wolves, facing the moon, were doing
howling.

17. その峰は雲の上にそびえてい
た。

Sono mine wa kumo no ue ni sobiete ita.
That peak was towering above the clouds.

18. 協力できたら嬉しいです。

Kyouryoku dekitara ureshii desu.
If I am able to cooperate, I will be pleased.
(to say "if *you* are able to cooperate, I will
be pleased," use "kyouroku dekite
moraeba, ureshii...")

19. 奇妙な伝染病が町を襲った。

Kimyou na densenbyou ga machi wo
osotta.
A strange infectious disease attacked the
town.

20. 彼らは石油を船に積み込ん
だ。

Karera wa sekiyu wo fune ni tsumikonda.
They loaded oil into the ship.

21. 図書館内では飲食禁止です。

Toshokan nai de wa inshoku kinshi desu.
In the library, eating and drinking are
prohibited.

22. 泥棒は犬が吠えるのを聞くと
すぐに逃げ去った。

Dorobou wa inu ga hoeru no wo kiku to
sugu ni nigesatta.
When the thief heard the dog barking, he
took flight right away.

Supplemental Reading Practice

After completing Chapter 42 of this book, you should be able to read the "Never Let Your Guard Down" article from the "Kona's Big Adventure" series in *Satori Reader*.

Chapter 43

New Kanji in this Chapter

# 945 伏 (3)	# 946 床 (3)	# 947 獲 (2)	# 948 狙 (1)
# 949 匂 (1)	# 950 闇 (1)	# 951 臓 (1)	# 952 斉 (1)

Vocabulary List with Mnemonics

from the Kanji Catalogue

伏せる	fuseru = to lay an object upside down or face down, to lie down, to cast one's eyes down; *the foolish seller made it a rule to lay his merchandise face down*
うつ伏せに	utsubuse ni = face down; *when I was utilizing the supermarket, I saw a boozed-up Segway driver and my niece lying face down on the floor*
降伏する	koufuku suru = to surrender; *when the corporal reached Fukuoka, he surrendered*
床	yuka = floor; *I keep my yucca on the floor*
床	toko = bed, floor; *after Tony Blair had a coronary, he spent a lot of time in bed or on the floor*
床屋	tokoya = barbershop; *Tony Blair drinks cola with his Yankee friends at the barbershop*
起床	kishou = rising, getting out of bed; *when the king stays by the shore, he rises early*
獲得する	kakutoku suru = to win or obtain; *that cactus is totally cool, and I hope to win it in a contest*
獲物	emono = game (hunting) or catch (fishing); *when Eskimos get mono (things) from hunting or fishing, we call them game or catch*
狙う	nerau = to aim; *she aimed the gun at the necklace that Raul Castro was wearing*
匂う	niou = to smell of; *that knee oil you are applying smells good*

Kanji Pronunciations

# 945 – fu, fuku, bu	# 946 – yuka, shou, toko	# 947 – kaku, e	# 948 – nera
# 949 – nio	# 950 – yami	# 951 – zou	# 952 – sei

匂い	nioi = fragrance, scent; from niou = to smell of
闇	yami = darkness; *the yaks meet in darkness*
暗闇	kurayami = darkness; from kurai = dark + yami = darkness
心臓	shinzou = the heart (organ); from shin = heart + zou = organ; *zou (elephants) have big internal organs*
内臓	naizou = internal organ, intestines; from nai = inside + zou = organ
一斉に	issei ni = all at once, at the same time, all together; *it's easy to say that you will do it if everyone else will do it at the same time*

from the Practice Sentences

売り上げ	uriage = sales; *if you try to sell urine to the aged, your sales will be poor*
心臓発作	shinzou hossa = heart attack; from shinzou = heart + hossa = attack or fit; *when the horse saw the snake, he had a fit*
第一人者	dai ichi ninsha = leading person; from dai ichi = the most, the best, first; + nin = person + sha = person
外科	geka = surgery; *Genghis Khan underwent surgery*
受験生	jukensei = examinee; from 受験する juken suru = to take an examination; *the juice that Ken bought helped him when he took the examination;* + sei = to live; cf. 受験者 jukensha = examinee
取りかかる	torikakaru = to launch or start; *the Tories' money kakaru (will be spent) to ensure that their boats will launch or start*
飛び込む	tobikomu = to jump or dive in; from tobu = to fly + komu = to crowd in
立ち上がる	tachiagaru = to stand up; from tatsu = to stand + agaru = to rise
見通し	mitoushi = outlook, perspective; *mitochondria shield this cell's nucleus, from our perspective*

from Satori Reader

先回り	sakimawari = going on ahead; from saki = tip + mawaru = to turn
待ち伏せる	machibuseru = to ambush; from matsu = to wait + buseru = fuseru = to lie down
追い込む	oikomu = to herd; from ou = to chase + komu = to crowd in
しとしと	shitoshito = gently (raining); *the sheep toy got damp when it rained gently*
羽ばたき	habataki = fluttering of wings; *on Halloween, the barber looked tacky as he fluttered his wings*
丸のみ	marunomi = swallowing whole; from maru = circle + nomu = to drink
飛び起きる	tobiokiru = to jump to one's feet; from tobu = to fly + okiru = to get up

よじ登る	yojinoboru = to scramble up; from yojireru = to be twisted; *the yogi's jeans had been attacked by a red rooster and looked twisted*; + noboru = to climb
先頭	sentou = vanguard, first; from sen = before, e.g., sensei = teacher + tou = head
勢い	ikioi = force, power, energy, spirit; *there is a lot of energy in the icky oil industry*

Practice Sentences

1. 彼は床に身を伏せた。

Kare wa toko ni mi wo fuseta.
He laid his body (i.e., he lay down) on the bed. (it's also OK to pronounce this "yuka ni mi wo fuseta," if he lay on the floor)

2. 彼の音楽は海外で人気を獲得している。

Kare no ongaku wa kaigai de ninki wo kakutoku shite iru.
His music is winning popularity in foreign countries.

3. 鳥を狙うには遠すぎる。

Tori wo nerau ni wa toosugiru.
As for for the purpose of to aim on the bird, it's too far. (i.e., too far away to shoot)

4. この匂いは何ですか。

Kono nioi wa nan desu ka.
What is this smell?

5. そこは深い闇だった。

Soko wa fukai yami datta.
As for that place, it was a deep darkness.

6. 胸の中に心臓がある。

Mune no naka ni shinzou ga aru.
The heart exists in the chest.

7. ベルが鳴ると、受験生は一斉に試験に取りかかった。

Beru ga naru to, jukensei wa issei ni shiken ni torikakatta.
When the bell rings, the test-taking people, all together, started the test.

8. うつ伏せになってください。

Utsubuse ni natte kudasai.
Please lie face down.

9. 床屋に行って髪を切る。

Tokoya ni itte kami wo kiru.
I'll go to the barbershop and cut my hair.

10. 日本の選手はメダルをいくつ獲得しましたか？

Nihon no senshuu wa medaru wo ikutsu kakutoku shimashita ka.
How many medals did the Japanese athletes win?

11. 今回は私も優勝を狙っていました。

Konkai wa watashi mo yuushou wo neratte imashita.
This time I also was aiming at the championship.

12. 何かが焦げてる匂いがする。

Nanika kogeteru nioi ga suru.
Something-is-burning smell does. (i.e., I smell something burning)

13. 真っ暗闇だ。

Makkura yami da.
It's pitch dark. (cf. 真っ黒 makkuro
= pitch black)

14. 彼は心臓発作で死んだ。

Kare wa shinzou hossa de shinda.
He died of a heart attack.

15. みんなで一斉に水に飛び込んだ。

Minna de issei ni mizu ni tobikonda.
Of everyone, all together, we jumped (or
dove) into the water.

16. 降伏するくらいなら死んだ方がましだ。

Koufuku suru kurai nara shinda hou ga
mashi da.
To surrender approximately case, it
would be better to die. (i.e., I'd rather die
than surrender)

17. あなたはいつも何時に起床しますか。

Anata wa itsumo nanji ni kishou shimasu
ka.
At what time do you usually get up?

18. 獲物が捕れなかった。

Emono ga torenakatta.
He couldn't get any game.

19. 売り上げ倍増を狙っていたが、見通しが甘かった。

Uriage baizou wo neratte ita ga, mitoushi
ga amakatta.
We were aiming on gross sales doubling,
but the outlook was sweet (i.e., overly
optimistic).

20. この食べ物は腐った匂いがします。

Kono tabemono wa kusatta nioi ga
shimasu.
This food does a rotted smell. (i.e., it
smells rotten)

21. 彼女は暗闇を恐れている。

Kanojo wa kurayami wo osorete iru.
She fears the darkness.

22. 彼は心臓外科の第一人者だ。

Kare wa shinzou geka no dai ichi ninsha
da.
He is a leading person in heart surgery.

23. 彼らは一斉に立ち上がった。

Karera wa issei ni tachiagata.
They all stood up at the same time.

24. 床をきれいに掃除してください。

Yuka wo kirei ni souji shite kudasai.
Please clean the floor cleanly.

Supplemental Reading Practice

After completing Chapter 43 of this book, you should be able to read the "Silent Hunter" and "Midnight Dash" articles from the "Kona's Big Adventure" series in *Satori Reader*.

Chapter 44

New Kanji in this Chapter

# 953 猛 (1)	# 954 程 (2)	# 955 祈 (2)	# 956 俺 (1)
# 957 苔 (1)	# 958 馬 (3)	# 959 嗅 (2)	# 960 態 (1)

Vocabulary List with Mnemonics

from the Kanji Catalogue

猛暑   mousho = fierce heat, heat wave; *Moses showed the people of Israel how to survive a heat wave in the wilderness*

猛勉強   moubenkyou = studying extra hard; from mou = fierce, strength; *the mole is fierce*; + benkyou = study

猛練習   mourenshuu = hard training; from mou = fierce, strength; *the mole is fierce*; + renshuu = practice

猛犬   mouken = savage dog; from mou = fierce, strength; *the mole is fierce*; + ken = dog; *Ken and Barbie have a dog*

程   hodo = extent, degree, limits, moderation, approximate time, about so much (usually spelled ほど); *the host doles out the drinks only to the extent necessary*

程度   teido = criterion, standard, extent; *the taste of the dough met the baker's standard*

祈る   inoru = to pray; *the innocent roosters prayed for peace*

俺   ore = I, me; *I live in Oregon*

苔   koke = moss, lichen; *the Coke in the kegs was stored under some moss*

馬   uma = horse; *this horse belongs to an Uruguayan man*

絵馬   ema = a drawing or painting of a horse; *the emancipated people made drawings of horses*

馬鹿   baka = stupid person, usually written バカ; *he may be a stupid person, but he has a baccalaureate degree*

木馬   mokuba = a wooden horse; from moku = wood + ba = horse; *there are a lot of horses in Barcelona*

競馬   keiba = horse racing; *I ate some cake in a bar while I watched horse racing*

Kanji Pronunciations

# 953 – mou	# 954 – hodo, tei	# 955 – ki, ino	# 956 – ore
# 957 – koke	# 958 – uma, ba, ma	# 959 – kyuu, ka	# 960 – tai

嗅覚　kyuukaku = sense of smell; *that cute guy named Karl the Kool-Aid vendor has a good sense of smell*

嗅ぐ　kagu = to sniff or smell; *that carpenter is goofy in that he smells wood before cutting it*

態度　taido = attitude; *the Thai doorman has a good attitude*

変態　hentai = pervert or perversion, metamorphosis (insect); *the hens are tired of those perverts*

from the Practice Sentences

過程　katei = process; *the dog caught his tail in the door while in the process of leaving*

感　kan = sensation, emotion, feeling; from kanjiru = to sense or feel

事態　jitai = situation, circumstance; *the Jeep's tire was flat, so we had to deal with that situation*

に違いない　ni chigainai = no doubt, certainly; from chigau = to differ; literally this means "to not differ" or "there will be no discrepancy"

期末　kimatsu = end of term (semester); *let's keep these mats until the end of the term*

大騒ぎ　oosawagi = a big fuss, uproar; from ookii = big + sawagu = to make a fuss

無実　mujitsu = innocence or innocent; *I saw a movie in which a jittery superstar proclaimed his innocence*

from Satori Reader

手遅れ　te okure = occurring too late; from te = hand + okure = to be delayed, suggesting that a hand was employed too late

鳴き声　nakigoe = an animal cry, howl, chirp; from naku = to bark, chirp or cry + goe = koe = voice; cf. 泣き声 nakigoe = a human cry, weeping

勝ち目　kachime = chance of success, odds; from katsu = to win + me = ordinal number, e.g., hitotsume no kado = the first corner

ふと　futo = accidentally, suddenly, casually; *the foolish Tory suddenly fell down*

反射的に　hanshatekini = reflexively; from hansha = reflection + teki = related to

ひたすら　hitasura = nothing but; *the Himalayan tanner's supervisor ran out of the room, and nothing but an apology could make him come back*

見下ろす　miorosu = to overlook (scenery); *the mean old rogue sued after he happened to overlook his neighbor trampling on his shrubs*

うろつく　urotsuku = to loiter or hover; from urouro = loitering, restlessly + tsuku = adhere

うなる　unaru = to groan or roar; *the Unabomber ruined the ambush when he groaned*

しめた！　shimeta = I've got it!, or all right!; *when the sheepherders met Tarzan, they said "all right!"*

つかの間 — tsuka no ma = a moment; *since he had it in a tsuitcase (suitcase) in the car, the Norwegian mariner only needed a moment to locate his umbrella*

うっすら — ussura = slightly, faintly, dimly; from usui = pale, thin, watery, light, weak

根比べ — konkurabe = a test of endurance; *Conan O'Brien wanted to kuraberu (compare) himself to his rival, so he set up a test of endurance*

見かける — mikakeru = to catch sight of; from mi = to see + kakeru = to begin to do something

ひっくり返す — hikkurikaesu = to turn over, to knock over; from hiku = to pull + kaesu = to turn something over, to return an item

カリカリ — karikari = crisp, crunchy; *Caribbean potato chips are crunchy*

とうてい — toutei = (cannot) possibly, no matter how; *the toast on the table cannot possibly satisfy my appetite, no matter how much butter I spread on it*

Practice Sentences

1. 猛犬に注意！
Mouken ni chuui.
To the savage dog, caution. (i.e., beware of the dog)

2. 過程が大切です。
Katei ga taisetsu desu.
The process is important.

3. 病気の回復を祈る。
Byouki no kaifuku wo inoru.
I pray on (i.e., for) recovery from the illness.

4. 俺の言う通りにするんだ。
Ore no iu toori ni surun da.
To my to-say way to-do thing it is. (i.e., you must do as I say)

5. 日本庭園の苔が美しい。
Nihon tei'en no koke ga utsukushii.
The formal Japanese garden's moss is beautiful.

6. 馬は草を食べる。
Uma wa kusa wo taberu.
Horses eat grass.

7. 嗅覚は五感の一つです。
Kyuukaku wa gokan no hitotsu desu.
The sense of smell is one of the five senses.

8. 緊急事態だ。
Kinkyuu jitai da.
It's an emergency situation.

9. 猛練習したに違いない。
Mourenshuu shita ni chigainai.
You certainly did hard training.

10. 早ければ早い程よい。
Hayakereba hayai hodo yoi.
If it's early, to the degree early, good. (i.e., the earlier the better; to say "the more," follow the eba form of a verb or i adjective with the plain speech form and then use hodo)

11. 馬を走らせています。
Uma wo hashirasete imasu.
He is making the horse run.

12. 成功を祈る。

Seikou wo inoru.
I pray on (i.e., for) success.

13. 俺、飯食うよ。

Ore, meshi kuu yo.
I will eat rice for sure. (man's rough speech; this means "I will eat now")

14. あの森にはたくさんの苔が生えている。

Ano mori ni wa takusan no koke ga haete iru.
As for in that forest, a lot of moss is growing.

15. 彼女は花の匂いを嗅いだ。

Kanojo wa hana no nioi wo kaida.
She smelled the flower's fragrance.

16. 彼は事態を知らなかった。

Kare wa jitai wo shiranakatta.
He was unaware of the situation.

17. 期末試験のため猛勉強をしている。

Kimatsu shiken no tame moubenkyou wo shite iru.
I am studying intensely for the end-of-semester exam.

18. 大騒ぎする程でもない。

Oosawagi suru hodo de mo nai.
To do a big fuss, to that degree even is not. (i.e., it's no big deal)

19. 幸運を祈ります。

Kou'un wo inorimasu.
I pray on (i.e., for) good luck.

20. 俺は無実だ。

Ore wa mujitsu da.
I am innocent.

21. この生け花は苔を使っています。

Kono ikebana wa koke wo tsukatte imasu.
This ikebana flower arrangement is using moss.

22. 馬鹿はやめろ！

Baka wa yamero!
Stop being ridiculous!

23. 食べ物の匂いを嗅ぐとお腹がすく。

Tabemono no nioi wo kagu to onaka ga suku.
When one smells the fragrance of the food, one gets hungry.

24. 彼に対する態度が変わった。

Kare ni tai suru taido ga kawatta.
To him, the to-confront attitude changed (i.e., my attitude toward him changed).

Supplemental Reading Practice

After completing Chapter 44 of this book, you should be able to read the "Flight," "Cornered," "Morning Light," and "Endurance Test" articles from the "Kona's Big Adventure" series in *Satori Reader*.

Chapter 45

New Kanji in this Chapter

# 961 命 (3)	# 962 令 (1)	# 963 洞 (2)	# 964 穴 (1)
# 965 謙 (1)	# 966 虚 (1)	# 967 嘘 (1)	# 968 荒 (3)

Vocabulary List with Mnemonics

from the Kanji Catalogue

命 — inochi = life, most precious possession or person; *these innocent children are my most precious possessions*

命じる — meijiru = to command or appoint; *in the Meiji era, people spread rumors about whom the emperor might appoint to high office*

命令 — meirei = a command or order; *the major rated his men according to how well they responded to his commands*

寿命 — ju'myou = life span; *the jubilant cat meowed when it learned that it would be given seven more lives, extending its lifespan*

号令 — gourei = a command or order; *the ghost raced around issuing commands*

洞察 — dousatsu = insight, discernment; *the doorman read satisfying Superman novels to enhance his insight into the criminal mind*

穴 — ana = hole; *the anatomy class studied the seven holes in a dog's head*

洞穴 — hora'ana = cave, den; from hora = cave; *the cave is home to rats*; + ana = hole

謙虚 — kenkyo = modesty; *when the Kennedys visited Kyoto, they noticed the modesty of the residents*

嘘 — uso = lie; *when you say that you have uber solar panels, that's a lie*

嘘をつく — uso wo tsuku = to tell a lie; from uso = lie + tsuku = to adhere

荒い — arai = violent, rough, rude; *when violent, rough and rude people assemble, a riot can break out*

荒野 — kouya = wilderness, the wild; *the coat of a yak is adapted to wilderness life*

荒らす — arasu = to lay waste, damage, devastate, break into, invade; *Arafat sued his enemies for damaging his car*

荒れる — areru = to be stormy or rough, to fall into ruin; *the American red rooster endured some stormy and rough weather as it crossed the road*

Kanji Pronunciations

# 961 – inochi, mei, myou	# 962 – rei	# 963 – dou, hora	# 964 – ana
# 965 – ken	# 966 – kyo	# 967 – uso	# 968 – ara, a, kou

from the Practice Sentences

厳守する — genshu suru = to observe strictly (regulations, etc.); _Genghis had shoes that had to be polished every day, and his instructions for doing so were observed strictly_

運命 — unmei = fate or destiny; _the unlucky maid had to face her destiny_

悪意 — aku'i = malice, ill will; from aku = evil + imi = meaning

隊長 — taichou = commanding officer; _the commanding officer was tired of his chores_

直ちに — tadachi ni = immediately; _a taxi dashed up and delivered the cheese immediately_

集合する — shuugou suru = to gather or assemble; _the top shooters in the golf club assembled_

突っ込む — tsukkomu = to thrust into or jump into; from tsu = to protrude; _my tsuitcase (suitcase) protruded into the aisle of the train;_ + komu = to crowd in

身につける — mi ni tsukeru = to take on, to learn or acquire knowledge, to wear clothes, etc.; from mi = body or person + tsukeru = to attach

ますます — masumasu = increasingly, more and more; _he is learning mas y mas (more and more, in Spanish)_

生まれながら — umare nagara = by nature, naturally, by birth; from umare = birth + nagara = while or at the same time

読者 — dokusha = a person who reads; from doku = reading; _this document is meant for reading;_ + sha = person

from Satori Reader

ぶつぶつ — butsubutsu = grunt, grumble, complaint; from butsu = thing; _it was butsubutsu (thing, thing, or "one thing after another"), and they made a complaint_

ひくつく — hikutsuku = to twitch; _sometimes heated Kool-Aid tsuku (adheres) to my nose and makes it twitch_

片目 — katame = one eye; from kata = one side; _I can only see one side of the catalog;_ + me = eye

つぶれる — tsubureru = to be smashed, become useless, go bankrupt; _the tsuitcase (suitcase) where I keep my booze was pushed over by a red rooster, and the bottles were smashed_

走り去る — hashirisaru = to run away; from hashiru = to run + saru = to leave

がくぜん — gakuzen = shock, astonishment, terror; _when I drank a gallon of Kool-Aid at one sitting, the Zen monk expressed shock_

Practice Sentences

1. この命令は厳守すべきだ。

Kono meirei wa genshu subeki da.
This order should be strictly observed.

2. これは私が洞穴の中で見つけたものです。

Kore wa watashi ga hora'ana no naka de mitsuketa mono desu.
These are things that I found in the cave.

3. 褒められても謙虚が大事。

Homerarete mo kenkyo ga daiji.
Even when being praised, modesty is important.

4. 運命って信じる？

Unmei tte shinjiru?
As for the one called fate, do you believe (i.e., do you believe in fate, or destiny)?

5. 悪意のない嘘だ。

Akui no nai uso da.
It's a lie without malice (i.e., a white lie).

6. 彼女は言葉使いが荒い。

Kanojo wa kotobazukai ga arai.
As for her, the use of words is rough (i.e., she uses impolite language).

7. そのままボートで洞穴に突っ込んで行った。

Sono mama booto de hora'ana ni tsukkonde itta.
That manner, in the boat, we thrust into the cave and went.

8. 隊長は部下に直ちに集合するように命令した。

Taichou wa buka ni tadachi ni shuugou suru you ni meirei shita.
The commanding officer ordered the subordinates to assemble immediately.

9. 謙虚さを身につけたら、あなたはもっといい人になるでしょう。

Kenkyosa wo mi ni tsuketara, anata wa motto ii hito ni naru deshou.
If you attach modesty to your person (i.e., if you take it on), you will probably become a better person.

10. 彼の命が危ない。

Kare no inochi ga abunai.
His life is in danger.

11. なぜ嘘をついたの？

Naze uso wo tsuita no?
Why did you tell a lie?

12. 海はますます荒れてきた。

Umi wa masumasu arete kita.
The ocean started to become more and more rough.

13. 彼は私に１人で行けと命令した。

Kare wa watashi ni hitori de ike to meirei shita.
He ordered me to go alone.

14. この小説は読者の洞察が必要です。

Kono shousetsu wa dokusha no dousatsu ga hitsuyou desu.
As for this novel, the reader's discernment is necessary.

15. 靴下に穴があいているよ。

Kutsushita ni ana ga aite iru yo.
A hole is opening in the sock, for sure.
(i.e., there's a hole in the sock)

16. 彼は生まれながら謙虚だ。

Kare wa umare nagara kenkyo da.
He is modest by nature.

17. 彼女は嘘が大嫌いだ。

Kanojo wa uso ga daikirai da.
She really hates lies.

18. 彼は運転が荒い。

Kare wa unten ga arai.
As for him, the driving is rough (i.e., he makes abrupt changes, etc.).

19. 日本人は寿命が長いと言われている。

Nihonjin wa jumyou ga nagai to iwarete iru.
Japanese people have a long life span, it is said on them.

Supplemental Reading Practice

After completing Chapter 45 of this book, you should be able to read the "Attitude Adjustment" article from the "Kona's Big Adventure" series in *Satori Reader*.

Chapter 46

New Kanji in this Chapter

# 969 共 (2)	# 970 異 (2)	# 971 驚 (2)	# 972 巣 (2)
# 973 崩 (2)	# 974 就 (2)	# 975 蹴 (1)	# 976 黄 (3)

Vocabulary List with Mnemonics

from the Kanji Catalogue

共に   tomo ni = together; *we are going to have <u>tomograms</u> of our <u>knees</u> done <u>together</u>*

共同の   kyoudou no = cooperative, communal; *in <u>Kyouto</u>, people build <u>doors</u> in a <u>cooperative</u> way*

共感   kyoukan = sympathy; *in <u>Kyouto</u>, if you have <u>cancer</u>, you get a lot of <u>sympathy</u>*

共通の   kyoutsuu no = common, mutual; *in <u>Kyouto</u>, everyone wears nice <u>tsuits</u> (suits) by <u>mutual</u> consent*

驚異   kyou'i = miracle, marvel; *in <u>Kyouto</u>, the <u>eagles</u> are a <u>marvel</u>*

異議   igi = objection; *I have an <u>objection</u> to <u>eating geese</u>*

異なる   kotonaru = to differ; *the <u>koto</u> (Japanese harp) that the <u>nanny ruined differed</u> from the one that she didn't touch*

驚く   odoroku = to be astonished; *I was <u>astonished</u> at the <u>odorous Kool</u>-Aid that they served*

精巣   seisou = testicle; from sei = vitality; *the <u>sage</u> has <u>vitality</u>;* + sou = nest; *the bird <u>soared</u> up to its <u>nest</u>*

卵巣   ransou = ovary; from ran = egg; *I eat <u>eggs</u> on my <u>ranch</u>;* + sou = nest; *the bird <u>soared</u> up to its <u>nest</u>*

巣   su = nest, animal habitat, cobweb, honeycomb, den; *<u>Superman</u> protected the <u>nest</u>*

崩す   kuzusu = to dismantle, pull down or destroy, to throw off balance, to change money; *rats <u>destroyed</u> the <u>cool zucchinis</u> that <u>Superman</u> grew*

崩れる   kuzureru = to collapse, be destroyed, lose shape; *we piled up some <u>cool zucchinis</u>, but a <u>red rooster</u> jumped on them and caused them to <u>collapse</u>*

就く   tsuku = to start, set out, obtain a position; *when I <u>started</u> on my trip, I brought along a <u>tsuitcase</u> (suitcase) of <u>Kool</u>-Aid*

Kanji Pronunciations

# 969 – tomo, kyou	# 970 – koto, i	# 971 – kyou, odoro	# 972 – sou, su
# 973 – hou, kuzu	# 974 – shuu, tsu	# 975 – ke	# 976 – ou, kou, ki

就職する	shuushoku suru = to find employment; *when your shoes shock you, they are telling you to find employment*
蹴る	keru = to kick; *my Keds (a brand of shoes) were ruined when I kicked a tarball*
蹴飛ばす	ketobasu = to kick away, to refuse curtly; from keru = to kick + tobasu = to fly or speed
卵黄	ran'ou = egg yolk; from ran = egg + ou = yellow; *oats are yellow*
黄金	ougon = gold; from ou = yellow; *oats are yellow;* + gon = gold; *that gong is made of gold*
黄砂	kousa = yellow dust from the Yellow River region, which blows to Japan; from kou = yellow; *corn is yellow;* + sa = sand; *the salaryman walked in the sand*
黄色	ki'iro = yellow; from ki = yellow; *my keys are yellow;* + iro = color
黄身	kimi = egg yolk; from ki = yellow; *my keys are yellow;* + mi = body

from the Practice Sentences

助け合う	tasukeau = to help each other, cooperate; from tasukeru = to help + au = to come together, match or suit
崩れ落ちる	kuzureochiru = to tumble down, to fall in; from kuzureru = to collapse + ochiru = to fall
驚くべき	odorokubeki = surprising, remarkable; from odoroku = to be astonished + beki = should
発見	hakken = discovery; *the harbor where the Kennedys kept their boats was the site of a discovery*
大小	daisho = large and small; from dai = large + sho = small; *I saw large and small people at the diet show*
教職	kyoushoku = the teaching profession; from kyoushitsu = classroom + shokugyou = occupation
横っ腹	yokoppara = side of the body, or flank; from yoko = side + para = hara = abdomen
異常	ijou = abnormal, bizarre; *the eels that Joan of Arc caught were abnormal and bizarre;* cf. 以上 ijou = not more than
クモ	kumo = spider; *the Kool-Aid that Moses drank had a spider in it*
言語	gengo = language; *Genghis had a goal to learn new languages*
ふさぐ	fusagu = block, to stop up, close; *they fuss and argue and block our way*
驚異的	kyou'iteki = marvelous, miraculous; from kyou'i = marvel, miracle + teki = related to

46-180

from Satori Reader

見逃す	minogasu = to overlook, to turn a blind eye to; *the mean old gas station owner overlooked the boy's shoplifting*
それどころか	soredokoroka = on the contrary; *on the contrary, the typical soldier from the Red army owns a Corolla car*; cf. それどころ soredokoro = not that much, used before a negative verb
込み上げる	komiageru = to fill (the heart), to well up (feelings or sensations); from komu = to crowd in + ageru = to raise
ズルズル	zuruzuru = sound or act of dragging, slipping, slithering; *on the zoo's roof, a snake was slithering around*
こすれる	kosureru = to be rubbed; *the Korean supervisor's red rooster likes to have his head rubbed*
パックリ	pakkuri = gaping (mouth); *Pac-Man waited for his curry with a gaping mouth*
ペロリと	perori to = eating up quickly; *when that person visited the Orient with Tony Blair, he ate his meals quickly*
飛び掛かる	tobikakaru = to leap at, to swoop down on; from tobu = to fly + kakaru = to be caught in, to hang, to spend (time or money)

Practice Sentences

1. 共に助け合いながら生きている。

Tomo ni tasukeai nagara ikite iru.
While mutually helping each other, we are living.

2. 何か異議がありますか？

Nanika igi ga arimasu ka.
Is there any objection?

3. みんなが驚く程、寿司を食べた。

Minna ga odoroku hodo, sushi wo tabeta.
To the degree that everyone will get astonished, he ate sushi. (i.e., he ate a lot)

4. この家はクモの巣でいっぱいです。

Kono ie wa kumo no su de ippai desu.
This house is full of spider webs.

5. 大きい地震があり積んでおいた箱が崩れ落ちてしまった。

Ookii jishin ga ari tsunde oita hako ga kuzure ochite shimatta.
Since a big earthquake exists, the were-piled-up-in-advance boxes tumbled down completely.

6. 国に帰りたくない訳ではないが、できれば日本で就職したいと思っている。

Kuni ni kaeritakunai wake de wa nai ga, dekireba nihon de shuushoku shitai to omotte iru.
To the country (i.e., my country) do not want to return reason it isn't (i.e., it isn't necessarily that; wake de wa nai = not necessarily), but if I am able, I'd like to find a job in Japan, I'm thinking.

7. ドアを蹴らないでください。

Doa wo keranai de kudasai.
Please don't kick the door.

8. 赤やら黄色やら、いろんな色の花が咲いている。

Aka yara kiiro yara, ironna iro no hana ga saite iru.
Red etc., yellow etc., various colors' flowers are blossoming. (yara = etcetera)

9. 音楽は世界の共通言語だ。

Ongaku wa sekai no kyoutsuu gengo da.
Music is the world's common language.

10. 僕の考えは君と異なる。

Boku no kangae wa kimi to kotonaru.
My thinking differs from yours.

11. これは驚くべき発見だ。

Kore wa odorokubeki hakken da.
This is a surprising discovery.

12. 鳥は巣を作る。

Tori wa su wo tsukuru.
Birds build nests.

13. 崖崩れが起き大小の岩が道路をふさいでいる。

Gake kuzure ga oki daisho no iwa ga douro wo fusaide iru.
Since the cliff collapse occurs, large and small size's rocks are blocking the road.

14. 彼女は教職に就いた。

Kanojo wa kyoushoku ni tsuita.
She got a position in the teaching profession.

15. あの男は私の横っ腹を蹴った。

Ano otoko wa watashi no yokoppara wo ketta.
That man over there kicked my side (or flank).

16. 娘は卵の黄身が大好きです。

Musume wa tamago no kimi ga daisuki desu.
My daughter loves egg yolks.

17. 三人、共に笑い始めました。

San'nin, tomo ni warai hajimemashita.
Three people, together, began to laugh.

18. 今年の夏は異常に暑い。

Kotoshi no natsu wa ijou ni atsui.
This summer is abnormally hot.

19. 卵巣にガンができていた。

Ransou ni gan ga dekite ita.
There was cancer in the ovary.

20. バランスを崩して倒れた。

Baransu wo kuzushite taoreta.
I lost my balance and fell.

21. 就職していない大学卒業生は4000人以上に及んでいる。

Shuushoku shite inai daigaku sotsugyou sei wa yonsen nin ijou ni oyonde iru.
As for not-finding-work university graduates, they extend to not less than 4,000 people.

22. ボールを蹴飛ばした。

Booru wo ketobashita.
I kicked the ball away.

23. そのクラウンは黄金でできています。

Sono kuraun wa ougon de dekite imasu.
That crown is made from gold.

24. 彼は驚異的な力で自動車を持ち上げた。

Kare wa kyou'iteki na chikara de jidousha wo mochiageta.
He lifted the car with marvelous force.

Supplemental Reading Practice

After completing Chapter 46 of this book, you should be able to read the "An Unpleasant Revelation," "Reprieve," and "Serpent" articles from the "Kona's Big Adventure" series in *Satori Reader*.

Chapter 47

New Kanji in this Chapter

# 977 救 (2)	# 978 疑 (2)	# 979 輝 (2)	# 980 肌 (1)
# 981 滑 (3)	# 982 覗 (1)	# 983 井 (3)	# 984 桜 (2)

Vocabulary List with Mnemonics

from the Kanji Catalogue

救う — suku'u = to rescue; *by suing the Kool-Aid industry, we can help to rescue some sugar addicts*

救い — sukui = help, hope; from suku'u = to rescue

救急車 — kyuukyuusha = ambulance; from kyuukyuu = first aid, emergency; *the shortage of cucumbers in Cuba is an emergency*; + sha = vehicle

救済 — kyuusai = help, rescue, relief; *Cuban scientists have organized a rescue effort*

疑う — utagau = to doubt or suspect; *in Utah, if you lose your gaudy jewelry, I doubt that you will get it back*

疑問 — gimon = a question or doubt; *the guitar-playing monkey was consumed by doubt*

疑惑 — giwaku = a suspicion or doubt; *some geese were recruited for the war against the Kool-Aid industry, but they had doubts about their mission*

輝く — kagayaku = to shine, glitter, sparkle; *when the cat in the garden saw the yak, its eyes sparkled*

光輝 — kouki = brightness, splendor; *the corporal polished the key to the prescribed level of brightness*

肌 — hada = skin, personality; *my Hawaiian daughter has good skin and a nice personality*

肌着 — hadagi = underwear; from hada = skin + giru = kiru = to wear

木肌 — kihada = bark of a tree; from ki = tree + hada = skin

滑る — suberu = to slide or slip, to fail an exam; *when submarines erupt from under the water, fish slide off the sides*

滑らかな — nameraka na = mellow, smooth (usually written なめらかな); *my nanny from Mexico is a rock artist, and she is mellow, with smooth skin*

Kanji Pronunciations

# 977 – kyuu, suku	# 978 – utaga, gi	# 979 – ki, kagaya	# 980 – hada
# 981 – sube, name, katsu	# 982 – nozo	# 983 – jou, i, ino	# 984 – sakura, zakura

円滑	enkatsu = smooth, harmonious; *my energetic cats engage in smooth and harmonious play*
覗く	nozoku = to peek or snoop; *I parked in the No Zone outside the Kool-Aid factory so that I could snoop on the activities inside*; cf. 除く nozoku = to remove
覗き込む	nozokikomu = to peer into; from nozoku = to snoop + komu = to crowd in
井戸	ido = water well; *the eastern door leads to a water well*
天井	tenjou = ceiling; *the tent that Joan of Arc slept in had a low ceiling*
桜	sakura = cherry; *the salaryman turned off his kuuraa (cooler, or air conditioner) before going out to see the cherry blossoms*
桜の花	sakura no hana = cherry blossoms; from sakura = cherry + hana = flower
夜桜見物	yozakura kenbutsu = going out to look at cherry blossoms in the evening; from yoru = night + zakura = sakura = cherry + kenbutsu = sightseeing

from the Practice Sentences

熱心	nesshin = enthusiastic; *the doctor was enthusiastic about treating diseases of the neck and the shin*
難民	nanmin = refugee; from nan = difficult, e.g., kon'nan = difficult; + shimin = citizen
輝かしい	kagayakashii = brilliant, bright, splendid; from kagayaku = to shine

from Satori Reader

バサバサ	basabasa = rustling, fluttering, flapping; *on Barcelona's sandy beaches, many birds make a fluttering sound*
クチバシ	kuchibashi = beak, bill; *the part of a woodpecker's kuchi (mouth) that it uses for bashing holes in trees is called its beak*
ひょっと	hyotto = possibly; *the Lone Ranger said "Hi-yo" when his toe encountered an object, which he thought was possibly a snake*; cf. ひょっとすると hyotto suru to = possibly, maybe
駆け下りる	kakeoriru = to run down (stairs, etc.); from kakeru = to run + oriru = to descend
はぐれる	hagureru = to lose sight of one's companions, to miss a chance; *in the hall, the goose and the red rooster lost sight of each other*
めちゃくちゃ	mechakucha = absurd, incoherent; *after taking the medicine, Prince Charles started his Kool-Aid chants, which were generally incoherent*
泣き出す	nakidasu = to burst into tears; from naku = to cry + dasu = to put out

どうにでもなれ	dou ni demo nare = let come what will; literally "to how, even though, become" (this is the imperative tense; to form the imperative tense of a "u" verb, add "e" to the verb root, i.e., the pre-u form)
思い切る	omoikiru = to cut off thought, i.e., to take the plunge and do something; from omou = to think + kiru = to cut
羽ばたく	habataku = to flap (wings); *the Hawaiian bat will attack you, flapping its wings*
飛び立つ	tobitatsu = to jump up, to fly away, to take off; from tobu = to fly + tatsu = to stand up
ワクワク	wakuwaku = trembling, nervous, excited; *when Washington drank Kool-Aid, he got excited*
まく	maku = to sow, sprinkle, scatter; *after the farmer got macular degeneration, he could no longer sow his fields*
なる	naru = to bear (fruit); *when fruit naru (becomes), the tree bears fruit*
張り切る	harikiru = to be in high spirits, enthusiastic, eager; *Prince Harry keeps his room clean because he is enthusiastic about cleanliness*
ゆったり	yuttari = comfortable, easy, loose; *in that comfortable, loose atmosphere, the youth tarried too long and missed the train*
真ん丸	manmaru = a perfect circle; from manjitsu = truth + maru = circle

Practice Sentences

1. 犬が人の命を救ったという記事を読んだ。

Inu ga hito no inochi wo sukutta to iu kiji wo yonda.
A dog rescued a person's life quote to-say article I read. (i.e., I read an article about a dog who saved a person)

2. 泥棒ではないかと警察に疑われた。

Dorobou de wa nai ka to keisatsu ni utagawareta.
A thief is not question quote by the police they suspected on me. (i.e., the police thought I might be a thief)

3. 太陽が輝いている。

Taiyou ga kagayaite iru.
The sun is shining.

4. 雨の日は床が滑りやすいので注意してください。

Ame no hi wa yuka ga suberi yasui node chuui shite kudasai.
As for rain's days, since the floor is easy to slip (i.e., slippery), please pay attention.

5. 最近、熱心に肌や髪の毛の手入れをする男性が増えたそうです。

Saikin, nesshin ni hada ya kaminoke no teire wo suru dansei ga fueta sou desu.
Recently, enthusiastically, skin-and-hair-etc.'s take-care-of men (i.e., men who are enthusiastically taking care of their skin, hair, etc.) increased, reportedly.

6. 部屋を覗き込んだ。

Heya wo nozokikonda.
I peeked into the room.

7. 三井産業との取引の仕事をさせたいと思う。

Mitsui sangyou to no torihiki no shigoto wo sasetai to omou.
I would like to be made to do some with-Mitsui-industries business deal's work、I think.

8. 暖かくなって桜が咲いたら、両親を呼んでこの町を案内したい。

Atatakaku natte sakura ga saitara, ryoushin wo yonde kono machi wo annai shitai.
When it gets warm and the cherries bloum, I want to call the parents and do guidance on this town (i.e., show it to them).

9. 救急車を呼んでください。

Kyuukyuusha wo yonde kudasai.
Please call an ambulance.

10. 疑問が解けました。

Gimon ga tokemashita.
The doubts resolved (i.e., they cleared up).

11. 海は太陽の光を受けて輝く。

Umi wa taiyou no hikari wo ukete kagayaku.
The ocean receives the sun's light and shines (ie., it glows or glitters).

12. 彼女の肌は滑らかです。

Kanojo no hada wa nameraka desu.
Her skin is smooth.

13. 雲の間から太陽が覗いています。

Kumo no aida kara taiyou ga nozoite imasu.
The sun is peeping from a gap in the clouds.

14. 天井を見上げた。

Tenjou wo miageta.
I looked up at the ceiling.

15. 桜が咲いたかと思うと、もう散り始めた。

Sakura ga saita ka to omou to, mou chirihajimeta.
The cherries blossomed, question quote if I think (i.e., as soon as they did so), already they are starting to scatter.

16. アフリカの難民が救いを求めている。

Afurika no nanmin ga sukui wo motomete iru.
African refugees are requesting help.

17. 彼が来るかは疑わしい。

Kare ga kuru ka wa utagawashii.
As for him, as for to come question, doubtful. (i.e., it's doubtful that he will come)

18. 君には輝かしい未来が待っているよ。

Kimi ni wa kagayakashii mirai ga matte iru yo.
As for to you, a brilliant future is waiting, for sure.

19. あの時、彼女の肌を優しく撫でていた。

Ano toki, kanojo no hada wo yasashiku nadete ita.
That time, I was gently stroking her skin.

20. 彼は中国語を知っていたので、計画を円滑に実行できた。

Kare wa chuugokugo wo shitte ita node, keikaku wo enkatsu ni jikkou dekita.
Since he knew the Chinese language, he was able to implement the plan smoothly.

21. 戸棚の中を覗いたらおいしそうなケーキがあった。

Todana no naka wo nozoitara oishisou na keeki ga atta.
When I peeked inside the cupboard, there was a delicious-looking cake.

22. その猫は井戸の中にいる。

Sono neko wa ido no naka ni iru.
That cat is inside the well.

23. 夜桜見物はとても楽しいです。

Yozakura kenbutsu wa totemo tanoshii desu.
Night-cherry sightseeing (i.e., viewing cherry blossoms at night) is very pleasant.

Supplemental Reading Practice

After completing Chapter 47 of this book, you should be able to read the "Wise Winged Giant," "A Kindness Returned," "Homeward Bound," and "Circling Shadow" articles from the "Kona's Big Adventure" series in *Satori Reader*.

Chapter 48

New Kanji in this Chapter

# 985 悠 (1)	# 986 抱 (2)	# 987 融 (1)	# 988 均 (1)
# 989 齢 (1)	# 990 刊 (1)	# 991 賞 (1)	# 992 躍 (1)

Vocabulary List with Mnemonics

from the Kanji Catalogue

悠々 — yuuyuu = quiet, calm, leisurely; *the youthful unicorn moved in a quiet, calm and leisurely way*

悠長 — yuuchou = leisurely, slow, deliberate, easy-going; *in the Yukon, I did my chores in a leisurely way*

悠久の — yuukyuu no = eternal; *after the unicorn was cured, it enjoyed eternal life*

抱く — daku = to embrace, hold or hug; *Dad drank some Kool-Aid and then embraced me*

抱きしめる — dakishimeru = to hug someone tightly; *from daku = to hug + shimeru = to close*

辛抱 — shinbou = endurance, patience; *the Shinto boy showed endurance and patience*

金融 — kinyuu = finance, money-lending; *the king cares about the youth of the country and is asking the banks to increase money-lending to them*

融合 — yuugou = fusion, adhesion, blending; *in the Yukon, our goal is a fusion of all cultures into one*

平均 — heikin = average, mean; *that halo-wearing king is just average*

年齢 — nenrei = age; *as the nen (years) race by we begin to show our age*

朝刊 — choukan = morning newspaper; *I choked on candy while reading the morning newspaper*

週刊誌 — shuukanshi = weekly magazine; *a shoe can shield your foot better than a weekly magazine*

刊行する — kankou suru = to publish; *the Canadian corporation publishes a newsletter*

受賞する — jushou suru = to win an award or prize; *at the jewelry show, I won a prize*

入賞する — nyuushou suru = to win an award or prize; *at the Nyuuyooku (New York) show, I won a prize*

Kanji Pronunciations

# 985 – yuu	# 986 – bou, da	# 987 – yuu	# 988 – kin
# 989 – rei	# 990 – kan	# 991 – shou	# 992 – yaku

躍進	yakushin = progress; *when the yakuza put new shingles on his house, people said that he was making progress*
活躍する	katsuyaku suru = to be active, implying successful or energetic activity; *the cats belonging to the yakuza were active all night;* cf. 活動する katsudou suru = to be active

from the Practice Sentences

融資する	yuushi suru = to finance or lend money; *the bank financed my Yukon sheep farm*
背丈	setake = height, stature; *the senator was a tall Kennedy whose height was remarkable*
値する	atai suru = to be worth it, to deserve it; *a Thai vacation is worth the money*
一躍	ichiyaku = suddenly, overnight; from ichi = one + yaku = leap; *the yakuza took a leap over the fence*
辛抱強い	shinbouzuyoi = patient; from shinbou = patience + zuyoi = tsuyoi = strong
危機	kiki = crisis, danger, risk; *the king had a key to the codes that were to be used in a crisis*
就学	shuugaku = attending school; *my parents gave me new shoes and a gallon of Kool-Aid for attending school*
新刊書	shinkansho = new publication; from shin = new + kankou suru = to publish + sho = document, e.g., jisho = dictionary
飛躍的に	hiyakuteki ni = rapidly; from hi = to fly, e.g., hikouki = airplane; + yaku = leap; *the yakuza took a leap over the fence;* + teki = related to
向上	koujou = improvement; from kou = to face, e.g., houkou = direction; + jou = above, e.g., jouzu = skillful
頭上	zujou = overhead; from zu = head, e.g., zutsuu = headache; + jou = above, e.g., jouzu = skillful
均一	kin'itsu = uniformity, equality; from kin = level, average; *our kindergarten is just average, since we try to keep everyone on the same level;* + itsu = one; *he eats one apple*
決定	kettei = a decision; *I can't make a decision about whether to buy a new kettle or a new table*
高齢	kourei = elderly; from kou = high, e.g., koukou = high school; + rei = age, e.g., nenrei = age
焼死する	shoushi suru = to burn to death; from shou = to burn; *the showroom burned down;* + shinu = to die
夕刊	yuukan = evening newspaper; from yuube = evening + kankou suru = to publish

from Satori Reader

降ろす
orosu = to let someone out of a vehicle; the transitive form of oriru = to get out of a vehicle

飛び上がる
tobiagaru = to fly up; from tobu = to fly + agaru = to rise

やがて
yagate = before long, soon; *the yard garbage is terrible, and before long the neighbors will start complaining*

ワシ
washi = eagle; *the eagle is standing on the washing machine*

ガミガミ
gamigami = nagging, griping; *the gambler will serve as a mediator to try to stop the griping*

つたう
tsutau = to go along, to climb up or down; *carrying a tsuitcase (suitcase) full of towels, he went along to the laundromat*

着地
chakuchi = landing; from chaku = to arrive, e.g., touchaku = arrival; + chi = ground, e.g., tochi = land, soil

しきりに
shikiri ni = often, frequently, eagerly; *the sheep and the kitty come around often*

抱き上げる
dakiageru = to hold up in one's arms; from daku = to hug + ageru = to raise

ゴシゴシ
goshigoshi = scrubbing, rubbing vigorously; *when we bathe the goats and the sheep, we subject them to vigorous scrubbing*

最終回
saishuukai = the last time, the final episode; from saishuu = the last; *the silent shooter was on his last legs*; + kai = times; *the kites rotate many times*

ふらつく
furatsuku = to wander aimlessly, to stagger, to waver; *after I got to furansu (France) with my tsuitcase (suitcase) full of Kool-Aid, I wandered aimlessly*

ぐるぐる
guruguru = turning round and round, going around in circles; *I keep going from guru to guru and feel like I'm going around in circles*

通用する
tsuuyou suru = to pass as, to pass muster; *with a tsuitcase (suitcase) full of yogurt, I will be able to pass as a salesman*

ふるさと
furusato = hometown, homeland; *it seemed foolish to ruin the satellite tower in my hometown*; this can also be spelled 故郷, # 1059, or ふる里, # 1060

from News in Slow Japanese

アーティスト
aatisuto = artist

アイドル
aidoru = idol, young star, TV personality

ヘヴィメタル
hevimetaru = heavy metal

見た目
mitame = appearance; from mita = saw + me = eyes

ミスマッチ	misumatchi = mismatch
ワールドツアー	waarudo tsuaa = world tour
同年	dounen = that year, the same year, the same age; from dou = the same; *we like the same doughnuts*; + nen = year
追加	tsuika = addition, supplement; *I have a Tsuidish (Swedish) car in addition to my Japanese one*
公演	kouen = public performance; from kou = public + ensou = to perform; cf. 公園 kouen = public park; 講演 kouen = lecture
人気ぶり	ninkiburi = so popular; from ninki = popular + buri = "it's like"; *a burrito is like a sandwich*; from buru = to assume the air of, behave like; *those Buddhists rule their monastery and behave like kings*
月刊誌	gekkanshi = monthly magazine; from getsu = month + kankou suru = to publish + shi = magazine, e.g., zasshi = magazine; cf. 週刊誌 shuukanshi = weekly magazine
ミュージカルアクト	myuujikaru akuto = musical act

Practice Sentences

1. 決して悠長な仕事ではない。

Kesshite yuuchou na shigoto de wa nai.
It isn't leisurely work at all.

2. 彼は服が汚れるのもかまわず、犬を抱きしめた。

Kare wa fuku ga yogoreru no mo kamawazu, inu wo dakishimeta.
As for him, the clothes will get dirty thing even not minding, he hugged the dog tightly.

3. 銀行はその会社に融資をした。

Ginkou wa sono kaisha ni yuushi wo shita.
The bank did financing for that company.

4. 彼は平均的な背丈だ。

Kare wa heikinteki na setake da.
He is of average height.

5. 私達は同じ年齢です。

Watashitachi wa onaji nenrei desu.
We are the same age.

6. 彼はその賞に値する。

Kare wa sono shou ni atai suru.
He deserves that award.

7. 駅で週刊誌を買った。

Eki de shuukanshi wo katta.
I bought a weekly magazine at the station.

8. 彼女は一躍有名になった。

Kanojo wa ichiyaku yumei ni natta.
She suddenly became famous.

9. 悠太さんは朝から晩まで１日中歩き回った。

Yuuta san wa asa kara ban made ichinichijuu arukimawatta.
Yuuta walked around all day from morning until evening.

10. 彼は辛抱強かった。

Kare wa shinbouzuyokatta.
He was patient.

11. 物価の上がり下がりが金融危機を引き起こした。

Bukka no agari sagari ga kin'yuu kiki wo hikiokoshita.
The rise and fall of prices caused a financial crisis.

12. 君の作文は平均よりも上だ。

Kimi no sakubun wa heikin yorimo ue da.
Your written composition, compared to the average, is above (i.e., it's above average).

13. 彼は就学できる年齢だ。

Kare wa shuugaku dekiru nenrei da.
He is old enough to go to school.

14. 新聞に新刊書の広告を出した。

Shinbun ni shinkansho no koukoku wo dashita.
I put an advertisement for the new publication in the newspaper.

15. 三位に入賞した。

San i ni nyuushou shita.
I won third prize.

16. １年間の留学で彼女のフランス語は飛躍的に向上した。

Ichinenkan no ryuugaku de kanojo no furansugo wa hiyakuteki ni koujou shita.
On the one-year duration's foreign study, her French improved rapidly.

17. あのタカは頭上を悠々と飛んでいる。

Ano taka wa zujou wo yuuyuu to tonde iru.
That falcon is flying calmly overhead.

18. 少女が人形を抱いている。

Shoujo ga ningyou wo daite iru.
The little girl is hugging the doll.

19. 金融サービスのコストはどの国でも高くなっている。

Kin'yuu saabisu no kosuto wa dono kuni demo takakunatte iru.
The cost of financial services is rising in every country.

20. 我が社は均一料金にすることに決定した。

Wagasha wa kin'itsu ryoukin ni suru koto ni kettei shita.
Our company decided on flat-rate pricing.

21. 高齢の女性が焼死した。

Kourei no josei ga shoushi shita.
An elderly woman burned to death.

22. 大変眠くて、夕刊も読めなかった。

Taihen nemukute, yuukan mo yomenakatta.
Since extremely sleepy, I couldn't even read the evening newspaper.

23. 彼はノーベル賞を受賞した。

Kare wa nooberu shou wo jushou shita.
He was awarded the Nobel prize.

24. 二人とも今日は大活躍だったみたいね。

Futari tomo kyou wa dai katsuyaku datta mitai ne.
Both of them seem to have been extremely active today, huh. (implying that they seemed to be very successful)

Supplemental Reading Practice

After completing Chapter 48 of this book, you should be able to read the "Farewell," "Reunion," and "A New Kona" articles from "Kona's Big Adventure," in *Satori Reader,* completing the Kona series.

A Different Reading Practice Resource

You may now start reading a different online resource, *News in Slow Japanese*, which you will find at NewsInSlowJapanese.com. Like *Satori Reader*, this is a subscription site, and we are not affiliated with it in any way. After completing Chapter 48 of this book, you should be able to read **Lesson 001, "Baby Metal."**

To get started, go to NewsInSlowJapanese.com and register for one-month access. Then scroll to the very bottom of the Home page, or almost any other page, where you will see a thin box extending horizontally across the screen with the title *"Scroll through all lessons and episodes."* Click inside this box and then scroll to a point approximately midway down, where you will see "LESSON 001: Baby Metal."

Click on this lesson and then click on the section titled "Step 2. Reading Practice." If you scroll down further, you will find the article "Baby Metal," which you can display with either pop-up, romaji or plain text. It's best to begin with **pop-up text**, since this option will allow you to hover your mouse over portions of the article to see explanations as you read.

Although there is no English translation provided for the entire article as such, if you click on the blue bar labeled "Vocabulary List," located just below the article, you will find English translations for most individual phrases. You will also want to listen to the audio playback features that are built into the site, since these provide important clues to the meanings of certain words and will help your listening skills.

News in Slow Japanese is an outstanding resource that can help you to learn Japanese. However, if you need to economize, you may choose to sign up for only a one-month subscription at first. During that time, you should save the written material for Lessons 001 through 045. This should include **three selections** from each lesson: 1) the Reading Practice material in the **romaji** version, 2) the same material in the **plain** version, and 3) the **Vocabulary List**.

When you have learned the kanji for a given lesson and are ready to start reading, if your subscription to *News in Slow Japanese* has expired, please print or display the material that you have saved in a fairly large font and read the **plain** version of the Reading Practice material, while using the romaji version and the Vocabulary List for reference.

Please note that, although the titles of the lessons are sometimes omitted from the romaji sections, the kana equivalents of the titles can be found in the "Vocabulary List" sections.

To clarify one potentially confusing phrase in "Baby Metal," the average age of the band members is 14.7 years.

Chapter 49

New Kanji in this Chapter

# 993 佐 (1)	# 994 賀 (1)	# 995 補 (2)	# 996 候 (1)
# 997 給 (1)	# 998 状 (1)	# 999 録 (1)	# 1000 更 (2)

Vocabulary List with Mnemonics

from the Kanji Catalogue

佐賀県 — saga ken = Saga Prefecture; *I met a sad gambler in Saga Prefecture*

大佐 — taisa = colonel; *the Thai salaryman dreamed of becoming a colonel*

補佐 — hosa = aid, help; *the hobo stood in the sand and waited for help*

祝賀 — shukuga = celebration; *during the celebration, we will shoot off fireworks and drink Kool-Aid in the garden*

祝賀会 — shukugakai = celebration; from shukuga = celebration + kaigi = meeting

賀状 — gajou = New Year's card; *the gambler and Joan of Arc always send each other New Year's cards*

年賀状 — nengajou = New Year's card; from nen = year + gajou = New Year's card

補給する — hokyuu suru = to supply or supplement; *we hope that Cuba will supplement our relief efforts in the Caribbean*

候補 — kouho = candidate; *the candidate came from a cohort of politicians who banded together*

補う — oginau = to supplement or compensate for; *an old guitar is now being offered to compensate him for his work*

気候 — kikou = climate; *the climate is so cold that it kills corn plants*

天候 — tenkou = weather; *thanks to the weather, we have tender corn this year*

給料 — kyuuryou = salary; *I use my salary to buy curios*

状態 — joutai = condition, circumstances, state; *under the circumstances, Joan was tired*

紹介状 — shoukaijou = letter of introduction; *although she showed it to the Kaiser, Joan didn't expect much from the letter of introduction*

記録 — kiroku = a record or document; *this document shows how they keep their roses cool*

Kanji Pronunciations

# 993 – sa	# 994 – ga	# 995 – ho, ogina	# 996 – kou
# 997 – kyuu	# 998 – jou	# 999 – roku	# 1000 – kou, sara

録音   rokuon = a sound recording; from roku = a recording; *when the robot sells you Kool-Aid, it makes a recording of the transaction*; + on = sound, e.g., ongaku = music

登録   touroku = registration, enrollment; *registration is held from too to roku (10 to 6)*

更に   sara ni = again, furthermore; *you put Saran wrap on your knee again*

変更   henkou = a change or alteration; *if the hens are cold, we have to make an alteration to their coop*

更新   koushin = renewal, improvement; *in Kobe, many shingles were changed during urban renewal*

from the Practice Sentences

書き上げる   kakiageru = to finish writing; from kaku = to write; + ageru = to finish, when used after a verb stem, e.g., shiageru = to finish doing

補助   hojo = assistance, support; *when she was at home, Joan gave assistance to her family*

自活   jikatsu = supporting one's self; from jibun = self + katsu = life, livelihood

兆候   choukou = symptom, sign; *Margaret Cho had a cold, judging from her symptoms*

月日   tsukihi = time, years; from tsuki = month + hi = day

内政面   naiseimen = domestic affairs, internal administration; *some nice sailing men are in charge of domestic affairs*

指名する   shimei suru = to appoint or nominate; from shi = finger; *the sheep bit my finger*; + mei = name, e.g., yuumei = famous

月給   gekkyuu = monthly salary; from getsu = month + kyuuryou = salary

病状   byoujou = condition related to health; from byouki = sick + joutai = condition

好転する   kouten suru = to improve; *the cold weather tends to improve in April*

路線   rosen = route (transportation); from ro = road, e.g. douro = road; + sen = line

白状する   hakujou suru = to confess or admit; *the hacker went to Joan of Arc to confess his crimes*

今更   ima sara = now, after a long time; at this late hour; from ima = now + sara ni = again, furthermore

昼寝   hirune = a nap; from hiru = noon + neru = to sleep

Practice Sentences

1. 佐知子さんを紹介しましょう。   Sachiko-san wo shoukai shimashou.
I shall introduce Sachiko.

2. 年賀状はもう全部書き上げましたか。
Nengajou wa mou zenbu kakiagemashita ka?
Have you already finished writing all of the New Year's cards?

3. 十八歳のとき彼は両親の補助なしで自活できた。
Juuhassai no toki kare wa ryoushin no hojo nashi de jikatsu dekita.
At 18 years of age, he was able to make a living by himself, without help from his parents.

4. インフレの兆候が見られる。
Infure no choukou ga mirareru.
Signs of inflation are visible.

5. 日本の会社では普通、夏と冬に給料の二三ヵ月分のボーナスが出ます。
Nihon no kaisha de wa futsuu, natsu to fuyu ni kyuuryou no nisan kagetsu bun no boonasu ga demasu.
As for at Japanese companies, ordinarily, in summer and winter, the salary's two or three month portion's bonus comes out.

6. 彼は世界記録を破った。
Kare wa sekai kiroku wo yabutta.
He broke the world record.

7. 更に一年の月日が過ぎた。
Sara ni ichinen no tsukihi ga sugita.
Again, a year's time passed by.

8. 彼は内政面で首相を補佐しています。
Kare wa naiseimen de shushou wo hosa shite imasu.
He is assisting the prime minister with domestic affairs.

9. その祝賀会でお酒を飲み過ぎました。
Sono shukugakai de osake wo nomisugimashita.
I drank too much sake at that celebration.

10. 戸川さんは市長候補に指名されています。
Togawa-san wa shichou kouho ni shimei sarete imasu.
Togawa is being nominated as a candidate for mayor.

11. 私の月給は三十万円です。
Watashi no gekkyuu wa sanjuuman'en desu.
My monthly salary is 300,000 yen.

12. 彼女の病状は少しずつ好転していた。
Kanojo no byoujou wa sukoshi zutsu kouten shite ita.
Her health condition was improving little by little.

13. この会話は録音されています。
Kono kaiwa wa rokuon sarete imasu.
This conversation is being recorded.

14. 地震で路線の変更がありました。

Jishin de rosen no henkou ga arimashita.
Due to the earthquake there was a change in the route.

15. 佐賀県は私のふるさとです。

Saga ken wa watashi no furusato desu.
Saga prefecture is my homeland.

16. 兵士たちは十分な食料と水を補給された。

Heishitachi wa juubun na shokuryou to mizu wo hokyuu sareta.
The soldiers were supplied with enough food and water.

17. 世界中の気候が変わっています。

Sekai juu no kikou ga kawatte imasu.
The climate throughout the world is changing.

18. 彼は人を殺した事を白状した。

Kare wa hito wo koroshita koto wo hakujou shita.
He confessed to having killed a person.

19. 明日は外国人登録に行くつもりなんです。

Ashita wa gaikokujin touroku ni ikutsumori nan desu.
As for tomorrow, I'm planning to go for the purpose of alien registration.

20. 今更どうしようもない事だ。

Ima sara dou shiyou mo nai koto da.
Now, at this late hour, it's how-we-shall-do even-not-exist thing. (i.e., there's nothing we can do now)

21. 彼は昼寝をして睡眠不足を補おうとした。

Kare wa hirune wo shite suimin busoku wo oginaou to shita.
Doing a nap, he tried to compensate for his lack of sleep.

Chapter 50

New Kanji in this Chapter

# 1001 挑 (2)	# 1002 沖 (1)	# 1003 縄 (2)	# 1004 府 (1)
# 1005 阪 (2)	# 1006 奈 (1)	# 1007 茨 (1)	# 1008 城 (3)

Vocabulary List with Mnemonics

from the Kanji Catalogue

挑戦する	chousen suru = to challenge; *the party chose a senator to challenge the president*
挑む	idomu = to challenge; *my eagle dozed as the movie stars challenged each other*
沖	oki = open sea, off the coast; *we ate old quiche out in the open sea*
縄	nawa = rope; *narco warlords use rope to tie up their opponents*
沖縄	Okinawa
縄文時代	joumon jidai = the Jomon period (14,000 – 300 BC); *we joked about finding a Monet painting dating from the Jomon period*
政府	seifu = government; *the government tries to ensure safe food*
都道府県	todoufuken = the 47 administrative divisions of Japan; *Tony Blair gave some dough and food to Ken for memorizing the administrative divisions of Japan*
大阪	oosaka = Osaka, large hill; from ookii = large + saka = hill; *we play sakkaa (soccer) on a hill*
阪神	hanshin = Osaka and Kobe; *Hansel visited Shinto temples in Osaka and Kobe*
奈良	Nara = ancient capital of Japan
神奈川県	Kanagawa Ken = a prefecture in Japan
茨城県	Ibaraki Ken = a prefecture in Japan
城	shiro = castle; *the sheep are roaming among the ruins of that castle*
荒城	koujou = ruined castle; from kouya = wilderness + jou = castle; *Joan of Arc stayed in that castle*
名城	meijou = famous castle; from mei = famous, e.g., yuumei = famous; + jou = castle; *Joan of Arc stayed in that castle*

Kanji Pronunciations

# 1001 – chou, ido	# 1002 – oki	# 1003 – nawa, jou	# 1004 – fu
# 1005 – saka, han	# 1006 – na	# 1007 – ibara	# 1008 – shiro, ki, jou

from the Practice Sentences

機関   kikan = engine, system, agency; *the key to curing this cancer is to follow the agency's guidelines*

古城   kojou = old castle; from ko = old; *that koala is old;* + jou = castle; *Joan of Arc stayed in that castle*

荒れ果てる   arehateru = to fall into ruin; *while arguing at the restaurant, I learned that the Harvard tennis team was spreading rumors that the campus was falling into ruin*

公用   kouyou = public business, official business; from kou = public, e.g., kouen = public park; + youji = errand

遠景   enkei = background, distant view; *some engineers were eating cake in the background*

安定   antei = stability; *my aunt's kitchen table was a symbol of stability*

from News in Slow Japanese

気球   kikyuu = balloon; from ki = air + kyuu = ball

太平洋   taiheiyou = Pacific Ocean; *the tide delivered a hated yogi who had floated across the Pacific Ocean*

横断する   oudan suru = to cross; *the old dancer crossed the stage*

飛行   hikou = aviation, flight, e.g., hikouki = airplane

着水   chakusui = landing on the water; from chaku = arrival, e.g., touchaku suru = to arrive; + sui = water, e.g., suiei = swimming

いずれ   izure = which, soon, someday, in the end; *the eagle zoo rescues birds which may someday be released back into the wild*

首都   shuto = capital city; from shu = chief, e.g., shusho = prime minister; + to = capital, e.g., kyouto = ancient capital of Japan

上位   joui = high rank; from jou = above, e.g., jouzu = skillful; + i = rank

観光客   kankoukyaku = tourist; from kankou = sightseeing; *sightseers will see canned corn;* + kyaku = customer

牛久   Ushiku = a town in Ibaraki prefecture

大仏   daibutsu = a large statue of Buddha; from dai = large + butsu = Buddha

ブロンズ   buronzu = bronze

立像   ritsuzou = standing statue; from kiritsu suru = to stand up; + zou = image or shape, e.g., butsuzou = statue or image of Buddha

最大   saidai = biggest, maximum; *the science of dieting helps the biggest people*

自由   jiyuu = freedom, liberty; *the genius used his money to buy freedom*

女神   megami = goddess, female deity; from me = female; *I know a female in Mexico;* + gami = kami = god

一目　　hitome = a glance or glimpse; from hitotsu = one + me = eye

次回　　jikai = next time; *the genie promised to bring me a kite the next time we meet*

Practice Sentences

1. もう一回挑戦してみたいです。
Mou ikkai chousen shite mitai desu.
I would like to challenge (i.e., test myself) one more time and see.

2. 沖縄の最低賃金は642円です。
Okinawa no saitei chingin wa roppyaku yonjuu ni en desu.
Okinawa's minimum wage is 642 yen.

3. 彼女は政府機関に勤めているのでしょう。
Kanojo wa seifu kikan ni tsutomete iru no deshou.
She is being employed by a government agency probably.

4. 姉は結婚して大阪に住んでいます。
Ane wa kekkon shite oosaka ni sunde imasu.
As for my older sister, she got married and lives in Osaka.

5. 奈良に鹿がたくさんいるよ。
Nara ni shika ga takusan iru yo.
There are a lot of deer in Nara, for sure.

6. 茨城では何月が一番暑いですか。
Ibaraki de wa nan gatsu ga ichiban atsui desu ka.
As for of Ibaraki, what month is the hottest?

7. 彼女は私にテニスの試合を挑んだ。
Kanojo wa watashi ni tenisu no shiai wo idonda.
She challenged me to play a tennis match.

8. 風が止んだら沖まで船を出そう。
Kaze ga yandara oki made fune wo dasou.
When the wind stops, let's take the boat out to the open sea.

9. その古城は荒れ果てていた。
Sono kojou wa arehatete ita.
That old castle was in ruins.

10. この縄は丈夫だ。
Kono nawa wa joubu da.
This rope is strong.

11. 政府は今、困難に直面している。
Seifu wa ima, kon'nan ni chokumen shite iru.
The government is facing difficulty now.

12. 彼は公用で大阪に行った。
Kare wa kouyou de oosaka ni itta.
He went to Osaka on public (i.e., official) business.

13. 加奈子ちゃんは千葉から東京に通います。

Kanako-chan wa chiba kara toukyou ni kayoimasu.
Little Kanako commutes from Chiba to Tokyo.

14. 茨城県は東京から遠いですか。

Ibaraki ken wa toukyou kara tooi desu ka.
Is Ibaraki prefecture far from Tokyo?

15. 彼は何度か挑んだが成功しなかった。

Kare wa nandoka idonda ga seikou shinakatta.
He challenged (i.e., tried) several times, but he did not succeed.

16. 日本で一番南にある主な島は沖縄です。

Nihon de ichiban minami ni aru omo na shima wa okinawa desu.
In Japan, the principal island that is furthest south is Okinawa.

17. その絵の遠景に城がある。

Sono e no enkei ni shiro ga aru.
There is a castle in the background of that picture.

18. その国の政府は安定している。

Sono kuni no seifu wa antei shite iru.
The government of that country is stable.

19. 我が社は大阪に事務所を移した。

Wagasha wa oosaka ni jimusho wo utsushita.
Our company moved the office to Osaka.

20. 彼は来月、奈良を訪れるつもりだと言った。

Kare wa raigetsu, nara wo otozurerutsumori da to itta.
He said that he intends to visit Nara next month.

21. 成田空港は茨城県の南にあります。

Narita kuukou wa ibaraki ken no minami ni arimasu.
Narita airport is south of Ibaraki prefecture.

Supplemental Reading Practice

After completing Chapter 50 of this book, you should be able to read Lesson 002, "Taking on a Crossing of the Pacific in a Balloon" and Lesson 003, "Ushiku Daibutsu," in *News in Slow Japanese*.

If you find the 4th sentence in Lesson 002 a little difficult to understand, here is an explanation: *Futari wa* (the two people) *gasu kikyuu de* (by gas balloon) *taiheiyou oudan to* (a Pacific Ocean crossing and) *hikou kyori no* (a flying distance's) *saikou kiroku* (highest record) *koushin ni* (for the sake of improving) *chousen shimashita* (they challenged, or attempted).

Chapter 51

New Kanji in this Chapter

# 1009 挟 (1)	# 1010 省 (3)	# 1011 携 (2)	# 1012 帯 (2)
# 1013 滞 (1)	# 1014 在 (2)	# 1015 陸 (1)	# 1016 湾 (1)

Vocabulary List with Mnemonics

from the Kanji Catalogue

挟む	hasamu = to hold or place between, to pinch; *the handsome salaryman moved his chopsticks in such a way that they pinched his food*
挟まる	hasamaru = to get between, to get caught in; *the handsome salaryman ruined his shoe when he got it caught between two stones*
省く	habuku = to omit, to cut down (cost); *I will cut down on Hawaiian booze and Kool-Aid*
反省	hansei = scrutiny, self-scrutiny, regret; *Hansel sagely recognized that the birds were eating the crumbs and did self-scrutiny*
携わる	tazusawaru = to engage (in); *the tall zookeeper from Saskatchewan kept wasps in his room and was engaged in the science of entomology*
携える	tazusaeru = to carry with; *the tall zookeeper from Saskatchewan was erudite and he always carried an electronic dictionary with him*
携帯電話	keitaidenwa = a cellular phone; from keitai suru = to carry; *I bought a cane in Thailand and carried it home*; + denwa = phone
帯	obi = a kimono sash; *after Oprah drank beer, her kimono sash was too short*
所帯	shotai = household, family; *our household keeps a short tiger as a pet*
滞在する	taizai suru = to stay (at a hotel, etc.); *when I got tired in Zaire (former name of the Congo), I stayed at a hotel*
現在	genzai = nowadays, present time; *Genghis said that the zeitgeist (spirit of the age) at the present time was decadent*
在る	aru = to exist, usually spelled ある; *these architectural ruins exist in Egypt*; cf. 有る aru = to exist
陸	riku = land; *real Kool-Aid comes from a far-away land*

Kanji Pronunciations

# 1009 – hasa	# 1010 – shou, habu, sei	# 1011 – tazusa, kei	# 1012 – obi, tai
# 1013 – tai	# 1014 – zai, a	# 1015 – riku	# 1016 – wan

大陸	tairiku = continent, mainland (China); from tai = big + riku = land
離陸する	ririku suru = to take off (flight); from ri = to separate, e.g., rikon = divorce; + riku = land
陸軍	rikugun = army; from riku = land + gunjin = soldier
湾	wan = gulf, bay; I *wandered* down to the *bay*
台湾	taiwan = Taiwan

from the Practice Sentences

国務省	kokumushou = State Department; *I drank Coke at the movie show as I watched a film about the State Department*
時刻	jikoku = time, hour; from jikan = time + koku = to carve (into pieces); *I received some Coke for carving the roast*
最中	saichuu = in the midst of, during; *the scientist chewed gum during the meeting*
不在	fuzai = absence; from fu = negation + zai = to exist or stay, e.g., taizai suru = to stay (at a hotel, etc.)
滞納	tainou = deliquency (failure to pay); *the time for the nomads to pay their rent has passed, and they are in a state of delinquency*
着陸する	chakuriku suru = to land; from chaku = to arrive; *she drank champagne and Kool-Aid after she arrived*; + riku = land
湾岸	wangan = gulf coast; from wan = gulf or bay + gan = beach, e.g., kaigan = beach
湾岸戦争	wangan sensou = the Gulf War; from wangan = gulf coast + sensou = war
手間	tema = time, trouble; *termites in Massachusetts cause a lot of trouble*
長期間	choukikan = a long time; *when I was choking on candy, it took a long time for my friends to respond*
取り合わせ	toriawase = assortment, combination; from toru = to take + awaseru = to harmonize or put together
関東	kantou = the Kanto region, a district of Japan that encompasses seven prefectures, including Tokyo; from kan = to connect, e.g., kankei = relationship; + tou = east, e.g., Toukyou = eastern capital
地方	chihou = region, district; *the cheese we hope to eat will differ in each region*
上陸する	jouriku suru = to land, to hit (typhoon); from jou = above, e.g., jouzu = skillful; + riku = land
存在	sonzai = existence, presence; *Sony opened an office in Zaire (former name of the Congo) in order to have a presence there*

from News in Slow Japanese

四川省	shisenshou = Szechuan, or Sichuan, a province in China

おり	ori = a cage or cell; *when I was in a prison cell, I ate Oreo cookies*
隅っこ	sumikko = a corner, nook or recess; *sumisu-san (Mr. Smith) looked cozy in his chair in the corner*
引っ張る	hipparu = to pull toward oneself; from hiku = to pull + paru = haru = to stretch, pull or extend; *the harp was ruined when I stretched the strings too much*
見守る	mimamoru = to watch over, watch attentively; from miru = to watch + mamoru = to protect
およそ	oyoso = approximately; *the old yogurt that the soldiers ate was approximately a month past its expiration date*
救出する	kyuushutsu suru = to rescue or extricate; from kyuusai = help, rescue + shutsu = to put out, e.g., gaishutsu suru = to go out
経由	keiyu = via, by way of; *to get to my cave in the Yukon, I travel via a forest path*
ぶりに	buri ni = after an interval, e.g., ichinen buri ni = after one year's interval; *I gave a burrito to my niece, after an interval when she hadn't eaten one*
美味しい	oishii = delicious; this is an alternative spelling of おいしい; it can be read literally as 美(しい) utsukushii (beautiful) + (意)味 imi (taste)

Practice Sentences

1. 痛い！ドアに指挟んだ！
Itai! Doa ni yubi hasanda!
Ouch! I pinched my finger in the door!

2. 国務省で働いている。
Kokumushou de hataraite iru.
I am laboring in the State Department.

3. 携帯電話を持っていますか？
Keitai denwa wo motte imasu ka.
Do you have a mobile phone?

4. しばらくこのホテルに滞在します。
Shibaraku kono hoteru ni taizai shimasu.
I will stay in this hotel for awhile.

5. 飛行機は離陸したばかりだ。
Hikouki wa ririku shita bakari da.
The airplane just took off.

6. その空港は大阪湾にあります。
Sono kuukou wa oosaka wan ni arimasu.
That airport is in Osaka bay.

7. 現在の時刻は何時ですか。
Genzai no jikoku wa nan ji desu ka.
What is the current time of day?

8. 彼女は会話の最中に口を挟むことがよくある。
Kanojo wa kaiwa no saichuu ni kuchi wo hasamu koto ga yoku aru.
She often places her mouth in the middle of a conversation (i.e., she interrupts).

9. 社内運動会の反省会をすること
になりました。

Shanai undoukai no hanseikai wo suru
koto ni narimashita.
He was scheduled to do an inside-the-
company sports tournament's self-
scrutiny meeting.

10. 父は今不在です。

Chichi wa ima fuzai desu.
My father is absent now.

11. 明日、彼らは月に着陸する。

Ashita, karera wa tsuki ni chakuriku
suru.
Tomorrow they will land on the moon.

12. 携帯の電池が切れてしまった。

Keitai no denchi ga kirete shimatta.
The cell phone's battery ran down
completely.

13. 料金滞納で電話を止められた。

Ryoukin tainou de denwa wo tomerareta.
Due to fee delinquency (i.e., unpaid
bills), the phone (i.e., the service) was
stopped on me.

14. １９９０年に湾岸戦争が始まった。

Sen kyuuhyaku kyuujuu nen ni wangan
sensou ga hajimatta.
In 1990, the gulf shore war (i.e., the Gulf
War) began.

15. 彼は耳にペンを挟んだ。

Kare wa mimi ni pen wo hasanda.
He put a pen behind his ear.

16. それでだいぶ手間が省ける。

Sore de daibu tema ga habukeru.
That can save a lot of trouble.

17. 彼女の着物と帯の取り合わせ
がきれいですね。

Kanojo no kimono to obi no toriawase ga
kirei desu ne.
Her kimono and sashi combination is
pretty, huh.

18. できるだけ長期間滞在したい
と思っています。

Dekiru dake choukikan taizai shitai to
omotte imasu.
I would like to stay as long as possible,
I'm thinking.

19. 台風が関東地方に上陸した。

Taifuu ga kantou chihou ni jouriku shita.
The typhoon struck the Kantou region.

20. 台湾料理はインド料理ほど辛
くない。

Taiwan ryouri wa indo ryouri hodo
karakunai.
Compared to Indian food, Taiwanese
food is not as spicy.

21. 彼はそれ以来、宗教活動に携
わっている。

Kare wa sore irai shuukyou katsudou ni
tazusawatte iru.
Since then he is engaging in religious
activity.

22. 神は存在する。

Kami wa sonzai suru.
God exists.

Supplemental Reading Practice

After completing Chapter 51 of this book, you should be able to read Lesson 004, "Panda Wedged Between the Bars of a Cage," and Lesson 005, "Sakura's Spain Travel Journal" in *News in Slow Japanese*.

Chapter 52

New Kanji in this Chapter

# 1017 旧 (1)	# 1018 盛 (4)	# 1019 災 (2)	# 1020 乱 (2)
# 1021 暴 (2)	# 1022 爆 (1)	# 1023 縁 (1)	# 1024 怪 (3)

Vocabulary List with Mnemonics

from the Kanji Catalogue

旧正月   kyuu shougatsu = lunar New Year, or Chinese New Year; from kyuu = old times; *I remember the old times in Cuba*; + shougatsu = New Year

旧年   kyuunen = last year, used in formal writing; from kyuu = old times; *I remember the old times in Cuba*; + nen = year

盛る   moru = to fill or pile up; *Moses ruined the pool when he filled it with dirt*

盛んな   sakan na = active, enthusiastic, energetic, thriving; *drinking sake from a can is a thriving custom, and people who do it tend to be active and enthusiastic*

全盛   zensei = culmination, heyday, peak; *that Zen sage is at the peak of his powers*

盛大な   seidai na = grandiose, pompous, thriving, successful; *the sailors built a dike that was grandiose and successful*

震災   shinsai = great earthquake; from shin = to shake, e.g., jishin = earthquake; + sai = calamity; *silence is a calamity when it results from hearing loss*

火災   kasai = fire; from kaji = fire + sai = calamity; *silence is a calamity when it results from hearing loss*

災難   sainan = misfortune, disaster; from sai = calamity; *silence is a calamity when it results from hearing loss;* + nan = difficult, e.g., kon'nan = difficult

災い   wazawai = calamity, disaster; *wacky Zambian warriors from the east caused the calamity*

Kanji Pronunciations

# 1017 – kyuu	# 1018 – mo, saka, jou, sei	# 1019 – sai, wazawa	# 1020 – mida, ran
# 1021 – bou, aba	# 1022 – baku	# 1023 – en	# 1024 – aya, ke, kai

乱れる — midareru = to become chaotic, disrupted or windblown (hair); *after the mediator's daughter got a red rooster, the barnyard became chaotic*

乱暴な — ranbou na = violent, disorderly; *violent men ransacked the bowling alley*

暴れる — abareru = to become violent; *she abandoned her red rooster after it became violent*

爆弾 — bakudan = bomb; *in the back of the Uber car, the dancer concealed a bomb*

原爆 — genbaku = atomic bomb; an abbreviation of 原子爆弾 genshibakudan; from genshi = atom; *Genghis said that his sheets were made of atoms*; + bakudan = bomb

縁 — en = relation, bond, kinship, fate; *entertainers have a bond with their audience*

縁起 — engi = omen, sign of luck, origin, causation; *those energetic geese are a sign of luck and a good omen*

怪しい — ayashii = suspicious, doubtful; *the Ayatollah thought that some of the Shiites were of doubtful loyalty*

怪物 — kaibutsu = monster; from kai = mystery, suspicious; *the kite that appeared over my house seemed suspicious*; + doubutsu = animal

大怪我 — ookega = serious injury; from ookii = big + kega = injury; *a keg of apple juice fell on me and caused an injury*

from the Practice Sentences

旧友 — kyuuyuu = old friend; from kyuu = old times; *I remember the old times in Cuba*; + yuujin = friend

工業 — kougyou = industry; *in that industry, the workers get cold gyoza for lunch*

報知器 — houchiki = alarm; *our host had a cheeky son who kept setting off the fire alarm*

特権 — tokken = privilege; *the king's crown is a token of his privilege*

乱用する — ran'you suru = to abuse, misuse; *he misused a key, unlocked a door and ransacked the yogurt store*

暴力 — bouryoku = violence, brutality; from bou = violent; *bowling is a violent sport for the bowling pins*; + ryoku = force, power

一族 — ichizoku = family, household, relatives; from ichi = one + kazoku = family

大げさ — oogesa = exaggerated; *Obama guessed he had 10 apples, but it was an exaggerated estimate*

当時 — touji = those days, old days; *in those days, we often had to tow our Jeep*

かろうじて — karoujite = barely; *when I spilled Karo syrup on my jeans in Texas, I was barely able to scrub out the stain*

目に余る — me ni amaru = to be intolerable; from me ni = to the eyes + amaru = to be in excess; literally "to the eyes to be in excess"

爆発	bakuhatsu = an explosion or eruption; from bakudan = bomb + hatsu = discharge, departure, e.g., shuppatsu suru = to depart
大盛り	oomori = a large serving; from ookii = big + moru = to fill or pile up
転じる	tenjiru = to turn or shift; *the tenacious genius who ruled over the factory decided to shift its production to electric cars*
動乱	douran = disturbance, commotion; *during the disturbance, the crowd opened the door and ransacked the store*
暴れまわる	abaremawaru = to rampage, run riot; from abareru = to become violent + mawaru = to turn
投下する	touka suru = to throw down or drop; from tou = to throw; *I threw toast at my brother*; + ka = below, e.g., chikatetsu = subway
以前	izen = ago (suggesting a long time), before; *eastern Zen was popular before western Zen*

from News in Slow Japanese

東南アジア	tounan'ajia = southeast Asian; from tou = east, e.g, toukyou = eastern capital; + nan = south, e.g., nanbei = South America; + ajia = Asia
最終日	saishuubi = the last or final day; from saishuu = the last + bi = hi = day
無病	mubyou = in perfect health; from mu = negation + byouki = illness
息災	sokusai = good health; *as I soak in the tub, I sigh and wish for good health*
台南市	tainan shi = Tainan, a city in Taiwan
会場	kaijou = venue, site of an event; from kaigi = meeting + jou = place; *this place where I live is a joke*
発	hatsu = counter for gunshots or explosions; the pronunciation varies according to the number preceding it, e.g, ippatsu, nihatsu, sanpatsu, or manpatsu (1, 2, 3, or 10,000 explosions); *the explosion knocked the men's hats off*
爆竹	bakuchiku = firecracker; from bakudan = bomb + chiku = bamboo, e.g., chikurin = bamboo grove
放つ	hanatsu = to fire, to release, emit; a variation of 放す hanasu = to release
参加者	sankasha = participants; from sanka suru = to participate + sha = person
厚手	atsude = thick (paper, fabric, etc.); from atsui = thick + de = te = hand
ヘルメット	herumetto = helmet
花火	hanabi = fireworks; from hana = flower + bi = hi = fire
当たる	ataru = to hit; *a tall rooster fell from its perch and hit me*
怪我人	keganin = injured person; from kega = injury + nin = person

Practice Sentences

1. 旧友に招待された。

Kyuuyuu ni shoutai sareta.
I was invited by an old friend.

2. この町は、工業都市として盛んです。

Kono machi wa, kougyou toshi to shite sakan desu.
As for this town, in the capacity of an industrial city, it is thriving.

3. 火災報知器が鳴った。

Kasai houchiki ga natta.
The fire alarm rang.

4. 彼は特権を乱用した。

Kare wa tokken wo ranyou shita.
He abused his privilege.

5. 私たちは暴力が嫌いだ。

Watashitachi wa bouryoku ga kirai da.
We hate violence.

6. 戦争中たくさんの爆弾が落とされた。

Sensou chuu takusan no bakudan ga otosareta.
During the war, a lot of bombs were dropped.

7. 彼はその一族に縁がある。

Kare wa sono ichizoku ni en ga aru.
He is affiliated with that family.

8. 軽い怪我をしただけなのに、彼は大げさに騒いだ。

Karui kega wo shita dake na noni, kare wa oogesa ni sawaida.
A light injury he did only, even though it is, he made a fuss exaggeratedly.

9. 旧年中は大変お世話になりました。

Kyuunen chuu wa taihen osewa ni narimashita.
Throughout last year, greatly, honorable care developed (said on a New Year's card, meaning "thank you for your consideration during the year").

10. 当時その宗教は全盛だった。

Touji sono shuukyou wa zensei datta.
Those days, that religion was in its heyday.

11. 彼はかろうじて災難を逃れた。

Kare wa karoujite sainan wo nogareta.
He barely escaped the disaster.

12. 弟の乱暴はこの頃、目に余る。

Otouto no ranbou wa kono goro, me ni amaru.
Little brother's disorderliness is intolerable these days.

13. ガスタンクが突然爆発した。

Gasu tanku ga totsuzen bakuhatsu shita.
The gas tank exploded suddenly.

14. 縁起でもないこと言うなよ。

Engi demo nai koto iu na yo.
Don't say things that aren't even lucky, for sure. (i.e., don't say anything to bring us bad luck; na = "do not")

15. 彼が怪しいと思う。

Kare ga ayashii to omou.
He is suspicious, I think (i.e., I am suspicious of him).

16. 2018年の旧正月は2月16日となっています。

Nisen juuhachi nen no kyuu shougatsu wa nigatsu juu rokunichi tonatte imasu.
The Chinese New Year in 2018 will become (or, will be) February 16th.

17. ご飯は大盛りでお願いします。

Gohan wo oomori de onegai shimasu.
A large serving of rice, I beg you.

18. 災いを転じて福としなさい。

Wazawai wo tenjite fuku to shinasai.
On calamities, turn them and take them as fortune. (i.e., when life gives you lemons, make lemonade)

19. 動乱は3日間続いた。

Douran wa mikka kan tsuzuita.
The disturbance lasted for three days.

20. 部屋の中で暴れまわってはいけない。

Heya no naka de abaremawatte wa ikenai.
You must not rampage about in the room.

21. 1945年広島に原子爆弾が投下された。

Sen kyuuhyaku yonjuu go nen hiroshima ni genshi bakudan ga touka sareta.
In 1945 an atomic bomb was dropped in Hiroshima.

22. 7は縁起のいい番号だ。

Nana wa engi no ii bangou da.
Seven is a lucky number.

23. 以前恐ろしい怪物が住んでいた。

Izen osoroshii kaibutsu ga sunde ita.
A frightening monster was living in the past.

24. その知らせにひどく心が乱れた。

Sono shirase ni hidoku kokoro ga midareta.
My heart was terribly disrupted by that news (i.e. I was deeply upset).

Supplemental Reading Practice

After completing Chapter 52 of this book, you should be able to read Lesson 006, "A Dangerous Festival in Taiwan," in *News in Slow Japanese*.

Chapter 53

New Kanji in this Chapter

# 1025 松 (2)	# 1026 江 (2)	# 1027 講 (1)	# 1028 義 (1)
# 1029 推 (2)	# 1030 薦 (2)	# 1031 測 (2)	# 1032 再 (3)

Vocabulary List with Mnemonics

from the Kanji Catalogue

松	matsu = pine tree; *they put mats under the pine tree*
江戸	edo = old name for Tokyo; from e = bay; *this is an excellent bay*; + do = to = door
長江	choukou = Yangtze River in China; from chou = long; *she chose a long skirt*; + kou = creek; *it's cold in the creek*
講義	kougi = lecture; *the lecture was about Korean geese*
講堂	koudou = auditorium; from kougi = lecture + dou = hall, e.g., shokudou = dining hall
義理	giri = moral debt, limited duty to the outside world; *the captain felt giddy during the storm, but he had to do his limited duty*
義務	gimu = unlimited duty to the emperor, ancestors and descendants; *the geese on the moor must perform their unlimited duty to their offspring*
推薦する	suisen suru = to recommend; *a Swedish senator recommended tax cuts*
推測	suisoku = an assumption or guess; *when I fell off the swing and felt myself getting soaked, I made an assumption that I had fallen into a puddle*
推す	osu = to recommend; *for a more casual look, I recommend that you open your suit*
薦める	susumeru = to advise (this is usually spelled 勧める, # 698); *I advise Sue to attend summer school to get erudite*
測る	hakaru = to measure or gauge (this is usually spelled 計る, # 434); *at the hackathon we received rulers to measure our desktop space*
予測	yosoku = a prediction or supposition; *the yogi got soaked in the downpour which followed his prediction of rain*

Kanji Pronunciations

# 1025 – matsu, shou	# 1026 – e, kou	# 1027 – kou	# 1028 – gi
# 1029 – sui, o	# 1030 – susu, sen	# 1031 – haka, soku	# 1032 – sai, futata, sa

測定する
sokutei suru = to measure; *the rain soaked the tailor, but he kept on measuring his cloth*

再会する
saikai suru = to meet again; from sai = again; *the scientists performed the experiment again*; + kaigi = meeting

再開する
saikai suru = to reopen or resume; from sai = again; *the scientists performed the experiment again*; + kai = to open; *they opened the park so that people could fly kites*

再三
saisan = many times, again and again; from sai = again; *the scientists performed the experiment again*; + san = three

再び
futatabi = again; *he spilled food on the tatami mat, and the beast ate it again*

再来年
sarainen = the year after next; from sa = again; *I was sad that it happened again*; + rainen = next year

from the Practice Sentences

果たす
hatasu = to accomplish or realize; *when he was hatachi (20 years old) Superman visited Metropolis for the first time and realized his dream*

観月会
kangetsukai = a moon-viewing party; from kankou = sightseeing + getsu = moon + kaigi = meeting

実際のところ
jissai no tokoro = to tell the truth, as a matter of fact; from jissai = reality, fact + tokoro = moment or place

推理
suiri = speculation, inference; *there is speculation that Sweden will return the refugees*

推理小説
suiri shousetsu = a mystery or detective novel; from suiri = speculation + shousetsu = novel

再放送
saihousou = a re-broadcast; from sai = again; *the scientists performed the experiment again*; + housou = broadcast

つまり
tsumari = that is to say, in other words; *people who live on the tsuki (moon) tend to marry; in other words, it can get lonely up there*

民主
minshu = democracy, democratic; from shimin = citizen + shujin = master

主義
shugi = doctrine, rule, principle; from shujin = master + gi = justice, morality; *the geese benefit from the justice system*

民主主義
minshushugi = democracy; from minshu = democracy + shugi = doctrine or rule

理念
rinen = ideal, doctrine; *the reason my negative nephew quit school was that he adopted a doctrine of noncomformity*

温度計
ondokei = a thermometer; from ondo = temperature + kei = to measure or count, e.g., tokei = clock

器具
kigu = utensil, apparatus, device; *the king's goose wears a monitoring device*

立てる	tateru = to treat with respect, to give someone their due, among many other meanings; *Tarzan has a Texas rooster, and we treat it with respect*

from News in Slow Japanese

島根県	shimane ken = Shimane Prefecture; from shima = island + ne = root; *my roots are in the Netherlands*; + ken = prefecture
松江市	matsue shi = Matsue, a city in Shimane Prefecture; from matsu = pine tree + e = bay; *boats embark from the bay*; + shi = city
フォーゲル	foogeru = Vogel, the name of a park in Matsue
親近感	shinkinkan = a feeling of intimacy; from shin = intimate, e.g., ryoushin = parent; + kin = close, e.g., kinjo = neighborhood; + kanjiru = to feel
一時	ittoki = for a moment, for a while; from ichi = one + toki = time (this could also be read as ichiji = for a while, or as one o'clock, which could also be written 1 時)
見向きもせず	mimuki mo sezu = mimuki mo shinai = taking no notice, ignoring; from miru = to look + muku = to face toward; + sezu = shinai de = not doing
一途に	ichizu ni = wholehearted, earnest; from ichi = one + zu = route; *this is the route to the zoo*

Practice Sentences

1. 驚いたことには。松本さんが昨日亡くなったそうです。

Odoroita koto ni wa. Matsumotosan ga kinou nakunatta sou desu.
I was astonished. Matsumoto died yesterday, reportedly. (koto ni wa can be used to emphasize emotion)

2. 昔、人々は江戸から京都まで歩いていた。

Mukashi, hitobito wa edo kara kyouto made aruite ita.
In the old days, people were walking from Edo to Kyoto.

3. 講義を終わらせた。

Kougi wo owaraseta.
He ended the lecture.

4. 単なる推測だろう。

Tan'naru suisoku darou.
It's a mere guess, probably.

5. 何かお薦めの本はありますか。

Nanika osusume no hon wa arimasu ka.
Is there any book that you honorably recommend?

6. 彼女は義務を果たした。

Kanojo wa gimu wo hatashita.
She accomplished her unlimited duty.

7. 再来月は１２月だ。

Saraigetsu wa juunigatsu da.
The month after next is December.

8. 松山で生まれ育った。

Matsuyama de umaresodatta.
I was born and raised in Matsuyama.

9. 江戸時代には、観月会がとても人気だった。

Edo jidai ni wa, kangetsukai ga totemo ninki datta.
During the Edo period, moon-viewing parties were very popular.

10. 実際のところ、彼の講義は退屈であった。

Jissai no tokoro, kare no kougi wa taikutsu deatta.
As a matter of fact, his lecture was boring.

11. 推理小説を読むのが好きです。

Suiri shousetsu wo yomu no ga suki desu.
I like to read mystery novels.

12. 何が起こるか予測できない。

Nani ga okoru ka yosoku dekinai.
We are unable to predict whether something will occur. (this is an abbreviation of okoru ka dou ka)

13. この番組は再放送だ。

Kono bangumi wa saihousou da.
This program is a rerun.

14. 昔、私の家の前には大きな松の木があった。

Mukashi, watashi no ie no mae ni wa ookina matsu no ki ga atta.
In the old days, there was a big pine tree in front of my house.

15. 外国人の一団が江戸、つまり東京に到着した。

Gaikokujin no ichidan ga edo, tsumari toukyou ni touchaku shita.
A group of foreigners arrived at Edo, that is to say, Tokyo.

16. 講堂に入るとすぐに式が始まった。

Koudou ni hairu to sugu ni shiki ga hajimatta.
When I entered the auditorium, the ceremony began immediately.

17. 戦後日本では民主主義の理念が普及した。

Sengo nihon de wa minshushugi no rinen ga fukyuu shita.
After the war, the ideal of democracy spread in Japan.

18. このレストランは推薦できません。

Kono resutoran wa suisen dekimasen.
I cannot recommend this restaurant.

19. 温度計は温度を測る器具です。

Ondokei wa ondo wo hakaru kigu desu.
A thermometer is a tool to measure temperature.

20. もうすぐ授業が再開する。

Mou sugu jugyou ga saikai suru.
Pretty soon classes will resume.

21. 私は彼に義理を立てなけれ
ばならない。

Watashi wa kare ni giri wo tatenakereba
naranai.
As for me, to him, on limited duty, I
give him his due. (i.e., I must do right
by him)

22. 先生は私達にこの辞書を推
薦してくれた。

Sensei wa watashitachi ni kono jisho wo
suisen shite kureta.
The teacher recommended this
dictionary for us.

23. 彼は再びふるさとを訪れる
ことはなかった。

Kare wa futatabi furusato wo otozureru
koto wa nakatta.
He did not visit his homeland again.

Supplemental Reading Practice

After completing Chapter 53 of this book, you should be able to read Lesson 007,
"Penguin in Love," in *News in Slow Japanese.*

Chapter 54

New Kanji in this Chapter

# 1033 各 (2)	# 1034 繰 (1)	# 1035 是 (2)	# 1036 認 (2)
# 1037 遺 (2)	# 1038 総 (1)	# 1039 臣 (2)	# 1040 姫 (1)

Vocabulary List with Mnemonics

from the Kanji Catalogue

各 — kaku = each, every, either; *Karl the Kool-Aid vendor likes each variety of Kool-Aid*

各自の — kakuji no = each, one's own; from kaku = each + jibun = by oneself

各駅 — kakueki = each station; from kaku = each + eki = station

各国 — kakkoku = each country; from kakuji = each + koku = country

繰り返す — kurikaesu = to repeat, to do something over again; *when he gives me curry, I kaesu (give it back), and then we repeat this behavior*

是非とも — zehitomo = by all means; *I will go to the Zen temple for healing tomorrow, by all means*

是認 — ze'nin = approval; *the Zen monk said that the ninja met with his approval*

是程 — kore hodo = so much, this much, usually spelled これほど; from kore = this + hodo = about

確認 — kakunin = confirmation; *Karl the Kool-Aid vendor asked the ninja for confirmation of his order*

認める — mitomeru = to recognize or admit; *I admit that a good mediator can tomeru [stop] a strike*

遺産 — isan = inheritance, legacy, heritage; *it's easy for Santa Claus to brag about his legacy*

遺言 — yuigon = will, deathbed instructions; *some Yukon eagles that belonged to Gonzalez were bequeathed in the will*

総じて — soujite = in general, on the whole; *sombreros and jeans are accepted attire in Texas, in general*

Kanji Pronunciations

# 1033 – kaku, ka	# 1034 – ku	# 1035 – ze, kore	# 1036 – nin, mito
# 1037 – i, yui	# 1038 – sou	# 1039 – shin, jin	# 1040 – hime

総理   souri = prime minister; *the prime minister was targeted by a Soviet ring of spies;* cf. 首相 shushou = prime minister

総理大臣   souridaijin = prime minister; from souri = prime minister + dai = big + jin = minister; *the minister wore jeans on his days off*

総会   soukai = general meeting; from soujite = in general + kaigai = meeting

臣民   shinmin = royal subject; from shin = subject; *the Shinto priest was a loyal subject;* + min = citizen

姫   hime = princess; *the princess was attracted to he-men*

from the Practice Sentences

各地   kakuchi = every place, various places; from kaku = each, every + chi = ground, e.g., chikatetsu = subway

市場   shijou = market; *she jokes about the market;* this can also be read as ichiba = market; *I got my itchy bandana at the market*

広げる   hirogeru = to spread or expand, to unfold; *the hero and his guest ruined the carpet by unfolding it in the ocean*

遺書   isho = will; from isan = legacy + sho = document, e.g., jisho = dictionary

役   yaku = role, e.g., yaku ni tatsu = to make use of, to be useful

過ち   ayamachi = fault, mistake; *the Ayatollah got mad when the chief made a mistake*

総額   sougaku = total amount; from soujite = on the whole + gaku = a sum of money, e.g., kingaku = a sum of money

際   sai = when; *when I have nothing to say, I am silent*

立ち寄る   tachiyoru = to drop in for a short visit; from tatsu = to stand + yoru = to drop in

相続   souzoku = succession, inheritance; *when I lived in the Soviet zone, Kool-Aid was the only inheritance that I could expect*

座   za = seat, position; *he held an important position in Zambia*

引き継ぐ   hikitsugu = to succeed to, take over; from hiku = to pull + tsugu = to inherit

めいめい   meimei = each, individual; *the mayor mailed thank-you notes to each person who contributed to his campaign*

現段階   gendankai = present stage, current phase; *Genghis and the dancer fly kites during the current phase of their relationship*

において   ni oite = at or in; *my niece oiled her tennis racket at the gym*

遺言書   yuigonsho = written will; from yuigon = will + sho = document, e.g., jisho = dictionary

作成する   sakusei suru = to draw up (document), prepare, write, make produce; *the salaryman drank some Kool-Aid and consulted a sage before drawing up his will*

声明	seimei = declaration, statement; *the <u>sailors</u> and the <u>mayor</u> made a joint <u>statement</u>*

from News in Slow Japanese

学習	gakushuu = study, learning; from gaku = learning, + shuu = learning by repeating, e.g., renshuu = practice
再生	saisei = recyclying, rebirth, regeneration; *scientists <u>say</u> that <u>recycling</u> is good for the environment*
まねする	mane suru (an abbreviation of mane wo suru) = to imitate or copy; *that <u>map</u> of the Netherlands was <u>copied</u>*
再現する	saigen suru = to reproduce, replicate; *the <u>scientist</u> that <u>Genghis</u> hired was able to <u>reproduce</u> the results of the experiment*
取り入れる	tori'ireru = to harvest, take in, adopt, incorporate; from toru = to take + ireru = to put in

Practice Sentences

1. 彼女は日本の各地を旅してまわった。
Kanojo wa nihon no kakuchi wo tabi shite mawatta.
She traveled around on Japan's various places.

2. 彼女はそれを繰り返し説明した。
Kanojo wa sore wo kurikaeshi setsumei shita.
She explained that again.

3. 当社では是非ともヨーロッパへ市場を広げたいと考えております。
Tousha de wa zehitomo yooroppa e shijou wo hirogetai to kangaete orimasu.
As for at the designated company (i.e., our company), by all means, to Europe we want to expand the market, we are humbly thinking.

4. 二度確認しました。
Nido kakunin shimashita.
I confirmed it two times.

5. 彼は昨年遺書を書いた。
Kare wa sakunen isho wo kaita.
He wrote a will last year.

6. 総理大臣が昨日辞職した。
Souridaijin ga kinou jishoku shita.
The prime minister resigned yesterday.

7. 誰がお姫様の役を演じるの?
Dare ga ohimesama no yaku wo enjiru no?
Who will play the part of the princess?

8. 各駅停車をご利用のお客様は、次の駅でお乗り換えください。
Kakueki teisha wo go riyou no okyakusama wa, tsugi no eki de onorikae kudasai.
As for honorable customers who honorably use every station train-stopping (i.e., the local train), at the next station, please honorably transfer.

9. 同じ過ちを繰り返している。

Onaji ayamachi wo kurikaeshite iru.
I keep making the same mistake.

10. 総額はおよそ 50 ドル位だと 思います。

Sougaku wa oyoso gojuu doru gurai da to omoimasu.
The total amount is approximately $50, I think.

11. お買い物にお越しの際には是 非、お立ち寄りください。

Okaimono ni okoshi no sai ni wa zehi, otachiyori kudasai.
As for when you go for the purpose of honorable shopping, by all means, please drop by for a visit.

12. 僕の字が下手な事は認めるけ ど…

Boku no ji ga heta na koto wa mitomeru kedo...
My characters, as for unskillful things, I admit, but... (i.e., I don't write well)

13. 彼が父親の遺産を相続するだ ろう。

Kare ga chichioya no isan wo souzoku suru darou.
He will probably inherit his father's inheritance.

14. 小泉氏が森氏の総理大臣の座 を引き継いだ。

Koizumi shi ga mori shi no souridaijin no za wo hikitsuida.
Mr. Koizumi succeeded to Mr. Mori's prime minister's position.

15. 白雪姫ほどきれいな人はいま せん。

Shirayukihime hodo kirei na hito wa imasen.
Compared to White Snow Princess, prettier people don't exist.

16. そのチームの選手は各自のめ いめいのバットを持ってい る。

Sono chiimu no senshu wa kakuji no meimei no batto wo motte iru.
Each player on that team has his individual bat.

17. 総会は 9 時ちょうどに始まっ た。

Soukai wa kuji choudo ni hajimatta.
The general meeting began at exactly 9:00.

18. すみませんが、おっしゃった ことをもう 1 度繰り返してく ださいませんか。

Sumimasen ga, osshatta koto wo mo ichido kurikaeshite kudasaimasen ka.
Excuse me, but will you repeat what you honorably said one more time for me?

19. 現段階においては是認しにく いです。

Gendankai ni oite wa zenin shi nikui desu.
As for at the present stage, it is hard to approve.

20. まだ遺言書を作成していません。

Mada yuigonsho wo sakusei shite imasen.
I am still not drawing up a will (i.e., I haven't made one).

21. 総理大臣は明日、声明を発表する予定です。

Souridaijin wa ashita, seimei wo happyou suru yotei desu.
As for the prime minister, tomorrow there's a plan to announce a statement.

22. 姫路駅で降りなさい。

Himeji eki de orinasai.
Get off at Himeji station.

Supplemental Reading Practice

After completing Chapter 54 of this book, you should be able to read Lesson 008, "Shadowing," in *News in Slow Japanese*.

Chapter 55

New Kanji in this Chapter

# 1041 塗 (2)	# 1042 衣 (3)	# 1043 装 (3)	# 1044 弓 (2)
# 1045 矢 (1)	# 1046 印 (3)	# 1047 季 (1)	# 1048 節 (3)

Vocabulary List with Mnemonics

from the Kanji Catalogue

塗る	nuru = to paint, plaster, spread, smear; *I painted my new roof*
塗り替える	nurikaeru = to repaint, rewrite; from nuru = to paint + kaeru = to replace or exchange
衣服	ifuku = clothing; from i = clothes; *I buy new clothes for Easter*; + fuku = clothes, e.g., youfuku = Western clothes
衣類	irui = clothing; from i = clothes; *I buy new clothes for Easter*; + rui = variety, e.g., shurui = variety
浴衣	yukata = informal summer kimono; *the youthful kata (honorable person) wore a summer kimono*
衣	koromo = coating or breading (food), clothes; *the Corolla's motor had a coating of mud after the journey*
装置	souchi = equipment, device; *he sold cheap equipment*
装備	soubi = equipment; *the soda and beer were dispensed by some equipment*
服装	fukusou = outfit, dress style, attire; from fuku = clothes + souchi = equipment
装う	yosou = to serve or dish up; *the yogi asked the soldier to dish up the soup*
衣装	ishou = clothing, costume; *she bought a costume to wear to the Easter show*
弓	yumi = bow; *at the youth meeting, I saw many bows*
矢	ya = arrow; *I found an arrow in the yard*
弓矢	yumiya = bow and arrow; from yumi = bow + ya = arrow
弓道	kyuudou = archery; *in Cuba, there is a domed building devoted to archery*
矢印	yajirushi = arrow (on a map or sign); *the yacht and the Jeep were rushing after arrows on signs*

Kanji Pronunciations

# 1041 – nu, to	# 1042 – kata, i, koromo	# 1043 – sou, yoso, shou	# 1044 – yumi, kyuu
# 1045 – ya	# 1046 – shirushi, jirushi, in	# 1047 – ki	# 1048 – setsu, sechi, fushi

印   shirushi = sign, symbol, indication; *the Shiites were rushing to remove the symbols of Saddam from Iraq*

印象   inshou = impression; *the insects on the shore made an impression on me*

印象的   inshouteki = impressive; from inshou = impression + teki = related to

季節   kisetsu = season; *the king set up a super farm during the spring season*

四季   shiki = the four seasons; from shi = four + kisetsu = season

関節   kansetsu = joint (e.g., knee); *the cancer doctor set up a super clinic for joint problems*

節約する   setsuyaku suru = to economize; *I settled Sue and her yak in a small cottage in order to economize*

お節料理   osechi ryouri = food served during the New Year's holidays; *the old settlers ate cheese as their New Year's food*

節   fushi = knot (wood), joint (body), melody; *the food the sheep were eating caused their joints to swell*

from the Practice Sentences

張り   hari = tension, tone, will-power, pride; *the hairy archer increased the tension in the bow*

日焼け止め   hiyakedome = sunscreen; from hi = sun + yaku = to grill or toast + domeru = tomeru = to stop

自ら   mizukara = for one's self, personally; *the mizu (water) that I brought to the karaoke party was for myself*

Practice Sentences

1. 私はいつもパンにジャムを塗って食べます。

Watashi wa itsumo pan ni jamu wo nutte tabemasu.
I always paint jam to bread and eat. (i.e., I put jam on my bread)

2. 冬が近づいてきたので、暖かい衣類を買う時期だ。

Fuyu ga chikazuite kita node, atatakai irui wo kau jiki da.
Since winter is approaching and coming, it's the season to buy warm clothing.

3. 年をとっても、オシャレな服装をしていたい。

Toshi wo tottemo, oshare na fukusou wo shite itai.
Even though I take years (i.e., I get old), I am wanting to do a stylish dress style.

4. この弓は張りが強いです。

Kono yumi wa hari ga tsuyoi desu.
The tension in this bow is strong.

5. この矢印にそって進んでください。

Kono yajirushi ni sotte susunde kudasai.
In accordance with these arrows, please advance. (i.e., follow the arrows)

6. 花火の日には浴衣を着ている
   女性が多い。

Hanabi no hi ni wa yukata wo kite iru
josei ga ooi.
On fireworks' days yukata-wearing
women are numerous.

7. 冬は一番寒い季節です。

Fuyu wa ichiban samui kisetsu desu.
Winter is the coldest season.

8. 日焼け止めを塗りましたか。

Hiyakedome wo nurimashita ka.
Did you put sunscreen on?

9. その金が全て衣服に使われて
   しまった。

Sono kane ga subete ifuku ni tsukawarete
shimatta.
All of that money was completely used
on clothing.

10. これは電気を作る装置だ。

Kore wa denki wo tsukuru souchi da.
This is a device that produces electricity.

11. 矢のない弓は役に立たない。

Ya no nai yumi wa yaku ni tatanai.
A bow without arrows is useless.

12. 彼はなんと印象的な人なので
    しょう。

Kare wa nanto inshouteki na hito na no
deshou.
What an impressive person he is,
probably.

13. この季節に一人でいるのは嫌
    いだ。

Kono kisetsu ni hitori de iru no wa kirai
da.
I hate being alone at this season.

14. 天井を青く塗った。

Tenjou wo aoku nutta.
I painted the ceiling bluely (i.e., blue).

15. どういう衣装を子供たちに買
    ったのですか。

Dou iu ishou wo kodomotachi ni katta no
desu ka.
What sort of costumes did you buy for
the children?

16. 7歳の時、すでに自ら弓と矢
    を作った。

Nanasai no toki, sude ni mizukara yumi
to ya wo tsukutta.
At age 7, he already made a bow and
arrow by himself.

17. 母が私にお節料理の作り方を
    教えてくれた。

Haha ga watashi ni osechi ryouri no
tsukurikata wo oshiete kureta.
My mother taught me how to make
osechi cuisine (for New Year's).

18. 分からない単語に印をつけな
    さい。

Wakaranai tango ni shirushi wo
tsukenasai.
Attach marks to the words that you don't
understand.

19. 日本には四季があります。

Nihon ni wa shiki ga arimasu.
There are four seasons in Japan.

20. 給料が多くないので、毎日節約している。

Kyuuryou ga ookunai node, mainichi setsuyaku shite iru.
Since the salary isn't numerous, every day I'm economizing.

Chapter 56

New Kanji in this Chapter

# 1049 修 (3)	# 1050 般 (2)	# 1051 壁 (3)	# 1052 編 (3)
# 1053 評 (1)	# 1054 判 (2)	# 1055 猿 (3)	# 1056 芸 (1)

Vocabulary List with Mnemonics

from the Kanji Catalogue

修める	osameru = to learn or master; *Osama's men ruined his kitchen when they tried to master cooking*
修理	shuuri = repairs; *that shoe repair shop does all of the repairs on my shoes*
修行	shugyou = training, apprenticeship; *the shoe salesmen were fed gyoza during their training*
一般に	ippan ni = commonly, generally, usually; *my Easter pants are usually colorful*
一般的に	ippanteki ni = commonly, generally, usually; from ippan = usually + teki = related to
般若	han'nya = prajna, wisdom, insight into the nature of reality (Buddhism); *the handsome yak driver had achieved prajna*
壁	kabe = wall; *he threw the bottle of cabernet sauvignon against the wall*
壁画	hekiga = mural painting; *the heavy king sat in the garden and watched as the mural was painted*
編む	amu = to knit; *she knitted an amulet*
編集	henshuu = editing; *Henry VIII wore good shoes while editing his proclamations*
編集者	henshuusha = editor; from henshuu = editing + sha = person
短編	tanpen = short story or film; *the tank driver penned a short story about the war*
評判	hyouban = reputation, popularity, rumor; *"Hi-yo Silver" was banned, and this affected the Lone Ranger's reputation and popularity*
評価	hyouka = assessment, evaluation; *high yogurt prices caused a change in our evaluation of the market*
評価する	hyouka suru = to value, to appreciate; from hyouka = evaluation

Kanji Pronunciations

# 1049 – osa, shuu, shu	# 1050 – han, pan	# 1051 – kabe, heki, peki	# 1052 – hen, pen, a
# 1053 – hyou	# 1054 – han, ban	# 1055 – saru, zaru, en	# 1056 – gei

不評	fu'hyou = bad reputation or review, unpopularity; from fu = negation + hyouban = reputation
定評	teihyou = reputation, notoriety; from tei = to decide or fix, e.g., yotei = plan; + hyouban = reputation
判断	handan = judgment, decision; *to hand the dancer a victory was the judge's judgment and decision*
猿	saru = monkey; *Saruman kept a monkey as a pet*
日本猿	nihonzaru = Japanese macaque; from nihon = Japan + zaru = saru = monkey
類人猿	ruijin'en = ape; *Luigi's nephew enjoyed Mario's ape*
芸	gei = art or craft, animal trick; *arts, crafts and tricks were all a game to him*
芸術	geijutsu = art; *she gazes at the bay window that juts out from the house and declares it a kind of art*
芸術館	geijutsukan = art museum; from geijutsu = art + kan = large building, e.g., ryokan = Japanese inn
芸術家	geijutsuka = artist; from geijutsu = art + ka = person
芸者	geisha = geisha; from gei = art + sha = person

from the Practice Sentences

画家	gaka = painter; from ga = drawing or painting, e.g., manga = comics; + ka = person
一部	ichibu = a part or portion; from ichi = one + bu = part, e.g., zenbu = all
古代人	kodaijin = people from ancient times; from ko = old; *Corinth is an old city*; + dai = era, e.g., jidai = era; + jin = people
知能	chinou = intelligence, intellect; from chi = to know, e.g., chijin = acquaintance; + nouryoku = ability
絵画	kaiga = painting; *the Kaiser gallantly gave one of his paintings to a lady*
評論	hyouron = criticism, review; from hyouka = assessment + kouron = argument
外見	gaiken = appearance; from gai = outside, e.g., gaijin = foreigner; + ken = to look, e.g., haiken suru = to look humbly
職員	shokuin = staff, personnel; from shokugyou = occupation + in = group member
仕込む	shikomu = to train, to stock merchandise; *she communicates with people when she trains them*
公開	koukai = opening, or making available to the public; from kou = public, e.g., kouen = public park; + kai = open, e.g., kaihatsu = development
一般に公開	ippan ni koukai = open to the general public; from ippan ni = generally, usually + koukai = opening to the public

判明する	hanmei suru = to prove to be, to become clear; from handan = judgment + mei = bright or clear, e.g., setsumei = explanation

from News in Slow Japanese

平成	heisei = Heisei era beginning in 1989; from heiwa = peace, tranquility + sei = completion, e.g., seikou = success
大がかり	oogakari = large scale; *Oprah and the gambler carried debt on a large scale*
ふき直す	fukinaosu = to repair a roof; from fuku = to thatch a roof; *I'll give you some food and Kool-Aid if you thatch my roof*; + naosu = to repair
再開日	saikaibi = reopening day; from saikai suru = to reopen + bi = hi = day
初日	shonichi = first or opening day; from sho = to begin, e.g., saisho = the beginning; + nichi = day
観光地	kankouchi = tourist sites; from kankou = sightseeing + chi = ground, e.g., chikatetsu = subway
二本編	nihon hen = Japanese edition; from nihon = Japan + henshuu = editing
選定	sentei = selection; from sen = to choose, e.g., senkyou = election; + tei = to decide or fix, e.g., yotei = plan
見学	kengaku = inspection, field trip; from ken = to look, e.g., haiken suru = to look humbly; + gaku = learning, e.g., gakusei = student

Practice Sentences

1. その画家はパリへ修行に行った。
Sono gaka wa pari e shugyou ni itta.
The painter went to Paris for the purpose of training.

2. 韓国料理は一般的に辛い。
Kankoku ryouri wa ippanteki ni karai.
Korean food is usually spicy.

3. この壁画からは古代人の生活の一部を見ることができる。
Kono hekiga kara wa kodaijin no seikatsu no ichibu wo miru koto ga dekiru.
From the mural, we can see a part of the life of ancient people.

4. 家内がこのセーターを編んでくれたんです。
Kanai ga kono seetaa wo ande kuretan desu.
My wife knitted this sweater for me.

5. あのご兄弟は子供のときから頭が良くて評判でした。
Ano gokyoudai wa kodomo no toki kara atama ga yokute hyouban deshita.
As for those honorable brothers over there, since the child's time, heads were good (i.e., they were intelligent) and it was popularity.

6. 類人猿は知能が高い。
Ruijin'en wa chinou ga takai.
Apes have high intelligence.

7. この絵画は芸術作品です。

Kono kaiga wa geijutsu sakuhin desu.
This painting is a work of art.

8. 彼はすべての科目において良い結果を修めた。

Kare wa subete no kamoku ni oite yoi kekka wo osameta.
He mastered a good result in all subjects.
(ni oite = in, at, regarding)

9. 一般に男子は女子よりも足が速い。

Ippan ni danshi wa joshi yori mo ashi ga hayai.
Usually, boys, compared to girls, have fast legs. (i.e., they can run faster)

10. 壁の穴をふさいだ。

Kabe no ana wo fusaida.
I blocked the hole in the wall.

11. 編集者がそのパーティーに出席していた。

Henshuusha ga sono paatii ni shusseki shite ita.
The editor was attending that party.

12. 彼の評論は高く評価された。

Kare no hyouron wa takaku hyouka sareta.
His criticism was highly appreciated.

13. 人は中身より外見で判断されやすい。

Hito wa nakami yori gaiken de handan sare yasui.
People, compared to substance (i.e., their inner qualities), are judged easily by appearance.

14. 動物園から猿が逃げ出し、職員が追いかけて捕まえた。

Doubutsuen kara saru ga nigedashi, shokuin ga oikakete tsukamaeta.
From the zoo, a monkey ran away and put out, and the personnel chased and caught it.

15. その犬に芸を仕込んだ。

Sono inu ni gei wo shikonda.
I trained that dog to do tricks.

16. 家を修理しています。

Ie wo shuuri shite imasu.
I am repairing the house.

17. このプールは一般に公開されている。

Kono puuru wa ippan ni koukai sarete iru.
This pool is usually being opened (i.e., open) to the public.

18. 絵を壁に掛けた。

E wo kabe ni kaketa.
I hung the picture on the wall.

19. 短編を読んでいる。

Tanpen wo yonde iru.
I'm reading a short story.

20. 国会は多分この不評の法律を改正するだろう。

Kokkai wa tabun kono fu'hyou no houritsu wo kaisei suru darou.
Probably the Diet will amend this unpopular law, probably.

21. 彼が泥棒だと言うことが判明した。

Kare ga dorobou da to iu koto ga hanmei shita.
It was proved that he is a thief.

22. 猿も木から落ちる。

Saru mo ki kara ochiru.
Even monkeys fall from trees.

23. 彼女は若い芸術家と恋に落ちた。

Kanojo wa wakai geijutsuka to koi ni ochita.
She fell in love with a young artist.

Supplemental Reading Practice

After completing Chapter 56 of this book, you should be able to read Lesson 009, "Himeji Castle Reopens," in *News in Slow Japanese*.

Chapter 57

New Kanji in this Chapter

# 1057 虎 (1)	# 1058 劇 (1)	# 1059 郷 (3)	# 1060 里 (3)
# 1061 量 (2)	# 1062 幹 (2)	# 1063 央 (1)	# 1064 請 (2)

Vocabulary List with Mnemonics

from the Kanji Catalogue

虎   tora = tiger; *Tony Blair ran away from the tiger*

劇   geki = a play; *I saw the guests kissing during the play*

劇場   gekijou = a theater; from geki = play + jou = place, e.g., koujou = factory

歌劇   kageki = opera; from kashu = singer + geki = play

里   sato = hometown, village; *there is a satellite tower in the village*

郷里   kyouri = hometown; *is Kyouto really your hometown?*

故郷   kokyou = hometown (or furusato); *people in my hometown add Coke to their yogurt*; also pronounced furusato, which is often spelled ふるさと; *it seemed foolish to ruin the satellite tower in my hometown*

水郷   suigou = riverside or lakeside location; from sui = water, e.g. suiei = swimming; + gou = village; *there are goats in the village*

人里   hitozato = human habitation; from hito = people + zato = sato = village

量   ryou = quantity; *Pope Leo has a quantity of carnations*

大量   tairyou = large amount; from tai = big + ryou = quantity

量る   hakaru = to weigh; *the hackathon was ruined when someone decided to weigh all of the hackers*; cf. 計る hakaru = to measure

幹   miki = tree trunk; *Mickey Mouse can climb tree trunks*

幹部   kanbu = an executive; *that executive drinks only Canadian booze*

新幹線   shinkansen = bullet train; from shin = new, e.g., shinbun = newspaper; + kan = trunk or main; *Canada is our main export market*; + sen = line

中央   chuu'ou = center, middle; from chuu = middle + ou = middle; *we are sailing in the middle of the ocean*

Kanji Pronunciations

# 1057 – tora	# 1058 – geki	# 1059 – sato, kyou, gou	# 1060 – sato, zato, ri
# 1061 – ryou, haka	# 1062 – miki, kan	# 1063 – ou	# 1064 – sei, ko

請求	seikyuu = demand, request; *there is a <u>demand</u> for a <u>safe</u> <u>cure</u> for cancer*
申請する	shinsei suru = to apply for or request; *the <u>Shinto</u> <u>sailor</u> <u>requested</u> shore leave*
請う	kou = to beg or ask; *he <u>asked</u> for a <u>coat</u>*
請い求める	koimotomeru = to beg or request; from kou = to ask + motomeru = to ask, request or buy

from the Practice Sentences

便り	tayori = news, letter; *the <u>tall</u> <u>Yorkshire</u> man is <u>reading</u> his <u>letters</u>*
里心	satogokoro = homesickness, nostalgia (used with tsuku, e.g., satogokoro ga tsuku = to get homesick); from sato = hometown + gokoro = kokoro = heart
音量	onryou = sound volume; from ongaku = music + ryou = quantity
請求書	seikyuusho = invoice; from seikyuu = demand + sho = document, e.g., jisho = dictionary
広場	hiroba = plaza, town square; from hiroi = spacious + basho = place
主人公	shujinkou = hero, heroine, protagonist; from shu = main, e.g., shujin = master; + jin = person + kou = public
協議	kyougi = discussion, conference; *we had a <u>discussion</u> about <u>Kyou</u>to <u>geese</u>*
合計	goukei = sum, total; from gou = to match or harmonize; *our <u>goats</u> <u>match</u> each other*; + kei = to measure or count, e.g., tokei = clock

from News in Slow Japanese

復活	fukkatsu = revival, restoration; from fuku = to repeat, e.g., fukushuu = review; + katsu = life, e.g., seikatsu = life, livelihood
いっぱいで	ippai de = at the end of (a year, etc.); from ippai = full
閉園	heien = closing (park, etc.); from hei = to close; *we <u>close</u> the gate to people who want to harvest <u>hay</u>*; + en = park, e.g., kouen = park
繰り広げる	kurihirogeru = to unfold, to open; from kurikaesu = to repeat + hirogeru = to unfold
軍団	gundan = army corps; from gunjin = soldier + dantai = group
高齢化	koureika = aging; from kourei = elderly + ka = "ization," e.g., kindai = modern times, kindaika = modernization
後継者	koukeisha = a successor; *we will consume <u>cola</u> and <u>cake</u>, and then the <u>Shah</u> will name his <u>successor</u>*
一時	ichiji = for a while; from ichi = one + jikan = time (this can also be read as ichiji = one o'clock); cf. ひととき hitotoki = for a moment, for a while
通す	toosu = to pass something through; this is the transitive form of the verb 通る tooru = to pass through

消費	shouhi = consumption, expenditure; *the shoulder healed, thanks to my expenditures for physical therapy*
消費量	shouhiryou = amount of consumption; from shouhi = consumption + ryou = quantity
主食	shushoku = main food; from shu = main, e.g., shujin = master; + shokuji = meal
バングラディシュ	banguradishu = Bangladesh
ラオス	raosu = Laos
カンボジア	kanbojia = Cambodia
ベトナム	betonamu = Vietnam
意外	igai = unexpected; *the eating guide contained some unexpected advice*
キューバ	kyuuba = Cuba
中南米	chuunanbei = Central and South America; from chuu = middle + nanbei = South America
時速	jisoku = speed; from jikan = time + soku = fast, e.g., sokutatsu = express mail
有人	yuujin = manned, occupied, piloted; from yuu = to exist; *we exist in the Yukon*; + jin = person; cf. 友人 yuujin = friend
走行	soukou = running a wheeled vehicle; from sou = to run; *people used to run in the Soviet Union*; + kou = to go, e.g., ryokou = trip
鉄道	tetsudou = railroad, railway; from tetsu = iron + dou = way
最速	saisoku = fastest; from sai = the most, e.g., saikou = the best; + soku = fast; e.g., sokutatsu = express mail
リニア	rini'a = linear
名古屋	nagoya = Nagoya, a large city in Japan
開業	kaigyou = opening a business; from kai = to open; *we open the gate so that people can fly their kites*; + gyou = hard work, skills; e.g., kougyou = industry

Practice Sentences

1. 虎は肉食動物です。

Tora wa nikushoku doubutsu desu.
A tiger is a carniverous animal.

2. 劇場の裏に駐車場がある。

Gekijou no ura ni chuushajou ga aru.
There is a parking lot behind the theater.

3. この子犬は里心がついて泣いているんだ。

Kono koinu wa satogokoro ga tsuite naite irun da.
Since this puppy is homesick, it's crying.

4. どんなに忙しくても月に少なくとも一度は故郷の父母に便りをします。

Donna ni isogashikutemo tsuki ni sukunakutomo ichido wa furusato no chichihaha ni tayori wo shimasu.
No matter how busy I am, I write a letter to my hometown parents at least once a month. (this can also be read as *kokyou no chichihaha*)

5. 音量を下げてください。

Onryou wo sagete kudasai.
Please lower the sound volume.

6. 新幹線で行けば、あっという間に着いちゃうよ。

Shinkansen de ikeba, atto iu ma ni tsuichau yo.
If you go by bullet train, you will arrive completely in no time.

7. 公園の中央に池がある。

Kouen no chuu'ou ni ike ga aru.
There's a pond in the middle of the park.

8. これは電気代の請求書です。

Kore wa denkidai no seikyuusho desu.
This is the electricity cost's demand sheet (i.e., the electricity invoice).

9. 虎は大きな猫と呼ぶことができる。

Tora wa ookina neko to yobu koto ga dekiru.
One can call a tiger a big cat.

10. この歌劇は３幕からなる。

Kono kageki wa sanmaku kara naru.
This opera develops from (i.e., contains) three acts.

11. 私の郷里の町は海の隣です。

Watashi no kyouri no machi wa umi no tonari desu.
My hometown is next to the ocean.

12. 毎日何回も自分の体重を量るというダイエット方法があるそうです。

Mainichi nankaimo jibun no taijuu wo hakaru to iu daietto houhou ga aru sou desu.
Every day, many times, to weigh oneself's body weight, quote to say diet method exists reportedly. (i.e., reportedly there is a dieting method in which one weighs himself many times every day)

13. 彼らは木の幹を切り倒してボートを作った。

Karera wa ki no miki wo kiritaoshite booto wo tsukutta.
They cut down a tree trunk and made a boat.

14. 井戸はこの広場の中央にあります。

Ido wa kono hiroba no chuu'ou ni arimasu.
A well is in the center of this plaza.

15. ビザを申請した。

Biza wo shinsei shita.
I applied for a visa.

16. 動物園から一頭の虎が逃げ出した。

Doubutsuen kara ittou no tora ga nigedashita.
A tiger escaped from the zoo.

17. その劇は主人公の死で終わった。

Sono geki wa shujinkou no shi de owatta.
That play ended with the death of the main character.

18. どこへ行こうとも故郷のことは忘れない。

Doko e ikou tomo kokyou no koto wa wasurenai.
Wherever I go, I don't forget my hometown. (this could also be read *furusato* no koto)

19. 彼女は人里離れたところに住んでいます。

Kanojo wa hitozato hanareta tokoro ni sunde imasu.
She lives in a place that is separated from human habitation.

20. 日本は米国と大量な貿易をしている。

Nihon wa beikoku to tairyou na bou'eki wo shite iru.
Japan is doing a large amount of trade with the United States.

21. 彼はその問題について幹部の何人かと協議した。

Kare wa sono mondai ni tsuite kanbu no nan'ninka to kyougi shita.
He consulted with some of the executives about the problem.

22. 中央線で行った方が早いでしょう。

Chuu-ou sen de itta hou ga hayai deshou.
It would probably be quicker to go by the Chuo Line.

23. 請求書を合計してください。

Seikyuusho wo goukei shite kudasai.
Please total the invoice.

Supplemental Reading Practice

After completing Chapter 57 of this book, you should be able to read Lesson 010, "The Monkey School is Back," Lesson 011, "Rice Consumption," and Lesson 012, "603 kph: World's Fastest Train," in *News in Slow Japanese*.

Chapter 58

New Kanji in this Chapter

# 1065 老 (3)	# 1066 祉 (1)	# 1067 施 (3)	# 1068 設 (3)
# 1069 療 (1)	# 1070 与 (2)	# 1071 州 (2)	# 1072 孫 (2)

Vocabulary List with Mnemonics

from the Kanji Catalogue

老いる — o'iru = to grow old; *when he grew old, he kept old eagles in his room*

老人 — roujin = elderly person; *an elderly person may become a low jin (short person)*

老ける — fukeru = to age or lose one's youthful appearance; *the foolish Kennedy ruined his health and began to age*

福祉 — fukushi = welfare; *in Fukuoka, clean sheets are provided by the welfare department*

施す — hodokosu = to donate, perform, give time; *I will hold the door while my co-supervisor donates food to the beggars outside*

施設 — shisetsu = facility, institution, equipment; *the Shiites set up a super institution*

実施する — jisshi suru = to carry out or effect; *using a Jeep, we took the sheep to the pasture and carried out our orders*

お布施 — ofuse = honorable alms or offerings (e.g., given to monks); from o = honorable + fuse = offering; *the food we sent was an offering*

設ける — moukeru = to set up, establish; *we fed mostly ketchup to the rooster while we set up the chicken coop*

設備 — setsubi = equipment, facility; *I will setsumei suru (explain) why there are bees living in the facility*

設計 — sekkei = design or plan; *they are selling cakes with innovative designs*

設定する — settei suru = to set up; *they set the table and then set up the playhouse*

治療 — chiryou = medical treatment; *the cheese that Pope Leo blessed was effective as a medical treatment*

与える — ataeru = to give, award, cause; *if I attain erudition, I will give my goods to the poor*

Kanji Pronunciations

# 1065 – o, rou, fu	# 1066 – shi	# 1067 – se, hodoko, shi	# 1068 – se, mou, setsu
# 1069 – ryou	# 1070 – ata, yo	# 1071 – su, shuu	# 1072 – son, mago

三角州	sankakusu = a delta; from san = three + kaku = corner + su = sandbank; *Superman flew over the sandbank*
九州	kyuushuu = Kyushu (island)
賞与	shouyo = reward, bonus; *I will show the yodeler his bonus*
孫	mago = grandchild; *my grandchild scored a magnificent goal*
孫娘	magomusume = granddaughter; from mago = grandchild + musume = daughter
子孫	shison = descendant; *that Shiite who works for Sony is concerned about the welfare of his descendants*

from the Practice Sentences

老齢	rourei = advanced age; from roujin = elderly person + nenrei = age
社会	shakai = society; *the Shah and the Kaiser worked to improve society*
重要性	juuyousei = importance; from juuyou = important + sei = innate nature; *that sailor's innate nature makes him wander*
内地	naichi = inland area, mainland area of Japan, i.e., Honshu, Shikoku and Kyushu, as viewed from Hokkaido and Okinawa; from nai = inside + chi = ground or soil, e.g., chikatetsu = subway
強調する	kyouchou suru = to emphasize; *in Kyouto, he chose to emphasize his love of Japanese food*
宿泊	shukuhaku = lodging; from shuku = inn; *I wore my shoes from Kuwait to the inn*; + haku = to stay overnight, e.g., nihaku = a two-night stay
合衆国	gasshuukoku = a federal state; *the gambler took off his shoes and drank a Coke when he arrived in the federal state*
半紙	hanshi = common Japanese writing paper; literally, "half a paper"; *Hansel gave the Shiite some writing paper*
鉄橋	tekkyou = iron bridge, railroad bridge; from tetsu = iron + kyou = bridge; *a bridge was built in Kyouto*
建設	kensetsu = construction; from kenchiku = architecture + setsu = to set up, e.g., shisetsu = facility

from News in Slow Japanese

医療	iryou = medical treatment; from isha = doctor + chiryou = medical treatment
助手	joshu = assistant; *Joan of Arc's shoes were polished by her assistant*
出勤する	shukkin suru = to go to work; *we go to work shucking corn*
天使	tenshi = angel; from ten = sky, e.g., tenki = weather; + shi = servant, e.g., taishi = ambassador

Practice Sentences

1. 老齢で弱っている。

Rourei de yowatte iru.
He is weak from advanced age.

2. 彼がその車を設計した。

Kare ga sono kuruma wo sekkei shita.
He designed that car.

3. 彼女は社会福祉に携わっている。

Kanojo wa shakai fukushi ni tazusawatte iru.
She is engaged in social welfare.

4. この計画を実施するつもりです。

Kono keikaku wo jisshi surutsumori desu.
I intend to carry out this plan.

5. 彼は治療を断られた。

Kare wa chiryou wo kotowarareta.
He was refused medical treatment.

6. それを彼に与えなさい。

Sore wo kare ni ataenasai.
Give that to him.

7. 孫が生まれたという知らせを聞いた。

Mago ga umareta to iu shirase wo kiita.
I heard the news that my grandchild was born.

8. 本州は、北海道からは「内地」と呼ばれることもある。

Honshuu wa, hokkaidou kara wa "naichi" to yobareru koto mo aru.
As for Honshu, as for from Hokkaido, "inland area" it is sometimes also called.

9. 彼は老けて見える。

Kare wa fukete mieru.
He looks old.

10. 福祉の重要性はいくら強調してもしすぎるということはない。

Fukushi no juuyousei wa ikura kyouchou shite mo shisugiru to iu koto wa nai.
As for welfare's importance, how much one emphasizes it even, to overdo to-say thing doesn't exist (i.e., you can't over-emphasize it).

11. 宿泊施設を探しています。

Shukuhaku shisetsu wo sagashite imasu.
I am looking for a lodging facility.

12. 彼女は彼の足の骨折を治療した。

Kanojo wa kare no ashi no kossetsu wo chiryou shita.
She treated the fracture of his leg.

13. 時々お金を息子に与える。

Tokidoki okane wo musuko ni ataeru.
Sometimes I give money to my son.

14. 子孫にきれいな緑の地球を残したい。

Shison ni kirei na midori no chikyuu wo nokoshitai.
I want to leave a clean green Earth to my descendants.

15. アメリカ合衆国には 50 の州がある。

Amerika gasshuukoku ni wa gojuu no shuu ga aru.
In the America federal state there are 50 states.

16. 彼女は自分が老いているのを感じた。

Kanojo wa jibun ga oite iru no wo kanjita.
She felt herself growing old.

17. 人々の福祉に努力するのを自分の努めだと彼は見直した。

Hitobito no fukushi ni douryoku suru no wo jibun no tsutome da to kare wa minaoshita.
To the welfare of the people, to do effort is his effort, he realized. (i.e., he came to see that it was his duty to work for the people's welfare)

18. お布施を渡す時は、半紙に包んでもいいです。

Ofuse wo watasu toki wa, hanshi ni tsutsunde mo ii desu.
As for the time when you hand over an offering, it's all right to wrap it in writing paper.

19. その川には鉄橋がすでに建設中だ。

Sono kawa ni wa tekkyou ga sude ni kensetsuchuu da.
At that river an iron bridge is already under construction.

20. 病院で治療を受けている。

Byouin de chiryou wo ukete iru.
I'm receiving medical treatment at a hospital.

21. もうすぐ賞与がでるわね。

Mou sugu shouyo ga deru wa ne.
Pretty soon bonuses will come out, huh.

22. 彼は孫と一緒の時が一番楽しそうだ。

Kare wa mago to issho no toki ga ichiban tanoshisou da.
The time when he is together with his grandchild seems to be the most enjoyable.

23. 桜島という火山が九州の南にあります。

Sakurajima to iu kazan ga kyuushuu no minami ni arimasu.
The Sakurajima-called volcano exists in southern Kyushu.

24. この病院には新しい設備が備わっている。

Kono byouin ni wa atarashii setsubi ga sonawatte iru.
This hospital is equipped with new equipment.

Supplemental Reading Practice

After completing Chapter 58 of this book, you should be able to read Lesson 013, "The Teacup Poodle that Works at a Nursing Home," in *News in Slow Japanese*.

Chapter 59

New Kanji in this Chapter

# 1073 遭 (2)	# 1074 昏 (1)	# 1075 労 (1)	# 1076 叶 (1)
# 1077 王 (1)	# 1078 妃 (1)	# 1079 宮 (3)	# 1080 殿 (2)

Vocabulary List with Mnemonics

from the Kanji Catalogue

遭難 — sounan = accident, disaster, being stranded; *our sober nanny prevented a disaster*

遭う — au = to be involved (in an accident, etc.), to get caught in, encounter, meet; *the owl was involved in an accident*

昏睡 — konsui = coma, stupor; *the woman from the Congo drank the sweet potion and fell into a coma*

苦労 — kurou = hardship; *they are cool robots, but they are taking away jobs and causing hardship*

叶う — kanau = to come true or be fulfilled (referring to a wish or dream); *California is now a dream come true for many immigrants*

叶える — kanaeru = to grant or answer a request, to meet requirements; the transitive form of kanau = to be fulfilled

王様 — ousama = king; from ou = king; *the king is old*; + sama = very honorable

女王 — jo'ou = queen; from josei = female + ou = king

王子 — ouji = prince; from ou = king + ji = child; *the child rides in a Jeep*

王妃 — ouhi = queen; from ou = king + hi = queen; *the queen is a healer*

神宮 — jinguu = high-status (imperial) Shinto shrine; *the genius hired Goofy to guard the high-status shrine*

宮殿 — kyuuden = palace; *the cute dentist lives in a palace*

子宮 — shikyuu = uterus; *we took our sheep to Cuba to have surgery done on its uterus*

お宮参り — omiyamairi = shrine visit; from o = honorable + miya = palace or shrine; *she will meet the Yankees in a palace*; + mairu = to humbly go

殿様 — tonosama = daimyo, feudal lord; from tono = lord; *that lord is totally normal*; + sama = very honorable

Kanji Pronunciations

# 1073 – sou, a	# 1074 – kon	# 1075 – rou	# 1076 – kana
# 1077 – ou	# 1078 – hi	# 1079 – guu, kyuu, miya	# 1080 – den, tono

from the Practice Sentences

見つけ出す	mitsukedasu = to find out, discover, locate; from mitsukeru = to find + dasu = to put out
権力	kenryoku = authority; from ken'i = authority + ryoku = force
夕立	yuudachi = evening rain shower; *the youth ate damp cheese during an evening rain shower*
労働	roudou = manual labor; *when we use robots to make doors, we save a lot of manual labor*
重労働	juuroudou = heavy labor; from juu = heavy, e.g., taijuu = a person's weight; + roudou = manual labor
労働者	roudousha = laborer; from roudou = manual labor + sha = person
発育	hatsu'iku = development or growth (physical); *the hat Superman wore had ear cooties, which stunted his growth*
賃上げ	chin'age = wage increase; from chin = wages, fee, e.g., yachin = rent; + ageru = to raise
国王	koku'ou = king; from koku = country + ou = king
王位	ou'i = throne, crown; from ou = king + i = rank, e.g., dai ichi i = first place
王宮	oukyuu = royal palace; from ou = king + kyuuden = palace

from News in Slow Japanese

出来事	dekigoto = occurrence, event; from dekiru = to be able + goto = koto = thing
関わらず	kakawarazu = regardless, in spite of, nevertheless; *the cacao beans that Washington fed his rabbits in Zurich were not good for them; nevertheless I didn't interfere*
まだまだ	madamada = still more to come, not yet; from mada = still, not yet

Practice Sentences

1. 彼女は深い昏睡状態にいた。

Kanojo wa fukai konsui joutai ni ita.
She was in a deep comatose condition.

2. 彼らはその場所を見つけ出すのに苦労した。

Karera wa sono basho wo mitsukedasu noni kurou shita.
As for them, to find that place was hard. (noni = in order to do, and other meanings)

3. 夢を叶えるために、努力しよう。

Yume wo kanaeru tame ni, doryoku shiyou.
For the purpose of the dreams to be granted (i.e., to come true), let's do effort.

4. 王と王妃は権力を乱用した。

Ou to ouhi wa kenryoku wo ran'you shita.
The king and queen abused their authority.

5. それからあなたは二ヶ月間昏睡状態にいた。

Sore kara anata wa nikagetsukan konsui joutai ni ita.
And then, for two months' duration, you were in a comatose condition.

6. 彼は宮殿のような家に住んでいる。

Kare wa kyuuden no you na ie ni sunde iru.
He lives in a house like a palace.

7. 夕立に遭いました。

Yuudachi ni aimashita.
I encountered an evening shower.

8. 彼は重労働に慣れている。

Kare wa juuroudou ni narete iru.
He is used to heavy labor.

9. 望みは叶いましたか。

Nozomi wa kanaimashita ka.
Did the wish come true?

10. 王妃は王の側に立っていた。

Ouhi wa ou no soba ni tatte ita.
The queen was standing beside the king.

11. 赤ちゃんは子宮内で発育します。

Akachan wa shikyuunai de hatsu'iku shimasu.
Babies develop inside the uterus.

12. 友人は残念ながら交通事故に遭って、昏睡状態になってしまった。

Yuujin wa zannen nagara koutsuu jiko ni atte, konsui joutai ni natte shimatta.
Unfortunately my friend got involved in a traffic accident and completely developed a comatose state.

13. 労働者達は賃上げを要求した。

Roudoushatachi wa chin'age wo youkyuu shita.
The workers demanded a pay raise.

14. 世の中にはどんなに願っても叶わないことがあります。

Yo no naka ni wa donna ni negatte mo kanawanai koto ga arimasu.
As for in the world, whatever I pray for even, there are unfulfilled things (i.e., some wishes cannot be granted).

15. 宮殿には国王と王妃が住んでいる。

Kyuuden ni wa kokuou to ouhi ga sunde iru.
The king and queen live in a palace.

16. 彼らは山で遭難した。

Karera wa yama de sounan shita.
They were stranded in the mountains.

17. 社長はたくさんの苦労を乗り
越えて、今の会社を作った。

Shachou wa takusan no kurou wo
norikoete ima no kaisha wo tsukutta.
As for the president, he overcame a lot of
hardships and created the present-day
company.

18. 誰が王位を継ぐのですか。

Dare ga ou'i wo tsugu no desu ka.
Who will succeed to the throne?

19. バッキンガム宮殿は、今でも
実際に使われている数少ない
王宮の一つです。

Bakkingamu kyuuden wa, ima demo
jissai ni tsukawarete iru kazu sukunai
oukyuu no hitotsu desu.
Buckingham Palace, even now truly
being used, it is one of the numbers-few
royal palaces. (i.e., it is one of the few
royal palaces being used currently)

Supplemental Reading Practice

After completing Chapter 59 of this book, you should be able to read Lesson 014,
"Graduating College Along with Two Grandkids at 80," in *News in Slow Japanese*.

Chapter 60

New Kanji in this Chapter

# 1081 崎 (1)	# 1082 批 (1)	# 1083 摘 (2)	# 1084 跳 (2)
# 1085 症 (1)	# 1086 版 (2)	# 1087 翻 (1)	# 1088 著 (3)

Vocabulary List with Mnemonics

from the Kanji Catalogue

川崎 — Kawasaki = a city in Japan; from kawa = river + saki = promontory

長崎 — Nagasaki = a city in Japan; from nagai = long + saki = promontory

批判 — hihan = criticism; *the hero was handsome, but he received a lot of criticism*

批評 — hihyou = review, remark, criticism; *the hero said "Hi-yo Silver," and this remark was mentioned in the reviews and criticisms that he received*

指摘 — shiteki = pointing out, identification; *the Shiite techie was responsible for the identification of the computer virus*

摘む — tsumu = to pick tea, cotton, etc.; *I will pick flowers and put them in the tsuitcase (suitcase) that I'm taking to the moon*

跳ねる — haneru = to jump or hop, to splash; *Hansel is an erudite guy who likes to jump*

跳ぶ — tobu = to jump or leap; *Tony Blair wears boots when he jumps;* cf. 飛ぶ tobu = to fly

跳び箱 — tobibako = a vaulting box; from tobu = to jump + bako = hako = box

症状 — shoujou = symptoms, condition of a patient; *I will show Joan of Arc my list of symptoms*

感染症 — kansenshou = infectious disease; from kansen = infection + shoujou = symptoms

版画 — hanga = woodblock print; *he keeps his woodblock print in an airplane hanger*

出版 — shuppan = publication; *this is a publication about shoes and pants*

翻訳 — hon'yaku = translation; *in Honduras, a yak herder earns money by doing translations*

著す — arawasu = to write or publish; *Yasser Arafat washed his suit and then sat down to write a book*

Kanji Pronunciations

# 1081 – saki	# 1082 – hi	# 1083 – teki, tsu	# 1084 – ha, to
# 1085 – shou	# 1086 – han, pan	# 1087 – hon	# 1088 – cho, arawa, ichijiru

著しい ichijirushii = remarkable, conspicuous; *at ichiji (1:00) he was rushing, which was remarkable and conspicuous*

著者 chosha = author; *he chose a lady with a shawl to be the author of his biography*

著名 chomei = famous; *Margaret Cho's maid became famous*

from the Practice Sentences

縄跳び nawatobi = skipping rope; from nawa = rope + tobu = to jump

恐怖 kyoufu = fear, dread, horror; *in Kyouto I met a fool who filled me with dread*

恐怖症 kyoufushou = morbid fear, phobia; from kyoufu = dread + shoujou = symptoms

好評 kouhyou = favorable review, good reception; from kou = to like, e.g., koubutsu = favorite food; + hyouban = reputation

狭心症 kyoushinshou = angina (pain due to narrowing of the heart arteries), heart attack; from kyou = narrow; *the apartments in Kyouto are narrow*; + shin = heart + shoujou = symptoms; cf. 心臓発作 shinzou hossa = heart attack

出版社 shuppansha = publisher; from shuppan = publication + kaisha = company

英作文 eisakubun = English composition; from eigo = English + sakubun = composition

跳び上がる tobiagaru = to jump up; from tobu = to jump + agaru = to rise

不眠症 fuminshou = insomnia; from fu = negation + suimin = sleep + shoujou = symptoms

低下する teika suru = to decrease; *if you use tasers on the cats, their numbers will decrease*

from News in Slow Japanese

英国 igirisu = England (usually pronounced eikoku, from eigo = English + koku = country); igirisu is usually spelled イギリス

大分 ooita = Oita, a city and prefecture on the island of Kyushu

高崎山 Takasakiyama = name of a zoo in Oita city

すっかり sukkari = thoroughly, completely; *Superman carries out his duties completely*

会見 kaiken = meeting, interview; from kaigi = meeting + haiken suru = to humbly see

王室 oushitsu = royal family; from ou = king + shitsu = room

Practice Sentences

1. 川崎にはたくさんの工場があります。

Kawasaki ni wa takusan no koujou ga arimasu.
There are a lot of factories in Kawasaki.

2. 私を批判し続けないでください。

Watashi wo hihan shi tsuzukenaide kudasai.
Please don't continue to criticize me.

3. 庭の花を摘んだ。

Niwa no hana wo tsunda.
I picked the garden's flower.

4. プールの横で縄跳びをしている女の子は花子ちゃんです。

Puuru no yoko de nawatobi wo shite iru onna no ko wa Hanako chan desu.
The girl beside the pool skipping rope is little Hanako.

5. 私は犬恐怖症だ。

Watashi wa inu kyoufushou da.
As for me, it's a morbid fear of dogs.

6. その本は 1689 年に出版された。

Sono hon wa sen roppyaku hachijuu kyuu nen ni shuppan sareta.
That book was published in 1689.

7. あなたは翻訳者ですか。

Anata wa hon'yaku sha desu ka.
Are you a translator?

8. 有名作家は又ベストセラーを著した。

Yuumei sakka wa mata besuto seraa wo arawashita.
The famous author wrote a best-seller again.

9. 長崎は美しい港町です。

Nagasaki wa utsukushii minatomachi desu.
Nagasaki is a beautiful port city.

10. 劇の批評はとても好評だった。

Geki no hihyou wa totemo kouhyou datta.
The play's reviews were very favorable reviews.

11. ご指摘有難うございます。

Goshiteki arigatou gozaimasu.
Thanks a lot for your honorable pointing-out (i.e., for your advice).

12. 池の魚が跳ねた。

Ike no sakana ga haneta.
The pond's fish jumped.

13. 僕は狭心症の発作が時々起こります。

Boku wa kyoushinshou no hossa ga tokidoki okorimasu.
As for me, attacks of angina (chest pain due to heart disease) sometimes occur.

14. 出版社へその本 1 冊注文してくれませんか。

Shuppansha e sono hon issatsu chumon shite kuremasen ka.
Won't you order a copy of that book from the publisher for me?

15. この本の翻訳ができるか自身がない。

Kono hon no hon'yaku ga dekiru ka jishin ga nai.
I am not confident that I will be able to translate this book.

16. この物語の著者は誰ですか。

Kono monogatari no chosha wa dare desu ka.
Who is the author of this story?

17. 私は長崎を案内するために彼らと一緒に行きました。

Watashi wa nagasaki wo annai suru tame ni karera to issho ni ikimashita.
I went with them in order to guide them around Nagasaki.

18. あなたにはこの人たちを批判する権利はない。

Anata ni wa kono hitotachi wo hihan suru kenri wa nai.
You have no right to criticize these people.

19. 先生は私の英作文の間違いをいくつか指摘した。

Sensei wa watashi no eisakubun no machigai wo ikutsuka shiteki shita.
The teacher pointed out several mistakes in my English composition.

20. 猫は驚いて跳び上がった。

Neko wa odoroite tobiagatta.
The cat was surprised and jumped up.

21. 私は不眠症で困っています。

Watashi wa fuminshou de komatte imasu.
I am being inconvenienced by insomnia.

22. 友達に版画を売っているいい店を教えてもらいました。

Tomodachi ni hanga wo utte iru ii mise wo oshiete moraimashita.
A friend told me about a good store that is selling woodblock prints.

23. このドイツ語を翻訳していただけませんか。

Kono doitsugo wo hon'yaku shite itadakemasen ka.
Can you translate this German for me?

24. 最近の子供たちの体力は著しく低下している。

Saikin no komodotachi no tairyoku wa ichijirushiku teika shite iru.
Recently, children's stamina is decreasing remarkably.

Supplemental Reading Practice

After completing Chapter 60 of this book, you should be able to read Lesson 015, "Japan's Charlotte," in *News in Slow Japanese*.

Chapter 61

New Kanji in this Chapter

# 1089 樹 (2)	# 1090 訓 (1)	# 1091 筆 (4)	# 1092 鉛 (2)
# 1093 児 (3)	# 1094 童 (1)	# 1095 奄 (1)	# 1096 底 (3)

Vocabulary List with Mnemonics

from the Kanji Catalogue

樹木	jumoku = trees; from ju = tree; *we get juice from orange trees*; + moku = wood, e.g., mokusei = made of wood
直樹	naoki = a man's given name
訓練	kunren = training; *the cunning rent collector came while the soldier was in training*
教訓	kyoukun = moral, teaching, lesson; *in Kyouto, my cunning teacher taught me a lesson*
筆	fude = writing brush; *the foolish dentist brushed his teeth with a writing brush*
毛筆	mouhitsu = writing or painting brush; *Moses hits you with a writing brush when you talk in class*
鉛筆	enpitsu = pencil; *after he got a new pencil, the engineer peeled the paint off and dropped it into his tsoup (soup)*
筆者	hissha = writer; *the writer lived in a hideous shack*
鉛	namari = lead (an element); *the narco named Mario uses lead bullets*
小児科	shounika = pediatrics; from shou = small, e.g., shougakkou = elementary school; + ni = child; *I kneel to speak to the child*; + kagaku = science
児童	jidou = child; *a child is sitting in a Jeep door*; cf. 自動 jidou = automatic
孤児	koji = orphan; from kodoku = solitude + jidou = child
鹿児島	Kagoshima = a city in Kyushu
童話	douwa = fairy tale; from jidou = child + wa = to speak, e.g., kaiwa = conversation
奄美大島	Amami Ooshima = an island between Kyushu and Okinawa; from Amamikyu, the creation goddess of the Ryukyu Islands, + ookii = large + shima = island
底	soko = bottom; *I sold my coal when the price reached the bottom*

Kanji Pronunciations

# 1089 – ju, ki	# 1090 – kun	# 1091 – fude, hitsu, pitsu, hi	# 1092 – namari, en
# 1093 – ni, go, ji	# 1094 – dou	# 1095 – ama	# 1096 – soko, zoko, tei

靴底　　kutsuzoko = the sole of a shoe; from kutsu = shoe + zoko = soko = bottom

海底　　kaitei = bottom of the sea; from kai = ocean, e.g., kaigai = overseas; + tei = bottom; *I taped my shoe at the bottom*

from the Practice Sentences

防火　　bouka = fire prevention, fireproofing; from bouei = defense + kaji = fire

入場　　nyuujou = admission (to a theater, etc.); from nyuu = to enter, e.g., nyuugaku = to enter a school; + jou = place, e.g., kinjou = neighborhood

果樹園　kajuen = an orchard; from ka = fruit; *I carved some fruit*; + ju = tree; *we get juice from orange trees*; + en = park, e.g., kouen = park

価値　　kachi = value; *he's catching a lot of balls, and we recognize his value to the team*

転がる　korogaru = to roll, fall over, lie down; from korobu = to fall over + garu = to show signs of doing something, e.g., ikitagaru = to show signs of wanting to go

切り倒す　kiritaosu = to cut down; from kiru = to cut + taosu = to knock down

切り開く　kirihiraku = to clear land, to open up; from kiru = to cut + hiraku = to open

批評家　hihyouka = a critic; from hihyou = criticism + ka = person

明らか　akiraka = obvious; *it's obvious that a key to the locker is needed*

神童　　shindou = a child prodigy; from shin = mind, e.g., seishin = mind or spirit + jidou = child

くっつく　kuttsuku = to adhere to, keep close to; from kutsu = shoe + tsuku = to adhere

from News in Slow Japanese

自閉症　jiheishou = autism; from jibun = self + hei = to close, e.g., heiten = closed store; + shou = symptoms

飛び跳ねる　tobihaneru = to hop; from tobu = to fly + haneru = to hop

突破する　toppa suru = to break through; from totsuzen = sudden + pa = to break or tear; *the padre broke the bread for communion*

20ヶ国　nijuukakoku = 20 countries; this small ヶ ka can often be seen in counting words, e.g., 2ヶ月 nikagetsu = 2 months

筆談　　hitsudan = communicating in writing; from mouhitsu = writing brush + soudan = consultation

なりに　nari ni = in a person's own way or style; *the nanny reads to my niece in her own way*

身近　　mijika = close at hand, closely related; from mi = body or person + jika = chika = close

Practice Sentences

1. 村上春樹の本を読みました
   か。

   Murakami haruki no hon wo
   yomimashita ka.
   Did you read Haruki Murakami's book?

2. 私たちは昨日防火訓練をし
   た。

   Watashitachi wa kinou bouka kunren wo
   shita.
   We did fire-prevention drills yesterday.

3. 彼は鉛筆で真っ直ぐな線を描
   いた。

   Kare wa enpitsu de massugu na sen wo
   kaita.
   He drew a straight line with a pencil.
   (OK to pronounce this "egaita," instead
   of "kaita")

4. 児童は入場無料です。

   Jidou wa nyuujou muryou desu.
   For children, admission is free.

5. 船から奄美大島が良く見えま
   した。

   Fune kara, amami ooshima ga yoku
   miemashita.
   From the boat, Amami Ooshima island
   could be seen well.

6. 彼女は心の底から笑った。

   Kanojo wa kokoro no soko kara waratta.
   She laughed from the bottom of her
   heart.

7. 彼は果樹園を経営している。

   Kare wa kajuen wo keiei shite iru.
   He is managing an orchard.

8. その教訓は覚えておく価値が
   ある。

   Sono kyoukun wa oboete oku kachi ga
   aru.
   As for that moral, it has remember-in-
   advance value (i.e., it's worth
   remembering).

9. 鉛筆が私の机の端から転がり
   落ちた。

   Enpitsu ga watashi no tsukue no hashi
   kara korogari ochita.
   The pencil rolled down from the edge of
   my desk.

10. 彼女はその孤児の世話をした
    そうです。

    Kanojo wa sono koji no sewa wo shita
    sou desu.
    Reportedly she performed the care of that
    orphan.

11. この童話は七歳の子が読むの
    に十分やさしい。

    Kono douwa wa nanasai no ko ga yomu
    noni juubun yasashii.
    As for this fairy tale, for the sake of a 7-
    year-old child to read, it is easy enough.

12. 奄美大島の海岸で、きれいな
    貝を拾った。

    Amami ooshima no kaigan de, kirei na
    kai wo hirotta.
    On Amami Ooshima island's beach, I
    picked up a pretty shell.

13. 船は海底に沈んだ。
Fune wa kaitei ni shizunda.
The ship sank to the bottom of the sea.

14. 樹木が切り倒され土地が切り開かれている。
Jumoku ga kiritaosare tochi ga kirihirakarete iru.
The trees are cut down, and the land is cleared.

15. 彼の失敗は私にとって良い教訓になりました。
Kare no shippai wa watashi ni totte yoi kyoukun ni narimashita.
As for his failure, it became a good lesson for me.

16. この記事の筆者は有名な批評家だ。
Kono kiji no hissha wa yuumei na hihyouka da.
The author of this article is a famous critic.

17. これは鉛のように重い。
Kore wa namari no you ni omoi.
This is heavy, like lead.

18. 鹿児島は九州の一番南にあります。
Kagoshima wa kyuushuu no ichiban minami ni arimasu.
Kagoshima is in Kyushu's farthest south.

19. 彼女は明らかに神童である。
Kanojo wa akiraka ni shindou de aru.
She is obviously a child prodigy.

20. 奄美大島に観光で行ったことがある。
Amami ooshima ni kankou de itta koto ga aru.
I have been to Amami Ooshima island for sightseeing.

21. ガムが靴底にくっついた。
Gamu ga kutsuzoko ni kuttsuita.
The gum stuck to the sole of the shoe.

22. 筆で字を書くのは難しい。
Fude de ji wo kaku no wa muzukashii.
It's difficult to write characters with a brush.

Supplemental Reading Practice

After completing Chapter 61 of this book, you should be able to read Lesson 016, "The Reason I Jump," in *News in Slow Japanese*.

Chapter 62

New Kanji in this Chapter

# 1097 径 (1)	# 1098 種 (2)	# 1099 酎 (1)	# 1100 沢 (3)
# 1101 蒸 (2)	# 1102 芋 (1)	# 1103 麦 (3)	# 1104 粉 (3)

Vocabulary List with Mnemonics

from the Kanji Catalogue

直径　chokkei = diameter; *I choked on a piece of cake because its diameter was too large*

半径　hankei = radius; from han = half + chokkei = diameter

種　tane = seed; *I keep my seeds in tan eggshells*

種類　shurui = variety, type; *the shoes that Louie wears are of several types*

人種　jinshu = race of people; from jin = person + shurui = type

一種の　isshu no = a kind of, a type of; from ichi = one + shurui = type

焼酎　shouchuu = a Japanese spirit distilled from sweet potatoes, rice, etc.; *showpeople choose to drink shouchuu*

沢村　Sawamura = a family name; from sawa = swamp; *I saw water in the swamp*; + mura = village

金沢　Kanazawa = a city in Honshu

光沢　koutaku = luster; *cold tap water and Kool-Aid will put the luster back into your silverware*

沢山　takusan = many or much (usually written たくさん)

蒸気　jouki = vapor, steam; *I was only joking when I said that I saw steam coming out of your ears*

蒸発　jouhatsu = evaporation; from jou = steam; *Joan of Arc used steam to cook her vegetables*; + hatsu = departure, e.g. shuppatsu = departure

蒸す　musu = to steam, to be hot and humid; *in the movie, Superman steamed his food*

蒸し暑い　mushiatsui = hot and humid; from musu = to steam + atsui = hot

芋　imo = potato; *eating potatoes stimulates positive emotions*

Kanji Pronunciations

# 1097 – kei	# 1098 – tane, shu	# 1099 – chuu	# 1100 – sawa, zawa, taku
# 1101 – jou, mu	# 1102 – imo	# 1103 – baku, ba, mugi	# 1104 – kona, ko, fun

じゃが芋   jagaimo = Irish potato, usually written ジャガイモ; *Mick Jagger's aunt has an emotional attachment to Irish potatoes*

麦   mugi = barley, wheat; *we had to move our gear to make room for the barley*

粉   kona = flour, powder; *Conan O'Brien cooks with flour*

小麦   komugi = wheat; from ko = small + mugi = barley

小麦粉   komugiko = wheat flour; from komugi = wheat + kona = flour

花粉   kafun = pollen; from ka = flower, e.g., kabin = vase; + fun = powder; *that powder on your nose looks funny*

from the Practice Sentences

花粉症   kafunshou = hay fever; from kafun = pollen + shoujou = symptoms

円周   enshuu = circumference; from en = circle; *en (yen) coins are circular*; + shuu = circumference, e.g., isshuu = tour, round trip

老化   rouka = aging; from roujin = elderly person + ka = -ization; e.g., kindai = modern times, kindaika = modernization

居酒屋   izakaya = a pub or bar; from i = dwelling, e.g., ima = living room; + zakaya = sakaya = liquor store

近頃   chikagoro = recently, lately, nowadays; from chikai = close + goro = approximate time

水蒸気   suijouki = water vapor; from sui = water, e.g., suiei = swimming; + jouki = vapor

固まり   katamari = mass, lump; from katamaru = to harden

焼き芋   yaki imo = roasted sweet potato; from yaku = to grill + imo = potato

産物   sanbutsu = product; from sangyou = industry + butsu = thing

大麦   oomugi = barley; from ookii = big + mugi = barley

from News in Slow Japanese

ミステリー   misuterii = mystery

サークル   saakuru = circle

出現する   shutsugen suru = to appear; from shutsu = to put out, e.g., gaishutsu suru = to go out; + genjitsu = reality

二重   nijuu = double; from ni = two + juu = heavy, e.g., taijuu = a person's weight; cf. 二十 nijuu = twenty

オス   osu = a male (animal); *the old supervisor had a male cat*

フグ   fugu = a blowfish or puffer fish; *a food that Goofy liked was puffer fish*

メス	mesu = a female (animal); *the Mexican supervisor had a female cat*
産卵	sanran = egg-laying, spawning; from san = products, e.g., seisan = production + ran = egg; *I got these eggs at the ranch*
新種	shinshu = new species or variety; from shin = new + shurui = type
立大	ritsudai = private university; from ritsu = to stand + daigaku = university
州立大	shuuritsudai = state university; from shuu = large area or state, e.g., Kyuushuu = an island in Japan; + ritsudai = private university
国際	kokusai = international; *Coke is advertised on signs in international airports*
生物	seibutsu = living creature; from seikatsu = life + butsu = thing
生物種	seibutsushu = species; from seibutsu = living creature + shurui = type
探査	tansa = probe, inquiry, investigation; from tanken = exploration + chousa = investigation
研究所	kenkyuujo = research institute, laboratory; from kenkyuu = research + jo = place, e.g., kinjo = neighborhood

Practice Sentences

1. 円周から直径が計算できますか。

Enshuu kara chokkei ga keisan dekimasu ka.
Can you calculate the diameter from the circumference?

2. 老化現象の一種です。

Rouka genshou no isshu desu.
It's a type of aging phenomenon.

3. 居酒屋に行くと焼酎を飲まずにはいられない。

Izakaya ni iku to shouchuu wo nomazuni wa irarenai.
When I go to a pub, I can't help drinking shochu.

4. 金沢は静かな町です。

Kanazawa wa shizuka na machi desu.
Kanazawa is a quiet town.

5. 蒸した芋が食べたい。

Mushita imo ga tabetai.
I want to eat steamed potatoes.

6. 小麦粉を戸棚に入れてください。

Komugiko wo todana ni irete kudasai.
Please put the wheat flour in the cupboard.

7. この丸の半径は３センチです。

Kono maru no hankei wa san senchi desu.
The radius of this circle is 3 centimeters.

8. 鶏に餌として種を与えている。

Niwatori ni esa to shite tane wo ataete iru.
I am giving seeds to the chickens as animal food.

9. 夕べは焼酎を飲みすぎました。

Yuube wa shouchuu wo nomisugimashita.
As for last night, I drank too much shochu.

10. この指輪は光沢を失った。

Kono yubiwa wa koutaku wo ushinatta.
This ring lost its luster.

11. ここで小麦を作っています。

Koko de komugi wo tsukutte imasu.
We are growing wheat here.

12. 雲は水蒸気の固まりである。

Kumo wa suijouki no katamari de aru.
A cloud is a mass of water vapor.

13. じゃが芋とにんじんと玉ねぎを入れました。

Jagaimo to ninjin to tamanegi wo iremashita.
I inserted potatoes, carrots and onions.

14. 近頃は沢山の人が花粉症を持っている。

Chikagoro wa takusan no hito ga kafunshou wo motte iru.
Recently a lot of people have hay fever.

15. 直径は半径の２倍の長さがある。

Chokkei wa hankei no nibai no nagasa ga aru.
The diameter is twice the length of the radius.

16. アメリカの魚の種類は日本ほど多くありません。

Amerika no sakana no shurui wa nihon hodo ooku arimasen.
The fish varieties in America, compared to Japan, are less numerous.

17. 公園で桜の花を見ながら焼酎を飲むのは初めてだった。

Kouen de sakura no hana wo mi nagara shouchuu wo nomu no wa hajimete datta.
In a park, while looking at cherry blossoms, as for to drink shochu, it was the first time.

18. いい友達が沢山できて幸せです。

Ii tomodachi ga takusan dekite shiawase desu.
Because many good friends are possible, it's happiness.

19. 夕べは蒸し暑かったから一晩中クーラーを点けていました。

Yuube wa mushiatsukatta kara hitoban juu kuuraa wo tsukete imashita.
As for last night, since it was muggy, all night long the air conditioner was turned on. (the use of tsukete rather than tsuite implies that the *speaker* turned it on)

20. 焼き芋が一番好きです。

Yaki imo ga ichiban suki desu.
I like roasted sweet potato the best.

21. 大麦は我が社の主な産物です。

Oomugi wa wagasha no omo na sanbutsu desu.
Barley is the main product of our company.

22. 粉と卵二個を入れてください。

Kona to tamago niko wo irete kudasai.
Please insert the flour and two eggs.

Supplemental Reading Practice

After completing Chapter 62 of this book, you should be able to read Lesson 017, "The Mystery Circles of Amami Oshima," in *News in Slow Japanese*.

Chapter 63

New Kanji in this Chapter

# 1105 農 (1)	# 1106 濃 (2)	# 1107 虜 (2)	# 1108 造 (2)
# 1109 募 (2)	# 1110 催 (2)	# 1111 跡 (2)	# 1112 清 (2)

Vocabulary List with Mnemonics

from the Kanji Catalogue

農業   nougyou = agriculture; *the workers in <u>agriculture</u> received <u>no gyouza</u>*

農家   nouka = farmer, farmhouse; *the <u>No</u>rwegian <u>car</u>penter became a <u>farmer</u>*

農夫   noufu = farmer; *that <u>farmer</u> is <u>no fool</u>*

濃い   koi = dark, thick, strong, dense; *this <u>coin</u> is <u>dark, thick, strong</u> and <u>dense</u>*

濃度   noudo = concentration; *the <u>No</u>rwegian bread <u>dough</u> has a high <u>concentration</u> of sugar*

虜   toriko = captive, prisoner; *the <u>Tory</u> corporal captured a <u>prisoner</u>*

捕虜   horyo = prisoner of war, captive; *<u>Ho</u>mer and Pope <u>Leo</u> were taken <u>prisoner</u>*

造る   tsukuru = to create or make (this is more commonly spelled 作る); *I carried a <u>tsui</u>tcase (suitcase) of <u>Kool</u>-Aid to my <u>room</u> and <u>created</u> some refreshing drinks*

造り酒屋   tsukurizakaya = a sake brewery; from tsukuru = to make + zakaya = sakaya = liquor store

製造   seizou = manufacturing, production; *we conduct <u>manufacturing</u> in a <u>safe zone</u>*

改造   kaizou = remodeling; *the <u>Kai</u>ser created a <u>zone</u> in which architectural <u>remodeling</u> was allowed*

募る   tsunoru = to advertise, recruit, intensify; *the <u>tsu</u>perior (superior) <u>No</u>rwegians in the <u>room</u> planned <u>to recruit</u> people for their cause*

応募   oubo = application, subscription; *he completed an <u>application</u> to work on <u>O</u>prah's <u>boat</u>*

開催する   kaisai suru = to hold a meeting or open an exhibition; *the <u>kind</u> p<u>sy</u>chologists will <u>hold a meeting</u>*

催す   moyo'osu = to hold an event; *a <u>mo</u>tormouth <u>yo</u>gi opened a <u>s</u>upermarket and <u>held an event</u> to mark the occasion*

Kanji Pronunciations

# 1105 – nou	# 1106 – ko, nou	# 1107 – toriko, ryo	# 1108 – tsuku, zou
# 1109 – tsuno, bo	# 1110 – moyo'o, sai	# 1111 – seki, ato	# 1112 – sei, kiyo

催し	moyo'oshi = an event or meeting; from moyo'osu = to hold an event
奇跡	kiseki = miracle, wonder, marvel; *the key to selling quiche is to tell customers that its effects are a marvel*
跡	ato = trace, track, ruin; *the artificial tomatoes contain a trace of chemicals*
清掃	seisou = cleaning; *sailors and soldiers do a lot of cleaning*
清い	kiyoi = clear, pure; *the king is a yogurt eater who likes pure food*
清らかな	kiyoraka na = clean, pure, chaste; *the king's yogurt lacks calcium, but it is pure*
清める	kiyomeru = to purify or cleanse; *the king's yogurt is made in a messy room, but later it is purified*
清水	kiyomizu = spring water, pure water; from kiyoi = pure + mizu = water

from the Practice Sentences

農産物	nousanbutsu = agricultural produce; from nougyou = agriculture + sangyou = industry + butsu = thing
緑茶	ryokucha = green tea; from ryoku = green; *Pope Leo drinks Kool-Aid that is green*; + cha = tea
寺院	ji'in = Buddhist temple; from ji = temple; *that temple has a Jeep*; + in = institution, e.g., byouin = hospital
木造	mokuzou = wooden construction; from moku = wood + seizou = manufacturing
まとめて	matomete = all together, all at once; *the magnificent toads left for Mexico and Texas all together and all at once*
清算する	seisan suru = to settle (an account) or clear (a debt); *a sailor delivered the sand and settled the account*; cf. 生産する seisan suru = to produce
幸い	saiwai = lucky, happy; *the scientist's wife was happy*
農場	noujou = a farm; from nougyou = agriculture + jou = place, e.g., koujou = factory
仕事場	shigotoba = a workshop, construction site; from shigoto = work + basho = place
募金	bokin = fundraising; *Bo Peep went to the kindergarten to do some fundraising*
跡形	atokata = trace, vestige; from ato = trace or track; *artificial tomatoes contain a trace of chemicals*; + kata = shape; *a catapult has a distinctive shape*

from News in Slow Japanese

蒸留	jouryuu = distillation; *Joan of Arc reused her brother's still for her alcohol distillation business*
蒸留酒	jouryuushu = distilled liquor; from jouryuu = distillation + shu = alcohol; *I spilled alcohol on my shoes*
濃さ	kosa = consistency, darkness, thickness, density; from koi = dark, thick, dense + sa = a suffix that makes a noun from an adjective

口当たり	kuchiatari = taste; from kuchi = mouth + atari = just, right, reasonable; *the <u>Atari</u> game system employed the <u>right</u> technology for its era*
在住	zaijuu = residence; *due to the local <u>zeitgeist</u> (spirit of the age) and the orange <u>juice</u>, I am taking up <u>residence</u> in Florida*
中心	chuushin = center, core, focus; from chuu = middle + shin = heart, mind
CM	shi emu = commercial or advertisement; an abbreviation commonly used in Japan for TV commercials
がん治療	gan chiryou = cancer treatment; from gan = cancer + chiryou = medical treatment
かつら	katsura = a wig; *the man eating ton <u>katsu</u> and <u>ramen</u> is wearing a <u>wig</u>*
選手権	senshuken = championship; from senshu = athlete + kenri = right or privilege
首都	shuto = capital city; from shu = neck or chief, e.g., shushou = prime minister; + toshi = city
位置	ichi = position, location, situation; from i = rank; *the guy ringing the <u>Easter</u> bell has a high <u>rank</u>*; + chi = to place; *we <u>place</u> <u>cheese</u> at the back of our shelves*
設置	secchi = establishment, installation; from settei suru = to set up + chi = to place; *we <u>place</u> <u>cheese</u> at the back of our shelves*
変身	henshin = transformation; from hen = to change something; *owning a <u>hen</u> <u>changed</u> my life*; + shin = body or flesh; *the <u>Shinto</u> priest takes care of his <u>body</u>*
観戦	kansen = watching a game, observing; *the <u>Canadian</u> <u>sen</u>ators were <u>watching a game</u>*; cf. 感染 kansen = infection
観戦者	kansensha = spectator; from kansen = watching a game + sha = person
暇つぶし	himatsubushi = killing time; from hima = free time + tsubusu = to smash, block or waste; *the agents <u>smashed</u> the <u>tsu</u>itcase (suitcase) full of <u>booze</u> in front of their supervisor*
利用者	riyousha = user; from riyou = utilization + sha = person

Practice Sentences

1. 濃い緑茶を飲みすぎている。

Koi ryokucha wo nomisugite iru.
I'm drinking too much strong green tea.

2. わが国の主な農産物は米であ
る。

Wagakuni no omo na nousanbutsu wa kome de aru.
Our country's main agricultural product is rice.

3. 彼らは捕虜になった。

Karera wa horyo ni natta.
They became prisoners.

4. 日本の寺院の大半は木造で作
られている。

Nihon no ji'in no taihan wa mokuzou de tsukurarete iru.
Most Japanese temples are made of wooden construction.

5. 応募書類を記入してくださ
い。

Oubo shorui wo ki'nyuu shite kudasai.
Please fill out the application form.

6. 会議は今日の午後開催され
る。

Kaigi wa kyou no gogo kaisai sareru.
The meeting will be held this afternoon.

7. 足に子供の頃、怪我をした跡
が残っている。

Ashi ni kodomo no koro kega wo shita
ato ga nokotte iru.
There's a mark remaining on my leg
from an injury I sustained as a child.

8. チェックアウトのときにまと
めて清算してください。

Chekkauto no toki ni matomete seisan
shite kudasai.
At checkout time, please settle it
(financially) all at once.

9. 農家から卵と牛乳を買った。

Nouka kara tamago to gyuunyuu wo
katta.
I bought eggs and milk from a farmer.

10. このスープは美味しいけど、
ちょっと味が濃いかな。

Kono suupu wa oishii kedo, chotto aji ga
koi kana.
This soup is delicious, but the taste is a
little strong, I wonder.

11. 捕虜になっても威厳はあっ
た。

Horyo ni nattemo igen wa atta.
Even though he was captured, he had
dignity.

12. この飛行機はフランスで製造
されました。

Kono hikouki wa furansu de seizou
saremashita.
This airplane was manufactured in
France.

13. 新聞の広告に応募して職を得
た。

Shinbun no koukoku ni oubo shite shoku
wo eta.
I applied to (i.e., responded to) a newspaper advertisement and received a job.

14. 彼女は来週パーティーを催
す。

Kanojo wa raishuu paatii wo moyo'osu.
She will hold a party next week.

15. それはまさに奇跡だった。

Sore wa masa ni kiseki datta.
That was really a marvel.

16. 心の清い人達は幸いである。

Kokoro no kiyoi hitotachi wa saiwai de
aru.
People who are pure of heart are happy.

17. 農場で働いている。

Noujou de hataraite iru.
I'm laboring on a farm.

18. 「濃度が高い」状態を「濃い」と言います。

"Noudo ga takai" joutai wo "koi" to iimasu.
The "concentration is high" condition is called "dense." (i.e., that's what "dense" means)

19. 捕虜は、「いつ帰れるのか」と聞きました。

Horyo wa "itsu kaereru no ka" to kikimashita.
The prisoner asked, "When will I be able to return?"

20. 地下室を仕事場に改造した。

Chikashitsu wo shigotoba ni kaizou shita.
We remodeled the basement into a workshop.

21. 共同募金は、都道府県ごとに行われています。

Kyoudou bokin wa, todoufuken goto ni okonawarete imasu.
Cooperative fundraising is carried out for each of the administrative divisions (Tokyo, Hokkaido, Osaka, Kyoto and the various prefectures).

22. 今日の催しのチケットはありますか。

Kyou no moyo'oshi no chiketto wa arimasu ka.
Are there any tickets for today's event?

23. 彼は跡形もなく消えたんだ。

Kare wa atokata mo naku kietan da.
He disappeared without even a trace.

24. あなたに一ドルを払えば清算がつく。

Anata ni ichidoru wo haraeba seisan ga tsuku.
If I pay you one dollar, the account will settle.

Supplemental Reading Practice

After completing Chapter 63 of this book, you should be able to read Lesson 018, "The Shochu Handout," Lesson 019, "The Boy Who Kept Growing his Hair Out, Even After Being Called a Girl," and Lesson 020, "Bus Stop Transformed into Soccer Goal," in *News in Slow Japanese*.

Chapter 64

New Kanji in this Chapter

# 1113 収 (2)	# 1114 拭 (2)	# 1115 賛 (1)	# 1116 型 (3)
# 1117 典 (1)	# 1118 侍 (1)	# 1119 洪 (1)	# 1120 遇 (1)

Vocabulary List with Mnemonics

from the Kanji Catalogue

収める — osameru = to put away (in a closet), conclude, pay a bill; this can also be spelled 納める, # 705; *when Osama met Ruth, he was putting away the dishes and paying the bills*

回収する — kaishuu suru = to recover, recall, collect (bills or trash); *the Kaiser's shoe was recovered after he lost it*

収入 — shuunyuu = income; *people shun you if your income is low*

拭う — nuguu = to wipe; *I have to wipe up after that neutered goose*

拭く — fuku = to wipe or mop; *I mopped the floor in Fukuoka*

賛成 — sansei = agreement; *when I met Santa at Safeway, he signed an agreement with me*

絶賛する — zessan suru = to praise highly; *the Zen monk who played Santa praised the audience highly*

型 — kata = form (e.g., dance), posture, style; *it's important to show the right form when using a catapult*

髪型 — kamigata = hair style (this can also be written 髪形, # 573); from kami = hair + gata = kata = form

典型 — tenkei = type, model, representative; *these ten canines are representative of the dog species*

典型的な — tenkeiteki na = typical; from tenkei = representative + teki = related to

辞典 — jiten = dictionary; *the genius read ten dictionaries*

百科 — hyakka = many objects (for study); from hyaku = one hundred + ka = section or category, e.g., kyoukasho = textbook

百科事典 — hyakkajiten = encyclopedia; from hyakka = many objects + jiten = dictionary

Kanji Pronunciations

# 1113 – osa, shuu	# 1114 – nugu, fu	# 1115 – san	# 1116 – kata, gata, kei
# 1117 – ten	# 1118 – samurai	# 1119 – kou	# 1120 – guu

古典 — koten = classical work, classic; *the <u>Co</u>lombian <u>ten</u>nis player was reading a <u>classic</u>*

侍 — samurai = Japanese warrior; *I'm <u>sad</u> because a <u>Moo</u>nie took my <u>ri</u>ce and gave it to a <u>Japanese</u> <u>warrior</u>*

洪水 — kouzui = flood; *a <u>Co</u>lombian <u>zoo</u> in the <u>east</u> was affected by a <u>flood</u>*

遭遇する — souguu suru = to encounter; *the <u>soldier's</u> <u>goose</u> <u>encountered</u> a fox*

待遇 — taiguu = treatment (of customer), salary and benefits; *the <u>treatment</u> of the <u>Thai</u> <u>goose</u> was fair*

from the Practice Sentences

収集 — shuushuu = collection; *the <u>shooter's</u> <u>shoe</u>s were combined into a <u>collection</u>*

天災 — tensai = natural disaster; from ten'nen = natural + sainan = disaster; cf. 天才 tensai = genius

境遇 — kyouguu = circumstances, environment; *in <u>Kyou</u>to, the <u>goo</u>se enjoyed a good <u>environment</u>*

吸収する — kyuushuu suru = to absorb or digest; *on <u>Kyuushuu</u> island, I watched a sponge <u>absorb</u> a bowl of water*

賞賛する — shousan suru = to praise, exalt, admire, commend; *<u>show</u> <u>Santa</u> how much you <u>admire</u> him*

英和辞典 — eiwa jiten = English-Japanese dictionary; from eigo = English + wa = Japanese, e.g., washoku = Japanese food; + jiten = dictionary

不作 — fusaku = poor harvest; from fu = negation + sakuhin = creation

収容する — shuuyou suru = to accommodate or take in; *when he saw the <u>shooting</u> star, the <u>yogi</u> decided to <u>accomodate</u> us*

型紙 — katagami = pattern paper (for dressmaking); from kata = form + gami = kami = paper

賛同する — sandou suru = to approve or endorse; *<u>Santa's</u> <u>doughnuts</u> were <u>approved</u> by everyone*

小型車 — kogatasha = a compact car; from ko = small + gata = kata = form + jidousha = car

行方 — yu'kue = whereabouts, location; *the <u>you</u>th sold some <u>Kool</u>-Aid to the <u>en</u>gineer, but he didn't reveal its <u>location</u>*

現代 — gendai = modern times, nowadays; *<u>Gen</u>ghis would be put on a <u>diet</u> if he lived <u>nowadays</u>*

不明 — fumei = unknown, uncertain; from fu = negation + mei = bright, obvious, e.g., setsumei = explanation

from News in Slow Japanese

記者 — kisha = reporter; *the Irish <u>reporter</u> <u>keeps</u> a <u>sha</u>mrock in her purse*

車内 — shanai = inside a train or car; from densha = train + nai = inside; cf. 社内 shanai = inside a company

置き場	okiba = storage space; from oku = to place + basho = place
当り	atari = per, apiece, when used as a suffix; this can also be spelled 当たり; *my brother and I had one Atari game apiece*; cf. 当たり atari = a hit or success; cf. 当たり前 atarimae = just or right, reasonable, natural, proper
手際	tegiwa = skill, performance, tact; *Tennessee geese swim on water and have skill in catching fish*
良さ	yosa = merit, virtue; from yoi = good + sa, a suffix that creates a noun from an adjective
旅行者	ryokousha = traveler; from ryoukou = travel + sha = person
乗務員	joumuin = crew member (of a vehicle); from joumu = transport-related work; *when Joan of Arc was in the mood, she did transport-related work*; + in = member
ちょんまげ	chonmage = topknot (hair style for samurai or sumo wrestler); *after I chose negativity, Ma (mother) and her guest tied a topknot in my hair*
ヘア	hea = hair
もともと	motomoto = originally, from the outset; from 元 moto = origin
きっかけ	kikkake = excuse, catalyst, motive, impetus; *the king's call to Kennedy was the catalyst for the decision*
和む	nagomu = to be softened, to calm down; *the nagging ghost was in a mood to calm down*; cf. 慰める nagusameru = to console or divert
結う	yuu = to tie up, braid, fasten (hair); *in the Yukon, people tie up their hair*

Practice Sentences

1. 私の趣味は切手の収集です。

Watashi no shumi wa kitte no shuushuu desu.
My hobby is stamp collecting.

2. 足を拭きなさい。

Ashi wo fukinasai.
Wipe your feet.

3. この計画はあなたさえ賛成してくれればまとまるのよ。

Kono keikaku wa anata sae sansei shite kurereba matomaru no yo.
As for this plan, if only you agree and give, it will settle for sure.

4. 彼は典型的な日本人だ。

Kare wa tenkeiteki na nihonjin da.
He's a typical Japanese person.

5. 侍の道は厳しかった。

Samurai no michi wa kibishikatta.
The way of the samurai was strict.

6. 地震や洪水は天災です。

Jishin ya kouzui wa tensai desu.
Earthquakes and floods, etc., are natural disasters.

7. 私は今あなたを助けられる境遇ではない。

Watashi wa ima anata wo tasukerareru kyouguu de wa nai.
As for me, now, to be able to help you circumstances are not (i.e., I can't help you now).

8. 黒い紙は光を吸収する。

Kuroi kami wa hikari wo kyuushuu suru.
Black paper absorbs light.

9. 母は病気の子供の顔をタオルで拭ってやった。

Haha wa byouki no kodomo no kao wo taoru de nugutte yatta.
My mother wiped the sick child's face with a towel and gave.

10. 誰もが彼を賞賛する。

Dare mo ga kare wo shousan suru.
Everyone admires him.

11. 英和辞典を買った。

Eiwa jiten wo katta.
I bought an English-Japanese dictionary.

12. 僕には侍の血が流れている。

Boku ni wa samurai no chi ga nagarete iru.
Samurai blood flows in me.

13. 洪水のため米は不作だった。

Kouzui no tame kome wa fusaku datta.
Due to the flood, the rice was a poor harvest.

14. この前学校の帰りに古本屋に寄ったら長い間探してた本に遭遇した。

Kono mae gakkou no kaeri ni furuhonya ni yottara nagai aida sagashiteta hon ni souguu shita.
Recently, when I dropped by a used bookstore on the way home from school, I encountered a book that I had been looking for for a long time.

15. このホテルは500人の客を収容できる。

Kono hoteru wa gohyaku nin no kyaku wo shuuyou dekiru.
This hotel can accommodate 500 guests.

16. この洋服の型紙をもらえますか。

Kono youfuku no katagami wo moraemasu ka.
Could I get this paper clothing pattern?

17. バスタオルで体を拭いた。

Basu taoru de karada wo fuita.
I wiped my body with a bath towel.

18. 私達は彼の意見に賛同するのは簡単なことだ。

Watashitachi wa kare no iken ni sandou suru no wa kantan na koto da.
It's a simple thing for us to endorse his opinion.

19. 小型車を借りたいのですが。

Kogatasha wo karitai no desu ga.
I'd like to rent a compact car, but...

20. 日本の古典が大好きだ。

Nihon no koten ga daisuki da.
I love the Japanese classics.

21. 現代の日本に侍はいません。

Gendai no nihon ni samurai wa imasen.
There are no samurai in contemporary Japan.

22. 洪水で３人の人が行方不明に
なった。

Kouzui de san'nin no hito ga yukue fumei ni natta.
Due to the flood, three people became whereabouts-unclear (i.e., missing).

23. 彼はもっとよい待遇を受ける
権利がある。

Kare wa motto yoi taiguu wo ukeru kenri ga aru.
He has a right to receive better treatment.

Supplemental Reading Practice

After completing Chapter 64, you should be able to read Lesson 021, "The Seven-Minute Miracle," and Lesson 022, "Samurai Taxi Driver," in *News in Slow Japanese*.

Chapter 65

New Kanji in this Chapter

# 1121 妓 (1)	# 1122 誕 (1)	# 1123 称 (1)	# 1124 列 (2)
# 1125 統 (1)	# 1126 領 (1)	# 1127 慢 (1)	# 1128 嵐 (1)

Vocabulary List with Mnemonics

from the Kanji Catalogue

舞妓   maiko = an apprentice geisha, a dancing girl; *a miner from Kobe met an apprentice geisha*

芸妓   geiko = 芸者 geisha; *the gay coder was infatuated with a geisha*

誕生する   tanjou suru = to be born; *the tanner joked that he was born at the tannery*

誕生日   tanjoubi = birthday; from tanjou suru = to be born + bi = hi = day

対称   taishou = symmetry; *the tiger showed off its symmetry*

対称性   taishousei = symmetry; *the tiger showed the sailors its symmetry*

対称的な   taishouteki na = symmetrical; from taishou = symmetry + teki = related to

通称   tsuushou = a nickname or alias, popular name; *Tsuuper (Super) Shorty is his nickname*

列   retsu = line; *my retro suit has prominent lines on it*

配列   hairetsu = arrangement, disposition; *Heidi's retro suits were hung up in a particular arrangement*

列車   ressha = train; from retsu = line + sha = vehicle

統一   tou'itsu = standardization, unification; from tou = to unify; *Tony Blair unified his party*; + itsu = one

統計   toukei = statistics; *here are the statistics regarding the total number of cakes sold*; cf. 時計 tokei = clock

大統領   daitouryou = president (of a country); *the diver told Pope Leo that he was searching for the president, who had disappeared from a boat*

領土   ryoudo = territory; *while Pope Leo was dozing, the enemy invaded his territory*

領収書   ryoushuusho = receipt; *Pope Leo went to a shoe show and saved his receipt*

Kanji Pronunciations

# 1121 – ko	# 1122 – tan	# 1123 – shou	# 1124 – retsu, re
# 1125 – tou	# 1126 – ryou	# 1127 – man	# 1128 – arashi

自慢   jiman = pride, boast; *the G-man (government man) had pride*

我慢   gaman = patience, endurance; *the garbage man has patience and endurance*

嵐   arashi = storm; *an Arab who is a Shiite was caught in a storm*

from the Practice Sentences

置き屋   okiya = geisha house; *the old king's yacht was being used as a geisha house*

衣食住   ishokujuu = clothing, food & shelter (the necessities of life); from ifuku = clothing + shokuji = meal + juusho = address

左右   sayuu = left and right; *the sad youth did not know left from right*

一緒   issho = together, identical, at the same time; *the Easter shows were identical, and they were held at the same time*

辞任する   jinin suru = to resign from a position; *the genius was a ninja who had resigned his position*

静まる   shizumaru = to become calm or quiet; from shizuka = quiet + maru = round, completely

芸舞妓   geimaiko = geisha and maiko; from geisha + maiko

生命   seimei = life or existence; *the sailor and the mailman both enjoyed life*

通称名   tsuushoumei = nickname or alias; from tsuushou = nickname + mei = name, e.g., yuumei = famous

様々   samazama = various; *the Good Samaritan and his Zambian friend Max were involved in various plans*

慢心   manshin = pride, self-conceit; *the mansion's shingles were a source of pride*

半玉   hangyoku = apprentice or child geisha; *Hansel gave some gyoza and Kool-Aid to the child geisha*

好む   konomu = to like or prefer; *Superman liked the way the women hid their cold noses on the moon*

物語る   monogataru = to tell or indicate; the verb associated with monogatari = story

北方   hoppou = northward; from ho = north; *I hope we go north for the summer*; + pou = hou = direction

from News in Slow Japanese

愛好   aikou = love, adoration; from aijou = love + kou = favorite, e.g., koubutsu = favorite food

愛好者   aikousha = fan, enthusiast; from aikou = adoration + sha = person

内装   naisou = interior, interior design; *the nice socialist was interested in interior design*

味わう   ajiwau = to taste, savor, relish; *as she savored the cake, she said, "this aji (taste) is wow!"*

空間   kuukan = space; from kuuki = air + kan = between, e.g., jikan = time

Practice Sentences

1. 舞妓さんになってからも置き屋さんが衣食住の世話をします。

Maiko-san ni natte kara mo okiyasan ga ishokujuu no sewa wo shimasu.
After becoming a maiko as well, the geisha house will take care of food, clothing and shelter.

2. 子供の誕生日に何をやろうか。

Kodomo no tanjoubi ni nani wo yarou ka.
What shall we give for the child's birthday? (man's speech)

3. 「対称的」は、左右の形や配列が左右一緒だということ。

"Taishouteki" wa, sayuu no katachi ya hairetsu ga sayuu issho da to iu koto.
As for "symmetrical," left-and-right's shape and arrangement, etc., are the same left and right, quote to say thing. (i.e., that's what "symmetrical" means)

4. 彼は大統領を辞任した。

Kare wa daitouryou wo jinin shita.
He resigned the presidency.

5. 熱くてもエアコンがないので、我慢をするしかない。

Atsukutemo eakon ga nai node, gaman wo suru shika nai.
Even though it's hot, since an air conditioner doesn't exist, except to-put-up-with doesn't exist (i.e., we have to put up with it).

6. 嵐は静まった。

Arashi wa shizumatta.
The storm calmed down.

7. 芸舞妓さんと遊びをしたりおしゃべりをしたりして楽しみます。

Geimaiko-san to asobi wo shitari oshaberi wo shitari shite tanoshimimasu.
With geisha and maiko, play, etc., chatter, etc., they (i.e., the customers) enjoy themselves.

8. 生命はいつ誕生したのですか。

Seimei wa itsu tanjou shita no desu ka.
When was life born (i.e., when did it begin)?

9. 通称名登録も必要ですか。

Tsuushoumei touroku mo hitsuyou desu ka.
Is it also necessary to register a nickname?

10. 列車は加速した。

Ressha wa kasoku shita.
The train accelerated.

11. 彼は様々のグループを統一し
ようとした。

Kare wa samazama no guruupu wo
touitsu shiyou to shita.
He tried to unify the various groups.

12. 領収書をいただけますか。

Ryoushuusho wo itadakemasu ka.
May I get a receipt?

13. 慢心してはいけません！

Manshin shite wa ikemasen!
You must not be conceited (i.e., don't
rest on your laurels)!

14. 嵐で停電した。

Arashi de teiden shita.
Due to the storm, there was a power
outage.

15. 関東では舞妓を半玉、芸妓を
芸者と呼びます。

Kantou de wa maiko wo hangyoku, geiko
wo geisha to yobimasu.
As for in Kanto (the region around
Tokyo), they call maiko "hangyoku" and
geiko "geisha."

16. 彼らは最初の子供の誕生を喜
んだ。

Karera wa saisho no kodomo no tanjou
wo yorokonda.
They were delighted at the birth of their
first child.

17. 左右対称性が高い顔が好まれ
ます。

Sayuu taishousei ga takai kao ga
konomaremasu.
Faces with high (i.e., a lot of) left-and-
right symmetry are preferred.

18. 私は列の最後だ。

Watashi wa retsu no saigo da.
I am the last in line.

19. 統計はすべてを物語るとは限
らない。

Toukei wa subete wo monogataru to wa
kagiranai.
As for statistics, as for the one called "to
tell everything," it isn't limited (i.e., they
don't necessarily tell the whole story).

20. ２月７日は日本では北方領土
の日です。

Nigatsu nanoka wa nihon de wa hoppou
ryoudo no hi desu.
In Japan, February 7 is Northern
Territories' Day.

21. この店の自慢料理はなんです
か。

Kono mise no jiman ryouri wa nan desu
ka.
What is the "pride cuisine" (i.e., the
specialty) of this restaurant?

22. この風は嵐の前兆だ。

Kono kaze wa arashi no zenchou da.
This wind is a portent of a storm.

Supplemental Reading Practice

After completing Chapter 65, you should be able to read Lesson 023, "Otaku Room,"
in *News in Slow Japanese*.

Chapter 66

New Kanji in this Chapter

# 1129 幻 (2)	# 1130 坂 (2)	# 1131 級 (1)	# 1132 等 (4)
# 1133 技 (2)	# 1134 房 (2)	# 1135 粒 (2)	# 1136 眺 (2)

Vocabulary List with Mnemonics

from the Kanji Catalogue

幻想	gensou = fantasy, illusion; *Genghis and his soldiers were fooled by an illusion*
幻覚	genkaku = hallucination; *Genghis drank the cactus juice and had hallucinations*
幻	maboroshi = illusion, vision; *a mariner got into a boat and was rowing a sheep across a lake when he saw a vision*
坂	saka = slope, hill; *we play sakkaa (soccer) on that hill*
下り坂	kudarizaka = downward slope; from kudaru = to go down + saka = hill
級	kyuu = class, level, grade; *those cute girls are in the 3rd grade class*
高級	koukyuu = high class or quality; from kou = high, e.g., koukou = high school; + kyuu = class
同級生	doukyuusei = classmate; from dou = same; *your doughnut is the same flavor as mine*; + kyuu = class + sei = to live
等級	toukyuu = grade, ranking; from tou = equivalent; *taking the toll road is equivalent to taking the train*; + kyuu = level or grade
上等	joutou = excellent, very good; *Joan of Arc's tomatoes are excellent*
平等	byoudou = equal; *the beer that I ordered was by the door, but I had an equal amount in the refrigerator*
等しい	hitoshii = same, equal; *the number of hito (people) who own sheep is equal to the number who own cattle*
等々	nadonado = etcetera; from nado = etcetera
技	waza = skill, technique; *the warlord zapped me with a taser to show his technique*
技術	gijutsu = technology, technique, skill; *this guitar juts out in various places, demonstrating the technique of its maker*

Kanji Pronunciations

# 1129 – gen, maboroshi	# 1130 – saka, zaka	# 1131 – kyuu	# 1132 – tou, dou, hito, nado
# 1133 – waza, gi	# 1134 – bou, fusa	# 1135 – tsubu, ryuu	# 1136 – naga, chou

競技   kyougi = athletic competition; *in <u>Kyouto</u>, I carried my <u>guitar</u> during an <u>athletic competition</u>*

暖房   danbou = heating, heater; *the <u>dancer</u> <u>boasted</u> about her space <u>heater</u>*

冷房   reibou = air conditioning; *the <u>racer</u> <u>boasted</u> about his <u>air</u> <u>conditioning</u>*

女房   nyoubou = one's wife; *when we <u>need yogurt</u> for our <u>boy</u>, <u>my wife</u> buys some*

房   fusa = a bunch, cluster, tassel; *<u>food is satisfying</u> when it comes in <u>bunches</u>*

粒   tsubu = grains, drops, counter for tiny particles; *the <u>tsupervisor's</u> (supervisor's) <u>boots</u> were covered with <u>drops</u> of water*

雨粒   amatsubu = raindrop; from ama = ame = rain + tsubu = drop

粒子   ryuushi = a particle or grain; *we <u>reuse</u> our <u>sheets</u> after removing every <u>particle</u> of dirt from them*

眺める   nagameru = to gaze or look at; *<u>Nagaina</u> checks her <u>meeru</u> (e-mail) and <u>gazes</u> at it*

眺め   nagame = a view; from nagameru = to gaze at

眺望   choubou = a view; *I <u>chose</u> a <u>boat</u> with big windows so that I could enjoy the <u>views</u>*

from the Practice Sentences

上り坂   noborizaka = uphill slope; from noboru = to climb + zaka = saka = hill

坂道   sakamichi = uphill path; from saka = hill + michi = path

ぶどう   budou = grapes; *the <u>boot</u> by the <u>door</u> is full of <u>grapes</u>*

駆け上がる   kakeagaru = to run up; from kakeru = to run + agaru = to rise

大粒   ootsubu = large drop, large grain; from ookii = big + tsubu = drop or grain

ごく小さい   gokuchiisai = very small; from goku = extremely; *the gold <u>Kool</u>-Aid is <u>extremely</u> delicious*; + chiisai = small

from News in Slow Japanese

定期   teiki = routine, regularity; *my <u>routine</u> is to <u>taste</u> <u>quiche</u> before serving it*

定期的に   teikiteki ni = at fixed intervals; from teiki = routine + teki = related to

嵐山   Arashiyama = a district in Kyoto; from arashi = storm + yama = mountain

ステーキ店   suteeki ten = steak shop; from steak + ten = store, e.g., ten'in = store clerk

和牛   wagyuu = Wagyu beef, Japanese beef; from wa = Japanese, e.g., washoku = Japanese food; + gyuunyuu = beef

村沢牛   murasawa gyuu = a type of wagyu beef produced in Nagano prefecture; from mura = village + sawa = swamp + gyuunyuu = beef

松坂牛   matsuzaka gyuu = a type of wagyu beef produced in Mie prefecture; from matsu = pine tree + zaka = saka = hill + gyuunyuu = beef

地名	chimei = place name; chimei no (or na) = famous; from chi = ground, e.g., chikatetsu = subway; + mei = name, e.g., yuumei = famous
生産者	seisansha = producer; from seisan suru = to produce + sha = person
高評	kouhyou = favorable review, high reputation; from kou = high, e.g., koukou = high school; + hyouban = reputation
高評価	kouhyouka = highly rated, well-liked; from kouhyou = high reputation + kachi = value
高める	takameru = to raise; from takai = high
高め	takame = on the high side; from takameru = to raise
キウイ	kiui = kiwi fruit
高品質	kouhinshitsu = high quality; from kou = high, e.g., koukou = high school; + hinshitsu = quality
開発	kaihatsu = development, exploitation; *the Kaiser's hatsus (hats) were purchased with money he made from development and exploitation*
初競り	hatsuseri = opening of an auction; *our hats are a serious concern when we dress up for the opening of an auction*
個人	kojin = individual, private, personal; *whether or not to go to court wearing jeans is a personal decision*
個人的	kojinteki = personal, self-centered; from kojin = personal + teki = related to
気軽	kigaru = carefree, lighthearted; from ki = spirit + garui = karui = light
たくましい	takumashii = strong, dependable; *when he is using tap water to make Kool-Aid and mashing potatoes, my husband seems strong and dependable*
視線	shisen = gaze; *the sheepish senator gazed into her eyes*
何気に	nanige ni = inadvertently, without knowing; *the nanny's guest didn't see my niece and inadvertently stepped on her foot*; cf. 何気ない nanigenai = casual, nonchalant
仕草	shigusa = gesture, mannerism; *that sheep farmer and those goofy saxophone players have some strange mannerisms*
急増	kyuuzou = sudden increase; from kyuu ni = suddenly + zou = to increase, e.g., baizou suru = to double

Practice Sentences

1. 幻覚が見えると言っている。

Genkaku ga mieru to itte iru.
She is saying that hallucinations are visible (i.e., she is seeing them).

2. この道は上り坂になっている。

Kono michi wa noborizaka ni natte iru.
This road is becoming an uphill slope.

3. そんな高級なホテルには泊ま
   ったことがない。

Sonna koukyuu na hoteru ni wa tomatta koto ga nai.
As for to such a high-class hotel, I have never stayed.

4. 我々は法の下で平等である。

Wareware wa hou no shita de byoudou de aru.
We are all equal under the law.

5. さぁ、最後の競技だ。

Saa, saigo no kyougi da.
Well, it's the last athletic competition.

6. 今日は外は風が強くて寒いけ
   れど部屋の中は暖房が入って
   いて暖かいですね。

Kyou wa, soto wa kaze ga tsuyokute samui keredo heya no naka wa danbou ga haitte ite atatakai desu ne.
As for today, as for outside, the wind is strong and cold, but as for inside of the room, a heater is being entered, and it's warm, huh.

7. 空が暗くなったかと思うと大
   粒の雨が降り出した。

Sora ga kuraku natta ka to omou to ootsubu no ame ga furidashita.
The sky became dark, as soon as, large raindrops' rain fell/put out. (i.e., as soon as the sky got dark, it started to rain heavily)

8. ガイドブックによるとあのホ
   テルは眺めがいいらしい。

Gaidobukku ni yoru to ano hoteru wa nagame ga ii rashii.
According to the guidebook, that hotel has a good view, it appears.

9. 安全なんて幻想だ。

Anzen nante gensou da.
Safety, such a thing, it's an illusion.

10. 険しい坂道を登るのは、若い
    人でも大変だ。

Kewashii sakamichi wo noboru no wa, wakai hito demo taihen da.
As for to climb a steep uphill path, even though young people, it's terrible.

11. 息子はＡ級試験で３科目に合
    格した。

Musuko wa A kyuu shiken de san kamoku ni goukaku shita.
My son passed three subjects by an "A" test level.

12. １ドルは100セントに等し
    い。

Ichi doru wa hyaku sento ni hitoshii.
A dollar is equal to 100 cents.

13. その手術をするには、高度な
    技術が必要だ。

Sono shujutsu wo suru ni wa, koudo na gijutsu ga hitsuyou da.
In order to do that surgery, advanced skill is necessary.

14. 彼女は坂を駆け上った。

Kanojo wa saka wo kakeagatta.
She ran up the hill.

15. 女房は読売新聞へ勤める事になった。

Nyoubou wa yomiuri shinbun e tsutomeru koto ni natta.
My wife became employed at the Yomiuri newspaper.

16. ２粒の涙が彼女の頬を流れ落ちた。

Nitsubu no namida ga kanojo no hoo wo nagareochita.
Two tear drops flowed and fell on her cheeks.

17. 鳥が頭上を飛んでいくのを眺めるのが好きです。

Tori ga zujou wo tonde iku no wo nagameru no ga suki desu.
I like to watch the birds flying and going overhead.

18. どちらにしてもあれは幻だ。

Dochira ni shite mo are wa maboroshi da.
Whichever you choose even (i.e., one way or the other), that is an illusion.

19. 彼は同級生と仲がいい。

Kare wa doukyuusei to naka ga ii.
He gets along well with his classmates.

20. 父親の誕生日に上等なワインを買った。

Chichioya no tanjoubi ni joutou na wain wo katta.
I bought an excellent wine for my father's birthday.

21. 柔道では力より技の方が大切である。

Juudou de wa chikara yori waza no hou ga taisetsu de aru.
In judo, compared to force, skill is more important.

22. 私は市場でリンゴを３個とぶどうを２房、デザート用に買った。

Watashi wa ichiba de ringo wo sanko to budou wo nifusa, dezaato you ni katta.
I bought 3 apples and 2 bunches of grapes at the market for dessert.

23. 空気中のごく小さい粒子がガンのもとになることがある。

Kuuki chuu no goku chiisai ryuushi ga gan no moto ni naru koto ga aru.
Very small particles in the air are sometimes the basis of developing cancer.

24. 地下歩道を抜けたところが眺望スペース入口です。

Chika hodou wo nuketa tokoro ga choubou supeesu iriguchi desu.
The place you passed on the underground walkway is the entrance to the viewing space.

Supplemental Reading Practice

After completing Chapter 66, you should be able to read Lesson 024, "Most Popular Restaurant of 2015," Lesson 025, "Ruby Roman," and Lesson 026, "The Gorilla that is Too Handsome," in *News in Slow Japanese*.

Chapter 67

New Kanji in this Chapter

# 1137 秒 (1)	# 1138 針 (2)	# 1139 効 (2)	# 1140 免 (2)
# 1141 許 (2)	# 1142 疫 (1)	# 1143 樋 (2)	# 1144 箸 (2)

Vocabulary List with Mnemonics

from the Kanji Catalogue

一秒　　ichibyou = a second (1/60 minute); from ichi = one + byou = second; *the bee owner sees a bee fly by every second*

秒針　　byoushin = the second hand on a clock; from byou = second + shin = needle; *the Shinto priest gave me a needle*

針　　　hari = needle; *Prince Harry is good with needles*

方針　　houshin = policy, principle, direction; from hou = direction + shin = needle

効く　　kiku = to be effective; *if you kiku (listen) to the doctor's instructions, the medicine will be effective*

効果　　kouka = effect; *the cold car had an effect on the children;* cf. 結果 kekka = effect

効力　　kouryoku = an effect; from kouka = effect + ryoku = power; cf. 協力 kyouryoku = cooperation

免許　　menkyo = license; *the men went to Kyoto to get a license*

免除　　menjo = exemption; *the men asked Joan of Arc to help them get an exemption from military service*

免状　　menjou = diploma, license; *the men joked that their diplomas were written with disappearing ink*

免疫　　men'eki = immunity; *she was exposed to meningitis at the eki (station), but she has immunity*

免れる　manugareru = to be exempted from, to avoid; *the manual that the gambler wrote about red roosters avoided the topic of sex*

許す　　yurusu = to forgive, accept, permit; *after the youths used a ruse on Superman, he forgave them*

許可　　kyoka = permission, approval; *I have permission to drive a Kyoto car*

Kanji Pronunciations

# 1137 – byou	# 1138 – hari, shin	# 1139 – ki, kou	# 1140 – men, manuga
# 1141 – yuru, kyo	# 1142 – eki	# 1143 – hi, doi	# 1144 – hashi, bashi

疫病 — ekibyou = plague, epidemic; from eki = epidemic; *an excellent king healed people during the epidemic*; + byouki = illness

樋口 — Higuchi = family name; from hi = water pipe; *during the heat wave, I cooled off with water from a water pipe*; + guchi = kuchi = mouth

雨樋 — amadoi = rain gutter; from ama = ame = rain + doi = gutter; *my doily was flushed down the gutter*

箸 — hashi = chopsticks; *I eat hash made from eels, using chopsticks*

割り箸 — waribashi = splittable (disposable) chopsticks; from waru = to break glass or wood + bashi = hashi = chopsticks

from the Practice Sentences

針仕事 — harishigoto = sewing, needlework; from hari = needle + shigoto = work

免税 — menzei = tax exemption; from menjo = exemption + zeikin = taxes

手つき — tetsuki = manner of using the hands; from te = hand + tsukau = to use

有効な — yuukou na = valid, effective; *the youthful co-ed had a valid and effective plan*

入力 — nyuuryoku = computer input, data entry; from nyuu = to enter, e.g., nyuugaku = entering school; + ryoku = power

危うく — ayauku = barely, almost; *the Ayatollah called an Uber car to bring Kool-Aid for the party, and it arrived barely in time*

はしか — hashika = measles; *while we were hashing out our problems in the car, I noticed a spot of measles on my arm*

from News in Slow Japanese

解消 — kaishou = reduction, cancellation, resolution; *the Kaiser came to the shore and worked out a resolution to the sailor's strike*

免疫力 — men'eki ryoku = immunity; from men'eki = immune + ryoku = power

緊張感 — kinchoukan = tension, nervousness; from kinchou = tension + kanjiru = to feel

解かれる — tokareru = to get solved or untied; the passive form of 解く toku = to untie, solve, undo, work out, dispel

不安感 — fuankan = an uneasy feeling, sense of anxiety; from fuan = anxiety, uneasiness + kanjiru = to feel

安心感 — anshinkan = a sense of security; from anshin = peace of mind, relief + kanjiru = to feel

そうめん — soumen = thin white noodles; *the Soviet men ate white noodles*

流し — nagashi = flowing; also = kitchen sink; from nagasu = to flush, drain, pour, wash away

竹製 — takesei = made from bamboo; from take = bamboo + seihin = finished product

すくう	sukuu = to scoop up or ladle; _Superman went to the Kool-Aid pitcher and scooped up a drink_; cf. 救う sukuu = to rescue
上手く	umaku = skillfully, usually spelled うまく ; from umai = skillful
キャッチする	kyacchi suru = to catch
アジ	aji = horse mackerel; _the aristocratic genius prefers horse mackerel_
乗り切る	norikiru = to get through or ride across; from noru = to board a vehicle + kiru = to cut

Practice Sentences

1. 光は１秒間に地球を７回半回ります。

Hikari wa ichibyoukan ni chikyuu wo nanakai han mawarimasu.
Light circles around the earth 7 ½ times per second.

2. 彼女は針仕事が上手だ。

Kanojo wa harishigoto ga jouzu da.
She is skillful at needlework.

3. 中国の薬で風邪に良く効くらしいですよ。

Chuugoku no kusuri de kaze ni yoku kiku rashii desu yo.
It's Chinese medicine, and it seems to have a good effect on colds, for sure.

4. 運転免許はお持ちですか。

Unten menkyo wa omochi desu ka.
Are you honorably holding (i.e., do you possess) a driver's license?

5. 古代では疫病でたくさんの人が死んだ。

Kodai de wa ekibyou de takusan no hito ga shinda.
In ancient times many people died of the plague.

6. 雨樋修理がかかる費用をお伝えいたします。

Amadoi shuuri ga kakaru hiyou wo otsutae itashimasu.
I will humbly inform you about rain gutter repair to-spend expenses.

7. 和食のレストランへ行くたびに、割り箸を家へもって帰ります。

Washoku no resutoran e iku tabi ni, waribashi wo uchi e motte kaerimasu.
On occasions when I eat at Japanese restaurants, I take splittable chopsticks home.

8. 彼は数秒待ってドアを開けた。

Kare wa suubyou matte doa wo aketa.
He waited a few seconds and then opened the door.

9. 個人情報を公開しないのが私たちの方針です。

Kojin jouhou wo koukai shinai no ga watashitachi no houshin desu.
It is our policy not to disclose personal information.

10. ここは免税店ですか。

Koko wa menzei ten desu ka.
Is this a tax-free shop?

11. 疫病が発生した。

Ekibyou ga hassei shita.
An epidemic broke out.

12. 彼の発言は逆効果になった。

Kare no hatsugen wa gyaku kouka ni natta.
His remarks had the opposite effect (from what was expected).

13. ここに駐車するには許可が必要です。

Koko ni chuusha suru ni wa kyoka ga hitsuyou desu.
Permission is necessary in order to park here.

14. 雨樋が詰まって草が生えてるなら早めのお掃除が必要です。

Amadoi ga tsumatte kusa ga haeteru nara hayame no osouji ga hitsuyou desu.
In the case that the rain gutters are clogged and the grass is growing, early honorable cleaning is necessary.

15. 彼は不器用な手つきで箸を使っていた。

Kare wa bukiyou na tetsuki de hashi wo tsukatte ita.
He was using chopsticks in a clumsy hand-use manner.

16. 彼は 100 メートルを 12 秒以内で走ることができます。

Kare wa hyaku meetoru wo juuni byou inai de hashiru koto ga dekimasu.
He can run 100 meters within 12 seconds.

17. 時計の針を進めた。

Tokei no hari wo susumeta.
I advanced the hands of the clock.

18. 有効なメールアドレスを入力してください。

Yuukou na meeru adoresu wo nyuuryoku shite kudasai.
Please enter a valid email address.

19. 彼は危うく死を免れた。

Kare wa ayauku shi wo manugareta.
He barely avoided death.

20. 失敗は許されない。

Shippai wa yurusarenai.
As for the mistake, it can't be forgiven.

21. 樋口さんは箸を使ってそばを食べます。

Higuchi san wa hashi wo tsukatte soba wo tabemasu.
Higuchi eats thin buckwheat noodles using chopsticks.

22. 家の子供はみな、はしかに免疫がある。

Uchi no kodomo wa mina, hashika ni men'eki ga aru.
All of our children are immune to measles.

Supplemental Reading Practice

After completing Chapter 67, you should be able to read Lesson 027, "The Magical Power of Hugs," and Lesson 028, "Nagashi Aji," in *News in Slow Japanese*.

Chapter 68

New Kanji in this Chapter

# 1145 志 (3)	# 1146 軒 (2)	# 1147 激 (2)	# 1148 減 (2)
# 1149 処 (2)	# 1150 証 (1)	# 1151 拠 (2)	# 1152 唱 (2)

Vocabulary List with Mnemonics

from the Kanji Catalogue

志	kokorozashi = kokoroza = ambition, wish, goal; *a man with his kokoro (heart) set on Zambian sheep has an ambition to market wool*
志望	shibou = ambition, wish, goal; *when the first sheep was born, my ambition was to raise a large herd*
一軒	ikken = one house; from ichi = one + ken = house; *Ken and Barbie live in a house*
軒	noki = eaves; *it's normal to keep out of the rain by standing under the eaves*
過激な	kageki na = aggressive, radical; from ka = excessively; *Karl Marx was excessively studious;* + geki = intense; *the guest who took our keys was intense*
激戦	gekisen = fierce competition or battle; from geki = intense; *the guest who took our keys was intense;* + sensou = war
激しい	hageshii = fierce, tempestuous, crowded (traffic), frequent (change); *our Hawaiian guest was a Shiite with a fierce demeanor*
減少	genshou = a decrease; *Genghis showed how a tax decrease could help the people*
激減	gekigen = sharp decrease; from geki = intense; *the guest who took our keys was intense;* + genshou = a decrease
加減する	kagen suru = to moderate, downgrade; *the carpenter that Genghis hired downgraded his plans for the new palace*
半減する	hangen suru = to reduce by half; from hanbun = half + genshou = decrease
減る	heru = to reduce, lose (weight); *the herald ruined his health when he lost weight*

Kanji Pronunciations

# 1145 – kokoroza, kokorozashi, shi	# 1146 – ken, noki	# 1147 – hage, geki	# 1148 – gen, he
# 1149 – dokoro, sho	# 1150 – shou	# 1151 – kyo, ko	# 1152 – shou, tona

お食事処	oshokujidokoro = restaurant (Japanese style); from oshokuji = honorable meal + dokoro = place; *the doorman's Corolla was in that place*
処理する	shori suru= to deal with, handle, eliminate; *Shorty deals with our garbage*
対処する	taisho suru = to deal with, implying that one solves a problem; *at the Thai show, I had to deal with many problems*; cf. 対応する taiou suru = to address
処分	shobun = disposal, expulsion, punishment; *after my expulsion, I had to move from the shore to the boondocks*
証拠	shouko = evidence, proof, testimony; *the short Colombian gave testimony*
証明	shoumei = proof, identification; *I showed the mayor my identification card*
拠点	kyoten = position, location, base, point; *the Kyoto tennis club is at this location*
根拠	konkyo = basis or foundation (of a belief, etc.); *Conan O'Brien went to Kyoto and discovered a basis for the rumor*
合唱団	gasshoudan = chorus goup, choir; from gasshou = chorus; *it was a ghastly show, but I sang in the chorus*; + dantai = group
独唱	dokushou = solo singing; from dokushin = single, unmarried; + shou = to sing energetically, e.g. gasshou = chorus
唱える	tonaeru = to advocate or recite; *the tonal quality of the erudite attorney's voice impressed everyone as she advocated for justice*

from the Practice Sentences

激痛	gekitsuu = intense, sharp pain; from geki = intense; *the guest who took our key was intense*; + tsuu = pain, e.g. zutsuu = headache
折り曲げる	orimageru = to bend or fold down; from oru = to break or fold + mageru = to twist; *the magician gets the rooster to twist his head around*
証言	shougen = testimony; *although time was short, Genghis listened to the testimony*
真相	shinsou = truth, real situation; *the Shinto priest soberly contemplated the truth*
本拠地	honkyochi = headquarters, base; from honkyo = base; *we moved our base from Hong Kong to Kyoto;* + chi = ground, e.g., chikatetsu = subway
歌唱	kashou = song, singing; from kashu = singer + shou = to sing, e.g., dokushou = solo singing
歌唱法	kashouhou = the laws or rules of singing; from kashou = singing + houritsu = law
意志	ishi = will, willpower; *the eastern Shiites had a lot of willpower*
火事	kaji = fire; *he was cagey when they asked him about the fire*
全焼する	zenshou suru = to burn completely; from zen = entire + shou = to burn; *I burn wood by the shore*
減税	genzei = tax reduction; from genshou = a decrease + zeikin = tax

苦情　kujou = a complaint; *although it was cool, Job had complaints about the heat*

暗証番号　anshou bangou = code number; from an = dark; *ants live in the dark*; + shoumei = proof, identification + bangou = number

主張　shuchou = assertion, claim; *the shooter choked when he was asked about his claim that he acted alone*; cf. 出張 shutchou = business trip

一角　ikkaku = corner, section, point; from ichi = one + kaku = corner, e.g., shikaku = a square or rectangle

酒好き　sakezuki = a drinker, someone who likes sake; from sake + zuki = suki = to like

不服　fufuku = dissatisfaction, complaint; *the foolish guy from Fukuoka was full of complaints*

from News in Slow Japanese

三毛猫　mikeneko = calico cat, a cat with three colors of fur; from mittsu = three + ke = hair or fur + neko = cat

天国　tengoku = heaven, paradise; from ten = sky, e.g., tenki = weather; + goku = koku = country

旅立つ　tabidatsu = to begin a trip, to pass away; from tabi = trip + datsu = tatsu = to stand

明神　myoujin = a gracious deity; from myou = bright; *the cat meows in the bright sun*; + jin = god, e.g., jinja = a Shinto shrine

後任　kounin = successor, replacement; from kou = later, e.g., koukai = regret; + nin = responsibility, e.g., shunin = person in charge

寝室　shinshitsu = bedroom; from shin = to sleep; *I say Shinto prayers before I sleep*; + shitsu = room

一軒家　ikkenya = detached house; from ikken = one house + ya = house

住宅　juutaku = residence, house; from juusho = address + otaku = home

こだわる　kodawaru = to be particular about, to be fixated on; *I am particular about the Kodak warranty for the ruined camera*

職人　shokunin = craftsperson, artisan; from shokugyou = occupation + nin = person

目指す　mezasu = to aim at; *sitting in the mezzanine of the theater, Sue decided to aim at a career in the opera*

受講生　jukousei = students attending lectures; from jukou = attending lectures; *the junior corporal spends his time attending lectures*; + sei = to live

料理人　ryourinin = chef or cook; from ryouri = cuisine + nin = person

経営者　kei'eisha = business manager or owner; from kei'ei = management + sha = person

一人前　ichininmae = becoming adult, coming of age; *ichinin mae (before one person, i.e., before you can become a complete person), you must come of age*

離島　ritou = isolated island; from ri = to separate, e.g., rikon = divorce; + tou = island, e.g., hantou = peninsula

入団
資格

nyuudan = enrollment; from nyuu = to enter + dantai = group

shikaku = credentials, qualifications; *when my sheep bumped into the cactus, I found a veterinarian with good credentials*; cf. 四角 shikaku = square or rectangle

Practice Sentences

1. 第一志望の大学に合格して、どんなに嬉しかったことか。

Daiichi shibou no daigaku ni goukaku shite, donna ni ureshikatta koto ka.
To the number one ambition's (i.e., my first-choice) university, acceptance do, and how pleased I was! (donna ni followed by koto ka = "how much!")

2. みんなでもう一軒行きませんか。

Minna de mou ikken ikimasen ka.
With everyone, won't you go to one more house (i.e., one more bar)?

3. 肩に激痛を感じた。

Kata ni gekitsuu wo kanjita.
I felt a severe pain in my shoulder.

4. 最近、タバコを吸う人が減りましたね。

Saikin, tabako wo suu hito ga herimashita ne.
Recently people who smoke tobacco decreased, huh.

5. この書類は、機械で処理しますから、折り曲げないでください。

Kono shorui wa, kikai de shori shimasu kara, orimagenai de kudasai.
Since we will get rid of these documents by means of a machine, please don't fold them.

6. 彼の証言は真相に近い。

Kare no shougen wa shinsou ni chikai.
His testimony is close to the truth.

7. 我が社の本拠地は東京にあります。

Wagasha no honkyochi wa toukyou ni arimasu.
Our company's headquarters are in Tokyo.

8. 彼女は私達に歌唱法を教えてくれた。

Kanojo wa watashitachi ni kashouhou wo oshiete kureta.
She taught us singing rules and gave.

9. 彼は意志が弱い。

Kare wa ishi ga yowai.
He has weak willpower.

10. ２軒目の家がその火事で全焼した。

Niken me no ie ga sono kaji de zenshou shita.
Two houses were burned completely in that fire.

11. 君の考えは少し過激だ。

Kimi no kangae wa sukoshi kageki da.
Your idea is a little radical.

12. 彼は減税を唱えた。

Kare wa genzei wo tonaeta.
He advocated tax cuts.

13. お客さんから苦情を受けた
ら、すぐ対処するべきだ。

Okyakusan kara kujou wo uketara, sugu
taisho suru beki da.
If you receive a complaint from an
honorable customer, you should deal
with it soon.

14. 暗証番号を忘れちゃった！

Anshou bangou wo wasurechatta!
I completely forgot the pin number!

15. これらの主張には科学的な根
拠がない。

Korera no shuchou ni wa kagakuteki na
konkyo ga nai.
There is no scientific basis for these
claims.

16. 彼女は女優になることを志し
た。

Kanojo wa joyuu ni naru koto wo
kokoroza shita.
She did (i.e., had) an ambition to become
an actress.

17. 通りに面した軒下に出す簡単
な店で食べました。

Toori ni men shita noki shita ni dasu
kantan na mise de tabemashita.
I ate at a simple shop which faced the
street, put out under the eaves.

18. 激しくドアをノックする音で
彼は目が覚めた。

Hageshiku doa wo nokku suru oto de
kare wa me ga sameta.
Due to a fiercely knocking sound on the
door, he woke up.

19. この国の人口は徐々に減少し
ている。

Kono kuni no jinkou wa jojo ni genshou
shite iru.
This country's population is gradually
decreasing.

20. お食事処の一角に、お酒好き
にはたまらない「プレミアム
焼酎コーナー」を見つけた。

Oshokujidokoro no ikkaku ni, osakezuki
ni wa tamaranai "puremiamu shouchuu
koonaa" wo mitsuketa.
In the corner of the restaurant, I found a
"Premium Shochu Corner" which is
irresistible to honorable sake lovers.

21. 新たな証拠を発見した。

Arata na shouko wo hakken shita.
I discovered fresh evidence.

22. その決定に不服を唱えた。

Sono kettei ni fufuku wo tonaeta.
I expressed dissatisfaction with the
decision.

Supplemental Reading Practice

After completing Chapter 68, you should be able to read Lesson 029, "The New
Station Master" (with the exception of 鐵 tetsu, a fairly obscure kanji which you don't
need to learn at this point, found on the first line of the lesson). You should also be able

to read Lesson 030, "Tiny House," Lesson 031, "Sushi Academy," and Lesson 032, "KBG84," in *News in Slow Japanese*

Chapter 69

New Kanji in this Chapter

# 1153 満 (2)	# 1154 杉 (1)	# 1155 制 (1)	# 1156 提 (1)
# 1157 甲 (1)	# 1158 羅 (1)	# 1159 徳 (1)	# 1160 祥 (1)

Vocabulary List with Mnemonics

from the Kanji Catalogue

満員	man'in = full house, no vacancy; *the man who works inside the hotel says that there is no vacancy*
満腹	manpuku = full stomach; *that man, who is poor, drank a lot of Kool-Aid and ended up with a full stomach*
満足	manzoku = satisfaction; *the man who drank Zooey's Kool-Aid reported satisfaction*
不満	fuman = dissatisfaction; from fu = negation + manzoku = satisfaction
満ちる	michiru = to become full; *in Michigan I ruined my appetite when I became full of potato chips*
杉	sugi = Japanese cedar tree; *Superman's geese gathered under some Japanese cedar trees*
制度	seido = system or regime; *that sailor's doughnuts are made using a special system*
制服	seifuku = a uniform; from seido = system + fuku = clothes
提出する	teishutsu suru = to hand in or submit; *if that taser shoots me, I will submit my resignation*
前提	zentei = premise, prerequisite; *the Zen tape describes the prerequisites for meditation*
甲羅	koura = shell; *she poured cola on the turtle's shell*
足の甲	ashi no kou = top of the foot; from ashi = foot + the possessive no + koura = shell

Kanji Pronunciations

# 1153 – mi, man	# 1154 – sugi	# 1155 – sei	# 1156 – tei
# 1157 – kou	# 1158 – ra	# 1159 – toku	# 1160 – shou

道徳	doutoku = morality, moral, ethics; *he consumes only <u>doughnuts</u>, <u>tofu</u> and <u>Kool</u>-Aid, since he questions the <u>morality</u> of eating meat*
美徳	bitoku = virtue; from bi = beautiful, e.g., bijin = a beautiful woman; + doutoku = morality
発祥	hasshou = origin; *the <u>harbor</u> and <u>show</u> business are among the <u>origins</u> of New York's wealth*
不祥事	fushouji = scandal; *when the <u>foolish</u> <u>short</u> guy stole a <u>Jeep</u>, he caused a <u>scandal</u>*

from the Practice Sentences

大木	taiboku = a big tree; *the <u>Thai</u> <u>bowler</u> drank <u>Kool</u>-Aid under a <u>big tree</u>*
日給	nikkyuu = daily wage; from nichi = day + kyuuryou = salary, wages
人事課	jinjika = personnel department; from jin = people + ji = intangible thing; *genius is an <u>intangible</u> <u>thing</u>*; + ka = section, e.g., kachou = section manager
かにみそ	kanimiso = miso-like paste found in a crab's intestinal area; from kani = crab + miso = fermented bean paste
甲羅焼き	koura yaki = baked in the shell; from koura = shell + yaku = to bake
不道徳	fudoutoku = immoral; from fu = negation + doutoku = moral
ほのかな	honoka na = faint, dim, slight; *she <u>holds</u> her <u>nose</u> when a <u>candle</u> is lit, but she still smells a <u>faint</u> odor*
やすらぐ	yasuragu = to feel at peace; *after drinking <u>yak</u> soup at the <u>ranch</u> with <u>Goofy</u>, I <u>felt</u> <u>at peace</u>*
やすらぎ	yasuragi = peace of mind, tranquillity; from yasuragu = to feel at peace
公立	kouritsu = public; *the <u>corporation</u> received a <u>written</u> <u>suggestion</u> that it allow <u>public</u> access to some of its facilities*
こわれかかる	kowarekakaru = to begin to break down; from kowareru = to break, intransitive, + kakaru = to start
提案	teian = proposal; *the <u>tape</u> that Queen <u>Anne</u> sent contained her <u>proposals</u>*
固い	katai = hard; *the <u>car</u>'s <u>tires</u> got <u>hard</u> after I inflated them*; cf. 固体 kotai = solid
道徳上	doutokujou = morally, from a moral point of view; from doutoku = moral + jou = above, e.g., jouzu = skillful
制限	seigen = limit, restriction; *Carl <u>Sagan</u> put <u>restrictions</u> on his family's credit card use*
越す	kosu = to exceed, pass, cross, move (residence); *the <u>co</u>-supervisor <u>crossed</u> a line when he ridiculed the boss*

辞表	jihyou = written resignation; *when he got hit by a Jeep, the Lone Ranger said "Hi-yo" and submitted his written resignation*
物事	monogoto = thing, everything; from mono = thing + goto = koto = thing
成り立ち	naritachi = origin, structure, the way something came about; from naritatsu = to materialize
探求する	tankyuu suru = to pursue or search for; *the tanned Cubans searched for gold*
手の甲	te no kou = back of the hand; from te = hand + the possessive no + koura = shell

from News in Slow Japanese

限定	gentei = restriction, limit; *Genghis taped the restrictions on a wall*; cf. 制限 seigen = restriction, limit
満喫	mankitsu = fully enjoying, having enough food and drink; *the man who was engaged in kitsuen (smoking) was fully enjoying himself*
移住する	ijuu suru = to migrate or immigrate; from idou suru = to move an object + juusho = address
移住者	ijuusha = immigrant, migrant; from ijuu suru = to immigrate + sha = person
市町村	shichouson = cities, towns, villages; from toshi = city + chou = town; *I chose to live in this town*; + son = village; *they sing songs in that village*
アピール	apiiru = appeal, in the sense of being attractive to people
提供する	teikyou suru = to offer, provide or sponsor; *I will take you to Kyouto if you will provide the meals*
有給	yuukyuu = an abbreviation of 有給休暇　yuukyuukyuuka = paid vacation; from yuu = to exist; *the Yukon exists*; + kyuuryou = salary + kyuuka = vacation
遅め	osome = late, slow; from osoi = late, slow

Practice Sentences

1. 少年は満腹になった。

Shounen wa manpuku ni natta.
The boy became full.

2. 昔そこには杉の大木があった。

Mukashi soko ni wa sugi no taiboku ga atta.
In olden days, there was a big cedar tree there.

3. 彼らはその制度を改めた。

Karera wa sono seido wo aratameta.
They changed that system.

4. この書類は人事課に提出する
には及ばない。

Kono shorui wa jinjika ni teishutsu suru
ni wa oyobanai.
As for these documents, to the personnel
department, as for to submit, it doesn't
reach. (i.e., we don't have to submit
them)

5. かにみそ甲羅焼きを食べたこ
とがありますか。

Kanimiso koura yaki wo tabeta koto ga
arimasu ka.
Have you ever eaten miso with crab
innards baked in a shell?

6. 彼は不道徳な男だ。

Kare wa fudoutoku na otoko da.
He is an immoral man.

7. バレンシアはパエリア発祥の
地として知られている。

Barenshia wa paeria hasshou no chi to
shite shirarete iru.
Valencia is known as the birthplace of
paella. (to shite = as, in the role)

8. どのバスも満員だ。

Dono basu mo man'in da.
All of the buses are full.

9. 杉から匂うほのかな香りは人
をリラックスさせ、やすらぎ
を与えてくれます。

Sugi kara niou honoka na kaori wa hito
wo rirakkusu sase, yasuragi wo ataete
kuremasu.
From the cedar, it smells of a faint odor
that makes people relax and bestows
tranquility and gives.

10. 公立学校制度はこわれかかっ
ています。

Kouritsu gakkou seido wa kowarekakatte
imasu.
The public school system is starting to
break down.

11. 提案があります。

Teian ga arimasu.
There is (i.e., here is) a proposal.

12. カメの甲羅は固いです。

Kame no koura wa katai desu.
A turtle's shell is hard.

13. それは道徳上の問題だ。

Sore wa doutokujou no mondai da.
That is a moral question.

14. 彼の心は苦しみに満ちてい
る。

Kare no kokoro wa kurushimi ni michite
iru.
His heart is being filled with pain.

15. あの会社は過去に不祥事を起
こしたことがある。

Ano kaisha wa kako ni fushouji wo
okoshita koto ga aru.
That company has caused a scandal in
the past.

16. 森の中で一番高い杉は 56 メ
ートルもある。

Mori no naka de ichiban takai sugi wa
gojuuroku meetoru mo aru.
The highest cedar in the interior of the
forest is all of 56 meters.

17. その車は制限速度を越している。

Sono kuruma wa seigen sokudo wo koshite iru.
That car is exceeding the speed limit.

18. 辞表を提出した。

Jihyou wo teishutsu shita.
I handed in a written resignation.

19. かに甲羅グラタンはとてもおいしいです。

Kani koura guratan wa totemo oishii desu.
Crab shell gratin is very delicious.

20. 正直は美徳の一つです。

Shoujiki wa bitoku no hitotsu desu.
Honesty is one of the virtues.

21. ある物事の発祥を知るためには、その成り立ちを探求する必要がある。

Aru monogoto no hasshou wo shiru tame ni wa, sono naritachi wo tankyuu suru hitsuyou ga aru.
In order to know the origin of a thing, it is necessary to search for the way it came about.

22. 彼はガラスの破片で右手の甲に怪我をした。

Kare wa garasu no hahen de migi te no kou ni kega wo shita.
He did an injury to the back of his right hand by glass fragments.

Supplemental Reading Practice

After completing Chapter 69, you should be able to read Lesson 033, "Short Term Living in Hokkaido," and Lesson 034, "Sakura's Hawaii Travel Journal," in *News in Slow Japanese.*

Chapter 70

New Kanji in this Chapter

# 1161 勘 (1)	# 1162 弁 (1)	# 1163 護 (1)	# 1164 看 (1)
# 1165 婦 (1)	# 1166 板 (3)	# 1167 盆 (1)	# 1168 鬼 (2)

Vocabulary List with Mnemonics

from the Kanji Catalogue

勘弁   kanben = pardon, forgiveness; *I left the candy on the bench, but I hope that you can grant me forgiveness*

勘違い   kanchigai = misunderstanding, wrong guess; from kan = perception; *the public's perception of Canada is positive*; + chigai = difference

勘定   kanjou = bill, check, calculation; *in Canada, we joked about who should pick up the check*

弁護士   bengoshi = lawyer; *we hired a lawyer for the benefit of our goats and sheep*

弁当   bentou = box lunch; *I asked Benjamin Franklin to put some tofu in my box lunch*

名古屋弁   nagoyaben = Nagoya dialect; from Nagoya + ben = dialect; *my knowledge of the local dialect benefited me*

弁解   benkai = excuse, justification; *I made up an excuse for the benefit of the Kaiser*

看護婦   kangofu = female nurse; *the female nurse can go to the funeral*

看板   kanban = signboard; *the signboard states that candy is banned here*

婦人   fujin = woman; *on Mt. Fuji's north slope, a woman lives*

主婦   shufu = housewife; *that housewife will shoot you in the foot*

夫婦   fuufu = married couple; *that married couple may be foolish, but they make good food*

鉄板焼き   teppanyaki = food grilled on an iron griddle; from tetsu = iron + pan = plank or plate; *that pan is made from metal plates*; + yaku = to cook

板   ita = (wooden) board or (metal) plate; *I sawed a board for my Italian friend*

お盆   Obon = a Buddhist summer festival when ancestors are worshipped; *we visit our ancestor's old bones at a temple during the Buddhist summer festival*

Kanji Pronunciations

# 1161 – kan	# 1162 – ben	# 1163 – go	# 1164 – kan
# 1165 – fu	# 1166 – ban, ita, pan	# 1167 – bon	# 1168 – oni, ki

盆踊り — bonodori = a dance performed at Obon; from Bon = summer festival + odori = dance

鬼 — oni = devil, cruel person; *that devil is owning a cow*

殺人鬼 — satsujinki = killer, cutthroat; *I read a satisfying Superman novel about a genius who used a skeleton key to uncover evidence about a killer*

from the Practice Sentences

白衣 — hakui = white uniform; from haku = white, e.g., hakuhatsu = white hair; + ifuku = clothing

黒板 — kokuban = blackboard; *Coke is banned from the space near the blackboard*

駅弁 — ekiben = boxed lunch sold at train station; from eki = station + bentou = boxed lunch

探り当てる — saguriateru = to find out; from saguru = to probe, grope, look for + ateru = to hit, touch or win

人食い — hitokui = cannibalism, man-eating; from hito = person + kuu = to eat

年中行事 — nenjuugyouji = an annual event; from nen = year + juu = chuu = inside + gyouji = event

from News in Slow Japanese

叶わぬ — kanawanu = an archaic way of saying kanawazu = kanawanai = will not be fulfilled; from kanau = to come true or be fulfilled

カエル — kaeru = a frog; *the frog always kaeru (returns) to his home*

求愛 — kyuuai = courting; *the cute ice cream salesman was courting me*

キス — kisu = a kiss

せまる — semaru = to come close, to urge; *he urged me to sell magazines about roosters*

失恋 — shitsuren = unrequited love, lost love; from shitsu = to lose, e.g. shitsugyousha = unemployed people; + ren'ai = romantic love

見合い — miai = an arranged marriage meeting; from miru = to look + au = to match

出会える — deaeru = to be able to meet; the potential tense of deau = to meet; from deru = to go out + au = to meet

Practice Sentences

1. 息子はまだ若いということで勘弁してもらった。

Musuko wa mada wakai to iu koto de kanben shite moratta.
Due to the fact that my son is still young, (someone) forgave and we received.

2. 看護婦は白衣を着ている。

Kangofu wa hakui wo kite iru.
The female nurse is wearing a white uniform.

3. 黒板を見なさい。

Kokuban wo minasai.
Look at the blackboard.

4. お盆には大勢の人が田舎に帰るから電車や道路が込んで大変なの。

Obon ni wa oozei no hito ga inaka ni kaeru kara densha ya douro ga konde taihen na no.
As for at Obon, since a lot of people return to the hometowns, trains and roads, etc., get crowded, and it's terrible.

5. 来年のことを言えば鬼が笑う。

Rainen no koto wo ieba oni ga warau.
If you speak of next year's things, the devil will laugh.

6. お昼は駅弁にしよう。

Ohiru wa ekiben ni shiyou.
For honorable noon (i.e., lunch), let's choose a station boxed luch.

7. 看護婦は静脈を探り当てた。

Kangofu wa joumyaku wo saguriateta.
The nurse found (probed and hit) a vein.

8. 彼女の家の床は全部板でできている。

Kanojo no ie no yuka wa zenbu ita de dekite iru.
The floors of her house are all made of wooden boards.

9. みんなで盆踊りというダンスをするのよ。

Minna de bonodori to iu dansu wo suru no yo.
With everyone, we do the bonodori-called dance, for sure.

10. 森に行ったら、人食い鬼に気をつけてください！

Mori ni ittara hitokui oni ni ki wo tsukete kudasai!
If you go to the forest, watch out for the man-eating devils!

11. お勘定をお願いします。

Okanjou wo onegai shimasu.
The honorable check, I beg you.

12. 弁護士はみんな嘘つきだ。

Bengoshi wa minna usotsuki da.
Lawyers are all liars.

13. あの看板がよく読めないんです。

Ano kanban ga yoku yomenain desu.
That signboard over there is unable to be read well (i.e., I can't read it).

14. 私達は夫婦です。

Watashitachi wa fuufu desu.
We are husband and wife.

15. お盆は仏教の年中行事で、8月13日から15日まで行われます。

Obon wa bukkyou no nenjuugyouji de, hachigatsu juusan nichi kara juugo nichi made okonawaremasu.
Obon is a Buddhist annual event, and it's held from August 13 until August 15.

16. 彼女は殺人鬼から逃れようとして必死に走った。

Kanojo wa satsujinki kara nogareyou to shite hisshi ni hashitta.
Trying to escape from the murderer, she ran desperately.

17. あの老婦人は誰ですか？

Ano roufujin wa dare desu ka.
Who is that old woman?

18. 鉄板焼きとすき焼きとどっちの方が好きですか。

Teppanyaki to sukiyaki to dotchi no hou ga suki desu ka.
Do you prefer teppanyaki (grilled food) or sukiyaki (boiled food)?

19. う〜ん、どっか勘違いしてるかな？

Un, dokka kanchigai shiteru kana?
Well, I wonder if I'm misunderstanding something?

Supplemental Reading Practice

After completing Chapter 70, you should be able to read Lesson 035, "Chacha's Unrequited Love," in *News in Slow Japanese*.

Chapter 71

New Kanji in this Chapter

# 1169 魅 (1)	# 1170 倉 (2)	# 1171 創 (1)	# 1172 穀 (1)
# 1173 締 (3)	# 1174 偉 (2)	# 1175 載 (1)	# 1176 阿 (1)

Vocabulary List with Mnemonics

from the Kanji Catalogue

魅力	miryoku = attractiveness, charm; *after my meal, I drank some of Pope Leo's Kool-Aid and was delighted by its charm*
魅力的な	miryokuteki na = fascinating, charming; from miryoku = charm + teki = related to
倉庫	souko = warehouse; *the soldiers' coats were kept in a warehouse*
倉	kura = storehouse; *I have a storehouse where I keep kuuraa (air conditioners)*
創造	souzou = creation; *in the Soviet zone, scientists were assigned the creation of new weapons*
創立する	souritsu suru = to establish; *the soldiers received a written suggestion to establish a base*
創設する	sousetsu suru = to found, establish; from souzou = creation + shisetsu = facility or institution
独創性	dokusousei = originality, creativity; *the documentary about soldiers and sailors demonstrated their creativity in solving problems*
穀倉	kokusou = granary; *the Coke that the soldiers drink is stored in the granary*
穀物	kokumotsu = grain, cereal; *the Coke is in a storehouse behind the moats, together with the grain*
締める	shimeru = to fasten (seatbelt), tie (necktie), strangle, tighten (transitive); *when I fly my plane and look at the shimmering roofs below, I tighten my seat belt*
締まる	shimaru = to tighten (intransitive); the intransitive form of shimeru = to fasten
締め切り	shimekiri = closing, deadline; from shimeru = to strangle + kiru = to cut
戸締まり	tojimari = fastening doors; from to = door + jimari = shimari = fastening
偉人	ijin = an exceptional person; *the easygoing genius is an exceptional person*
偉大	idai = great, grand; *the eagle's dive from the sky was great*

Kanji Pronunciations

# 1169 – mi	# 1170 – sou, kura	# 1171 – sou	# 1172 – koku
# 1173 – shimari, ji, shi	# 1174 – i, era	# 1175 – no	# 1176 – a

偉い — erai = great, excellent, eminent, distinguished; *it was an error to throw ice at that distinguished woman*

載る — noru = to be printed or placed on; *it's normal for rumors to be printed in that newspaper*

載せる — noseru = to publish, to put on top of; the transitive form of noru = to be printed or placed on

阿波踊り — Awa Odori = a dance festival held during Obon in Tokushima City; *I was awakened by the odori (dance) festival*

from the Practice Sentences

周年 — shuunen = anniversary; from shuu = lap, e.g., isshuu = one lap; + nen = year

優れた — sugureta = excellent; *Superman has a goofy reputation at the tavern, but he's excellent in a crisis*

名称 — meishou = name, title; *the major came on shore and told us his name*

近年 — kin'nen = recent years; from kin = close, e.g., kinjo = neighborhood; + nen = year; cf. 禁煙 kin'en = no smoking

流布 — rufu = dissemination, circulation; *the ruined food was taken out of circulation*

独特 — dokutoku = unique, original, characteristic; from dokusousei = originality + toku = special

落ち込み — ochikomi = a decline; from ochiru = to fall + komu = to crowd into

急速に — kyuusoku ni = rapidly, promptly; from kyuu ni = suddenly + sassoku = immediately

予想 — yosou = expectation; *the yoga class met the soldier's expectations*

すいません — suimasen = an abbreviation of sumimasen = sorry, excuse me

はかり — hakari = a scale; from hakaru = to weigh

魅せられる — miserareru = to be enchanted or fascinated; *we made a meal from the selfish rancher's red rooster and were fascinated by the flavor*

果実 — kajitsu = berry, nut, fruit; *let's call the jittery superstar and give him these berries*

常食 — joushoku = staple food; *Joan of Arc shocked us when she refused her staple food*

from News in Slow Japanese

伝統 — dentou = tradition, heritage; *the dentist toasted his heritage*; cf. 電灯 dentou = electric light

芸能 — geinou = entertainment, performance; *the gay Norwegians put on a performance*

イベント — ibento = event

実る
minoru = to bear fruit, ripen; *we ate a <u>meal</u> in the <u>Nor</u>wegians' <u>room</u> consisting of fruit that was about to <u>ripen</u>*

ジャーナリスト
jaanarisuto = journalist

熱気
nekki = hot air, intensity, zeal; from netsu = fever + ki = air

包まれる
tsutsumareru = to be enveloped by; the passive tense of tsutsumu = to wrap up

踊り子
odoriko = dancer (usually female); from odoru = to dance + ko = child

広める
hiromeru = to publicize, propagate, spread; from hiroi = spacious

１分間
ippunkan = one minute duration; from ippun = one minute + kan = duration

遠ぼえ
tooboe = alternative spelling of 遠吠え tooboe = howling

ワールドレコーズ
waarudo rekoozu = world records

酒造所
shuzousho = a brewery, distillery (usually spelled and pronounced 酒造場 shuzoujou); from shuzou = sake brewing; *I bought some <u>shoes</u> in the Canal <u>Zone</u>, and then I learned <u>sake brewing</u>*; + basho = place

取締役
torishimariyaku = a company director, board member; from toru = to take + shimaru = to tighten + yaku = service, e.g., yaku ni tatsu = to be of service

代表取締役
daihyoutorishimariyaku = representative director (a director chosen by a board to represent it); from daihyou = representative + torishimariyaku = board member

議論
giron = discussion, controversy, argument; *the <u>gee</u>se that <u>Ron</u>ald Reagan kept in his yard caused some <u>controversy</u>*

Practice Sentences

1. 彼女は魅力的だ。
Kanojo wa miryokuteki da.
She is charming.

2. ホテルに寄って、高倉さんをお連れしましょう。
Hoteru ni yotte, takakura san wo otsure shimashou.
Let's stop at the hotel and take Takakura along.

3. 私たちの学校は創立して５０周年になります。
Watashitachi no gakkou wa souritsu shite gojuushuunen ni narimasu.
As for our school, being established, it becomes (or is) the 50th anniversary.

4. 隣の人の土地は自分の土地より優れた穀物を産出する。
Tonari no hito no tochi wa jibun no tochi yori sugureta kokumotsu wo sanshutsu suru.
Compared to my land, the neighbor's land yields more excellent grain.

5. シートベルトをお締めくださ
い。

Shiitoberuto wo oshime kudasai.
Please honorably fasten your seat belt.

6. 偉大な芸術家の作品が並んで
いた。

Idai na geijutsuka no sakuhin ga narande ita.
Great artists' works of art were lining up (i.e., there were a lot of them).

7. この雑誌には、教育問題につ
いての興味深い記事が載って
いる。

Kono zasshi ni wa, kyouiku mondai ni tsuite no kyoumibukai kiji ga notte iru.
As for in this magazine, deeply interesting articles about educatonal problems are being published.

8. 「阿波踊り」の名称がさほど
古い物でなく近年流布したこ
とがわかる。

"Awa odori" no meishou ga sahodo furui mono de naku kin'nen rufu shita koto ga wakaru.
We understand that the "Awa Odori" name, not being a very old thing, has been disseminated in recent years.

9. その絵には独特の魅力があ
る。

Sono e ni wa dokutoku no miryoku ga aru.
That picture has unique charm.

10. 車を倉庫に入れてください。

Kuruma wo souko ni irete kudasai.
Please put the car into the warehouse.

11. 彼は他の誰よりも独創性があ
る。

Kare wa hoka no dare yori mo dokusousei ga aru.
As for him, compared to anyone else, he has originality (i.e., he is more original than anyone else).

12. 穀物生産の落ち込みによっ
て、中国は急速に世界有数の
穀物輸入国となることが予想
される。

Kokumotsu seisan no ochikomi ni yotte, chuugoku wa kyuusoku ni sekai yuusuu no kokumotsu yu'nyuu koku tonaru koto ga yosou sareru.
Due to a decline in grain production, China is expected to rapidly become the world's prominent grain importing country.

13. 締め切りまでにあまり時間が
無くてすいません。

Shimekiri made ni amari jikan ga nakute suimasen.
Since there isn't much time by (i.e., until) the deadline, I'm sorry.

14. 偉人というものは若い頃に苦
労した人が多い。

Ijin to iu mono wa wakai koro ni kurou shita hito ga ooi.
As for those who are called exceptional people, during their youth, many people suffered.

15. 荷物をはかりの上に載せてく
ださい。

Nimotsu wo hakari no ue ni nosete kudasai.
Please put the luggage on the scale.

16. 「阿波踊り」が有名で、最近
では全国でも夏祭りとして催
しされている。

"Awa odori" ga yuumei de, saikin de wa zenkoku de mo natsu matsuri to shite moyo'oshi sarete iru.
"Awa Odori" is famous, and recently the event is held as a summer festival in the entire country also. (to shite = as, in this context)

17. 彼らは血と暴力に魅せられて
いる。

Karera wa chi to bouryoku ni miserarete iru.
They are fascinated with blood and violence.

18. 倉庫には家具の他に何もなか
った。

Souko ni wa kagu no hoka ni nanimo nakatta.
In the warehouse, except for furniture, there was nothing.

19. 神は天と地を創造した。

Kami wa ten to chi wo souzou shita.
God created the sky and the earth.

20. 戸締まりをするのを忘れる
な。

Tojimari wo suru no wo wasureru na.
Don't forget to fasten the door.

21. 彼は自分を偉い人だと思って
いる。

Kare wa jibun wo erai hito da to omotte iru.
He thinks that he is an eminent person. (jibun ga, also OK, not as good; wo is used because jibun is the object of omou)

22. 彼女の行いが新聞に載った。

Kanojo no okonai ga shinbun ni notta.
Her activities were published in the newspaper.

23. 阿波踊りは徳島県（旧阿波
国）を発祥とする盆踊りであ
る。

Awa odori wa tokushima ken (kyuu awakoku) wo hasshou to suru bonodori de aru.
Awa Odori is a Bon dance that we regard as originating on (or in) Tokushima Prefecture [previously Awa Country]. (to suru = to regard as, in this context)

24. 鳥は小さな果実と穀物の種を
常食としている。

Tori wa chiisana kajitsu to kokumotsu no tane wo joushoku to shite iru.
Birds are having small berries and grain seeds as a staple food. (joushoku to suru = to have as a staple food)

Supplemental Reading Practice

After completing Chapter 71, you should be able to read Lesson 036, "Awa Odori in Paris," and Lesson 037, "An Amazing Guiness Record," in *News in Slow Japanese.*

Chapter 72

New Kanji in this Chapter

# 1177 援 (1)	# 1178 箕 (1)	# 1179 滝 (1)	# 1180 脂 (2)
# 1181 悩 (2)	# 1182 河 (3)	# 1183 焚 (1)	# 1184 梨 (1)

Vocabulary List with Mnemonics

from the Kanji Catalogue

応援 — ouen = support; *the older engineers give support to the younger ones*

援助 — enjo = assistance, support; *I enjoy the support of my family*

救援 — kyuuen = rescue; *a Cuban engineer was responsible for my rescue*

声援 — seien = support, cheering; *the sailors' enthusiasm could be seen in their cheering*

箕面市 — Minooshi = Minoh city, north of Osaka; *I caught some minnows in Minoh*

滝 — taki = waterfall, cascade; *we were talking about a waterfall*

脂 — abura = fat; *that Abu Dhabi ram has a lot of fat on its bones*; cf. 油 abura = oil, # 942

悩む — nayamu = to be troubled or worried; *while I was taking a nap in the yard, the earth moved, and I got worried*

悩み — nayami = distress, worry; from nayamu = to be troubled or worried

苦悩 — kunou = agony, anguish; *when Kool-Aid went up my nose, I was in agony*

河口 — kakou = mouth of a river; *that car turned a corner and ended up in the mouth of a river*

運河 — unga = canal; *undoubtedly the gamblers will help us to pay for a canal*

河 — kawa = river (usually spelled 川); *the river supplies water for a car wash*

Kanji Pronunciations

# 1177 – en	# 1178 – mi	# 1179 – taki	# 1180 – abura, shi
# 1181 – naya, nou	# 1182 – ka, ga, kawa	# 1183 – ta	# 1184 – nashi

焚き火	takibi = bonfire; *that <u>tacky</u> <u>bee</u> flew into the <u>bonfire</u>*
焚く	taku = to burn (wood); *<u>Tarzan</u> drinks <u>Kool</u>-Aid while he <u>burns</u> <u>wood</u>*
梨	nashi = pear tree, or a pear; *when he saw that <u>pear</u>, he started <u>gnash</u>ing his teeth*; cf. なし nashi = without

from the Practice Sentences

支援	shien = support; *the <u>sheep</u> <u>encouraged</u> me, and I appreciated their <u>support</u>*
中部	chuubu = center (e.g., the center of a town), middle, heart; from chuu = middle + bu = section or part, e.g., buchou = section manager
山間地	sankanchi = a place among the mountains; from san = mountain + kan = between, e.g., jikan = time; + chi = ground or soil
脂っぽい	aburappoi = greasy, fatty, oily; *the <u>abura</u> (fat) on the table <u>points</u> to the conclusion that some <u>greasy</u> food was eaten here*
通り抜ける	toorinukeru = to pass through; from tooru = to pass througu + nukeru = to go through
名勝	meishou = a place of scenic beauty; *in the month of <u>May</u>, they <u>showed</u> me several <u>places</u> of <u>scenic</u> <u>beauty</u>*
小屋	koya = cabin, hut; from ko = small + ya = house or store
脂身	aburami = fatty meat; *the <u>abura</u> (fat) in this <u>meat</u> makes it <u>fatty</u> <u>meat</u>*
銀河	ginga = Milky Way, galaxy; from gin = silver + ga = river, e.g., unga = canal
申し出る	moushideru = to offer or volunteer; from mousu = to humbly speak + deru = to emerge
有数	yuusuu = prominent; from yuumei = famous + suuji = numeral
名高い	nadakai = famous; from namae = name + dakai = takai = high
脂ぎる	aburagiru = to become greasy or oily; *the <u>abura</u> (fat) got into the <u>gears</u>, and now they are <u>greasy</u>*
お火焚き祭	ohitaki matsuri = a Kyoto-area festival, held during the 11th lunar month, in which bonfires are burned at shrines; from ohi = honorable fire + taku = to burn wood + matsuri = festival
際に	sai ni = in case of, at that time; *if you study <u>science</u> with my <u>niece</u>, behave yourself <u>at</u> <u>that</u> <u>time</u>*

from News in Slow Japanese

イケメン	ikemen = good-looking guy, hunk; *I <u>eat</u> <u>ketchup</u> with those <u>men</u>, who are all <u>good</u>-<u>looking</u> <u>guys</u>*
公式	koushiki = formula; *in <u>Korea</u> I often used the <u>shift</u> <u>key</u> when I typed <u>formulas</u>*

公式な koushiki na (or no) = official; *our official policy is to proceed in accordance with a koushiki (formula)*

写真集 shashinshuu = a collection of photos, a photo album; from shashin = photograph + shuu = to gather; *Imelda Marcos gathered shoes*

発売する hatsubai suru = to sell, put on the market; from hatsu = departure, e.g., toukyou hatsu = departing from Tokyo; + bai = to sell, e.g., hanbai = sales

名言 meigen = a wise or famous saying; from yuumei = famous + gengo = language

りりしい ririshii = manly, dignified, gallant; *the reason that I retreated from the Shiites is that they all looked so manly*

まなざし manazashi = a look or gaze; *when the manager went to Zambia, the sheep caught his attention, and he directed a look in their direction*

格好よい kakkoyoi = good-looking, stylish (usually spelled かっこよい); from kakko = form, appearance + yoi = good

紅葉 kouyou (or momi'ji) = autumn colors, fall leaves; if pronounced momiji, this refers to maple trees or their leaves; *when the autumn colors peaked, it was cold, and we practiced yoga; we had a momentary meeting in the Jeep under the maple tree leaves*

国定 kokutei = state-sponsored, national; from koku = country + shitei = designation

脂っこい aburakkoi = greasy, fatty; *the abura (fat) on the coin made it greasy*

ぱりっと paritto = crisp, crunchy, modern, classy; *in Pari (Paris), the toast is crisp*

食感 shokkan = texture of food; from shokuji = meal + kanjiru = to feel

手間 tema = a lot of time or trouble; from te = hand + ma = duration, e.g., mamonaku = before long

口にする kuchi ni suru = to taste, eat, speak of; literally "to do to the mouth"

伝統的 dentouteki = traditional; from dentou = tradition + teki = related to

注目 chuumoku = attention; *if you chew moku (wood), you will get attention*

広まる hiromaru = to pervade or become widespread; from hiroi = spacious + maru = round, whole

グラマラス guramarasu = glamorous

山梨県 yamanashi ken = Yamanashi prefecture; literally "mountain pear prefecture"

河口湖 kawaguchi ko = Kawaguchi Lake; literally "river mouth lake"

くつろぎ kutsurogi = ease, relaxation, comfort; *take off your kutsu (shoes), roll up your gear, and enjoy some relaxation*

Practice Sentences

1. 皆様のご支援にお礼を申し上げたいと思います。

Minasama no goshien ni orei wo moshiagetai to omoimasu.
I would like to humbly express gratitude for honorable everyone's honorable support, I think.

2. 中部から北部にかけては山間地に箕面滝がある。

Chuubu kara hokubu ni kakete wa sankanchi ni minoo taki ga aru.
From the center, extending to the northern parts, among the mountains, Minoh Falls exists.

3. 男性の方が女性より肌が脂っぽいって本当ですか？

Dansei no hou ga josei yori hada ga aburappoi tte hontou desu ka.
Is it true that men have more greasy skin, compared to women?

4. 彼らは重税に悩まされた。

Karera wa juuzei ni nayamasareta.
They were troubled with heavy taxes.

5. 船はパナマ運河を通り抜けた。

Fune wa panama unga wo toorinuketa.
The ship passed through the Panama Canal.

6. 焚き火のあとがあるから誰かがここでキャンプをしていたらしい。

Takibi no ato ga aru kara dareka ga koko de kyanpu wo shite ita rashii.
Since the after-effects of a campfire exist, someone was camping here, it seems.

7. 山梨県の梨はとてもおいしい。

Yamanashi ken no nashi wa totemo oisihii.
The pears from Yamanashi Prefecture are very delicious.

8. そのチームはファンの応援に応えて優勝した。

Sono chiimu wa fan no ouen ni kotaete yuushou shita.
As for that team, responding to the fans' support, they did a victory.

9. 箕面山は国指定の名勝です。

Minoozan wa kuni shitei no meishou desu.
Minoh Mountain is a country-designated famous scenic spot.

10. 彼は滝の近くの小さな小屋にたった一人で住んでいる。

Kare wa taki no chikaku no chiisana koya ni tatta hitori de sunde iru.
He lives by all by himself in a small cabin near a waterfall. (tatta = only)

11. 肉から脂身を取りなさい。

Niku kara aburami wo torinasai.
Trim the fatty meat from the meat.

12. これでまた、私の悩みが増える。

Kore de mata, watashi no nayami ga fueru.
As a result of this, my troubles will increase again.

13. 私たちは銀河に住んでいますよ。

Watashitachi wa ginga ni sunde imasu yo.
We live in the Milky Way galaxy, for sure.

14. 寒かったので火を焚きました。

Samukatta node hi wo takimashita.
Since it was cold, I lit a fire.

15. 庭の梨がよく実った。

Niwa no nashi ga yoku minotta.
The pear tree in the garden is bearing fruit well. (this is the exclamatory tense)

16. 彼らは援助を申し出た。

Karera wa enjo wo moushideta.
They offered assistance.

17. 箕面市は大阪府北部に位置する市です。

Minoo shi wa oosakafu hokubu ni ichi suru shi desu.
Minoh city is a city that is situated in Osaka Prefecture's northern parts.

18. ナイアガラの滝は世界有数の観光地として名高いです。

Naiagara no taki wa sekai yuusuu no kankouchi to shite nadakai desu.
Niagara Falls, in the capacity of a world-prominent tourist spot, is famous.

19. 彼の顔が脂ぎっていた。

Kare no kao ga aburagitte ita.
His face was greasy.

20. 何で人生はこんなに苦悩でいっぱいなんだ？

Nande jinsei wa konna ni kunou de ippai nan da?
Why is life so full of suffering?

21. 東京は荒川の河口にある。

Toukyou wa arakawa no kakou ni aru.
Tokyo is at the mouth of the Ara River.

22. お火焚き祭に行った際には是非参加してみてください。

Ohitaki matsuri ni itta sai ni wa zehi sanka shite mite kudasai.
When you went (i.e., after going) to the festival of honorable fire-building, by all means please participate and see.

23. この梨はいい香りがする。

Kono nashi wa ii kaori ga suru.
This pear has a nice smell.

Supplemental Reading Practice

After completing Chapter 72, you should be able to read Lesson 038, "Too Handsome Gorilla (continued)," Lesson 039, "Maple Leaf Tempura," and Lesson 040, "Glamping," in *News in Slow Japanese*. Note that, in the "Glamping" lesson, the name of the "glamping facility" is given as "Hoshinoya Fuji." This can be understood by dividing it into two parts: "Hoshinoya" is just a name, but it could mean "Star's Shop." "Fuji" denotes the Hoshinoya resort located near Mt. Fuji. There are other Hoshinoya resorts in Tokyo, Kyoto, etc.

Chapter 73

New Kanji in this Chapter

# 1185 幅 (1)	# 1186 茂 (1)	# 1187 秘 (2)	# 1188 密 (3)
# 1189 綿 (2)	# 1190 蔵 (2)	# 1191 胴 (1)	# 1192 操 (2)

Vocabulary List with Mnemonics

from the Kanji Catalogue

幅   haba = width; *the Hawaiian barber is concerned about the width of her rice paddy*

茂る   shigeru = to grow thickly; *the sheep at Gettysburg ruin the grass that grows thickly in the fields*

神秘   shinpi = a mystery; *the Shinto priest peeked into the room in an effort to unravel the mystery*

秘密   himitsu = a secret; *it's a secret that he meets you*

秘書   hisho = a secretary; *the secretary goes to Hispanic shows*

綿密な   menmitsu na = detailed, meticulous; *the men will meet Superman to show him their detailed plan*

密会   mikkai = secret meeting; *when I meet the Kaiser, it's always a secret meeting*

密かに   hisoka ni = secretly, behind the scenes; *the hero sold his car secretly*

綿   wata (or men) = cotton; *the warlord targeted the cotton farm for extortion;* this can also be pronounced men; *the men wear cotton shirts*

木綿   momen = cotton; *the moment that cotton prices went up, I sold my stock*

冷蔵庫   reizouko = refrigerator; *I raced Zooey to get a cola from the refrigerator*

蔵書   zousho = a book collection or library; *Zooey showed me her book collection*

Kanji Pronunciations

# 1185 – haba	# 1186 – shige	# 1187 – pi, hi	# 1188 – mitsu, mi, hiso
# 1189 – wata, men	# 1190 – kura, zou	# 1191 – dou	# 1192 – ayatsu, sou

蔵	kura = a storehouse (this can also be written 倉, #1170); *I keep kuuraa (coolers) in my storehouse*
胴体	doutai = body, torso; *having a doughnut time every day makes your torso expand*
操る	ayatsuru = to control, manipulate, handle; *the Ayatollah's tsuitcase (suitcase) was ruined when the airline handled it*
操作	sousa = operation (of a machine); *I'm so sad that I have to waste my time on the operation of this machine*
体操	taisou = gymnastics, exercise; from tai = body, e.g. taionkei = body thermometer; + sousa = operation

from the Practice Sentences

肩幅	katahaba = width of the shoulders; from kata = shoulder + haba = width
雑草	zassou = weeds; *the Zambian soldier cut down some weeds*
生い茂る	oishigeru = to grow thickly; from ou = to grow; *as kids get older, they grow*; + shigeru = to grow thickly
男手	otokode = male help, man's handwriting; from otoko = male + de = te = hand
茂み	shigemi = bush; from shigeru = to grow thickly
相当	soutou = considerable, very large, appropriate; *my sore toe is a considerable problem*
相当数	soutousuu = a considerable number; from soutou = considerable + suuji = numeral
頭部	toubu = head; *Tony Blair's boot flew off and hit me on the head*
手足	teashi = hands and feet, limbs; from te = hand + ashi = foot or leg
部分	bubun = a part of something; *this boot that belonged to Daniel Boone is a part of history*
エンドユーザー	endoyuuzaa = end user
生かす	ikasu = to make the most of, to keep alive; *before Easter, I casually asked my wife if she was going to make the most of the opportunity to wear her new dress*
幅広い	habahiroi = extensive, broad; from haba = wide + hiroi = spacious
こんもり	konmori = thickly, densely; *Conan O'Brien visited the mori (forest) because he heard that it contained trees that grew thickly*
差し込む	sashikomu = shine in, flow in; *the sad sheep komu (crowd in) when they flow into their pens at the end of the day*
外部	gaibu = the outside world, exterior; from gai = outside, e.g., gaijin = foreigner; + bubun = part

食品 — shokuhin = food products; from shokuji = meal + seihin = product

腐敗 — fuhai = decomposition, decay, corruption; *the food that we hide outside the refrigerator might be prone to decay*

使者 — shisha = emissary, messenger; from shiyou suru = to use + sha = person; cf. 支社 shisha = branch office

見解 — kenkai = viewpoint; *Senator Kennedy and the Kaiser had different viewpoints*

いくらか — ikuraka = somewhat, a little; from ikura = how much + ka = question

from News in Slow Japanese

天橋立 — Amanohashidate = a famous sandbar in Kyoto Prefecture that is said to resemble a bridge to heaven; from ama = sky + the possessive no (unwritten) + hashi = bridge + dateru = tateru = to stand up or raise

日本海 — nihonkai = the sea of Japan; from nihon = Japan + kai = ocean

宮津 — Miya'zu = a town in Tokyo Prefecture; *we will meet some yaks at the zoo in Miyazu*

砂浜 — sunahama = sandy beach; from suna = sand + hamabe = beach

一体 — ittai = one body or unit, what on earth!; from ichi = one + tai = body, e.g. taionkei = body thermometer

神秘的 — shinpiteki = mysterious; from shinpi = mystery + teki = related to

細長い — hosonagai = long and narrow; from hosoi = narrow + nagai = long

片道 — katamichi = one-way (trip); from katahou = one side + michi = way

Practice Sentences

1. 彼は肩幅が広い。
Kare wa katahaba ga hiroi.
His shoulders are broad.

2. 庭には雑草が生い茂っていた。
Niwa ni wa zassou ga oishigette ita.
Weeds were growing thickly in the garden.

3. 彼は今、政治家の秘書です。
Kare wa ima, seijika no hisho desu.
Now he's a politician's secretary.

4. 私たちは密会を開いた。
Watashitachi wa mikkai wo hiraita.
We opened (i.e., held) a secret meeting.

5. このシャツは綿 100％です。
Kono shatsu wa men hyaku paasento desu.
This shirt is 100% cotton.

6. 今、冷蔵庫にりんごが一つも入っていません。

Ima, reizouko ni ringo ga hitotsu mo haitte imasen.
Now there isn't even one apple in the refrigerator.

7. その犬は非常に長い胴体と短い足を持っている。

Sono inu wa hijou ni nagai doutai to mijikai ashi wo motte iru.
That dog has an extremely long torso and short legs.

8. 彼は体操が得意だ。

Kare wa taisou ga tokui da.
Gymnastics are his strong point.

9. やっぱり男手があると作業の幅が広がるねぇ。

Yappari otokode ga aru to sagyou no haba ga hirogaru nee.
After all, when male help exists, the breadth of the work expands, huh.

10. 何かが茂みの後ろで動いている。

Nanika ga shigemi no ushiro de ugoite iru.
Something is moving behind the bushes.

11. 秘密を守れますか。

Himitsu wo mamoremasu ka.
Can you protect (i.e., keep) a secret?

12. 綿は水を吸収する。

Wata wa mizu wo kyuushuu suru.
Cotton absorbs water. (men wa, also OK)

13. 彼は相当数の蔵書を集めた。

Kare wa soutousuu no zousho wo atsumeta.
He collected a considerable library.

14. 頭部と手足を除いた部分を胴体と言います。

Toubu to teashi wo nozoita bubun wo doutai to iimasu.
The part that excluded (i.e., excludes) the head and the limbs is called the torso.

15. 私たちの運命は星に操られていると思いますか？

Watashitachi no unmei wa hoshi ni ayatsurarete iru to omoimasu ka.
Do you think that our destiny is controlled by the stars?

16. 私どもは経験と技術を生かし、エンドユーザーに幅広いサービスを提供いたします。

Watashidomo wa keiken to gijutsu wo ikashi, endoyuuzaa ni habahiroi saabisu wo teikyou itashimasu.
Making the most of our experience and skill, we humbly provide extensive services to the end users.

17. こんもりと茂った木々の葉を通して日光が差し込んだ。

Konmori to shigetta kigi no ha wo tooshite nikkou ga sashikonda.
Penetrating the leaves of the thickly grown trees, sunlight shone in. (konmori "to" = "with" thickly or "of" thickly)

18. 秘密が外部に漏れた。

Himitsu ga gaibu ni moreta.
The secret leaked to the outside world.

19. 冷蔵庫は食品の腐敗を防ぐ。

Reizouko wa shokuhin no fuhai wo fusegu.
A refrigerator prevents the decay of food products.

20. 肩は胴体の一部と言えます。

Kata wa doutai no ichibu to iemasu.
The shoulders can be said to be a part of the torso.

21. 使者は京都へ密かに出発した。

Shisha wa kyouto e hisoka ni shuppatsu shita.
The messenger secretly departed to Kyoto.

22. この機械の操作は私には難しすぎる。

Kono kikai no sousa wa watashi ni wa muzukashisugiru.
The operation of this machine is too difficult for me.

23. 綿密に言うと、彼の見解は私とはいくらか異なる。

Menmitsu ni iu to, kare no kenkai wa watashi to wa ikuraka kotonaru.
Speaking in detail, his view differs somewhat from mine.

Supplemental Reading Practice

After completing Chapter 73, you should be able to read Lesson 041, "Aminohashidate," in *News in Slow Japanese.*

Chapter 74

New Kanji in this Chapter

# 1193 滅 (3)	# 1194 慮 (1)	# 1195 抵 (1)	# 1196 抗 (1)
# 1197 盤 (1)	# 1198 基 (2)	# 1199 販 (1)	# 1200 綱 (1)

Vocabulary List with Mnemonics

from the Kanji Catalogue

絶滅   zetsumetsu = extinction; *I was wearing my Zen tsuit (suit) when I met Superman, and he warned me about the possible extinction of the human race*

破滅   hametsu = devastation, ruin; *the Harvard delegation met Superman to see if he could prevent the devastation of their campus*

不滅の   fumetsu no = immortal, eternal; *the foolish guy met Superman and asked him for eternal life*

滅入る   me'iru = to feel depressed; *when I see that these men iru (exist) outside my house, I feel depressed*

滅ぼす   horobosu = to ruin or destroy; *my horoscope suggests that I buy a boat soon, since a flood is coming which will ruin our town*

配慮   hairyo = consideration, concern; *Heidi and Pope Leo show concern for others*

考慮   kouryo = consideration; *a corporation sent me some yogurt and asked me to give it my consideration*

遠慮   enryo = hesitation, reserve, restraint, modesty; *we have to encourage Pope Leo because he shows too much hesitation*

抵抗   teikou = resistance, opposition; *the tailor and his co-workers are leading the resistance*

抵当   teitou = mortgage; *it will take Tony Blair years to pay off his mortgage*

抗議   kougi = protest; *I will join a protest against the treatment of Korean geese*

反抗   hankou = rebellion, defiance, resistance; *Hansel stands against the corporations in defiance*

対抗する   taikou suru = to oppose or fight; *the Thai corporations oppose our plan*

吸盤   kyuuban = suction cup, sucker; *the Cuban used a suction cup to attach a cross to his windshield*

Kanji Pronunciations

# 1193 – metsu, me, horo	# 1194 – ryo	# 1195 – tei	# 1196 – kou
# 1197 – ban	# 1198 – moto, ki	# 1199 – han	# 1200 – tsuna

基盤	kiban = foundation, basis; *I have a <u>key</u> to the <u>bank</u>, so we can go inside and examine its <u>foundation</u>*
基ずく	motozuku = to be based on; *that <u>motorized</u> <u>zoo</u> <u>coops</u> up its animals efficiently <u>based</u> <u>on</u> its computer-controlled gate*s
に基づいて	ni motozuite = based on, according to; from motozuku = to be based on
基準	kijun = criterion, standard; *the <u>key</u> to <u>jungle</u> survival is to equip yourself according to <u>criteria</u> published by the survival industry*
基金	kikin = fund; *the <u>key</u> that the <u>king</u> keeps in his pocket unlocks the safe that contains documents about the <u>fund</u>*
基地	kichi = base; *our <u>base</u> has a <u>kitschy</u> vibe*
販売	hanbai = sales, marketing; *<u>Hansel</u> <u>buys</u> his cars from the <u>sales</u> department*
自働販売機	jidouhanbaiki = vending machine; from jidou = automatic + hanbai = sales + kikai = machine
綱	tsuna = a rope, cord, cable; *I survived the <u>tsuna</u>mi by holding onto a <u>rope</u>*
綱引き	tsunahiki = tug of war; from tsuna = rope + hiku = to pull

from the Practice Sentences

幻滅	genmetsu = disillusionment; *when <u>Genghis</u> <u>met</u> <u>Superman</u>, he felt <u>disillusionment</u>*
抵抗力	teikouryoku = power of resistance; from teikou = resistance + ryoku = power
空飛ぶ円盤	soratobu enban = flying saucer; from sora = sky + tobu = to fly + en = round; *ichi<u>en</u> (one yen) is <u>round</u>*; + ban = shallow bowl; *I mash <u>bananas</u> in this <u>shallow</u> <u>bowl</u>*
未満	miman = under, less than, used as a suffix; *the <u>meterman</u> is <u>less</u> <u>than</u> five feet tall*
なき	naki = lacking, less, without, used as a suffix; *she has a <u>knack</u> for eating <u>without</u> utensils*; cf. なし nashi = without; cf. ぬき nuki = without
羅針盤	rashinban = compass; from rashin = compass needle; *the <u>rabbit</u> hunter asked a <u>Shin</u>to priest for a <u>compass</u> <u>needle</u>*; + ban = shallow bowl; *I mash <u>bananas</u> in this <u>shallow</u> <u>bowl</u>*
販売部	hanbaibu = sales department; from hanbai = sales + bubun = a part of something

from News in Slow Japanese

シリーズ	shiriizu = series
登場する	toujou suru = to enter (a stage or story); *<u>Tony Blair</u> and <u>Joan</u> of Arc <u>entered</u> the story at different times*
愛称	aishou = a pet name; *at the <u>ice</u> <u>show</u>, some of the skaters had <u>pet</u> <u>names</u>*
R2 型	R2 gata = R2 model or style; from gata = style, e.g., kamigata = hair style

ほぼ　　　　　　　　hobo = almost, about; *the hobo had traveled almost all the way home*

実物大　　　　　　　jitsubutsu dai = actual size; from jitsubutsu = real thing + dai = big

リモコン　　　　　　rimokon = remote control

停止　　　　　　　　teishi = stopping; from tei = stopping, e.g., basutei = bus stop; + shi = to stop; *the sheep stopped when it reached the fence*

回転　　　　　　　　kaiten = rotation; *that kite has a tendency to do excessive rotation*

点滅する　　　　　　tenmetsu suru = to go on and off, to blink; *when the tennis coach met Superman, the lights in the house began to blink*

電子　　　　　　　　denshi = electron, electronic; from denki = electricity + shi = child; *the child is sleeping between the sheets*

音声　　　　　　　　onsei = voice; from on = sound, e.g., ongaku = music; + sei = voice; *I prefer to go there in a sailboat, so that I will be able to hear your voice*

受注　　　　　　　　juchuu = receiving an order; *the junior clerk chews gum while he receives orders*

発注　　　　　　　　hacchuu = placing an order; *the harbormaster will choose when to place the order*

取り組む　　　　　　torikumu = to deal with, wrestle with; from toru = to take + kumu = to assemble or make a plan

レーン　　　　　　　reen = lane

つるつる　　　　　　tsurutsuru = smooth, slippery; *my tsuitcase (suitcase) will be ruined, I cried, as it slid down the slippery cliff*

表面　　　　　　　　hyoumen = surface, exterior; *the Lone Ranger said "Hi-yo" when he saw the men who were on the surface of the moon*

なめらか　　　　　　nameraka = smooth; *my nanny from Mexico is a rock artist, and her skin is smooth*; this can also be written 滑らか, # 981

つや　　　　　　　　tsuya = luster, glaze, polish; *the tsuitcase (suitcase) the Yankee carried had a shiny luster*

表現する　　　　　　hyougen suru = to express or describe; *the Lone Ranger said "Hi-yo" when he saw Genghis, to express his delight*

青森県　　　　　　　aomori ken = Aomori Prefecture, at the northern tip of Honshu Island

最強　　　　　　　　saikyou = strongest, utmost; *the silent guy from Kyouto is strong*

大会　　　　　　　　taikai = convention, tournament, rally; from tai = big + kaigi = meeting

引っ張り合う　　　　hippariau = to pull from both ends, to play tug of war; from hipparu = to pull + au = to match or come together

くっきり　　　　　　kukkiri = clearly; *my cool kitty clearly enjoys attention*

盛り上がる   moriagaru = to swell, rise, get excited; from moru = to fill or pile up + agaru = to rise

Practice Sentences

1. 私たちはその結果に幻滅した。

Watashitachi wa sono kekka ni genmetsu shita.
We were disillusioned with that result.

2. 彼女は個人的な配慮をした。

Kanojo wa kojinteki na hairyo wo shita.
She gave it her personal consideration.

3. 誰も抵抗できない。

Daremo teikou dekinai.
No one can resist.

4. 彼女の書いた日記が本の基盤となった。

Kanojo no kaita nikki ga hon no kiban tonatta.
The diary that she wrote became the basis of a book.

5. この自動販売機、動かないんですが。

Kono jidou hanbaiki, ugokanain desu ga.
This vending machine is not moving (i.e., not working), but...

6. 綱が張りすぎて切れた。

Tsuna ga harisugite kireta.
Due to excessive stretching, the rope broke.

7. ちょっと気が滅入るなあ。

Chotto ki ga me'iru naa.
I'm a little depressed.

8. 果物をご遠慮なく。

Kudamono wo goenryonaku.
On the fruit, without honorable hesitation (i.e., feel free to have some fruit).

9. このビタミンは病気に対する抵抗力を強めます。

Kono bitamin wa byouki ni tai suru teikouryoku wo tsyomemasu.
This vitamin strengthens resistance against disease.

10. 空飛ぶ円盤だと思った。

Soratobu enban da to omotta.
I thought it was a flying saucer.

11. 私たちは過去のデータに基づいて予測している。

Watashitachi wa kako no deeta ni motozuite yosoku shite iru.
We are making predictions in accordance with past data.

12. 二十歳未満の方への販売をお断りしております。

Hatachi miman no kata e no hanbai wo okotowari shite orimasu.
To less than 20-year-old's people, their sales we are humbly refusing (i.e., we don't sell to people less than age 20).

13. 運動会の綱引きで優勝した。

Undoukai no tsunahiki de yuushou shita.
We won a victory in the sports tournament's tug of war.

14. 彼は酒で身を滅ぼした。

Kare wa sake de mi wo horoboshita.
He ruined his body with drinking.

15. 解決法をただ今考慮中です。

Kaiketsu hou wo tadaima kouryo chuu desu.
On a settlement method, at present it's in the middle of consideration (i.e., I'm currently considering how to settle it).

16. 家を抵当に入れました。

Ie wo teitou ni iremashita.
I went into a mortgage on the house (i.e., I mortgaged it).

17. 抗議した者は皆, 職を失った。

Kougi shita mono wa mina, shoku wo ushinatta.
As for the people who protested, all lost their jobs.

18. 宗教なき社会は羅針盤のない船のようなものである。

Shuukyou naki shakai wa rashinban no nai fune no you na mono de aru.
A society without religion is like a ship without a compass.

19. 彼が販売部の責任者です。

Kare ga hanbaibu no sekinin sha desu.
He is the responsible person for the sales department (i.e., he manages it).

20. 彼は綱から手を放して川に落ちた。

Kare wa tsuna kara te wo hanashite kawa ni ochita.
He released his hand from the rope and fell into the river.

Supplemental Reading Practice

After completing Chapter 74, you should be able to read Lesson 042, "R2D2 Transforms into a Refrigerator," Lesson 043, "Copenhagen Rush Hour," and Lesson 044, "Smoothest Bald Head," in *News in Slow Japanese*.

Chapter 75

New Kanji in this Chapter

# 1201 霧 (2)	# 1202 囲 (3)	# 1203 飾 (2)	# 1204 詣 (3)
# 1205 寛 (1)	# 1206 副 (1)	# 1207 互 (2)	# 1208 尊 (2)

Vocabulary List with Mnemonics

from the Kanji Catalogue

霧囲気	fun'iki (usually pronounced fu'inki) = atmosphere, ambience, mood, air; *those fools are winking at me, and it's affecting the ambience of the party*
囲む	kakomu = to surround or circle; *the carpentry corporation moved some stones when they built a fence to surround the well*
周囲	shuu'i = surroundings; *I shoo eagles away if they appear in my surroundings*
飾る	kazaru = to decorate; *in Kazakhstan, I heard a rumor that you decorate houses*
装飾	soushoku = decoration; *the soldier showed up with Kool-Aid while we were putting up the decorations*
詣でる	mouderu = to make a pilgrimage or visit a temple or shrine; *Moses and his dentist ruined their clothes when they visited a temple and fell into the pond*
詣で	moude = a temple or shrine visit; from mouderu = to visit a temple or shrine
初詣	hatsumoude = first shrine visit of the year (this can also be spelled 初詣で); from hatsu = the first time; *we are wearing our hats for the first time this season*; + moude = shrine visit
造詣	zoukei = knowledge, mastery; *in the Canal Zone, the best cakes are made by those with a mastery of baking*
寛大	kandai = understanding, lenient, tolerant, generous, broad-minded; *we gave him a Canadian dime because he was tolerant and generous*
寛容	kanyou = tolerance, open-mindedness, forbearance, generosity; *that Canadian yogi shows considerable tolerance and generosity*
副作用	fukusayou = a side-effect; *in Fukuoka a salaryman ate yogurt and suffered some side-effects*
副産物	fukusanbutsu = a byproduct; *in Fukuoka sandals and boots can be made from byproducts of the leather industry*

Kanji Pronunciations

# 1201 – fun, fu	# 1202 – kako, i, in	# 1203 – kaza, shoku	# 1204 – mou, moude, kei
# 1205 – kan	# 1206 – fuku	# 1207 – go, taga	# 1208 – son, touto

副住職 fukujuushoku = vice-priest; *in <u>Fuku</u>oka a <u>jury</u> <u>shocked</u> the community by finding a <u>vice-priest</u> guilty*

相互 sougo = each other, one another, mutuality; *the <u>soldiers</u> and the <u>gh</u>osts watched out for <u>one</u> <u>another</u>*

相互に sougo ni = mutually; from sougo = each other, mutuality

互い tagai = each other, one another; *if you both speak <u>Tagalog</u>, it will be <u>eas</u>y to communicate with <u>each</u> <u>other</u>*

互いに tagai ni = with each other, mutually, reciprocally; from tagai = each other

尊重する sonchou suru = to respect or value; *the <u>Son</u>y corporation <u>chose</u> to <u>value</u> its employees*

尊敬する sonkei suru = to respect; *the <u>Son</u>y corporation gives its employees <u>cakes</u> to show that it <u>respects</u> them*

尊い toutoi = sacred, important, valuable; *that <u>tortoise</u> <u>toy</u> is <u>valuable</u>*

from the Practice Sentences

造詣深い zoukeifukai (this can also be pronounced zoukeibukai) = scholarship, learning; from zoukei = knowledge, mastery + fukai = deep

くつろぐ kutsurogu = to relax or make oneself at home; *I take off my <u>kutsu</u> (shoes) and <u>roll</u> around with my <u>goose</u> when I want <u>to</u> <u>relax</u>*

気取る kidoru = to put on airs; from ki = spirit or air + doru = toru = to take

成長 seichou = growth; *the <u>Safeway</u> corporation <u>chose</u> a leader who promised <u>growth</u>*

新年 shin'nen = New Year; from shin = new, e.g., shinsen = fresh; + nen = year

お参り omairi = a humble visit to a shrine, grave, etc; from mairu = to humbly go

寛容さ kanyousa = tolerance, generosity; from kanyou = tolerance, generosity + sa = a suffix that makes a noun out of another word

副次的 fukujiteki = secondary; *in <u>Fuku</u>oka, genial <u>techies</u> are thought to be of <u>secondary</u> importance*

宗教心 shuukyoushin = piety, religious feeling; from shuukyou = religion + shin = heart or mind, e.g., shinpai = worry

主産物 shusanbutsu = a main product; from shu = main, e.g., shujin = master; + sanbutsu = product

製造過程 seizoukatei = manufacturing process; from seizou = manufacturing + katei = process

必然 hitsuzen = inevitable, necessary; from hitsuyou = necessary + shizen = nature

必然性 hitsuzensei = inevitability, necessity; from hitsuzen = inevitable, necessary + sei = innate nature, e.g., dansei = male

必然的	hitsuzenteki = inevitable, necessary; from hitsuzen = inevitable, necessary + teki = related to
物品	buppin = article, things, goods; from butsu = thing + pin = hin = goods, e.g., seihin = manufactured goods
引力	inryoku = gravitation; from in = to pull; *the innocent child pulled on his mother's skirt*; + ryoku = force
物体	buttai = object or body (in physics); from butsu = thing + tai = body, e.g., taijuu = body weight
引き付ける 引き付け合う	hikutsukeru = to attract, draw, pull; from hiku = to pull + tsukeru = to attach hikitsukeau = to pull together; from hikutsukeru = to pull + au = to fit or match

from News in Slow Japanese

街	machi = boulevard, avenue, town; *we wore matching outfits on the boulevard*; cf. 町 machi = town
飾り付け	kazaritsuke = decoration, arrangement; from kazaru = to decorate + tsukeru = to attach
一色	isshoku = one color, same tendency, everyone caught up in the same thing; from ichi = one + shoku = color; *she was shocked by the color of his face*
宗教感	shuukyoukan = religious feelings; from shuukyou = religion + kanjiru = to feel
寛容性	kanyousei = tolerance; from kanyou = tolerance + sei = innate nature, e.g., dansei = male

Practice Sentences

1. この場所は不思議な雰囲気が ある。

Kono basho wa fushigi na fu'inki ga aru.
There is a mysterious atmosphere in this place.

2. 部屋に花を飾りましょう。

Heya ni hana wo kazarimashou.
Let's decorate the room with flowers.

3. 日本文化に造詣深いことはい いことです。

Nihon bunka ni zoukeifukai koto wa ii koto desu.
Scholarship about Japanese culture is a good thing.

4. 祖父は、大勢の孫たちに囲ま れて、幸せそうです。

Sofu wa, oozei no magotachi ni kakomarete, shiawase sou desu.
My grandfather is surrounded by many grandchildren, and he appears happy.

5. 彼は寛大な人だ。

Kare wa kandai na hito da.
He is a generous person.

6. この薬に副作用はありません。

Kono kusuri ni fukusayou wa arimasen.
By (i.e., from) this medicine there are no side-effects.

7. お互いにどんなに忙しくても一年に一度は会おうと言っているんです。

Otagai ni donna ni isogashikutemo ichinen ni ichido wa aou to itte irun desu.
Mutually, no matter how busy, as for once a year, we shall meet, we are saying.

8. 私は、ある先生を大変尊敬しています。

Watashi wa, aru sensei wo taihen sonkei shite imasu.
I am respecting a certain teacher very much.

9. 彼女は皆をくつろいだ気分にさせる気取らない雰囲気を持っていた。

Kanojo wa mina wo kutsuroida kibun ni saseru kidoranai fu'inki wo motte ita.
She had an unassuming air that gave everyone a relaxed feeling.

10. ひな祭りというのは三月三日にひな人形を飾って女の子の成長を祝う。

Hinamatsuri to iu no wa sangatsu mikka ni hina ningyou wo kazatte onna no ko no seichou wo iwau.
As for the one called the Hina festival, on March 3, we decorate Hina dolls, and we celebrate girls' growth.

11. 初詣でとは新年に神社にお参りすることです。

Hatsumoude to wa shin'nen ni jinja ni omairi suru koto desu.
The one called Hatsumode is a visit to a shrine on New Year's.

12. 彼は周囲の期待に応えて頑張った。

Kare wa shuui no kitai ni kotaete ganbatta.
He responded to the anticipations of the surroundings (i.e., the people around him) and did his best.

13. 子供に対するときは寛容さを失ってはいけません。

Kodomo ni tai suru toki wa kan'yousa wo ushinatte wa ikemasen.
When you are confronting children, you must not lose tolerance.

14. この問題は副次的な重要性を持つに過ぎない。

Kono mondai wa fukujiteki na juyou sei wo motsu ni suginai.
This problem has no more than secondary importance.

15. 二社が互いに競争している。

Nisha ga tagai ni kyousou shite iru.
The two companies are competing against each other.

16. 愛ほど尊いものはない。

Ai hodo toutoi mono wa nai.
Compared to love, there is nothing more precious.

17. あなたの家はとても居心地の
よい雰囲気ですね。

Anata no ie wa totemo igokochi no yoi
fu'inki desu ne.
As for your house, it's a very good
feeling atmosphere.

18. 装飾は人類と共に常に存在し
てきました。

Soushoku wa jinrui to tomoni tsune ni
sonzai shite kimashita.
Ornaments have constantly existed and
come together with the human race.

19. 神社詣でに毎年行きます。

Jinja moude ni maitoshi ikimasu.
I go for the purpose of a shrine visit
every year.

20. 彼は他の人の宗教心には寛大
である。

Kare wa hoka no hito no shuukyoushin ni
wa kandai de aru.
He has tolerance of the religious feelings
of other people.

21. 副産物は、主産物の製造過程
から必然的に発生する物品で
ある。

Fukusanbutsu wa shusanbutsu no seizou
katei kara hitsuzenteki ni hassei suru
buppin de aru.
Byproducts are things that are inevitably
generated from the manufacturing
process of main products.

22. 引力とは物体が相互に引き付
け合う自然界の力のことであ
る。

Inryoku to wa buttai ga sougo ni
hikitsuke'au shizenkai no chikara no koto
de aru.
As for the one called gravity, it's the
force of Nature that mutually pulls
objects together.

23. 彼はまったく他人の気持ちを
尊重しないの。

Kare wa mattaku ta'nin no kimochi wo
sonchou shinai no.
He doesn't respect other people's
feelings at all.

Supplemental Reading Practice

After completing Chapter 75, you should be able to read Lesson 045, "Japanese Buddhism," in *News in Slow Japanese*.

This page intentionally left blank.

How to Read the Listings in the Kanji Catalogue

The listing for 飲 (to drink) is reproduced in the left column for illustration purposes. See the column on the right for explanations of the material found in the different sections of the listing.

399. 飲

PRONUNCIATIONS:
no, in

MEANINGS: to drink or swallow

EXAMPLES: 飲む nomu = to drink or swallow; 飲食 inshoku = drinking and eating

DESCRIPTION: on the left, 食(べる) taberu (to eat, # 398); on the right, an oil derrick which drinks oil from the ground

CUES: when the Nomads on the Moon 食 (eat), they 飲む nomu (drink) oil from the ground and then act Insane

COMPARE: (ご)飯 gohan = meal, cooked rice, # 400

PRONUNCIATIONS: Please note that, in some cases, a pronunciation is italicized, indicating that it is "exceptional." See the discussion of exceptional pronunciations on page 517.

MEANINGS: These are not intended to suggest that the kanji can necessarily be used by itself in Japanese writing. Many kanji, including this one, must be used in combination with other characters.

EXAMPLES: These are words that illustrate the use of this kanji, with their pronunciations and meanings.

DESCRIPTION: In this section, we describe the kanji as an image. 飲 contains two radicals. The radical on the left is 食, which is a kanji in its own right (# 398). Although 食 means "to eat," it isn't used as a word by itself, so we show it as part of the word 食(べる). The reason that we enclose べる in parentheses is to indicate that it isn't really important here. The emphasis is on 食 as a component of 飲.

The radical on the right resembles an oil derrick, in our opinion.

CUES: "Cues" are verbal retrieval cues, or homophones, that match the pronunciations of the kanji. You will find two Cues in this sentence: "**No**mads on the Moon" and "**In**sane." Please compare these Cues to the pronunciations shown in the first section. Note that only the primary Cues "**No**" and "**In**," which match the pronunciations of the kanji itself, are shown in bold capitalized text. The secondary Cue "Moon," which is intended to help you to remember the "mu" sound in the word "nomu," is simply capitalized.

The **CUES** section also demonstrates the use of at least one word that contains the kanji under discussion. In this example, that word is "飲む **no**mu." The pronunciation of the kanji is shown in bold underlined text.

COMPARE: In this section we call attention to other kanji that are similar to the kanji under discussion, either because their images are similar, as in this example, or because their pronunciations are the same. The parentheses around ご suggest that ご is *not* the focus of this comparison. Instead, the focus is on 飯.

Kanji Catalogue

Part One

Simple Shapes

1. 一 **PRONUNCIATIONS: ichi, hito, itsu, *tsui* MEANING: one EXAMPLES:** 一 ichi = one; 一つ hitotsu = one item; 一人 hitori = one person; 唯一の yui'itsu no = only, exclusive; 一日 tsuitachi = 1st of the month; 一日 ichinichi = one day **CUES:** I wrote the number 一 **ichi** (one) on my arm, and my skin became **Itchy**; HiroHito is 一人 **hito**ri (one person), and he **Eats** 一つの **hito**tsu no (one) **Sweet** apple on 一日 **tsui**tachi (the 1st of the month)

2. 二 **PRONUNCIATIONS: ni, futa, *futsu*, ha MEANING: two EXAMPLES:** 二 ni = two; 二つ futatsu = two items; 二人 futari = two people; 二日 futsuka = the 2nd of the month, two days; 二十日 hatsuka = the 20th of the month; 二十歳 hatachi = 20 years old **CUES:** my **Nie**ce is 第二位 dai **ni** i (number two rank) in her class; I bought 二つの **futa**tsu no (two) **Full Ta**nks of helium and dropped one on my **Foots** (feet) on 二日 **futsu**ka (the 2nd of the month) and the other on my **Hat**s on 二十日 **ha**tsuka (the 20th of the month)

3. 三 **PRONUNCIATIONS: san, mitsu, mi, *sha* MEANING: three EXAMPLES:** 三 san = three; 三つ mittsu = three items; 三日 mikka = 3rd of the month; 三越 Mitsukoshi = name of a department store; 三味線 shamisen = three-stringed Japanese lute **CUES: San**ta's hat cost 三ドル **san**doru (three dollars); when my family **Meets** him, we feed him a **Meal**, and he gives us 三つ **mi**ttsu no (three) presents to **Share**

4. 回 **PRONUNCIATIONS: kai, mawa MEANINGS: times, to rotate EXAMPLES:** 三回 sankai = three times; 回る mawaru = to turn, intransitive; 回す mawasu = to turn, transitive **DESCRIPTION:** this looks like a square kite **CUES:** I wash **Ki**tes in **Ma**donna's **Wa**shing machine and watch them 回る **mawa**ru (rotate) many 回 **kai** (times)

5. 品 **PRONUNCIATIONS: pin, shina, hin MEANINGS: goods, grade, class EXAMPLES:** 返品 henpin = returned goods; 品物 shinamono = merchandise; 品質 hinshitsu = quality **DESCRIPTION:** three boxes **CUES:** these three **Pin**k boxes contain **Shin**y **A**rtistic 品物 **shina**mono (goods) for **Hin**dus

6. 四 **PRONUNCIATIONS: yon, yo, shi MEANING: four EXAMPLES:** 四 yon = four; 四つ yottsu = four items; 四日 yokka = 4th of the month; 四方 shihou = all four directions **DESCRIPTION:** this looks like the floor diagram of a house; it has four sides but is divided into three spaces **CUES:** over **Yon**der, there are 四件の **yon**ken no (four) houses occupied by **Yo**delers, who perform 四つの **yo**ttsu no (four) songs and take care of **Sheep** during all 四季 **shi**ki (four seasons)

7. 呂 **PRONUNCIATION: ro MEANINGS: spine, backbone EXAMPLE:** 風呂 furo = bath, bathhouse, bathtub **DESCRIPTION:** this resembles two stacked vertebrae **CUES:** when I **Row**, my vertebrae stick out; afterwards I put on my **Robe** and walk to the 風呂 fu**ro** (bath)

322

8. 中 **PRONUNCIATIONS: chuu, naka, juu**
MEANINGS: inside, middle
EXAMPLES: 散歩中 sanpo chuu = in the middle of a walk; 真ん中 mannaka = middle; 中村 Nakamura = a family name; 一日中 ichinichijuu = all day long
DESCRIPTION: this kanji resembles yakitori (skewered chicken) **CUES:** 中村さん **Naka**mura-san (Mr. Nakamura) **Chew**s on some yakitori 中 **naka** (inside) his car parked outside the **Na**tional **Ca**thedral and drinks **Juice** **COMPARE:** 申(す) mousu = to humbly say, # 10

9. 虫 **PRONUNCIATIONS: mushi, chuu**
MEANING: insect **EXAMPLES:** 虫 mushi = worm, insect, bug; 害虫 gaichuu = harmful insects **DESCRIPTION:** 中 naka (inside, # 8) with an insect on the ground below **CUES:** I heard a **Mushy** song about this 虫 **mushi** (insect), which lies on the ground and tries to go 中 (inside) a house to **Chew** up the furniture

10. 申 **PRONUNCIATIONS: mou, moushi, shin MEANING:** to humbly say **EXAMPLES:** 申す mousu = to humbly speak; 申込書 moushikomisho = application form; 申請する shinsei suru = to apply or request **DESCRIPTION:** two lips stitched together **CUES: Mo**ses 申す **mou**su (speaks humbly) after his lips are stitched together with thread on a **Mor**mon **Sh**ip by a **Shin**to priest **COMPARE:** 中 naka = inside, middle, # 9

11. 立 **PRONUNCIATIONS: ta, ri, ritsu, da, *dachi* MEANING:** to stand **EXAMPLES:** 立つ tatsu = to stand; 立派 rippa = splendid; 起立する kiritsu suru = to stand up; 目立つ medatsu = to stand out; 夕立 yuudachi = evening rain shower **DESCRIPTION:** a tattletale standing on two shaky legs **CUES:** this **Ta**ttletale 立つ **ta**tsu (stands) and faces his critics, who **Ri**dicule him for wearing **Ritz**y clothes and for driving an old **Da**tsun and eating **Da**mp **Chee**se

12. 泣 **PRONUNCIATIONS: na, kyuu**
MEANING: to cry **EXAMPLE:** 泣く naku = to cry; 号泣 goukyuu = lamentations, wailing **DESCRIPTION:** on the left, a water radical, suggesting a connection with water, like crying; on the right, 立(つ) tatsu (to stand, # 11) **CUES:** when **Na**ncy is **C**ooped up in the house, she 立 (stands) and 泣く **na**ku (cries), and she looks **C**ute **ALSO COMPARE:** 位 kurai = rank, # 270

13. 人 **PRONUNCIATIONS: hito, bito[1], to, nin, jin, ri, *na* MEANING:** person **EXAMPLES:** 人 hito = person; 恋人 koibito = lover; 玄人 kurouto = expert, professional; 素人 shirouto = amateur; 人間 ningen = human being; 日本人 nihonjin = Japanese person; 一人 hitori = 1 person; 大人 otona = adult **DESCRIPTION:** a symmetrical person with two long legs **CUES:** Hiro**Hito** was a 人 **hito** (person) with long legs and **To**es who admired **Nin**jas and who wore **Jean**s when he wanted to look **Rea**lly **Na**tural **COMPARE:** 入(る) hairu = to enter, #14; 八 hachi = eight, # 15

14. 入 **PRONUNCIATIONS: hai, nyuu, i**
MEANINGS: to enter, to put into **EXAMPLES:** 入る hairu = to enter; 入学 nyuugaku = entering a school; 入れる ireru = to put into; 気に入る ki ni iru = to like **DESCRIPTION:** compared to 人 hito (person, # 13), 入 is more asymmetrical, with a line at the top extending to the left, suggesting wind-swept hair **CUES:** this 人 (person) with wind-swept hair 入る **hai**ru (enters) the house and says "**Hi** Ruth" before giving her some asymmetrical fruit from **Nyuu**yooku (New York) that was **I**rradiated to kill germs

---

[1] "Bito" follows the rules of rendaku (see p. 516). The superscript [1] indicates that we don't provide a separate retrieval cue for it.

15. 八 **PRONUNCIATIONS: hachi, you, ya, ha MEANING:** eight **EXAMPLES:** 八 hachi = eight; 八日 youka = the 8th of the month, eight days; 八つ yattsu = eight items; 八百 happyaku = eight hundred **DESCRIPTION:** 八 resembles the Eiffel tower; in addition, both "Eiffel" and "eight" start with "ei" **CUES:** as we left to see the Eiffel tower, 八 **hachi** (eight) chicks were **Hat**ching from **Yo**lks on our **Ya**cht in the **Ha**rbor **COMPARE:** 人 hito = person, # 13

16. 公 **PRONUNCIATIONS: kou, ooyake, ku MEANING:** public **EXAMPLES:** 公園 kouen = park; 公 ooyake = public; 公家 kuge = the Imperial court **DESCRIPTION:** at the top, 八 hachi (eight,# 15); at the bottom, the katakana character ム mu (the sound made by a cow) **CUES:** in the 公園 **kou**en (park), there are 八 (eight) ム (cows) with thick **Co**ats, and several **O**ld **Yak**s, for 公の **ooyake** no (public) use on **Coo**ler days

17. 六 **PRONUNCIATIONS: roku, mui, mu, *ro* MEANING:** six **EXAMPLES:** 六人 rokunin = six people; 六日 muika = the 6th of the month, six days; 六つ muttsu = six objects; 六本木 Roppongi = a district in Tokyo **DESCRIPTION:** a mother with a wide skirt **CUES:** confined in the **Lock**up, a mother hen gathers 六 **roku** (six) chicks under her skirt, to keep them away from **Muy** (very, in Spanish) hungry **Moo**nies who might want to **Roa**st them

18. 十 **PRONUNCIATIONS: *ta, too, juu, ju, ji, tsu* MEANINGS:** ten, full **EXAMPLES:** 二十歳 hatachi = 20 years old ; 十 too = 10; 十日 tooka = 10 days, the 10th of the month; 十 juu = 10; 十分 juubun = enough; 十分 juppun, also pronounced jippun, = 10 minutes; 二十日 hatsuka = the 20th of the month **NOTE:** 十分 juubun (enough) and 十分 juppun, also

pronounced jippun (10 minutes), are written in the same way **DESCRIPTION:** this looks like a "t" which is the first letter of the word "ten" in English and the word "too" in romaji **CUES:** we have 十 **juu** (ten) **T**all cans of **T**omato **J**uice in the **Jee**p, in a **Tsu**itcase (suitcase)

19. 高 **PRONUNCIATIONS: taka, kou, daka MEANINGS:** high, tall, expensive **EXAMPLES:** 高い takai = high, tall, expensive; 高校 koukou = high school; 円高 endaka = rise in the yen's value **DESCRIPTION:** a tower made from tall cans, with a roof on top **CUES:** these **T**all **C**ans have been stacked to create a 高い **taka**i (tall) **K**orean tower in **Dakha**, with a roof

20. 七 **PRONUNCIATIONS: nana, shichi, nano MEANING:** seven **EXAMPLES:** 七つ nanatsu = seven items; 七時 shichiji = 7:00; 七日 nanoka = 7th of the month, seven days **DESCRIPTION:** this is an upside-down 7 **CUES:** **N**ancy's **N**anny gave her 七 **nana** (seven) bites of **Sh**eep **Chee**se for taking a **Na**p with **N**orma

21. 宅 **PRONUNCIATION: taku MEANINGS:** house, home **EXAMPLES:** お宅 otaku = your honorable home; 帰宅 kitaku = the return home **DESCRIPTION:** at the top, a bad haircut; at the bottom, 七 shichi (seven, # 20), wearing a hat **CUE:** in this 宅 **taku** (home), 七 (seven) **T**all people are **Coo**ped up, wearing hats to hide their bad haircuts **COMPARE:** 民 min = people, # 375

22. 千 **PRONUNCIATIONS: sen, chi, zen MEANING:** thousand **EXAMPLES:** 千 sen = 1,000; 千葉 Chiba = name of a prefecture in Japan; 三千 sanzen = 3,000 **DESCRIPTION:** this resembles the katakana character チ chi, which could stand for cheese **CUES:** a **Sen**ator keeps 千 **sen** (1,000) blocks of **Chee**se at the **Zen** center

23. 手 PRONUNCIATIONS: te, de[1], shu, ta, zu, *ma* MEANING: hand EXAMPLES: 右手

migi te = right hand; 派手 hade = flashy, colorful; 運転手 untenshu = driver; 下手 heta = unskillful; 上手 jouzu = skillful; 上手い umai = delicious, skillful (usually written うまい) DESCRIPTION: a hand belonging to Ted Cruz, with six fingers at the top and a wrist curving to the left at the bottom CUES: when Ted Shooed away a Tarantula in Zurich, his Ma noticed that his 手 **te** (hand) has six fingers

24. 又 PRONUNCIATION: mata

MEANING: again EXAMPLES: 又 mata = again; 又は mata wa = alternatively DESCRIPTION: a simple table belonging to a matador CUE: the Matador liked this table so much that he bought it 又 **mata** (again)

COMPARE: 文 bun = sentence, # 25

25. 文 PRONUNCIATIONS: mon, bun, bumi MEANINGS: sentence, script, culture

EXAMPLES: 文句 monku = complaint; 文 bun = sentence; 文化 bunka = culture; 恋文 koibumi = love letter DESCRIPTION: an object, possibly a cultural artifact, on 又 ("again," # 24), but this resembles a simple table CUES: a Monk says that Daniel Boone's business is Booming, and as a result he has donated an artifact reflecting his 文化 **bun**ka (culture) which we are displaying on this 又 (table)

26. 支 PRONUNCIATIONS: shi, sasa, tsuka MEANINGS: to support; a branch

EXAMPLES: 支社 shisha = branch office; 支店 shiten = branch store; 支持する shiji suru = to support; 支える sasaeru = to support; 差し支え sashitsukae = hindrance, inconvenience, trouble DESCRIPTION: at the top, 士 shi (man, warrior, # 66), which helps us to pronounce this; at the bottom, 又 mata ("again," # 24), but this resembles springy legs CUES: according to our

sales spreadSheets, this 士 (man) with 又 (springy legs) who works at our 支社 **shi**sha (branch office) is selling lots of Salty Sandwiches, ever since we sent him a Tsuitcase (suitcase) of Caffeine COMPARE: 枝 eda = branch, # 128

27. 卒 PRONUNCIATIONS: sotsu, so MEANINGS: to end, sudden EXAMPLES:

卒業 sotsugyou = graduation; 卒倒する sottou suru = to faint or swoon DESCRIPTION: a double-breasted kimono, hanging from a hanger CUES: Sottish Superman wore a double-breasted kimono to his 卒業 **sotsu**gyou (graduation), where he sang a Solo

28. 卵 PRONUNCIATIONS: tamago, ran

MEANING: egg EXAMPLES: 卵 tamago = egg; ゆで卵 yudetamago = boiled egg; 卵黄 ran'ou = egg yolk DESCRIPTION: two eggs containing yolks CUE: I will eat these two 卵 **tamago** (eggs) with Tamales and Goat cheese on my Ranch

29. 点 PRONUNCIATIONS: *ta*, tsu, ten MEANINGS: spot, dot EXAMPLES:

点てる tateru = to perform the tea ceremony; 点く tsuku = to ignite or turn on, intransitive; 点ける tsukeru = to ignite or turn on, transitive; 点 ten = score; 百点 hyakuten = 100 points DESCRIPTION: a portable cannon, which is small enough to be stored in a tsuitcase (suitcase), on a walking platform CUES: a Tall starter removes this small portable cannon from his Tsuitcase (suitcase), aims it at the starting 点 **ten** (dot) and 点ける **tsu**keru (ignites) it to signal the start of a Tennis match

30. 久 PRONUNCIATIONS: kyuu, hisa, ku MEANINGS: long time, lasting

EXAMPLES: 永久に eikyuu ni = forever, permanently; 久しぶり hisashiburi = after a long time; 屋久島 Yakushima = an island south of Kyushu DESCRIPTION: a cute dancer with a ponytail CUES: this Cute dancer asks for a man's sash, but she waits until after His Sash Is Buried under the chicken **Coop** 久しぶり **hisa**shiburi (for a long time)

31. 当 PRONUNCIATIONS: tou, *ata*, a MEANINGS: just, right EXAMPLES: 本当 hontou = truth; 当然 touzen = naturally, deservedly; 当り atari = per, apiece, used as a suffix (this can also be written 当たり); 当たり前の atarimae no = right, reasonable, natural; 手当て teate = medical treatment; 突き当たり tsukiatari = T-intersection

DESCRIPTION: at the top, a switch with three prongs; at the bottom, a tool with three toes for dividing toast CUES: this is a tool with a three-pronged switch and three **Toe**s which will 当然 **tou**zen (naturally) divide **Toa**st in an 当たり前の **a**tarimae no (reasonable) way, and they are using it at the **Atari** company to prevent **A**rguments

Sun

32. 日 PRONUNCIATIONS: hi, nichi, bi, ka, jitsu, *you, ni, nou, su, ta, tachi, te* MEANINGS: day, sun EXAMPLES: 日にち hinichi = date; 一日 ichinichi = one day; 日曜日 nichiyoubi = Sunday; 二日 futsuka = the 2nd day of the month, 2 days; 二十日 hatsuka = the 20th of the month; 平日 heijitsu = week day; 今日 kyou = today; 日本 Nihon = Japan; 日光 Nikkou = sunshine, a town and a national park in Japan; 昨日 kinou = yesterday; 明日 asu = tomorrow; 明日 ashita = tomorrow; 一日 tsuitachi = the first day of the month; 明後日 asatte = the day after tomorrow, usually written あさって NOTE: ichinichi and tsuitachi are both written 一日; also, asu and ashita are both written 明日 DESCRIPTION: a rectangle divided into two halves CUES: 日光 **ni**kkou (sunshine) brings **Heat** to the **Nich**es near the **Bea**ch, where we **Call** on **Ji**ttery **S**uperintendants, **Yo**gis and **N**eanderthals with long **N**oses to

Supervise **Ta**xi drivers who are at**Tach**ing roof signs to their **Texas**-sized cabs

33. 昔 PRONUNCIATIONS: mukashi, seki, jaku MEANINGS: old days, ancient times EXAMPLE: 昔 mukashi = olden times; 昔日 sekijitsu = old times; 今昔 konjaku = past and present DESCRIPTION: at the top, bushes; at the bottom, 日 hi (sun, # 32) CUES: nowadays old people fund **M**useums with **C**ash, but in 昔 **mukashi** (the olden days), all they had was the 日 (sun), a couple of bushes, and a **S**elfish **K**ing named **Jack**

34. 早 PRONUNCIATIONS: haya, baya[1], sou, sa MEANING: early EXAMPLES: 早い hayai = early; 素早い subayai = speedy, nimble; 早退 soutai = leaving early; 早速 sassoku = immediately, sudden DESCRIPTION: a 日 hi (sun, # 32) on an unstable base; this resembles a spinning top CUES: Prince **Harry**'s **Y**acht features a spinning top that was **S**old in **Sa**skatchewan and spins 早い **haya**i (early) in the morning

COMPARE: 速(い) hayai = fast, # 359

35. 晩 PRONUNCIATION: ban MEANING: evening EXAMPLE: 今晩 konban = this evening DESCRIPTION: the vertical 日 hi (sun, # 32) on the left is cancelled by the horizontal 日 on sturdy legs on the right, causing things to be dark; there's a fish head on top of the 日 on the right, and there are long banana tree roots below it

CUE: we eat fish and **Ban**anas in the 晩 **ban** (evening), when 日 (suns) cancel each other, and it's dark

COMPARE: 映画 eiga = movie, # 36

36. 映 PRONUNCIATIONS: utsu, ei, ha

MEANINGS: to be imaged, to be reflected
EXAMPLES: 映す utsusu = to project on a screen, or to be reflected; 映画 eiga = movie; 映える haeru = to shine or look attractive
DESCRIPTION: these two 日 hi (suns, # 32) do not cancel each other, as they do in 晩 ban (evening, # 35); instead, the 日 on the right is a movie screen on a stand, and the projector utilizes the 日 on the left **CUES:** by Utilizing this 日 (Sun) on the left, we can 映す **utsu**su (project) 映画 **eiga** (movies) about **A**pes in **Ha**waii onto the screen on the right **ALSO COMPARE:** 英(語) eigo = the English language, # 43

37. 晴 PRONUNCIATIONS: ha, ba, sei, har

MEANING: to clear up **EXAMPLES:** 晴れる hareru = to clear up, to be sunny, to refresh (spirits), to be cleared (of a suspicion); 素晴らしい subarashii = wonderful; 晴天 seiten = fair weather; 春海通り Harumi Doori = name of a street in Tokyo
DESCRIPTION: on the left, 日 hi (sun, # 32); on the right, 青(い) aoi (blue, # 155)
CUES: in Hawaii, when the weather 晴れる **ha**reru (clears up), we see this 日 (sun) next to a 青 (blue) sky, and we can sit in a **Ba**r and watch **Sai**ls moving out in the **Har**bor
COMPARE: 暗(い) kurai = dark, # 268

38. 暖 PRONUNCIATIONS: atata, dan

MEANING: warm (atmosphere) **EXAMPLES:** 暖かい atatakai = warm (atmosphere); 暖める atatameru = to warm up the atmosphere, transitive; 暖房 danbou = heating, heater
DESCRIPTION: on the left, 日 hi (sun, # 32); on the lower right, 友(達) tomodachi (friend, # 459), who radiates waves of heat above his head **CUES:** my 友 (friend) **A**taturk with a **Ta**n radiates heat as he sits in this 暖かい **atata**kai (warm) 日 (sun) and waits for **Dan**'s Boy
COMPARE: 温(かい) atatakai = warm (objects), # 257; 温(める) atatameru = to warm up an object, such as water, # 257

39. 円 PRONUNCIATIONS: en, maru, maro

MEANINGS: yen, round, circle
EXAMPLES: 千円 sen'en = 1,000 yen; 円い marui = round; 円やか maroyaka = round, mild taste, mellow **DESCRIPTION:** 日 hi (sun, # 32) on its side, with legs **CUES:** 千円 sen'**en** (1,000-yen) coins are 円い **maru**i (round) like the 日 (sun); if they grow legs, they will be able to dance and **E**ntertain people who are **Maro**oned in **Mar**s **O**rbit **COMPARE:** 丸(い) marui = round, # 866, which is the kanji that is usually used to spell marui = round

40. 声 PRONUNCIATIONS: koe, sei

MEANING: voice **EXAMPLES:** 声 koe = voice; 声援 seien = cheering, support **DESCRIPTION:** at the top, 士 shi (man, warrior, # 66); below that, 日 hi (day, or sun, # 32) on its side, with a handle on the left, resembling a co-ed holding a mask, with openings for her eyes **CUES:** this 士 (man)'s girlfriend is a **Co-E**d who wears a mask when they go **Sai**ling; the mask doesn't block her mouth or affect her 声 **koe** (voice)

41. 昨 PRONUNCIATIONS: ki, saku

MEANINGS: yesterday, previous **EXAMPLES:** 昨日 kinou = yesterday; 昨晩 sakuban = last night **DESCRIPTION:** on the left, 日 hi (sun, # 32); on the right, this is a serrated axe, reportedly **CUES:** 昨日 **ki**nou (yesterday) I left this serrated axe and my **Ki**ndle in a **Sa**ck out in the 日 (sun)
COMPARE: 作(文) sakubun = written composition, # 482

42. 最 PRONUNCIATIONS: sai, mo, motto

MEANING: the most **EXAMPLES:** 最近 saikin = recently; 最初 saisho = the first; 最高 saikou = the best; 最上 saijou = the best;

最悪 saiaku = the worst; 最後 saigo = the last; 最寄の moyori no =nearest, neighboring; 最早 mohaya = by now, no longer; 最も mottomo = the most **DESCRIPTION:** at the top, 日 hi (day, or sun, # 32), which looks like a large sign on a platform; at the lower left, 耳 mimi (ears); at the lower right, 又 mata ("again"), but this resembles a simple table **CUES:** 最近 **sai**kin (recently), when this **Sign** is turned on, I sit at my 又 (table), and my 耳 (ears) can hear some **Moa**ning from behind the sign and also the traffic on the **Motor**way

43. 英 **PRONUNCIATION: ei**
MEANINGS: English, excellent **EXAMPLES:** 英語 eigo = the English language; 英雄 eiyuu = hero **DESCRIPTION:** at the top, a plant radical, consisting of a horizontal line intersected by two short verticals; in the middle, a horizontal 日 hi (sun, # 32) on legs, like a movie screen on a stand **CUE:** this movie screen shows an 英語 **ei**go (English language) movie about **A**pes and the plants they eat

COMPARE: 映(画) eiga = movie, # 36

44. 白 **PRONUNCIATIONS: shiro, haku, shira MEANING:** white **EXAMPLES:** 白い shiroi = white; 白髪 hakuhatsu = grey or white hair; 白髪 shiraga = grey or white hair **NOTE:** hakuhatsu and shiraga are both written 白髪 **DESCRIPTION:** 日 hi (sun, # 32) with a ray of light emerging from the top **CUES:** a light from this 日 (sun) shines on 白い **shiro**i (white) **Sheep** that **Roam** near a **Hacker**'s convention on a **Sheep Ranch** **COMPARE:** 自(分) jibun = one's self, # 55

45. 的 **PRONUNCIATIONS: teki, mato**
MEANINGS: target, having characteristics of **EXAMPLES:** 目的 mokuteki = purpose, 日本的 nihonteki = having the characteristics of Japan; 自動的な jidouteki na = automatic; 的 mato = target, center of attention **DESCRIPTION:** on the left, 白(い) shiroi (white, # 44); on the right, a giant hook **CUES:** this giant hook attaches to a 白 (white) **Techie** with the 目的 moku**teki** (purpose) of dragging him offstage for having stepped on **Ma's Toes COMPARE:** 約(束) yakusoku = promise, appointment, # 225

46. 泊 **PRONUNCIATIONS: haku, paku[1], to MEANING:** to stay overnight **EXAMPLES:** 二泊 nihaku = a 2-night stay; 三泊 sanpaku = a 3-night stay; 泊まる tomaru = to stay overnight **DESCRIPTION:** on the left, a water radical (see # 12); on the right, 白(い) shiroi (white, # 44) **CUES:** a **Hack** writer will 泊まる **to**maru (spend the night) in a 白 (white) hotel by the water and listen to the croaking of the **Toa**ds **COMPARE:** 泉 izumi = spring, # 252

47. 百 **PRONUNCIATIONS: hyaku, byaku[1], pyaku[1], o, *hya* MEANING:** hundred **EXAMPLES:** 百 hyaku = 100; 三百 sanbyaku = 300; 八百 happyaku = 800; 八百長 ya'ochou = a rigged affair; 八百屋 ya'oya = green grocer; 百科 hyakka = many objects **DESCRIPTION:** this looks like a hacker's limousine seen from the back, with an antenna **CUE:** Himalayan **Ya**k owners traveled in 百 **hyaku** (100) **O**range limousines as they ate **Heal**ing **Ya**ms **COMPARE:** 首 kubi = neck, # 56; 白(い) shiroi = white, # 44; 面(白い) omoshiroi = interesting, # 282

48. 星 **PRONUNCIATIONS: hoshi, sei**
MEANING: star **EXAMPLE:** 星 hoshi = star; 星座 seiza = constellation **DESCRIPTION:** 日 hi (sun, # 32) is shining above 生(きる) ikiru (to live, # 208) **CUES:** a 星 **hoshi** (star) is a 日 (sun) that 生 (lives), admired by **H**orses and **S**heep as they eat **S**age grass

49. 昼 PRONUNCIATIONS: **hiru, piru[1], chuu** MEANINGS: daytime, noon EXAMPLES: 昼 hiru = noon; 昼間 hiruma = daytime; 真っ昼間 mappiruma = broad daylight; 昼食 chuushoku = lunch DESCRIPTION: 日 hi (sun, # 32) under a heavy roof, but 日 resembles a gasoline pump here CUES: since it gets so hot at 昼 **hiru** (noon), the **H**eat has **R**uined this gas pump under a heavy roof, where I **Chew** my 昼食 **chuu**shoku (lunch) COMPARE: 午 go = noon, # 207

50. 母 PRONUNCIATIONS: **haha, bo, *kaa*, ba, *omo*** MEANING: mother EXAMPLES: 母 haha = mother; 祖母 sobo = grandmother; お母さん okaasan = honorable mother; 乳母 uba = wet nurse; 伯母さん obasan = aunt, middle-aged woman; 母屋 omoya = main building or main room; お祖母さん obaasan = grandmother NOTE: it isn't practical to divide the 祖母 baa in obaa-san into two component pronunciations, so this word must be learned as a combination of the two kanji DESCRIPTION: a modified 日 hi (day, or sun, # 32), this is said to have originally represented a mother's breasts CUES: this is a 母 **haha** (mother) who frequently says "**Ha Ha**" and comes from a **B**oring town in **C**alifornia with only one **Bar** and an **O**ld **M**otorcycle

Eye

51. 目 PRONUNCIATIONS: **me, moku, boku** MEANING: eye EXAMPLES: 目 me = eye; 目上 meue = one's superior; 目的 mokuteki = purpose; 注目 chuumoku = attention; 面目ない menbokunai = ashamed DESCRIPTION: 日 hi (day, # 32) with an additional horizontal line, resembling a refrigerator CUES: among refrigerator **M**echanics with big 目 **me** (eyes), the one who came to our house is the **M**ost **C**ool; he takes his annual **B**onus as **K**ool-**A**id

COMPARE: 耳 mimi = ear, # 57; 木(曜日) mokuyoubi = Thursday, # 118

52. 着 PRONUNCIATIONS: **ki, tsu, gi, chaku** MEANINGS: to arrive, to put clothes on EXAMPLES: 着る kiru = to wear clothes; 着物 kimono; 着く tsuku = to arrive; 着ける tsukeru = to wear (accessories); 水着 mizugi = swimsuit; 着席 chakuseki = taking a seat DESCRIPTION: at the top, 羊 hitsuji (sheep, not included in this Catalogue) which has a head with two horns and two ears, on a body with four legs; in this kanji, 羊 is missing its tail; below 羊, a platform, with a line extending down to the left, suggesting a trailing gown; at the bottom, 目 me (eyes, # 51) belonging to King Rudolph CUES: **King** Rudolf's 目 (eyes) widen when he sees this 羊 (sheep), which 着る **ki**ru (wears) a trailing gown and 着く **tsu**ku (arrives) at the palace with its **Tsu**itcase (suitcase), followed by some **G**eese, where it drinks a lot of **Ch**ampagne and **K**ool-**A**id

53. 見 PRONUNCIATIONS: **mi, ken** MEANINGS: to see, to look EXAMPLES: 見る miru = to look at or see; 拝見する haiken suru = to humbly look at or see DESCRIPTION: 目 me (eye, # 51) on sturdy legs CUES: this 目 (eye) on sturdy legs 見る **mi**ru (looks) in a **M**irror and 見る **mi**ru (sees) **Ken** and Barbie

54. 覚 PRONUNCIATIONS: **obo, sa, za[1], zama, kaku** MEANINGS: to memorize, realize, wake up EXAMPLES: 覚える oboeru = to memorize; 目が覚める me ga sameru = to wake up; 目覚める mezameru = to wake up; 目覚しい mezamashii = outstanding, striking, spectactular; 覚悟する kakugo suru = to be prepared for something unwelcome DESCRIPTION: at the top, three old boys on a roof; at the bottom 見(る) miru (to see, # 53) CUES: these three **O**ld **B**oys on a roof 覚える **obo**eru (memorize) **O**boe music; if you 見 (look) up, you can see a **S**amurai, his **Z**ambian friend **M**ax, and **K**arl the **K**ool-Aid vendor **COMPARE:** (食)堂 shokudou = dining hall, # 64

55. 自 PRONUNCIATIONS: ji, mizuka, shi, ono MEANING: self EXAMPLES: 自分

jibun = by oneself, on one's own; 自ら mizukara = personally, on one's own initiative; 自然 shizen = nature; 自ずから onozukara = naturally **DESCRIPTION:** 目 me (eyes, # 51), with a tiny "self" standing at the top **CUES:** my 目 (eyes) are good, so I can drive the **J**eep 自分で **ji**bun de (by myself), after giving **M**izu (water) to the **C**at, and visiting some **S**heep in **O**ld **N**orway **COMPARE:** 白(い) shiroi = white, # 44

56. 首 PRONUNCIATIONS: kubi, shu

MEANINGS: neck, chief, top **EXAMPLES:** 首 kubi = neck; 首相 shushou = prime minister **DESCRIPTION:** in this kanji, 目 me (eye, # 51) can be viewed as a person's body; above the body is a narrow neck; above the neck is a compressed head with two antennae **CUES:** this head with antennae, supported by a narrow 首 **kubi** (neck), peers over the wall of its **C**ubicle and **S**hoos co-workers away **COMPARE:** 百 hyaku = hundred, # 47; 道 michi = street, # 349

57. 耳 PRONUNCIATIONS: mimi, ji

MEANING: ear **EXAMPLES:** 耳 mimi = ear; 耳鼻科 jibika = ENT specialist **DESCRIPTION:** 目 me (eye, # 51) with five additional projections at the corners, one of which could be an ear lobe **CUES:** **M**imi sits in the **J**eep, showing off her 耳 **mimi** (ears) which **M**imic, or resemble, 目 (eyes)

58. 取 PRONUNCIATIONS: to, shu, tori

MEANING: to take **EXAMPLES:** 取る toru = to take or get; 受け取る uketoru = to receive; 取得する shutoku suru = to acquire; 取引 torihiki = business deal **DESCRIPTION:** on the left, 耳 mimi (ear, # 57); on the right 又 mata (again, # 24), which resembles a simple table **CUES:** this 耳 (ear) is going to 取(る) **to**ru (take) a **T**orpedo from this 又 (table) and use it to **S**hoot a **T**ory **COMPARE:** 恥(ずかしい) hazukashii = embarrassed, shy, # 309

Dirt

59. 土 PRONUNCIATIONS: tsuchi, to, mi, do MEANING: dirt EXAMPLES: 土田

Tsuchida = family name; 土地 tochi = land; お土産 omiyage = souvenir; 土曜日 doyoubi = Saturday **DESCRIPTION:** compared to (兵)士 heishi (soldier, # 66), 土 has shorter arms **CUES:** this kanji points up to the moon, where **T**suki **Chee**se (moon cheese) is as common as 土 **tsuchi** (dirt), and **To**ads conduct **M**eetings under moon **D**omes **ALSO COMPARE:** 月 tsuki = moon, # 148

60. 塩 PRONUNCIATIONS: shio, en

MEANING: salt **EXAMPLES:** 塩 shio = salt; 塩分 enbun = salt content **DESCRIPTION:** on the left, 土 tsuchi (dirt, # 59), suggesting earth where salt is collected via evaporation; at the upper right, a short crutch suspended over a block of salt; at the lower right, 皿 sara (bowl, # 567) **CUES:** after we break this 塩 **shio** (salt) block with this **S**hort crutch, it trickles into the 皿 (bowl), and we **En**joy eating it **COMPARE:** 温(かい) atatakai = warm (object), # 257

61. 増 PRONUNCIATIONS: fu, zou, ma

MEANING: to increase EXAMPLES: 増える fueru = to increase; 倍増する baizou suru = to double; 増す masu = to increase or grow

DESCRIPTION: on the left, 土 tsuchi (dirt, # 59); at the upper right, this looks like a Cheshire cat's face, with ears above two big square eyes and two big square teeth; at the bottom right, 日 hi (day, or sun, # 32), but this must be the cat's body

CUES: the number of cats living in the 土 (dirt) will 増える **fu**eru (increase) if we give them cat **Food**, and some may have to be sent to an animal **Zo**ne on Mars COMPARE: 猫 neko = cat, # 72; 贈(る) okuru = to give a present, # 84; 横 yoko = side, # 135

62. 室 PRONUNCIATIONS: shitsu, shi, muro MEANINGS: room, cellar EXAMPLE: 室内 shitsunai = indoors; 至福 shifuku = supreme bliss; 室町 muromachi = Japanese era ending in 1573 DESCRIPTION: at the top, a bad haircut; in the middle, a leg pedaling a bicycle; at the bottom 土 tsuchi (dirt, # 59) CUES: I keep this bicycle, my **Sheets** and a **Sheep** in this 室 **shitsu** (room), which features a floor of 土 (dirt) and **Murderous Rogues** with bad haircuts for roommates

COMPARE: 屋 ya = store, # 63

63. 屋 PRONUNCIATIONS: ya, oku
MEANINGS: house, store EXAMPLES: 本屋 honya = bookstore; 部屋 heya = room; 屋根 yane = roof; 屋上 okujou = rooftop

DESCRIPTION: compared to 室 shitsu (room, # 62), this kanji replaces the bad haircut with a heavy yak-proof double roof, attached to a lean-to CUES: since I live in a land of falling yaks, the addition of a heavy **Y**ak-proof 屋根 **ya**ne (roof) and an **Oak** lean-to has allowed me to convert my simple 室 (room) into a more durable (部)屋 he**ya** (room)

64. 堂 PRONUNCIATION: dou
MEANINGS: hall, grand building EXAMPLE: 食堂 shokudou = dining hall DESCRIPTION: at the top, a roof decorated with three characters; in the middle, kuchi 口 (mouth, # 426), which resembles a hall; at the bottom, 土 tsuchi (dirt, # 59), suggesting a mound of dirt CUE: this 食堂 shoku**dou** (dining hall) in the **Dominican Republic** is built on a mound of 土 (dirt) and decorated with three characters on the roof COMPARE: 覚(える) oboeru = to memorize, # 54

65. 熱 PRONUNCIATIONS: atsu, netsu, ne MEANINGS: hot objects, fever
EXAMPLES: 熱い atsui = hot (objects); 熱 netsu = fever; 熱心に nesshin ni = enthu-

siastically DESCRIPTION: in the upper left, 土 tsuchi (dirt, # 59) appears twice, once on a platform and again below the platform; this suggests items that grow in dirt, like vegetables; in the upper right, 九 kyuu (nine, # 111), with a slash across its left leg; at the bottom, a hot fire CUES: these 九 (nine) vegetables, which were grown in 土 (dirt) and then slashed with a knife, are being cooked by a fire **At Su**perman's house and are 熱い **atsu**i (hot); they will **Net Su**perman a profit when he sells them **Next** door COMPARE: 暑(い) atsui = hot atmosphere, # 278; 厚(い) atsui = thick, # 185; (大)勢 oozei = a crowd, # 110

Warrior
66. 士 PRONUNCIATIONS: shi, ji[1]

MEANINGS: man, warrior EXAMPLES: 武士 bushi = samurai, warrior; 兵士 heishi = soldier; 紳士 shinshi = gentleman; 富士山 fujisan = Mt. Fuji DESCRIPTION: compared to 土 tsuchi (dirt, # 59), 士 has a longer horizontal line at the top
CUE: this 兵士 hei**shi** (soldier) needs long arms in order to catch **Sheep** ALSO COMPARE: 仕(事) shigoto = work, # 67; 使(用) shiyou = use, employment, # 480

67. 仕 PRONUNCIATIONS: shi, tsuka, ji
MEANINGS: work, service EXAMPLES:
仕事 shigoto = work; 仕様 shiyou =
means, method; 仕える tsukaeru = to serve;
給仕 kyuuji = service, waiter/waitress
DESCRIPTION: a man with a slanted hat standing
with a 士 shi (man, warrior, # 66), which helps us
to pronounce this CUES: this man with a slanted
hat does 仕事 shigoto (work) for the 士 (man) on
the right, washing his **Shee**ts, and carrying them
around in a **Tsu**itcase (suitcase) in the **Car**, which is
a **Jeep** COMPARE: 使(用) shiyou = use,
employment, # 480; 私(用の) shiyou no =
private, # 510

Rice Paddy

68. 田 PRONUNCIATIONS: ta, da, den,
ina MEANINGS: rice paddies, field
EXAMPLES: 田中 Tanaka = family name;
田んぼ tanbo = rice paddy; 上田 Ueda =
family name; 田園 den'en = pastoral, rural;
田舎 inaka = countryside, home town
DESCRIPTION: a square rice paddy divided into
four sections CUES: 田中さん tanaka-san
(Mr. Tanaka) does the **Tango** on a **Dar**k night in
Denmark at a 田んぼ tanbo (rice paddy), but
this is considered **Ina**ppropriate behavior

69. 界 PRONUNCIATION: kai
MEANING: world EXAMPLE: 世界 sekai =
the world DESCRIPTION: at the top, 田 (rice
paddy, # 68), but this resembles a square kite; at the
bottom, an arrow pointing up
CUE: we shoot a **Kite** up into the sky, where it will
be seen by 世界 se**kai** (the world)

70. 町 PRONUNCIATIONS: machi, chou
MEANING: town EXAMPLES: 町 machi =
town; 町名 choumei = town name or street name
DESCRIPTION: on the left, 田 (rice paddy, # 68);
on the right, this J-shaped radical is said to be a nail
CUES: this 田 (rice paddy) and this nail can be
seen near a rice-producing 町 **machi** (town), where

people nail covers on boxes of rice and where some
employees wear **Matchi**ng outfits while they do their
Chores

71. 留 PRONUNCIATIONS: ryuu, ru, to,
todo MEANING: absence EXAMPLES: 留学
ryuugaku = foreign study; 留守 rusu = absence
from home; 留める tomeru = to fasten, button or
attach; 留まる todomaru = to stay
DESCRIPTION: at the top left, a backpack; at the
top right, 刀 katana (sword, # 102); at the bottom,
田 (rice paddy, # 68) CUES: Robert E. **Lee U**ses
his 刀 (sword) to **Ru**le over a 田 (rice paddy) in
Tokyo where the **Toa**ds **Doze**, but since he is taking
his backpack and leaving for 留学 **ryuu**gaku
(foreign study), he will soon be 留守 **ru**su (absent
from home)
COMPARE: 貿(易) boueki = trade, # 85

72. 猫 PRONUNCIATION: neko
MEANING: cat EXAMPLES: 猫 neko = cat;
子猫 koneko = kitten DESCRIPTION: on the
left, a woman contorting her body; on the right, a
plant radical (see # 43) above 田 (rice paddy, # 68);
the two radicals on the right look like a Cheshire cat
with prominent eye whiskers at the top, two large
square eyes, two large square teeth and a short neck
CUE: this woman loves her 猫 **neko** (cat) with a
short **Neck** and will contort herself to please it
COMPARE: 狭(い) semai = narrow, # 194; 増
(える) fueru = to increase, # 61; 贈(る) okuru
= to give a present, # 84; 横 yoko = side, # 135

73. 由 PRONUNCIATIONS: yuu, yu, yui
MEANING: reason EXAMPLES: 理由 riyuu =
reason; 経由で keiyu de = via, by way of;
由緒 yuisho = a history or lineage
DESCRIPTION: at the top, a unit of rice, possibly a
metric ton; at the bottom, 田 (rice paddy, # 68)
CUES: there is a **U**nit of rice at the top of this 田
(rice paddy), and the 理由 ri**yuu** (reason) is that a
Youth is bringing a truck to take the rice to the
Yukon **E**aster feast

74. 届 PRONUNCIATION: todo

MEANINGS: to reach, to deliver EXAMPLES: 届ける todokeru = to deliver, transitive; 届く todoku = to reach, to be received DESCRIPTION: at the top, a double roof, which could belong to the Tokyo Dome; under the roof, (理)由 riyuu (reason, # 73) CUE: the 由 (reason) that I can't 届ける todokeru (deliver) the package is that the Tokyo Dome collapsed on me, and I'm stuck under this double roof COMPARE: 戻(る) modoru = to return to a place, # 75

75. 戻 PRONUNCIATION: modo

MEANINGS: to return, revert EXAMPLES: 戻る modoru = to return to a place; 戻す modosu = to give something back DESCRIPTION: on the left, a lean-to with a double roof, and a layer of snow on top; under the roof, 大(きい) ookii (big, # 188) is a modest doorman CUE: the 大 (big) Modest Doorman and Ruth want to 戻る modoru (return) to their duties, but they're stuck under this double roof with a layer of snow on top COMPARE: 届(ける) todokeru = to deliver, # 74

76. 黒 PRONUNCIATIONS: kuro, guro[1], koku MEANINGS: black EXAMPLES: 黒い kuroi = black; 目黒 Meguro = a ward in Tokyo; 黒板 kokuban = blackboard DESCRIPTION: a 田 (rice paddy, # 68) on 土 tsuchi (dirt, # 59) with a fire at the bottom CUES: since there's a fire under the 土 (dirt) that supports this 田 (rice paddy), the paddy will turn 黒い kuroi (black), thanks to Kooky Roy Rogers, who tried to put out the flames with a can of Coke

77. 画 PRONUNCIATIONS: ga, kaku

MEANINGS: drawing, painting EXAMPLES: 映画 eiga = movie; 漫画 manga = comics; 計画 keikaku = plan DESCRIPTION: a 田 (rice paddy, # 68), which is connected to a handle and carried in a box CUES: a Gambler is making an 映画 eiga (movie) which is set in a 田 (rice paddy), and when he shows us this model of the paddy with a handle, which he keeps in a box, he Cackles about his 計画 keikaku (plans) COMPARE: 両(方) ryouhou = both, # 579; 面(白い) omoshiroi = interesting, # 282

78. 理 PRONUNCIATION: ri

MEANINGS: reason, rational EXAMPLES: 理由 riyuu = reason; 料理 ryouri = cooking DESCRIPTION: on the left, a reasonable 王 ou (king, # 1077); on the right, 田 (rice paddy, # 68), above 土 tsuchi (dirt, # 59) CUE: this 王 (king), who is a Reasonable guy, has his 理由 riyuu (reasons) for managing his 田 (rice paddy) and 土 (dirt) in the way that he does

79. 隅 PRONUNCIATION: sumi

MEANING: inside corner EXAMPLE: 引き出しの隅 hikidashi no sumi = inside corner of a drawer DESCRIPTION: on the left, ß beta from the Greek alphabet, suggesting a Greek citizen named Sumisu (Smith); on the right, 田 (rice paddy, # 68) growing from a pot, with roots below CUE: the roots of this 田 (rice paddy) in a pot are growing more vigorously in the right upper 隅 sumi (inside corner), since they are trying to avoid the ß (Greek) observer Sumisu-san (Mr. Smith) on the left

80. 魚 PRONUNCIATIONS: sakana, zakana[1], uo, gyo MEANING: fish EXAMPLES: 魚 sakana = fish; 小魚 kozakana = small fish; 魚 uo = fish; 金魚 kingyo = goldfish DESCRIPTION: at the top, a fish head; in the middle, 田 (rice paddy, # 68), which looks like scales on a fish; at the bottom, four legs CUES: we have a Sack of Canadian 魚 sakana (fish) like this that we caught in the Uber Ocean; they are covered with scales, each of them has four legs, and we will use them to make fish Gyoza

81. 角 PRONUNCIATIONS: kado, kaku, tsuno MEANING: outside corner EXAMPLES: 角 kado = outside corner; 四角い shikakui = square, rectangular; 角 tsuno = horn, antler, feeler

DESCRIPTION: compared to 魚 sakana (fish, # 80), this fish has lost two of its legs CUES: this poor 魚 (fish) lost two legs after catching them in a Car Door at a 角 **kado** (corner) near a Cactus farm, where he keeps a Tsuitcase (suitcase) full of Notebooks ALSO COMPARE: 負(ける) makeru = to lose, # 87

82. 曲 PRONUNCIATIONS: ma, kyoku
MEANINGS: to bend, musical tune EXAMPLES: 曲がる magaru = to bend or turn; 曲 kyoku = song, musical composition DESCRIPTION: this six-paddy group of 田 (rice paddies, # 68) has a two-pronged switch at the top, and it resembles a stringed musical instrument
CUES: I read an article in a Magazine about how to 曲がる **ma**garu (bend) this instrument in different directions using the switch at the top, and this allows me to play various 曲 **kyoku** (songs) for the Kyoto Kool-Aid Club

Money Chest
83. 貝 PRONUNCIATION: kai

MEANINGS: shell, shellfish EXAMPLE: 貝 kai = shell DESCRIPTION: a three-drawer money chest belonging to the Kaiser, supported by two legs

CUE: the Kaiser keeps his 貝 **kai** (shells) in this three-drawer money chest COMPARE: (道)具 dougu = tool, # 100, which is a three-drawer cabinet on a *table* supported by two legs

84. 贈 PRONUNCIATIONS: oku, zou
MEANING: to give a present EXAMPLES: 贈る okuru = to give a present; 贈り物 okurimono = a present; 贈呈 zoutei = a presentation (of a gift, etc.) DESCRIPTION: on the left, a 貝 kai (shell, money chest, # 83) made from oak; at the upper right, 田 (rice paddy, # 68) with two ears above it, but this resembles a Cheshire cat with two square eyes above two square teeth; at the lower right, 日 hi (sun, # 32), but this must be the cat's body CUES: I will 贈る **oku**ru (give) some cat food from this Oak 貝 (money chest) on the left to the cat on the right, which is confined to the pet Zone of our house

COMPARE: 送(る) okuru = to send out, # 348; 増(える) fueru = to increase, # 61; 猫 neko = cat, # 72; 横 yoko = side, # 135

85. 貿 PRONUNCIATION: bou
MEANING: to trade EXAMPLE: 貿易 boueki = trade DESCRIPTION: a backpack and a 刀 katana (sword, # 102) on top of 貝 kai (shell, money chest, # 83) CUE: I have this backpack and this 刀 (sword) on top of my three-drawer 貝 (money chest), and I would like to 貿易する **bou**eki suru (trade) them for a Bowling ball that I saw outside the Eki (station) COMPARE: 留(守) rusu = absence from home, # 71

86. 質 PRONUNCIATIONS: shitsu, shichi
MEANINGS: contents, quality, to inquire
EXAMPLES: 質問 shitsumon = question; 品質 hinshitsu = product quality; 質屋 shichiya = pawnshop DESCRIPTION: two pairs of pliers on top of 貝 kai (shell, money chest, # 83) CUES: I bought these two pairs of pliers with money from my three-drawer 貝 (money chest) and was told that they have 品質 hin**shitsu** (product quality), but my 質問 **shitsu**mon (question) is, will you give me some Sheets that I can wrap them in, in exchange for some Sheep Cheese?

87. 負 PRONUNCIATIONS: fu, o, ma
MEANINGS: to lose, to owe, to bear, to be wounded EXAMPLES: 負債 fusai = debt; 負う ou = to be indebted to, or to bear respon-sibility; 負ける makeru = to lose; 負かす makasu = to defeat DESCRIPTION: a foolish guy keeps a mackerel head, which has no value, on top of his 貝 kai (shell, money chest, # 83)
CUES: the Fool who Owns this Mackerel head which he keeps on his 貝 (money chest) accepted it as payment for a 負債 **fu**sai (debt) and 負けた **ma**keta (lost) money
COMPARE: 角 kado = outside corner, # 81

88. 員　PRONUNCIATION: in

MEANINGS: member of group, official
EXAMPLE: 会社員 kaishain = company employee **DESCRIPTION:** a hat, suggesting membership in a group, on top of 貝 kai (shell, money chest, # 83)

CUE: 員 <u>in</u> (members) are **I**nsiders, who have three-drawer 貝 (money chests) and wear hats

89. 買　PRONUNCIATIONS: ka, bai

MEANING: to buy **EXAMPLES:** 買う kau = to buy; 買い手 kaite = buyer; 売買 baibai = buying and selling **DESCRIPTION:** at the top, three eyes, suggesting an ability to see the prices of things like cars and bikes in the future; at the bottom, 貝 kai (shell, money chest, # 83)

CUES: this three-drawer 貝 (money chest) has three eyes and can see the future; it allows me to 買う <u>ka</u>u (buy) **C**ars and **B**ikes at bargain prices

90. 貸　PRONUNCIATIONS: ka, tai

MEANING: to lend **EXAMPLES:** 貸す kasu = to lend; 賃貸 chintai = lease, rental **DESCRIPTION:** at the upper left, a casual upright guy; at the upper right, a bending person, who looks anxious; at the bottom, 貝 kai (shell, money chest, # 83) **CUES:** the upright stance of the **C**asual guy on the left side of this 貝 (money chest) suggests that he 貸す <u>ka</u>su (lends) money, perhaps for buying **T**ires, to the bending person on the right **COMPARE:** 借(りる) kariru = to borrow, # 485

91. 資　PRONUNCIATION: shi

MEANINGS: resources, capital **EXAMPLES:** 資料 shiryou = literature, documents; 資金 shikin = funds, capital **DESCRIPTION:** at the top, 次 tsugi (next, # 536); at the bottom, 貝 kai (shell, money chest, # 83), which suggests investment capital **CUES:** first, I earn 資金 <u>shi</u>kin (capital) from my **S**heep farm; 次 (next), I save it in this three-drawer 貝 (money chest) **COMPARE:**

(家)賃 yachin = rent, #707; (佐)賀(県) sagaken = Saga Prefecture, # 994

92. 慣　PRONUNCIATIONS: na, kan

MEANING: to get used to **EXAMPLES:** 慣れる nareru = to get used to; 習慣 shuukan = customs, habits **DESCRIPTION:** on the left, an man standing erect; on the upper right, 田 (rice paddy, # 68) with a horizontal line drawn through it, which is said to represent a string of coins; on the lower right, 貝 kai (shell, money chest, # 83) **CUES:** this erect man on the left **N**arrates a story about how he 慣れた <u>na</u>reta (got used to) the string of coins which, in accordance with his 習慣 shuu<u>kan</u> (custom), he kept on his 貝 (money chest), until he used it to buy some **C**andy **COMPARE:** 帽(子) boushi = hat, # 243

93. 頭　PRONUNCIATIONS: atama, zu, tou, kashira　MEANINGS: head, top, counter for a large animal

EXAMPLES: 頭 atama = head; 頭痛 zutsuu = headache; 牛五頭 ushi gotou = five cows; 頭文字 kashira moji = first character of a word **DESCRIPTION:** on the left, a square head on a stand, covered by a cloth; on the right, 貝 kai (shell, money chest, # 83) with a platform mounted on top, where the head could fit **CUES:** this square 頭 <u>atama</u> (head) on the left was removed from his platform on the right for repair after he was **A**ttacked by his **Ma**, at the **Z**oo, for stepping on her **To**es while she was **Ca**shing a check for a **R**abbi, and he is resting on the stand on the left, where he has been covered with a cloth

94. 願　PRONUNCIATIONS: nega, gan

MEANINGS: to wish, a prayer **EXAMPLES:** 願う negau = to wish or beg; 願望 ganbou = wish, longing **DESCRIPTION:** on the left, a lean-to; inside the lean-to, 白(い) shiroi (white, # 44) at the top, and 小(さい) chiisai (small, # 253) at the bottom; on the right, 貝 kai (shell, money chest, # 83) with a platform where a head belongs, but the head is missing, as seen in 頭 atama (head, # 93) **CUES:** losing his head has had a **Neg**ative effect on this 小 (small) 白 (white) guy in the lean-to, and

he 願う **nega**u (begs) **Gan**dalf to find it
COMPARE: 顔 kao = face, # 95; 頃 koro = approximate time, # 96; (書)類 shorui = documents, # 97; 頼(む) tanomu = to request, # 98; 原(因) gen'in = cause, # 888

95. 顔 PRONUNCIATIONS: kao, gao[1], gan MEANING: face EXAMPLES: 顔 kao = face; 笑顔 egao = smiling face; 洗顔 sengan = face washing **DESCRIPTION:** at the upper left, a cow bell; at the lower left, three wrinkles inside a lean-to, suggesting the face of an old cow; on the right, 貝 kai (shell, money chest, # 83) with a platform on top where a face could fit **CUES:** these wrinkles at the lower left belong to the 顔 **kao** (face) of an old **Cow** that wears a cow bell; **Gan**dalf has removed it from its platform on top of the 貝 (money chest) for cleaning **COMPARE:** 頭 atama = head, # 93; 願(う) negau = to wish or beg, # 94; 頃 koro = approximate time, # 96; (書)類 shorui = documents, # 97; 頼(む) tanomu = to request, # 98

96. 頃 PRONUNCIATIONS: koro, goro
MEANINGS: about (referring to time)
EXAMPLE: 頃 koro = approximate time, often pronounced goro **DESCRIPTION:** on the left, the katakana character ヒ hi which which stands for ヒーロー (hero); on the right, 貝 kai (shell, money chest, # 83) with a platform where a head belongs, but the head is missing, as seen in 頭 atama (head, # 93), suggesting the need for a coroner **CUES:** the **Cor**oner on the left, who is a ヒ (hero), is examining this headless guy on the right, who was found near a merry-**Go-Ro**und, because he has to conduct an autopsy **COMPARE:** 願(う) negau = to wish or beg, # 94; 顔 kao = face, # 95; (書)類 shorui = documents, # 97; 頼(む) tanomu = to request,# 98

97. 類 PRONUNCIATION: rui
MEANINGS: sort, variety **EXAMPLES:** 書類 shorui = documents; 衣類 irui = clothes; 種類 shurui = variety **DESCRIPTION:** at the upper left, 米 kome (uncooked rice, # 326); at the lower left, 大(きい) ookii (big, # 188); taken together, these two radicals imply a big rice harvest; on the right, 貝 kai (shell, money chest, # 83) with a platform on top, which looks like Louis XVI without his head **CUE:** a 大 (big) harvest of 米 (rice) came in, and we want to Show **Louis** some 書類 sho**rui** (documents) about the harvest, but where is his head? **COMPARE:** 頭 atama = head, # 93; 願(う) negau = to wish or beg, # 94; 顔 kao = face, # 95; 頃 koro = approximate time, # 96; 頼(む) tanomu = to request, # 98

98. 頼 PRONUNCIATIONS: tano, tayo, rai MEANINGS: trust, request EXAMPLES: 頼む tanomu = to request, beg, ask, entrust to; 頼る tayoru = to rely on, depend on; 依頼 irai = request, commission **DESCRIPTION:** on the left, (約)束 yakusoku (appointment, # 99), which resembles a tangy orange 木 ki (tree, # 118) that is wearing glasses; on the right, 貝 kai (money chest, # 83), with a platform on top but no head, who keeps some tissue paper in one of her three drawers **CUES:** this is a glasses-wearing **T**angy **O**range 木 (tree) who 頼む **tano**mu (asks) the headless 貝 (money chest) for tissue paper to clean his glasses, since he 頼る **tayo**ru (depends) on her supply; he will give her some **T**angy **Y**ogurt and some **Ri**ce in return **COMPARE:** 頭 atama = head, # 93; 願(う) negau = to wish or beg, # 94; 顔 kao = face, # 95; 頃 koro = approximate time, # 96; (書)類 shorui = documents, # 97

99. 束 PRONUNCIATIONS: taba, soku, *tsuka* MEANINGS: bundle, sheaf EXAMPLES:

束ねる tabaneru = to bundle; 約束 yakusoku = promise, appointment; 束の間 tsuka no ma = moment DESCRIPTION: a 木 ki (tree, # 118) wearing glasses CUES: this is a 木 (tree) who has to wear glasses in order to watch his yak; seeing that the yak is dirty from rolling in TanBark, he has made 約束 yaku**soku** (appointment) for some Yak **Soak**ing, but he left the reminder notice in his **Tsui**tcase (suitcase) in the Car COMPARE: 東 higashi = east, # 508; 速(達) sokutatsu = express mail, # 359; 頼(む) tanomu = to request, # 98

Table Cabinet
100. 具 PRONUNCIATION: gu

MEANINGS: to equip, tool EXAMPLES: 道具 dougu = tool; 具体的に gutaiteki ni = concretely; 具合 guai = condition DESCRIPTION: unlike 貝 kai (shell, money chest, # 83) and other similar kanji, this consists of a cabinet on a *table* supported by two legs CUE: I keep 道具 dou**gu** (tools) in my cabinet on a table, together with the **Goo** that I use to grease them

101. 真 PRONUNCIATIONS: makoto, ma, shin MEANINGS: truth, genuine

EXAMPLES: 真 makoto = truth, sincerity; 真面目な majime na = sincere; 真ん中 mannaka = middle; 真っ直ぐ massugu = straight; 写真 shashin = photograph; 真実 shinjitsu = truth; 真理 shinri = truth

DESCRIPTION: compared to 具 gu (tool, # 100) which resembles a simple table cabinet, this kanji adds a machine with a shiny antenna at the top CUES: this cabinet on a table contains strings for **Ma**'s **Koto** (Japanese harp), and it has a **Machine** with a **Shin**y antenna at the top, which delivers 真実の **shin**jitsu no (true) news about 真面目な **ma**jime na (sincere) people

Sword
102. 刀 PRONUNCIATIONS: katana, tou, *chi* MEANINGS: sword, knife EXAMPLES:

刀 katana = sword; 短刀 tantou = dagger; 太刀 tachi = long sword DESCRIPTION: compared to 力 chikara (force, # 107), 刀 is missing a handle at the top, suggesting a blade without a handle CUES: I bought this 刀 **katana** (sword) from a **Cata**logue store in **Na**gasaki in order to cut my **Toe**nails; it was **Cheap**, but it's missing its handle ALSO COMPARE: 九 kyuu = nine, # 111; 万 man = ten thousand, # 113; 方 kata = honorable person, # 114

103. 切 PRONUNCIATIONS: ki, gi[1], setsu, sai MEANINGS: to cut, serious, earnest

EXAMPLES: 切る kiru = to cut; 横切る yokogiru = to cut across; 親切 shinsetsu = kind; 大切 taisetsu = important; 一切 issai = everything in affirmative sentences, nothing or never in negative sentences DESCRIPTION: on the left, 七 shichi (seven, # 20); on the right, a 刀 katana (sword, # 102), belonging to a friend of King Rudolph CUES: it takes 七 (seven) people to 切る **ki**ru (cut) with this big 刀 (sword); when you buy one, **K**ing Rudolph, who is very 大切 tai**setsu** (important), **Sets U** up with a seller, but you have to **Sign** a contract

104. 初 PRONUNCIATIONS: haji, sho, hatsu MEANINGS: for the first time, to begin

EXAMPLES: 初めて hajimete = for the first time; 最初 saisho = the beginning; 初恋 hatsukoi = first love DESCRIPTION: on the left, a happy man named Jimmy Carter, with a thin hat and big lips; on the right 刀 katana (sword, # 102) CUES: **Happy Jimmy**, who has a thin hat and big lips projecting to the right, kisses his 刀 (sword) before his 初めての **haji**mete no (first) battle and **Shows** it to his admirers, after which all of the people remove their **Hats** COMPARE: 始(める) hajimeru = to begin, # 540.

105. 分 PRONUNCIATIONS: **bun, pun, ita, wa, fun** MEANINGS: to divide, to understand, minute EXAMPLES: 十分 juubun = enough (this can also be read as juppun, or jippun, = 10 minutes); 大分 ooita = Oita, a prefecture in Kyushu; 分かる wakaru = to understand; 分かれる wakareru = to branch off; 五分 gofun = 5 minutes DESCRIPTION: at the top, 八 hachi (eight, # 15); at the bottom, a 刀 katana (sword, # 102) belonging to Daniel Boone CUES: when Daniel **Boone** lived in the **Pun**jab, he tried to 分かる **wa**karu (understand) an **Ita**lian magnet by using this 刀 (sword) to cut it into 八 (eight) parts, which then 分かれた **wa**kareta (separated) from one another; this was **Wac**ky but **Fun**

106. 召 PRONUNCIATION: **me** MEANING: to eat EXAMPLE: 召し上がる meshiagaru = to honorably eat DESCRIPTION: 刀 katana (sword, # 102) over 口 kuchi (mouth, # 426) CUE: this person makes a **Me**ss as he 召し上がる **me**shiagaru (honorably eats) with his 口 (mouth), after cutting his food with his 刀 (sword)

107. 力 PRONUNCIATIONS: **chikara, riki, ryoku** MEANINGS: strength, power, force EXAMPLES: 力 chikara = force; 力作 rikisaku = masterpiece; 努力 doryoku = effort DESCRIPTION: compared to 九 kyuu (nine, # 111), 力, like the city of Chicago, is in motion to the right; compared to 刀 katana (sword, # 102), 力 has a handle for control CUES: in **Chica**go **Ra**mbo showed his motorcycle's 力 **chikara** (force) to **Ri**cky, controlling it with this handle, before Pope **Leo Cut** him off with a popemobile ALSO COMPARE: the katakana character 力 ka; 万 man = ten thousand, # 113; 方 kata = honorable person, # 114

108. 助 PRONUNCIATIONS: **tasu, jo, suke** MEANING: to help EXAMPLES: 助ける tasukeru = to help; 助手 joshu = assistant; 飲助 nomisuke = heavy drinker DESCRIPTION: on the left, a tall 目 me (eyes, # 51); on the right, an even taller 力 chikara (force, # 107) CUES: good 目 (eyes) and 力 (force) are necessary in order to 助ける **tasu**keru (help) people with their problems, and this **Tall Su**perintendent of schools has both qualities, allowing him to help people like **Jo**an of Arc obtain **Su**perior **Ke**ttles

109. 男 PRONUNCIATIONS: **otoko, dan, o, nan** MEANING: male EXAMPLES: 男の子 otoko no ko = boy; 男性 dansei = man; 正男 Masao = a boy's given name; 長男 chounan = first-born son DESCRIPTION: at the top, 田 (rice paddy, # 68); at the bottom, 力 chikara (force, # 107); this kanji appears to be dancing CUES: this 男性 **dan**sei (man), who is wearing an **O**ttoman-era **Co**at, demonstrates his 力 (force) by **Dan**cing in a 田 (rice paddy) with its **O**wner, **Na**ncy

110. 勢 PRONUNCIATIONS: **zei, sei, ikio** MEANINGS: vigor, power EXAMPLES: 大勢 oozei = many people; 勢力 seiryoku = power, influence; 勢い ikioi = power, energy DESCRIPTION: at the upper left, 土 tsuchi (dirt, # 59) appears twice, separated by some sturdy legs; this suggests items that grow in dirt, like vegetables; at the upper right, 九 kyuu (nine, # 111), with a slash across its left leg; at the bottom, 力 chikara (force, # 107) CUES: **Za**ne Grey had the 力 (force) to produce 九 (nine) kinds of **Sa**fe vegetables which grow in 土 (dirt) and provide food for 大勢の oo**zei** no (many) people in the **Icky Oi**l industry COMPARE: 熱(い) atsui = hot objects, # 65

111. 九 **PRONUNCIATIONS: kyuu, ku, kokono MEANING:** nine **EXAMPLES:** 九 kyuu = nine; 九月 kugatsu = September; 九つ kokonotsu = nine objects **DESCRIPTION:** compared to 力 chikara (force, # 107), 九 kyuu, like Cuba, doesn't seem as eager to move toward the right **CUES:** this **Cu**ban guy with 九 **kyuu** (nine) **Kooky** kids eats a lot of **Co**conuts and seems laid-back **ALSO COMPARE:** 刀 katana = sword, # 102; 万 man = ten thousand, # 113; 方 kata = honorable person, # 114

112. 究 **PRONUNCIATION: kyuu MEANING:** to investigate thoroughly **EXAMPLES:** 研究 kenkyuu = research; 研究者 kenkyuusha = researcher **DESCRIPTION:** at the top, a soaring bird; at the bottom, 九 kyuu (nine, # 111), which helps us to pronounce this **CUES:** when the 研究 ken**kyuu** (research) on **Cu**te kittens was completed, the 九 **Kyuu** (nine) 研究者 ken**kyuu**sha (researchers) soared with excitement **COMPARE:** 空 sora = sky, # 248

113. 万 **PRONUNCIATIONS: ban, man MEANING:** ten thousand **EXAMPLES:** 万事 banji = everything; 二万 niman = 20,000 **DESCRIPTION:** compared to 力 chikara (force, # 107), 万 has a flat top; compared to 刀 katana (sword, # 102), 万 has a neck, allowing its flat top to swivel **CUES:** **Ban**kers in **Man**ila use 万 **man**'s swiveling flat top to count 一万円 ichi**man**'en (10,000 yen) bills **ALSO COMPARE:** 九 kyuu = nine, # 111; 方 kata = honorable person, # 114

114. 方 **PRONUNCIATIONS: kue, kata, gata[1], hou, pou[1] MEANINGS:** honorable person, direction, method **EXAMPLES:** 行方 yukue = whereabouts; 方 kata = honorable person; 読み方 yomikata = reading method; 夕方 yuugata = evening; 方がいい hou ga ii = it would be better; 一方で ippou de = on the other side **DESCRIPTION:** 万 man (ten thousand, # 113) wears a flat hat on his neck, but 方 wears a nicer hat **CUES:** the nice hat that this 方 **kata** (honorable person) is wearing is his 方 **kata** (method) of impressing people; during a **Que**st, if there is a **Cata**strophe you can count on him to **Hold** you tightly **ALSO COMPARE:** 刀 katana = sword, # 102; 力 chikara = force, # 107; 九 kyuu = nine, # 111

115. 族 **PRONUNCIATION: zoku MEANINGS:** family, tribe **EXAMPLE:** 家族 kazoku = family **DESCRIPTION:** on the left, a 方 kata (honorable person, # 114) named Zooey; on the right, a crutch held up by her father, an American Indian chief, who is wearing a war bonnet **CUES:** this 家族 ka**zoku** (family) of disabled American Indian 方 (honorable people) drinks mostly beer, but **Zo**oey drinks **Ko**ol-Aid **COMPARE:** 旅(行) ryokou = trip, # 116; 知(る) shiru = to know, # 323; 短(い) mijikai = short, # 324; 医(者) isha = doctor, # 325

116. 旅 **PRONUNCIATIONS: ryo, tabi MEANINGS:** trip, to travel **EXAMPLES:** 旅行する ryokou suru = to travel; 旅館 ryokan = a Japanese inn; 旅 tabi = trip, travel **DESCRIPTION:** on the left, a 方 kata (honorable person, # 114) named Pope Leo; on the right, compared to (家)族 kazoku (family, # 115), the American Indian chief has been replaced by the legs of a crutch-carrying person, who appears to be stepping out on a journey **CUES:** this 方 (honorable person) named Pope **Leo** and his crutch-carrying companion will 旅行する **ryo**kou suru (travel) and are taking the first step on their 旅 **tabi** (trip) with their **Tabby** cat

117. 放 **PRONUNCIATIONS: hou, hana, pana[1] MEANINGS:** to emit, release **EXAMPLES:** 放送 housou = broadcasting;

食べ放題 tabehoudai = all you can eat; 放す hanasu = to release; 開けっ放し akeppanashi = left open **DESCRIPTION:** on the left, a 方 kata (honorable person, # 114) named Hopeful Hannah; the bottom half of 方 resembles an h, which helps us to pronounce this; on the right, a dancer with a ponytail **CUES:** this Hopeful 方 (honorable person) named **Hannah** wants to 放送する **hou**sou suru (broadcast) information about dancers like this, and she will also work to 放す **hana**su (release) any dancers that are in prison **COMPARE:** 話(す) hanasu = to talk, # 433; (家)族 kazoku = family, # 115; 旅 tabi = travel, # 116

Tree

118. 木 PRONUNCIATIONS: gi, ki, moku, boku, ko, *mo* MEANINGS: wood, tree

EXAMPLES: 六本木 roppongi = district in Tokyo; 木の実 kinomi = nut, fruit, berry; 木曜日 mokuyoubi = Thursday; 土木 doboku = public works, civil engineering; 木の葉 konoha = leaf; 木綿 momen = cotton **DESCRIPTION:** a tree with a central trunk and four branches **CUES:** when you return with your **Guitar** and take out your house **Key**, this 木 **ki** (tree) in the front yard reminds you to buy **More Kool-Aid**, but not the **Boring Kool-Aid**, since that's no better than **Cola**, and to **Mow** the lawn **COMPARE:** 本 hon = book, # 123; 末 matsu = end, # 119; 目(的) mokuteki = purpose, # 51

119. 末 PRONUNCIATIONS: sue, matsu, ma MEANING: end

EXAMPLES: 末っ子 suekko = youngest child; 週末 shuumatsu = weekend; 末期 makki = the hour of death **DESCRIPTION:** 木 ki (tree, # 118) with two pairs of branches; the longer branches in 末 are at the top, since trees reach for the sky on (週)末 shuumatsu (weekends); compare this to 未(来) mirai (future, # 672), in which the longer branches are at the bottom **CUES:** people on **Suede Mats** sit around this **M**agnificent tree with an extra pair of branches, which are longer at the top since it reaches for the sky on 週末 shuu**matsu** (weekends) **ALSO COMPARE:** 本 hon = book, # 123

120. 案 PRONUNCIATION: an

MEANINGS: plan, idea **EXAMPLES:** 案内する annai suru = to show around; 案 an = proposal, idea; 提案 teian = proposal **DESCRIPTION:** at the top, 安(い) yasui, (inexpensive, # 236); at the bottom, a 木 ki (tree, # 118) belonging to Queen Anne **CUE:** Queen **Anne** will 案内する **an**nai suru (show us around) and demonstrate her 案 **an** (proposal) for living in a 安 (inexpensive) way in treetops **COMPARE:** 安(心) anshin = relief, # 236; 柔(らかい) yawarakai = soft, # 546

121. 菜 PRONUNCIATIONS: na, sai

MEANINGS: vegetable, side dish **EXAMPLES:** 菜っ葉 nappa = green leafy vegetables; 野菜 yasai = vegetable **DESCRIPTION:** at the top, a plant radical (see # 43), suggesting vegetables; in the middle, four lines which could represent a barbecue grate; at the bottom, 木 ki (wood, # 118) **CUES:** during the Vietnam war, people cooked **N**atural 野菜 ya**sai** (vegetables) over fires fueled by 木 (wood) in **S**aigon

122. 休 PRONUNCIATIONS: yasu, kyuu

MEANING: rest **EXAMPLES:** 休む yasumu = to rest; 休暇 kyuuka = vacation **DESCRIPTION:** a man with a slanted hat, resting against a 木 ki (tree, # 118) **CUES:** this man with a slanted hat 休む **yasu**mu (rests) against a 木 (tree) and drinks **Yak Soup**; he's taking a 休暇 **kyuu**ka (vacation) with his **Cute Cat** **COMPARE:** 体 karada = body, # 124

123. 本 PRONUNCIATIONS: **hon, moto, pon, bon** MEANINGS: book, a counter for long thin objects, main, true, real EXAMPLES: 本屋 honya = bookstore; 四本 yonhon = four bottles; 山本 Yamamoto = a family name; 一本 ippon = one bottle; 何本 nanbon = how many bottles DESCRIPTION: a 木 ki (tree, # 118) in Honduras, with a horizontal line across the lower trunk, which could represent an open book CUES: the 本 **hon** (book) near the bottom of this 木 (tree) in **Hon**duras tells the story of a **Motor**cycle that ran into a **Pon**y and broke its **Bon**es COMPARE: 体 karada = body, # 124

124. 体 PRONUNCIATIONS: **karada, tai, tei** MEANING: body EXAMPLES: 体 karada = body; 身体 shintai = the human body; 体裁 teisai = appearance, looks DESCRIPTION: on the left, a man with a slanted hat; on the right, 本 hon (book, # 123) CUES: this man with a slanted hat wanted to read this 本 (book) about **Cara**cas' **Da**rk underworld on a plane, but his 体 **karada** (body) got **T**ired, and he fell asleep during **Take**-off COMPARE: 休(む) yasumu = to rest, # 122

125. 林 PRONUNCIATIONS: **hayashi, rin, bayashi** MEANING: grove EXAMPLES: 林 hayashi = grove; 森林 shinrin = forest; 小林 Kobayashi = a family name DESCRIPTION: two 木 ki (trees, # 118) CUES: **Hay** is growing in **Ash**land near this 林 **hayashi** (grove) of 木 (trees) with **Wrin**kled bark, where **Ba**ts, **Ya**ks and **Shee**p roam

126. 磨 PRONUNCIATIONS: **miga, su, ma** MEANINGS: grind, polish, scour, brush EXAMPLES: 磨く migaku = to brush; 歯磨き hamigaki = toothpaste, brushing one's teeth; 磨る suru = to grind; 研磨 kenma = grinding, abrading, polishing DESCRIPTION: on the left and top, a lean-to; inside the lean-to, a picture of a 林 hayashi (grove, # 125); under this picture, 石 ishi (stone, # 458), but this resembles a toilet CUES: a **Mee**k **Ga**kusei (student) 磨く **miga**ku (brushes) his teeth in this outhouse in **Su**dan, where his **Ma** put a picture of a 林 (grove) over the 石 (toilet)

127. 森 PRONUNCIATIONS: **mori, shin** MEANING: forest EXAMPLES: 森 mori = forest; 森林 shinrin = forest DESCRIPTION: three 木 ki (trees, # 118) CUES: **Mau**ree**n** likes to visit the three 木 (trees) in this 森 **mori** (forest) and worship the **Shin**tou spirits there

128. 枝 PRONUNCIATIONS: **eda, ji** MEANING: branch EXAMPLES: 枝 eda = branch; 枝豆 edamame = soybeans served in the pod; 爪楊枝 tsumayouji = toothpick DESCRIPTION: on the left, an apple 木 ki (tree, # 118); on the right, 支 shi (branch, # 26), but this looks like a 又 (car jack) lifting a branch CUE: an editor uses this 又 (car jack) to lift an 枝 **eda** (branch) and line it up with an existing one on the **Ed**itor's **Apple** 木 (tree), and he's considered a **Genius** COMPARE: 枚 mai = counter for flat thin objects, # 129; (学)校 gakkou = school, # 130; 技 waza = skill, # 1133

129. 枚 PRONUNCIATION: **mai** MEANING: counter for flat thin objects EXAMPLE: 紙二枚 kami nimai = two sheets of paper DESCRIPTION: on the left, a 木 ki (tree, # 118); on the right, a dancer with a ponytail CUE: this dancer on the right is a **Mi**ser who rations paper that she makes from 木 (trees) like this; if you ask her for some, she says, "何枚 nan**mai** (how many sheets) do you need?" COMPARE: 枝 eda = branch, # 128; (学)校 gakkou = school, # 130

130. 校 PRONUNCIATION: kou

MEANING: school EXAMPLE: 学校 gakkou = school DESCRIPTION: on the left, 木 ki (tree, # 118); on the right, 交 kou (crossing, # 144), which helps us to pronounce this CUES: this 学校 gak**kou** (school) is near a 交 (crossing), and it's usually Cold because it's shaded by a 木 (tree) COMPARE: 枝 eda = branch, # 128; 枚 mai = counter for flat, thin objects, # 129

131. 村 PRONUNCIATIONS: son, mura

MEANING: village EXAMPLES: 村長 sonchou = village mayor; 村 mura = village DESCRIPTION: this is a mural showing, on the left, a 木 ki (tree, # 118) and, on the right, a kneeling guy, who has dropped a piece of gum on the ground CUES: my Son painted this Mural which depicts a 村 **mura** (village), with a 木 (tree) on the left and this kneeling guy on the right; the kneeling guy has dropped a piece of gum on the ground COMPARE: 付(ける) tsukeru = to attach or stick, # 132

132. 付 PRONUNCIATIONS: tsu, zu, fu, tsuke MEANINGS: to adhere, to issue

EXAMPLES: 付ける tsukeru = to attach or stick, transitive; 付く tsuku = to adhere, intransitive; 事付け kotozuke = message; 寄付 kifu = donation; 受付 uketsuke = reception DESCRIPTION: on the left, a man with a slanted hat wearing a nice tsuit (suit); on the right, a kneeling guy, who has dropped a piece of gum on the ground CUES: this man with a slanted hat, who is wearing a nice Tsuit (suit), went to Zurich and warned this Foolish kneeling guy that the piece of gum might 付く **tsu**ku (adhere) to the guy's shoe or to his TsuitKeis (suitcase) COMPARE: 村 mura = village, # 131; (切)符 kippu = ticket, # 133

133. 符 PRONUNCIATIONS: pu, fu

MEANING: tag EXAMPLE: 切符 kippu = ticket; 護符 gofu = talisman, charm DESCRIPTION: at the top, two short 竹 take (bamboo, # 134) which look like clamps; at the bottom, 付く tsuku (to adhere, # 132), which includes a man with a slanted hat CUES: this man with a slanted hat, whose name is Putin, Foolishly clamped some 切符 kip**pu** (tickets) together with 竹 (bamboo) clamps, and now they 付 (adhere) to each other COMPARE: 村 mura = village, # 131; 笑(う) warau = to laugh, # 199; 第 dai = order, # 530

134. 竹 PRONUNCIATIONS: take, chiku

MEANING: bamboo EXAMPLES: 竹の子 takenoko = bamboo shoot; 竹林 chikurin = bamboo grove DESCRIPTION: the two radicals used to write 竹 take (bamboo) are said to be identical, even though the one on the right curves under at the bottom; each of them contains a horizontal line at the top, unlike the radical on the left side of 付 tsu (to adhere, # 132) CUES: these two cowboys, viewed from the side, each with his hat pushed back on his head, are admiring some 竹 **take** (bamboo) which they may Take home; the cowboy in front is kneeling, and both are eating Chicken Cutlets

135. 横 PRONUNCIATIONS: yoko, ou

MEANINGS: sideways, crooked EXAMPLES: 横 yoko = side; 横切る yokogiru = to cross or cut across; 横断する oudan suru = to cross (a street, etc.) DESCRIPTION: at the left, 木 ki (tree, # 118); at the right, a Cheshire cat belonging to Yoko Ono, with a plant radical (see # 43) at the top resembling prominent eye whiskers and, below that, two large eyes, two large teeth, and extended front paws CUES: Yoko Ono's cat is 横 **yoko** (beside) this 木 (tree) COMPARE: 増(える) fueru = to increase, # 61; 贈(る) okuru = to give a present, # 84; 構(う) kamau = to mind, #141; 猫 neko = cat, # 72

136. 様 **PRONUNCIATIONS: you, sama**
MEANINGS: appearance, honorific form of address
EXAMPLES: 様子 yousu = condition, state;
お客様 okyakusama = very honorable customer
DESCRIPTION: on the left, a 木 ki (tree, # 118);
on the upper right, 羊 hitsuji (sheep, not included in
this Catalogue), an animal with 2 horns, 2 ears, 4
legs, and a tail – but the tail is absent here; on the
lower right, 水 mizu (water, # 251)
CUES: a **Yo**gurt seller named **Yo**landa 様 **sama**
(very honorable **Yo**landa) will rescue this 羊
(sheep) that is drowning in 水 (water) beside this
木 (tree) because she is a Good **Sama**ritan
COMPARE: 機 ki = machine, # 137

137. 機 **PRONUNCIATIONS: ki, hata**
MEANING: machine **EXAMPLES:** 機械 kikai
= machine; 飛行機 hikouki = airplane;
機織り hataori = weaving, weaver
DESCRIPTION: on the left, 木 ki (wood, # 118),
which helps us to pronounce this; on the upper right,
two 糸 (skeet shooters, #219); at the lower right, a
platform supported by legs and transected by a
halberd (combination lance and axe) **CUES:** this
機械 ki**kai** (machine), which can **Ki**ck you in the
Eye, consists of 木 **Ki** (wood) and a halberd, it's
held together with **Ha**waiian **Tar**, and it supports two
糸 (skeet shooters)
COMPARE: 様 sama = honorific form of address,
136; 械 kai = machine, # 138

138. 械 **PRONUNCIATION: kai**
MEANINGS: machine, gadget **EXAMPLE:**
機械 kikai = machine **DESCRIPTION:** on the
left, 木 ki (wood, # 118); on the right, a halberd
(combination lance and axe); in the center,
reportedly, two hands tied together, i.e., a set of
handcuffs **CUE:** the **Kai**ser owned this 機械
ki**kai** (machine) made from 木 (wood), featuring
wooden handcuffs and a halberd to deal with
criminals **COMPARE:** 機 ki = machine, # 137

139. 橋 **PRONUNCIATIONS: hashi,**
bashi[1], kyou MEANING: bridge **EXAMPLES:**
橋 hashi = bridge; 新橋 Shinbashi = district in
Tokyo; 歩道橋 hodoukyou = pedestrian bridge
DESCRIPTION: on the left, 木 ki (wood,
118); on the right, a pregnant woman walking on
what appears to be a bridge
CUES: this pregnant woman walks across a 橋
hashi (bridge) built with **Hashi** (chopsticks) made
from 木 (wood) in **Kyou**to

140. 机 **PRONUNCIATIONS: ki, tsukue**
MEANING: desk **EXAMPLES:** 机上 kijou =
on the desk, theoretical, academic; 机 tsukue = desk
DESCRIPTION: on the left, 木 ki (wood, # 118);
on the right, a finished desk, which is high enough to
accommodate a tsuitcase (suitcase) below it
CUES: if we put a tsuitcase (suitcase) containing
Kimonos under a 机 **tsukue** (desk) made from 木
(wood), the desk will be **Tsuit**Case no **U**e (above the
suitcase)

141. 構 **PRONUNCIATIONS: kou, kama,**
gama MEANINGS: fine, to mind **EXAMPLES:**
結構 kekkou = fine, splendid, considerably;
構う kamau = to mind or care about; 心構え
kokorogamae = a mental attitude **DESCRIPTION:**
on the left, 木 ki (wood, # 118); on the upper right,
some bushes; on the lower right, 円 en (yen, # 39)
with two additional lines drawn through it for extra
support, suggesting a strong building
CUES: the people in **Ko**be used 木 (wood) when
they built this 結構な kek**kou** na (fine) structure
with bushes on the roof; since they 構う **kama**u
(care about) strong buildings, they consulted the
Kama Sutra, spent a lot of 円 (yen), and
strengthened the building with additional lateral
supports so that it would provide protection from
Gamma rays **COMPARE:** 横 yoko = side, # 135

142. 箱 PRONUNCIATIONS: hako,

bako[1] MEANING: box EXAMPLES: 箱 hako
= box; 靴箱 kutsubako = shoe box
DESCRIPTION: on the lower left, 木 ki (wood,
118); at the top, shortened 竹 take (bamboo,
134), resembling clamps; on the lower right, 目
me (eye, # 51), but this resembles a finished box
CUE: a 箱 **hako** (box) made from 木 (wood) and
竹 (bamboo) is on the lower right, and it contains a
Hat and a **Co**at

Crossing
143. 父 PRONUNCIATIONS: chichi, *tou,*
fu, *ji* MEANING: father EXAMPLES: 父
chichi = father; お父さん otousan = honorable
father; 祖父 sofu = grandfather; 伯父さん
ojisan = uncle; お祖父さん ojiisan =
grandfather NOTE: it isn't practical to divide the
祖父 jii in the word ojiisan into two component
pronunciations, so this word must be learned as a
combination of the two kanji
DESCRIPTION: a father with thick eyebrows,
sitting with crossed legs CUES: this 父 **chichi**
(father) has thick eyebrows, sits with crossed legs,
dresses in a **Chichi** (chic) way, smokes **T**obacco,
cooks good **Fo**od, and drives a **Jee**p

144. 交 PRONUNCIATIONS: kou, maji,
ka MEANINGS: crossing, mingling
EXAMPLES: 交通 koutsuu = traffic; 交差点
kousaten = traffic intersection; 交わる majiwaru
= to keep company with; 交わす kawasu = to
exchange DESCRIPTION: crossed roads under
六 roku (six, # 17) CUES: this 交差点
kousaten (traffic intersection) of 六 (six) roads in
Korea has **Ma**gic traffic signals that keep **Ca**rs from
colliding

145. 郊 PRONUNCIATION: kou
MEANING: suburb EXAMPLE: 郊外 kougai =
suburbs DESCRIPTION: on the left, 交 kou
(crossing, # 144), which helps us to pronounce this;
on the right, ß beta from the Greek alphabet CUE:
this ß (Greek) guy lives near a 交 (crossing) in the
郊外 **kou**gai (suburbs), and he's a **Co**ld **G**uy,
since his house is unheated

Mountain
146. 山 PRONUNCIATIONS: yama, san,
zan MEANING: mountain EXAMPLES:
山登り yamanobori = mountain climbing;
富士山 fujisan = Mt. Fuji; 火山 kazan =
volcano DESCRIPTION: this mountain resembles
a volcano with lava spewing from the top
CUES: a **Ya**k with **Ma**gic friends, including **Sa**nta
Claus, lives on this volcanic 山 **yama** (mountain) in
Zan**z**ibar

147. 出 PRONUNCIATIONS: shutsu, da,
sui, de, shu MEANINGS: to leave, to put out
EXAMPLES: 外出する gaishutsu suru = to go
out; 出す dasu = to put out; 出納 suitou =
accounts; 出る deru = to leave or go out; 出席
shusseki = attendance; 出張 shutchou = business
trip DESCRIPTION: two 山 yama (mountains,
146), suggesting two volcanoes CUES: these two
volcanoes 出す **da**su (put out) lava, which 出る
deru (emerges), **Shoo**ts up into the air, **Da**shes down
the slopes and burns a **Swee**t **De**butante's **Sho**es

Moon
148. 月 PRONUNCIATIONS: tsuki, ge,
getsu, gatsu MEANINGS: moon EXAMPLES:
毎月 maitsuki = every month; 月給 gekkyuu =
monthly salary; 月曜日 getsuyoubi = Monday;
二月 nigatsu = February DESCRIPTION: 日
hi (day, or sun, # 32) with two asymmetrical legs
CUES: I packed a **Tsu**itcase (suitcase) for a **K**ing
named **Ge**nghis to take to the 月 **tsuki** (moon),
where he hopes to **Ge**t **Su**per rich by **Ga**thering **Soo**t
from moon volcanoes

149. 勝 PRONUNCIATIONS: **shou, ka, masa** MEANINGS: to win, victory EXAMPLES: 優勝 yuushou = victory, championship; 勝つ katsu = to win; 勝る masaru = to outclass, to outdo DESCRIPTION: on the left, 月 tsuki (moon, # 148); on the upper right, a complex radical that resembles a bonfire; on the lower right, 力 chikara (force, # 107) CUES: in order to put on a **Show** and achieve a 優勝 yuu**shou** (victory), this 月 (moon) **Sho**ne its light with 力 (force) to ignite this bonfire, and it 勝つ た **ka**tta (won) a **Ca**talogue and a **Massa**ge

150. 服 PRONUNCIATION: **fuku, puku**[1] MEANING: clothes EXAMPLE: 洋服 youfuku = Western clothes; 屈服する kuppuku suru = to surrender DESCRIPTION: on the left, 月 tsuki (moon, # 148); on the right, a dressing room, with a hook for hanging clothes; inside the dressing room, 又 mata ("again," # 24), but this resembles a simple dressing table CUE: I will try on some 洋服 you**fuku** (Western clothes) by the light of this 月 (moon) in **Fuku**oka, near a 又 (table), in a dressing room with a clothes hook COMPARE: 報(告) houkoku = report, # 386

151. 育 PRONUNCIATIONS: **soda, iku, haguku** MEANING: to bring up or raise a child EXAMPLES: 育てる sodateru = to raise; 教育 kyouiku = education; 育む hagukumu = to nourish, nurture DESCRIPTION: at the top, a pedaling leg, wearing a pointy hat; at the bottom, 月 tsuki (moon, # 148) CUES: this cyclist with a pointy hat sits on the 月 (moon), thinking that giving **Soda** is **T**errible when one 育てる **soda**teru (raises) a child, and that a child's 教育 kyou**iku** (education) should be mostly about **Ear Co**oties and how to **Hatch** a **Goose** in a **Coop**

152. 背 PRONUNCIATIONS: **hai, se, sei, somu** MEANINGS: back, height EXAMPLES: 背景 haikei = background, setting; 背が高い se ga takai = the height is tall; 背中 senaka = the back of the body; 背 sei = height; 背く somuku = to rebel against, disobey DESCRIPTION: 北 kita (north, # 373) on top of a 月 tsuki (moon, # 148), but 北 could be two people sitting back-to-back, comparing their sitting heights CUES: in a **High** place on the 北 (north) side of the 月 (moon), these two **Se**cretaries sit back-to-back and **Say** that they are the same 背 **sei** (height) which they find **So Mo**ving COMPARE: 皆 mina = all, everyone, # 597

153. 胃 PRONUNCIATION: **i** MEANING: stomach EXAMPLES: 胃 i = stomach; 胃癌 igan = stomach cancer DESCRIPTION: at the top, a 田 (rice paddy, # 68); at the bottom, 月 tsuki (moon, # 148) CUE: in Iraq, a man in a 田 (rice paddy) rubs his 胃 **i** (stomach) while gazing at the 月 (moon)

154. 明 PRONUNCIATIONS: **aka, ashi, aki, a, mei, min, myou** MEANINGS: bright, obvious, tomorrow EXAMPLES: 明るい akarui = bright, cheerful; 明日 ashita = tomorrow; 明らかな akiraka na = obvious; 明日 asu = tomorrow; 明後日 asatte = the day after tomorrow, usually written あさって; 明ける akeru = to end or expire, or to start; 説明 setsumei = explanation; 明朝体 minchoutai = Ming dynasty, or Ming-style font; 明日 myou-nichi = tomorrow; 明後日 myougonichi = the day after tomorrow NOTE: ashita, asu and myounichi are all written 明日, and they all have the same meaning; *also,* asatte and myougonichi are both written 明後日 and have the same meaning DESCRIPTION: on the left, 日 hi (day, or sun,

32); on the right, 月 tsuki (moon, # 148)

CUES: when the 日 (sun) and 月 (moon) shine together, the sky is 明るい **aka**rui (bright), and we can expect someone to come to the Ac**a**demy 明日 **ashi**ta (tomorrow) and give an **A**shy ashtray, **A Key** and some **A**nchovies to **M**ay, our **M**ean cat, who will **M**eow in response **COMPARE:** 朝 asa = morning, # 291

155. 青 PRONUNCIATIONS: ao, sei, *sao*

MEANINGS: blue, fresh **EXAMPLES:** 青い aoi = blue; 青年 seinen = young man; 真っ青な massao na = deep blue, ghastly pale

DESCRIPTION: at the top, compared to 土 tsuchi (dirt, # 59), this radical has an extra horizontal line, where an owl might perch; at the bottom, 月 tsuki (moon, # 148) **CUES:** an **O**wl perched on top of this 月 (moon) sees an 青い **ao**i (blue) sky and feels **S**afe but still makes a **S**our face **COMPARE:** 情(報) jouhou = information, news, # 156; 表 omote = surface, front, outside, # 582

156. 情 PRONUNCIATIONS: nasa, jou

MEANINGS: emotion, feelings **EXAMPLES:** 情けない nasakenai = disappointing, regrettable; 愛情 aijou = love; 情報 jouhou = information, news **DESCRIPTION:** on the left, an erect astronaut from NASA named Joan of Arc; on the right 青(い) aoi (blue, # 155)

CUES: NASA sent **Joan** the astronaut some 情けない **nasa**kenai (regrettable) 情報 **jou**hou (information), and she is feeling 青 (blue)

157. 前 PRONUNCIATIONS: mae, zen, sen

MEANINGS: front, before **EXAMPLES:** 二年前 ninen mae = two years ago; 駅前 eki mae = in front of the station; 午前九時 gozen kuji = 9:00 a.m.; 先祖 senzo = ancestor **DESCRIPTION:** on the top, an upside-down bench, with its legs sticking up; on the lower left, 月 tsuki (moon, # 148); on the lower right, the katakana character リ Ri, who is a maestro **CUES:** this 月 (moon) and リ Ri the **Mae**stro are carrying a bench to a **Zen** temple at the Zen Cen**ter**, but the 月 is standing 前 **mae** (in front of) リ and will get to the temple 前 **mae** (before) リ

158. 消 PRONUNCIATIONS: ke, ki, shou

MEANINGS: to disappear, to erase **EXAMPLES:** 消す kesu = to erase, turn off, extinguish, wipe out; 消える kieru = to go out (referring to, e.g., a fire); 消火器 shoukaki = fire extinguisher; 消化 shouka = digestion (food and information); 消防署 shoubousho = firehouse **DESCRIPTION:** on the left, a water radical (see # 12); on the right, 3 prongs, which resemble a switch, on 月 tsuki (moon, # 148) **CUES: Ke**n lives on the 月 (moon), where there is a 3-pronged switch that can 消す **ke**su (turn off) the water flow to Barbie, who lives in **Kie**v, where they have good **Shou**s **COMPARE:** 決(して) kesshite = never, # 180

159. 散 PRONUNCIATIONS: chi, san

MEANING: to disperse **EXAMPLES:** 散る chiru = to disperse or scatter; 散歩 sanpo = a walk **DESCRIPTION:** on the upper left, some bushes; on the lower left, 月 tsuki (moon, # 148); on the right, a dancer with a ponytail **CUES:** this **Chee**rful dancer is going for a 散歩 **san**po (walk) in **San**d near some bushes by the light of the 月 (moon)

Evening

160. 夕 PRONUNCIATION: yuu

MEANING: evening **EXAMPLES:** 夕方 yuugata = evening; 夕べ yuube = last night **DESCRIPTION:** this is a half 月 tsuki (moon, # 148), or a lesser moon, shining in the Yukon **CUE:** this 夕 (half moon, or lesser moon) shines above the **Yu**kon during the 夕方 **yuu**gata (evening) **COMPARE:** the katakana 夕 ta

161. 多 **PRONUNCIATIONS: oo, ta**
MEANING: many **EXAMPLES:** 多い
ooi = a lot; 多分 tabun = probably
DESCRIPTION: two 夕 yuu (lesser moons,
160) **CUES:** there are 多い <u>oo</u>i (many) Old
夕 (lesser moons) orbiting Jupiter, and I saw them
on my **T**ablet computer

162. 名 **PRONUNCIATIONS: na, mei,
myou MEANING:** name **EXAMPLES:** 名前
namae = name; 有名 yuumei = famous; 名字
myouji = family name **DESCRIPTION:** on the
upper left, 夕 yuu (lesser moon, # 160); on the
lower right, 口 kuchi (mouth, # 426), which
resembles a card with names written on it
CUES: Napoleon's **M**aestro (teacher, in Spanish)
has a **M**aid who went into a **M**eeting in **Y**osemite,
wrote her 名前 <u>na</u>mae (name) on this 口 (card)
and hung it from a 有名 yuu<u>mei</u> (famous) 夕
(lesser moon)

163. 外 **PRONUNCIATIONS: soto, hoka,
gai, hazu, ge MEANING:** outside **EXAMPLES:**
外 soto = outside; 外に hoka ni = besides, in
addition; 外人 gaijin = foreigner; 外す hazusu
= to remove; 外科 geka = surgery (medical
specialty) **NOTE:** both soto and hoka are written
外 **DESCRIPTION:** on the left, 夕 yuu (evening,
160); on the right, a radical that resembles the
katakana character ト to, which reminds us of
tomatoes **CUES:** in order to get ト (tomatoes) in
the 夕 (evening), Justice **Soto**mayor has to go 外
<u>soto</u> (outside) the **H**ockey **A**rena and find a **Gui**de,
who wears a **H**at and a **Z**oot suit, and looks **Gay**
COMPARE: 他(の) hoka no = another
(undefined) object, # 505

164. 死 **PRONUNCIATIONS: shi, ji**
MEANINGS: to die, death **EXAMPLES:** 死ぬ
shinu = to die; 死亡 shibou = death; 早死に
hayajini = early death, dying young
DESCRIPTION: at the top, a lid which could be a

sheet; on the left, 夕 yuu (evening, # 160); on the
right, the katakana character ヒ hi, which resembles
a body curled up in a casket **CUES:** if a person
死ぬ <u>shi</u>nu (dies) in the 夕 (evening), they put the
ヒ (body) under this **Sheet** and place it in a **Jeep**
COMPARE: 列 retsu = line, # 1124

165. 夢 **PRONUNCIATIONS: yume, mu**
MEANING: dream **EXAMPLES:** 夢 yume =
dream; 悪夢 akumu = nightmare
DESCRIPTION: at the top, a plant radical (see
43); in the middle, three eyes; at the bottom, 夕
yuu (evening, # 160), which helps us to pronounce
this **CUES:** my 夢 <u>yume</u> (dreams) come from a
third eye in my forehead and concern plants
from **U**tah and **Me**xico that bloom in the 夕
(evening) when the **Moon** is shining

Master
166. 主 **PRONUNCIATIONS: shu, omo,
nushi, zu MEANINGS:** lord, master, proprietor,
main **EXAMPLES:** 主人 shujin = husband,
master, landlord, landlady, proprietor, host or
hostess; 主婦 shufu = housewife; 主な omo
na = main, chief; 地主 jinushi = land owner;
坊主 bouzu = Buddhist monk **DESCRIPTION:**
a man with broad shoulders, two arms and two legs,
wearing a tiny cap **CUES:** this 主人 <u>shu</u>jin
(master) wears a little cap, and he has nice **Shoes**; he
uses an **O**ld **M**obile phone, his house has **New**
Shingles, and he likes to visit the **Zoo**
COMPARE: 玉 tama = ball, jewel, # 169; 王 ou
= king, # 1077

167. 住 **PRONUNCIATIONS: juu, su**
MEANING: to reside **EXAMPLES:** 住所
juusho = address; 住む sumu = to reside
DESCRIPTION: on the left, a man with a slanted
hat; on the right, 主 shu (master, # 166)
CUES: this man with a slanted hat, who drinks a lot
of **J**uice, graduated **Su**mma cum laude; he stands
with his 主 (master) outside a house where they
both 住む <u>su</u>mu (reside)

COMPARE: 主任 shunin = foreman, # 166 and # 483; 注(意) chuui = caution, # 168

168. 注 PRONUNCIATIONS: chuu, soso

MEANINGS: to pour carefully, to pay attention
EXAMPLES: 注文する chuumon suru = to order; 注意する chuui suru = to warn; 注ぐ sosogu = to pour **DESCRIPTION:** on the left, a water radical (see # 12); on the right, 主 shu (master, # 166) **CUES:** while Chewing gum, this 主 (master) 注ぐ sosogu (pours) water and often spills it, causing the carpet to become So Soggy, so 注意してください chuui shite kudasai (please be careful)

COMPARE: 住(む) sumu = to reside, # 167

169. 玉 PRONUNCIATIONS: dama, tama, gyoku MEANINGS: a round object, a jewel EXAMPLES: 10 円玉 juuen dama = ten-yen coin; 玉 tama = ball, jewel; 玉ねぎ tamanegi = onion; 玉座 gyokuza = throne DESCRIPTION: reportedly this represents a vertical string of three jewels, but apparently one fell off the string CUES: people from Damascus who like Tamales sometimes pay for them with strings of 玉 tama (jewels) like this one, but other Syrians prefer to eat Gyoza with Kool-Aid COMPARE: 主(人) shujin = husband, # 166; 国 kuni = country, # 170; 球 tama = bulb, # 606, which helps us to pronounce this; 王 ou = king, # 1077

170. 国 PRONUNCIATIONS: kuni, koku, goku, ko MEANINGS: country EXAMPLES: 国 kuni = country; 韓国 kankoku = South Korea; 中国 chuugoku = China; 国会 kokkai = Diet (legislature) DESCRIPTION: a 玉 tama (jewel, # 169) in a box CUES: my 国 kuni (country) is like a 玉 (jewel) in a box, and it's full of Cunning people who drink a lot of Coke and Gold Kool-Aid, and dig up a lot of Coal COMPARE: (公)園 kouen = park, # 279; 困(る) komaru = to be inconvenienced, # 280

Above & Below

171. 上 PRONUNCIATIONS: ue, a, jou, kami, uwa, nobo, u MEANINGS: up, above, to raise, to give EXAMPLES: 上 ue = up; 上げる ageru = to give, or to raise something up; 上手 jouzu = skillful; 川上 kawakami = upriver; 上着 uwagi = outer garment; 上る noboru = to go up; 上手い umai = skillful, delicious (usually written うまい) DESCRIPTION: compared to 土 tsuchi (dirt, # 59), 上 is asymmetrical and looks like a waiter holding a tray CUES: our Ueitaa (waiters) live 上 ue (above) the ground, from which they 上る noboru (rise) asymmetrically; working like Ants, they tell Jokes to Commies, they sleep in Uber Wagons, and Nobody in Uruguay can match them ALSO COMPARE: 登(る) noboru = to climb,# 297; 下 shita = below, # 172; 止(める) tomeru = to stop, transitive, # 173

172. 下 PRONUNCIATIONS: shita, moto, sa, ge, kuda, shimo, o, ka, he MEANINGS: down, below, to hang down, to lower EXAMPLES: 下着 shitagi = undergarment; 足下 ashimoto = underfoot; 下げる sageru = to lower, transitive, or to hang down; 下がる sagaru = to hang, intransitive; to step back, or go down; 下品な gehin na = vulgar; 下る kudaru = to descend; 下さる kudasaru = to give to me; 川下 kawashimo = downstream; 下ろす orosu = to withdraw money; 地下鉄 chikatetsu = subway; 下手 heta = unskillful

DESCRIPTION: compared to 不 fu (negation, # 176), 下 is asymmetrical

CUES: Shigella live in Tarballs 下 shita (below) ground, from which they 下る kudaru (descend) asymmetrically in Motorboats; when their spirits Sag, they Get assistance from barraCudas and Shimon Peres, who Oblige them to Call 911 for serious problems but Help them with minor issues

ALSO COMPARE: 上 ue = above, # 171

173. 止 PRONUNCIATIONS: to, ya, shi, do MEANING: to stop EXAMPLES: 止まる tomaru = to stop, intransitive; 止める tomeru = to stop, transitive; 止める yameru = to stop doing something, to give up; 中止する chuushi suru = to cancel; 通行止め tsuukoudome = road closed NOTE: tomeru and yameru are both written 止める DESCRIPTION: this resembles a barrier built to keep traffic out of a farm CUES: we put up this barrier so that cars will 止まる tomaru (stop) before they run into our Tomato and Yam farm; Sheep also cannot enter, due to a Domestic dispute COMPARE: 正(し い) tadashii = correct, # 174; 上(げる) ageru = to give to someone of equal or higher status, # 171; 辞(める) yameru = to resign a position, # 387

174. 正 PRONUNCIATIONS: tada, shou, sei, masa MEANING: correct EXAMPLES: 正しい tadashii = correct; 正直な shoujiki na = honest; 正解 seikai = correct answer; 正夢 masayume = a dream come true DESCRIPTION: 止(まる) tomaru (to stop, # 173), with a cap added at the top CUES: if a car 止 (stops) and everything is 正しい tadashii (correct), a Taxi Dashes up, and the driver places a cap on top of the 止 (barrier), Showing that it is Safe for the car to proceed to the Massage parlor

175. 政 PRONUNCIATION: sei MEANINGS: politics, government EXAMPLES: 政治 seiji = politics, government; 政治家 seijika = politician DESCRIPTION: on the left, 正(しい) tadashii (correct, # 174); on the right, a dancer with a ponytail CUE: 政治家 seijika (politicans) should pass 正 (correct) laws to encourage the development of Safe Jeeps for dancers like this

176. 不 PRONUNCIATIONS: bu, fu MEANING: negation EXAMPLES: 運動不足 undoubusoku = not enough exercise; 不便 fuben = inconvenient; 不足 fusoku = insufficiency DESCRIPTION: compared to 下 shita (below, # 172), 不 descends into the ground symmetrically, like a carrot divided into three parts CUES: while walking around in my Boots, I come across this symmetrical three-part carrot, but it's 不足 fusoku (insufficient) as a Food source

Knee

177. 年 PRONUNCIATIONS: nen, toshi MEANING: year EXAMPLES: 三年 sannen = three years; 今年 kotoshi = this year DESCRIPTION: a disabled negative nephew is sitting facing left, with a knee protruding and a crutch over his head CUES: my Negative Nephew is disabled and has been sitting here for a 年 nen (year), holding a crutch, playing with his Toy Sheep and waiting for help COMPARE: 念 nen = thought, # 314

178. 降 PRONUNCIATIONS: o, fu, kou, bu MEANINGS: to precipitate, to step down EXAMPLES: 降りる oriru = to get off a train etc.; 降る furu = to rain or snow; 下降 kakou = descent; 小降り koburi = light rain DESCRIPTION: on the left, ß beta, a character from the Greek alphabet; on the upper right, a dancer with a ponytail; on the lower right, a character similar to 年 nen (year, # 177), sitting facing left, with a knee protruding CUES: this dancer with a ponytail 降りる oriru (gets off) a ß (Greek) ship and leaps over this sitting figure to get some Oreos, but then the rain 降る furu (precipitates) Furiously, she gets Cold, and she puts on her Boots

179. 五 PRONUNCIATIONS: go, itsu MEANING: five EXAMPLES: 五人 gonin = five people; 五つ itsutsu = five items DESCRIPTION: unlike 年 nen (year, # 177) and 降(る) furu (to precipitate, # 178), the knee in 五

faces to the right; 五 contains five straight lines but is written with four strokes; it resembles a golfer staring down a fairway **CUES:** 五 **go** (five) **G**olfers wearing **I**talian **Su**its are staring down a fairway

180. 決 **PRONUNCIATIONS: ki, ketsu, ke MEANINGS:** to decide, to do decisively **EXAMPLES:** 決める kimeru = to decide or arrange; 決まる kimaru = to be decided or arranged; 解決 kaiketsu = settlement, resolution, solution; 決して kesshite = never **DESCRIPTION:** on the left, a water radical (see # 12); on the right, compared to the left-facing knees in 年 nen (year, # 177) and 降(る) furu (to precipitate, # 178), this knee is facing right and is mounted on a stand, resembling a tiller for steering a boat **CUES:** a pilot, who is wearing a **K**imono, moves this tiller when he 決める **ki**meru (decides) to turn the boat in the water, and he pours from a **K**ettle into his **S**oup, which he 決して **ke**sshite (never) shares with **K**en and Barbie **ALSO COMPARE:** 消(す) kesu = to erase, turn off, # 158

181. 片 **PRONUNCIATIONS: kata, pen, hen MEANINGS:** one side, piece **EXAMPLES:** 片方 katahou = one side, the other side, one of a pair; 片手 katate = one hand or arm; 片付ける katazukeru = to put in order; 一片 ippen = a slice or piece; 破片 hahen = shard, fragment **DESCRIPTION:** a person kneeling, holding a tray and looking to one side **CUES:** this person, who is kneeling on one knee, holds out a tray with a **Cata**logue of **Pen**s on it, but a **Hen** that is watching can only see 片方 **kata**hou (one side) of it **COMPARE:** 方 kata = method, or honorable person, # 114

Child

182. 子 **PRONUNCIATIONS: su, ko, go[1], shi, ji[1] MEANING:** child **EXAMPLES:** 様子 yousu = condition; 子供 kodomo = child; 迷子 maigo = a lost person; 男子 danshi = boy;

王子 ouji = prince **DESCRIPTION:** a thin cold child, with a flat head **CUES:** this thin 子 **ko** (child) from **Su**dan gets **C**old at night and sleeps under a **Sheep**skin **COMPARE:** 字 ji = character, # 183

183. 字 **PRONUNCIATION: ji MEANING:** character **EXAMPLE:** 漢字 kanji = kanji **DESCRIPTION:** at the top, a had haircut; at the bottom, 子 ko (child, # 182) **CUE:** this 子 (child) is a **G**enius with a bad haircut who writes excellent 字 **ji** (characters) **COMPARE:** 学 gaku = learning, # 184

184. 学 **PRONUNCIATIONS: gaku, ga, mana MEANINGS:** study, learning, science **EXAMPLES:** 学のある人 gaku no aru hito = a learned person; 学校 gakkou = school; 学ぶ manabu = to learn **DESCRIPTION:** at the top, a roof with three characters protruding from it; at the bottom, 子 ko (child, # 182) **CUES:** this **Ga**wky Uruguayan 子 (child) had the **Ga**ll to write three characters on the roof of the 学校 **ga**kkou (school) after he **Ma**naged to 学ぶ **mana**bu (learn) them **COMPARE:** 字 ji = character, # 183

185. 厚 **PRONUNCIATIONS: atsu, kou MEANING:** thick **EXAMPLES:** 厚い atsui = thick; 濃厚 noukou = density, concentration **DESCRIPTION:** on the left, a lean-to belonging to Superman; under the lean-to, 日 hi (sun, # 32), which looks like a heavy weight resting on 子 ko (child, # 182) **CUES:** this poor 子 (child) is getting crushed under a heavy 日 (weight) At Superman's lean-to, and he will likely become somewhat 厚い **atsu**i (thick, i.e., wide) as a result, but he will just have to **C**ope with that **COMPARE:** 暑(い) atsui = hot atmosphere, # 278; 熱(い) atsui = hot objects, # 65

186. 乳 **PRONUNCIATIONS: nyuu, chichi, *u*, chi MEANING:** milk **EXAMPLES:** 牛乳 gyuunyuu = cow's milk; 乳 chichi = milk; 乳母 uba = wet nurse; 乳首 chikubi = nipple **DESCRIPTION:** on the upper left, a few drops of milk; on the lower left, a 子 ko (child, # 182); on the right, a breast **CUES:** this 子 (child) at a mother's breast is drinking 乳 **nyuu** (milk) in **Nyuu**yooku (New York), while **Chichi** (father) looks on and eats **U**ber crackers and **Chee**se **COMPARE:** 父 chichi = father, # 143

187. 教 **PRONUNCIATIONS: oshi, kyou, oso MEANING:** to teach **EXAMPLES:** 教える oshieru = to teach; 教室 kyoushitsu = classroom; 教わる osowaru = to be taught **DESCRIPTION:** this is a situation that concerns OSHA (the Occupational Safety and Health Administration): on the upper left, 土 tsuchi (dirt, # 59); below that, a pair of scissors; below the scissors, 子 ko (child, # 182); on the right, a dancer with a ponytail **CUES:** OSHA **I**nforms and 教える **oshi**eru (teaches) this 子 (child) and this dancer in **Kyou**to that they should stay out of the 土 (dirt), not play with scissors and not eat **O**ld **Soy** sauce

Big

188. 大 **PRONUNCIATIONS: tai, oo, dai, oto, yama MEANING:** big **EXAMPLES:** 大変 taihen = terrible; 大きい ookii = big; 大学 daigaku = university; 大人 otona = adult; 大和 yamato = ancient Japan **DESCRIPTION:** 大 is a big character expanding in all directions, who is very tired **CUES:** this 大きい **oo**kii (big) man is **T**ired and **O**verweight, and he lives on a **D**iet of **O**ld **T**omatoes near a **Yama** (mountain)

189. 天 **PRONUNCIATIONS: ama, ten MEANINGS:** sky, heavens **EXAMPLES:** 天の川 ama no gawa = Milky Way; 天国 tengoku = heaven; 天気 tenki = weather **DESCRIPTION:** compared to 大(きい) ookii (big, # 188), this has a tent above it

CUES: in the Ama**z**on, the 天 **ama** (sky) is like this **Tent** over a 大 (big) forest

190. 犬 **PRONUNCIATIONS: inu, ken MEANING:** dog **EXAMPLES:** 犬 inu = dog; 番犬 banken = watchdog **DESCRIPTION:** 大(きい) ookii (big, # 188), with a ball above its right arm **CUES:** this 犬 **inu** (dog), which is 大 (big) and belongs to the **Inu**it tribe, chases a ball that **Ken** threw to Barbie

191. 太 **PRONUNCIATIONS: futo, buto[1], tai, ta MEANINGS:** to get fat, big, thick **EXAMPLES:** 太る futoru = to get fat; 小太り kobutori = plump; 太陽 taiyou = the sun; 太郎 tarou = a boy's given name **DESCRIPTION:** 大(きい) ookii (big, # 188), with a ball near its left leg **CUES:** since this 大 (big) person 太る **futo**ru (gets fat) to the point that he has to sleep on a **Futo**n with Ruth, he can only chase balls near the floor, he **Ti**res easily, and he worries about the **Ta**r in his cigarettes

192. 喫 **PRONUNCIATIONS: kitsu, ki MEANING:** to consume or smoke **EXAMPLES:** 喫煙 kitsuen = smoking; 喫茶店 kissaten = coffee house **DESCRIPTION:** at the top left, 口 kuchi (mouth, # 426), suggesting smoking; in the upper center, 主 shu (master, # 166); on the upper right, 刀 katana (sword, # 102); at the bottom, 大(きい) ookii (big, # 188) **CUES:** I feel like a 大 (big) 主 (master) when I make cigarettes using a **Kit** that I got from **Superman**, and I cut them in the **Kit**chen with this 刀 (sword), before smoking them through my 口 (mouth) at a 喫茶店 **kis**saten (coffee shop)

193. 咲 **PRONUNCIATIONS: sa, za MEANING:** to blossom or bloom **EXAMPLES:** 咲く saku = to blossom or bloom; 早咲き hayazaki = early blooming **DESCRIPTION:** on the left, 口 kuchi (mouth, # 426); on the right,

大(きい) ookii (big, # 188), with several extra lines added near the top, suggesting blossoms **CUES:** this 大 (big) tree 咲く <u>sa</u>ku (blossoms), and we keep the flowers in a **Sack**; **Z**ach makes tea from the blossoms, and we savor it in our 口 (mouths) **COMPARE:** 呼(ぶ) yobu = to call out, to summon, # 428; 味 aji = taste, # 245

194. 狭 PRONUNCIATIONS: sema, kyou, seba MEANING: narrow EXAMPLE: 狭い

semai = narrow, cramped; 狭小 kyoushou = cramped, narrow, confined; 狭める sebameru = to narrow or reduce **DESCRIPTION:** on the left, a person contorting her body; on the right, 大(きい) ookii (big, # 188) with four extra arms, suggesting a very big person **CUES:** inside a **Sem**i-truck near **Kyou**to, these two people are trying to pass each other in a 狭い <u>sema</u>i (narrow) space; the lady on the left contorts her body in order to accommodate the very 大 (big) person on the right, who **Se**lls **Ba**rbed wire **COMPARE:** 猫 neko = cat, # 72

195. 実 PRONUNCIATIONS: jitsu, ji, mi, mino MEANINGS: real, fruit EXAMPLES:

実は jitsu wa = as a matter of fact; 実行 jikkou = practice, action, deed, performance, implementation; 木の実 kinomi = nut, fruit, berry; 実る minoru = to bear fruit or ripen **DESCRIPTION:** at the top, a bad haircut; in the middle, 士 shi (man, warrior, # 66); at the bottom, 大(きい) ookii (big, # 188) **CUES:** this 大 (big) 士 (man) is a **J**ittery **S**uperstar with a bad haircut and a **Jee**p who raises 実の <u>jitsu</u> no (real) 木の実 kino<u>mi</u> (nuts) and shares **Mea**ls with a **M**inotaur

196. 険 PRONUNCIATIONS: kewa, ken MEANINGS: steep, danger EXAMPLES:

険しい kewashii = steep; 危険 kiken = danger; 保険 hoken = insurance

DESCRIPTION: on the left, ß from the Greek alphabet; at the top right, a steep roof; under the roof, 大(きい) ookii (big, # 188), intersected by a horizontal keg, with a handle at the top **CUES:** this is a laundromat with a horizontally placed 大 (big) **K**eg stuck inside a **Wa**shing machine; the roof is too 険しい <u>kewa</u>shii (steep) to allow the ß (Greek) guy named **Ken** to climb the roof, grab the handle and fix the problem for Barbie **COMPARE:** (試)験 shiken = exam, # 382

197. 漢 PRONUNCIATION: kan

MEANING: Chinese **EXAMPLE:** 漢字 kanji = Chinese character **DESCRIPTION:** on the left, a water radical (see # 12); at the upper right, a plant radical (see # 43); at the middle right, a pair of reading glasses; at the bottom right, 大(きい) ookii (big, # 188), with an extra pair of arms **CUE:** Chinese people come from over the water, they are fond of plants, they often wear glasses, they have 大 (big) hearts, and they print 漢字 <u>kan</u>ji (Chinese characters) on their **Can**dy wrappers **COMPARE:** 難(しい) muzukashii = difficult, # 198

198. 難 PRONUNCIATIONS: nan, muzuka, gato, gata, niku MEANING: difficulty

EXAMPLES: 困難 kon'nan = difficulty; 難しい muzukashii = difficult; 有難う arigatou = thank you; 有難い arigatai = grateful, but this is usually written ありがたい; 難い nikui = difficult to do, e.g., 読み難い yominikui = difficult to read, but this is usually written 読みにくい **DESCRIPTION:** on the left, 漢 kan (Chinese, # 197), without its water radical; on the right, a cage **CUES:** **Nan**cy is a 漢 (Chinese) person who wants to help the cats in this cage, which is 難しい <u>muzuka</u>shii (difficult) to penetrate; she wants to put a **Muzzle** on **Z**uckerberg's **Cat**, which is inside the cage, along with another **Gato** (male cat, in Spanish), a **Gata** (female cat, in Spanish), and her **Niec**e from **Ku**wait **COMPARE:** 誰 dare = who, # 440

199. 笑 **PRONUNCIATIONS: wara, e, shou MEANINGS:** to smile or laugh **EXAMPLES:** 笑う warau = to laugh; 笑顔 egao = smiling face; 爆笑 bakushou = burst of laughter **DESCRIPTION:** at the top, short 竹 take (bamboo, # 134) which resemble clamps; at the bottom, 大(きい) ookii (big, # 188), wearing a flat hat **CUES:** this 大 (big) **W**arrior named **R**aul **C**astro has 竹 (bamboo) clamps pinned to his eyebrows, and they made me 笑う **wara**u (laugh) during his **E**xcellent **Show COMPARE:** 第 dai = order, # 530; (切)符 kippu = ticket, # 133

Cage

200. 曜 **PRONUNCIATION: you MEANING:** day of the week **EXAMPLE:** 日曜日 nichiyoubi = Sunday **DESCRIPTION:** on the left, a 日 hi (sun, # 32) shining in Yosemite; on the upper right, feathers, suggesting a bird; on the lower right, a cage **CUE:** every 曜日 **you**bi (day of the week) in **Y**osemite, the 日 (sun) shines on this bird in a cage **COMPARE:** (洗)濯 sentaku = laundry, # 201

201. 濯 **PRONUNCIATION: taku MEANINGS:** laundry, wash **EXAMPLE:** 洗濯 sentaku = laundry **DESCRIPTION:** on the left, a water radical (see # 12); on the upper right, feathers, suggesting a bird; on the lower right, a cage **CUE:** using **T**ap water and **K**ool-Aid, we wash this bird in a cage whenever we do the 洗濯 sen**taku** (laundry) **COMPARE:** 曜 you = day of the week, # 200

202. 集 **PRONUNCIATIONS: atsu, shuu, tsudo MEANINGS:** to collect, gather, congregate **EXAMPLES:** 集める atsumeru = to collect, transitive; 集まる atsumaru = to congregate, intransitive; 集合 shuugou = gathering, assembly, meeting; 集う tsudou = to gather or meet **DESCRIPTION:** at the top, a cage; at the bottom, 木 ki (tree, # 118) **CUES:** this cage has been placed in a 木 (tree) to 集める **atsu**meru (collect) **A**tsui (hot) flying **M**ermaids, who travel without **S**hoes and carry **Tsui**tcases (suitcases) full of **D**ough (money)

203. 進 **PRONUNCIATIONS: susu, susumu, shin, jin**[1] **MEANING:** to move forward **EXAMPLES:** 進む susumu = to advance, make progress; 進める susumeru = to advance or promote, transitive; 進 Susumu = a boy's given name; 進出する shinshutsu suru = to advance or expand; 精進料理 shoujinryouri = vegetarian cuisine, as eaten by Buddhist monks **DESCRIPTION:** at the left and the bottom, a snail; at the right, riding on the snail, a cage **CUES:** **S**uperman's **S**ummer **Mu**sic program is like this cage on a snail which 進む **susu**mu (advances) slowly and collects donations for a **Shin**tou shrine **COMPARE:** 勧(める) susumeru = to advise, # 698

204. 準 **PRONUNCIATION: jun MEANINGS:** standard, preparation **EXAMPLE:** 準備 junbi = preparation **DESCRIPTION:** at the upper left, a water radical (see # 12); at the upper right, a cage, which resembles a fish trap; at the bottom 十 juu (ten, # 18) **CUE:** 十 (ten) fishermen are placing their fish traps in water as 準備 **jun**bi (preparation) for **Jun**gle fishing

Cow

205. 牛 **PRONUNCIATIONS: gyuu, ushi MEANING:** cow **EXAMPLES:** 牛肉 gyuuniku = beef; 牛 ushi = cow **DESCRIPTION:** a depiction of the front half of a cow, seen from above; at the top, the head; below that, the horns, with an enlarged horn on the left; below that, the front legs and the anterior trunk of the body **CUES:** a **G**uatemalan **You**th, who is an **U**sher at an **I**ndian theatre, owns this 牛 **ushi** (cow) with one horn that is bigger than the other **COMPARE:** 午 go = noon, # 207

206. 失 **PRONUNCIATIONS: shitsu, ushina, shi MEANINGS:** to lose; to slip away **EXAMPLES:** 失礼 shitsurei = discourtesy; 失業者 shitsugyousha = unemployed people; 失う ushinau = to lose; 失敗する shippai suru = to fail **DESCRIPTION:** a fusion between 牛 ushi (cow, # 205) and 大(きい) ookii (big, # 188) **CUES:** this 大 (big) 牛 (cow) often steps on our **Sheets**, and she is 失礼 **shitsu**rei (rude), but we have an **Ushi** (cow) **Now**, and also a **Sheep**, and we don't want to 失う **ushina**u (lose) them **COMPARE:** 矢 ya = arrow, # 1045

207. 午 **PRONUNCIATION: go**

MEANING: noon **EXAMPLES:** 午前 gozen = in the morning; 午後 gogo = in the afternoon **DESCRIPTION:** compared to 牛 ushi (cow, # 205), this cow is missing her head **CUE:** this 牛 (cow) hides her head at 午 **go** (noon), when the **Go**lden sun shines brightest **ALSO COMPARE:** 昼 hiru = noon, # 49

208. 生 **PRONUNCIATIONS: i, u, sei, shou, jou, nama, fu, ha, o MEANINGS:** to be born, to live **EXAMPLES:** 生きる ikiru = to live; 生まれる umareru = to be born; 先生 sensei = teacher; 一生 isshou = a lifetime; 誕生日 tanjoubi = birthday; 生 nama = raw; 芝生 shibafu = lawn; 生える haeru = to grow or sprout; 生い茂る oishigeru = to grow thickly **DESCRIPTION:** at the top, 牛 ushi (cow, # 205); at the bottom, 土 tsuchi (dirt, # 59) **CUES:** after this 牛 (cow) 生まれる **u**mareru (is born), it rises out of the 土 (dirt), and it 生きる **i**kiru (lives), befriending **Ea**gles, driving for **U**ber, **Sa**ving its money, and going to **Sho**ws with **Jo**e Nama**th** and his **Fo**olish **Ha**cker friends, until finally it gets **O**ld **COMPARE:** 性 sei = gender, # 209

209. 性 **PRONUNCIATIONS: saga, sei, shou MEANINGS:** innate nature, sex, gender

EXAMPLES: 性 saga = one's nature, or custom; 性 sei = gender; 男性 dansei = man, male; 女性 josei = woman, female; 性格 seikaku = personality, character; 性能 seinou = efficiency; 相性 aishou = affinity, compatibility **DESCRIPTION:** on the left, an erect radical which could be a chromosome; on the right, 生(まれる) umareru (to be born, # 208) **CUES: Saga**cious scientists often **Say** that chromosomes like this one on the left determine one's 性 **sei** (gender) at the time one 生 (is born), and they can **Show** us these chromosomes under a microscope

210. 産 **PRONUNCIATIONS: san, u, ubu, yage MEANINGS:** to give birth, to produce **EXAMPLES:** 産業 sangyou = industry; 産む umu = to give birth, produce, lay an egg; 産着 ubugi = baby clothes; お土産 omiyage = souvenir **DESCRIPTION:** at the top, a bell resting on a lean-to, which is a sanitarium; inside the lean-to, 生(きる) ikiru (to live, # 208) **CUES:** this **San**itarium has a bell on the roof, which rings to announce that medical researchers 生 (live) inside and will create a 産業 **san**gyou (industry) that 産む **u**mu (gives birth) to treatments for **O**ozing wounds caused by poorly fitting **Uru**guayan **Boo**ts, such as **Yam** and Ge**kko**-based ointments

Plants

211. 花 **PRONUNCIATIONS: hana, bana[1], ka MEANING:** flower **EXAMPLES:** お花見 ohanami = honorable flower viewing; 生け花 ikebana = Japanese flower arrangement; 花粉 kafun = pollen **DESCRIPTION:** at the top, a plant radical (see # 43); at the bottom, 化(学) kagaku (chemistry, # 487), which resembles some asymmetrical flowers but also looks like a map of Canada; i.e., on the left, we see a straight west coast, topped by Alaska, while on the right we see Hudson Bay and the Maritime provinces **CUES: Hannah**'s asymmetrical 花 **hana** (flowers) grow in **Ca**nada **COMPARE:** 茶 cha = tea, # 212

212. 茶 PRONUNCIATIONS: cha, sa

MEANING: tea EXAMPLES: お茶 ocha = honorable tea; 喫茶店 kissaten = cafe DESCRIPTION: at the top, a plant radical (see # 43); at the bottom, a symmetrical bush growing under a roof CUES: Prince Charles' 茶 **cha** (tea) bushes grow in small houses and are symmetrical, since he **Sa**ws them back every year COMPARE: 花 hana = flower, # 211

Temple

213. 寺 PRONUNCIATIONS: tera, dera[1], ji MEANING: temple EXAMPLES: 寺 tera = temple; 清水寺 Kiyomizudera = a temple in Kyoto; 寺院 ji'in = temple DESCRIPTION: at the top, 土 tsuchi (dirt, # 59), which resembles a cross; at the bottom, an asymmetrical structure with a terrace at the top, suggesting that a building has been built into the side of a hill

CUES: this 寺 **tera** (temple), which is built into the side of a hill, features a 土 (cross) at the top, as well as a **Terra**ce and a **Jeep** COMPARE: 守(る) mamoru = to protect, # 214

214. 守 PRONUNCIATIONS: su, mori, mamo, shu MEANINGS: to protect, guard or defend EXAMPLES: 留守 rusu = absence from a house; 子守 komori = nanny, baby sitter; 守る mamoru = to protect; 守備 shubi = defense, garrisoning DESCRIPTION: at the top, a bad haircut; at the bottom, an asymmetrical support structure, suggesting that a building has been built into the side of a hill; compared to 寺 tera (temple, # 213), the cross at the top has been replaced by a bad haircut CUES: while the monks were 留守 ru**su** (absent), **S**uperman and **Maure**en removed the 土 (cross) from this 寺 (temple), added a stronger roof that resembles a bad haircut in order to 守る **mamo**ru (protect) it from falling **Mamm**oths, and tied it down with **Sho**elaces

215. 時 PRONUNCIATIONS: ji, *to*, toki

MEANING: time EXAMPLES: 時間 jikan = time; 時計 tokei = clock, or watch; 時 toki = time DESCRIPTION: on the left, 日 hi (sun, # 32); on the right, 寺 tera (temple, # 213)

CUES: the 日 (sun) shines on this 寺 (temple), and the temple's sundial tells the 時 **toki** (time), which is 一時 ichi**ji** (1:00), suggesting that we can go out to the temple's **Jeep**, smoke **To**bacco and eat **Cake**, and then enjoy some **To**ast with **Qui**che

216. 持 PRONUNCIATIONS: mo, ji MEANINGS: to hold or possess EXAMPLES: 持つ motsu = to hold or have; 持参する jisan suru = to bring or take; 支持する shiji suru = to support DESCRIPTION: on the left, a kneeling guy; on the right, 寺 tera (temple, # 213) CUES: this kneeling guy crawls up to one of the 寺 (temple)'s **Mo**ats to say that he 持 **mo**tsu (has) a **Jeep** that he wants to give to the monks COMPARE: 待(つ) matsu = to wait, # 217

217. 待 PRONUNCIATIONS: ma, tai MEANINGS: to wait or handle EXAMPLES: 待つ matsu = to wait; 招待 shoutai = invitation DESCRIPTION: on the left, a man with two hats; on the right, 寺 tera (temple, # 213) CUES: this man with two hats 待 **ma**tsu (waits) at the 寺 (temple) and asks for some **Mat**s to sit on, since he has traveled a long way and is **Tired** COMPARE: 持(つ) motsu = to hold or have, # 216; 得(る) eru = to get, # 706

218. 特 PRONUNCIATIONS: toku, to MEANINGS: special, notable EXAMPLES: 特に toku ni = especially; 特別 tokubetsu = special; 特急 tokkyuu = special express train DESCRIPTION: on the left, 牛 ushi (cow, # 205); on the right, 寺 tera (temple, # 213) CUES: this 特別な **toku**betsu na (special) 牛 (cow) on the left is **Totally Cool**, and it was given to this 寺 (temple) by a **To**ny Blair

Skeet Shooter

219. 糸 **PRONUNCIATIONS: ito, shi**

MEANING: thread **EXAMPLES:** 糸 ito = thread, yarn; 糸目 itome = stitches; 金糸 kinshi = golden thread **DESCRIPTION:** a gun mounted on a three-legged platform; this resembles a skeet shooter, a machine that launches clay targets into the air for target practice **CUE:** this skeet shooter has been repaired with 糸 **ito** (thread), and we use it to fire at the mosqu**I**tos who bite our **Sheep**

220. 細 **PRONUNCIATIONS: hoso, boso, koma, sai MEANINGS:** slender, detail **EXAMPLES:** 細い hosoi = thin; 心細い kokorobosoi = downhearted; 細かい komakai = minute, small; 詳細 shousai = details **DESCRIPTION:** on the left, a 糸 (skeet shooter, # 219); on the right, 田 (rice paddy, # 68) **CUES:** a **H**ome-schooled **S**oldier, who is just a **B**oy **S**oldier, and who is in a **Coma**, is **S**ilent as this 糸 (skeet shooter) shoots at the 細い **hoso**i (narrow) 田 (rice paddy) where he is hiding, leaving trails of smoke which are quite 細い **koma**kai (small)

221. 紙 **PRONUNCIATIONS: kami, gami[1], shi MEANING:** paper **EXAMPLES:** 紙 kami = paper; 折り紙 origami = Japanese paper-folding craft; 紙幣 shihei = paper money **DESCRIPTION:** on the left, a 糸 (skeet shooter , # 219); on the right, a pavilion with a flat roof **CUES:** this 糸 (skeet shooter) is firing skeets onto the flat 紙 **kami** (paper) roof of a pavilion, since it is occupied by **Commie**s (Communists) who are using **Shi**elds to protect themselves **COMPARE:** 低(い) hikui = low, # 222; 神 kami = god, # 273; (女)将 okami = landlady, # 374; 髪 kami = hair, # 501; (彼)氏 kareshi = boyfriend, # 709

222. 低 **PRONUNCIATIONS: hiku, tei MEANINGS:** low, short in stature **EXAMPLES:** 低い hikui = low; 最低 saitei = the worst **DESCRIPTION:** on the left, a guy with a slanted hat; on the right, a pavilion with a flat roof, as seen in 紙 kami (paper, # 221), but this pavilion is elevated on a flat rock **CUES:** this guy with a slanted hat has the **Hiccup**s and is too 低い **hiku**i (low) to see over the 紙 (paper) pavilion, which has been **Ta**ped to a flat rock

223. 絵 **PRONUNCIATIONS: kai, e MEANINGS:** picture, drawing, painting **EXAMPLES:** 絵画 kaiga = painting; 絵本 ehon = picture book **DESCRIPTION:** on the left, a 糸 (skeet shooter, # 219); on the right, 会(議) kaigi (meeting, # 293), which helps us to pronounce this **CUES:** this 糸 (skeet shooter) will have a 会 (meeting) with the **Kai**ser to paint his 絵画 **kai**ga (painting), and he will produce an **E**xcellent 絵 **e** (picture) **COMPARE:** 給(料) kyuuryou = salary, # 997

224. 経 **PRONUNCIATIONS: kyou, ta, kei, he MEANING:** to pass through **EXAMPLES:** 経文 kyoumon = sutras, scriptures; 経つ tatsu = to elapse or pass, referring to time; 経験 keiken = experience; 経済 keizai = economics; 経る heru = to pass (time), to go through or by way of **DESCRIPTION:** on the left, a 糸 (skeet shooter, # 219); on the upper right, 又 mata ("again," # 24), but this resembles a dog groomer's table; on the lower right, 土 tsuchi (dirt, # 59) **CUES:** this 糸 (skeet shooter) gets some 経験 **kei**ken (experience) by shooting toward a dog groomer's 又 (table) on some 土 (dirt) in **Kyou**to, where the dogs wear dog **Tag**s, sit in **Ca**ges, and **Hel**p themselves to dog food **COMPARE:** 軽(い) karui = light (weight), # 289; 結(果) kekka = result, # 231

225. 約 PRONUNCIATION: **yaku**
MEANINGS: approximately, to promise, to shorten
EXAMPLES: 予約 yoyaku = reservation;
約束 yakusoku = promise; 契約 keiyaku =
contract; 約一年 yaku ichinen = approximately
one year DESCRIPTION: on the left, a 糸 (skeet
shooter, # 219); on the right, a giant hook
CUE: this giant hook, made from a **Yak** horn, grabs
a 糸 (skeet shooter) and binds him to his 契約
kei**yaku** (contract) COMPARE: 的 teki = having
the characteristics of, # 45

226. 続 PRONUNCIATIONS: **tsuzu, zoku**
MEANING: to continue EXAMPLES: 続く
tsuzuku = to continue, intransitive; 接続
setsuzoku = connection DESCRIPTION: on the
left, a 糸 (skeet shooter, # 219); on the right,
売(る) uru (to sell, # 425), which features a 士
shi (man, or warrior, # 66) on a sturdy platform, who
left his tsuitcase (suitcase) back at the zoo CUES:
this 糸 (skeet shooter) will 続く **tsuzu**ku
(continue) shooting skeets at this 士 (man) on the
platform, and the 士 (man) will 続く **tsuzu**ku
(continue) to get more skeets from his **Tsu**itcase
(suitcase) at the **Zoo** and then 売 (sell) them to the
糸 (skeet shooter), as **Z**ombies in **Ku**wait watch on
TV COMPARE: 読(む) yomu = to read, # 432

227. 緑 PRONUNCIATIONS: **midori,**
ryoku MEANING: green EXAMPLES: 緑
midori = green; 緑茶 ryokucha = green tea
DESCRIPTION: on the left, a 糸 (skeet shooter,
219); on the upper right, a green flag; on the
lower right, this resembles 水 mizu (water, # 251)
but is different; it is said to represent an animal, with
a head, a tail and four legs CUES: this 糸 (skeet
shooter) fires at a 緑 **midori** (green) flag on a
Miniature **D**ory that is carrying this animal, while
Pope **Leo** drinks **Kool**-Aid and 緑茶 **ryoku**cha
(green tea) COMPARE: 線 sen (line), # 228

228. 線 PRONUNCIATION: **sen**
MEANING: line EXAMPLES: 線 sen = line;
二番線 nibansen = Track Number Two;
山手線 yamanote sen = Yamanote line
DESCRIPTION: on the left, a 糸 (skeet shooter,
219); on the right, 泉 izumi (fountain, # 252)
which consists of 白(い) shiroi (white, # 44)
above 水 mizu (water, # 251) CUE: Senator 白
(White) is drowning in 水 (water), and this 糸
(skeet shooter) shoots a 線 **sen** (line) to save him
COMPARE: 緑 midori = green, # 227;
(温)泉 onsen = hot spring, # 252

229. 練 PRONUNCIATIONS: **ren, ne**
MEANINGS: to practice or train EXAMPLES:
練習する renshuu suru = to practice; 練る
neru = to knead or plan carefully DESCRIPTION:
on the left, a 糸 (skeet shooter, # 219); on the right,
東 higashi (east, # 508) CUES: this 糸 (skeet
shooter) 練習 **ren**shuu suru (practices) shooting
東 (east), since that's where its enemy the **Rent**
collector lives in **Ne**braska

230. 絡 PRONUNCIATIONS: **kara, raku**
MEANING: to get entangled with EXAMPLE:
絡まる karamaru = to become entangled in;
連絡する renraku suru = to contact
DESCRIPTION: on the left, a 糸 (skeet shooter,
219); on the right, a dancer with a ponytail leaping
over a box full of karaoke equipment
CUES: someone 連絡する ren**raku** suru
(contacts) this dancer with a ponytail about the
approach of a 糸 (skeet shooter), and while she is
escaping by leaping over this box of **Kara**oke
equipment, she **Rak**es it with her toes
COMPARE: 終(わる) owaru = to finish,
233; 落(語) rakugo = Japanese comic story
telling, # 526; 楽 raku = pleasure, # 520

231. 結 **PRONUNCIATIONS: ke, musu, yu, ketsu MEANINGS:** to tie, bind, organize, fasten **EXAMPLES:** 結果 kekka = result; 結婚 kekkon = marriage; 結局 kekkyoku = after all; 結ぶ musubu = bind, connect, conclude, organize, e.g., 手を結ぶ te wo musubu = to join hands; 髪を結う kami wo yuu = to put up the hair; 団結 danketsu = unity, combination **DESCRIPTION:** on the left, a 糸 (skeet shooter, # 219); on the upper right, 士 shi (man, or warrior, # 66); on the lower right, 口 kuchi (mouth, # 426) **CUES:** this 糸 (skeet shooter) will 結婚する **ke**kkon suru (marry) this 士 (man), who is a **Ke**nnedy with **Mus**cles who lives in the **Yu**kon and who likes to put **Ket**chup in his **Soup**, and the 結果 **ke**kka (result) is that they will have to learn to control their 口 (mouths) **COMPARE:** 経(験) keiken = experience, # 224

232. 緒 **PRONUNCIATIONS: cho, o, sho MEANINGS:** rope, beginning **EXAMPLES:** 情緒 joucho = emotion; 鼻緒 hanao = straps of geta (wooden clogs); 一緒に issho ni = together **DESCRIPTION:** on the left, a 糸 (skeet shooter, # 219); on the right, 者 mono (person, # 276) **CUES:** this 糸 (skeet shooter) has **Cho**sen this **O**lder 者 (person) to marry, and she **Sho**ws up, and they are 一緒に is**sho** ni (together) at last

233. 終 **PRONUNCIATIONS: o, shuu MEANINGS:** to end or finish **EXAMPLES:** 終わる owaru = to finish, intransitive; 終える oeru = to finish, transitive; 最終電車 saishuu densha= last train **DESCRIPTION:** on the left, a 糸 (skeet shooter, # 219); on the right, 冬 fuyu (winter, # 234) **CUES:** this 糸 (skeet shooter)'s contract 終わる **o**waru (finishes) when 冬 (winter arrives), and he goes back to **O**hio, in

order to **Shoot** at his old enemies **COMPARE:** (連)絡 renraku = contact, # 230

234. 冬 **PRONUNCIATIONS: tou, fuyu MEANING:** winter **EXAMPLES:** 冬期 touki = winter; 冬 fuyu = winter **DESCRIPTION:** a dancer with a pony tail jumps over a patch of ice **CUES:** this dancer with a ponytail escapes some **To**ries by taking a big leap over a patch of ice in 冬 **fuyu** (winter); I **Fooled You**, she cries **COMPARE:** 終(わる) owaru = to finish, # 233; 久(しぶり) hisashiburi = after a long time, # 30

Female

235. 女 **PRONUNCIATIONS: onna, jo, o, me, nyou, ma MEANING:** female **EXAMPLES:** 女の人 onna no hito = woman; 女性 josei = woman; 女将 okami = mistress, landlady, hostess, proprietress; 乙女 otome = maiden; 女房 nyoubou = one's wife; 海女 ama = fisherwoman, female pearl diver **DESCRIPTION:** at the top, a reclining horizontal cross; at the bottom, an X-shaped figure that resembles a person, carrying the cross **CUES:** an **O**ld **Na**sty taskmaster is forcing some 女の人 **onna** no hito (women) named **Jo**an of Arc and **O**prah to carry this cross to **Me**xico, but they will **Need Yo**gurt if they are going to make it as far as the **Ma**ll

236. 安 **PRONUNCIATIONS: an, yasu MEANINGS:** inexpensive, secure, peaceful **EXAMPLES:** 安心する anshin suru = to feel relieved; 安い yasui = cheap **DESCRIPTION:** at the top, a bad haircut; at the bottom, an 女 onna (female, # 235) named Anne **CUES:** Queen **Anne** is a 女 (female) with a bad haircut who gives us 安心 **an**shin (relief) by cooking 安い **yasu**i (cheap) **Yak Soup COMPARE:** 案 an = plan, idea, # 120; 休(む) yasumu = to rest, # 122

237. 妻 **PRONUNCIATIONS: tsuma, sai**

MEANING: wife **EXAMPLES:** 妻 tsuma = wife; 夫妻 fusai = married couple **DESCRIPTION:** at the top, a cross with a comb intersecting it; at the bottom, 女 onna (female, # 235) **CUES:** this 妻 <u>tsuma</u> (wife) is a 女 (female) and a **Ts**uper (**super**) **Ma** who is a **S**cientist, and she wears a cross and a comb in her hair

238. 要 **PRONUNCIATIONS: kaname, you, i MEANING:** important **EXAMPLES:** 肝心要 kanjin kaname = the main point; 要するに you suru ni = in short; 必要 hitsuyou = necessary; 要る iru = to need **DESCRIPTION:** at the top, three eyes suspended from a platform; at the bottom, 女 onna (female, # 235) **CUES:** because she has three eyes, this 女 (female) **Cana**dian **Mai**d knows all of the 必要 hits<u>you</u> (necessary) things that her employer 要る <u>i</u>ru (needs) to eat, such as **Y**ogurt and **E**els **COMPARE:** 悪(い) warui = bad, # 313

239. 好 **PRONUNCIATIONS: su, zu[1], kono, kou MEANING:** to like **EXAMPLES:** 好きです suki desu = I like it; 好き zuki = enthusiast, used as a suffix, e.g., ryokouzuki = travel lover; 好む konomu = to like or favor; 好物 koubutsu = favorite food **DESCRIPTION:** on the left, an 女 onna (female, # 235); on the right, 子 ko (children, # 182) **CUES: Su**perman 好き <u>su</u>ki (likes) the way that 女 (females) and 子 (children) hide their **C**old **N**oses in their **Co**ats during the winter

240. 婚 **PRONUNCIATION: kon**

MEANING: marriage **EXAMPLE:** 結婚 kekkon = marriage **DESCRIPTION:** on the left, 女 onna (female, # 235); on the upper right, the paper pavilion from 紙 kami (paper, # 221); on the lower right, a 日 hi (sun, # 32) shining in the Congo **CUE:** this 女 (female) from the **Con**go will 結婚する kek<u>kon</u> suru (marry), and she is writing wedding invitations on 紙 (paper) in the bright 日 (sun) **COMPARE:** 昏(睡) konsui = stupor, # 1074, which helps us to pronounce this

241. 姉 **PRONUNCIATIONS: ane, *nee*, shi MEANING:** older sister **EXAMPLES:** 姉 ane = older sister; お姉さん oneesan = honorable older sister; 姉妹 shimai = sisters **DESCRIPTION:** on the left, 女 onna (female, # 235); on the right, 市 shi (city, # 242), which looks like a spinning lady with wide hips **CUES:** compared to 妹 (little sister, # 244), this 姉 <u>ane</u> (big sister) has wider hips, tells more **A**necdotes, eats more **N**ectarines, and is more **C**hic, since she lives in the 市 (city)

242. 市 **PRONUNCIATIONS: shi, ichi**
MEANINGS: market, city, municipal **EXAMPLES:** 都市 toshi = city; 市長 shichou = mayor; 市場 ichiba = market **DESCRIPTION:** a spinning lady with wide hips who owns sheep and wears a pointy hat **CUES:** this lady has wide hips and spins around the 都市 to<u>shi</u> (city) looking for her **Sh**eep who are **I**tching to see her **COMPARE:** 姉 ane = older sister, # 241

243. 帽 **PRONUNCIATION: bou**

MEANINGS: cap, headgear **EXAMPLE:** 帽子 boushi = hat **DESCRIPTION:** on the left, Bo Peep, a spinning lady with wide hips; compared to 市 shi (city, # 242), she is not wearing a pointy hat; on the upper right, 日 hi (sun, # 32); on the lower right, 目 me (eye, # 51); 日 and 目 resemble two tall hats **CUES: Bo** Peep is trying to decide between these two **Bo**dacious 帽子 <u>bou</u>shi (hats) **ALSO COMPARE:** 慣(れる) nareru = to get used to, # 92

244. 妹 PRONUNCIATIONS: **imouto, mai** MEANING: younger sister **EXAMPLES:** 妹 imouto = younger sister; 姉妹 shimai = sisters **DESCRIPTION:** on the left, 女 onna (female, # 235); on the right, 木 ki (tree, # 118), with an extra horizontal line forming two arms, representing a little sister **CUES:** compared to 姉 (big sister, # 241), 妹 **imouto** (little sister) has narrow hips, she has relatively **Immo**bile **Toes** which make it difficult for her to spin, and she plays with **Mice**

ALSO COMPARE: 味 aji = taste, # 245

245. 味 PRONUNCIATIONS: **aji, mi, *i*** MEANING: taste **EXAMPLES:** 味 aji = taste; 意味 imi = meaning; 趣味 shumi = hobby; 地味な jimi na = subdued, inconspicuous, unattractive; 美味しい oishii = delicious (this is usually written おいしい)

DESCRIPTION: on the left, 口 kuchi (mouth, # 426), but this resembles a mirror; on the right, 妹 (little sister, # 244), without her female radical **CUES:** 妹 (little sister) is **Ag**ing, but when she looks in this 口 (**Mirror**), she sees that she still has good 味 **aji** (taste) in her **E**astern clothes

COMPARE: 咲(く) saku = to blossom, # 193

Crafted Object

246. 工 PRONUNCIATIONS: **kou, ku** MEANING: crafted object **EXAMPLES:** 工場 koujou = factory, 大工 daiku = carpenter **DESCRIPTION:** an I-beam, seen on end **CUES:** this 工 **kou** (crafted object) resembles an I-beam, seen on end, which is used inside **Coal** mines and in **Co**oling towers **COMPARE:** the katakana character エ e

247. 紅 PRONUNCIATIONS: **kou, beni, *momi*** MEANINGS: scarlet, red **EXAMPLES:** 紅茶 koucha = black tea; 紅 beni = red, rouge, lipstick; 口紅 kuchibeni = lipstick; 紅葉 momiji = Japanese maple, autumn colors **DESCRIPTION:** on the left, a 糸 skeet shooter (# 219); on the right, 工 kou (crafted object, # 246), which helps us to pronounce this **CUES:** this 糸 (skeet shooter) shoots 紅茶 **kou**cha (black tea) at the 工 (crafted object), who works in a **Coal** mine, but the crafted object just applies her 口紅 kuchi**beni** (lipstick) and leaves for **Beni**hana (a chain of teppanyaki restaurants) to attend a **M**otorcycle club **Mee**ting

248. 空 PRONUNCIATIONS: **su, a, muna, kuu, kara, sora, zora[1]** MEANINGS: sky, empty **EXAMPLES:** 空く suku = to become empty; 空く aku = to become vacant; 空き地 akichi = vacant lot; 空しい munashii = empty, fruitless; 空港 kuukou = airport; 空車 kuusha = free taxi; 空 kara = empty; 空 sora = sky; 夜空 yozora = night sky **NOTE:** suku and aku are both written 空く; in addition, kara and sora are both written 空 **DESCRIPTION:** at the top, a super-sized soaring albatross; at the bottom, 工 kou (crafted object, # 246), which could be part of a vacant cooling tower **CUES:** this **S**uper-sized **A**lbatross, whose **M**ood is **N**asty, rebounds from an 空いている **a**ite iru (vacant) 工 (crafted object) **Co**oling tower near the 空港 **kuu**kou (airport) in **Cara**cas and **Soar**s into the 空 **sora** (sky)

249. 式 PRONUNCIATION: **shiki** MEANINGS: ceremony, formula **EXAMPLE:** 結婚式 kekkon shiki = wedding ceremony

DESCRIPTION: a tall woman leans over a 工 kou (crafted object, # 246) **CUE:** this tall woman, who is participating in a 式 **shiki** (ceremony), leans over a 工 (crafted object), and she sees that it is a **Shift** Key **COMPARE:** 試(験) shiken = examination, # 436

Water

250. 川 PRONUNCIATIONS: **kawa, sen, gawa** MEANING: river EXAMPLES: 川 kawa = river; 河川 kasen = river; 小川 ogawa = brook DESCRIPTION: a flowing river CUES: this 川 **kawa** (river) supplies water for a **Car Wa**sh in the **Cen**ter of a town, where there is a **Gas War**

251. 水 PRONUNCIATIONS: **mizu, sui, zui**[1] MEANING: water EXAMPLES: 水 mizu = water; 水曜日 suiyoubi = Wednesday; 洪水 kouzui = flood DESCRIPTION: a waterfall flowing between two cliffs at a miniature zoo

CUES: outside the cafeteria at a **Miniature Zoo**, 水 **mizu** (water) was flowing between these two cliffs, and we ordered **Swee**t Yogurt

COMPARE: 小(さい) chiisai = small, # 253

252. 泉 PRONUNCIATIONS: **sen, izumi** MEANING: fountain EXAMPLES: 温泉 onsen = hot spring; 泉 izumi = spring (of water) DESCRIPTION: at the top, 白(い) shiroi (white, # 44); at the bottom, 水 mizu (water, # 251) CUES: **Sen**ator 白 (White) bathed in an 温泉 on**sen** (hot spring) which was supplied by this 水 (water) from a natural 泉 **izumi** (spring) at the **Ea**gle **Zoo** in **Mi**chigan COMPARE: 線 sen = line, # 228; 泊(まる) tomaru = to spend the night, # 46

253. 小 PRONUNCIATIONS: **chii, shou, ko, o,** *a* MEANING: small EXAMPLES: 小さい chiisai = small; 小学校 shougakkou = elementary school; 小鳥 kotori = little bird; 小川 ogawa = brook; 小豆 azuki = red bean DESCRIPTION: like 水 mizu (water, # 251), 小 contains a central line with a curve at the bottom, but the secondary lines surrounding this middle line are smaller and straighter in 小, which resembles a chimpanzee wearng a coat CUES: this 小さい **chii**sai (small) **Chi**mpanzee Signed up and then

Showed up wearing a **Coat** at a 小学校 **shou**gakkou (elementary school) in **O**saka, where it majored in **Art** COMPARE: 川 kawa = river, # 250; 少(々) shoushou = a little, # 254, which helps us to pronounce this

254. 少 PRONUNCIATIONS: **suku, suko, shou** MEANING: small amount EXAMPLES: 少ない sukunai = a little; 少し sukoshi = a little; 少々 shoushou = a little DESCRIPTION: this kanji adds a disparaging slash to 小(学校) shougakkou (elementary school, # 253), which helps us to pronounce this, suggesting that something is 少ない **suku**nai (a few) or 少し **suko**shi (a little)

CUES: our **Succu**lent plants are 少ない **suku**nai (few), but **Super**man and his **Co**-workers got 少し **suko**shi (a little) pleasure from them when they came to our 小 (small) plant **Show**

255. 泳 PRONUNCIATIONS: *oyo, ei* MEANING: to swim EXAMPLES: 泳ぐ oyogu = to swim; 水泳 suiei = swimming DESCRIPTION: on the left, a water radical (see # 12), suggesting swimming; on the right, 水 mizu (water, # 251), with two small lines added above it; this suggests two kinds of water CUES: **O**prah eats **Yo**gurt before she 泳ぐ **oyo**gu (swims) in salt water, and she drinks **A**le before her 水泳 su**iei** (swimming) sessions in fresh water

256. 浴 PRONUNCIATIONS: *yu, a, yoku* MEANING: to bathe EXAMPLES: 浴衣 yukata = summer kimono; 浴びる abiru = to bathe; 浴室 yokushitsu = bathroom DESCRIPTION: on the left, a water radical (see # 12); on the right, a bathroom containing a bathtub, with water vapor rising from the top, which looks like a good place to drink a biiru (beer) CUES: a **You**thful person puts on a 浴衣 **yu**kata (summer robe), drinks **A** Biiru (a beer), and 浴びる **a**biru (bathes) in this **Yoku** (well)-made 浴室 **yoku**shitsu (bathroom), which has water vapor rising from the roof

COMPARE: (内)容 naiyou = content, # 296; 欲(しい) hoshii = desire, # 535; 裕(福) yuufuku = rich, # 660

257. 温 PRONUNCIATIONS: atata, on

MEANING: warm objects EXAMPLES: 温かい atatakai = warm (water, etc.); 温める atatameru = to heat up water, etc., transitive; 温度 ondo = temperature; 温泉 onsen = hot spring DESCRIPTION: on the left, a water radical (see # 12); on the upper right, a warm 日 hi (sun, # 32) shining; on the lower right, 皿 sara (bowl, # 567) CUES: Ataturk with a Tan is the Owner of this bathhouse, where the 日 (sun) shines on water in a 皿 (bowl) and produces 温かい **atata**kai (warm) water vapor

COMPARE: 暖(かい) atatakai = warm atmosphere, # 38; 塩 shio = salt, # 60

258. 薄 PRONUNCIATIONS: usu, haku

MEANINGS: dilute, thin, weak EXAMPLES: 薄い usui = pale, thin, light, watery, dilute, weak (taste); 薄情 hakujou = cruel, heartless, uncaring DESCRIPTION: on the left, a water radical (see # 12); at the top, a plant radical (see # 43); at the lower right, 寺 tera (temple, # 213), but 田 (rice paddy, # 68) has been inserted into the middle of 寺 CUES: combining water with rice, this 寺 (temple)'s 田 (rice paddy) is producing 薄い **usu**i (thin) rice tea appropriate for Usurers and Hackers

259. 済 PRONUNCIATIONS: sai, su, zai

MEANING: to finish EXAMPLES: 救済 kyuusai = help, rescue, relief; 済む sumu = to end (intransitive), to manage, to do without; 済ます sumasu = to finish, transitive; 経済 keizai = economy DESCRIPTION: on the left, a water radical (see # 12), which suggests an ocean; on the right, 又 mata ("again," # 24) wearing a pointy hat, above a truncated 月 tsuki (moon, # 148)

CUES: 又 ("again"), who is wearing a pointy hat, is a **S**cientist who graduated **Su**mma cum laude but who is still trying to 済ます **su**masu (finish) her dissertation on 月 (moon) phenomena, and she is happy to discover this truncated moon shining near the ocean in **Zai**re

260. 活 PRONUNCIATIONS: katsu, ka

MEANINGS: life, lively, activity EXAMPLES: 生活 seikatsu = life, livelihood; 活躍 katsuyaku = great efforts; 活気 kakki = liveliness DESCRIPTION: on the left, a water radical (see # 12); on the upper right, a forked tongue; on the lower right, 口 kuchi (mouth, # 426)

CUES: my 生活 sei**katsu** (livelihood) is to cook Safe ton **Katsu** (breaded pork cutlet) and **C**abbage, and I add this water to the sauce and taste it with this forked tongue before serving it

Rain

261. 雨 PRONUNCIATIONS: ame, u, ama, same, *yu* MEANING: rain

EXAMPLES: 大雨 ooame = heavy rain; 雨量 uryou = amount of rain; 雨傘 amagasa = Japanese umbrella; 小雨 kosame = light rain or drizzle; 梅雨 tsuyu = rainy season DESCRIPTION: this resembles rain drops on two window panes CUES: in **Am**erican **U**rban areas, the amount of 雨 **ame** (rain) that is seen on window panes varies depending on the location, and the same is true in the **Ama**zon, over the **Sa**lt mines of **Me**xico, and in the **Yu**kon

262. 雪 PRONUNCIATIONS: setsu, yuki, *buki* MEANING: snow

EXAMPLES: 新雪 shinsetsu = new snow; 雪 yuki = snow; 吹雪 fubuki = snowstorm DESCRIPTION: at the top, 雨 ame (rain, # 261); at the bottom, there are three layers of ice CUES: since there are three layers of ice on the ground, this 雨 (rain) must be 雪 **yuki** (snow), which some of our **S**ettlement's **S**uper pioneers say is **Yuck**y, and that's why they are **Book**ing vacations in Florida COMPARE: 電(気) denki = electricity, # 263

263. 電 **PRONUNCIATION: den**

MEANING: electricity **EXAMPLES:** 電気

denki = electricity **DESCRIPTION:** at the top, 雨

ame (rain, # 261); at the bottom, 田 (rice paddy, # 68), with a wire emerging from it, suggesting an electrical transformer

CUE: a wire is emerging from the transformer under this 雨 (rain), suggesting that 電気 **den**ki (electricity) is being generated from lightning strikes in **Den**mark **COMPARE:** 雪 yuki = snow, # 262

264. 雲 **PRONUNCIATIONS: un, kumo, gumo[1] MEANING:** cloud **EXAMPLE:** 雲海

unkai = sea of clouds; 雲 kumo = cloud; 雨雲 amagumo = rain cloud **DESCRIPTION:** at the top, 雨 ame (rain, # 261); at the bottom, Governor Cuomo's leg pedaling a bicycle **CUE:** these 雲 **kumo** (clouds) suggest that 雨 (rain) is coming, so **U**ndoubtedly Governor **Cu**omo had better pedal his bike home quickly **COMPARE:** 曇(り) kumori = cloudy, not included in this Catalogue, which adds a small 日 hi (sun, # 32) to the top of 雲

265. 震 **PRONUNCIATIONS: shin, furu MEANINGS:** to tremble or shake **EXAMPLES:** 地震 jishin = earthquake; 震える furueru = to tremble **DESCRIPTION:** at the top, 雨 ame (rain, # 261); at the bottom, a Shintou shrine which is a lean-to containing a rug, supported by the katakana character エ and the letter Y

CUES: this 雨 (rain) is falling during a 地震 ji**shin** (earthquake), and since only エ and Y are supporting the lean-to and rug that make up this **Shin**tou shrine, it will 震える **furu**eru (tremble) and collapse into **Fu**ll-blown **Ru**in

Sound

266. 音 **PRONUNCIATIONS: oto, on, in, ne MEANING:** sound **EXAMPLES:** 音 oto = sound; 音楽 ongaku = music; 母音 boin = vowel; 音色 neiro = timbre **DESCRIPTION:** at

the top, 立(つ) tatsu = to stand, # 11, but this resembles an Ottoman-era bell; at the bottom, 日 hi (day, # 32), which resembles a two-drawer cabinet **CUES:** during the **Otto**man era, people discovered that this bell on a two-drawer 日 (cabinet) full of **On**ions makes an **In**credible 音 **oto** (sound) which annoys the **Ne**ighbors **COMPARE:** 暗(い) kurai = dark, # 268

267. 部 **PRONUNCIATIONS: he, be, bu MEANINGS:** part, section **EXAMPLES:** 部屋 heya = room; 子供部屋 kodomobeya = child's room 全部 zenbu = entirely; 部長 buchou = division manager **DESCRIPTION:** on the left, compared to 音 oto (sound, # 266), this bell is on a box instead of a cabinet; on the right, ß from the Greek alphabet, suggesting that Helen, a Greek citizen, owns the bell **CUES:** **He**len is a ß (Greek) 部長 **bu**chou (division manager) who keeps this **Be**ll on a box in her 部屋 **he**ya (room) for **Bu**ddhist ceremonies

268. 暗 **PRONUNCIATIONS: kura, an MEANING:** dark **EXAMPLES:** 暗い kurai = dark; 暗示 anji = hint **DESCRIPTION:** on the left, 日 hi (sun, # 32); on the right, 音 oto (sound, # 266), which features a bell on a cabinet, where curry rice is stored **CUES:** even when the 日 (sun) shines on this bell, there are 暗い **kura**i (dark) places in the cabinet below it, where we keep **Cu**rry **Ra**men, but **An**ts are getting into it **COMPARE:** 晴(れる) hareru = to clear up, # 37

269. 倍 **PRONUNCIATION: bai MEANINGS:** to double or multiply **EXAMPLES:** 三倍の sanbai no = three times as much; 倍増する baizou suru = to double **DESCRIPTION:** on the left, a man with a slanted hat; on the right, a bell on a box **CUE:** this man will **Bu**y the bell on the box and resell it for 倍増 **bai**zou (double) the price **COMPARE:** 部(屋) heya = room, # 267; 音 oto = sound, # 266

270. 位 **PRONUNCIATIONS: i, kurai, gurai[1] MEANINGS:** rank, place, approximately **EXAMPLES:** 第一位 dai ichi i = first place; 位 kurai = rank; どれ位 doregurai = how far (or long, many, much) **DESCRIPTION:** on the left, a man with a slanted hat; on the right, 立(つ) tatsu (to stand, # 11), which resembles an Easter bell **CUES:** this man with a slanted hat who plays this **Ea**ster bell won 第一位 dai ichi **i** (first place) in a bell-ringing competition, received a prize of **Ku**waiti **R**ice, and was awarded a high 位 **kurai** (rank) **COMPARE:** 泣(く) naku = to cry, # 12; 暗(い) kurai = dark, # 268; 音 oto = sound, # 266; 意(味) imi = meaning, # 317

Shah

271. 社 **PRONUNCIATIONS: sha, yashiro, ja MEANINGS:** shrine, company of people **EXAMPLES:** 会社 kaisha = company; 社 yashiro = a Shinto shrine; 神社 jinja = a Shinto shrine **DESCRIPTION:** on the left, the Shah; on the right, 土 tsuchi (dirt, # 59) **CUES:** this **Sh**ah is looking at this 土 (dirt), on which **Y**aks and **Sh**eep **Roa**m, where he plans to build a 会社 kai**sha** (company) with **J**ack Nicholson

272. 祖 **PRONUNCIATIONS: so, zo[1], jii, baa MEANING:** ancestral **EXAMPLES:** 祖父 sofu = grandfather; 祖母 sobo = grandmother; 祖先 sosen = ancestor; 先祖 senzo = ancestor; お祖父さん ojiisan = grandfather; お祖母さん obaasan = grandmother **NOTE:** it isn't practical to divide the 祖父 jii in ojiisan and the 祖母 baa in obaasan into two component pronunciations, so these words must be learned as combinations of kanji; also, we don't provide Cues for jii or baa **DESCRIPTION:** on the left, the Shah (see # 271); on the right, 目 me (eye # 51) on a base, resembling a solar panel **CUE:** this Shah is praying at the tomb of his 祖父 **so**fu (grandfather), which looks like a 目 (**So**lar panel)

273. 神 **PRONUNCIATIONS: kou, jin, shin, kami, gami[1], ka, mi MEANINGS:** gods, mind, soul **EXAMPLES:** 神戸 Koube = a city in Japan; 神社 jinja = shintou shrine; 神道 Shintou = a Japanese religion; 神 kami = god; 女神 megami = goddess; 神奈川 Kanagawa = a prefecture in Japan; お神酒 omiki = sake offered to the gods **DESCRIPTION:** on the left, the Shah (see # 271), wearing skinny jeans; on the right, what appears to be a car but, compared to 車 kuruma (car, # 283), this car is missing its wheels **CUES:** the Shah, who is feeling **C**old, stands in his skinny **J**eans praying to this **Sh**iny car without wheels which he regards as a 神 **kami** (god), but a **Commie** (Communist) is waiting to **C**all him to a **M**eeting **COMPARE:** 押(す) osu = to push, # 592; 紙 kami = paper, # 221; (女)将 okami = mistress, landlady, # 374; 髪 kami = hair, # 501

274. 祝 **PRONUNCIATIONS: iwa, shuku, shuu MEANING:** to celebrate **EXAMPLES:** 祝う iwau = to celebrate; 祝日 shukujitsu = national holiday; 祝儀 shuugi = celebration, wedding, gratuity **DESCRIPTION:** on the left, the Shah (see # 271); on the right, 兄 ani (big brother, # 420) **CUES:** this Shah **iwa**u 祝う (celebrates) with this 兄 (big brother); they are happy that eels are on the menu and say "**E**els? **Wow!**" as they **Sh**uck corn for the feast and **Sh**oot off fireworks

275. 礼 **PRONUNCIATION: rei MEANINGS:** to bow; propriety; a gift in token of gratitude **EXAMPLES:** お礼 orei = gratitude, thanks; 礼 rei = a bow, or gratitude; 失礼 shitsurei = discourtesy **DESCRIPTION:** on the left, the Shah (see # 271); on the right, the letter L, for "Lady" **CUE:** this Shah feels お礼 o**rei** (gratitude) to this **L**ady, who helped him after the Shah was 失礼 shitsu**rei** (rude) to her

Person

276. 者 PRONUNCIATIONS: mono, sha, ja[1] MEANING: person EXAMPLES: 悪者 warumono = villain; 学者 gakusha = scholar; 金の亡者 kane no mouja = a money-grubbing person DESCRIPTION: at the top, 土 tsuchi (dirt, # 59); in the middle, a pair of scissors; at the bottom, 日 hi (sun, # 32), which resembles a two-drawer cabinet CUES: this 者 **mono** (person) is playing a **Mono**tonous game with some 土 (dirt) and the **Sharp** scissors that he keeps in this 日 (cabinet)

277. 都 PRONUNCIATIONS: tsu, to, miyako MEANING: capital EXAMPLES: 都合 tsugou = circumstances, convenience; 都市 toshi = city; 京都 Kyouto = city in Japan; 都 miyako = capital DESCRIPTION: on the left, 者 mono (person, # 276), who plays with scissors as if they were toys; on the right, ß beta, from the Greek alphabet, suggesting that this is a Greek 者 (person) CUES: 都合がいい **tsu**gou ga ii (it is convenient) for this ß (Greek) 者 (person) to carry a **Tsu**itcase (suitcase) containing scissors to the big 都市 **to**shi (city), where he hopes to buy better **Toys** and **Meet Yak Ow**ners

278. 暑 PRONUNCIATIONS: sho, atsu MEANING: hot atmosphere EXAMPLES: 暑中 shochuu = mid-summer, hot season; 暑い日 atsui hi = hot day DESCRIPTION: at the top, 日 hi (sun, # 32); at the bottom, a 者 mono (person, # 276) named Superman CUE: compared to 者 (person), this kanji has an extra 日 (sun) at the top, which **Shows** us that the weather **At** **Su**perman's house is doubly 暑い **atsu**i (hot) ALSO COMPARE: 熱(い) atsui = hot objects, # 65; 厚(い) atsui = thick, # 185

Complicated Boxes

279. 園 PRONUNCIATIONS: en, zono, sono MEANINGS: park, spacious garden EXAMPLES: 公園 kouen = park; 花園 hanazono = flower garden; 園子 Sonoko = a girl's given name DESCRIPTION: on the perimeter, a fence, suggesting a park; at the top, 土 tsuchi (dirt, # 59); at the bottom, a machine on a tripod, with a speaker extending to the right, which could be a megaphone CUES: an **En**gineer is using this megaphone to tell children playing in the 土 (dirt) in the 公園 kou**en** (park) to enter the **Z**one to the **N**orth, and have **Son**ograms done COMPARE: 遠(い) tooi = far, # 351, or 遠(慮) enryo = reserve, # 351, which helps us to pronounce this; 国 kuni = country, # 170; 困(る) komaru = to be inconvenienced, # 280

280. 困 PRONUNCIATIONS: koma, kon MEANING: in trouble EXAMPLES: 困る komaru = to be troubled, inconvenienced; 困難 kon'nan = difficult DESCRIPTION: a 木 ki (tree, # 118) stuck in a box CUES: while this 木 (tree) was in a **Coma**, someone built a box around it, so that it 困っている **koma**tte iru (is in trouble), and **Con**an O'Brien says that this is a 困難な **kon**'nan na (difficult) situation COMPARE: 国 kuni = country, # 170; (公)園 kouen = park, # 279

281. 図 PRONUNCIATIONS: zu, to, haka MEANINGS: drawing, to plan EXAMPLES: 図 zu = drawing; 地図 chizu = map; 図書館 toshokan = library; 図る hakaru = to plot or attempt DESCRIPTION: a framed drawing of two people riding on a giraffe CUES: this is a 図 **zu** (drawing) of two people riding on a giraffe, returning from the **Zoo**, where they saw some **To**ads, to the 図書館 **to**shokan (library), where there is going to be a **Hack**athon COMPARE: 以(下) ika (less than), # 601

282. 面 PRONUNCIATIONS: omo, *ji*, **men,** *noo*, **tsura** MEANINGS: mask, face, features EXAMPLES: 面白い omoshiroi = interesting; 真面目な majime na = sincere; 面倒 mendou = annoyance; 地面 jimen = the surface of the earth, the ground; 箕面市 Minooshi = a city north of Osaka; 面 tsura = a face DESCRIPTION: this resembles an old limousine with an antenna, seen from the back, with 目 me (eye, # 51) imprinted on it CUES: this **O**ld **M**o**t**orcar is a **J**eep, and the working 目 (eye) on its back panel is an 面白い <u>omo</u>shiroi (interesting) innovation that protects it from 面倒な <u>men</u>dou na (annoying) **M**en without **D**ough (money) from the **N**orth who might want to **Tsu**e (sue) the **R**appers who ride in it COMPARE: (映)画 eiga = movie, # 77

Car

283. 車 PRONUNCIATIONS: kuruma, **sha** MEANING: car EXAMPLES: 車 kuruma = car, wheel; 自転車 jitensha = bicycle DESCRIPTION: a two-wheeled car seen from the top, with a wheel on each side, which belongs to the Shah CUES: this **C**urvy, **R**oomy, **M**agnificent 車 <u>kuruma</u> (car) belongs to the **Shah** COMPARE: 重(い) omoi = heavy, # 284

284. 重 PRONUNCIATIONS: omo, kasa, **chou, juu, e** MEANINGS: heavy, layer EXAMPLES: 重い omoi = heavy; 重ねる kasaneru = to pile up; 慎重な shinchou na = cautious, prudent; 体重 taijuu = a person's weight; 紙一重 kamihito'e = paper-thin (difference) DESCRIPTION: a 車 kuruma (car, # 283), with extra hubcaps added to each wheel CUES: this 車 (car) is 重い <u>omo</u>i (heavy) because **O**ld **M**oses added extra hubcaps to each wheel, and **Casa**nova and Margaret **Cho** 重ねる <u>kasa</u>neru (pile up) even more weight by adding **J**uice and **E**ggs to the trunk

285. 転 PRONUNCIATIONS: koro, ten MEANING: to roll EXAMPLES: 転ぶ korobu = to fall; 自転車 jitensha = bicycle DESCRIPTION: on the left, a 車 sha (vehicle, # 283); on the right, a pedaling leg, with a line above it suggesting a bicycle basket CUES: this 車 (vehicle) with a pedaling leg, suggests a 自転車 ji<u>ten</u>sha (bicycle), from which one may 転ぶ <u>koro</u>bu (fall down) if one's **Coro**nary arteries **B**urst while riding in **Ten**nessee COMPARE: 伝(える) tsutaeru = to convey, # 345; (自)動(車) jidousha = car, # 286

286. 動 PRONUNCIATIONS: dou, ugo MEANING: to move EXAMPLES: 自動車 jidousha = car; 動く ugoku = to move, intransitive; 動かす ugokasu = to move, transitive DESCRIPTION: on the left, 重(い) omoi (heavy, # 284); on the right, 力 chikara (force, # 107) CUES: this is a 重 (heavy) 自動車 ji<u>dou</u>sha (car) which 動く <u>ugo</u>ku (moves) under its own 力 (force) to escape **D**oberman dogs and **U**ber **Go**phers COMPARE: (自)転(車) jitensha = bicycle, # 285; 働(く) hataraku = to labor, # 287

287. 働 PRONUNCIATIONS: hatara, dou MEANINGS: to work, operate EXAMPLES: 働く hataraku = to labor; 労働者 roudousha = laborer DESCRIPTION: on the left, a man with a slanted hat; on the right, 動(く) ugoku (to move, # 286) which includes the radical 重(い) omoi (heavy, # 284) CUES: as this man with a slanted hat 働く <u>hatara</u>ku (labors) making **H**ats for **Ara**bs, he 動 (moves) 重 (heavy) hats from one place to another and gets paid good **Dou**gh (money) for doing so

288. 輸 PRONUNCIATION: yu

MEANING: to transport EXAMPLES: 輸入 する yunyuu suru= to import; 輸出する yushutsu suru = to export DESCRIPTION: on the left, a 車 kuruma (car, # 283); at the top right, a peaked roof suggesting a house in the Yukon; at the lower right, 月 tsuki (month, # 148) and the katakana character リ Ri

CUE: リ Ri, working from this house in the **Yu**kon, 輸入する **yu**nyuu suru (imports) 車 (cars) like this one every 月 (month)

289. 軽 PRONUNCIATIONS: karu, garu[1], kei, karo MEANING: light weight

EXAMPLES: 軽い karui = light; 尻軽な shirigaru na = frivolous, of loose morals; 軽自動 車 keijidousha = a lightweight car; 軽やか karoyaka = light, easy, minor DESCRIPTION: on the left, 車 kuruma (car, # 283); on the right, 又 mata ("again," # 24), but this resembles an athlete leaping over 土 tsuchi (dirt, # 59) CUES: like **Caru**so, who was said to have a light voice, this 又 (athlete) is 軽い **karu**i (light) enough to jump out of a 車 (car) and over a pile of 土 (dirt), even after eating a whole **Ca**ke and a bag of **Carro**ts COMPARE: 経(験) keiken = experience, # 224

290. 乾 PRONUNCIATIONS: kawa, kan

MEANING: to get dry EXAMPLES: 乾く kawaku = to get dry; 乾電池 kandenchi = dry cell battery DESCRIPTION: the radical on the left is not the same as 車 kuruma (car, # 283), since the axle doesn't travel all the way through, so let's call this a California wagon; on the right, a snake holding a crutch CUES: this disabled snake is lurking outside our **Ca**lifornia **Wa**gon, so let's stay inside, where 乾いている **kawa**ite iru (it's dry), and we can eat from **Can**s COMPARE: 朝 asa = morning, # 291; 渇(く) kawaku = to get thirsty, not included in this Catalogue, e.g., 喉が渇く nodo ga kawaku = to get thirsty

291. 朝 PRONUNCIATIONS: *sa, chou,*

asa MEANING: morning EXAMPLES: 今朝 kesa = this morning; 朝食 choushoku = breakfast; 朝 asa = morning DESCRIPTION: the radical on the left is not the same as 車 kuruma (car, # 283), since the axle doesn't travel all the way through, so let's call this a wagon; on the right, 月 tsuki (moon, # 148) CUES: I'm sitting in this wagon in the early 朝 **asa** (morning), watching the 月 (moon) fade away, feeling **S**ad that I was **Cho**sen for early morning watch duty, and hoping that the day will get warm **ASA**P

COMPARE: 明(日) ashita = tomorrow, # 154; 乾(く) kawaku = to get dry, # 290

Now

292. 今 PRONUNCIATIONS: ima, kon, k,

ko, ke MEANING: now EXAMPLES: 今 ima = now; 今度 kondo = this time, next time; 今日 kyou = today; 今年 kotoshi = this year; 今朝 kesa = this morning DESCRIPTION: at the top, a roof, with a ceiling under it; at the bottom, the number 7 CUES: I**ma**gine that 今 **ima** (now) it is 7 o'clock, and it's time for the **Co**nductor to turn the **K**ey, start the **Co**mmuter train and settle back to drink a **Ke**g of beer COMPARE: 会(う) au = to meet, # 293; 合(う) au = to harmonize, # 294

293. 会 PRONUNCIATIONS: kai, gai, e,

a MEANING: to meet (people) EXAMPLES: 会社 kaisha = company; 会議 kaigi = meeting; 運送会社 unsougaisha = moving company; 会得する etoku suru = to grasp, understand, master; 会う au = to meet someone DESCRIPTION: at the top, a roof, with a ceiling under it, but this could be a Kaiser's hat; at the bottom, a leg pedaling a bicycle in Austria CUES: the **Kai**ser will travel by bike in order to 会う **a**u (meet) a **Gui**de, who is an **E**xpert and will take him to a 会議 **kai**gi (meeting) in **A**ustria

COMPARE: 今 ima = now, # 292; 合(う) au = to harmonize, # 294

294. 合 PRONUNCIATIONS: **ai, gou, a, ga** MEANING: to match or harmonize, to come together EXAMPLES: 具合 guai = condition, state; 都合 tsugou = circumstances, convenience; 合う au = to come together, to match or suit; 合わせる awaseru = to put together, combine or harmonize; 合戦 gassen = battle DESCRIPTION: at the top, a roof, with a ceiling under it, but this could be a lid for a box; at the bottom, an ice-cold box CUES: this kanji shows a lid fitting neatly on a 口 (box) under a roof, suggesting that our plans to market Ice-cold Goat milk will 合う **a**u (come together) in Australia, if 都合がいい tsu**gou** ga ii (circumstances are good), and if we can buy Gas for our milk trucks COMPARE: 今 ima = now, # 292; 会(う) au = to meet, # 293

295. 答 PRONUNCIATIONS: **kota, tou** MEANING: to answer a question EXAMPLE: 答える kotaeru = to reply; 回答 kaitou = answer, response DESCRIPTION: at the top, two shortened 竹 take (bamboo, # 134), which could represent a question on the left and a corresponding answer on the right; at the bottom, 合(う) au (to match or suit, # 294) CUE: when I met with my Colorado Tax attorney in this little house and asked about my Tobacco investments, her 答え **kota**e (answer), which 合 (matched) my needs, was to invest in 竹 (bamboo) instead COMPARE: (内)容 naiyou = content, # 296

296. 容 PRONUNCIATION: **you** MEANINGS: content, to let in EXAMPLE: 内容 naiyou = content DESCRIPTION: at the top, a hovering bird; at the bottom, a box containing yogurt, with a roof; compared to 合(う) au (match, # 294) and 答(え) kotae (answer, # 295), there is no lid above the box, leaving the contents exposed CUE: this hovering bird is trying to get into the 内容 nai**you** (contents) of this box under a roof, which consist of Yogurt ALSO COMPARE: 浴(びる) abiru = to bathe, # 256; 溶(岩)

yougan = lava, # 815, which helps us to pronounce this

Bench Hats
297. 登 PRONUNCIATIONS: **nobo, to, tou** MEANING: to climb EXAMPLES: 登る noboru = to climb; 登山 tozan = mountain climbing; 登録 touroku = registration; 登頂する touchou suru = to reach the summit DESCRIPTION: at the top left and top right, two radicals that resemble upside-down benches; let's call them bench hats; at the bottom, a climber with a big 口 kuchi (mouth), standing on a broad base CUES: this climber with a big 口 (mouth), who wears two bench hats, can 登る **nobo**ru (climb) like **Nob**ody else, but certain **Tor**toises can also climb well COMPARE: 上(る) noboru = to rise, # 171; 発(表) happyou = presentation, # 298

298. 発 PRONUNCIATIONS: **ha, hatsu, patsu**[1]**, ho** MEANINGS: departure, to disclose EXAMPLES: 発表 happyou = presentation; 発明 hatsumei = invention; 東京発 toukyou hatsu = departing from Tokyo; 出発する shuppatsu suru = to depart; 発作 hossa = attack or fit, e.g., 心臓発作 shinzou hossa = heart attack DESCRIPTION: at the top left and top right, two radicals that resemble upside-down benches; let's call them bench hats; at the bottom, a happy expansive guy with a long right leg and a protruding toe on his right foot CUES: this **Ha**ppy Yodeler, wearing two bench **Hats**, gives a 発表 **ha**ppyou (presentation) with his right leg extended, but the sock on his right foot has a **Ho**le in it, exposing his toe COMPARE: 登(る) noboru = to climb, # 297

Peaked Roof

299. 冷 **PRONUNCIATIONS: rei, tsume, hi, sa MEANING:** cold object (not cold atmosphere) **EXAMPLES:** 冷蔵庫 reizouko =refrigerator; 冷たい tsumetai = cold object; 冷やす hiyasu = to chill; 冷める sameru = to cool off **DESCRIPTION:** on the left, a water radical (see # 12) which suggests rain; on the right, a house with a peaked roof and a wobbly table on the ground floor, which we rent from Melvin **CUES:** this table in Mel's house is shaky because one of the legs is too long, and when it **R**ains, the walls are 冷たい **tsume**tai (cold), so we will **Tsue** (sue) **Me**lvin to get him to **H**eat the house, and use a **Sa**w to shorten the table leg **COMPARE:** 命令 meirei = a command, # 961 and # 962

300. 全 **PRONUNCIATIONS: matta, sube, zen MEANINGS:** all, entire **EXAMPLES:** 全く mattaku = entirely; 全て subete = all, everything; 全部 zenbu = all, everything; **DESCRIPTION:** at the top, a Zen temple with a peaked roof; under the roof, 王 ou (king, # 1077); compared to 金 kane (money, # 301), 全 is missing two short slanting lines at the bottom **CUES:** a **Mata**dor and a **Sub**editor come to this **Zen** temple to talk about 全部 **zen**bu (everything) with the 王 (king) **ALSO COMPARE:** 主(人) shujin = master, # 166

301. 金 **PRONUNCIATIONS: kin, kon, gon[1], kane, kana, gin MEANINGS:** money, gold, metal **EXAMPLES:** 金曜日 kinyoubi = Friday; 金属 kinzoku = metal; 金剛力 kongouriki = superhuman strength; 黄金 ougon = gold; お金 okane = money; 金物 kanamono = hardware; 賃金 chingin = wages **DESCRIPTION:** this is a well-supported symmetrical house that could be a kindergarten; compared to 全 zen (everything, # 300), 金 includes an additional slanting line on each side of the ground floor, which may represent money or gold belonging to the kindergarten **CUES:** my teacher at this **Kin**dergarten in the **Con**go gave me some

お金 **o**kane (money) to buy some **Can**adian **E**ggs, some **Cana**ries and some **Gin**kgo leaves

302. 銀 **PRONUNCIATION: gin MEANING:** silver **EXAMPLES:** 銀行 ginkou = bank; 銀 gin = silver **DESCRIPTION:** on the left, 金 kane (money, # 301); at the top right, 日 hi (sun, # 32); at the bottom right, the letters L and y which remind us of "friendly" **CUE:** when I went to the 銀行 **gin**kou (bank) to get 金 (money) for **Gin,** this friend**Ly** 日 (sun) was shining **COMPARE:** 良(い) yoi = good, # 303

303. 良 **PRONUNCIATIONS: ryou, yo, i, ra MEANING:** good **EXAMPLES:** 良好 ryoukou = favorable, satisfactory; 不良 furyou = delinquent, poor condition; 良い yoi = good; 良い ii = good, usually written いい; 良かった yokatta = it was good; 奈良 Nara = a city in Japan; 野良 nora = field, farm **NOTE:** yoi and ii are both written 良い **DESCRIPTION:** at the top, 白(い) shiroi (white, # 44); at the bottom, the letters L and y which remind us of "friendly" **CUES:** Pope **Leo** is a friend**Ly** 白 (white) guy who is a **Y**ogurt **E**ater, and he's a 良い **yo**i (good) person who also eats a lot of **Ra**men (egg noodles) **COMPARE:** 銀 gin = silver, # 302; 長(い) nagai = long, # 502

304. 鉄 **PRONUNCIATIONS: te, de[1], tetsu MEANING:** iron **EXAMPLES:** 鉄砲 teppou = gun; 豆鉄砲 mamedeppou = peashooter; 地下鉄 chikatetsu = subway; 鉄製 tetsusei = made of iron **DESCRIPTION:** on the left, 金 kane (metal, # 301); on the right, 失(礼) shitsurei (discourtesy, # 206) which is a fusion of 牛 ushi (cow, # 205) and 大きい ookii (big, # 188) **CUE:** this 大 (big) 牛 (cow) stepped on some rusty 金 (metal) in **T**exas, and needed a

Tetanus shot which **Su**perman gave her via a 鉄 **tetsu** (iron) needle

305. 館 PRONUNCIATIONS: kan, yakata

MEANING: large building **EXAMPLES:**
旅館 ryokan = Japanese inn; 図書館 toshokan
= library; 館 yakata = mansion, palace

DESCRIPTION: on the left, 食(事) shokuji
(meal, # 398); on the right, a two-story building,
under a roof that resembles a bad haircut

CUES: this is a 旅館 ryo**kan** (Japanese inn),
where 食 (meals) are made on the left, and the two-
story dormitory on the right is lighted by **Ca**ndles to
discourage **Yak Att**acks during the night

COMPARE: 追(う) ou = to chase, # 821;
(警)官 keikan = policeman, # 880

Heart

306. 心 PRONUNCIATIONS: kokoro, shin, koko, goko MEANINGS: heart, mind

EXAMPLES: 心 kokoro = heart; 心配する
shinpai suru = to worry; 心地 kokochi = feeling,
sensation, mood; 居心地 igokochi = the way one
feels in a particular ambience **DESCRIPTION:** the
small line on the left represents one ventricle of a
heart, the large curved line represents the other
ventricle, and the two lines at the upper right
represent shingles, protecting the heart of a man
named Roy Rogers **CUES:** don't throw **Co**conuts at
Roy's **Shin**gles, since you may damage his 心
kokoro (heart); instead eat your **Co**conuts over on
the **Go**ld **Coa**st

307. 必 PRONUNCIATIONS: kanara, hi, hitsu MEANINGS: without fail, necessary

EXAMPLES: 必ず kanarazu = without fail;
必死に hisshi = desperately, frantically;必要
hitsuyou = necessary

DESCRIPTION: a 心 kokoro (heart, # 306)
belonging to a Canadian rat, sliced in half
CUES: if you want the **Cana**dian **Ra**t from the Zoo
to expire 必ず **kanara**zu (without fail), it is 必
要 **hitsu**you (necessary) to be a **He**ro and slice its
心 (heart) in two, before it **Hits U** with its tail

308. 思 PRONUNCIATIONS: omo, shi

MEANINGS: to think, thought **EXAMPLE:**
思う omou = to think/feel; 思想 shisou =
thought, idea **DESCRIPTION:** at the top,
田 tanbo (rice paddy, # 68); at the bottom, 心
kokoro (heart, # 306), but these could be four legs on
a sheep **CUES:** **O**saka **M**osquitoes breed in 田
(rice paddies), and we 思う **omo**u (think) that they
bite four-legged **Sheep**

309. 恥 PRONUNCIATIONS: ha, haji

MEANINGS: shame, dishonor **EXAMPLES:**
恥ずかしい hazukashii = embarrassed, shy,
ashamed; 恥 haji = shame, dishonor

DESCRIPTION: on the left, 耳 mimi (ears,
57); on the right, 心 kokoro (heart, # 306)

CUES: it's 恥ずかしい **ha**zukashii (embar-
rassing) that 耳 (ears) are located next to 心
(hearts) in a back room at Prince **Ha**rry's **Z**oo, which
is **Ca**shing in on body parts, according to **Ha**cker
Jimmy Carter

310. 忘 PRONUNCIATIONS: wasu, bou

MEANING: to forget **EXAMPLES:** 忘れる
wasureru = to forget; 忘年会 bounenkai = end-
of-year party **DESCRIPTION:** at the top, a fish
hook; at the bottom, 心 kokoro (heart, # 306)
CUES: after a **Wa**r in the **Su**ez canal involving
patrol **Bo**ats, a wizard put this fish hook into my 心
(heart) to make me 忘れる **wasu**reru (forget) it

COMPARE: 荒(い) arai = violent, # 968

311. 窓 PRONUNCIATIONS: mado, sou

MEANING: window **EXAMPLES:** 窓 mado =
window; 同窓会 dousoukai = reunion of
graduates **DESCRIPTION:** at the top, a bird
soaring; in the middle, ム mu (the sound made by a
cow), so the bird must be a cowbird; at the bottom,
心 kokoro (heart, # 306) **CUES:** when I was
living in a **Ma**rs **D**ome, I looked through a 窓 **mado**
(window) and saw this **S**oaring ム (cow) bird,
causing my 心 (heart) to flutter

312. 急 **PRONUNCIATIONS: kyuu, iso**
MEANING: to hurry or rush **EXAMPLES:**
急に kyuu ni = suddenly; 急ぐ isogu = to hurry
DESCRIPTION: at the top, a cute fish head that
seems isolated; in the middle, some stream-lining,
suggesting speed; at the bottom, 心 kokoro (heart,
306) **CUES:** this Cute fish is Isolated from the
others, but he has a lot of 心 (heart), and 急に
kyuu ni (suddenly) he can 急ぐ **iso**gu (hurry)

313. 悪 **PRONUNCIATIONS: waru, aku,**
a, o MEANING: bad **EXAMPLES:** 悪い
warui = bad; 悪 aku = evil; 悪しからず
ashikarazu = don't take it badly; 嫌悪 ken'o =
hatred, disgust **DESCRIPTION:** at the top, three
eyes, sandwiched between two platforms; at the
bottom, 心 kokoro (heart, # 306)
CUES: War **Ru**ined the health of this three-eyed
pirate with a 悪い **waru**i (bad) 心 (heart), but he
is getting **Acu**puncture treatments from his **A**unt in
Osaka
COMPARE: 要(る) iru = to need, # 238

314. 念 **PRONUNCIATION: nen**
MEANINGS: thought, to ponder **EXAMPLES:**
残念 zannen = too bad; 信念 shinnen = belief
DESCRIPTION: at the top, 今 ima (now, # 292);
at the bottom, 心 kokoro (heart, # 306); together
they look like a negative nephew, moving to the right
CUE: 今 (now), my **N**egative **N**ephew's 心
(heart) is driving him to the right of the political
spectrum, and that's 残念 zan**nen** (too bad)
COMPARE: 年 nen = year, # 177

315. 息 **PRONUNCIATIONS: musu, i, iki,**
soku MEANINGS: son, breath, respiration
EXAMPLES: 息子 musuko = son; 息吹 ibuki
= breath; 息吹く ibuku = to breathe; 息 iki =
breath, respiration; 休息 kyuusoku = rest, relief,
relaxation **DESCRIPTION:** at the top, 自 ji (self,
55), which resembles a rib cage or perhaps a
stringed musical instrument; at the bottom, 心

kokoro (heart, # 306) **CUES:** my 自 (self)'s
息子 **musu**ko (son) is a **M**usical **U**ber driver, and
he has a good 心 (heart), but he's so thin that you
can see his ribs, he has big **Ea**rs, his 息 **iki** (breath)
is **I**cky, and he's always **S**oaked with sweat

316. 娘 **PRONUNCIATION: musume**
MEANINGS: daughter, young woman
EXAMPLE: 娘 musume = daughter
DESCRIPTION: on the left, 女 onna (female,
235); on the right, 良(い) yoi (good, # 303)
CUE: our 娘 **musume** (daughter) is a 女 (female)
and she's a 良 (good) girl who worked at the
Museum during the **Summer**

317. 意 **PRONUNCIATION: i**
MEANINGS: meaning, intention, mind
EXAMPLES: 意味 imi = meaning; 意見 iken
= opinion **DESCRIPTION:** at the top, 音 oto
(sound, # 266); at the bottom, 心 kokoro (heart,
306) **CUE:** this 音 (sound) in my 心 (heart)
sounds **E**erie and must have some kind of 意味
imi (meaning)
COMPARE: 億 oku = 100 million, # 318;
(第一)位 dai ichi i = first place, # 270

318. 億 **PRONUNCIATION: oku**
MEANING: one hundred million **EXAMPLE:**
五億 go oku = 500 million **DESCRIPTION:** on
the left, a man with a slanted hat; on the right,
意(味) imi (meaning, # 317), which features a
bell at the top **CUE:** this man with a slanted hat is
ringing 意 (meaning)'s bell, which can play 一億
の ichi**oku** no (100 million) **O**ld **Kool**-Aid jingles

319. 怒 **PRONUNCIATIONS: oko, ika, do**
MEANING: angry **EXAMPLES:** 怒る okoru =
to get angry; 怒り ikari = anger, fury; 激怒
gekido = fury, outrage **DESCRIPTION:** at the
upper left, 女 onna (female, # 235); at the upper
right, 又 mata ("again," # 24), but this resembles a

leaping athlete named Oklahoma Ruth; at the bottom, 心 kokoro (heart, # 306)

CUES: OklahOma Ruth is a 女 (female) and an 又 (athlete) with a 心 (heart) who 怒った okotta (got angry) at Icarus, the Dope who flew too close to the sun **COMPARE:** 努(める) tsutomeru = to make an effort, # 519

X's

320. 区 PRONUNCIATION: ku

MEANINGS: ward, section **EXAMPLES:** 区役所 kuyakusho = ward office; 区別する kubetsu suru = to distinguish or differentiate **DESCRIPTION:** a building in Kuwait that is open on one side, resembling a storefront, containing an X **CUE:** this 区役所 kuyakusho (ward office) in Kuwait is a storefront, and X marks the spot where citizens from the ward are served **COMPARE:** 医 i = medicine, # 325

321. 気 PRONUNCIATIONS: ki, ge, gi, ke, ku MEANINGS: spirit, air EXAMPLES:

天気 tenki = weather; 気持ち kimochi = feeling; 何気ない nanigenai = casual; 風邪気味 kazegimi = a bit of a cold (upper respiratory infection); 寒気 samuke = a chill; 意気地 ikuji = self-respect **DESCRIPTION:** at the top and to the right, a lean-to with a triple roof; at the bottom, an X representing the spirit of a king

CUES: the 気 ki (spirit) of a King, Genghis Khan, who played the Guitar in Kenya and Kuwait, is represented by this X and is protected by this lean-to with a triple roof

322. 歳 PRONUNCIATIONS: sai, zai[1], sei, chi MEANINGS: age, year EXAMPLE: 十六歳 juurokusai = 16 years old; 万歳 banzai = "10,000 years," i.e., "long live!"; お歳暮 oseibo = year-end gift; 二十歳 hatachi = 20 years old

DESCRIPTION: at the top, 止(まる) tomaru (to stop, # 173); below 止, a lean-to supported by a long halberd (combination lance and axe); on the lower left, a nail flanked by two pieces of gum; this kanji resembles a math problem in division, as seen

in constructions like 3 |12x = 4x

CUES: 歳 sai (age) is a number, and it is divisible, but I remain Silent about my age and 止 (stop) before I Say it, lest people Cheat me

American Indian Chief

323. 知 PRONUNCIATIONS: shi, chi

MEANINGS: to know; knowledge **EXAMPLES:** 知る shiru = to know; 知らせる shiraseru = to inform; 知り合い shiriai = acquaintance; 知識 chishiki = knowledge; 知人 chijin = acquaintance **DESCRIPTION:** on the left, an American Indian chief, wearing a war bonnet; on the right, the 口 kuchi (mouth, # 426) of a sheep **CUES:** this American Indian chief is a veterinary dentist specializing in Sheep who 知る shiru (knows) a lot about the 口 (mouth), and his prices are Cheap

COMPARE: 短(い) mijikai = short, # 324

324. 短 PRONUNCIATIONS: mijika, tan

MEANING: short **EXAMPLES:** 短い mijikai = short; 長短 choutan = length **DESCRIPTION:** on the left, a midget American Indian chief, wearing a war bonnet; on the right, a gasoline pump **CUES:** this American Indian chief is a Midget who owns a Jeep Car; he has a good Tan, but he is too 短い mijikai (short) to see over this gas pump

COMPARE: 知(る) shiru = to know, # 323

325. 医 PRONUNCIATION: i

MEANING: medicine **EXAMPLES:** 医者 isha = medical doctor **DESCRIPTION:** an American Indian chief, wearing a war bonnet, in a building that is open on one side **CUE:** this American Indian chief is an 医者 isha (doctor) with Eagle eyes, staring out of his storefront clinic, which is open on one side **COMPARE:** 区(役所) kuyakusho = ward office, # 320

Uncooked Rice

326. 米 **PRONUNCIATIONS: yone, kome, bei, mai MEANINGS:** rice, America **EXAMPLES:** 米酢 yonezu = rice vinegar; 米 kome = uncooked rice; 米国 beikoku = U.S.A.; 白米 hakumai = white rice **DESCRIPTION:** this resembles an eight-sided comet **CUES:** a **Y**ogi in the **Ne**therlands can arrange these 米 **kome** (uncooked rice) grains into an eight-sided **Comet**, **Ba**ke them in an oven and feed them to **Mi**ce **COMPARE:** 来(る) kuru = to come, # 327; 奥(さん) okusan = someone else's wife, # 532; 歯 ha = tooth, # 533

327. 来 **PRONUNCIATIONS: ki, ko, ku, rai MEANINGS:** to come, next **EXAMPLES:** 来ます kimasu = to come; 来ない konai = will not come; 来る kuru = to come; 来年 rainen = next year; 来日する rainichi suru = to visit Japan **DESCRIPTION:** compared to 米 kome (rice, # 326), this adds a horizontal line at the top, which could be a package of Kool-Aid **CUES:** the **Key** to getting the **Co**ders to 来る **ku**ru (come) for dinner 来週 **rai**shuu (next week) is to promise to serve plenty of **Kool**-Aid with our 米 (**Rice**)

328. 番 **PRONUNCIATION: ban MEANINGS:** watch, turn, order **EXAMPLES:** 一番 ichiban = number one; 交番 kouban = police box; 番号 bangou = number **DESCRIPTION:** at the top, 米 kome (rice, # 326), with a slash drawn over it; at the bottom, a 田 (rice paddy, # 68) in Bangladesh **CUE:** the horizontal slash at the top indicates that it's the 番 **ban** (turn) of this 田 (rice paddy) in **Ba**ngladesh to supply 米 (rice)

329. 隣 **PRONUNCIATIONS: rin, tonari MEANINGS:** neighbor, next door **EXAMPLES:** 隣人 rinjin = neighbor; 隣 tonari = next door **DESCRIPTION:** on the left, ß beta from the Greek alphabet; at the top, 米 kome (rice, # 326); at the bottom left, 夕(方) yuugata (evening, # 160); at the bottom right, a left-facing knee, suggesting a sitting person **CUES:** this **Lean** ß (Greek) named Tobias of **Na**rita lives 学校の隣 gakkou no **tonari** (next door to a school) and sits in the 夕 (evenings), sorting through his 米 (rice) **COMPARE:** 降(りる) oriru = to exit a vehicle, # 178

Sheep

330. 洋 **PRONUNCIATION: you MEANINGS:** ocean, abroad **EXAMPLES:** 西洋 seiyou = the western part of the world; 洋服 youfuku = Western clothes; 東洋 touyou = the eastern part of the world **DESCRIPTION:** on the left, a water radical (see # 12); on the right, 羊 hitsuji (sheep, not included in this Catalogue), an animal that has two horns, two ears, four legs and a tail; compared to 半 han (half, middle, # 331), 羊 hitsuji (sheep) has two back legs plus an open Y at the top, which could stand for 洋 **you** (abroad) **CUE:** 西洋 sei**you** (the western part of the world) is across the water, where a lot of people keep 羊 (sheep) and eat **Yo**gurt **COMPARE:** 遅(い) osoi = late, # 350

331. 半 **PRONUNCIATIONS: naka, han MEANINGS:** half, middle **EXAMPLES:** 半ば nakaba = half, the middle; 一時半 ichijihan = half past 1:00; 半分 hanbun = half, or a ½ share **DESCRIPTION:** compared to 羊 hitsuji (sheep, not included in this Catalogue), 半 adds a vertical line at the top but removes the sheep's two back legs **CUES:** if you stare at this kanji and have the **Kna**ck of **A**bandoning useless thought, **Han**sel says that you will see that the bottom 半分 **han**bun (half) of this 羊 (sheep) is absent

332. 業 PRONUNCIATIONS: gyou, gou, waza MEANINGS: hard work, skills EXAMPLES: 卒業 sotsugyou = graduation; 工業 kougyou = industry; 授業 jugyou = class; 自業自得 jigoujitoku = paying for one's mistakes; 仕業 shiwaza = deeds, acts DESCRIPTION: at the bottom, 木 ki (tree, # 118); above this tree are several extra branches, capped by a tray carrying four lights, resembling a Christmas tree CUES: 卒業 sotsu**gyou** (graduation) is a celebration that reminds us of Christmas 木 (trees) and Christmas, since graduation is a time when we can eat **Gyo**za (pot stickers) made with **Goa**t meat and **Wa**tch **Za**chary open his graduation presents COMPARE: 僕 boku = I (male), # 333

333. 僕 PRONUNCIATIONS: boku, shimobe MEANING: I (male) EXAMPLE: 僕 boku = I (male); 僕 shimobe = manservant, menial DESCRIPTION: on the left, a man with a slanted hat, who is bony; on the right, compared to 業 gyou (hard work, # 332), this radical is missing its central trunk at the bottom CUE: 僕 **boku** (I) am a **Bo**ny **Koo**l-Aid salesman, and ever since I cut the central trunk from 業 gyou (hard work), I stay in bed, wearing my slanted hat and wishing that my **Shee**ts had **Mo**re **Be**lls on them

Man with a Double Hat
334. 行 PRONUNCIATIONS: i, kou, okona, gyou, yu MEANINGS: to go, carry out, conduct a business EXAMPLES: 行く iku = to go; 銀行 ginkou = bank; 行う okonau = to conduct; 行事 gyouji = event; 東京行き toukyou yuki = bound for Tokyo DESCRIPTION: on the right, a man from Italy with a double hat; on the right, this J-shaped radical is a nail, with a line above it which could represent a hammer CUES: this man with a double hat from Italy has a **Co**ld, but he will 行く **i**ku (go) to **Oklah**O**ma** **No**w, carrying a hammer and a nail, to get some **Gyo**za for the **Yu**le celebration

335. 後 PRONUNCIATIONS: ushi, go, ato, nochi, kou, *sa* MEANINGS: behind, later, rear EXAMPLES: 後ろ ushiro = behind; 午後 gogo = afternoon; 後で ato de = later; 後ほど nochihodo = afterward, later; 後悔 koukai = regret; 明後日 asatte = the day after tomorrow, usually written あさって DESCRIPTION: on the left, a man with a double hat; on the right, a dancer with a ponytail who is an usher, holding a gun over her head, similar to the gun of a 糸 (skeet shooter, # 219) CUES: next to this man with the double hat, we see a dancer who is an **Ush**er from **Iran**, pointing a gun to the 後ろ **ushi**ro (rear); she will spend **Go**ld in the 午後 go**go** (afternoon) to buy an **Ato**mic clock, and 後で **ato** de (later) she will eat some g**No**cchi and drink some **Co**la with some **Sa**murai COMPARE: 係(り) kakari = person in charge, # 492

Every
336. 毎 PRONUNCIATIONS: mai, goto MEANING: every EXAMPLES: 毎週 maishuu = every week; 三日毎に mikka goto ni = every three days DESCRIPTION: at the top, a crutch belonging to Michael Jackson; at the bottom, 田 (rice paddy, # 68) CUES: 毎日 **mai**nichi (every day), **Mi**chael grabs a crutch, loads the **Goa**ts into the **To**yota, and goes out to a 田 (rice paddy) COMPARE: 海 umi = ocean, # 337

337. 海 PRONUNCIATIONS: umi, kai, a, *una* MEANINGS: ocean, sea, beach EXAMPLES: 海 umi = ocean; 海外 kaigai = overseas; 海女 ama = fisherwoman, female pearl diver; 海原 unabara = ocean DESCRIPTION: on the left, a water radical (see # 12), suggesting the ocean; on the right, 毎 mai (every, # 336) CUES: 毎 (every) year I go to the 海 **umi** (ocean) to watch **U**ber **Mi**litary exercises with the **Kai**ser and eat **A**pples, but I am **Un**affected by the show

What

338. 何 **PRONUNCIATIONS: ka, nan, nani MEANING: what EXAMPLES:**
幾何学 kikagaku = geometry; 何人 nannin = how many people; 何 nani = what
DESCRIPTION: on the left, a man with a slanted hat watching over a box under a lean-to
CUES: seeing this box in the lean-to where they park their **Car**, **Nan**cy and her **Nan**ny ask the man with a slanted hat, "何ですか **nan** desu ka" (what is it?) **COMPARE:** 同(じ) onaji = the same, # 339; 向(こう) mukou = opposite (side), # 340; 伺(う) ukagau = to humbly visit, # 341; 荷(物) nimotsu = luggage, # 342

339. 同 **PRONUNCIATIONS: ona, dou MEANINGS: the same, the said EXAMPLES:**
同じ onaji = the same; 同情 doujou = sympathy, pity **DESCRIPTION:** compared to 何 nani (what, # 338), this kanji is 同じ **ona**ji (the same) on both the right and the left, i.e., its lean-to is symmetrical, and there is a line above the box **CUES:** the line above this box in a symmetrical lean-to, which is 同じ **ona**ji (the same) on the left and on the right, represents an **O**ld **Na**sty **D**oughnut
ALSO COMPARE: 向(こう) mukou = opposite (side), # 340; 伺(う) ukagau = to humbly visit, # 341

340. 向 **PRONUNCIATIONS: mu, kou, nata MEANINGS: to face, opposite side**
EXAMPLES: 向く muku = to face toward; 向かう mukau = to go toward; 向こう mukou = the other side; 方向 houkou = direction; 日向 hinata = sunny place, in the sun
DESCRIPTION: compared to 同 ona (the same, # 339), the line above this box has moved to the opposite side of the upper fence
CUES: the ground is **M**ucky and **C**old on the 向こう **mu**kou (opposite) side of the upper fence, where the **Na**zi **Ta**lent contest is held
ALSO COMPARE: 何 nani = what, # 338; 伺(う) ukagau = to humbly visit, # 341

341. 伺 **PRONUNCIATION: ukaga**
MEANINGS: to pay respects, visit, inquire
EXAMPLE: 伺う ukagau = to ask humbly, to visit humbly **DESCRIPTION:** compared to 何 nani (what, # 338), there is a line above the box **CUE:** a man with a slanted hat, who is an **U**ber **Cali**fornia **Gambler**, 伺う **ukaga**u (humbly visits) in order to 伺う **ukaga**u (humbly inquire) about this line above this box before betting on the contents of the box
ALSO COMPARE: 同(じ) onaji = the same, # 339; 向(く) muku = to face toward, # 340

342. 荷 **PRONUNCIATIONS: ni, ka MEANINGS: to carry, luggage EXAMPLES:**
荷物 nimotsu = luggage; 出荷する shukka suru = to ship or send **DESCRIPTION:** at the top, a plant radical (see # 43); at the bottom, 何 nani (what, # 338) **CUES:** Question: 何 (what) is your **Nie**ce carrying in her 荷物 **ni**motsu (luggage)? Answer: it's **Ca**bbage, which is plant material.

Bicycle

343. 去 **PRONUNCIATIONS: kyo, sa, ko MEANINGS: to leave, past EXAMPLES:**
去年 kyonen = last year; 去る saru = to leave; 過去 kako = the past **DESCRIPTION:** at the top, 土 tsuchi (dirt, # 59), which looks like a cross; at the bottom, the katakana character ム mu under a horizontal line, which looks like a pedaling leg
CUES: after buying a bicycle in **Kyo**to 去年 **kyo**nen (last year), **Sar**uman decided to 去る **sar**u (depart), so he put on this 土 (cross) and ム (pedaled) his bike to **Ko**be, where he had lived in the 過去 ka**ko** (past)
COMPARE: 法(律) houritsu = law, # 344

344. 法 **PRONUNCIATIONS: hou, pou**
MEANING: law EXAMPLES: 法律 houritsu = law; 方法 houhou = method; 文法 bunpou = grammar, syntax **DESCRIPTION:** on the left, a water radical (see # 12); on the right, 去(る) saru

(to leave, # 343), which reminds us of Saruman wearing a cross and riding a bike **CUES:** Saruman 去 (leaves), but since there's a **Ho**le in the bridge, his ム (bike) falls into the water, and he decides to pass a 法律 **hou**ritsu (law) telling the **Po**lice to prohibit bikes on the bridge

345. 伝 PRONUNCIATIONS: den, tsuta, tsuda MEANINGS: to convey, transmit, hand down EXAMPLES: 伝言 dengon = message; 伝える tsutaeru = to convey or hand down; 手伝う tetsudau = to help DESCRIPTION: on the left, a man with a slanted hat from Denmark; at the top right, two horizontal lines which could represent a bicycle's basket; at the bottom right, a ム (pedaling leg), suggesting a bicycle

CUES: this man with a slanted hat from **Den**mark rides a ム (bike) with a 伝言 **den**gon (message) in the basket which he will 伝える **tsuta**eru (convey); he usually wears a **Tsu**it (suit) and **T**ai**ls**, but the **Tsu**it got **Dam**aged

Snail

346. 週 PRONUNCIATION: shuu
MEANING: week **EXAMPLE:** 来週 raishuu = next week **DESCRIPTION:** on the lower left, a snail; the snail carries a tent containing 土 tsuchi (dirt, # 59) near the top and a package containing shoes at the bottom, hidden under the dirt

CUE: our **Sho**es arrive 毎週 mai**shuu** (every week) in this box hidden under some 土 (dirt), carried in a tent on a snail **COMPARE:** 調(べる) shiraberu = to check, # 441

347. 達 PRONUNCIATIONS: tachi, dachi, ta, tatsu MEANINGS: plural, friend
EXAMPLES: 人達 hitotachi = people; 友達 tomodachi = friend; 達成 tassei = achievement; 速達 sokutatsu = express mail **DESCRIPTION:** on the lower left, a snail; on the snail, a tower with five levels for attaching notices

CUES: this snail carries a tower with five levels, enough to hold many 人達 hito**tachi** (people), who are at**Tach**ing political notices with **Da**rk **Chee**se to this **Ta**ll tower; this is titsu for **Tatsu**, since the other political party is doing the same thing

to them **COMPARE:** 幸(せ) shiawase = happiness, # 385, which has only four levels and no snail

348. 送 PRONUNCIATIONS: oku, sou
MEANING: to send **EXAMPLES:** 送る okuru = to send, or to drop off; 放送 housou = broadcast **DESCRIPTION:** on the lower left, a snail; on the snail, an 大(きい) ookii (big, # 188) person named Oklahoma's Uber Ruth, wearing a hat with two antennae **CUES:** on this snail, Oklahoma's Uber Ruth, a 大 (big) person wearing antennae, runs left and right, 送る **oku**ru (sends out) packages, and 放送する hou**sou** suru (broadcasts) Sordid electronic messages with her antennae

349. 道 PRONUNCIATIONS: dou, michi, tou MEANINGS: road, street, direction
EXAMPLES: 道路 douro = road; 道 michi = street; 神道 shintou = a Japanese religion **DESCRIPTION:** on the lower left, a snail from Michigan; on the snail, 首 kubi (neck, # 56)

CUES: this snail is carrying 首 (neck) to its **Dor**mitory, but there is a bottle- 首 (neck) in this 道 **michi** (street) in **Michi**gan caused by a **To**ad accident **COMPARE:** 通(る) tooru = to pass through, # 365, spelled with "oo" rather than "ou"

350. 遅 PRONUNCIATIONS: oso, oku, chi MEANINGS: slow, late EXAMPLES:
遅い osoi = late, slow; 遅れる okureru = to be delayed; 遅刻する chikoku suru = to be tardy **DESCRIPTION:** on the lower left, a snail, which is carrying a lean-to with a double roof; under the lean-to, Oscar the oily 羊 hitsuji (sheep, not included in this Catalogue – an animal with two horns, two ears, four legs and a tail), who is returning from the oil fields **CUES:** this snail carries Oscar the **O**ily 羊 (sheep), plus a double roof above Oscar, causing the snail to move slowly, and it appears that Oscar will be 遅い **oso**i (late) to work, he will 遅れる **oku**reru (be delayed) to the **Occ**ult museum, and he will 遅刻する **chi**koku suru (be tardy) on his trip to the **Chee**se factory

351. 遠 PRONUNCIATIONS: too, en, doo

MEANING: distant, far EXAMPLES: 遠い tooi = far; 遠慮 enryo = reserve; 待ち遠しい machidooshii = long for, look forward to DESCRIPTION: on the lower left, a snail; at the top, 土 tsuchi (dirt, # 59), but this looks like a t, which could stand for "tooi" (distant); at the bottom, a machine on a tripod, with a speaker extending to the right, which could be a toy megaphone CUES: this snail carries a megaphone, hidden under some 土 (dirt), which looks like a **T**oy but which an advertiser can use to speak to people in 遠い **too**i (distant) places, **En**couraging them to eat **Dough**nuts COMPARE: (公)園 kouen = park, # 279, which helps us to pronounce this

352. 選 PRONUNCIATIONS: sen, era

MEANING: to choose EXAMPLES: 選挙 senkyo = election; 選手 senshuu = athlete; 選ぶ erabu = to choose DESCRIPTION: on the lower left, a snail; on the snail's back, at the top, two backward S's, which may represent two backward people running for senator in the era of Bush, elevated on a high platform

CUES: this snail is a 選挙 **sen**kyo (election) van, carrying two backward candidates for the **Sen**ate on a high platform, from which one had to 選ぶ **era**bu (choose) during the **Era** of Bush COMPARE: 替(える) kaeru = to replace or to exchange money, # 551

353. 連 PRONUNCIATIONS: ren, tsu, tsura MEANINGS: linking, accompanying

EXAMPLES: 連絡する renraku suru = to contact; 連れて行く tsurete iku = to bring a person along; 連なる tsuranaru = to stand in a row DESCRIPTION: on the lower left, a snail; above the snail, a rental 車 kuruma (car, # 283)

CUES: my **Ren**tal 車 (car) broke down, and after I 連絡した **ren**raku shita (contacted) the agency, they sent this snail to pick up the car, after which they 連れて行った **tsu**rete itta (took me along) to my destination, but I left my **Tsu**itcase (suitcase) containing my **Tsu**it (suit) and my **Ra**men

in the car

COMPARE: 運(ぶ) hakobu = to carry, # 354

354. 運 PRONUNCIATIONS: hako, un

MEANINGS: to transport, luck EXAMPLES: 運ぶ hakobu = to carry or transport; 運動 undou = exercise, 運転する unten suru = to operate or drive; 運 un = luck, fortune DESCRIPTION: on the lower left, a snail; on the snail, 車 kuruma (car, # 283), covered by a lid

CUES: this snail can 運ぶ **hako**bu (carry) this 車 (car), and the car can 運ぶ **hako**bu (carry) this lid, which also serves as a **Hat** on **C**old days; **Un**doubtedly the hat will also protect us from rain when we 運動する **un**dou suru (exercise)

COMPARE: 連(絡) renraku = contact, # 353

355. 違 PRONUNCIATIONS: chiga, i

MEANINGS: to differ, wrong EXAMPLES: 違う chigau = different; 違反 ihan = violation, offense DESCRIPTION: on the lower left, a snail, carrying a radical that looks about the same whether it is right side up or upside down; reportedly this represents two feet facing in opposite directions

CUES: these two feet on a snail are 違う **chiga**u (different) in that they face in opposite directions; both feet have been been bitten up by **Chig**gers and Ants, not to mention **E**els

356. 返 PRONUNCIATIONS: kae, gae[1], hen MEANING: to return something

EXAMPLES: 返す kaesu = to return an item; 寝返る negaeru = to betray; 返事 henji = reply DESCRIPTION: on the lower left, a snail; on the right, a large F over a smaller X

CUES: when I get an F on my paper, or have it marked with an X, I put it on this snail and 返す **kae**su (return it) to the teacher, but the teacher **C**alls Esther, my mother, and sends the paper back to us on a **Hen** COMPARE: (ご)飯 gohan = meal, cooked rice, # 400

357. 込 **PRONUNCIATIONS: ko, komi**
MEANING: to get crowded **EXAMPLES:** 込む
komu = to get crowded; 申込書 moushikomisho
= application form **DESCRIPTION:** on the lower
left, a commuter snail; on the right, 入(る) hairu
(to enter, # 14) **CUES:** many people 入 (enter)
this snail bus in order to **C**ommute to work, but it
込む **ko**mu (gets crowded), often **C**omically so
NOTE: Japanese people are more likely to use an
alternative spelling, 混む, for komu when it
appears by itself and means "to get crowded"; they
use 込む in compound words, like 飛び込む
tobikomu = to dive

358. 迎 **PRONUNCIATIONS: muka, gei**
MEANING: to welcome **EXAMPLES:**
迎える mukaeru = to greet/welcome;
歓迎する kangei suru = to welcome
DESCRIPTION: on the lower left, a snail; on the
snail, two standing figures who could be Moonies
CUES: two **Moo**nies **Ca**ll to potential donors as they
ride on this snail to the station, where they will
迎える **muka**eru (greet and welcome) a
colleague **Gai**ly

359. 速 **PRONUNCIATIONS: haya, soku,**
sumi MEANING: fast **EXAMPLES:** 速い
hayai = fast; 速達 sokutatsu = express mail;
高速道路 kousokudouro = expressway;
早速 sassoku = immediately; 速やかな
sumiyaka na = swift **DESCRIPTION:** on the lower
left, a snail heading to Prince Harry's yacht; riding
on the snail, 束 soku (bundle, # 99), which helps us
to pronounce this **CUES:** this 束 (bundle), which
looks like a tree wearing glasses, is 速い **haya**i
(fast), in spite of using a snail for transport, since his
glasses allow him to see far ahead and avoid
obstacles; he is heading to Prince **Har**ry's **Y**acht,
where he will **So**ak in the tub with **Sumi**su-san (Mr.
Smith) **COMPARE:** 早(い) hayai = early, # 34

360. 遊 **PRONUNCIATIONS: aso, yuu**
MEANINGS: to play, have fun **EXAMPLES:**
遊ぶ asobu = to play; 遊園地 yuuenchi =
playground **DESCRIPTION:** on the lower left, a
snail; above the snail, 方 kata (honorable people,
114), a crutch, and 子 ko (child, # 182)
CUES: an **Asso**ciate **Boo**t maker allows his
handicapped 子 (child) to 遊ぶ **aso**bu (play) with
these 方 (honorable people) on snails in the **Yu**kon

361. 過 **PRONUNCIATIONS: su, ka,**
ayama MEANINGS: to pass through, excessively
EXAMPLES: 食べ過ぎる tabesugiru = to
overeat; 過ぎる sugiru = to pass by; 過去
kako = the past; 過ち ayamachi = fault, error
DESCRIPTION: on the lower left, a snail; on the
right, two boxes which each contain a smaller
package holding Superman's geese; in the upper box,
the inner package has slipped out of place
CUES: I placed these two packages containing
Superman's **G**eese into the center of larger boxes for
transport on this snail, but I やり過ぎた
yari**sug**ita (overdid it) by piling them so high, and
the package that was in the center of the upper box
slipped out of place, resulting in a **Ca**cophony of
honking, and the **Aya**tollah got **Mad**

362. 辺 **PRONUNCIATIONS: hen, ata,**
nabe, be MEANINGS: area, around, peripheral,
edge **EXAMPLES:** この辺 kono hen = around
here; その辺り sono atari = around there;
田辺 Tanabe = family name; 水辺 mizube =
waterside **DESCRIPTION:** on the lower left, a
snail; on the right, a 刀 katana (sword, # 102) used
to guard hens **CUES:** I keep my 刀 (sword) on the
back of this snail when guarding the **Hen**s in this
hen 辺 (area) near the **Ata**ri company; **N**ancy and
Betty are my favorites, and then there is **Be**tsy

363. 建 **PRONUNCIATIONS: ta, tate, kon, ken MEANING:** to erect a building **EXAMPLES:** 建てる tateru = to build; 建物 tatemono = building; 建立 konryuu = act of building a temple or monument, etc.; 建築 kenchiku = architecture **DESCRIPTION:** the radical seen at the lower left of this kanji is different from the snail radical seen earlier in this section; we call it a "3x snail," since it consists of a 3 intersected at the bottom to form an X; on the right, a three-fingered hand has been placed across the top of a telegraph pole, and this is similar to the three-fingered hand in 書く kaku (to write, # 415)

CUES: before they 建てる **ta**teru (erect) a **T**axi garage for a **T**all **T**echie who is a **C**onehead, **K**en and Barbie must review their plans 3x and 書 (write) them down

Fence

364. 用 **PRONUNCIATIONS: you, mochi MEANINGS:** errand, to use **EXAMPLES:** 用事 youji = errand; 利用する riyou suru = to use; 用いる mochi'iru = to use **DESCRIPTION:** a Japanese fence, made from pieces of bamboo and tied together with rope **CUES:** we will 利用する ri**you** suru (use) this fence to enclose a cow, so that we can make our own **Y**ogurt and stop **Mooch**ing from the neighbors

365. 通 **PRONUNCIATIONS: too, tsuu, doo, kayo MEANING:** to pass through **EXAMPLES:** 通る tooru = to pass through; 通り toori = street, way; 通学する tsuugaku suru = to commute to school; 通り doori = in accordance with, Avenue; 通う kayou = to commute **DESCRIPTION:** on the lower left, a snail; at the upper right, the katakana character マ ma, which represents a mammoth; at the lower right, 用 you (errand, # 364) which resembles a fence **CUES:** this マ (mammoth) on (or perhaps inside) this 用 (fence) 通う **kayo**u (commutes) on this snail to its job at a lakeside hotel, where マ (mammoths) 通る **too**ru (pass through) the lobby **T**owing **Tsu**itcases (suitcases), guests arrive in

Dories, and **C**oyotes roam the grounds **COMPARE:** 踊(る) odoru = to dance, # 366; 痛(い) itai = painful, # 368; 道 tou, or dou, = road, street, direction, # 349

366. 踊 **PRONUNCIATIONS: you, odo MEANINGS:** to dance or skip **EXAMPLE:** 舞踊 buyou = dancing; 踊る odoru = to dance **DESCRIPTION:** on the left, a square head on 正(しい) tadashii (correct, # 174), suggesting a correct gentleman; on the right, the katakana character マ ma, which represents a mammoth, on 用 you (errand, # 364), which resembles a fence **CUES:** this 正 (correct) gentleman goes behind this 用 (fence), removes the **Y**oke of a マ (mammoth) and 踊る **odo**ru (dances) with it, which leaves a distinctive **Od**or of mammoth on the gentleman **COMPARE:** 通(う) kayou = to commute, # 365; 痛(い) itai = painful, # 368

367. 備 **PRONUNCIATIONS: sona, bi MEANINGS:** to be prepared or equipped with **EXAMPLES:** 備える sonaeru = to prepare, have, be equipped with; 準備 junbi = preparation; 設備 setsubi = equipment, facility **DESCRIPTION:** on the left, a man with a slanted hat; at the top right, some bushes above a lean-to; at the bottom right, 用 you (errand, # 364), which resembles a fence **CUES:** this man with a slanted hat uses **Son**ar to monitor the **Bi**ngo games that are held in his 設備 setsu**bi** (facility), which is a lean-to under a roof garden, with a 用 (fence) around it

Vertical Bed

368. 痛 **PRONUNCIATIONS: ita, tsuu MEANING:** pain **EXAMPLES:** 痛い itai = painful; 頭痛 zutsuu = headache **DESCRIPTION:** on the upper left, a bed shown vertically, with legs pointing to the left and a headboard at the top; in the bed, 用 you (errand, # 364), which resembles a fence, with the katakana character マ ma, which represents a mammoth, above it **CUES:** this マ (mammoth) on this 用

(fence), who comes from **Ita**ly and is wearing a **Tsu**it (suit), is being squeezed against this headboard, which 痛い <u>itai</u> (hurts)

COMPARE: 通(う) kayou = to commute, # 365; 踊(る) odoru = to dance, # 366

369. 病 PRONUNCIATIONS: ya, byou, yamai MEANINGS: illness, disease, sick

EXAMPLES: 病む yamu = to fall sick; 病気 byouki = illness; 病 yamai = illness; DESCRIPTION: on the upper left, a bed shown vertically, with legs pointing to the left and a headboard at the top; inside the bed, 内 uchi (within, # 396), suspended from a horizontal beam, resembling a chest x-ray of a yak, with ribs superimposed on lungs CUES: this 内 (chest x-ray) of a **Ya**k in a bed suggests a 病気 <u>byou</u>ki (illness) which could be **B.O.** (bacterial overgrowth), or maybe just an allergy to **Ya**k **M**ites

370. 疲 PRONUNCIATIONS: tsuka, hi MEANINGS: to get tired, fatigue EXAMPLES: 疲れる tsukareru = to get tired; 疲労 hirou = fatigue, weariness DESCRIPTION: on the upper left, a bed shown vertically, with legs pointing to the left and a headboard at the top; in the bed, at the top, an arrow pointing to the right, intersected by a vertical line, representing a guy named Straight Arrow, who has a long cape that trails down to the end of the bed on the left; at the bottom, 又 mata ("again," # 24), but this looks like Straight Arrow's springy legs CUES: Straight Arrow 疲れた <u>tsuka</u>reta (got tired) and is sleeping in this bed; he left his **Tsu**it (suit) in the **Car**, but he's still wearing his **Hero**'s cape COMPARE: 彼 kare = he, # 371

371. 彼 PRONUNCIATIONS: kare, kano

MEANINGS: he, she EXAMPLES: 彼 kare = he; 彼女 kanojo = she DESCRIPTION: on the left, a man with a double hat; at the upper right, an arrow pointing to the right, intersected by a vertical line, representing a guy named Straight Arrow, who has a long cape on the left that trails down to the floor; at the lower right, 又 mata ("again," # 24), but this looks like Straight Arrow's springy legs CUES: this man with a double hat and Straight Arrow are males who eat a lot of **Kare**e (curry) made with **Cano**la oil, and either of them can be

referred to as 彼 <u>kare</u> (he) COMPARE: 疲(れる) tsukareru = to get tired, # 370

372. 寝 PRONUNCIATIONS: ne, shin MEANINGS: to sleep or lie down EXAMPLES: 寝る neru = to go to bed, to sleep; 寝室 shinshitsu = bedroom DESCRIPTION: on the left, a bed shown vertically; at the top, a bad haircut; on the right, long hair belonging to Nervous Ruth, streaming to the left, above a platform that is resting on 又 mata ("again," # 24), but this looks like Ruth's springy legs CUES: Nervous Ruth, who has a bad haircut, <u>ne</u>ru 寝る (sleeps) in this bed, with her long hair falling to the left, after saying her **Shin**to prayers COMPARE: 眠(る) nemuru = to sleep, # 376

373. 北 PRONUNCIATIONS: kita, ho, hoku, boku[1] MEANING: north EXAMPLES: 北 kita = north; 北海道 hokkaidou = Hokkaido; 北方 hoppou = northward; 北部 hokubu = the northern part; 敗北 haiboku = defeat DESCRIPTION: on the left, a bed, shown vertically; on the right, the katakana character ヒ hi, which resembles a person lying in the bed; together, these two radicals seem to point north CUES: a **K**ing reviews his **Tax** code while lying in this bed, with his head pointing 北 <u>kita</u> (north), where he keeps a **Home** at the North Pole, and the **Home** is **Cool**

374. 将 PRONUNCIATIONS: *kami*, shou MEANINGS: future, army general EXAMPLES: 女将 okami = mistress, landlady, hostess, proprietress; 将来 shourai = future; 大将 taishou = a general in the military DESCRIPTION: on the left, a bed shown vertically; at the upper right, several floating lines that suggest dreams floating in the air; at the lower right, a Commie (Communist) lying in this bed, with an object next to her feet, which could be *Das Kapital* CUES: a **Commie**, who is lying on this bed, sees visions of the 将来 <u>shou</u>rai (future) dancing above her head; she believes that these dreams **Show** Life as it will be after the Revolution COMPARE: 紙 kami = paper, # 221; 神 kami = god, # 273; 髪 kami = hair, # 501

Citizen

375. 民 PRONUNCIATIONS: min, tami

MEANING: people **EXAMPLES:** 市民 shimin = citizen; 民 tami = the people, a nation **DESCRIPTION:** on the upper left, a lean-to with a double roof; at the lower right, a mean bending person trying to squeeze into it **CUES:** these 市民 shi**min** (citizens) are squeezed into their lean-to's like sardines in a can, which is why they are so **Mean** and carry **Tommy** guns **COMPARE:** 眠(る) nemuru = to sleep, # 376; 宅 taku = home, # 21

376. 眠 PRONUNCIATIONS: nemu, min

MEANING: to sleep **EXAMPLES:** 眠る nemuru = to sleep; 眠い nemui = sleepy; 睡眠を取る suimin wo toru = to get some sleep **DESCRIPTION:** on the left, 目 me (eye, # 51); on the right, (市)民 shimin (citizen, # 375), which helps us to pronounce this **CUES:** the 目 (eyes) of this 民 (citizen) are wide open, and he can't 眠る **nemu**ru (sleep), because his **N**eighbors' **Mu**sic **R**uins his rest, and this makes him **Mean ALSO COMPARE:** 寝(る) neru = to sleep, # 372

Festival

377. 祭 PRONUNCIATIONS: sai, matsu, matsuri MEANINGS: festival, to worship

EXAMPLES: 祭日 saijitsu = holiday; 祭る matsuru = to worship; 祭 matsuri = festival **DESCRIPTION:** a spinning pavilion with a peaked roof; on the left roof, a three-legged bench; on the right roof, a slice of pizza **CUES:** as we admired this spinning pavilion decorated for a **S**cientific 祭 **matsu**ri (festival), we sat on a **Mat** that **Su**perman had **R**epaired and enjoyed seeing the three-legged bench and the pizza slice on the roof **COMPARE:** 途(中) tochuu = on the way, # 378; (国)際 kokusai = international, # 379

378. 途 PRONUNCIATIONS: to, *zu*

MEANINGS: route, way **EXAMPLE:** 途中 tochuu = on the way; 一途に ichizu ni = wholeheartedly **DESCRIPTION:** on the lower left, a snail; at the upper right, a pavilion spinning like a tornado, with a peaked roof; unlike 祭 matsu (festival, # 377), this pavilion carries no decorations **CUES:** a snail carries this pavilion which spins like a **T**ornado 途中 **to**chuu (on the way) to the **Z**oo

379. 際 PRONUNCIATIONS: sai, giwa, kiwa MEANINGS: contact, edge of an area

EXAMPLES: 国際 kokusai = international; 手際 tegiwa = skill; 際立つ kiwadatsu = to stand out or be conspicuous **DESCRIPTION:** on the left, ß from the Greek alphabet, suggesting Greek science; on the right, 祭 matsuri (festival, # 377) **CUES:** this 祭 (festival) has a 国際 koku**sai** (international) flavor; it includes exhibits on ß (Greek) **S**cience and **G**eeky **W**arriors, and it is **K**eenly **W**atched by the world

Horse

380. 駅 PRONUNCIATION: eki

MEANING: train station **EXAMPLE:** 東京駅 toukyou eki = Tokyo station **DESCRIPTION:** on the left, 馬 uma (horse, # 958); on the right, the square mounted high above the ground reportedly represents a "watchful eye" **CUE:** this reminds us of the old custom of changing 馬 (horses) at the royal 駅 **eki** (station) under the watchful eye of Edward the **K**ing **COMPARE:** 訳 wake = reason, # 437

381. 駐 PRONUNCIATION: chuu

MEANING: to park a vehicle **EXAMPLES:** 駐車する chuusha suru = to park a vehicle **DESCRIPTION:** on the left, 馬 uma (horse, # 958); on the right, 主(人) shujin (master, # 166) **CUE:** this 主 (master) 駐車する **chuu**sha suru (parks) this 馬 (horse) and carriage, while the horse **Chew**s hay

382. 験 PRONUNCIATION: ken

MEANING: to examine **EXAMPLES:** 試験 shiken = examination; 経験 keiken = experience **DESCRIPTION:** on the left, 馬 uma (horse,

958); on the right, a laundromat with a peaked roof, containing a keg stuck sideways in a washing machine **CUES:** Ken and his 馬 (horse) have arrived from the **Ken**tucky Derby to visit Barbie, and he will 経験する kei**ken** suru (experience) the stuck-keg problem when he does his laundry **COMPARE:** 険(しい) kewashii = steep, # 196

Needle

383. 親 **PRONUNCIATIONS: oya, shin, shita MEANINGS:** parent, intimate **EXAMPLES:** 親 oya = parent; 両親 ryoushin = parents; 親しい shitashii = intimate, close **DESCRIPTION:** on the left, 木 ki (tree, # 118) topped by an additional pair of branches and a bell which, taken together, resemble a needle with a syringe; on the right, 見(る) miru (to look, # 53) **CUES:** when 親 **oya** (parents) say **Oya**suminasai (good night) to their kids, they should 見 (look) at their beds and check for **Shi**ny needles like this and for **Shiny Tacks** **COMPARE:** 新 shin = new, # 389

384. 辛 **PRONUNCIATIONS: kara, shin, tsura MEANINGS:** spicy, bitter, hot, salty **EXAMPLES:** 辛い karai = spicy, hot; 香辛料 koushinryou = spices; 辛い tsurai = painful, tormenting **NOTE:** karai and tsurai are both written 辛い **DESCRIPTION:** a needle and syringe; compared to the needle in 新 shin (new, # 389), 辛 is missing two handles near the bottom; when viewed as a tower, 辛 has three levels **CUES:** while singing **Kara**oke and eating 辛い **kara**i (spicy) food on a **Shin**gle at a dude ranch, I found this needle in the food, so I **Tsu**ed the **Ran**ch **ALSO COMPARE:** 幸(せ) shiawase = happiness, # 385, which has four levels

385. 幸 **PRONUNCIATIONS: shiawa, sachi, saiwa, kou MEANINGS:** happiness, good luck **EXAMPLES:** 幸せ shiawase = happiness; 幸子 Sachiko = a girl's given name; 幸い saiwai = lucky, happy; 幸福 koufuku = happiness

DESCRIPTION: 幸 has four levels, compared to 辛(い) karai (spicy, # 384), which has three levels; also, 幸 has an antenna at the top **CUES:** I live in a **Shia** country torn by **War**, and there are some **Sa**d **Chi**ldren here, and a lot of 辛 (spicy) food, but if I can take **Si**lent **Wa**lks, fight off **Co**lds, and keep this antenna on my roof, that means 幸せ **shiawa**se (happiness) for me, and I feel 幸い **saiwa**i (lucky) **ALSO COMPARE:** 達 tachi (plural, # 347), where the tower has 5 levels

386. 報 **PRONUNCIATIONS: hou, muku MEANINGS:** report, news **EXAMPLES:** 報告 houkoku = report; 予報 yohou = forecast; 報いる mukuiru = to reward or repay **DESCRIPTION:** on the left, 幸(せ) shiawase (happiness, # 385), resembling a syringe with a needle; on the right, a dressing room, with a hook at the top for hanging clothes and a table at the bottom **CUES:** we received a 報告 **hou**koku (report) about a **Hor**net with a 幸 (needle)-like stinger near the **Hook** in the dressing room, but the **Moo**nie who reported it had been drinking too much **Kool**-Aid **COMPARE:** 服 fuku = clothes, # 150

387. 辞 **PRONUNCIATIONS: ji, ya MEANINGS:** word, to resign **EXAMPLES:** 辞書 jisho = dictionary; 辞める yameru = to resign a position **DESCRIPTION:** on the left, 口 kuchi (mouth, # 426), with a forked tongue emerging from it; on the right, 辛(い) karai (spicy, # 384) **CUES:** Jimmy Carter Showed us this forked tongue after he finished his work tasting **Ya**m dishes and said that the recipes were too 辛 (spicy) for him, so he will start working on a 辞書 **ji**sho (dictionary) project and 辞める **ya**meru (resign) from his tasting job **COMPARE:** (生)活 seikatsu = livelihood, # 260; 止(める) yameru = to stop doing something, to give up, # 173; 話(す) hanasu = to speak, # 433

388. 南 **PRONUNCIATIONS: minami, nan MEANING:** south **EXAMPLES:** 南 minami = south; 南米 nanbei = South America **DESCRIPTION:** at the sides and top, a weather station, with an antenna on top; inside the weather station, a needle pointing south **CUES:** in this weather station located near the **Mina**ret of **Mi**ckey's mosque, the compass needle points 南 **minami** (south), rather than north, according to his **Nan**ny

Pliers

389. 新 **PRONUNCIATIONS: atara, shin, ara MEANINGS:** new, fresh **EXAMPLES:** 新しい atarashii = new, fresh; 新聞 shinbun = newspaper; 新たな arata na = new, fresh **DESCRIPTION:** on the left, 木 ki (tree, # 118) topped by an additional pair of branches and a bell; this resembles a shiny syringe and needle; on the right, a pair of pliers **CUES:** I store my **Atara**x (allergy medicine) with this 新しい **atara**shii (new) **Shi**ny needle and this pair of **Ara**bian pliers **COMPARE:** 親 shin = parent, # 383

390. 近 **PRONUNCIATIONS: chika, jika[1], kin MEANING:** near, close **EXAMPLES:** 近い chikai = close; 身近 mijika = close at hand, closely related; 近所 kinjo = neighborhood; 最近 saikin = recently **DESCRIPTION:** on the lower left, a snail from Chicago; on the snail, a pair of pliers **CUES:** this snail is an electrician from **Chica**go who carries a pair of pliers that he uses on wires that are 近い **chika**i (near) the **Kin**dergarten where he works

391. 所 **PRONUNCIATIONS: tokoro, dokoro[1], jo, sho MEANING:** place **EXAMPLES:** 所 tokoro = place; 台所 daidokoro = kitchen; 近所 kinjo = neighborhood; 場所 basho = place **DESCRIPTION:** on the left, under a roof, a P, which could stand for a "**P**lace" belonging to Tony Blair; on the right, a pair of pliers **CUES:** after **T**ony had a **Coronary**, **Joan** of Arc used these pliers to fix up his 所 **tokoro** (Place) for a **Sho**w

Old

392. 古 **PRONUNCIATIONS: furu, go, ko MEANINGS:** old, referring to things **EXAMPLES:** 古い furui = old; 名古屋 Nagoya = city in Japan; 古代 kodai = ancient times **DESCRIPTION:** a box with a cross on it **CUES:** I was **Fu**rious when they **Ru**ined this 古い **furu**i (old) tomb with a **Go**ld cross on top, where a **Ko**ala was buried

393. 苦 **PRONUNCIATIONS: niga, ku, kuru MEANINGS:** bitter, painful **EXAMPLES:** 苦い nigai = hard, painful; 苦手 nigate = weak point; 苦労 kurou = hardship; 苦しい kurushii = hard, painful **DESCRIPTION:** at the top, a plant radical (see # 43), representing Nigerian apple trees; at the bottom, 古(い) furui (old, # 392), which resembles a tomb with a cross on it **CUES:** it's 苦い **niga**i (bitter) to see these 古 (old) tombs overgrown with **Ni**gerian **A**pple trees, and it's even worse when rac**Coo**ns dig up the levee, and the river's **Cu**rrent **Ru**ins the cemetery

394. 故 **PRONUNCIATIONS: furu, ko, yue MEANINGS:** past, to cause **EXAMPLES:** 故郷 furusato = hometown (usually written ふるさと); 事故 jiko = accident; 故障 koshou = breakdown; 故に yue ni = therefore **DESCRIPTION:** on the left, 古(い) furui (old, # 392); on the right, a dancer with a ponytail **CUES:** due to a **Fo**olish **Roo**ster, an 古 (old) car from **Co**lombia was involved in a 事故 ji**ko** (accident), and now this dancer has to fly home by **U.A.** (United Airlines)

395. 個 **PRONUNCIATION: ko MEANINGS:** individual, counter for eggs, etc. **EXAMPLES:** 卵三個 tamago sanko = three eggs; 個人 kojin = individual **DESCRIPTION:** on the left, a man with a slanted hat; on the right, 古(い) furui (old, # 392), inside a cold box **CUE:** this man with a slanted hat keeps 卵一個 tamago ik**ko** (one egg) in this **Co**ld box, but the egg is getting 古 (old)

ALSO COMPARE: 週 shuu = week, # 346; 固(体) kotai = solid, # 731, which helps us to pronounce this

Inside

396. 内 PRONUNCIATIONS: nai, uchi, dai **MEANING:** inside **EXAMPLES:** 国内 kokunai = inside the country; 家内 kanai = my wife; その内に sono uchi ni = before long; 境内 keidai = grounds (of a temple)
DESCRIPTION: a person extending her head through a hole in the roof of a building
CUES: this 家内 ka**nai** (wife) with a **Kni**fe and some **U**ber **Chee**se, who is 内 **uchi** (inside) a dwelling, puts her head through a hole in the roof and complains about her **Di**et **COMPARE:** 家 uchi = home, # 405; 病(気) byouki = illness, # 369; 肉 niku = meat, # 397

397. 肉 PRONUNCIATION: niku

MEANING: meat **EXAMPLE:** 肉 niku = meat **DESCRIPTION:** these look like ribs on an chest x-ray, surrounded by meat
CUE: my **Ni**ece in **Ku**wait sent us this 肉 **niku** (meat) which was x-rayed in Customs
COMPARE: 内 uchi = within, # 396

Eat

398. 食 PRONUNCIATIONS: ta, shoku, ku, jiki **MEANING:** to eat **EXAMPLES:** 食べる taberu = to eat; 食事 shokuji = meal; 食う kuu = to eat (rough speech); 餌食 ejiki = victim, prey **DESCRIPTION:** at the top, a peaked roof, suggesting a tavern; at the bottom, 良(い) yoi (good, # 303), suggesting good food **CUES:** after I 食べた **ta**beta (ate) some 良 (good) food in this **T**avern, I **Sho**wed some **Ko**ol-Aid packages to my **Ku**waiti friends, but then I lost my **Jee**p **Key**s
COMPARE: 娘 musume = daughter, # 316; 飲(む) nomu = to drink, # 399; (ご)飯 gohan = meal, cooked rice, # 400

399. 飲 PRONUNCIATIONS: no, in
MEANINGS: to drink or swallow **EXAMPLES:** 飲む nomu = to drink or swallow; 飲食 inshoku = drinking and eating **DESCRIPTION:** on the left, 食(べる) taberu (to eat, # 398); on the right, an oil derrick which drinks oil from the ground **CUES:** when the **N**omads on the Moon 食 (eat), they 飲む **no**mu (drink) oil from the ground and then act **In**sane **COMPARE:** (ご)飯 gohan = meal, cooked rice, # 400

400. 飯 PRONUNCIATIONS: han, pan[1], meshi **MEANING:** a meal **EXAMPLES:** ご飯 gohan = meal, cooked rice; 残飯 zanpan = leftover food; 冷や飯 hiyameshi = cold rice **DESCRIPTION:** on the left, 食(事) shokuji (meal, # 398); on the right, an X under an F **CUES:** this ご飯 go**han** (cooked rice) 食 (meal) that **Han**sel made is **Mes**sy, and it gets an **F**; we're also marking it with an **X** **COMPARE:** 返(す) kaesu = to return something, # 356

Various

401. 物 PRONUNCIATIONS: motsu, butsu, bu, mono **MEANINGS:** stuff, tangible things **EXAMPLES:** 荷物 nimotsu = luggage; 動物 doubutsu = animal; 物価 bukka = price of goods; 物 mono = thing **DESCRIPTION:** on the left, 牛 ushi (cow, # 205); on the right, this radical reportedly represents a variety of streamers, or "assorted things," which may produce a monotonous sound when the wind blows **CUES:** when we sit by the castle **Mo**ats, 牛 (cows), old **Bo**ots, empty **Boo**ze bottles and other assorted 物 **mono** (things) make **Mono**tonous noise in the wind

384

402. 易 PRONUNCIATIONS: yasa, eki, i MEANINGS: easy, fortune telling EXAMPLES: 易しい yasashii = easy; 貿易 boueki = trade; 安易な an'i na = easy DESCRIPTION: at the top, 日 hi (sun, # 32); at the bottom, a variety of streamers which reportedly represent simple, various things, implying that things under the sun are simple and easy CUES: a Yakuza Saw a Shiite in the Eki (station) and told him that writing 日 (sun) and some streamers to form the word 易しい yasashii (easy) is Easy, compared to writing 優しい yasashii (kind, # 528) ALSO COMPARE: 場(所) basho = place, # 403; 湯 yu = hot water, # 404; 駅 eki = station, # 380

403. 場 PRONUNCIATIONS: jou, ba MEANING: place EXAMPLES: 会場 kaijou = site of an event; 場所 basho = place DESCRIPTION: on the left, 土 tsuchi (dirt, # 59) conveys the idea of place; on the right, 易(しい) yasashii (easy, # 402), with wide roots like those of banana trees CUES: Joan of Arc likes Bananas, and it's 易 (easy) for her to grow them in this 場所 basho (place), since they love 土 (dirt) COMPARE: 湯 yu = hot water, # 404

404. 湯 PRONUNCIATIONS: yu, tou MEANINGS: hot water, hot bath EXAMPLES: お湯 oyu = honorable hot water; 熱湯 nettou = boiling water DESCRIPTION: on the left, a water radical (see # 12); on the right, 易(しい) yasashii (easy, # 402), with long roots like those of yucca plants CUES: growing Yucca plants is 易 (easy), since they love water; after giving them some, I relax in 湯 yu (hot water), and stretch my Toes COMPARE: 場(所) basho = place, # 403

405. 家 PRONUNCIATIONS: ie, uchi, ke, ka, ya MEANINGS: house, person EXAMPLES: 家 ie = house; 家 uchi = home, but Japanese people usually spell this うち, to avoid confusion with ie (house); 田中家 tanakake = the Tanaka family; 家族 kazoku = family; 家内 kanai = my wife; 家主 yanushi = landlord DESCRIPTION: at the top, a bad haircut; at the bottom, this radical is also found in 豚 buta (pork, not included in this Catalogue); it is not the same as the radicals seen in 物 mono (thing, # 401) and in 易(しい) yasashii (easy, # 402), although they are similar CUES: a Yellow 豚 (pig) lives in this 家 ie (house), where they make Uber Cheese, Ken parks his Car, and Barbie grows Yams

Rocker-bottom

406. 参 PRONUNCIATIONS: mai, san MEANINGS: to humbly come or go, to visit a temple or shrine EXAMPLES: 参る mairu = to humbly come or go; 参加 sanka = participation DESCRIPTION: at the top, the katakana character ム mu (the sound made by a cow); at the bottom, a rocker-bottom shoe CUES: wobbling on rocker-bottom shoes, this ム (cow) travels many Mairu (miles) as she 参ります mairimasu (humbly goes) to San Francisco COMPARE: 珍(しい) mezurashii = unusual, rare, # 407

407. 珍 PRONUNCIATIONS: mezura, chin MEANINGS: rare, strange EXAMPLE: 珍しい mezurashii = unusual, rare; 珍味 chinmi = delicacy, danties DESCRIPTION: on the left, 王 ou (king, # 1077); on the right, a rocker-bottom shoe CUES: when this 王 (king) visited a 珍しい mezurashii (unusual) Mexican Zoo to see Raccoons, he wore rocker-bottom shoes like this one, but he fell and hurt his Chin COMPARE: 参(る) mairu = to humbly come or go, # 406

408. 歩 PRONUNCIATIONS: **aru, ayu, po, ho** MEANINGS: to walk, step EXAMPLES: 歩く aruku = to walk; 歩み ayumi = walking, step, history, record; 散歩する sanpo suru = to walk; 歩道 hodou = sidewalk DESCRIPTION: at the top, 止(める) tomeru (to stop, # 173); at the bottom, 少(し) sukoshi (a little, # 254); together these resemble a rocker-bottom shoe with an ankle above it CUES: wearing rocker-bottom shoes in **Aru**ba, I will 歩く **aru**ku (walk) for the Clean Air Trust fundraiser, together with **A You**th I know, in order to help 止 (stop) **P**ollution 少 (a little), near my **H**ome

Gate

409. 門 PRONUNCIATIONS: **mon, kado** MEANINGS: gate, doors EXAMPLE: 門 mon = gate; 門出する kadode suru = to leave one's home, to start in life DESCRIPTION: two swinging doors that form a gate CUES: a **M**on**k** watches this 門 **mon** (gate) near a **C**athedral **D**ome

410. 問 PRONUNCIATIONS: **mon, ton, to** MEANINGS: to question or inquire EXAMPLES: 問題 mondai = a problem; 質問 shitsumon = a question; 問屋 tonya = wholesaler; 問う tou = to ask, question, inquire, to charge (with a crime) DESCRIPTION: compared to 門 mon (gate, # 409), this adds 口 kuchi (mouth, # 426), but 口 could be a painting CUES: when we hang this **Mon**et 口 (painting) under this gate, the **Ton**e of the colors changes, but this is only a small 問題 **mon**dai (problem), compared to things like **T**ornados

411. 間 PRONUNCIATIONS: **ma, ken, aida, gen, kan** MEANINGS: duration of time, between EXAMPLES: 間違える machigaeru = to make a mistake; 間もなく mamonaku = before long; 世間 seken = society, other people; 間 aida = duration, between; 人間 ningen = human being; 時間 jikan = time, hour

DESCRIPTION: compared to 門 mon (gate, # 409), this adds 日 hi (day, or sun, # 32), suggesting time CUES: standing near this 門 (gate) at the **Ma**ll, **Ken**, Barbie's friend **Ida**, and **Gen**ghis **Khan** measure the 間 **aida** (duration) of time by watching the shadows the 日 (sun) casts on the ground ALSO COMPARE: 聞(く) kiku = to hear or ask, # 412

412. 聞 PRONUNCIATIONS: **bun, ki, gi**[1] MEANINGS: to listen, hear, ask EXAMPLES: 新聞 shinbun = newspaper; 聞く kiku = to hear or ask; 人聞き hitogiki = reputation DESCRIPTION: compared to 門 mon (gate, # 409), this adds 耳 mimi (ears, # 57) CUES: sitting under this 門 (gate) out in the **Boon**docks, we open our 耳 (ears) to 聞く **ki**ku (listen) to gossip, we 聞く **ki**ku (ask) each other questions, and we read 新聞 shin**bun** (newspapers) on our **Ki**ndles ALSO COMPARE: 間 aida = duration, between, # 411

413. 開 PRONUNCIATIONS: **a, kai, hira** MEANINGS: to open, to begin EXAMPLES: 開ける akeru = to open, transitive; 開く aku = to open, intransitive; 開発 kaihatsu = development; 開く hiraku = to open or unfold, transitive NOTE: both aku and hiraku are written 開く DESCRIPTION: compared to 門 mon (gate, # 409), 開 adds a man named Achilles in the gate, who has a welcoming stance CUES: **A**chilles is standing in this gate with a welcoming stance, signaling that he will 開ける **a**keru (open) the gate so that people may bring their **Ki**tes inside, where they can **Hear Ra**p music COMPARE: 閉(める) shimeru = to close, transitive, # 414

414. 閉 PRONUNCIATIONS: to, shi, hei
MEANING: to close EXAMPLES: 閉じる
tojiru = to close; 閉める shimeru = to close,
transitive; 閉鎖する heisa suru = to close down
DESCRIPTION: compared to 門 mon (gate,
409), 閉 adds Tony Blair standing in the gate,
who has a forbidding stance CUES: Tony Blair
stands in this gate and extends a leg like a **Shie**ld to
block passage, signifying that the gate 閉まっ
ている shimatte iru (is closed) to people who
want to harvest **Hay** ALSO COMPARE:
開(ける) akeru = to open, # 413

Trident

415. 書 PRONUNCIATIONS: ka, sho
MEANING: to write EXAMPLES: 書く kaku
= to write; 辞書 jisho = dictionary
DESCRIPTION: at the top, a three-fingered hand
that resembles a trident is grasping a vertical brush,
which is writing on a table supported by a two-
drawer cabinet
CUES: I'm using this brush and writing table to
書く kaku (write) a story about the time I took a
Camel from **Kuwait** to a Broadway **Show**

416. 事 PRONUNCIATIONS: koto, goto,
ji MEANINGS: an intangible thing or matter
EXAMPLES: 事 koto = matter; 仕事 shigoto =
work; 用事 youji = errand DESCRIPTION:
this vertical line with a curve at the bottom is a very
tall **t** which represents an academic **t**est; it is
intersected by a rectangle near the top, representing a
test sheet, and by a stabbing trident near the bottom,
suggesting the consequences of failure to pass the
test CUES: this represents a test about 事 koto
(intangible things), such as **Koto** (Japanese harp)
music, **Ghost Toes** and **Genius**
COMPARE: 言(葉) kotoba = words, # 430

417. 律 PRONUNCIATIONS: ritsu, richi
MEANING: law EXAMPLES: 法律 houritsu =
law; 律儀な richigi na = conscientious
DESCRIPTION: on the left, a man with a double
hat named Richie; on the right, a telephone pole; the
three-fingered trident near the top of the pole is

pointed at the man, as though threatening him
CUES: 法律 houritsu (laws) are more than
Written Suggestions; they threaten men like **Richie**
with tridents like this if they don't obey
COMPARE: 静(か) shizuka = quiet, # 418; 君
kimi = you, # 419

418. 静 PRONUNCIATIONS: shizu, jou,
sei MEANINGS: quiet, serene EXAMPLES:
静か shizuka = quiet, serene; 静脈 joumyaku =
vein; 安静 ansei = rest DESCRIPTION: on the
left, 青(い) aoi (blue, # 155); on the right, a
monster with a fish head that someone has stabbed
with a trident CUES: the sky is 青 (blue), and it's
静か shizuka (quiet), now that a **Sheep** herder
from **Zurich** has stabbed this fish monster, and **Joan**
of Arc is **Safe** COMPARE: 君 kimi = you,
419; (法)律 houritsu = law, # 417

419. 君 PRONUNCIATIONS: kun, kimi
MEANING: suffix for (usually) male names of
younger people EXAMPLES: 石田君 ishida
kun = young man Ishida; 君 kimi = you (informal
male speech) DESCRIPTION: at the top, someone
named Kimmy has been stabbed in the face with a
trident; at the bottom, 口 kuchi (mouth, # 426)
CUES: "Hey 君 kimi (you)! A **Cunning** person
has stabbed **Kimmy** with this trident, and his 口
(mouth) is wide open."
COMPARE: (法)律 houritsu = law, # 417;
静(か) shizuka = quiet, # 418

Sturdy Legs

420. 兄 PRONUNCIATIONS: ani, *nii*,
kyou, kei MEANINGS: older brother, male elder
EXAMPLES: 兄 ani = my older brother;
お兄さん oniisan = your older brother;
兄弟 kyoudai = siblings; 父兄 fukei = parents,
guardians DESCRIPTION: this square head on
sturdy legs could belong to an animal
CUES: 兄 ani (older brother) has a square 口
(head) and sturdy legs, and he ate like an **A**ni**mal**
when he visited his **Nie**ce in **Kyou**to, where she
offered him some **Cake**

421. 元 **PRONUNCIATIONS: moto, gen, gan MEANINGS:** base, origin, source
EXAMPLES: 元 moto = base, origin, source; 元気 genki = cheerful, healthy; 元日 ganjitsu = January 1 **DESCRIPTION:** a table on sturdy legs, with a strong line over it **CUES:** this sturdy table suggests a solid 元 **moto** (base or source) for a 元気な **gen**ki na (healthy) lifestyle, such as the ones exemplified by the **Mo**torcycle gang led by **Gen**ghis Khan and **Gan**dalf

422. 先 **PRONUNCIATIONS: sen, ma, saki MEANINGS:** previous, before
EXAMPLES: 先生 sensei = teacher; 先ず mazu = first of all; 先 saki = tip, point, first, future; 先に saki ni = ahead, formerly, beyond; 先ほど sakihodo = a while ago **DESCRIPTION:** a senator, standing on a platform with sturdy legs, holding a shield on the left **CUES:** this **Sen**ator, who used to be a 先生 **sen**sei (teacher), is standing on a platform with sturdy legs at the **Ma**ll and holding a shield, which he keeps in a **Sack** that he bought in India, to shield himself from accusations about things that happened 先ほど **saki**hodo (a while ago) **COMPARE:** 洗(う) arau = to wash, # 423; (報)告 houkoku = report, # 429

423. 洗 **PRONUNCIATIONS: sen, ara MEANING:** to wash with water **EXAMPLES:** 洗濯 sentaku = laundry; 洗う arau = to wash **DESCRIPTION:** on the left, a water radical; on the right, 先 sen (previous, # 422), which helps us to pronounce this **CUES:** this **Sen**ator, who returned from Saudi **Ara**bia 先 (previously), stands on a platform with sturdy legs; he holds his shield out to the water on the left and 洗う **ara**u (washes) it **COMPARE:** (報)告 houkoku = report, # 429

424. 院 **PRONUNCIATION: in MEANING:** institution **EXAMPLE:** 病院 byouin = hospital **DESCRIPTION:** on the left, ß beta from the Greek alphabet; at the upper right, a roof which resembles bad haircut; at the lower right 元 moto (base, # 421) **CUE:** ß (Greek) doctors with bad haircuts put a roof on this sturdy 元 (base) and made a 病院 byou**in** (hospital) for people with **In**dustrial injuries

425. 売 **PRONUNCIATIONS: u, bai, uri MEANING:** to sell **EXAMPLES:** 売る uru = to sell; 販売 hanbai = sales; 読売 Yomiuri = name of a newspaper **DESCRIPTION:** at the top, a statue of a (兵)士 heishi (soldier, # 66) made from uranium; at the bottom, a base with sturdy legs, similar to 元 moto (base, # 421) **CUES:** we 売る **u**ru (sell) this **U**ranium 士 (soldier) statue mounted on a sturdy 元 (base), which you may also **Bu**y from our 販売機 han**bai**ki (vending machines) located near the **Ur**inals in the bathrooms **COMPARE:** 読(む) yomu = to read, # 432

Mouth

426. 口 **PRONUNCIATIONS: kuchi, ku, kou, guchi MEANING:** mouth **EXAMPLES:** 口 kuchi = mouth; 口説く kudoku = to persuade, seduce or make advances; 人口 jinkou = popula-tion; 入り口 iriguchi = entrance **DESCRIPTION:** a square mouth **CUES:** in **Ku**wait they eat **Chee**se and drink **Kool**-Aid with their 口 **kuchi** (mouths), and they carry Cola in **Gucci** handbags **COMPARE:** the katakana character ロ ro

427. 吸 **PRONUNCIATIONS: su, kyuu MEANING:** to suck **EXAMPLES:** タバコを吸う tabako wo suu = to smoke tobacco; 吸収する kyuushuu suru = to digest
DESCRIPTION: on the left, 口 kuchi (mouth, # 426); on the right, a graph of breathing patterns **CUES:** this mouth on the left and this graph of breathing patterns on the right remind us of a baby named **Sue** who cannot 吸う **su**u (suck) properly but is very **Cute COMPARE:** 吹(く) fuku = to blow, breathe, whistle, # 537

428. 呼 **PRONUNCIATIONS: yo, ko**
MEANINGS: to call out, exhale **EXAMPLES:**
呼ぶ yobu = to call out, to summon; 呼び名
yobina = given name, alias; 呼吸 kokyuu =
breathing, respiration **DESCRIPTION:** on the left,
口 kuchi (mouth, # 426); on the right, a person
throwing up her arms in frustration as she calls a
tardy companion **CUES:** I open my 口 (mouth)
when I 呼ぶ **yo**bu (call out) to say that the **Y**ogurt
Burned, together with my **C**oat **COMPARE:**
咲(く) saku = to blossom, # 193

429. 告 **PRONUNCIATIONS: koku, tsu**
MEANINGS: to proclaim, to inform
EXAMPLES: 広告 koukoku = advertisement;
報告 houkoku = report; 告げる tsugeru = to
inform **DESCRIPTION:** at the top, a person
extending a shield to the left; at the bottom, 口
kuchi (mouth, # 426) **CUES:** this big 口 (mouth)
speaks 広告 kou**koku** (advertisements), and the
person above it holds out a shield to demonstrate that
drinking **C**oke, as well as consuming **Ts**oup (soup)
with **G**uests, can shield us from unpopularity
COMPARE: 先 saki = previously, # 422;
洗(う) arau = to wash, # 423

430. 言 **PRONUNCIATIONS: i, koto, gen,**
gon MEANINGS: words, to say **EXAMPLES:**
言う iu = to speak; 言葉 kotoba = words;
言語 gengo = language; 伝言 dengon =
message **DESCRIPTION:** at the top, four
horizontal lines that represent words; at the bottom,
口 kuchi (mouth, # 426) **CUES:** an **I**ndian from
Utah uses this 口 (mouth) to 言う **i**u (speak) four
言葉 **koto**ba (words) about **Koto** (intransitive
things) to **Gen**ghis Khan, but soon the words are
Gone **COMPARE:** 事 koto = intransitive things,
416

431. 信 **PRONUNCIATION: shin**
MEANINGS: to believe, to trust, letter
EXAMPLES: 信じる shinjiru = to believe;
信号 shingou = stoplight; 信念 shinnen =

belief; 信徒 shinto = a follower or believer
DESCRIPTION: on the left, a man with a slanted
hat; on the right, 言(う) iu (to speak, # 430)
CUE: this man with a slanted hat 信じる
shinjiru (believes) in **Shin**tou, and he 言 (speaks)
about his 信念 **shin**nen (beliefs) **COMPARE:**
神(道) Shintou = a Japanese religion, # 273

432. 読 **PRONUNCIATIONS: doku, yo,**
tou, do, yomi MEANING: reading
EXAMPLES: 読書 dokusho = reading; 読む
yomu = to read; 句読点 kutouten = punctuation
marks; 読経 dokyou = sutra chanting; 読(解)
dokkai = reading comprehension; 読売 Yomiuri =
name of a newspaper **DESCRIPTION:** on the left,
言(う) iu (to speak, # 430); on the right, 売
(る) uru (to sell, # 425) **CUES:** in a **D**ocumentary
about **Yo**semite, a man stands on his **To**es, 読む
yomu (reads) from a transcript and 言 (speaks) in
order to 売 (sell) a hotel room with a nice view of
Half **Do**me, where one can practice **Yo**ga and **M**eet
single people **COMPARE:** 続(く) tsuzuku = to
continue, # 226

433. 話 **PRONUNCIATIONS: hana,**
hanashi, banashi[1], wa MEANING: to speak
EXAMPLES: 話す hanasu = to talk; 話 hanashi
= story; 昔話 mukashibanashi = folklore; 会話
kaiwa = conversation **DESCRIPTION:** on the left,
言(う) iu (to speak, # 430); at the upper right, a
forked tongue; at the lower right, 口 kuchi (mouth,
426) **CUES:** when **Hannah** 話す **hana**su
(talks), she 言 (speaks); meanwhile, **Hannah**'s
Sheep lick salt with forked tongues that project from
their 口 (mouths) and **Wa**lk around
COMPARE: (生)活 seikatsu = livelihood, # 260;
辞(書) jisho = dictionary, # 387

434. 計 PRONUNCIATIONS: haka, kei MEANINGS: to measure or count EXAMPLES: 計る hakaru = to measure; 時計 tokei = clock, watch; 計画 keikaku = plan DESCRIPTION: on the left, 言(う) iu (to speak, # 430); on the right, 十 juu (ten, # 18) CUES: I 言 (speak) about my 計画 keikaku (plan) to buy a 時計 tokei (clock) with the 十 (ten) dollars I earned in the last **Hacka**thon, which we held in a **Cave**

435. 語 PRONUNCIATIONS: go, kata, gata[1], *gatari* MEANINGS: words, to talk EXAMPLES: 英語 eigo = English; 語る kataru = to talk; 物語る monogataru = to tell or indicate; 物語 monogatari = story

DESCRIPTION: on the left, 言(う) iu (to say, # 430); on the right, 五 go (five, # 179), which helps us to pronounce this, standing on a box and resembling a golfer staring down a fairway CUES: this man knows 五 **Go** (five) words in 英語 ei**go** (English), but he only likes to 語る **kata**ru (talk) about **Golf**; he 言 (says) that he has to stand on a 口 (box) and stare because he has **Cata**racts, and he drinks **Gatari**de instead of Gatorade

436. 試 PRONUNCIATIONS: tame, shi, kokoro MEANINGS: to test, a trial EXAMPLES: 試す tamesu = to attempt; 試験 shiken = examination; 試みる kokoromiru = to attempt DESCRIPTION: on the left, 言(葉) kotoba (words, # 430); on the right, 式 shiki (ceremony, # 249), which resembles a tall woman leaning over a shift key CUES: this tall woman, who prefers **Tall Men**, raises **Sheep**, and has a big **Kokoro** (heart), 試す **tame**su (tries) to leap over 言 (words) during a 式 (ceremony) which is a 試験 **shi**ken (test) for her dance class

437. 訳 PRONUNCIATIONS: wake, yaku MEANINGS: reason, translation EXAMPLES: 訳 wake = reason, interpretation; 言い訳 iiwake = excuse; 通訳 tsuuyaku = interpreter, interpretation DESCRIPTION: on the left, 言(葉) kotoba (words, # 430); on the right, a square eye on long legs; we called this a "watchful eye" when describing 駅 eki (station, # 380), but it could also be considered a "wakeful eye" CUES: the 訳 **wake** (reason) that this **Wake**ful eye is watching these 言 (words) is to check the accuracy of the 通訳 tsuu**yaku** (interpretation) being done for a **Yaku**za (gangster)

438. 議 PRONUNCIATION: gi MEANING: to discuss EXAMPLE: 会議 kaigi = meeting DESCRIPTION: on the left, 言(う) iu (to speak, # 430); at the top right, 羊 hitsuji (sheep, not included in this Catalogue), which has both horns, both ears and all four legs, but is missing its tail; at the lower right, a kneeling guy and a halberd (combination lance and axe), incorporating an X, which represents the missing tail CUE: the purpose of this 会議 kai**gi** (meeting) is to 言 (speak) about the family of **Gee**se that ran off with this 羊 (sheep)'s tail, represented by an X, after the kneeling guy cut it off with his halberd

439. 説 PRONUNCIATIONS: setsu, zetsu[1], zei, to MEANINGS: to explain, opinion EXAMPLES: 説明 setsumei = explanation; 小説 shousetsu = novel; 演説 enzetsu = a speech; 遊説 yuuzei = election campaign; 説く toku = to explain, persuade, preach DESCRIPTION: on the left, 言(う) iu (to speak, # 430); on the right, 兄 ani (older brother, # 420), wearing rabbit ears CUES: this 兄 (older brother), who is wearing rabbit ears, 説明する **setsu**mei suru (explains) and 言 (speaks) about how he **Set** up a **Su**per rabbit farm, with help from some **Za**ny **To**ries

440. 誰 PRONUNCIATION: dare
MEANING: who EXAMPLES: 誰 dare = who
DESCRIPTION: on the left, 言(う) iu (to speak,
430); on the right, a cage CUE: 誰 **dare** (who)
Dares to 言 (speak) from this cage? COMPARE:
難(しい) muzukashii = difficult, # 198

441. 調 PRONUNCIATIONS: chou, shira
MEANINGS: to investigate, condition
EXAMPLES: 調子 choushi = condition;
調べる shiraberu = to check DESCRIPTION:
on the left, 言(う) iu (to speak, # 430); on the
right, a tent; inside the tent, 土 tsuchi (dirt, # 59)
above 口 kuchi (mouth, # 426), which resembles a
box CUES: people 言 (say) that a detective has
been **Cho**sen to 調べる **shira**beru (check) this
box hidden below the 土 (dirt) inside the tent to see
whether it contains **Sh**eep or **R**abbit food
COMPARE: 週 shuu = week, # 346

442. 研 PRONUNCIATIONS: ken, to
MEANINGS: to hone, to sharpen by grinding
EXAMPLES: 研究 kenkyuu = research; 研ぐ
togu = to sharpen, to wash rice DESCRIPTION:
on the left, 石 ishi (stone, # 458); on the right, a tall
person named Ken who is standing on his toes
CUES: **Ken** is a tall researcher who does 研究
kenkyuu (research) into kidney 石 (stones), with
help from Barbie, and this keeps him on his **T**oes

Fire

443. 火 PRONUNCIATIONS: hi, bi[1], ka
MEANING: fire EXAMPLES: 火 hi = fire;
花火 hanabi = fireworks; 火事 kaji = fire;
火曜日 kayoubi = Tuesday
DESCRIPTION: 人 hito (person, # 13) with
flames leaping from both sides
CUES: this 人 (person) got lost in the **H**imalayas
and used a signal 火 **hi** (fire) to **C**all for help

444. 灰 PRONUNCIATIONS: hai, kai
MEANING: ash EXAMPLES: 灰 hai = ash;
灰色 hai'iro = grey; 石灰岩 sekkaigan =
limestone DESCRIPTION: on the upper left, a
lean-to; inside the lean-to, a high 火 hi (fire,
443) CUE: if you light a **H**igh 火 (fire) inside
this lean-to, you will generate 灰 **hai** (ash) and
make the inside of the lean-to 灰色 **hai'**iro (grey),
and the **Kai**ser will get mad

445. 秋 PRONUNCIATIONS: aki, shuu
MEANING: autumn EXAMPLES: 秋 aki =
autumn; 晩秋 banshuu = late fall
DESCRIPTION: on the left, 禾 (a grain plant with
a ripe head); on the right, 火 hi (fire, # 443)
CUES: **Achi**lles visited us in 秋 **aki** (autumn)
to admire this ripe 禾 (grain) and our 火 (fire)-like
leaves, and also to show us his new **Sho**es

446. 焼 PRONUNCIATIONS: ya, shou,
jou[1] MEANING: to burn EXAMPLES: 焼く
yaku = to grill, toast, etc.; 焼き鳥 yakitori =
grilled skewered chicken; 焼却 shoukyaku =
incineration; 芋焼酎 imojouchuu = sweet potato
shochu DESCRIPTION: on the left, 火 hi (fire,
443); on the right, 元 moto (base, # 421),
supporting three pieces of chicken on skewers
CUES: 焼き鳥 **ya**kitori (grilled chicken) is
grilled with this 火 (fire) on a 元 (base) and often
eaten by **Ya**kuza (gangsters) during movie **Sho**ws

447. 赤 PRONUNCIATIONS: aka, ka,
seki MEANING: red EXAMPLES: 赤い akai
= red; 赤ちゃん akachan = baby; 真っ赤
makka = bright red; 赤道 sekidou = equator
DESCRIPTION: at the top, 土 tsuchi (dirt,
59); at the bottom, a fire CUES: this fire under
some 土 (dirt) at the **Aca**demy Awards is 赤い
akai (red), it's about to start a **Ca**r fire, and the
smoke from it is causing a **Se**ki (cough)

COMPARE: 咳 seki = cough, not included in this Catalogue

448. 光 PRONUNCIATIONS: hika, hikari, kou MEANING: light EXAMPLES: 光 hikari = light; 光る hikaru = to shine, glitter, stand out; 日光 nikkou = sunlight; also, 日光 Nikkou = a town in Japan DESCRIPTION: three streams of light emerging from a fire on a sturdy base, similar to 元 moto (base, # 421)

CUES: the Hick Karl and his friend, the Hick Carrie, who were feeling Cold, lit this fire that 光る hikaru (shines) on a sturdy 元 (base)

Foot

449. 足 PRONUNCIATIONS: ashi, a, ta, soku, zoku[1] MEANINGS: leg, foot, to suffice EXAMPLES: 足 ashi = leg or foot; 足立 Adachi = a ward in Tokyo; 足りる tariru = to suffice; 不足 fusoku = insufficient; 満足 manzoku = satisfaction DESCRIPTION: at the bottom left, a foot radical; above the foot, a square that resembles a kneecap, connecting to the foot via a "T" turned on its side, which may represent the Tibia CUES: I tripped on an Ashy ashcan and hurt this 足 ashi (leg), and the Accident 足りた tarita (sufficed) to keep me from going to work at the Tariff office; I then saw an Uber car and kicked water at it to Soak the Uber, but my efforts were 不足 fusoku (insufficient)

450. 走 PRONUNCIATIONS: hashi, sou MEANING: to run EXAMPLES: 走る hashiru = to run; 脱走 dassou = desertion, escape DESCRIPTION: at the bottom, a big foot radical; above the foot, horizontal lines representing knees, hips, and shoulders CUES: after smoking Hashish in the Soviet Union, this guy with big feet could really 走る hashiru (run)

COMPARE: 足 ashi = leg or foot, # 449

451. 徒 PRONUNCIATION: to MEANINGS: follower, pupil EXAMPLES: 生徒 seito = student; 信徒 shinto = follower, believer DESCRIPTION: on the left, a man with a double hat, who resembles 行(く) iku (to go, # 334); on the right, 走(る) hashiru (to run, # 450) CUE: after he finishes his Toast, a 生徒 seito (student) 走 (runs) after his teacher, and they 行 (go) to school

452. 起 PRONUNCIATIONS: o, ki, gi[1] MEANINGS: to get up, to arise EXAMPLES: 起きる okiru = to get up; 起こす okosu = to wake someone up; 起こる okoru = to occur, to happen; 起立する kiritsu suru = to stand up; 縁起 engi = omen, luck

DESCRIPTION: at the left and bottom, 走(る) hashiru (to run, # 450), which incorporates a foot at the bottom; on the right, a snake from Okinawa CUES: if I'm camping in Okinawa and this snake appears at the end of my foot, I 起きる okiru (get up), grab my Keys and 走 (run)

453. 越 PRONUNCIATIONS: ko, e, koshi, etsu MEANINGS: to cross or go over EXAMPLES: 引っ越す hikkosu = to move one's residence; 越える koeru = to go across; 越権 ekken = going beyond authority, abuse of confidence; 三越 Mitsukoshi = name of a department store; 超越する chouetsu suru = to stand out or transcend DESCRIPTION: at the left and bottom, 走(る) hashiru (to run, # 450); on the right, a halberd (a combination of an axe and a lance), belonging to a Coast Guardsman CUES: this Coast Guardsman has 引っ越した hikkoshita (moved his residence), and he 走 (runs) with his halberd, since now he has to 越える koeru (go across) town in order to Embark with his Co-Shipmates, carrying some Etchings from Sudan

454. 題 PRONUNCIATION: dai

MEANINGS: title, topic **EXAMPLES:** 問題 mondai = problem; 題名 daimei = title; 話題 wadai = topic **DESCRIPTION:** at the bottom, a foot radical, which looks like a boat; on the left end of the boat, a lantern; on the right end of the boat, a boatman who is missing his head, as seen in the radical on the right in 頭 atama (head, # 93)

CUE: the 話題 wa**dai** (topic) of today's discussion is this headless boatman who will ferry me across the River Styx after I **Die**; this sounds like a real 問題 mon**dai** (problem)

455. 定 PRONUNCIATIONS: jou, tei, sada MEANINGS: to decide, to be fixed

EXAMPLES: 勘定 kanjou = bill, check, calculation; 予定 yotei = plan; 定年 teinen = retirement age; 定める sadameru = to decide or prescribe **DESCRIPTION:** at the top, a bad haircut; in the middle, a taser weapon; at the bottom, a foot radical **CUES:** **Jo**an of Arc had a 予定 yo**tei** (plan) to mount a **Ta**ser on this foot and hide from **Sadda**m under this bad haircut

Hugging
456. 左 PRONUNCIATIONS: hidari, sa

MEANING: left **EXAMPLES:** 左手 hidari te = left hand; 左折 sasetsu = left turn **DESCRIPTION:** on the left, a hugging person named Robert E. Lee; on the right, 工 kou (crafted object, # 246) **CUES:** when Robert E. Lee makes this 工 (crafted object), he needs to hug it with his 左 **hidari** (left) arm, but that's difficult now, since a **Hide**A**way** bed hit **Lee**'s left arm after a **Sa**xophone player bumped into it

COMPARE: 右 migi = right, # 457

457. 右 PRONUNCIATIONS: migi, u, yuu MEANING: right EXAMPLES: 右側

migigawa = right side; 右折 usetsu = right turn; 左右 sayuu = left and right **DESCRIPTION:** on the left, a hugging person; on the right, 口 kuchi (mouth, # 426) **CUES:** I use my 右 **migi** (right) hand to grasp food and bring it to my 口 (mouth), but some **Mean Gee**se and an **U**ber strike in the **Yu**kon are making it hard for me to focus on eating

COMPARE: 左 hidari = left, # 456; 石 ishi = stone, # 458; 若(い) wakai = young, # 461

458. 石 PRONUNCIATIONS: ishi, seki, shaku, se, koku MEANING: stone

EXAMPLES: 小石 koishi = pebble; 一石 isseki = one stone; 磁石 jishaku = magnet; 石鹸 sekken = soap; 石 koku = a unit of rice, approx. 278 liters **DESCRIPTION:** compared to 右 migi (right, # 457), 石 ishi is missing a vertical line at the top, and it seems that someone may have removed a seat from its roof **CUES:** compared to 右 (right), a seat is missing from the top of this 石 **ishi** (stone), because an **In**donesian **Sh**ip was ordered by a **Se**lfish **K**ing to transport it to a **Sh**ack for a **Se**cretary to sit on while she drinks a **Co**ke

459. 友 PRONUNCIATIONS: yuu, tomo

MEANING: friend **EXAMPLES:** 友人 yuujin = friend; 友達 tomodachi = friend **DESCRIPTION:** on the left, a hugging person; on the right, 又 mata ("again," # 24), but this resembles a simple table **CUES:** my **You**thful 友達 **tomo**dachi (friend) is hugging this 又 (table) that he made; **Tomo**rrow he will make another one for me

460. 有 PRONUNCIATIONS: a, ari, yuu MEANINGS: to exist, to have EXAMPLES:

有る aru = to exist (usually written ある); 有難う arigatou = thank you; 有名 yuumei = famous **DESCRIPTION:** on the left, a hugging person; on the right, 月 tsuki (moon, # 148) **CUES:** **A**rthur, an **Ari**stocrat from the **Yu**kon, symbolically hugs this 有名 **yuu**mei (famous) 月 (moon) which 有る **a**ru (exists), and he says 有難う **ari**gatou (thank you)

461. 若 PRONUNCIATIONS: waka, jaku, nya MEANING: young EXAMPLE: 若い

wakai = young; 若年 jakunen = youth, an early age; 般若 han'nya = prajna, wisdom
DESCRIPTION: at the top, a plant radical; at the bottom, 右 migi (right, # 457)

CUES: when I was 若い **waka**i (young), I played **Whack-A**-mole with **Jack** Nicholson under these bushes on the 右 (right) side of our house, and we whacked the moles with the **Knee** bones of **Ya**ks

462. 存 PRONUNCIATIONS: zon, son

MEANINGS: to sustain, to humbly know or think
EXAMPLES: 存じる zonjiru = to humbly know; 存在 sonzai = existence, presence
DESCRIPTION: on the left, a hugging person, plus an additional vertical line; on the right, 子 ko (child, # 182) CUES: when I'm in the **Zon**e, I hug this 子 (child), who plays games that are made by **Son**y, as I 存じる **zon**jiru (humbly know)

463. 怖 PRONUNCIATIONS: kowa, fu

MEANINGS: dreadful, to be frightened
EXAMPLES: 怖い kowai = afraid, scary; 恐怖 kyoufu = fear, horror DESCRIPTION: on the left, an erect guy who could be a koala; on the upper right, a hugging person; on the lower right, Bo Peep, as seen in 帽(子) boushi (hat, # 243)
CUES: the erect guy on the left is a **Koa**la, and I **Foo**lishly hug my friend Bo Peep because I'm 怖い **kowa**i (scared) COMPARE: (毛)布 moufu = blanket, # 687, which helps us to pronounce this

West

464. 西 PRONUNCIATIONS: nishi, zai, sei, sui MEANING: west EXAMPLES: 西

nishi = west; 東西 touzai = East and West; 西欧 seiou = Western Europe; 西瓜 suika = watermelon DESCRIPTION: at the top, a balcony in Zaire (former name of the Congo) supported by two legs; at the bottom, 四 yon (four, # 6)

CUES: Nietzche lived in this house with 四 (four) sides and high balconies in 西 **nishi** (west) Zaire, where he felt Safer than he did in Sweden
COMPARE: 酒 sake, # 465

465. 酒 PRONUNCIATIONS: ki, sake, zake[1], shu, saka, zaka[1] MEANING: alcohol

EXAMPLES: お神酒 omiki = sake offered to the gods; 酒 sake = alcoholic beverage; 冷酒 hiyazake = cold sake, but this is usually pronounced "reishu"; 日本酒 nihonshu = Japanese sake; 洋酒 youshu = foreign liquor; 酒屋 sakaya = liquor store; 居酒屋 izakaya = a bar or pub
DESCRIPTION: on the left, a water radical, suggesting liquid; on the right, 西 nishi (west, # 464), with an added basement

CUES: while drinking 酒 **sake** and eating **Qui**che in the basement of this house, I **Saw Kay** on the 西 (west) side, so I put on my **Shoe**s and went outside to play **Sakkaa** (soccer)

466. 配 PRONUNCIATIONS: kuba, hai, pai MEANINGS: to distribute, hand out, arrange

EXAMPLES: 配る kubaru = to deliver, distribute, hand out; 宅配便 takuhaibin = home delivery; 心配する shinpai suru = to worry

DESCRIPTION: on the left, 酒 sake (# 465), missing its water radical; on the right, a twisted backwards letter "S"
CUES: a **Cool B**armaid named **Hei**di has brought a **Pie** to this house with a 酒 (sake) cellar, but since no one is at home, she is twisted with 心配 shin**pai** (worry) that it will spoil

Kangaroo

467. 汚 PRONUNCIATIONS: o, yogo, kitana, kega MEANINGS: dirty, soiled
EXAMPLES: 汚水 osui = sewage; 汚い kitanai = dirty; 汚す yogosu = to soil; 汚す kegasu = to sully or disgrace NOTE: both yogosu and kegasu are written 汚す DESCRIPTION: on the left, a water radical; on the right, a kangaroo from oosutorariya (Australia), with a powerful leg for jumping
CUES: this kangaroo from Oosutorariya (Australia) jumps away from 汚水 osui (sewage), causing me to spill Yogurt made from Goat's milk on my Suit and 汚す yogosu (soil) it; the kangaroo also bumps into a Kitten At Night and gets it 汚い kitanai (dirty), and it spills a Kega (keg of) beer

468. 写 PRONUNCIATIONS: utsu, sha, ja¹ MEANING: to copy EXAMPLES: 写す utsusu = to copy; 写真 shashin = photograph; 青写真 aojashin = blueprint DESCRIPTION: at the top, a roof; at the bottom, a kangaroo, up to his calves in water,with a powerful leg for jumping
CUES: this kangaroo flooded the darkroom while trying to 写す utsusu (copy) some 写真 shashin (photos) of people Utilizing Supermarkets, which he wanted to take back to his Shack

469. 考 PRONUNCIATIONS: kanga, kou MEANING: to think thoroughly EXAMPLES: 考える kangaeru = to think; 思考 shikou = consideration, thought DESCRIPTION: compared to 者 mono (person, # 276), this kanji has powerful legs like a kangaroo and, like 者, it plays with scissors CUES: this Kangaroo is a 者 (person) who 考える kangaeru (thinks) about how to Cope with the cuts that he gets from scissors, but he continues to play with them

470. 号 PRONUNCIATION: gou
MEANINGS: to call in a loud voice, number
EXAMPLES: 番号 bangou = number; 信号 shingou = traffic light; 六号車 rokugousha = car number six DESCRIPTION: at the top, 口 kuchi (mouth, # 426); at the bottom, a kangaroo with a powerful leg for kicking, which resembles a soccer player who can score goals CUE: this 口 (mouth) at the top represents a 番号 bangou (number, i.e., the number "0") which this kangaroo soccer player wears on his uniform when he scores Goals

Feathers

471. 弱 PRONUNCIATIONS: yowa, jaku
MEANING: weak EXAMPLES: 弱い yowai = weak; 弱点 jakuten = weak point, weakness
DESCRIPTION: these two radicals represent feathers, reportedly CUES: these two feathers that Your Wife and Jack Nicholson placed next to each other are 弱い yowai (weak)

472. 習 PRONUNCIATIONS: nara, shuu
MEANINGS: to learn, learning by repeating
EXAMPLES: 習う narau = to learn; 練習 renshuu = practice; 習字 shuuji = calligraphy practice DESCRIPTION: at the top, these two radicals represent feathers, reportedly; at the bottom, 白(い) shiroi (white, # 44) CUES: these two feathers plus 白 (white) suggest that a 白 (white) bird was using its feathers to 習う narau (learn) to fly in Nara, until someone threw a Shoe at it

Fish Head

473. 色 PRONUNCIATIONS: iro, shiki, shoku MEANINGS: color, amorous
EXAMPLES: 茶色 chairo = brown; 景色 keshiki = view; 血色 kesshoku = complexion
DESCRIPTION: at the top, a fish head; in the middle, a horizontal 日 hi (day, or sun, # 32), but this looks like two eyes; at the bottom, a snake CUES: this snake with two eyes and a fish head has an 色 iro (color) like Iron; it is sitting up high and has a good 景色 keshiki (view) of a Shiite King, who lives by the Shore in Kuwait

474. 勉 PRONUNCIATION: ben
MEANING: exerting oneself EXAMPLE:
勉強 benkyou = study DESCRIPTION: at the
upper left, a fish head; below this, a horizontal 日
hi (day, or sun, # 32), but this looks like two eyes; at
the lower left, two long tentacles, one of them bent,
possibly belonging to an octopus; at the right, 力
chikara (force or power, # 107)
CUE: this octopus **Ben**ds a tentacle and kneels,
using his 力 (power) of concentration to
勉強する **ben**kyou suru (study)

475. 触 PRONUNCIATIONS: fu, sawa,
shoku MEANINGS: contact, touch, feel
EXAMPLES: 触れる fureru = to touch (usually
unintentional, includes contact with air or electric
current); 触る sawaru = to touch (usually
intentional, not including contact with air or electric
current); 接触する sesshoku suru = to touch or
contact DESCRIPTION: at the upper left, a fish
head; below this, 田 (rice paddy, # 68), on legs,
which resembles a person's body; on the right, 虫
mushi (insect, # 9) CUES: this **F**oolish fish-head
guy is sidling up to 触る **sawa**ru (touch) the 虫
(insect) which he **Saw Wa**lking down the road, but
he will get **Shock**ed by its stinger

Pull

476. 引 PRONUNCIATIONS: hi, in, hiki,
biki[1] MEANING: to pull EXAMPLES: 引く
hiku = to pull; 引っ越す hikkosu = to move;
引力 inryoku = attraction, gravitational pull,
magnetism; 取引 torihiki = business deal;
割引 waribiki = discount DESCRIPTION: on
the left, a bow, reportedly, but this could also be a
twisted hickory tree; on the right, a rope CUES:
since this **H**ickory tree was twisted, I 引いた
hiita (pulled) it down with this rope, but the rope
Injured my skin, and now I have a **Hickey**

477. 張 PRONUNCIATIONS: chou, ha,
pa, ba[1] MEANINGS: to stretch, pull or extend
EXAMPLES: 出張 shutchou = business trip;
張り合う hariau = to compete or contend with;

引っ張る hipparu = to pull; 頑張る
ganbaru = to do one's best DESCRIPTION: on the
left, a bow, reportedly, but this could represent
something twisted; on the right, 長(い) nagai
(long, # 502); together, these two radicals remind us
of a long twisted story
CUES: on 出張 shut**chou** (business trips),
businessmen who are **Cho**sen by their managers sit
around the **Har**bor, beg each other's **Par**don, and tell
長 (long) twisted stories while they 引っ張る
hip**paru** (pull) on their noses
COMPARE: 引(く) hiku = to pull, # 476

478. 強 PRONUNCIATIONS: tsuyo,
kyou, gou, shi MEANINGS: strong, to force
EXAMPLES: 強い tsuyoi = strong; 勉強
benkyou = study; 強引 gouin = coercive, high-
handed; 強いる shi'iru = to force
DESCRIPTION: on the left, a bow, reportedly,
which resembles 引(く) hiku (to pull, # 476); at
the upper right, the katakana character ム mu; at
the lower right, 虫 mushi (insect, # 9), but these two
radicals on the right, taken together, look like a
barbell CUES: my **Tsui**tcase (suitcase) is **Yoi**
(good), but it popped open, and this barbell that I
was carrying in it fell into a hole in **Kyou**to; it will
take a 強い **tsuyo**i (strong) person, or maybe a big
Goat or a **Shee**p, to 引 (pull) it out

479. 風 PRONUNCIATIONS: fuu, fu,
kaze, kaza, ka MEANINGS: wind, manner, style
EXAMPLES: 台風 taifuu = typhoon; 日本風
nihon fuu = Japanese style; 風呂 furo = hot bath;
風 kaze = wind; 風向き kazamuki = wind
direction; 風邪 kaze = upper respiratory infection
DESCRIPTION: the continuous line on the left, top
and right side of this kanji suggests wind, blowing
from left to right; under this line of wind, a 虫
mushi (insect, # 9) is wearing a flat hat and seems to
be dropping into someone's food CUES: when a
台風 tai**fuu** (typhoon) occurs, it creates 風 **kaze**
(wind) which may blow these 虫 (insects) into our
Food or damage the **Ca**zette (cassette) collection
from **Kaza**khstan which we keep in the **Ca**r
COMPARE: 凧 tako = kite, # 767

Man with a Slanted Hat

480. 使 **PRONUNCIATIONS: tsuka, shi**
MEANINGS: to use; servant **EXAMPLES:**
使う tsukau = to use; 使用 shiyou = use,
employment; 大使 taishi = ambassador
DESCRIPTION: on the left, a man with a slanted
hat; on the right, a servant wearing ordinary glasses,
rather than the bifocals seen in 便(利) benri
(convenient), # 481 **CUES:** this man with a slanted
hat 使う **tsuka**u (uses) this servant, who wears
ordinary glasses (not bifocals), and has a **T**suitcase
(suitcase) in his **C**ar, where he keeps fresh **Sheet**s
COMPARE: (兵)士 heishi = soldier, # 66;
仕(様) shiyou = means, method, # 67;
私(用の) shiyou no = private, # 510

481. 便 **PRONUNCIATIONS: tayo, ben,**
bin MEANINGS: service, convenient
EXAMPLES: 便り tayori = news, letter;
便利 benri = convenient; 郵便 yuubin = mail
DESCRIPTION: on the left, a tall Yorkshire man
with a slanted hat; on the right, a servant named Ben
Franklin; compared to 使う tsukau (to use, # 480),
Ben is wearing bifocals, which he invented
CUES: this man with a slanted hat is a **T**all
Yorkshire man, with a servant named **Ben** who
wears bifocals, which are 便利 **ben**ri (convenient)
when reading small print in **Bin**go instructions

482. 作 **PRONUNCIATIONS: tsuku, saku,**
sa MEANINGS: to create or make
EXAMPLES: 作る tsukuru = to make; 作文
sakubun = written composition; 作品 sakuhin =
creation, work of art or literature; 作家 sakka =
writer; 発作 hossa = attack or fit, e.g., 心臓発
作 shinzou hossa = heart attack **DESCRIPTION:**
on the left, a man with a slanted hat; on the right,
reportedly this is a serrated axe, small enough to fit
into a tsuitcase (suitcase) from Kuwait
CUES: this man with a slanted hat is using this
serrated axe that he carried in his **T**suitcase
(suitcase) from **Ku**wait to 作る **tsuku**ru (make) a
作品 **saku**hin (creation), which he will keep in a
Sack whenever he is playing the **S**axophone
COMPARE: 昨(晩) sakuban = last night, # 41

483. 任 **PRONUNCIATIONS: maka, nin**
MEANINGS: to take up a burden; responsibility
EXAMPLES: 任せる makaseru = to entrust;
主任 shunin = foreman **DESCRIPTION:** on the
left, a man with a slanted hat; on the right, 王 ou
(king, # 1077) which looks like pieces of macaroni
arranged in a pattern **CUES:** this man with a
slanted hat will 任せる **maka**seru (entrust)
responsibility for this **Maca**roni to the 主任
shu**nin** (foreman), since he's a **Nin**ja
COMPARE: 住(む) sumu = to reside, # 167

484. 価 **PRONUNCIATIONS: ka, atai**
MEANINGS: value, price **EXAMPLES:** 物価
bukka = price; 価値 kachi = value; 価 atai =
value, price **DESCRIPTION:** on the left, a man
with a slanted hat; on the right, a carry-on suitcase
with its handle extended **CUES:** this man is
Calculating the 物価 buk**ka** (price) of this **Carry**-
on suitcase that **A Thai** guy is selling
COMPARE: 値 atai = value, price, # 571

485. 借 **PRONUNCIATIONS: ka, shaku,**
sha MEANING: to borrow **EXAMPLES:**
借りる kariru = to borrow or rent; 借家
shakuya = rented house; 借金 shakkin = debt
DESCRIPTION: on the left, a man with a slanted
hat; on the right, 昔 mukashi (olden days, # 33),
which looks like a bank teller's window
CUES: in 昔 (the olden days), this man with a
slanted hat stood outside a 昔 (bank teller's
window) to 借りる **ka**riru (borrow) money
which he **C**arried home to his **Shack** in **Sha**nghai

486. 供 **PRONUNCIATIONS: domo, kyou,**
ku, tomo, sona MEANINGS: together, both
EXAMPLES: 子供 kodomo = child; 提供す
る teikyou suru = to offer, provide, sponsor;
供物 kumotsu = offering; お供する otomo
suru = to accompany; 備える sonaeru = to offer
at an altar **DESCRIPTION:** on the left, a man with
a slanted hat; on the right, some bushes balanced on
a dome **CUES:** this man watches as 子供

ko**domo** (children) play in bushes balanced on a **Dome** in **Kyou**to, and he offers them **Kool**-Aid in exchange for getting **Tomo**grams of their **Knees**, or at least some **Sonar** exams

487. 化 PRONUNCIATIONS: ke, ba, ka

MEANING: to change EXAMPLES: 化粧 keshou = makeup; 化かす bakasu = to bewitch or enchant; 化学 kagaku = chemistry; 文化 bunka = culture DESCRIPTION: on the left, a man with a slanted hat; on the right, the katakana character ヒ hi; these two radicals resemble a map of Canada, i.e., on the left, we see a straight west coast, topped by Alaska; on the right, we see Hudson Bay and the Maritime provinces

CUES: **Ke**n creates 化粧 **ke**shou (makeup) for **Ba**rbie at his job in the 化学 **ka**gaku (chemistry) industry in **Ca**nada COMPARE: 科(学) kagaku = science, # 511; 花 hana = flower, # 211

488. 件 PRONUNCIATION: ken

MEANINGS: case, matter, counter for houses EXAMPLES: その件 sono ken = the matter being discussed; 事件 jiken = incident; 四件 yonken = four houses DESCRIPTION: on the left, a man with a slanted hat named Ken; on the right, 牛 ushi (cow, # 205) CUES: this man with a slanted hat named **Ken** investigates a 事件 ji**ken** (incident) at the **Ken**tucky Derby involving Barbie's 牛 (cow)

489. 夜 PRONUNCIATIONS: yoru, yo, ya

MEANING: night EXAMPLES: 夜 yoru = night; 夜中 yonaka = middle of the night; 今夜 konya = tonight DESCRIPTION: at the top, a roof with a chimney; at the lower left, a man with a slanted hat; at the lower right, this appears to be a yoke designed to fit around the neck of a yak CUES: this man eats **Yo**gurt under his **Roof** at 夜 **yo**ru (night), and then he repairs this **Yo**ke for his **Yak** COMPARE: 宿(題) shukudai = homework, # 491

490. 側 PRONUNCIATIONS: gawa, soba, soku MEANINGS: side, close by EXAMPLES: 右側 migigawa = right side; 側に soba ni = close to; however, 側 soba is usually written そば, to avoid confusion with gawa; 側面 sokumen = side, aspect DESCRIPTION: on the left, a man with a slanted hat; in the middle, 貝 kai (shell, # 83); on the right, the katakana character リ Ri CUES: this man with a slanted hat and リ Ri are on opposite 側 **gawa** (sides) of 貝 (shell), but there is a **Ga**udy **Wa**gon 側に **soba** ni (close by), at which they are both able to buy **Soba** (noodles) **Soa**ked in broth

491. 宿 PRONUNCIATIONS: shuku, yado, juku MEANING: inn EXAMPLES: 宿題 shukudai = homework; 宿 yado = inn; 新宿 Shinjuku = a ward in Tokyo DESCRIPTION: at the top, a bad haircut; at the lower left, a man with a slanted hat; at the lower right, 百 hyaku (hundred, # 47) CUES: 百 (one hundred) guys with bad haircuts showed up to help this man with a slanted hat do his 宿題 **shuku**dai (homework); the guys, who are wearing **Shoes** from **Ku**wait, are staying at the 宿 **yado** (inn), in the **Ya**rd by the **Do**or, next to the **Juke**box COMPARE: 夜 yoru = night, # 489

492. 係 PRONUNCIATIONS: kakari, kei, kaka MEANING: person in charge EXAMPLES: 係 kakari = person in charge; 関係 kankei = relationship; 係り kakari = duty DESCRIPTION: on the left, a man with a slanted hat; on the right, a 糸 (skeet shooter, # 219), with a cape draped across his head

CUES: this man with a slanted hat is a 係員 **kakari** in (person in charge), and he shows that he **Can Carry** his weight in his 関係 kan**kei** (relationship) with the 糸 (skeet shooter) by giving him a **Cape** and some **Caca**o beans

Lean-to

493. 店 PRONUNCIATIONS: mise, ten
MEANINGS: shop, store
EXAMPLES: 店 mise = store; 店員 ten'in = store clerk; 喫茶店 kissaten = coffee shop
DESCRIPTION: on the upper left, a lean-to; inside the lean-to, a well with a handle
CUES: this is a Miserable 店 **mise** (store) under a lean-to, where people come to buy well water from a 店員 **ten**'in (store clerk) who also plays Tennis

494. 広 PRONUNCIATIONS: hiro, biro, kou MEANINGS: spacious, wide EXAMPLES:
広い hiroi = wide, spacious; 背広 sebiro = man's suit; 広告 koukoku = advertisement
DESCRIPTION: on the upper left, a lean-to, with a small sign on the top; inside the lean-to, the katakana character ム mu (the sound made by a cow) CUES: this ム (cow) has a 広い **hiro**i (wide and spacious) lean-to; the sign at the top says that it is intended for Heroes who eat a lot of Bean Rolls (burritos) and drink Cola

495. 庭 PRONUNCIATIONS: niwa, tei
MEANING: garden EXAMPLES: 庭 niwa = garden; 裏庭 uraniwa = back yard; 庭園 teien = formal Japanese garden DESCRIPTION: on the upper left, a lean-to; inside the lean-to, the radical at the lower left is different from the snail radical seen in many kanji, e.g., 週 shuu (week, # 346); we can call it a "3x snail," since it consists of a 3 intersected at the bottom to form an X; let's also call it a wagon, since an 王 ou (king, # 1077) is riding in it
CUES: this 王 (king) likes neon lighting, and he rides in his Neon-lit Wagon under a lean-to in his 庭 **niwa** (garden), where he is guarded with Tasers

496. 席 PRONUNCIATIONS: se, seki
MEANING: seat EXAMPLES: 寄席 yose = an entertainment hall; 席 seki = seat; 出席 shusseki suru = to attend; 座席 zaseki = the seat of a chair DESCRIPTION: on the upper left, a lean-to; inside the lean-to, an infant seat resting on a three-legged stool which resembles a Segway
CUES: before feeding the baby, I put him in this infant 席 **seki** (seat) on top of a Segway in this lean-to, but he has a Seki (cough) and can't eat
COMPARE: 両(方) ryouhou = both, # 579; 座(る) suwaru = to sit on a zabuton, # 497; 咳 seki = cough, not included in this Catalogue

497. 座 PRONUNCIATIONS: za, suwa
MEANINGS: to sit, seat EXAMPLES:
座布団 zabuton = floor cushion for sitting; 口座 kouza = account (bank); 座る suwaru = to sit on a zabuton DESCRIPTION: on the upper left, a lean-to; inside the lean-to, 土 tsuchi (dirt, # 59); on each side of the upper deck of 土 (dirt), a person is sitting CUES: if you 座る **suwa**ru (sit) on this 土 (dirt) in a restaurant in Zambia, they serve you Soup and Water
COMPARE: 席 seki = seat, # 496

498. 度 PRONUNCIATIONS: do, tabi, taku MEANINGS: time, degree EXAMPLES:
今度 kondo = this time or next time; 百度 hyakudo = 100 degrees; 転勤の度 tenkin no tabi = transfer's occasion; 支度 shitaku = preparation DESCRIPTION: on the upper left, a lean-to belonging to Dorothy; inside the lean-to, a pot of food over 又 mata ("again," # 24), but this resembles a simple table
CUES: 毎度 mai**do** (every time) Dorothy prepares a pot of food for the Wizard of Oz in her lean-to, she also feeds it to her Tabby cat at this 又 (table), together with Tap water and Kool-Aid

499. 渡 PRONUNCIATIONS: wata, to
MEANINGS: to cross, to hand over EXAMPLES:
渡る wataru = to cross; 渡す watasu = to hand over; 渡米 tobei = going to America
DESCRIPTION: on the left, a water radical; on the right, 度 do (time, # 498) CUES: every 度 (time) that Napoleon would 渡る **wata**ru (cross) this water at Waterloo, he had to 渡す **wata**su (hand) money to a Toll collector

500. 岸 PRONUNCIATIONS: gan, kishi

MEANINGS: beach, shore **EXAMPLES:** 海岸 kaigan = beach; 岸 kishi = beach, shore **DESCRIPTION:** at the top, 山 yama (mountain, # 146); below 山, a kitschy lean-to; inside the lean-to, a telephone pole **CUES: Gand**alf visits a 海岸 kai**gan** (beach) under this 山 (mountain), and talks on the telephone in a **Kitschy** lean-to

Hair

501. 髪 PRONUNCIATIONS: kami, hatsu, *ga* MEANING: hair EXAMPLES: 髪 kami = hair; 白髪 hakuhatsu = white or grey hair; 白髪 shiraga = white or grey hair NOTE:

hakuhatsu and shiraga are both written 白

DESCRIPTION: on the upper left, 長(い) nagai (long, # 502); on the upper right, three lines suggesting hair strands; at the bottom, 友(達) tomodachi (friend, # 459)

CUES: this 友 (friend), who is a **Cam**bodian Immigrant, has 長 (long) 髪 **kami** (hair) which she covers with **Hats** that she bought in **Gaza**

COMPARE: 紙 kami = paper, # 221; 神 kami = god, # 273; (女)将 okami = landlady, # 374

502. 長 PRONUNCIATIONS: naga, chou

MEANINGS: long, chief, principal **EXAMPLES:** 長い nagai = long; 社長 shachou = company president **DESCRIPTION:** at the top, long flowing hair; at the bottom; the letters L and y which remind us of "friendly" **CUES:** this friend**Ly** 社長 sha**chou** (president) with long hair owns **Naga**ina, a 長い **naga**i (long) cobra who was **Cho**sen to represent her tribe

COMPARE: (出)張 shutchou = business trip, # 477; 良(い) yoi = good, # 303

Scorpion

503. 地 PRONUNCIATIONS: ji, chi

MEANINGS: ground, soil **EXAMPLES:** 地震 jishin = earthquake; 地下鉄 chikatetsu = subway **DESCRIPTION:** on the left, 土 tsuchi (dirt, # 59); on the right, this is reportedly a scorpion, with a long stinging tail **CUES:** **J**ittery scorpions live in the 土 (dirt) under the 地 **chi** (ground), where they eat **Chee**se **COMPARE:** 池 ike = pond, # 504; 他 hoka = another, # 505

504. 池 PRONUNCIATIONS: ike, chi

MEANING: pond **EXAMPLES:** 池 ike = pond; 乾電池 kandenchi = battery **DESCRIPTION:** on the left, a water radical (see # 12); on the right, this is reportedly a scorpion, with a long stinging tail **CUES:** scorpions lived under the water near the 池 **ike** (pond) on **Ike's** (Eisenhower's) farm and ate his **Chee**se **COMPARE:** 地 chi = ground, # 503; 他 hoka = another, # 505

505. 他 PRONUNCIATIONS: hoka, ta

MEANING: others **EXAMPLES:** 他の hoka no = another (undefined) object; 他人 ta'nin = other people, outsiders **DESCRIPTION:** on the left, a man with a slanted hat; on the right, this is reportedly a scorpion, with a long stinging tail **CUES:** ordinary men with flat hats ride in unmarked vehicles, but 他の **hoka** no (other) men with slanted hats ride in **Hopped-up Ca**rs marked with scorpion decals, which is why they are considered 他人 **ta**nin (outsiders), in spite of their nice **Tans**

COMPARE: 外(に) hoka ni = besides, # 163; 別(の) betsu no = another (defined) object, # 561; 地 chi = ground, # 503; 池 ike = pond, # 504

Skirts

506. 春 PRONUNCIATIONS: haru, shun MEANING: spring

EXAMPLE: 春休み haruyasumi = spring break; 晩春 banshun = late spring DESCRIPTION: at the top, a 人 hito (person, # 13), with the number 三 san (three, # 3) inscribed across it; at the bottom, 日 hi (sun, # 32), which appears to be under the skirts of 人 CUES: during the first 春 **haru** (spring) when King **Ha**rold **Ru**led, many 人 (people) gave birth to 三つ子 mitsugo (triplets), with 日 (sun)-like (i.e., sunny) dispositions, but the king **Shun**ned those babies

507. 寒 PRONUNCIATIONS: samu, kan MEANING: cold atmosphere

EXAMPLES: 寒い samui = cold atmosphere; 寒気 kanki = a chill, but this can also be pronounced "samuke" DESCRIPTION: at the top, a bad haircut; under the roof, a samurai's wife, wearing a corset, with legs spread apart, sheltering some children under her skirt CUES: when it's 寒い **samu**i (cold), this **Samu**rai's wife, who lives in **Ca**nada and has a bad haircut, gathers her children under her skirt

East

508. 東 PRONUNCIATIONS: higashi, tou MEANING: east

EXAMPLES: 東 higashi = east; 東京 toukyou = Tokyo DESCRIPTION: 日 hi (sun, # 32) seen behind a 木 ki (tree, # 118) in the morning, telling us that this tree is east of us CUES: in a **High Gash** on the 東 **higashi** (east) side of this 木 (tree) in 東京 **tou**kyou (Tokyo), there is a family of tree **Toa**ds that watches the 日 (sun) rise COMPARE: 乗(る) noru = to get aboard or ride, # 509; 果(物) kudamono = fruit, # 587, in which a 田 (rice paddy) appears *above* a 木 (tree)

509. 乗 PRONUNCIATIONS: jou, no MEANINGS: to ride, to get aboard

EXAMPLES: 乗客 joukyaku = passenger; 乗る noru = to get aboard or ride DESCRIPTION: compared to 東 higashi (east, # 508), 乗 has a roof on top, suggesting a vehicle with a roof; the structure overlapping the 木 ki (tree, # 118) in 乗 has protrusions on both sides, suggesting that it is a vehicle, not the sun that is seen behind the tree in 東 (east) CUES: **Joa**n of Arc is waiting because she wants to be a 乗客 **jou**kyaku (passenger) on the vehicle behind this 木 (tree), but when she tries to 乗る **no**ru (board), there is **No** Room

Grain Plants

510. 私 PRONUNCIATIONS: watakushi, watashi, shi MEANINGS: I, personal, private

EXAMPLES: 私 watakushi = I; 私 watashi = I; 私用の shiyou no = private DESCRIPTION: on the left, 禾 (a grain plant with a ripe head); on the right, the katakana character ム mu, which resembles an arm bent to claim what belongs to me CUES: 私 **watakushi** (I) am a **Wa**shington **Takushii** (taxi) driver, and I use a lawyer named **Wa**llace to create **Tax Shi**elds for my **Shee**p farm, where I ム (bend my arm) to clutch this 禾 (ripe grain) that is mine COMPARE: 仕(様) shiyou = means, method, # 67; 使(用) shiyou = use, employment, # 480; 払(う) harau = to buy, # 591

511. 科 PRONUNCIATION: ka MEANINGS: section, category

EXAMPLES: 化学 kagaku = science; 科学者 kagakusha = scientist; 教科書 kyoukasho = textbook; 歯科 shika = dentistry DESCRIPTION: on the left, 禾 (a grain plant with a ripe head), but let's call this a scientist with a flat-top haircut; on the right, a shelf holding two bottles of calcium CUE: this 科学者 **ka**gakusha (scientist) with a flat-top haircut searches this shelf for some **Ca**lcium to use in his research COMPARE: 化(学) kagaku = chemistry, # 487; 料(理) ryouri = cuisine, # 512; 課 ka = section, # 587

512. 料 PRONUNCIATION: ryou
MEANINGS: food, fee, provisions
EXAMPLES: 料理 ryouri = cuisine; 無料 muryou = free of charge; 料金 ryoukin = fee
DESCRIPTION: on the left, 米 kome (uncooked rice, # 326), but this resembles Pope Leo, a pet owner with messy hair; on the right, a shelf holding two cans of food   CUE: Pope Leo, a fuzzy-haired pet owner, is about to open one of two cans of pet 料理 ryouri (cuisine) on this shelf   COMPARE: 科(学) kagaku = science, # 511

513. 和 PRONUNCIATIONS: wa, yawa, nago, o, *yori, to*   MEANING: harmony
EXAMPLES: 和食 washoku = Japanese food; 温和 onwa = mild, calm, gentle; 和らぐ yawaragu = to soften or become less severe; 和む nagomu = to be softened, to calm down; 和尚 oshou = Buddhist priest; 日和 hiyori = weather, climatic conditions; 大和 yamato = ancient Japan
DESCRIPTION: on the left, 禾 (a grain plant with a ripe head); on the right, 口 kuchi (mouth, # 426), suggesting eating   CUES: when this 禾 (grain plant) gets ripe, we eat 和食 washoku (Japanese food) served from a Wagon, experience 平和 heiwa (peace), Yawn and Wash the dishes, but sometimes we are bothered by Nagging Ghosts from Old times who claim that Yogi's can Lead by wiggling their Toes

Capital
514. 京 PRONUNCIATIONS: kyou, kei
MEANING: capital   EXAMPLES: 京都 kyouto = Kyoto; 東京 toukyou = Tokyo; 京阪 keihan = Kyoto-Osaka   DESCRIPTION: a castle with a roof and a chimney, set on a hill   CUES: the Key that the Yodeler gave me fits this castle on a hill in 京都 kyouto (Kyoto), which features a Cave underground   COMPARE: 涼(しい) suzushii = cool, # 515

515. 涼 PRONUNCIATIONS: ryou, suzu
MEANINGS: cool   EXAMPLE: 涼風 ryoufuu = a cool breeze; 涼しい suzushii = cool
DESCRIPTION: on the left, a water radical; on the right, 京 kyou (capital, # 514)
CUES: when it rains in the 京 (capital), it gets 涼しい suzushii (cool), and it's a good time for Pope Leo to fry some of Superman's Zucchini

516. 景 PRONUNCIATIONS: ke, kei
MEANINGS: fine view, scene
EXAMPLES: 景色 keshiki = view, scenery; 風景 fuukei = view, scenery, landscape
DESCRIPTION: at the top, 日 hi (sun, # 32); at the bottom, 京 kyou (capital, # 514)
CUES: when the 日 (sun) shines above the 京 (capital), the 景色 keshiki (scenery) is lovely, and we drink from a Keg provided by our Shiite King and eat Cake

Tsutomeru
517. 勤 PRONUNCIATIONS: tsuto, kin
MEANINGS: to be employed, to serve
EXAMPLES: 勤める tsutomeru = to be employed; 通勤する tsuukin suru = to commute to work; 出勤する shukkin suru = to attend work   DESCRIPTION: at the upper left, a plant radical (see # 43); at the lower left, a sincere man wearing glasses; on the right, 力 chikara (force, # 107)   CUES: this sincere man wearing glasses with plants dangling over his head Tsuki Tomeru (moon parks) his moon buggy at the place where he 勤めている tsutomete iru (is being employed), and he expends a lot of 力 (force) taking care of plants at a moon Kindergarten
COMPARE: 務(める) tsutomeru = to discharge one's duty, # 518; 努(める) tsutomeru = to make an effort, # 519; 野(菜) yasai = vegetable, # 545; 漢(字) kanji = Chinese character, # 197; 難(しい) muzukashii = difficult, # 198

518. 務 PRONUNCIATIONS: **mu, tsuto**
MEANING: to discharge one's duty **EXAMPLES:**
公務員 koumuin = public servant; 事務所
jimusho = office; 務める tsutomeru = to
discharge one's duty **DESCRIPTION:** this is a
portrait of the workers at an office on the moon: at
the upper left, the katakana character マ ma,
representing Ma (mother); at the lower left, a barbed
nail; at the upper right, a dancer with a ponytail; at
the lower right, 力 chikara (force, # 107) **CUES:**
マ (Ma), a guy with a barbed wit, a dancer, and a
guy with 力 (force) work at a 事務所 ji**mu**sho
(office) on the **Moon**, where they **Tsuki Tomeru**
(moon park) their moon buggies and then **tsuto**meru
務める (discharge their duties) **COMPARE:**
勤(める) tsutomeru = to be employed, # 517;
努(める) tsutomeru = to make an effort, # 519

519. 努 PRONUNCIATIONS: **tsuto, do**
MEANING: to try hard **EXAMPLES:** 努める
tsutomeru = to make an effort; 努力 doryoku =
effort **DESCRIPTION:** at the upper left, 女 onna
(female, # 235); at the upper right, 又 mata
("again," # 24), but this resembles a table where
doughnuts are made; at the bottom, 力 ryoku (force,
107) **CUES:** this 女 (female) **Tsuki Tomeru**
(moon parks) her moon buggy and 努める
tsutomeru (makes an effort) for her job on the moon,
where she expends 努力 d**o**ryoku (effort) making
Doughnuts on a 又 (table) **COMPARE:**
勤(める) tsutomeru = to be employed, # 517;
務(める) tsutomeru = to discharge one's duty,
518; 怒(る) okoru = to get angry, # 319

Pleasant
520. 楽 PRONUNCIATIONS: **tano, gaku,
raku, *ra, gura*** MEANINGS: happy, enjoyable,
without difficulty **EXAMPLES:** 楽しい
tanoshii = pleasant; 音楽 ongaku = music; 楽
raku = comfort, pleasure, relief; 楽観 rakkan =

optimism; 神楽 kagura = sacred Shinto music and
dance **DESCRIPTION:** a tall Norwegian has
installed a loudspeaker at the top of a 木 ki (tree,
118), and music is emerging from it
CUES: a loudspeaker which a **T**all **N**orwegian has
mounted on this 木 (tree) plays 楽しい **tano**shii
(pleasant) 音楽 on**gaku** (music) for **Gaku**sei
(students) during **Rack**etball games at a **Ra**nch,
where they play with **Goofy Ra**dicals
COMPARE: 薬 kusuri = medicine, # 521; 絡
raku = contact, # 230; 落(語) rakugo = Japanese
comic story telling, # 526

521. 薬 PRONUNCIATIONS: **kusuri,
gusuri[1], ya, yaku** MEANINGS: medicine,
pharmaceutical **EXAMPLES:** 薬 kusuri =
medicine; 眠り薬 nemurigusuri = sleeping
medicine; 薬局 yakkyoku = pharmacy; 薬品
yakuhin = medicine, drug **DESCRIPTION:** at the
top, a plant radical (see # 43); at the bottom,
楽(しい) tanoshii (pleasant, # 520) **CUES:** 薬
kusuri (medicines), which a doctor will prescribe
after a **Cursory** exam, come from plants like **Ya**ms
and sometimes have 楽 (pleasant) side-effects, such
as causing people to **Yak** (talk) too much

Dancer
522. 夏 PRONUNCIATIONS: **natsu, ka,
ge** MEANING: summer **EXAMPLES:** 夏 natsu
= summer; 初夏 shoka = early summer; 夏至
geshi = summer solstice **DESCRIPTION:** at the
top, a radical similar to 百 hyaku (hundred, # 47),
but with one additional horizontal line; like 百, this
resembles a limousine with an antenna, seen from the
back; at the bottom, a dancer with a ponytail
CUES: in 夏 **natsu** (summer), this dancer with a
ponytail wears a **Nat**ty **Suit** and is driven in a
limousine **Ca**r to **Ge**ttysburg
COMPARE: 愛 ai = love, # 523

523. 愛 PRONUNCIATIONS: ai, me, mana, ito MEANING: love EXAMPLES:
愛しています ai shite imasu = I love you;
愛情 aijou = love; 愛でる mederu = to love or admire; 愛弟子 manadeshi = favorite student;
愛しい itoshii = lovely, dear, beloved
DESCRIPTION: at the top, the upper portion of 受(ける) ukeru (to take an exam, # 577), which resembles a cloth covering three exam booklets on a tablecloth; in the middle, 心 kokoro (heart, # 306); at the bottom, a dancer with a ponytail CUE: this dancer with a ponytail is an Ice dancer from Mexico who studies Management, and eats Eels and Tomatoes, and when she 受 (takes) her exams, she puts a lot of 心 (heart) into them because of the 愛情 **ai**jou (love) that she feels for knowledge
COMPARE: 夏 natsu = summer, # 522

524. 客 PRONUNCIATIONS: kyaku, kaku MEANINGS: guest, customer
EXAMPLES: お客 okyaku = honorable guest; 観客 kankyaku = audience; 乗客 joukyaku = passenger; 旅客 ryokaku = passenger, traveler
DESCRIPTION: at the top, a bad haircut; in the middle, a leaping dancer with a ponytail; at the bottom, a box CUE: this dancer with a ponytail, who has a bad haircut, leaps over a box of Kool-Aid for a 客 **kyaku** (customer) who is a Kayaker named Karl the Kool-Aid vendor COMPARE: (連)絡 renraku = contact, # 230; (道)路 douro = road, # 525; 各(駅) kakueki = each station, # 1033, which helps us to pronounce this

525. 路 PRONUNCIATIONS: ro, ji
MEANING: road EXAMPLE: 道路 douro = road; 旅路 tabiji = journey DESCRIPTION: on the left, a square head above 正(しい) tadashii (correct, # 174), suggesting a correct gentleman, as seen in 踊(る) odoru (to dance, # 366); on the right, a dancer with a ponytail leaping over a box, as seen in 客 kyaku (customer, # 524)
CUES: this 正 (correct) gentleman and this dancer with a ponytail who leaps over boxes are Roaming on a 道路 dou**ro** (road), looking for a Jeep
COMPARE: 絡 raku = contact, # 230; 落(す) otosu = to drop, # 526

526. 落 PRONUNCIATIONS: o, raku MEANINGS: to fall or drop EXAMPLES:
落ちる ochiru = to fall; 落とす otosu = to knock down or drop; 落語 rakugo = Japanese comic story telling DESCRIPTION: at the top, a plant radical (see # 43); on the lower left, a water radical (see # 12); on the lower right, a dancer with a ponytail, leaping over a box of old cheese CUES: when this dancer jumps over a box of Old Cheese to escape a flood, her head Rakes some leaves and 落とす **o**tosu (knocks them down) so that they 落ちる **o**chiru (fall), and her toes Rake the box as well, scratching it
COMPARE: (連)絡 renraku = contact, # 230; 楽 raku = comfort, pleasure, relief, # 520; 客 kyaku = customer, # 524; 路 ro = road, # 525

527. 復 PRONUNCIATIONS: fuku, puku[1], fu MEANINGS: again, to repeat EXAMPLES:
復習 fukushuu = review; 回復 kaifuku = recovery; 反復 hanpuku = repetition;
復活 fukkatsu = revival, rebirth, restoration
DESCRIPTION: this is a pleasant scene from Fukuoka: on the left, a man in a double hat, who is a therapist; at the top right, a crutch; at the middle right, 日 hi (sun, # 32); at the bottom right, a dancer with a ponytail
CUE: in Fukuoka, this injured dancer works with this therapist; she uses crutches, she sits in the 日 (sun), she eats good Food, and she experiences 回復 kai**fuku** (recovery)

528. 優 **PRONUNCIATIONS: yasa, yuu, sugu MEANINGS:** actor, excellent, graceful **EXAMPLES:** 優しい yasashii = kind; 優秀 yuushuu = excellent; 優勝 yuushou = victory; 優れる sugureru = to excel **DESCRIPTION:** on the left, a man with a slanted hat; at the top right, a radical that looks like 百 hyaku (hundred, # 47) but with one more horizontal line, resembling a limousine with an antenna; at the middle right, 心 kokoro (heart, # 306); at the bottom right, a youthful dancer with a ponytail **CUES:** this man with a slanted hat is 優しい **yasa**shii (kind), he wears a **Y**ankee **Sa**sh, he rides in a 優秀な **yuu**shuu na (excellent) limousine, he acts from his 心 (heart), his girlfriend is a **Yo**uthful dancer with a ponytail, and they will **Soo**n buy a **Goo**se

Twisted

529. 弟 **PRONUNCIATIONS: otouto, dai, tei, de MEANING:** younger brother **EXAMPLES:** 弟 otouto = younger brother; 兄弟 kyoudai = sibling; 子弟 shitei = younger people; 弟子 deshi = disciple, apprentice **DESCRIPTION:** younger brother, wearing two antennae on his head, appears to have twisted himself around a 木 ki (tree, # 118), which is missing a branch on the lower right **CUES:** this 弟 **otouto** (younger brother) eats only **O**ld **T**oma**T**oes, which is a strange **Di**et, and he has twisted himself around a 木 (tree) which he wants to make into a **T**able for a **De**butante **COMPARE:** 第 dai = order, number, # 530, which helps us to pronounce this

530. 第 **PRONUNCIATION: dai MEANING:** order **EXAMPLES:** 第三課 daisanka = section number three; 次第に shidai ni = gradually; 次第で shidai de = depending on **DESCRIPTION:** at the top, 竹 take (bamboo, # 134), which resembles two clamps; at the bottom, 弟 otouto (younger brother, # 529), without his antennae **CUE:** this 弟 (younger brother) has two

竹 (bamboo) clamps in his hair, indicating that he is 第二 **dai** ni (Number Two) in line at Weight Watchers; he wants to go on a **Di**et, and he will get to the front of the queue 次第に shi**dai** ni (gradually) **COMPARE:** (切)符 kippu = ticket, # 133; 笑(う) warau = to laugh, # 199

531. 沸 **PRONUNCIATIONS: wa, fu MEANINGS:** to seethe, boil **EXAMPLES:** 沸く waku = to boil, intransitive; 沸かす wakasu = to boil, transitive; 沸騰する futtou suru = to boil **DESCRIPTION:** on the left, a water radical; on the right, twisted radiator pipes **CUES:** **Wat**er is **C**ool before it enters these twisted pipes, but then it 沸く **wa**ku (boils) and cooks our **F**ood

Deep Inside

532. 奥 **PRONUNCIATIONS: oku, ou MEANING:** deep inside **EXAMPLES:** 奥の方 oku no hou = toward the back; 奥さん okusan = someone else's wife; 奥義 ougi = secrets, mysteries **DESCRIPTION:** a box containing 米 kome (uncooked rice, # 326) on top of a two-legged table **CUES:** an 奥さん **oku**san (honorable wife) who went to **O**klahoma **U**niversity stores 米 (rice) by placing it 奥の方 **oku** no hou (toward the back) of this **O**ak box on two legs **COMPARE:** 歯 ha = tooth, # 533

533. 歯 **PRONUNCIATIONS: ha, ba, shi MEANING:** tooth **EXAMPLES:** 歯 ha = tooth; 虫歯 mushiba = decayed tooth; 歯科 shika = dentistry **DESCRIPTION:** at the top, 止(める) tomeru (to stop, # 173); at the bottom, 米 kome (uncooked rice, # 326), in a box; together these radicals resemble irregular teeth arising from a gum containing dental roots **CUES:** my two 歯 **ha** (teeth) can be seen above this gum line, with the roots below, and they are rather irregular, since my false 歯 **ha** (teeth) are in the **Ha**ll at a **Ba**r, where my **Shee**pdog left them **COMPARE:** 奥(さん) okusan = someone else's wife, # 532

Oil Derrick

534. 歌 PRONUNCIATIONS: **ka, uta**
MEANINGS: to sing, a song EXAMPLES:
歌手 kashu = singer ; 歌う utau = to sing
DESCRIPTION: on the left, two song sheets hanging from racks; on the right, an oil derrick from Utah CUES: this oil derrick is a 歌手 **ka**shu (singer) who likes to eat **Ca**shew nuts, and she reads from a music stand with two song sheets when she 歌う **uta**u (sings) in **Ut**ah

535. 欲 PRONUNCIATIONS: **ho, yoku**
MEANINGS: greed, wanting more EXAMPLES:
欲しい hoshii = to desire ; 欲張り yokubari = greed; 食欲 shokuyoku = appetite
DESCRIPTION: at the upper left, some droplets of water; at the lower left, a yoku (well) made house; on the right, an oil derrick CUES: this oil derrick 欲しい **ho**shii (desires) a **H**orse that she saw on a **S**hip, as well as this **Yoku** (well) made house, which she is drooling over

536. 次 PRONUNCIATIONS: **shi, tsugi, ji, tsu** MEANING: next EXAMPLES: 次第に shidai ni = gradually; 次に tsugi ni = next; 次回に jikai ni = next time; 取り次ぐ toritsugu = to convey or transmit DESCRIPTION: on the left, a water radical; on the right, an oil derrick CUES: this oil derrick is trying to pump this water, but a **S**heep herder spilled **Ts**oup (soup) into its **Ge**ars; 次に **tsugi** ni (next), a **J**eep driver wearing a **Ts**uit (suit) will try to get it working again

537. 吹 PRONUNCIATIONS: **fu, sui**
MEANINGS: to blow, to breathe EXAMPLE:
吹く fuku = to blow, breathe, whistle; 吹奏楽 suisougaku = music from wind instruments
DESCRIPTION: on the left, 口 kuchi (mouth, # 426); on the right, an oil derrick in Fukuoka CUES: in **Fu**kuoka, this oil derrick drinks oil and then 吹く **fu**ku (blows) it out through its 口 (mouth), because it isn't **Sw**eet enough
COMPARE: 吸(う) suu = to suck, # 427; 服 fuku = clothes, # 150; 復(習) fukushuu = review, # 527

Platform

538. 台 PRONUNCIATIONS: **dai, tai**
MEANING: platform EXAMPLES: 台 dai = platform; 台所 daidokoro = kitchen; 二台 nidai = two machines, cars etc.; 台風 taifuu = typhoon DESCRIPTION: at the top, the katakana character ム mu (the sound made by a cow); at the bottom 口 kuchi (mouth, # 426), but this could be a platform CUES: this ム (cow) rests on a 台 **dai** (platform); she is on a **D**iet, and she is **T**ired of it

539. 治 PRONUNCIATIONS: **nao, chi, osa, ji** MEANINGS: to govern, control, cure EXAMPLES: 治す naosu = to heal; 治る naoru = to recover from illness; 治安 chian = safety; 治める osameru = to govern or reign; 政治 seiji = politics DESCRIPTION: on the left, a water radical; on the right, 台 dai (platform, # 538), which consists of ム mu (the sound made by a cow) above a 口 kuchi (mouth, # 426)
CUES: **Nao**mi 治した **nao**shita (cured) this ム (cow) on a platform **Ch**eaply by mixing medicine with water and squirting it into its 口 (mouth), but **Osa**ma bin Laden **Je**ered her efforts
COMPARE: 直(す) naosu = to correct, repair or restore, # 570

540. 始 PRONUNCIATIONS: **haji, shi**
MEANING: to begin EXAMPLES: 始める hajimeru = to begin; 開始する kaishi suru = to begin DESCRIPTION: on the left, 女 onna (female, # 235); on the right; 台 dai (stand, # 538)
CUES: this 女 (female) leaves her **H**at in her **J**eep and 始める **haji**meru (begins) her job by approaching the 台 (stand) where she must examine **S**heep COMPARE: 初(めて) hajimete = for the first time, # 104

Hanging Bucket

541. 甘 **PRONUNCIATIONS: ama, kan**
MEANING: sweet **EXAMPLES:** 甘い amai =
sweet; 甘味所 kanmidokoro = a cafe featuring
Japanese-style sweets **DESCRIPTION:** a bucket
hanging from a rod, half-full of liquid
CUES: **Ama**nda bought this half-full bucket of
甘い **ama**i (sweet) molasses and made **Candy**

542. 世 **PRONUNCIATIONS: se, yo, sei**
MEANINGS: a world, a generation **EXAMPLES:**
世界 sekai = the world; 世話をする sewa
wo suru = to take care of; 世の中 yo no naka =
life, society, world; 世紀 seiki = century
DESCRIPTION: a bucket hanging from a rod
supported by a stand **CUES:** since the 世界 **se**kai
(world) is hanging in this bucket and might fall any
Second, people are consulting **Yo**gis to find out how
to keep it **Sa**fe

543. 葉 **PRONUNCIATIONS: ha, you, ba,**
ji **MEANING:** leaf **EXAMPLES:** 葉 ha = leaf;
紅葉 kouyou = autumn colors; 言葉 kotoba =
word; 紅葉 momiji = Japanese maple, autumn
colors **DESCRIPTION:** at the top, a plant radical
(see # 43); in the middle, 世 se (world, # 542)
which includes a hanging bucket; at the bottom, a
木 ki (tree, # 118) in Hawaii
CUES: in **Ha**waii, a **Yo**gi came out of a **Ba**r and saw
these 葉 **ha** (leaves) hanging over a bucket on a 木
(tree) next to his **Jee**p

Rotated M

544. 予 **PRONUNCIATION: yo**
MEANINGS: to prepare, preliminary
EXAMPLES: 予定 yotei = plan, schedule;
予約 yoyaku = reservation **DESCRIPTION:** an
M rotated 45° to the right, representing Mom,
balanced on a nail **CUE:** this M (Mom) has good
balance, and she has a 予定 **yo**tei (plan) to make
予約 **yo**yaku (reservations) for a **Yo**ga class
COMPARE: 野(菜) yasai = vegetable, # 545;
柔(道) juudou = judo, # 546

545. 野 **PRONUNCIATIONS: no, ya**
MEANINGS: field, outside, outsider
EXAMPLES: 野原 nohara = field; 野村
Nomura = a family name; 野菜 yasai = vegetable;
野球 yakyuu = baseball **DESCRIPTION:** at the
upper left, 田 (rice paddy, # 68); at the lower left,
土 tsuchi (dirt, # 59); together these resemble a
sincere guy wearing bifocals; on the right, 予(定)
yotei (plan, # 544), resembling an M rotated 45° to
the right, which reminds us of a mom, balanced on a
nail **CUES:** this sincere guy with bifocals and his
M (mom) live in **No**rway, and they have a plan to
grow some 野菜 **ya**sai (vegetables) for their **Ya**k
COMPARE: 勤(める) tsutomeru = to be
employed, # 517; 漢(字) kanji = Chinese
character, # 197; 難(しい) muzukashii =
difficult, # 198; 予(定) yotei = plan, # 544;
柔(道) juudou = judo, # 546

546. 柔 **PRONUNCIATIONS: nyuu, juu,**
yawa MEANINGS: tender, gentleness, softness
EXAMPLES: 柔和 nyuuwa = gentleness,
mildness; 柔道 juudou = judo; 柔らかい
yawarakai = soft, tender, limp **DESCRIPTION:** at
the top, an M rotated 45° to the right, which
represents Mom; at the bottom, 木 ki (tree, # 118)
CUES: this M (Mom) from **Nyuu**yooku (New
York) knows 柔道 **juu**dou and can climb a 木
(tree) although she knows that this activity is rather
Juvenile; she is 柔らかい **yawa**rakai (tender
and soft) and always gives her **Ya**k **Wa**ter
COMPARE: 予(定) yotei = plan, # 544; 案 an =
proposal, idea, # 120; 野(菜) yasai = vegetable,
545

Snake

547. 危 **PRONUNCIATIONS: abu, ki, aya**
MEANING: danger **EXAMPLES:** 危ない
abunai = dangerous; 危険 kiken = danger;
危うい ayaui = dangerous, risky
DESCRIPTION: at the top, an abused fish head;

under the fish head, a lean-to; under the lean-to, a snake **CUES:** this fish head, who has been **Ab**used, sits on a lean-to and tries to escape the 危ない **abu**nai (dangerous) snake lurking inside, which has already **Ki**lled Ken but spared Barbie and the **Aya**tollah

548. 包 PRONUNCIATIONS: hou, tsutsu, zutsu MEANING: to wrap EXAMPLES: 包装 housou = wrapping; 包む tsutsumu = to wrap; 小包 kozutsumi = a package sent by mail DESCRIPTION: at the top, J-shaped packaging; below, contents shaped like a backward "S"

CUES: our **Ho**stess will 包む **tsutsu**mu (wrap) this J-shaped or S-shaped package, which contains **Tsu**its (suits) piled on **Tsu**its, including **Zoot Su**its for our **Mee**ting

549. 港 PRONUNCIATIONS: kou, minato MEANING: port EXAMPLES: 空港 kuukou = airport; 港 minato = port DESCRIPTION: on the left, a water radical; at the upper right, a broad tower on sturdy legs; at the bottom right, a snake **CUES:** at this 港 **minato** (port) in **Co**logne, which is controlled by **Mighty NATO**, there is a tower on the upper right that supports cranes used to load ships, and there is a snake on the lower right, swimming in the water on the left

550. 記 PRONUNCIATIONS: ki, shiru

MEANING: to record **EXAMPLES:** 記事 kiji = newspaper article; 日記 nikki = diary; 記入 kinyuu = entry, filling in forms; 記す shirusu = to record or write **DESCRIPTION:** on the left, 言(葉) kotoba (words, # 430); on the right, a killer snake **CUES:** I read a 記事 **ki**ji (article) containing a lot of 言 (words) about this snake that tried to **Ki**ll Jimmy Carter and the **Shee**p that escaped to the **Roof**

Kaeru & Kawaru
551. 替 PRONUNCIATIONS: ka, gae, ga
MEANINGS: to replace, or to exchange money
EXAMPLES: 替える kaeru = to replace or exchange money; 両替 ryougae = money

exchange; 着替える kigaeru = to change clothes **DESCRIPTION:** at the top, two 夫 otto (husbands, # 614) named Carl Ericson and Guy Ericson; at the bottom, 日 hi (sun, # 32) **CUES:** since **Ca**rl Ericson and **Gu**y Ericson are two 夫 otto (husbands) who are almost identical, there is no **Gap** between them as they stand in the 日 (sun), and we can 替える **ka**eru (exchange) one for the other **COMPARE:** 選(ぶ) erabu = to choose, # 352

552. 代 PRONUNCIATIONS: dai, ka, yo, shiro, tai MEANINGS: people changing, generations EXAMPLES: 時代 jidai = era; 代わる kawaru = to take the place of; 代わりに kawari ni = in place of; 千代田 Chiyoda = a ward in Tokyo; 身代金 minoshirokin = ransom; 永代 eitai = permanence, eternity **DESCRIPTION:** on the left, the man with a slanted hat is the president; on the right, the woman leaning on him is the vice president **CUES:** if this man with a slanted hat **Di**es, this leaning woman will start a new 時代 ji**dai** (era) in government; she will **Ca**ll the War department, 代わる **ka**waru (take the place) of the president, and order people to eat more **Yo**gurt and to wear **Sheep**skin **Ro**bes or **Ti**ger pelts

553. 変 PRONUNCIATIONS: hen, ka
MEANINGS: to change something; strange, extraordinary **EXAMPLES:** 変な hen na = strange; 大変 taihen = terrible; 変える kaeru = to change, transitive; 変わる kawaru = to change, intransitive **DESCRIPTION:** at the top, a swooping hen; at the bottom, a dancer with a ponytail **CUES:** I just saw a 変な **hen** na (strange) sight: a large **Hen** swooped down over this dancer with a ponytail and tried to 変える **ka**eru (change) her; let's **Ca**ll Erudite Eric to witness this

408

554. 換 PRONUNCIATIONS: **ka, kan**
MEANINGS: to replace or exchange
EXAMPLES: 乗り換える norikaeru = to
change trains; 交換する koukan suru = to
exchange DESCRIPTION: on the left, an erudite
kneeling guy; on the right, a Canadian general with
a fish head, who wears two decorations on his chest
CUES: we have **C**alled this **E**rudite kneeling guy to
換える **ka**eru (exchange) the decoration on the
right side of this **Cana**dian general's chest for the
one on the left

Bird
555. 鳥 PRONUNCIATIONS: **tori, chou**
MEANING: bird EXAMPLES: 小鳥 kotori =
small bird; 白鳥 hakuchou = swan
DESCRIPTION: this 鳥 tori (bird) has a little tuft
on its head, feathers, and strangely, five toes
CUES: this 鳥 **tori** (bird) with five toes belongs to
a **Tory** who was **Cho**sen to serve in Parliament
COMPARE: 島 shima = island, # 556; 馬 uma =
horse, # 958

556. 島 PRONUNCIATIONS: **shima,**
jima[1], tou MEANING: island EXAMPLES: 島
shima = island; 広島 Hiroshima = city in Japan;
桜島 Sakurajima = a volcano in southern Kyushu;
半島 hantou = peninsula DESCRIPTION:
compared to 鳥 tori (bird, # 555), four of the bird's
toes have been replaced by 山 yama (mountain,
146) CUES: 鳥 (birds) that live on 山
(mountains) that arise on 島 **shima** (islands), such
as this one near Hiro**Shima**, sometimes lose their
Toes to predators

Yak or Sword on a Table
557. 役 PRONUNCIATIONS: **yaku, eki**
MEANINGS: role, service EXAMPLES:
役に立つ yaku ni tatsu = to make use of;
区役所 kuyakusho = ward office; 兵役 heieki
= military service DESCRIPTION: on the left, a
man with a double hat; on the right, π (the Greek
letter pi, which represents a pious yak here), standing

on 又 mata ("again,"# 24), but this resembles a
simple table CUES: this man with a double hat is
performing a 役 **yaku** (service) by taking care of
this π (Yak), which is standing on this 又 (table) in
an **Eki** (station)
COMPARE: 投(げる) nageru = to throw,
558; 段(々) dandan = gradually, # 559

558. 投 PRONUNCIATIONS: **tou, na**
MEANING: to throw EXAMPLES: 投資
toushi = investment; 投げる nageru = to throw
DESCRIPTION: on the left, a kneeling guy; on the
right, π (the Greek letter pi), standing on 又 mata
("again," # 24), but this resembles a table
CUES: this kneeling guy wants to make some **T**oast
and has been **Na**gging π to **G**et off the 又 (table);
next, he plans to 投げる **na**geru (throw) π off
COMPARE: 役 yaku = role, service, # 557;
段(々) dandan = gradually, # 559

559. 段 PRONUNCIATION: **dan**
MEANINGS: step, paragraph, case EXAMPLES:
階段 kaidan = stairs; 段々 dandan = gradually;
普段 fudan = usual, every day DESCRIPTION:
on the left, a ladder with four steps; on the right, π
(the Greek letter pi), which is a pious yak belonging
to a dancer, standing on a 又 mata ("again," # 24),
but this resembles a simple table CUE: a **Dan**cer
uses these 階段 kai**dan** (steps) on the left to climb
up and down and give food to the π (yak) on the 又
(table) COMPARE: 役 yaku = role, service,
557; 投(げる) nageru = to throw, # 558;
作(る) tsukuru = to make, # 482

560. 招 PRONUNCIATIONS: **mane, shou**
MEANING: to invite EXAMPLES: 招く
maneku = to invite; 招待 shoutai = invitation
DESCRIPTION: on the left, a kneeling guy; on the
right, a 刀 katana (sword, # 102) on a box
CUES: this kneeling guy wants to write a letter to
招く **mane**ku (invite) a **Manne**quin to a

Broadway **Show**, but first he has to remove the 刀 (sword) from his writing 口 (box) **COMPARE:** 投(げる) nageru = to throw, # 558

Ri

561. 別 PRONUNCIATIONS: betsu, waka, be MEANING: to separate EXAMPLES:
別に betsu ni = particularly; 別の betsu no = another (defined) object; 別れる wakareru = to separate; 別居 bekkyo = separation of family members DESCRIPTION: on the left, Betsy, who has a square head resting on 万 man (ten thousand, # 113); on the right, the katakana character リ Ri CUES: Betsy with her square head doesn't like リ Ri with his pointy toes 別に **betsu** ni (particularly), and they 別れる **waka**reru (break up) after リ Ri **W**alks on the **C**at and **B**ends its tail COMPARE: 他(の) hoka no = another (undefined) object, # 505

562. 割 PRONUNCIATIONS: wa, wari, katsu, sa MEANINGS: to divide, apportion EXAMPLES: 割る waru = to break glass and wood, transitive; 割れる wareru = to break, intransitive; 4割る2 yon waru ni = 4 divided by 2; 割に wari ni = relatively; 分割する bunkatsu suru = to divide or split; 時間を割く jikan wo saku = to make time for DESCRIPTION: on the left, 王 ou (king, # 1077), wearing a wide crown; he is standing on a box, which might be a warrior's tomb; on the right, the katakana character リ Ri, which looks like some kind of tool CUES: this 王 (king), wearing a wide crown, is **W**alking on a **W**arrior's tomb with his **C**ats, eating **S**ardines and digging with the リ Ri tool, trying to 割る **wa**ru (break) the tomb

563. 倒 PRONUNCIATIONS: tao, tou, dou MEANINGS: overthrow, fall, collapse, breakdown, become bankrupt EXAMPLES: 倒れる taoreru = to fall, collapse, drop, fall senseless; 倒す taosu = to bring down, knock down, defeat; 倒産 tousan = bankruptcy; 面倒 mendou = annoyance, difficulty, care DESCRIPTION: on the left, a man with a slanted hat; in the center, a tower composed of a pedaling leg balanced on 土 tsuchi (dirt, # 59); on the right, the katakana character リ Ri CUES: if either this man or リ Ri moves, the **Tow**er will 倒れる **tao**reru (fall), and that will cause **T**otal 面倒 men**dou** (annoyance) to the people who paid good **Dough** (money) to put it up

564. 利 PRONUNCIATIONS: ri MEANINGS: useful, sharp EXAMPLES: 利用する riyou suru = to use; 便利 benri = convenient; 有利 yuuri = advantageous; 利益 rieki = profit DESCRIPTION: on the left, 禾 (a grain plant with a ripe head); on the right, the katakana character リ Ri, which tells us how to pronounce this CUES: リ Ri 利用する **ri**you suru (uses) this 禾 (ripe grain) to make meals

565. 刻 PRONUNCIATIONS: koku, kiza MEANINGS: to tick away, to cut into pieces EXAMPLES: 遅刻する chikoku suru = to be tardy; 時刻 jikoku = time; 刻む kizamu = to cut, mince, carve DESCRIPTION: on the left, this is said to be the skeleton of a wild boar; on the right, the katakana character リ Ri CUES: after リ Ri carved up this boar, he stopped to drink a **Coke**, and to **K**id **Za**ch about not helping him, and therefore he will 遅刻する chi**koku** suru (be tardy)

566. 帰 PRONUNCIATIONS: kae, ki MEANINGS: to go home, to return EXAMPLES: 帰る kaeru = to return home; 帰宅 kitaku = a return to one's home DESCRIPTION: on the left, the katakana character リ Ri; at the upper right, long hair streaming to the left; at the lower right, the face of an elephant, with low-hanging ears and a long trunk CUES: as リ Ri watches, a **C**at **E**nters my home, and I will 帰る **kae**ru (return), riding this elephant, with my long hair streaming to the left, to **K**ick the cat out

Vertical Storage

567. 皿 PRONUNCIATIONS: sara, zara[1]

MEANING: plate, dish, saucer EXAMPLES: 皿 sara = plate, dish or saucer; 大皿 oozara = large dish DESCRIPTION: three rolls of Saran wrap, positioned vertically on a shelf

CUE: I put my left-over food on 皿 **sara** (plates) and cover it with this **Saran** wrap

COMPARE: 温(かい) atatakai = warm object, # 257; 冊 satsu = counter for books, # 568

568. 冊 PRONUNCIATION: satsu

MEANING: counter for books EXAMPLE: 三冊 sansatsu = three books DESCRIPTION: a box divided into six compartments for storing satisfying Superman novels CUE: only six 冊 **satsu** (volumes) of **S**atisfying **S**uperman novels will fit into this bookcase

COMPARE: 皿 sara = plate or dish, # 567

Shelf Storage

569. 置 PRONUNCIATIONS: o, chi

MEANINGS: to place, to leave something

EXAMPLES: 置く oku = to place something; 位置 ichi = position

DESCRIPTION: at the top, a thick double handle, with the upper level divided into three sections; below this, a three-drawer oak box; at the bottom, a shelf with a back wall, seen from the side CUES: we use this thick double-handled tool to 置く **o**ku (place) heavy items, like **O**ak storage boxes of **Ch**eese, at the backs of our shelves

COMPARE: 直(す) naosu (to correct, #570)

570. 直 PRONUNCIATIONS: nao, su, jiki, jika, choku, cho, tada MEANINGS: straight, direct, to correct EXAMPLES: 直す naosu = to correct or repair something; 真っ直ぐ massugu = straight; 正直 shoujiki = honest; 直に jika ni = directly; 直面 chokumen = confrontation; 直行便 chokkoubin = nonstop flight; 直ちに tadachi ni = immediately DESCRIPTION: at the top, a thin handle; below this, a three-drawer box; at the bottom, a shelf with a back wall, seen from the side CUES: **Na**omi and **Su**perman say that if we

use this thin-handled tool to place lighter items, like **Jeep Keys** for our **Jeep Car**, and Margaret **Ch**o's **Kool**-Aid packets, at the backs of our shelves, we can 直す **nao**su (correct) our storage problems and simplify our **Ch**ores, and we think that they are **Tada**shii (correct) COMPARE: 置(く) oku = to place, # 569; 治(す) naosu = to heal, # 539; 値(段) nedan = price, # 571; 正(しい) tadashii = correct, # 174

571. 値 PRONUNCIATIONS: atai, chi, ne

MEANING: value EXAMPLES: 値 atai = value, price; 価値 kachi = value; 値段 nedan = price DESCRIPTION: on the left, a man with a slanted hat; on the right, 直(す) naosu (to correct, #570), which looks like a thin handle on a box, stored at the back of a shelf

CUES: this man with a slanted hat, who is **A Thai** person, thinks that, in order to 直 (correct) our storage policy, we should store our **Ch**eap lightweight items, like **N**ecklaces, in this box with a thin handle at the back of this shelf, but the 値段 **ne**dan (prices) that he charges for his advice are high COMPARE: 価 atai = value, price, # 484

572. 県 PRONUNCIATION: ken

MEANING: prefecture EXAMPLE: 県 ken = prefecture; 広島県 hiroshima ken = Hiroshima prefecture DESCRIPTION: compared to 直(す) naosu (to correct, # 570), this shelf that Ken & Barbie designed has three legs and can walk around; for that reason, they have no need for a handle at the top of the three-drawer box CUE: **Ken** and Barbie like to move around in their 県 **ken** (prefecture), and they keep their maps in this three-drawer box on a three-legged self-propelled shelf

Tower

573. 形 PRONUNCIATIONS: katachi, gyou, kei, kata, gata[1] MEANING: shape

EXAMPLES: 形 katachi = shape; 人形 ningyou = doll; 形態 keitai = form, shape, system; 形見 katami = keepsake, memento; 髪形 kamigata = hair style DESCRIPTION: on the left, a tower, which could be part of a catapult; on the right, these three lines look like spare cords for the catapult **CUES:** this tower 形 **katachi** (shape) is part of a **Cat**apult for launching **Chee**se at enemies who steal our **Gyo**za and **Ca**ke, and it can be bought from a **Cat**alog

574. 飛 PRONUNCIATIONS: hi, to

MEANING: to fly **EXAMPLES:** 飛行機 hikouki = airplane; 飛ぶ tobu = to fly **DESCRIPTION:** on the left, a toy tower that is slightly different from the one found in 形 katachi (shape, # 573); on the right, two propellers, suggesting that a toy airplane may be perched on this tower **CUES:** when these two propellers start turning, you will **Hear** a whirring sound, and a **Toy** 飛行機 **hi**kouki (airplane) will start to 飛ぶ **to**bu (fly) from this toy tower

Vertical Lines
575. 並 PRONUNCIATIONS: nara, hei, nami MEANINGS: to line up; row

EXAMPLES: 並ぶ narabu = to line up, intransitive; 並べる naraberu = to line up, transitive; 並列 heiretsu = arrangement, parallel, abreast; 並の nami no = ordinary, usual **DESCRIPTION:** various lines on a temple wall in Nara, most of which line up fairly well; compared to 普(通) futsuu (ordinary, # 576), the stove at the bottom is missing

CUES: these lines **nara**bu 並ぶ (line up) on the wall of a temple in **Nara,** spelling a **H**ateful message, and the authorities will soon be **Nam**ing the culprit

576. 普 PRONUNCIATION: fu
MEANINGS: universal, ordinary **EXAMPLES:** 普通 futsuu = ordinarily, usually, generally; 普段 fudan no = usual, casual, everyday **DESCRIPTION:** at the top, 並(ぶ) narabu (to line up, # 575), but this looks like four burners on a stove for cooking food, with the two center burners producing a higher flame; at the bottom, 日 hi (sun, # 32), but this is the body of the stove

CUE: this is just a 普通 **fu**tsuu (ordinary) stove, with four burners for cooking **Food**

577. 受 PRONUNCIATIONS: u, uke, ju

MEANING: to receive **EXAMPLES:** 受ける ukeru = to receive, to take or pass an exam or class; 受付 uketsuke = reception; 受験する juken suru = to take an academic exam **DESCRIPTION:** at the top, a cloth covering three exam booklets; below that, a tablecloth; at the bottom, 又 mata ("again," # 24), an exam table **CUES:** when you 受ける **u**keru (take or receive) an exam in Uruguay or in the **U.K.**, three exam booklets are covered with cloth and placed on top of a tablecloth covering this 又 (table), on which you may keep a bottle of **Juice** **COMPARE:** 授(業) jugyou = class, # 578; 愛 ai = love, # 523

578. 授 PRONUNCIATIONS: ju, sazu
MEANINGS: to grant or bestow **EXAMPLES:** 授業 jugyou = class instruction; 教授 kyouju = professor; 授かる sazukaru = to be endowed with, be blessed with **DESCRIPTION:** on the left, a kneeling guy; on the right, 受(ける) ukeru (to take, or pass, an exam or class, # 577)

CUES: this kneeling guy is a 教授 kyou**ju** (professor) who drinks **Juice** in his 授業 **ju**gyou (class) while his students 受 (take) an exam about the animals living in the **San Diego Zoo** **COMPARE:** 愛 ai = love, # 523

579. 両 PRONUNCIATION: ryou

MEANINGS: both, two **EXAMPLES:** 両方 ryouhou = both; 両親 ryoushin = both parents **DESCRIPTION:** this resembles a chairlift seat, hanging from a cable **CUE:** 両方 **ryo**hou (both) Pope **Leo** and his Hobo friend can fit onto this chair lift seat when they go skiing **COMPARE:** 席 seki (seat), # 496; (映)画 eiga = movie, # 77

エ & Y

580. 製 PRONUNCIATION: sei

MEANING: to manufacture **EXAMPLES:** 日本製 nihonsei = Japanese product; 製品 seihin = finished product; 手製の tesei no = handmade, homemade **DESCRIPTION:** above the line, 牛 ushi (cow, # 205) sits on a revolving chair, next to リ Ri the supervisor; below the line, the katakana character エ and the letter Y are the workers in the factory **CUES:** following orders given by the 牛 (cow) and リ Ri, エ and Y manufacture 製品 seihin (finished products) to be sold at **Sa**feway stores **COMPARE:** 制(度) seido = system, # 1155, which helps us to pronounce this

581. 袋 PRONUNCIATIONS: bi, fukuro, bukuro[1]

MEANINGS: sack, bag, pouch **EXAMPLES:** 足袋 tabi = Japanese-style socks; 袋 fukuro = sack, bag; 手袋 tebukuro = gloves; 紙袋 kamibukuro = paper bag **DESCRIPTION:** above the line, the katakana character イ and the leaning woman from 式 shiki (ceremony, # 249); below the line, the katakana character エ and the letter Y are the workers in a factory in Fukuoka **CUES:** エ and Y manufacture 袋 fukuro (bags) for the upper class, including イ and the woman from 式, who use them to carry **Bee**r on **Fuku**oka **Roa**ds

582. 表 PRONUNCIATIONS: omote, pyou, arawa, hyou, byou[1]

MEANINGS: surface, outside, front, to make public **EXAMPLES:** 表 omote = surface, front, outside; 発表する happyou suru = to announce, publish, reveal, make a presentation; 表す arawasu = to signify, represent or express; 表現 hyougen = expression; 裏表紙 urabyoushi = back cover **DESCRIPTION:** above the line, a double cross above an omotel (honorable motel); below the line, the katakana character エ and the letter Y **CUES:** in this **Omote**l (honorable motel), there are many straight 表 omote (surfaces), such as the ones in the double cross seen on the roof; at the bottom, エ and Y are the owners and, like the Lone Ranger, they often greet guests from **Pyo**ngyang, or **Ara**b guests like **Wa**li and Sultan, by saying "**Hi-Yo**" **COMPARE:** 青(い) aoi = blue, # 155

Net

583. 無 PRONUNCIATIONS: mu, bu, na

MEANINGS: nothing, to not exist **EXAMPLES:** 無理 muri = impossible, unreasonable; 無料 muryou = free of charge; 無駄な muda na = useless, wasteful; 無事 buji = safety, peace, health, good condition; 無くす nakusu = to lose; 無くなる nakunaru = to run out or disappear; 無い nai = does not exist, usually written ない **DESCRIPTION:** a large net running on four legs; this could be a drunk wagon

CUES: **Mu**riel says that it's 無理 muri (impossible) for the **Boo**zers to escape from this net-like drunk wagon while it's running along, unless they have a **Kna**ck for doing so

584. 舞 PRONUNCIATIONS: ma, bu, mai

MEANING: to dance **EXAMPLES:** 見舞い mimai = visit to a sick person; 舞う mau = to dance; 舞台 butai = stage, setting, scene; 舞 mai = a dance **DESCRIPTION:** at the top, a net; at the lower left, 夕(方) yuugata (evening, # 160); on the lower right, a sitting person, with a knee extending to the left

CUES: **Ma** is caught in this net of illness, so I will お見舞いする omimai suru (pay a visit to a sick person) in the 夕 (evening), sit by her bedside, drink **Boo**ze, and listen to **Mi**chael **Ja**ckson music

Shaky Table

585. 亡 **PRONUNCIATIONS: na, bou, mou MEANINGS:** to pass away, to die **EXAMPLES:** 亡くなる nakunaru = to die; 死亡 shibou = death; 金の亡者 kane no mouja = a money-grubbing person **DESCRIPTION:** a shaky table; there's a **Kn**ack to balancing this shaky table; if we seat **Bo**no and **Mo**ses at it, it might fall on them, and they may 亡くなる **na**kunaru (die) **COMPARE:** 忙(しい) isogashii = busy, # 586

586. 忙 **PRONUNCIATIONS: isoga, bou MEANING:** busy **EXAMPLES:** 忙しい isogashii = busy; 多忙 tabou = very busy **DESCRIPTION:** on the left, an man standing erect; on the right, 亡(くなる) nakunaru (to die, # 585), which resembles a shaky table **CUES:** there is an **I**solated **Ga**dfly on this shaky table on a **Bo**at, and this man is 忙しい **iso**gashii (busy), trying to keep it all from falling down

Fruit

587. 果 **PRONUNCIATIONS: kuda, ha, ka MEANINGS:** fruit, reward **EXAMPLES:** 果物 kudamono = fruit; 果たす hatasu = to accomplish, realize, perform; 結果 kekka = result **DESCRIPTION:** at the top, 田 (rice paddy, # 68), which resembles four fruits available for harvesting; at the bottom, 木 ki (tree, # 118)

CUES: my **Co**ol **Da**d saw these four 果物 **kuda**mono (fruits) growing on a 木 (tree), so he **H**arvested them and **C**arved them up **COMPARE:** 課 ka = section, # 588; 菓(子) kashi = candy, # 589; 東 higashi = east, # 508, in which a 日 (sun) appears *behind* a 木 (tree)

588. 課 **PRONUNCIATION: ka MEANINGS:** to assign, lesson, section **EXAMPLES:** 課長 kachou = section manager; 第一課 dai ikka = section # 1 **DESCRIPTION:** on the left, 言(う) iu (to speak, # 430); on the right, 果(物) kudamono (fruit, # 587)

CUE: in his 課 **ka** (section) at a fruit company, Karl Marx, the 課長 **ka**chou (section manager), 言 (speaks) about this 果 (fruit) **ALSO COMPARE:** 菓子 kashi = candy, # 589

589. 菓 **PRONUNCIATIONS: ka, ga MEANING:** sweets **EXAMPLES:** お菓子 okashi = pastry, confectionery, candy; 和菓子 wagashi = Japanese sweets **DESCRIPTION:** at the top, a plant radical (see # 43); at the bottom, 果(物) kudamono (fruit, # 587); together these may suggest a cashew tree **CUES:** we often eat 菓子 **ka**shi (candy) that is made from **C**ashew nuts and 果 (fruit), but sometimes it gives us **Ga**s **COMPARE:** 課 ka = section, # 588

Kneeling Person

590. 打 **PRONUNCIATIONS: u, da MEANING:** to hit **EXAMPLES:** 打つ utsu = to hit or strike; 打ち合わせ uchiawase = a planning meeting; 打撃 dageki = shock, impact **DESCRIPTION:** on the left, a kneeling guy wearing an uber tsuit (suit); on the right, a nail, which looks like a dagger **CUES:** this kneeling guy is a gangster who wears **U**ber **Ts**uits (suits) and sometimes 打つ **u**tsu (strikes) his enemies with this **Da**gger

591. 払 **PRONUNCIATIONS: hara, bara**[1] **MEANINGS:** to pay, to brush away **EXAMPLES:** 払う harau = to pay; 支払い shiharai = payment; 着払い chakubarai = cash on delivery **DESCRIPTION:** on the left, a kneeling guy; on the right, the katakana character ム mu (the sound made by a cow when it is harassed) **CUE:** this kneeling guy is crawling over to see if he can 払う **hara**u (pay) for this ム (cow), which is being **Ha**rassed **COMPARE:** 私 watashi = I, # 510

592. 押 PRONUNCIATIONS: o, ou, oshi
MEANINGS: to press or push EXAMPLES:
押す osu = to push; 押収 oushuu = seizure,
confiscation; 押入れ oshi'ire = closet, which
can also be written 押し入れ
DESCRIPTION: on the left, a kneeling guy; on the
right, 田 (rice paddy, # 68), on a pole, but this looks
like a sign CUES: this Old kneeling guy 押す
osu (pushes) on this sign in Oosutorariya (Australia),
causing it to fall onto some Old Sheep
COMPARE: 神 kami = god, # 273

593. 拝 PRONUNCIATIONS: oga, hai
MEANINGS: to worship, to revere, to do something
humbly EXAMPLES: 拝む ogamu = to assume
the posture of prayer with hands held together, to
revere; 拝見する haiken suru = to humbly read
or see DESCRIPTION: on the left, a kneeling
person named Oprah; on the right, a high stalk of
flowers CUES: before Oprah Gambles, she kneels
and 拝む ogamu (prays humbly) to a god, and
since she is holding these flowers High, people say
that they 拝見する haiken suru (humbly see)
them

594. 捨 PRONUNCIATIONS: su, sha
MEANING: to throw away EXAMPLE:
捨てる suteru = to throw away; 四捨五入
する shishagonyuu suru = to round to the nearest
whole number DESCRIPTION: on the left, a
kneeling person named Superman; at the top right, a
peaked roof on a shack; at the middle right, 土
tsuchi (dirt, # 59), which resembles a cross; at the
bottom right, 口 kuchi (mouth, # 426), which could
be a platform for the cross
CUES: Superman is a Terrible person who is
crawling toward this Shack in order to 捨てる
suteru (throw away) this 土 (cross)
COMPARE: 拾(う) hirou = to pick up, # 595;
(田)舎 inaka = hometown, # 745

595. 拾 PRONUNCIATIONS: hiro, shuu
MEANING: to pick up EXAMPLE: 拾う hirou
= to pick up; 拾得する shuutoku suru = to

acquire or obtain DESCRIPTION: on the left, a
kneeling person who is a hero; at the top right, a
peaked roof; at the middle right, a horizontal line,
which could be a lid for a box; at the bottom right,
口 kuchi (mouth, # 426), which could be a box
CUES: this Hero is crawling toward the enemy's
storehouse and trying to 拾う hirou (pick up) a
口 (box) of Shoes COMPARE: 捨(てる)
suteru = to throw away, # 594

596. 掛 PRONUNCIATION: ka
MEANINGS: to hang, suspend, or depend
EXAMPLES: 掛ける kakeru = to hang (a
picture, etc.), to sit on a chair, to take (time or
money), to make a phone call, to multiply, to put on
(glasses), to pour or sprinkle, and many other
meanings DESCRIPTION: on the left, a kneeling
guy; in the middle, two 土 tsuchi (dirt, # 59), but
these look like chairs; on the right, the katakana
character ト to, which reminds us of a toboggan
CUE: this kneeling guy is a diplomat who
掛ける kakeru (hangs) two chairs on a wall next
to this ト (toboggan) at a Nordic diplomatic
reception and then Calls John Kerry

Everyone

597. 皆 PRONUNCIATIONS: kai, mina,
minna MEANINGS: all, everyone EXAMPLE:
皆目 kaimoku = utterly, altogether; 皆 mina =
everyone; 皆様 minnasama = very honorable
everyone DESCRIPTION: at the top, two people
are sitting facing in the same direction; at the bottom,
白(い) shiroi (white, # 44) CUES: 皆 mina
(everyone) has brought a Kite and is sitting on this
白 (white) snowy hill in Minasota (Minnesota)
COMPARE: 階(段) kaidan = stairs, # 598; 背
se = height, # 152

598. 階 PRONUNCIATION: kai
MEANINGS: story or floor of a building, counter
for stories or floors of a building EXAMPLES:
階段 kaidan = stairs; 四階 yonkai = the fourth
floor DESCRIPTION: on the left, the Greek letter
ß which represents a Greek guy with a kite; on the
right, 皆 mina (everyone, # 597) CUE: this ß
(Greek) guy, who owns a Kite, and 皆 (everyone)

else in our group live on the 三階 san**kai** (third floor) of our building

Nurse

599. 喜 **PRONUNCIATIONS: yoroko, ki**
MEANINGS: to feel pleased or happy
EXAMPLE: 喜ぶ yorokobu = to be delighted; 喜劇 kigeki = comedy **DESCRIPTION:** at the top, (兵)士 heishi (soldier, # 66) which resembles a cross worn by a nurse; in the middle, the nurse himself, wearing a white nurse's cap; at the bottom, a square which is the nurse's white coat
CUES: this nurse 喜ぶ **yorokobu** (gets delighted) in the **Yoro**pean (European) city of **Co**logne when a **King** gives him an award **COMPARE:** 嬉(しい) ureshii = pleased, # 600

600. 嬉 **PRONUNCIATION: ure**
MEANINGS: glad, pleased **EXAMPLES:** 嬉しい ureshii = pleased **DESCRIPTION:** on the left, 女 onna (female, # 235); on the right 喜(ぶ) yorokobu (to get delighted, # 599), which resembles a nurse wearing a cross and a white cap **CUES:** this 女 (female) 喜 (nurse) is 嬉しい **ureshii** (pleased) about her patient with kidney failure and the **Urea** **S**he is excreting (urea is a major component of urine)

Miscellaneous

601. 以 **PRONUNCIATIONS: i, mo**
MEANINGS: starting point, by means of
EXAMPLES: 以前に izen ni = a long time ago; 以後 igo = after, since, or from now on; 三人以上 sannin ijou = three people or more; 以下 ika = below, less than; 五分以内に gofun inai ni = within 5 minutes; 以外 igai = other than; 前以て maemotte = beforehand, in advance **DESCRIPTION:** this resembles someone sliding off the back of a giraffe **CUES:** this person used to ride a giraffe, a giant **E**el and a **M**otorcycle 以前に **i**zen ni (a long time ago)

602. 船 **PRONUNCIATIONS: fune, bune**[1], **funa, sen MEANINGS:** ship, boat **EXAMPLES:** 船 fune = ship, boat; 釣り船 tsuribune = fishing boat; 船便 funabin = ship mail; 船長 senchou = captain of a ship **DESCRIPTION:** on the left, a boat, seen from above, with a pointed prow and fore and aft compartments, but it is missing a stern in the back; on the right, 八 hachi (eight, # 15), above 口 kuchi (mouth, # 426), which could represent a dock **CUES:** this 船 **fune** (boat) is wide open at the rear, and it looks **Fune**y (funny) to **Fool**ish **Na**ncy, but there are 八 (eight) guys on the 口 (dock) who were **Sent** to work on the problem

603. 靴 **PRONUNCIATION: kutsu**
MEANING: shoe **EXAMPLE:** 靴 kutsu = shoe **DESCRIPTION:** on the left, this looks like a needle, with a syringe; on the right, 化(学) kagaku (chemistry, # 487), but this resembles a map of Canada – see # 487
CUE: these 靴 **kutsu** (shoes) that Superman bought in 化 (Canada) are too narrow, and it feels as though needles are **Cut**ting **S**uperman's feet

604. 寄 **PRONUNCIATIONS: yo, ki**
MEANINGS: to be inclined to, to stop by
EXAMPLES: 寄る yoru = to drop in at, to gather, to go closer; 年寄り toshiyori = elderly person; 寄付 kifu = donation **DESCRIPTION:** a pillar supporting a floor; above the floor, a big bird; under the floor, a box **CUES:** if you don't mind the big bird and want to 寄る **yo**ru (stop by) some **Yoru** (night), you can see this box containing 寄付 **kifu** (donations) under the floor, where we also **Keep Food** **COMPARE:** 夜 yoru = night, # 489; 奇(妙) kimyou = strange, # 854

605. 残 PRONUNCIATIONS: noko, *gori,*
zan MEANINGS: to remain, cruel EXAMPLES:
残る nokoru = to remain; 残す nokosu = to
leave behind; 名残 nagori = remnants, traces;
残念 zannen = regrettable; 残業 zangyou =
overtime DESCRIPTION: reportedly the radical
on the left is an axe, and the one on the right is a
halberd (combination lance and axe), sliced by four
cuts CUES: a Noble Code allows warriors to 残
す nokosu (leave behind) victims of **Gory** axe and
halberd attacks, but this is considered cruel and
残念 zannen (regrettable) behavior in **Zan**zibar

606. 球 PRONUNCIATIONS: kyuu, tama
MEANINGS: ball, sphere EXAMPLES: 野球
yakyuu = baseball; 地球 chikyuu = the Earth;
電気の球 denki no tama = lightbulb

DESCRIPTION: on the left, 玉 tama (ball, or
jewel, # 169), which looks like a cucumber and helps
us to pronounce this; on the right a tall **t**, with a **y**
under its right arm, which stands for "thank you";
the mark above the **t**'s right shoulder and the one to
the left of its foot may represent stray baseballs

CUES: I received this long 玉 (jewel), which looks
like a **C**ucumber, and I wrote, "**ty** (thank you) very
much for the jewel; I plan to sell it in order to buy
Tamales for my 野球 yakyuu (baseball) team"

607. 寿 PRONUNCIATIONS: su, ju,
kotobuki MEANINGS: life, longevity
EXAMPLES: 寿司 sushi = raw fish slices on
rice; 寿命 jumyou = lifespan, longevity; 寿
kotobuki = congratulations, felicitations (given at
weddings, New Year's, etc.) DESCRIPTION: at
the lower right, 寺 tera (temple, # 213), but the
cross at the top of 寺 is partially hidden beneath a
very long slanting **t**, which is superimposed on 寺
and may represent time CUES: the **S**upervisor of
the Sheep at this 寺 (temple) says that it's time to
eat 寿司 sushi with some **J**uice, but I'm practicing
for my **Koto** (Japanese harp) recital at **Buck**ingham
Palace

608. 司 PRONUNCIATIONS: shi,
tsukasado MEANINGS: official, to administer
EXAMPLES: 寿司 sushi = raw fish slices on
rice; 司会 shikai = master of ceremonies; 上司
joushi = one's superior (in a company); 司る
tsukasadoru = to rule, administer DESCRIPTION:
compared to 伺(う) ukagau (to visit or ask, # 341),
this is missing the man with a slanted hat, but it
retains the old nasty doughnut above the box inside a
lean-to CUES: after the man with the slanted hat
wanders off, his 上司 joushi (superior) removes
the old nasty doughnut from above this box looking
for **Sheep** food, but the box actually contains some
Tsoup (soup) that **Casa**nova found by the **Door**

ALSO COMPARE: (許)可 kyoka = permission,
615

Part Two

Chapter 1

609. 至 PRONUNCIATIONS: ita, shi
MEANING: to reach an end EXAMPLES:
至る itaru = to lead to, to reach, to result in;
至急 shikyuu = immediately, urgently;
至難の shinan no = extremely difficult
DESCRIPTION: at the top, a pedaling leg,
representing a bicycle; at the bottom, 土 tsuchi
(dirt, # 59) CUES: on the road that 至る itaru
(leads) to some **I**talian **R**uins, I saw a 至難の
shinan no (extremely difficult) situation: this bicycle
had collided with a **Sheep** from Cuba and was stuck
in some dirt COMPARE: 倒(れる) taoeru = to
fall down, # 563; 到(着する) touchaku suru =
to arrive, # 612

610. 極 PRONUNCIATIONS: kyoku, goku, kiwa MEANINGS: extreme, to culminate

EXAMPLES: 南極 nankyoku = the antarctic, South Pole; 極力 kyokuryoku = as much as possible, to the best of one's ability; 至極 shigoku = extremely; 極める kiwameru = to attain or master; 極めて kiwamete = extremely

DESCRIPTION: on the left, 木 ki (tree, # 118); on the right, a kangaroo leg, as seen in 考(える) kangaeru (to think, # 469); to the left of the leg, 口 kuchi (mouth, # 426), which resembles a chair; to the right of the leg, an X with a line above it, which could represent a folding table; at the bottom, a carpet CUES: at the Kyoto Kool-Aid club, on a cold night, this kangaroo sits on this chair near a table next to a 木 (tree) and drinks Gold Kool-Aid through his 口 (mouth) while pondering 極力 kyokuryoku (as much as possible) how to Keep Warm, which is 極めて kiwamete (extremely) difficult to do

611. 然 PRONUNCIATIONS: zen, nen MEANINGS: naturally, yes EXAMPLES:

全然 zenzen = not at all; 自然 shizen = nature; 当然 touzen = justly; 天然 ten'nen = natural DESCRIPTION: at the upper left, a three-legged bench with a rocker bottom, as seen in 祭(り) matsuri (festival, # 377); at the upper right, 犬 inu (dog, # 190); at the bottom, four vertical lines suggesting a hot fire CUES: as a Zen monk sits on this three-legged bench with a rocker bottom, watching his Negative Nephew play with a 犬 (dog) near a fire, he looks out at 自然 shizen (Nature) and sees it as 天然 ten'nen (natural)

COMPARE: 熱(い) atsui = hot (objects), # 65; 黙(る) damaru = to keep silent, # 836, in which the three-legged bench is replaced by a sincere guy

612. 到 PRONUNCIATION: tou

MEANING: to arrive EXAMPLES: 到着する touchaku suru = to arrive; 到来する tourai suru = to arrive; 到底 toutei (with negative) = not by any means, not at all DESCRIPTION: on the left, 至(急) shikyuu (immediately, # 609), consisting of a bike on some 土 (dirt); on the right, the katakana リ ri, which features a prominent toe at the bottom CUE: リ Ri 到着する touchaku suru (arrives) on this bicycle and 至 (immediately) uses his long Toes to clean 土 (dirt) from the tires COMPARE: 倒(れる) taoeru = to fall down, # 563

613. 丈 PRONUNCIATIONS: jou, take

MEANING: length EXAMPLES: 丈夫な joubu na = healthy, hearty, strong; 大丈夫 daijoubu = all right; 丈 take = size, height DESCRIPTION: compared to 大(きい) ookii (big, # 188), this guy's right hip has slipped out of its socket CUES: as a Joke, this 大 (big) right-wing guy likes to Take his right femur out of its socket; it looks dangerous, but he is 大丈夫 daijoubu (all right) ALSO COMPARE: 才(能) sainou = talent, # 617

614. 夫 PRONUNCIATIONS: otto, fuu, fu, bu MEANINGS: husband, man

EXAMPLES: 夫 otto = husband; 夫婦 fuufu = married couple; 工夫 kufuu = ingenuity; 水夫 suifu = sailor; 大丈夫 daijoubu = all right DESCRIPTION: 大(きい) ookii (big, # 188), with an extra pair of arms at the top CUES: during the Ottoman empire, an 夫 otto (husband) was often a 大 (big) guy with an extra pair of arms who Foolishly charged around the house with his Boots on COMPARE: 未(来) mirai = future, # 672, in which the extra pair of arms belongs to a 木 (tree); 天 ten (or ama) = sky, # 189

615. 可 PRONUNCIATION: ka

MEANINGS: possible, able **EXAMPLES:**
許可 kyoka = permission; 可愛い kawaii = cute (the "w" in kawaii is added for the sake of easy pronunciation); 不可能な fukanou na = impossible; 可能な kanou na = possible

DESCRIPTION: compared to 何 nani (what, # 338), the man with the slanted hat has wandered off **CUE:** the man with the slanted hat received 許可 kyoka (permission) to abandon 何 nani in order to work on his **Car** **ALSO COMPARE:** (寿)司 sushi, # 608, in which the man with a slanted hat abandons 伺(う) ukagau (to ask or visit humbly, # 341) in order to look for sushi, and his superior checks the box for **Sh**eep food

616. 能 PRONUNCIATION: nou

MEANING: ability **EXAMPLES:** 能力 nouryoku = ability; 有能な yuunou na = able, competent; 性能 seinou = performance, efficiency; 能 nou = Noh, old-style Japanese theater; 不可能な fukanou na = impossible

DESCRIPTION: at the upper left, the katakana ム mu, the sound made by a cow; at the lower left, 月 tsuki (moon, # 148); on the right, two stacked katakana ヒ hi's, representing "hear" and "heal" **CUE:** this ム (cow) on the 月 (moon) has the 能力 nouryoku (ability) to ヒ (hear) what we say and to ヒ (heal) our illnesses, but her **N**ose is stuffy, and she cannot smell us

....

Chapter 2
617. 才 PRONUNCIATION: sai

MEANINGS: age counter, talent **EXAMPLES:** 九十才 kyuujussai = 90 years old in casual writing; in formal writing, this would be written 九十歳; 才能 sainou = talent; 天才 tensai = genius **DESCRIPTION:** this is a kneeling guy whose left hip has slipped out of its socket **CUE:** this kneeling guy is a left-wing **Sci**entist whose left hip has slipped out of its socket, and since he is a

天才 tensai (genius), he can put it back by himself **COMPARE:** 丈(夫な) joubu na = healthy, # 613

618. 解 PRONUNCIATIONS: kai, to, ge

MEANINGS: to undo, to untie, to solve **EXAMPLES:** 理解 rikai = understanding; 解決 kaiketsu = solution; 読解 dokkai = reading comprehension; 解く toku = to solve or undo, transitive; 解ける tokeru = to untie or solve, intransitive; 解熱 ge'netsu = lowering a fever **DESCRIPTION:** on the left, the fish-head guy from 触(れる) fureru (to touch, # 475); at the upper right, 刀 katana (sword, # 102); at the lower right, 牛 ushi (cow, # 205) **CUES:** this fish-head guy is a **Kai**ser who has found that the 解決 kaiketsu (solution) to his financial problems is to sell 刀 (weapons) and 牛 (beef), as well as **T**omatoes and **Ge**ckos

619. 確 PRONUNCIATIONS: tashi, kaku

MEANINGS: certain, firm **EXAMPLES:** 確かに tashika ni = for sure, certainly; 確かめる tashikameru = to confirm; 正確 seikaku = precise; 確認 kakunin = confirmation

DESCRIPTION: on the left, 石 ishi (stone, # 458), but this could be a Tall Sheepherder; on the upper right, a swooping bird; on the lower right, the cage from 進(む) susumu (to advance, # 203), without its snail **CUES:** this swooping bird on the right sees a 石 (**T**all **Sh**eepherder) next to a cage in a **Ca**ctus patch, and it asks him to 確かめる tashikameru (confirm) whether this is a trap, using 正確 seikaku (precise) instruments **COMPARE:** 勧(める) susumeru = to advise, # 698

620. 卓 PRONUNCIATIONS: taku, ta

MEANINGS: table, desk, high **EXAMPLES:** 食卓 shokutaku = dining table; 卓球 takkyuu = pingpong **DESCRIPTION:** this appears to be the wagon from 朝 asa (morning, # 291), but the wheel at the top is broken **CUES:** sitting at a 食卓 shoku**taku** (dining table) while drinking **T**ap water and **K**ool-Aid, **Ta**rzan thinks about how to fix this wagon wheel

621. 超 PRONUNCIATION: chou

MEANINGS: ultra, super, over **EXAMPLES:** 超人的な choujinteki na = superhuman; 超満員 chouman'in = overcrowded **DESCRIPTION:** on the lower left, 走(る) hashiru (to run, # 450); on the upper right, a 刀 (sword, # 102) on a 口 (box, # 426) **CUE:** a 走 (runner) who is 超 **chou** (super) fast was **Cho**sen to carry this 刀 (sword) on a 口 (box) in a parade

622. 頑 PRONUNCIATION: gan

MEANING: stubborn **EXAMPLES:** 頑張る ganbaru = to persevere, to do one's best; 頑丈 ganjou = sturdy, strong; 頑固な ganko na = stubborn **DESCRIPTION:** on the left, 元 moto (base, origin, # 421); on the right, 貝 kai (shell, # 83), with a platform on top, where a head could fit, as seen in 頭 atama (head, # 93)

CUE: **Gan**dalf is a 頑固な **gan**ko na (stubborn) wizard who sometimes loses his 頭 (head), but he always 頑張る **gan**baru (does his best), since he operates from a reliable 元 (base) **ALSO COMPARE:** 願(う) negau = to beg, # 94; 顔 kao = face, # 95; 頃 koro = approximate time, # 96; (書)類 shorui = documents, # 97; 頼(む) tanomu = to request, # 98

623. 迷 PRONUNCIATIONS: *mai*, mei, mayo

MEANINGS: to be perplexed or lost **EXAMPLES:** 迷子 maigo = lost person; 迷信 meishin = superstition; 迷惑 meiwaku = trouble, annoyance; 迷う mayou = to lose direction **DESCRIPTION:** 米 kome (cooked rice, # 326), on a snail **CUES:** **M**ighty **M**ouse helps some **Mai**ds on snails who transport **Mayo**nnaise

and 米 (rice), but he often 迷う **mayo**u (loses direction), becomes a 迷子 **mai**go (lost person) and causes 迷惑 **mei**waku (inconvenience)

624. 惑 PRONUNCIATIONS: mado, waku

MEANING: to confuse **EXAMPLES:** 惑わす madowasu = to delude or seduce; 戸惑う tomadou = to be bewildered; 迷惑 meiwaku = trouble, annoyance; 当惑 touwaku = embarassment, bewilderment **DESCRIPTION:** at the upper right, a halberd (combination lance and axe); at the upper left, 口 kuchi (mouth, # 426) with a horizontal line under it, which could represent a window with piece of tape reinforcing the lower frame; at the bottom, 心 kokoro (heart, # 306) **CUES:** when I lived in a **Ma**rs **Do**me and we fought a **Wa**r against the **K**ool-**A**id industry, I had a brave 心 (heart) and was assigned to hold a halberd and look out the 口 (window) for people who might cause us 迷惑 mei**waku** (trouble) **COMPARE:** 感(じる) kanjiru = to feel, # 640, in which there is a lean-to, and the piece of tape is *above* a 口 (mouth); 窓 mado = window, # 311

··········

Chapter 3
625. 街 PRONUNCIATIONS: kai, machi, gai

MEANING: town **EXAMPLES:** 街道 kaidou = highway, path; 街角 machikado = street corner; 街灯 gaitou = street light; 地下街 chikagai = underground shopping mall **DESCRIPTION:** on the left and right 行(く) iku (to go, # 334); in the middle of 行, two piles of 土 tsuchi (dirt, # 59) **CUES:** when the **Kai**ser 行 (goes) around the 街角 **machi**kado (street corner), these two big **Match**ing piles of 土 (dirt) block the way, but the 街灯 **gai**tou (street light) **Gui**des him **COMPARE:** 町 machi = town, # 70

626. 灯 PRONUNCIATION: tou
MEANINGS: light, lamp, torch EXAMPLES:
街灯 gaitou = street light; 電灯 dentou =
electric light; 消灯時間 shoutoujikan = lights
out time DESCRIPTION: on the left, 火 hi (fire,
#443); on the right, 丁 tei (counter for guns, # 702),
but this could be a torch (flashlight)
CUE: the 丁 (Torch) on the right shines a 電
den**tou** (electric light), and the filaments in the bulb
glow like 火 (fire)

627. 停 PRONUNCIATION: tei
MEANINGS: halt, stopping
EXAMPLES: バス停 basutei = bus stop;
各駅停車 kakuekiteisha = local train
DESCRIPTION: on the left, a man with a slanted
hat; on the upper right, the upper half of 高(い)
takai (tall, # 19); on the lower right, a nail under a
roof CUE: the man with a slanted hat is a 高 (tall)
Tailor who sews with a nail under a roof at a バス
停 basu**tei** (bus stop)

628. 駄 PRONUNCIATIONS: ta, da
MEANING: pack horse EXAMPLES: 下駄
geta = Japanese clogs; 無駄な muda na =
useless, wasteful DESCRIPTION: on the left, 馬
uma (horse, # 958); on the right, 太(る) futoru (to
get fat, # 191)
CUES: **Tar**zan told his **Da**ughter to exercise this
太 (fat) 馬 (horse), since to do otherwise would be
無駄 mu**da** (useless and wasteful)

629. 汗 PRONUNCIATIONS: ase, kan
MEANING: sweat EXAMPLES: 汗をかく
ase wo kaku = to sweat; 発汗 hakkan =
perspiration DESCRIPTION: on the left, a water
radical; on the right, a telephone pole
CUES: **Ass**es (donkeys) 汗をかく **ase** wo
kaku (sweat) when we make them carry telephone
poles like this to **Can**ada

630. 周 PRONUNCIATIONS: mawa, shuu
MEANINGS: circumference, surface, lap
EXAMPLES: 周り mawari = surrounding;
周辺 shuuhen = neighborhood, vicinity, circumference; 一周 isshuu = round, tour
DESCRIPTION: compared to 週 shuu (week,
346), which helps us to pronounce this, the snail is
absent CUES: some Marine **Wa**rriors live in our
周辺 **shuu**hen (neighborhood); they have **Shoe**s
that they hide in this box under some 土 dirt in a
tent, and they don't need a snail to carry them
ALSO COMPARE: 回(る) mawaru = to rotate,
4; (お)巡(りさん) omawarisan =
policeman, # 778

631. 差 PRONUNCIATION: sa
MEANINGS: difference, gap EXAMPLES:
時差 jisa = time difference; 時差ボケ
jisaboke = jet lag; 交差点 kousaten = traffic
intersection; 差し上げる sashiageru = to give
humbly DESCRIPTION: compared to 着(く)
tsuku (to arrive, # 52), King Rudolf's 目 me (eyes)
have been replaced with the katakana エ (e) which
represents an Egg CUE: I 差し上げた
sashiageta (humbly gave) King Rudolf an エ (egg)
to rub in his eyes because he was suffering from
時差ボケ ji**sa**boke (jet lag), but the エ was
Salty

632. 慎 PRONUNCIATIONS: shin,
tsutsushi MEANINGS: careful, prudent
EXAMPLES: 慎重な shinchou na = careful,
prudent; 慎む tsutsushimu = to be discreet, to
refrain from DESCRIPTION: on the left, an erect
man; on the right, 真 shin (truth, # 101), which
helps us to pronounce this CUES: the erect man on
the left is a 慎重な **shin**chou na (prudent) **Shin**to
priest who seeks the 真 (truth), and he digs through
boxes of **Tsui**ts (suits), **Tsui**ts and **Shee**ts
....

Chapter 4

633. 成 PRONUNCIATIONS: sei, nari, na, jou

MEANINGS: to become, to be completed **EXAMPLES:** 成功 seikou = success; 完成 kansei = completion; 成り立つ naritatsu = to consist of, to materialize; 成田 Narita = city and airport near Tokyo; 成る naru = to consist of; 成仏する joubutsu suru = to enter Nirvana **DESCRIPTION:** on the left, 万 man (10,000, # 113), without its flat hat; on the right, a halberd (combination axe and lance) **CUES:** our **Sa**feway store is guarded by this **Na**sty **Ri**ng of 万 (10,000) **Na**zi guards armed with halberds, but **Joa**n of Arc says that it is a 成功 <u>sei</u>kou (success)

634. 功 PRONUNCIATION: kou

MEANINGS: merit, achievement **EXAMPLES:** 成功 seikou = success; 功績 kouseki = achievement **DESCRIPTION:** on the left, the katakana エ e which represents eggs; on the right, 力 chikara (force, # 107) **CUE:** if you want to 成功する sei<u>kou</u> suru (succeed) in the **Co**al business, you need to eat エ (eggs) for breakfast and expend a lot of 力 (force)

635. 継 PRONUNCIATIONS: tsu, kei

MEANINGS: inherit, succeed to **EXAMPLES:** 継ぐ tsugu = to succeed to, to inherit; 乗り継ぐ noritsugu = to connect to a different flight, train, etc.; 継ぎ目 tsugime = joint, seam; 継承する keishou suru = to succeed to **DESCRIPTION:** on the left, a 糸 skeet shooter (# 219); on the right, 米 kome (rice, # 326) on a shelf, which is used to make rice tsoup (soup) **CUES:** this 糸 (skeet shooter) is making 米 (rice) **T**soup (soup) on a shelf in the **Ca**ve where he lives, but one day he will 継ぐ <u>tsu</u>gu (inherit) the title of Chief Skeetshooter **COMPARE:** 断(る) kotowaru = to refuse, # 704

636. 単 PRONUNCIATION: tan

MEANINGS: simple, only **EXAMPLES:** 簡単 kantan = easy; 単語 tango = word; 単位 tan'i = credit (school) or unit; 単行本 tankoubon = special book, separate volume **DESCRIPTION:** 早(い) hayai (early, # 34), with three waves of heat streaming from its top **CUE:** since I arrived at the beach 早 (early), I had waves of heat rising from my head all day, and it was 簡単 kan<u>tan</u> (easy) to get a nice **Tan**

637. 余 PRONUNCIATIONS: ama, yo

MEANINGS: excess, leftover **EXAMPLES:** 余り amari = surplus, rest; 余る amaru = to be left over, to remain; 余計 yokei = excessive, all the more; 余分 yobun = surplus, extra **DESCRIPTION:** like 途(中) tochuu (on the way, # 378), 余 features a pavilion spinning like a tornado, but 余 is lacking a snail **CUES:** I was riding in a pavilion on a snail in the **Ama**zon, 途 (on the way) to pick up some **Yo**gurt, when I realized that the snail was 余計に <u>yo</u>kei ni (excessively) slow, and I got rid of it

638. 陣 PRONUNCIATION: jin

MEANINGS: battle array, ranks, camp, position **EXAMPLES:** 陣地 jinchi = encampment, position; 背水の陣 haisui no jin = back to the wall, last stand **DESCRIPTION:** on the left, ß beta from the Greek alphabet; on the right, 車 kuruma (car, # 283) **CUE:** this ß (Greek) soldier puts on his **Jeans**, gets in his 車 (car) and drives to his 陣地 <u>jin</u>chi (encampment)

639. 数 **PRONUNCIATIONS: kazo, kazu, zuu, suu** **MEANINGS:** number, to count **EXAMPLES:** 数える kazoeru = to count; 数 kazu = number; 人数 ninzuu = number of people; 数字 suuji = numeral, figure; 数学 suugaku = mathematics **DESCRIPTION:** on the upper left, 米 kome (rice, # 326); on the lower left, 女 onna (female, # 235); on the right, a dancer with a ponytail **CUES:** this 女 (female), who lives in a **Ca**sino **Zo**ne, **Casu**ally carries a bundle of 米 (rice) to this dancer, who lives at the **Zoo**, and asks her to 数える **kazo**eru (count) the 数 **kazu** (number) of grains, since the dancer is **Su**per at 数学 **suu**gaku (mathematics) **COMPARE:** 教(える) oshieru = to teach, # 187

640. 感 **PRONUNCIATION: kan** **MEANINGS:** to feel **EXAMPLES:** 感じる kanjiru = to feel; 感動する kandou suru = to be moved; 感心な kanshin na = impressive, admirable; 感じ kanji = impression, perception, feeling **DESCRIPTION:** on the upper left, a lean-to; under the lean-to, 口 kuchi (mouth, # 426), with a line over it representing a strip of tape; under 口, 心 kokoro (heart, # 306); on the right, a halberd (combination axe and lance) **CUE:** in **Ca**na**da**, when people are locked up in lean-to's, have their 口 (mouths) covered with tape, and are threatened with halberds, their 心 (hearts) beat rapidly, and they 感じる **kan**jiru (feel) anger **COMPARE:** (迷)惑 meiwaku (trouble), # 624, in which there is no lean-to, and the piece of tape is *under* 口

....

Chapter 5

641. 暮 **PRONUNCIATIONS: ku, bo, gu** **MEANINGS:** sunset, end of a year **EXAMPLES:** 暮らし kurashi = living, life; 暮らす kurasu = to make a living; 暮れ kure = year end, nightfall; お歳暮 oseibo = year end gift;

日暮れ higure = nightfall, dusk; 一人暮らし hitorigurashi = to live alone **DESCRIPTION:** at the top, a plant radical; below that, 日 hi (sun, # 32); below that, 大(きい) ookii (big, # 188), with a wide base; below that, another 日 (sun) **CUES:** this is a tale of two 日 (suns): the one at the top 暮らす **ku**rasu (makes a living) by shining light on plants, while the one at the bottom is 大 (big); the top sun drinks only **Ko**ol-Aid and is **Bo**ring, but the bottom sun is **Goo**fy **COMPARE:** 幕 maku = theater curtain, # 653, in which Bo Peep appears at the bottom; (応)募 oubo = application, # 1109, in which 力 chikara (force) appears at the bottom

642. 限 **PRONUNCIATIONS: gen, kagi** **MEANINGS:** limit, restrict, best of ability **EXAMPLES:** 限界 genkai = limit; 最低限 saiteigen = maximum; 最大限 saidaigen = maximum; 限る kagiru = to be limited to; 限らない kagiranai = not necessarily **DESCRIPTION:** on the left, ß beta from the Greek alphabet; on the right, 良(い) yoi (good, # 303), without its pointy hat **CUES:** this ß (Greek) guy named **Gen**ghis Khan is a 良 (good) hunter who can **Ca**ll **Gee**se, and there is no 限界 **gen**kai (limit) on his activities **COMPARE:** (屋)根 yane = roof, # 741

643. 貴 **PRONUNCIATIONS: ki, touto** **MEANING:** precious **EXAMPLES:** 貴重な kichou na = valuable; 貴ぶ toutobu = to value, respect **DESCRIPTION:** at the top, 中 naka (inside, # 8), resting on a platform; at the bottom, 貝 kai (shell, or three-drawer money chest, # 83), **CUES:** I keep 貴重な **ki**chou na (valuable) things, including my **Ke**ys and my **To**y **To**ads, in this three-drawer 貝 (money chest), and the 中 symbol above the chest reminds me that my valuables are 中 (inside)

644. 揃 PRONUNCIATION: soro

MEANINGS: to be complete, to be equal
EXAMPLES: 揃う sorou = to be complete, to be equal, to be the same, to assemble; 揃える soroeru = to arrange, prepare, make uniform
DESCRIPTION: on the left, a kneeling guy; on the right, 前 mae (before, # 157) CUE: this kneeling guy feels **Sorro**w that he left town 前 (before) the circus came, and he 揃う **soro**u (assembles) with other non-attendees to commiserate

645. 掃 PRONUNCIATIONS: sou, ha

MEANING: to sweep EXAMPLES: 掃除する souji suru = to clean; 掃く haku = to sweep; 掃き集める hakiatsumeru = to sweep up together DESCRIPTION: compared to 帰(る) kaeru (to return home, # 566), the katakana character リ Ri on the left has been replaced by this kneeling guy CUES: this kneeling guy will 帰 (return home), 掃く **ha**ku (sweep) the house, get on his knees, and use **Soap** to 掃除する **sou**ji suru (clean) his floors before the **Hacker** party ALSO COMPARE: 婦(人) fujin = woman, # 1165

646. 除 PRONUNCIATIONS: jo, nozo, ji

MEANING: to remove EXAMPLES: 削除する sakujo suru = to delete, eliminate; 除く nozoku = to remove; 掃除する souji suru = to clean DESCRIPTION: on the left, ß beta from the Greek alphabet; on the right, the spinning pavilion from 余(計) yokei (excessive, # 637), which belongs to Joan of Arc CUES: since this ß (Greek) guy is 余 (excessively) interested in **Joan of Arc** and her spinning pavilion, he drives to see her but ends up parking in the **No Zone**, from which a tow truck 除く **nozo**ku (removes) his **Jeep** COMPARE: 望(み) nozomi = hope, dream, wish, # 664; 徐(々に) jojo ni = gradually, # 904, in which the ß (Greek) guy has been replaced by a man with a slanted hat

647. 爪 PRONUNCIATIONS: tsuma, tsume

MEANINGS: nail, claw EXAMPLES: 爪楊枝 tsumayouji = toothpick; 爪 tsume = nail, claw; 爪きり tsumekiri = nail cutter DESCRIPTION: this resembles a toenail, cut square at the top, with long roots extending toward the bottom CUES: my **Tsuma** (wife) has long 爪 **tsume** (nails), and she uses them to open **Tsume**tai (cold) cartons of milk

648. 簡 PRONUNCIATION: kan

MEANING: simple and easy EXAMPLES: 簡単 kantan = simple and easy DESCRIPTION: at the top, 竹 take (bamboo, # 134); at the bottom 間 aida (duration, between, # 411), which depicts a 日 (sun, # 32) between gate posts CUE: in **Can**ada, people get **Tan**s 簡単に **kan**tan ni (easily) by hanging hammocks 間 (between) 竹 (bamboo) gate posts and lying in them on 日 (sunny) days

....

Chapter 6
649. 涙 PRONUNCIATION: namida

MEANINGS: tear, sympathy EXAMPLES: 涙 namida = tears DESCRIPTION: on the left, a water radical; on the right, 戻(る) modoru (to return, # 75) CUE: **Na**ncy has a **Mida**s touch and plenty of money, but when she 戻 (returns) to see all this water flooding her estate, her 涙 **namida** (tears) will flow

650. 煎 PRONUNCIATIONS: sen, i

MEANING: to boil EXAMPLES: 煎じる senjiru = to boil; 煎る iru = to roast or toast DESCRIPTION: at the top, 前 mae (before, # 157); at the bottom four flames suggesting a fire CUES: when our **Sen**ator came here 前 (before) the election, we were 煎じている **sen**jite iru (boiling) water over a fire and 煎って **i**tte (roasting) **Eels**

651. 身 PRONUNCIATIONS: shin, mi

MEANINGS: body, flesh EXAMPLES: 身長 shinchou = a person's height; 出身 shusshin = birthplace, hometown, alma mater; 身 mi = body, person, e.g., 一人身 hitori mi = one person; 親身に shinmi ni = kindly; 身元 mimoto = identity, lineage DESCRIPTION: 自(分) jibun (self, # 55), resting on a rickety chair, which is bisected and supported by a shiny sword CUES: when 自 (myself) climbs onto my rickety chair, people from my 出身 shus**shin** (birthplace) try to support me by driving a **Shin**y sword into the ground, so that my 身 **mi** (body) doesn't fall down, and they feed me **Mea**ls

652. 己 PRONUNCIATIONS: onore, ko

MEANING: self EXAMPLES: 己 onore = self; 利己的な rikoteki na = egotistic, self-centered; 利己主義 rikoshugi = egotism, selfishness DESCRIPTION: a snake CUES: this snake was the h**Onore**e at our awards ceremony, but its 己 **onore** (self) got **Cold**, so it went home

653. 幕 PRONUNCIATIONS: maku, baku

MEANINGS: curtain, drapery EXAMPLES: 幕 maku = theater curtain, act of a play; 字幕 jimaku = subtitle; 幕府 bakufu = shogunate administration DESCRIPTION: at the top, a plant radical; below that, 日 hi (sun, # 32); below that, 大(きい) ookii (big, # 188), with a wide base; below that, Bo Peep, as seen in 帽(子) boushi (hat, # 243) CUES: the 日 (sun) makes these plants grow, but it has caused 大 (big) problems for Bo Peep, who has **Mac**ular degeneration and spends her days behind closed 幕 **maku** (drapery) enjoying **Ba**li **Coo**lers COMPARE: 暮(らす) kurasu = to make a living, # 641, in which a 日 (sun) appears at the bottom; (応)募 oubo = application, # 1109, in which 力 chikara (force) appears at the bottom

654. 流 PRONUNCIATIONS: naga, ru, ryuu

MEANINGS: a stream, to flow EXAMPLES: 流す nagasu = to flush; 流れる nagareru = to flow; 流布 rufu = circulation, dissemination; 流行 ryuukou = vogue, fashion; 一流の ichiryuu no = first-rate; 風流な fuuryuu na = refined; 電流 denryuu = electric current DESCRIPTION: on the left, a water radical; at the upper right, a pedaling leg suggesting a cyclist; at the lower right, three legs CUES: when this cyclist encounters **Naga**ina (a snake from a Kipling story) in his **R**oom, he climbs onto this three-legged stool, empties his **Reu**sable water bottles onto her head, and watches the water 流れる **naga**reru (flow) COMPARE: 留(学) ryuugaku = foreign study, # 71

655. 韓 PRONUNCIATION: kan

MEANING: Korea EXAMPLES: 韓国 kankoku = S. Korea DESCRIPTION: on the left, the wagon from 朝 asa (morning, # 291); on the right, 違(う) chigau (to differ, # 355), without its snail CUE: in 韓国 **kan**koku (S. Korea), I rode in a wagon that was pulled by a **Kan**garoo, which was 違 (different) from what I expected

656. 費 PRONUNCIATIONS: tsui, hi

MEANING: to spend EXAMPLES: 費やす tsuiyasu = to spend time or money; 費用 hiyou = cost; 会費 kaihi = membership fee DESCRIPTION: at the top, 沸(く) waku (to boil, # 531), without its water radical; at the bottom, 貝 kai (shell, or three-drawer money chest, # 83) CUES: in order to make **Tsu**ite (sweet) candy, I 費やす **tsui**yasu (spend) money to buy a 沸 (boiler) for the top of my 貝 (money chest) and **Heat** up the ingredients; therefore my 費用 **hi**you (costs) are high

....

Chapter 7

657. 仲 **PRONUNCIATIONS: naka, chuu**

MEANING: relationship **EXAMPLES:** 仲 naka = relationship; 仲良し nakayoshi = close friend; 仲介 chuukai = mediation **DESCRIPTION:** on the left, a man with a slanted hat; on the right, 中 naka or chuu (inside, middle, # 8), which helps us with both of these pronunciations and which looks like yakitori (grilled chicken on a stick) **CUES:** this man with a slanted hat works at the National Cathedral and has a 仲 **naka** (relationship) with his 仲良し **naka**yoshi (close friend), and they both **Chew** 中 (chicken on a stick)

658. 紹 **PRONUNCIATION: shou**

MEANING: to introduce a person to someone **EXAMPLES:** 紹介 shoukai = introduction; 紹介状 shoukaijou = letter of introduction **DESCRIPTION:** compared to 招(待) shoutai (invitation, # 560), which helps us to pronounce this, the kneeling guy on the left has been replaced by a 糸 skeet shooter (# 219), but this kanji retains 刀 katana (sword, # 102), above 口 kuchi (mouth, # 426), which resembles a writing table **CUES:** a **Sho**gun asks a 糸 (skeet shooter) for a 紹介 **shou**kai (introduction) to the skeet shooter's daughter, and he places this 刀 (sword) on a 口 (table) to **Show** that he is serious about this **ALSO COMPARE:** 給(料) kyuuryou = salary, # 997

659. 介 **PRONUNCIATION: kai**

MEANINGS: to mediate, to help **EXAMPLES:** 紹介 shoukai = introduction; 仲介者 chuukaisha = mediator **DESCRIPTION:** this is an upwards-facing arrow; compared to (世)界 sekai (world, # 69), which helps us to pronounce this, it's missing the 田 (rice paddy) at the top

CUE: the **Kai**ser plans to serve as a 仲介者 chuu**kai**sha (mediator) in a moon dispute, but first we need to shoot him up into the sky

660. 裕 **PRONUNCIATION: yuu**

MEANINGS: abundant, rich **EXAMPLE:** 裕福な yuufuku na = rich, in the sense of affluent **DESCRIPTION:** on the left, happy Jimmy Carter, as seen in 初(めて) hajimete (for the first time, # 104); on the right, the sweating house from 欲(しい) hoshii (desire, # 535) **CUE:** happy Jimmy becomes 裕福 **yuu**fuku (rich) 初 (for the first time) and decides to buy this sweating house in the **Yu**kon **ALSO COMPARE:** 浴(衣) yukata = summer kimono, # 256

661. 福 **PRONUNCIATION: fuku**

MEANINGS: fortune, good luck **EXAMPLES:** 福 fuku = good luck, fortune; 幸福 koufuku = happiness **DESCRIPTION:** on the left, the Shah, as seen in (会)社 kaisha (company, # 271); on the upper right, 口 kuchi (mouth, # 426), with a strip of tape over it; at the lower right, 田 (rice paddy, # 68) **CUE:** this Shah had the 福 **fuku** (good luck) to find this 田 (rice paddy) in **Fuku**oka, but he doesn't want to talk about it before completing the sale, so he keeps his 口 (mouth) taped shut **COMPARE:** 富(士山) fujisan = Mt. Fuji, # 939; 幅 haba = width, # 1185

662. 羨 **PRONUNCIATIONS: sen, uraya**

MEANING: envy **EXAMPLES:** 羨望 senbou = envy; 羨ましい urayamashii = envious **DESCRIPTION:** at the top, 羊 hitsuji (sheep, not included in this Catalogue), missing its tail; at the bottom, 次 tsugi (next, # 536) **CUES:** a **Sen**ator has a big ranch where he keeps 羊 (sheep), and 次 (next) he finds **Ura**nium in the **Ya**rd, which makes other politicians feel even more 羨ましい **uraya**mashii (envious) **COMPARE:** 茨(城) ibaraki = a prefecture in Japan, # 1007, which replaces the 羊 (sheep) at the top with a plant radical

663. 希 PRONUNCIATION: ki

MEANINGS: rare, wish **EXAMPLE:** 希望 kibou = hope **DESCRIPTION:** at the top, an X; below the X, someone hugging Bo Peep, as seen in 帽(子) boushi (hat, # 243) **CUE:** I hug my friend Bo Peep in **Kiev**, while a mysterious X hovers overhead, and we have some 希望 **ki**bou (hope) that this X will turn out to be a good omen **COMPARE:** 布 nuno = cloth, # 687

664. 望

PRONUNCIATIONS: bou, nozo, mou
MEANINGS: to wish, to overlook (a view)
EXAMPLES: 希望 kibou = hope; 志望 shibou = ambition; 望み nozomi = hope, dream, wish; 所望 shomou = desire, wish, request
DESCRIPTION: at the upper left, 亡(くなる) nakunaru (to die, # 585); at the upper right, 月 tsuki (moon, # 148); at the bottom, 王 ou (king, # 1077)
CUES: this 王 (king) has a 志望 shi**bou** (ambition) to have his **B**ones buried on the 月 (moon) after he 亡 (dies), but when he summons **NASA** scientists to his palace to discuss this, they park in the **No Zo**ne next to the **Mo**at and get towed **COMPARE:** 除(く) nozoku = to remove, # 646

....

Chapter 8
665. 垢 PRONUNCIATIONS: kou, aka

MEANINGS: dirt, grime **EXAMPLES:** 歯垢 shikou = dental plaque ; 垢 aka = dirt
DESCRIPTION: on the left, 土 tsuchi (dirt, # 59); in the middle, an F; on the lower right, 口 kuchi (mouth, # 426) **CUES:** in **Colombia**, I attended an **Aca**demy that was constructed on 土 (dirt), but I learned that excessive 垢 **aka** (dirt) on my homework would cause me to get F's and that 歯垢 shi**kou** (dental plaque) can be caused by poor 口 (oral) hygiene

666. 離 PRONUNCIATIONS: hana, ri

MEANING: to separate **EXAMPLES:** 離れる hanareru = to part; 離婚 rikon = divorce; 距離 kyori = distance; 離陸する ririku suru = to take off (flight) **DESCRIPTION:** on the left, two stacked cans; the upper can contains an X and the lower one, which is upside-down, contains the katakana ム mu; on the right, a cage for fishing **CUES:** **Hannah** fishes with a cage on a **Reef** and catches X's and ム's, which she 離れる **hana**reru (separates) into two cans

667. 貯 PRONUNCIATIONS: cho, ta

MEANING: to save money or goods
EXAMPLES: 貯金 chokin = savings; 貯める tameru = to save (money)
DESCRIPTION: on the left, 貝 kai (shell, money chest, # 83); on the upper right, a bad haircut; on the lower right, a nail **CUES:** Margaret **Cho**, who has a bad haircut like this one, has a business which uses nails like this to nail **Tar**paper onto roofs, and she 貯める **ta**meru (saves) her 貯金 **cho**kin (savings) in this 貝 (money chest)

668. 旦 PRONUNCIATIONS: tan, dan

MEANINGS: dawn, early morning
EXAMPLES: 一旦 ittan = for a moment, once; 旦那 danna = master, husband; 旦那さん dannasan = male customer, master
DESCRIPTION: 日 hi (sun, # 32), with a line under it which could represent a dance floor **CUES:** since my 旦那 **dan**na (husband) spends time in the 日 (sun), he has a nice **Tan**, and he likes to **Da**nce on this floor
COMPARE: 担(当) tantou = charge (duty), # 729, which helps us to pronounce this

669. 那 PRONUNCIATION: na

MEANING: what? EXAMPLE: 旦那 danna = husband DESCRIPTION: on the left, 月 tsuki (moon, # 148), but all of the horizontal lines in 月 have been extended to the left; on the right, ß beta from the Greek alphabet CUE: when my ß (Greek) 旦那 dan**na** (husband) visited **Na**rnia, he saw a drawing of the 月 (moon), in which the artist had extended all of the horizontal lines to the left

670. 捕 PRONUNCIATIONS: to, ho, tsuka, tora MEANINGS: catch, capture, seize

EXAMPLES: 捕る toru = to catch; 捕虜 horyo = prisoner of war, captive; 捕まえる tsukamaeru = to capture or catch; 捕まる tsukamaru = to be caught; 捕らえる toraeru = to arrest, capture or understand DESCRIPTION: on the left, a kneeling guy; at the upper right, the top part of 犬 inu (dog, # 190) juggling a ball; at the lower right, 用(事) youji (errand, # 364), which resembles a fence CUES: this kneeling guy, who keeps this 犬 (dog) behind this 用 (fence), has a **To**e protruding from a **Ho**le in his sock, but he will get a leash from the **Tsui**tcase (suitcase) in his **Ca**r and take the 犬 (dog) out to 捕る **to**ru (catch) some **To**rtoises and **Ra**bbits COMPARE: 補(佐) hosa = aid, # 995, which helps us to pronounce this

671. 浮 PRONUNCIATIONS: u, uwa, fu, *uki* MEANING: to float EXAMPLES:

浮かぶ ukabu = to float, intransitive; 浮く uku = to float, transitive; 浮気 uwaki = extramarital affair; 浮つく uwatsuku = to be fickle or restless; 浮浪者 furousha = vagrant; 浮世 ukiyo = floating world, transitory life DESCRIPTION: on the left, a water radical; on the right, 学 gaku (learning, # 184), with a line at the top which could represent a shawl CUES: when an Uber car runs off a bridge and 浮かぶ **u**kabu (floats), people with 学 (learning) put shawls over

their heads and say "**U**ber was **Wa**rned" and "they are hiring **Foo**lish drivers," but other people say "**U**ber is the **Key** to our economy"

672. 未 PRONUNCIATIONS: ima, mi

MEANING: yet EXAMPLES: 未だに imada ni = even now, still, until this very day; 未来 mirai = future; 未開 mikai = primitive; 未経験 mikeiken = inexperienced

DESCRIPTION: 木 ki (tree, # 118), with an extra pair of branches; the lower branches are longer than the upper pair CUES: an **Ea**gle at the **Ma**ll 未だに imada ni (even now) perches on the shorter branches at the top of this tree, but in the 未来 **mi**rai (future), it will leave its perch to seek a **Mea**l COMPARE: (週)末 shuumatsu = weekend, # 119, in which the longer pair of branches is at the top, since trees reach for the sky on weekends; (意)味 imi = meaning, # 245, which includes a mirror; 夫 otto = husband, # 614, in which an extra pair of arms is seen on 大 (big) rather than on 木 (tree)

....

Chapter 9

673. 絶 PRONUNCIATIONS: ze, zetsu, ta

MEANINGS: to sever, discontinue EXAMPLES: 絶対に zettai ni = absolutely, by any means; 絶交する zekkou suru = to break off a relationship; 絶望 zetsubou = despair; 絶える taeru = to discontinue or cease DESCRIPTION: on the left, 糸 skeet shooter (# 219); on the right, 色 iro (color, # 473) CUES: this 糸 (skeet shooter) is a **Zen** monk who 絶対に **ze**ttai ni (absolutely) wants to wear a **Zen Tsui** (suit), but the tsuits they are selling are the wrong 色 (color) and don't fit him because he is too **Ta**ll

674. 対 PRONUNCIATIONS: tai, tsui

MEANINGS: opposing, pair EXAMPLES: 絶対に zettai ni = absolutely, by any means; 対して taishite = against, in contrast to, as opposed to, toward; 対する tai suru = to face toward, to confront; 対応する taiou suru = to address a problem; 対決する taiketsu suru = to confront; 対 tsui = pair, e.g., 対の tsui no = in a pair DESCRIPTION: on the upper left, a tire stop used in parking lots; on the lower left, an X; on the right, the kneeling guy seen in 村 mura (village, # 131), with a stick of gum on the ground nearby CUES: this kneeling guy, who comes from a 村 (village) and chews gum, 対する **tai** suru (opposes) **T**ire stops because he thinks they cause **T**ire damage, and he marks them all with **X**'s, but a **Tsui**dish (Swedish) parking lot attendant 対決す る **tai**ketsu suru (confronts) him about this practice

675. 悔 PRONUNCIATIONS: kai, ku, kuya MEANINGS: to regret, vexing

EXAMPLES: 後悔 koukai = regret; 悔い kui = regret; 悔やむ kuyamu = to regret, repent; 悔しい kuyashii = vexing, mortifying DESCRIPTION: on the left, an erect man; on the right, 毎 mai (every, # 336) CUES: this erect man is a **Kai**ser who feels 後悔 kou**kai** (regret) because 毎 (every) day he forgets to bring **K**ool-**A**id to his **Coo**ped-up **Ya**k, and this is 悔しい **kuya**shii (mortifying) COMPARE: 海 kai = ocean, # 337, which helps us to pronounce this

676. 宗 PRONUNCIATIONS: mune, sou, shuu MEANING: religious belief

EXAMPLES: 宗 mune = religion, sect; 宗家 souke = head of family, originator; 宗教 shuukyou = religion DESCRIPTION: at the top, a bad haircut; at the bottom, a spinning pavilion as seen in 祭(り) matsuri (festival, # 377) CUES: our 宗教 **shuu**kyou (religion) encourages

祭 (festivals) with spinning pavilions like this, and it attracts **M**oon **E**xperts with bad haircuts like this who promise to stay **S**ober and wear nice **Sho**es COMPARE: 余(り) amari = surplus, # 637

677. 応 PRONUNCIATIONS: kota, ou

MEANING: to respond willingly EXAMPLES: 応える kotaeru = to respond or affect; 応じる oujiru = to respond or comply with; 一応 ichiou = more or less, tentatively, for the time being; 応募 oubo = application, subscription; 応接室 ousetsu shitsu = reception room; 相応 sou'ou = appropriate, suitable DESCRIPTION: on the left and top, a lean-to with a small chimney on top; inside the lean-to, 心 kokoro (heart, # 306) CUES: my 心 (heart) is in this lean-to with a small chimney in N. Da**Kota**, where I plan to live while growing **O**ats, at least 一応 ichi**ou** (for the time being) COMPARE: 答える kotaeru = to answer, # 295

678. 仏 PRONUNCIATIONS: butsu, bu, hotoke MEANING: Buddha EXAMPLES:

仏壇 butsudan = Buddhist altar found in Japanese homes; 仏教 bukkyou = Buddhism; 仏 hotoke = Buddha DESCRIPTION: on the left, a man with a slanted hat; on the right, the katakana ム mu, which is the sound made by a cow CUES: my 仏教 **bu**kkyou (Buddhism) teacher wears a slanted hat, wears nice **B**oots, drinks **B**ooze and eats **H**ot**toke**eki (pancakes); he says that, if you want to become a 仏 **hotoke** (**B**uddha), you should never eat ム (cows)

679. 壇 PRONUNCIATION: dan

MEANING: stage EXAMPLES: 壇 dan = stage; 仏壇 butsudan = Buddhist altar found in Japanese homes DESCRIPTION: on the left, 土 tsuchi (dirt), # 59; on the upper right, a roof and chimney; below that, 回(る) mawaru (to rotate), # 4; below that, 日 hi (sun), # 32; at the bottom, a carpet; the items on the right resemble an older-model TV set with an antenna, resting on a cabinet on a carpet

CUES: **Dan**iel Boone sits in the **Dan**k 土 (dirt) to watch this TV which is next to the 仏壇 butsu**dan** (Buddhist altar) in his home

680. 反 PRONUNCIATIONS: han, so, tan
MEANINGS: to oppose, to reverse, cloth
EXAMPLES: 反対 hantai = opposition, the reverse; 反り返る sorikaeru = to bend back or warp; 反物 tanmono = cloth, textile
DESCRIPTION: at the top, an F; at the bottom, an X **CUES:** **Hans**el was に反対 ni **han**tai (in opposition to) the witch, and he had a plan to **Soak** her in a **Tan**k, but the plan was poor, and Gretel gave it a grade of F and marked it with an X
COMPARE: (ご)飯 gohan = meal, cooked rice, # 400, which helps us to pronounce this; 返(す) kaesu = to return something, # 356

··········

Chapter 10
681. 香 PRONUNCIATIONS: kou, kao
MEANINGS: incense, smell, perfume
EXAMPLES: 線香 senkou = incense stick; 香水 kousui = perfume; 香り kaori = fragrance, aroma **DESCRIPTION:** at the top, 木 ki (tree, # 118), wearing a jaunty hat; at the bottom, 日 hi (sun, # 32)
CUES: this 木 (tree) in **Colombia** puts on a jaunty hat and stands in the 日 (sun) with some **Cows**, enjoying the 香り **kao**ri (fragrance) of its flowers

682. 非 PRONUNCIATION: hi
MEANINGS: mistake, negative, wrong
EXAMPLES: 非常 hijou = emergency; 非常な hijou na = extreme, great; 非難 hinan = criticism, accusation, blame **DESCRIPTION:** reportedly, this represents two wings on opposite sides of a bird **CUE:** this bird is a **He**ro with two wings who can fly in a 非常 **hi**jou (emergency)
COMPARE: 兆 chou = trillion, # 849

683. 常 PRONUNCIATIONS: jou, tsune
MEANINGS: constant, always **EXAMPLES:** 非常 hijou = emergency; 非常な hijou na = extreme, great; 通常 tsuujou = usual; 常に tsune ni = always, continually **DESCRIPTION:** at the top, a hat with three antennae, as seen in 学 gaku (learning, # 184); below that, 口 kuchi (mouth, # 426), above a spinning base, like the one found in (都)市 toshi (city, # 242)
CUES: **Jo**an of Arc was a 学 (learned) person with a big 口 (mouth) who 市 (spun) from one hi**jou** 非常 (emergency) to another, but her life **Tsoon** (soon) Ended **ALSO COMPARE:** 営(業) eigyou = business, # 684

684. 営 PRONUNCIATIONS: ei, itona
MEANINGS: to conduct business, barracks
EXAMPLES: 経営 keiei = management; 営業 eigyou = business; 非営利 hieiri = nonprofit; 営む itonamu = to run a business
DESCRIPTION: at the top, three characters on a roof, as seen in 学 gaku (learning, # 184); at the bottom, (風)呂 furo (bath, # 7) **CUES:** honest Abe was a 学 (learned) man who used to sit in the 呂 (bath) and invent instruments with **Eerie Tonal** qualities, and he started an 営業 **ei**gyou (business) to sell them **COMPARE:** (非)常 hijou = emergency, # 683; 宮(殿) kyuuden = palace, # 1079

685. 漁 PRONUNCIATIONS: ryou, gyo
MEANING: to fish **EXAMPLES:** 漁 ryou = fishing; 漁師 ryoushi = fisherman; 漁業 gyogyou = fishing business **DESCRIPTION:** at the left, a water radical; at the right, 魚 sakana (fish, # 80) **CUES:** Pope **Leo** looked at this water, saw this 魚 (fish) and decided to start a 漁業 **gyo**gyou (fishing business) to sell fish **Gyoza**

686. 団 PRONUNCIATIONS: dan, ton
MEANING: a group of people **EXAMPLES:**
団体 dantai = group of people, an organization;
団結する danketsu suru = to unite or
consolidate; 布団 futon = floor cushion, or
Japanese bedding **DESCRIPTION:** the kneeling
guy seen in 付(く) tsuku (to stick, # 132) is stuck
inside a box, with a stick of gum on the ground
nearby **CUES:** this kneeling guy wants to **D**ance
and to eat **Ton** katsu (breaded pork) with his 団体
dantai (group), but he has gotten 付 (stuck) to the
gum that he dropped in this box
COMPARE: 困(る) komaru = to be inconvenienced, # 280, in which a *tree* is stuck in a box

687. 布 PRONUNCIATIONS: nuno, fu
MEANINGS: cloth, to spread **EXAMPLES:** 布
nuno = cloth; 布団 futon = floor cushion,
Japanese bedding; 毛布 moufu = blanket;
流布 rufu = circulation, dissemination
DESCRIPTION: a person hugging Bo Peep, as seen
in 帽(子) boushi (hat, # 243) **CUES:** I'm about
to get a **N**ew **No**se from a plastic surgeon, but I
don't want to look **Fo**olish, so I plan to hang out with
my friend Bo Peep and keep my face covered with
布 **nuno** (cloth) until the swelling goes down
COMPARE: (恐)怖 kyoufu = fear or horror,
# 463, which helps us to pronounce this; 希(望)
kibou = hope, # 663

688. 毛 PRONUNCIATIONS: mou, ke, ge
MEANING: hair **EXAMPLES:** 毛布 moufu =
blanket; 毛 ke = hair, fur, wool; 胸毛 munage =
chest hair **DESCRIPTION:** compared to 手 te
(hand, # 23), 毛 has a longer base which extends to
the right instead of the left
CUES: **Mo**ses was a right-wing guy who lived in
Kenya, slept under a 毛布 **mou**fu (blanket) with
Geckos, and had lots of 毛 **ke** (hair) growing on the
back of his 手 (hands)
....

Chapter 11
689. 巨 PRONUNCIATION: kyo
MEANING: huge **EXAMPLES:** 巨大 kyodai =
huge; 巨人 kyojin = a giant **DESCRIPTION:**
this looks like a child's swing set that has been
knocked onto its left side **CUE:** a 巨人 **kyo**jin
(giant) knocked over this swing set in **Kyo**to
COMPARE: 臣(民) shinmin = royal subject,
1039

690. 輪 PRONUNCIATIONS: rin, wa
MEANING: wheel **EXAMPLES:** 車輪 sharin =
wheel; 三輪車 sanrinsha = tricycle; 輪 wa =
round shape (ring, circle etc.); 内輪 uchiwa =
family or inner circle; 指輪 yubiwa = ring
DESCRIPTION: on the left, 車 kuruma (car,
283); on the upper right, a peaked roof with a
ceiling below; on the lower right, 冊 satsu (counter
for books, # 568); taken together, the radicals on the
right could represent a library
CUES: **Rin**go called a ride-Sha**Ring** service in order
to go to this 冊 (library), but a 車輪 sha**rin**
(wheel) fell off this 車 (car), and he had to **W**alk
COMPARE: 輸(入) yunyuu = to import, # 288,
in which 冊 satsu on the lower right is replaced by
月 tsuki (moon) and リ ri; (口)論 kouron =
argument, # 813, in which 車 (car) on the left is
replaced by 言(う) iu (to speak, # 430)

691. 指 PRONUNCIATIONS: yubi, shi,
sashi, sa, za[1] MEANING: finger **EXAMPLES:**
指 yubi = finger; 指先 yubisaki = fingertip;
指差す yubisasu = to point to (with finger);
指輪 yubiwa = ring; 指定席 shiteiseki =
reserved seat; 指図 sashizu = direction, command;
指す sasu = to point; 目指す mezasu = to aim
at **DESCRIPTION:** on the left, a kneeling guy;
on the upper right, the katakana ヒ hi, which
reminds us of a hero; on the lower right, 日 hi (sun,
32) **CUES:** this kneeling guy on the left works

with this ヒ (hero) on the right, who controls the **Yu**kon **Bee**f industry with one 指 **yubi** (finger); during the day, they kneel in the heat of the 日 (sun) watching **Shee**p, but at night they sleep on **Sa**tin **Shee**ts and dream of **Sa**skatchewan **COMPARE:** 脂(肪) shibou = fat, # 1180, which helps us to pronounce this

692. 廻 PRONUNCIATION: ne

MEANING: to revolve or turn **EXAMPLE:** 輪廻 rinne = samsara, cycle of death and rebirth **DESCRIPTION:** 回(る) mawaru (to rotate, # 4), riding on a snail **CUES:** I'm stuck in a box traveling on the back of this snail in the **Ne**therlands, 回 (rotating) back and forth and wondering whether my **Ne**xt life can be predicted, according to the doctrine of 輪廻 rin**ne** (samsara)

COMPARE: 転生 tenshou = reincarnation; 生まれ変わり umarekawari = reincarnation

693. 興 PRONUNCIATIONS: kyou, kou, oko MEANINGS: to raise or start

EXAMPLES: 興味 kyoumi = interest; 興奮 koufun = excitement; 興す okosu = to revive, to raise up **DESCRIPTION:** in the top center, 同(じ) onaji, # 339, with ladders added on both sides, similar to the one seen in (階)段 kaidan (stairs, # 559); at the bottom, a table with two legs **CUES:** in **Kyou**to you can find this store selling used clothing which is raised on two legs, with 同 (identical) 段 (stairs) on both sides providing access to the top of the building, where there are **C**ola machines, and since I have a 興味 **kyou**mi (interest) in **O**ld **C**oats, I shop there

694. 深 PRONUNCIATIONS: fuka, buka, shin MEANING: deep EXAMPLES: 深い

fukai = deep; 興味深い kyoumibukai = very interesting; 深夜 shinya = dead of night; 深刻 shinkoku = serious, grave **DESCRIPTION:** on the left, a water radical, suggesting swimming; at the upper right, a sturdy base that resembles 元 moto (base, # 421); at the bottom right, 木 ki (tree, # 118) **CUES:** a **F**oolish **C**ashier from **B**ucharest installed a sturdy 元 (base) at the top of a 木 (tree) and dove into the water below, but the water was 深い **fuka**i (deep), and a **Shin**to priest had to rescue him **COMPARE:** 探(す) sagasu = to search, # 699

695. 恋 PRONUNCIATIONS: koi, ren

MEANING: to be in love **EXAMPLES:** 恋 koi = love; 恋人 koibito = lover; 恋しい koishii = longed for, beloved; 恋愛 ren'ai = romantic love **DESCRIPTION:** at the top, a swooping hen, as seen in (大)変 taihen (terrible, # 553); at the bottom, 心 kokoro (heart, # 306)

CUES: this swooping hen is in 恋 **koi** (love) with this 心 (heart), and it's swooping down to give it a **Coi**n to help pay the **Ren**t

696. 職 PRONUNCIATIONS: shoku, sho

MEANINGS: job, employment **EXAMPLES:** 職業 shokugyou = occupation; 就職する shuushoku suru = to get a job; 職権 shokken = authority **DESCRIPTION:** on the left, 耳 mimi (ear, # 57); in the middle, 音 oto (sound, # 266); on the right, a halberd (combination axe and lance); together these radicals suggest a military musician **CUES:** I listen to 音 (sounds) with my 耳 (ears) while carrying this halberd, and it may **Shock** yo**U** to learn that my 職業 **shoku**gyou (occupation) is military musician, but wait until you see my **Show COMPARE:** 織(る) oru = to weave, # 753

....

Chapter 12

697. 伸 PRONUNCIATIONS: shin, no
MEANINGS: to expand, stretch, lengthen
EXAMPLES: 追伸 tsuishin = postscript;
伸ばす nobasu, transitive = to lengthen, stretch, develop, expand; 伸びる nobiru, intransitive = to lengthen, to be postponed DESCRIPTION: compared to 神 kami (god, # 273), the Shah on the left has been replaced by a man with a slanted hat CUES: a man with a slanted hat emerges from a Shinto shrine to find that his 車 (car) has no wheels; since there is No Basu (bus), he has to 伸ばす **no**basu (extend) his visit there ALSO COMPARE: 申(す) mousu = to humbly speak, # 10; 延(びる) nobiru = to lengthen, # 842

698. 勧 PRONUNCIATIONS: kan, susu
MEANINGS: to recommend, advise
EXAMPLES: 勧誘する kan'yuu suru = to invite or urge to join; 勧告 kankoku = recommendation, advice; 勧める susumeru = to advise or recommend DESCRIPTION: at the upper left, the upper portion of an American Indian chief, as seen in 知(る) shiru (to know, # 323), who is hugging the cage on the lower left; on the right 力 chikara (force, # 107) CUES: this American Indian chief is hugging a cage in a zoo, where a wild animal is being kept by 力 (force); the people of Canada are outraged about this, and the chief 勧める **susu**meru (recommends) that they Sue the Superintendent of the zoo COMPARE: 進(める) susumeru = to advance, transitive, # 203; 確(かめる) tashikameru = to confirm, # 619

699. 探 PRONUNCIATIONS: sagu, saga, tan MEANINGS: to search or look for
EXAMPLES: 探る saguru = to grope, look for, probe; 探す sagasu = to search or look for; 探険 tanken = exploration, expedition, # 196 (also written 探検 tanken, # 859) DESCRIPTION: on the left, a kneeling man; at the upper right, a sturdy base that resembles 元 moto (base, # 421); at the lower right, 木 ki (tree, # 118)
CUES: this kneeling guy wants to 探す **saga**su (look for) his Sad Goose, so he has Sagaciously set up this 元 (base) high in a 木 (tree), and he kneels there with binoculars, working on his Tan COMPARE: 深(い) fukai = deep, # 694

700. 改 PRONUNCIATIONS: arata, kai
MEANINGS: to renew, to change EXAMPLES:
改める aratameru = to change, correct; 改めて aratamete = again, anew, another time; 改正する kaisei suru = to revise, reform, amend DESCRIPTION: on the left, a snake; on the right, a dancer with a ponytail CUES: the Arab Tax collector on the right, who is a dancer, has gone out to fly her Kite, but 改めて **arata**mete (once again) she has encountered this big snake on the left

701. 関 PRONUNCIATIONS: kan, seki, kaka MEANINGS: relating, to connect, checkpoint EXAMPLES: 関係 kankei = relationship; 関する kan suru = to be related to, concerning; 玄関 genkan = front entry; 関所 sekisho = checkpoint; 関わる kakawaru = to be involved
DESCRIPTION: on the top and sides, 門 mon (gate, # 409); inside the gate, Oklahoma's Uber Ruth, as seen in 送(る) okuru (to send, # 348) CUES: Oklahoma's Uber Ruth is thinking of passing through this gate in order to pursue a 関係 **kan**kei (relationship) in Kansas; she has a Seki (cough) and can't decide whether she should go but finally decides to Call a Cab COMPARE: 開(く) aku = to open, transitive, # 413

702. 丁 PRONUNCIATIONS: chou, tei
MEANING: square block EXAMPLES:
丁目 choume = city block, district of a town; 丁寧 teinei = polite, courteous; 丁 tei = counter for guns, tools, leaves or cakes of something DESCRIPTION: reportedly, this represents a nail CUES: when I Choked on this nail, a 丁寧な **tei**nei na (polite) Tailor by saved me with a Heimlich maneuver

COMPARE: (電)灯 dentou = electric light, # 626; 町 machi = town, # 70

703. 寧 PRONUNCIATION: nei

MEANINGS: rather, probably EXAMPLES: 丁寧 teinei = polite, courteous

DESCRIPTION: at the top, a bad haircut; below that, 心 kokoro (heart, # 306); below that, 目 me (eye, # 51) turned horizontally, which could represent three eyes; at the bottom, 丁 tei (counter for guns, # 702), which resembles a nail

CUES: I have a 丁寧 teinei (polite) Neighbor with a bad haircut like this one, a good 心 (heart) and three eyes who tries to live with a small footprint, and therefore he balances his house on this Nail

704. 断 PRONUNCIATIONS: ta, kotowa, dan MEANING: to cut decisively EXAMPLES:

断つ tatsu = to cut off, discon-tinue; 断る kotowaru = to refuse; 中断 chuudan = interruption DESCRIPTION: on the lower left, a shelf seen from the side; on the shelf, 米 kome (uncooked rice, # 326); on the right, a tall pair of pliers CUES: this Tall pair of pliers is blocking access to a shelf full of rice which was intended to be the payment for a koto (Japanese harp), but the Koto is Warui (bad) and covered with Dandruff, and therefore the pliers 断る kotowaru (refuse) to accept it

COMPARE: 継(ぐ) tsugu = to inherit, # 635

....

Chapter 13

705. 納 PRONUNCIATIONS: nou, tou, osa, na MEANINGS: accept, deliver, finish

EXAMPLES: 納入 nounyuu = payment of taxes, etc, supply (of goods, etc.), delivery; 出納 suitou = receipts & expenditures; 納める osameru = to pay a bill, to put away (in a closet, etc.), to conclude; this can also be written 収める osameru, # 1113; 納まる osamaru = to be settled or solved; 納得する nattoku suru = to acquiesce, agree

DESCRIPTION: on the left, 糸 skeet shooter

(# 219); on the right, 内 uchi (inside, #396) which shows something projecting from a box CUES: this 糸 (skeet shooter) thinks that he sees either the Nose or a Toe of Osama, who is a Nasty man, protruding from 内 (inside) the box on the right, and he will 納める osameru (conclude) his mission by shooting him with a skeet COMPARE: 治(める) osameru = to govern or reign, # 539; 修(める) osameru = to learn or master, # 1049

706. 得 PRONUNCIATIONS: e, u, toku

MEANING: to gain EXAMPLES: 得る eru = to get, earn, understand, receive something; あり得る arieru = it's possible (this can also be pronounced ariuru); なし得る nashieru = to be able to do (this can also be pronounced nashiuru); 得 toku = gain, profit; 得意 tokui = pride, strong point DESCRIPTION: on the left, a man with a double hat; on the upper right, 日 hi (sun, # 32); on the lower right, the base of 寺 tera (temple, # 213), built into a hill

CUES: this man with a double hat thinks that cooking Eggs with the heat of this 日 (sun) on the top of a 寺 (temple) is Uber and Totally Cool, and he hopes to make a 得 toku (profit) from it

COMPARE: 待(つ) matsu = to wait, # 217

707. 賃 PRONUNCIATION: chin

MEANINGS: wages, fee, fare EXAMPLES: 家賃 yachin = rent; 電車賃 densha chin = train fare DESCRIPTION: on the upper left, a man with a slanted hat who is almost falling; on the upper right, 王 ou (king, # 1077); at the bottom, 貝 kai (shell, money chest, # 83)

CUE: this man with a slanted hat visits this 王 (king) and demands the 家賃 yachin (rent) for a palace that the king is using, but the king socks him on the Chin, and he falls off this money chest

COMPARE: 資(金) shikin = capital, # 91; (佐)賀(県) sagaken = Saga Prefecture, # 994

708. 税 PRONUNCIATION: zei

MEANINGS: tax, duty **EXAMPLE:** 税金

zeikin = tax, duty **DESCRIPTION:** on the left, 禾 (a grain plant with a ripe head); on the right, 兄 ani (older brother, # 420), wearing rabbit ears

CUE: while harvesting the 禾 (ripe grain) on the left, 兄 (older brother) put on rabbit ears and acted **Za**ny, until he realized that he would have to pay 税金 **zei**kin (taxes) on the grain

COMPARE: (遊)説 yuuzei = election campaign, # 439, which helps us to pronounce this

709. 氏 PRONUNCIATIONS: shi, uji

MEANING: surname **EXAMPLES:** 中村氏

nakamura shi = Mr. Nakamura; 彼氏 kareshi = boyfriend; 氏名 shimei = full name; 氏 uji = clan **DESCRIPTION:** this is a paper pavilion, as seen in 紙 kami (paper, # 221) **CUES:** my 彼氏 kare**shi** (boyfriend) made this 紙 (paper) pavilion out of **Shee**ts of paper, and he parks his **Uber Jee**p in it **ALSO COMPARE:** (市)民 shimin = citizen, # 375; 低(い) hikui = short, # 222

710. 慌 PRONUNCIATIONS: awa, kou

MEANING: to panic **EXAMPLES:** 慌てる awateru = to become confused, to panic, to be in a hurry; 恐慌 kyoukou = a panic

DESCRIPTION: on the left, an erect man; on the upper right, a plant radical; in the upper middle, a fish hook; on the lower right, three legs

CUES: this erect man on the left was **A**w**a**kened on a **C**old morning by this Terrorist with three legs who threw these plants and this fish hook at him, and he 慌てた **awa**teta (panicked) **COMPARE:** 荒(い) arai = violent, # 968

711. 期 PRONUNCIATIONS: ki, go

MEANINGS: period, to expect **EXAMPLES:** 時期 jiki = time, season; 期限 kigen = deadline; 学期 gakki = semester; 末期 matsugo = the hour of death, which also (this can also be pronounced makki) **DESCRIPTION:** on the upper left, a bucket as seen in 甘(い) amai (sweet, # 541), but with an additional compartment; on the lower left, a wide skirt as seen in 六 roku (six, # 17); on the right, 月 tsuki (moon, # 148) **CUES:** this woman on the left with a wide skirt makes 甘 (sweet) **Qui**che with **Goat**'s milk when the 月 (moon) is full, and she says that this is the right 時期 ji**ki** (season) for this activity

712. 素 PRONUNCIATIONS: su, so, shirou

MEANINGS: elementary, principle, uncovered **EXAMPLES:** 素晴らしい subarashii = wonderful, superb; 素早い subayai = nimble, speedy; 水素 suiso = hydrogen; 要素 youso = component, factor, element; 素人 shirouto = amateur **DESCRIPTION:** at the top, an owl's perch, as seen in 青(い) aoi (blue, # 155); at the bottom, 糸 skeet shooter (# 219)

CUES: **Su**perman 素早く **su**bayaku (speedily) **So**ared up and dropped an owl's perch on this 糸 (skeet shooter), but we pulled it off using **Shee**pdogs and **Ro**pes

....

Chapter 14

713. 訪 PRONUNCIATIONS: tazu, hou, otozu **MEANING:** to visit **EXAMPLES:**

訪ねる tazuneru = to visit; 訪問する houmon suru = to visit; 訪れる otozureru = to visit or arrive **DESCRIPTION:** on the left, 言(う) iu (to speak, # 430); on the right, a tall 方 kata (honorable person, # 114), also pronounced 方 hou (direction), which helps us to pronounce this

CUES: the 方 (honorable person) on the right, who is a **Ta**ll **Z**ookeeper, 言 (speaks) about the 方 (direction) in which the country is heading when he 訪ねる **tazu**neru (visits) my **H**ome to bring me an **O**toscope that I left at the **Z**oo

COMPARE: 尋ねる tazuneru = to ask, inquire, search for, not included in this Catalog

714. 加 PRONUNCIATIONS: **ka, kuwa**
MEANINGS: addition, increase, join, include
EXAMPLES: 参加 sanka = participation;
加える kuwaeru = to add or include
DESCRIPTION: on the left, 力 chikara (force,
107); on the right, 口 kuchi (mouth, # 426)
CUES: **Karl** Marx exerted a lot of 力 (force) to
swallow **Cool Wa**ter through his big 口 (mouth)
when he 参加した sa<u>nka</u> shita (cooperated)
with some research on water intoxication

715. 趣 PRONUNCIATIONS: **omomu,
omomuki, shu** MEANINGS: elegance, grace,
charm, attractive EXAMPLES: 趣く omomuku
= to go or tend toward; 趣がある omomuki ga
aru = it's tasteful; 趣味 shumi = hobby, taste
DESCRIPTION: on the lower left, 走(る)
hashiru (to run, # 450); on the upper right, 取(る)
toru (to take, # 58) CUES: when I 走 (run) after
alligators and 取 (take) their eggs, I often encounter
Old **M**osquitoes in **M**ucky swamps and lose my
Shoes, but this activity is my 趣味 **shu**mi (hobby)
COMPARE: 越(える) koeru = to go across,
453

716. 湖 PRONUNCIATIONS: **mizuumi,
ko** MEANING: lake EXAMPLES: 湖
mizu'umi = lake; 湖水 kosui = lake water
DESCRIPTION: on the left, a water radical; in the
middle, 古(い) furui (old, # 392); on the right,
月 tsuki (moon, # 148) CUES: this water in a 湖
<u>mizu'umi</u> (lake) is connected by a river to the **Mizu**
(water) in the **Umi** (ocean), and on **Cold** nights when
the 月 (moon) is out, I can see reflections of 古
(old) buildings on its surface

717. 距 PRONUNCIATION: **kyo**
MEANING: distance EXAMPLES: 距離
kyori = distance, range; 距骨 kyokotsu = talus (the
bone at the top of the foot that supports the tibia)
DESCRIPTION: on the left, reportedly this is a
simplification of 足 ashi (foot, # 449); on the right,
巨 kyo (huge, # 689), which helps us to pronounce
this CUE: I use my 巨 (huge) 足 (foot) to
measure 距離 <u>kyo</u>ri (distances) in **Kyo**to

718. 環 PRONUNCIATION: **kan**
MEANINGS: circle, round EXAMPLE: 環境
kankyou = environment, surroundings
DESCRIPTION: on the left, 王 ou (king, # 1077);
at the upper right, 目 me (eye, # 51) turned
horizontally, which could represent three eyes; at the
lower right, a machine on a tripod, as seen in
遠(い) tooi (far, # 351), which resembles a toy
megaphone, with a piece of cloth covering the top
CUE: this 王 (king) uses his three 目 (eyes) to
survey the 環境 <u>kan</u>kyou (environment) in
Canada while addressing the people with this toy
megaphone

719. 境 PRONUNCIATIONS: **kyou, sakai,
kei** MEANING: boundary EXAMPLES: 環境
kankyou = environment, surroundings; 境 sakai =
boundary, border; 境内 keidai = the grounds of a
temple DESCRIPTION: on the left, 土 tsuchi
(dirt, # 59); at the upper right, 音 oto (sound,
266); at the lower right, sturdy legs, as seen in 兄
ani (big brother, # 420)
CUES: if you go across this 土 (dirt) 境 <u>sakai</u>
(boundary) in **Kyou**to, you may hear loud 音
(sounds) made by policemen with sturdy legs, who
may **Sock** you in the **Eye** and put you in a **Cage**

720. 恵 PRONUNCIATIONS: e, megu, kei MEANINGS: blessing, grace EXAMPLES: 恵む megumu = to bless, show mercy, give money, etc.; 知恵 chie = wisdom, intelligence, idea; 恩恵 onkei = favor, benefit DESCRIPTION: at the top, too 十 (ten, # 18); at the bottom, 思(う) omou (to think, # 308) CUES: after gathering 十 (ten) Eggs, a Mexican Goose and a Cake for our meal, we 思 (think) that we 恵まれている megumarete iru (are being blessed)

....

Chapter 15

721. 豆 PRONUNCIATIONS: mame, zu, zuki, tou MEANING: bean EXAMPLES: 豆 mame = bean; 大豆 daizu = soybean; 小豆 azuki = red bean; 豆腐 toufu = bean curd DESCRIPTION: this is the climber from 登(録) touroku (registration, # 297), which helps us to pronounce this, without his bench hats, but it resembles a TV set with a cloth resting on top; it appears to be supported on a couple of toes CUES: some Mad Men (i.e., those who work on Madison Ave as advertisers) watch this TV set at a Zoo with a Zookeeper, supporting it with their Toes, and watching the advertisements they have created for 豆 mame (bean) products

COMPARE: 短(い) mijikai = short, # 324, in which we describe 豆 as a gasoline pump

722. 腐 PRONUNCIATIONS: kusa, fu MEANINGS: rot, decay, sour EXAMPLES: 腐る kusaru = to rot, spoil, be corrupted; 豆腐 toufu = bean curd DESCRIPTION: at the upper left, a lean-to, which could be a restaurant, with a chimney; under the roof, 付(く) tsuku (to attach, # 132); on the ground floor, 肉 niku (meat, # 397) CUES: we were eating a Cool Salad in this restaurant when we noticed that the 肉 (meat) that was 付 (attached) to the ceiling was beginning to 腐る kusaru (spoil), and we warned the owners about their Food storage practices

723. 孤 PRONUNCIATION: ko MEANINGS: orphan, alone EXAMPLES: 孤独 kodoku = solitude, isolation; 孤児 koji = orphan DESCRIPTION: on the left, 子 ko (child, # 182), which helps us to pronounce this; on the right, 爪 tsume (nail, claw, # 647), with a hammer on the ground just below it CUES: this poor 子 Ko (child) has long 爪 (nails) and Combs his hair with this hammer; no wonder that he lives in 孤独 kodoku (isolation)

724. 独 PRONUNCIATION: doku MEANINGS: alone, single EXAMPLES: 孤独 kodoku = solitude, isolation; 独立 dokuritsu = independence; 独身 dokushin = single, unmarried DESCRIPTION: on the left, a lady contorting her body, as seen in 猫 neko (cat, # 72); on the right, 虫 mushi (insect, # 9) CUE: I saw a Documentary about a lady who lives in 孤独 kodoku (isolation) because she is fond of 虫 (insects) and contorts herself for them COMPARE: 猫 neko = cat, # 72; 狭(い) semai = narrow, # 194; 犯(人) han'nin = criminal, # 901; 狩(る) karu = to hunt, # 923; 狙う nerau = to aim, # 948

725. 軍 PRONUNCIATION: gun MEANINGS: military, army EXAMPLES: 軍人 gunjin = soldier; 海軍 kaigun = navy; 陸軍 rikugun = army; 将軍 shougun = Shogun DESCRIPTION: a 車 kuruma (car) covered with a lid which can function as armor, without the snail that is seen in 運 hakobu (to carry, # 354) CUE: 軍人 gunjin (soldiers) carry Guns, they ride in armored 車 (cars) like this one, and they don't need snails to help them move around

726. 隊 PRONUNCIATION: tai MEANINGS: regiment, party, squad EXAMPLES: 軍隊 guntai = army; 兵隊 heitai = soldier DESCRIPTION: on the left, ß beta from the Greek alphabet; on the right, this resembles 家 ie (house, # 405), which suggests a pig under a roof, but the roof of this house is topped by a pair of ears belonging to a tiger **CUE:** this ß (Greek) 軍隊 gun**tai** (army) keeps a **Tiger** as a pet in a 家 (house), and its ears protrude from the roof

727. 奮 PRONUNCIATION: **fun**

MEANINGS: to muster up strength or be invigorated **EXAMPLES:** 興奮 koufun = excitement; 奮闘 futou = hard struggle, strenuous effort **DESCRIPTION:** at the top, an extra-wide 大(きい) ookii (big, # 188); in the middle, a cage; at the bottom, 田 (rice paddy, # 68) **CUE:** a 大 (big) guy dropped a cage into our 田 (rice paddy), causing some 興奮 kou**fun** (excitement), and we had **Fun** trying to fish it out

728. 闘 PRONUNCIATIONS: **tou, tataka**

MEANINGS: fight, war **EXAMPLES:** 奮闘 futou = hard struggle, strenuous effort; 闘う tatakau = to fight, make war **DESCRIPTION:** on the sides, 門 mon (gate, # 409); inside the gate, on the left, 豆 mame (bean, # 721); on the right, the kneeling guy from 付(く) tsuku (to stick or adhere, # 132) **CUES:** the 豆 (beans) in this 門 (gate) 付 (stick) to people's **Toes**, and a **Tall Taxi** driver **Called** me, asking me to remove them, but it will be a 奮闘 fun**tou** (hard struggle) to clean them up **COMPARE:** 戦(う) tatakau = to fight, # 933, which has the same meaning as 闘(う) tatakau; 戦う is the more common spelling

....

Chapter 16

729. 担 PRONUNCIATIONS: **nina, tan, katsu** MEANING: to carry (a burden)

EXAMPLES: 担う ninau = to carry or bear ; 担当 tantou = charge (duty); 担ぐ katsugu = to carry on one's shoulder **DESCRIPTION:** on the left, a kneeling person who represents Nancy Pelosi;

on the right, her 旦(那) danna (husband, # 668) **CUES:** Knee**ling** **N**ancy's 旦 (husband), who has a nice **Tan**, 担当する **tan**tou suru (takes charge of) preparing ton **Katsu** (breaded pork) for dinner

730. 端 PRONUNCIATIONS: **tan, hashi, pashi[1], pa** MEANINGS: edge, origin

EXAMPLES: 万端 bantan = all, everything; 端 hashi = end, edge, border; 端くれ hashikure = a scrap or piece, an unimportant person; 片っ端 katappashi = one side, one edge; 半端 hanpa = insufficient, incomplete, insincere **DESCRIPTION:** on the left, 立(つ) tatsu (to stand, # 11); at the upper right, 山 yama (mountain, # 146); at the lower right, the front of a limousine, with a vertically oriented grille and an antenna on the roof **CUES:** I 立 (stand) below a 山 (mountain) and admire my limousine, which looks as strong as a **Tan**k but is actually patched together with **Hashi** (chopsticks), and I wonder whether 万端 ban**tan** (all) of my friends will be able fit inside of it when we take it to a **Party**

731. 固 PRONUNCIATIONS: **ko, kata** MEANINGS: solid, firm EXAMPLES:

頑固な ganko na = stubborn; 固定する kotei suru = to rivet, fix, stabilize; 固体 kotai = solid; 固い katai = hard, firm, upright; 固める katameru = to harden, solidify, strengthen **DESCRIPTION:** on the perimeter, a box; inside the box, 古(い) furui (old, # 392) **CUES:** I keep a 古 (old) **C**odebook and a **C**ata**l**ogue in this box, which is made of 固体 **ko**tai (solid) plastic **COMPARE:** 個 ko = counter for eggs, etc., # 395, which helps us to pronounce this; 硬(い) katai = hard, not included in this Catalogue; 堅(い) katai = hard, not included in this Catalogue

732. 緊　PRONUNCIATION: kin

MEANING: tight　EXAMPLES: 緊張 kinchou
= tension　DESCRIPTION: at the upper left, 巨
kyo (huge, # 689), which resembles a child's swing
set turned on its side, but the swing ropes have been
tied on both sides to make the swing inoperable; at
the upper right, 又 mata (again, # 24), which
resembles a simple table; at the bottom, a 糸 skeet
shooter (# 219)
CUE: this 糸 (skeet shooter) is trying to juggle an
inoperable 巨 (swing set) and a 又 (table) at a
Kindergarten, and there is a lot of 緊張 kinchou
(tension) among the onlooking teachers

733. 愉　PRONUNCIATION: yu

MEANINGS: pleasure, happy　EXAMPLES:
愉快 yukai = pleasant, cheerful; 不愉快
fuyukai = unpleasant　DESCRIPTION: on the left,
an erect man; on the right, compared to 前 mae
(before, # 157), we see a roof at the top, instead of an
upside-down bench　CUE: this upright man owned
this 愉快 yukai (pleasant) house in the Yukon 前
(before), but the place where he lives now is
不愉快 fuyukai (unpleasant)

734. 快　PRONUNCIATIONS: kokoroyo, kai

MEANINGS: pleasant, cheerful
EXAMPLES: 快い kokoroyoi = pleasant,
comfortable; 愉快 yukai = pleasant, cheerful;
快速電車 kaisoku densha = express train;
全快する zenkai suru = to recover completely
(from illness)　DESCRIPTION: compared to 決
(める) kimeru (to arrange, # 180), the water
radical on the left has been replaced by an erect man
CUES: this erect man, whose Kokoro (heart) is Yoi
(good), and who is always 愉快 yukai (cheerful),
will 決 (arrange) to fly a Kite

735. 札　PRONUNCIATIONS: fuda, sa, satsu　MEANINGS: paper money, posted note

EXAMPLES: 値札 nefuda = price tag; 札幌
Sapporo = a city in Hokkaido; 千円札 sen'en

satsu = 1,000 yen bill　DESCRIPTION: on the left,
木 ki (tree, # 118); on the right, a breast, as seen in
乳 nyuu (milk, # 186)
CUES: a Foolish Dad needs some 札 satsu (bank
notes), so he plays a Saxophone in a band while
mom nurses their baby next to this 木 (tree) and
reads a Satisfying Superman novel

736. 鳩　PRONUNCIATION: hato

MEANINGS: pigeon, dove　EXAMPLES: 鳩
hato = pigeon, dove　DESCRIPTION: on the left,
九 kyuu (nine, # 111); on the right, 鳥 tori (bird,
555)　CUE: those 九 (nine) 鳥 (birds) eating
Ham and Toast are 鳩 hato (pigeons)
....

Chapter 17

737. 艦　PRONUNCIATION: kan

MEANING: warship　EXAMPLE: 軍艦 gunkan
= warship, battleship　DESCRIPTION: on the left,
the radical seen in fune 船 (boat, # 602), which
depicts a boat that is missing its stern; on the upper
right, an inoperable swing set lying on its side, as
seen in 緊(張) kinchou (tension, # 732), but this
can be seen as two cannons, and the horizontal lines
to the right of these can be seen as a crutch at the top
and a cannon shell at the bottom; at the lower right,
皿 sara (dish, # 567)　CUE: this 船 (boat) is
equipped with two Cannons firing crutches and
shells, and it appears to be a 軍艦 gunkan
(battleship) fighting over some 皿 (dishes)

738. 砲　PRONUNCIATIONS: hou, pou

MEANINGS: cannon, gun　EXAMPLES: 鉄砲
teppou = gun; 大砲 taihou = cannon; 砲火
houka = gunfire　DESCRIPTION: on the left, 石
ishi (stone, # 458); on the right, 包(む) tsutsumu
(to wrap, # 548)　CUES: a Hobo in Poland 包
(wrapped) some 石 (stones) in cloth and used a
大砲 taihou (cannon) to fire them toward me, so I
shot at him with a 鉄砲 teppou (gun)

739. 現 PRONUNCIATIONS: **gen, arawa**
MEANINGS: careful, prudent EXAMPLES:
現実 genjitsu = reality, fact; 現在 genzai = present time; 現金 genkin = cash; 現れる arawareru = to appear or to show up
DESCRIPTION: on the left, ou 王 (king, # 1077); on the right, 見(る) miru (to watch, # 53)
CUES: this 王 (king) is named **Gen**ghis Khan, and he asks an **Ar**ab **W**arrior to stand 見 (watch) in return for some 現金 **gen**kin (cash)
COMPARE: 理(由) riyuu = reason, # 78

740. 漏 PRONUNCIATIONS: **mo, rou**
MEANINGS: leak, escape EXAMPLES:
漏らす morasu = to let out, to omit; 漏電 rouden = electrical short circuit; 漏水 rousui = water leak DESCRIPTION: on the left, a water radical; in the middle, a tall P which represents St. Peter; on the lower right, 雨 ame (rain, # 261)
CUES: St. Peter was caught between water and 雨 (rain), and **M**oses told him that he needed to **R**ow his boat back to shore and 漏らす **mo**rasu (let out) some water from it

741. 根 PRONUNCIATIONS: **ne, kon**
MEANINGS: root, radical EXAMPLES: 屋根 yane = roof; 木の根 kinone = tree root; 根拠 konkyo = source or basis (of reasoning, etc.)
DESCRIPTION: on the left, a 木 ki (tree, # 118); on the right, 良(い) yoi (good, # 303), missing its pointy hat
CUES: this 良 (good) 木 (tree) is the 根拠 **kon**kyo (foundation) of the materials that we used to make the 屋根 ya**ne** (roofs) that we sell in the **N**etherlands and the **Co**ngo
COMPARE: 限(界) genkai = limit, # 642

742. 棚 PRONUNCIATIONS: **tana, dana**
MEANINGS: shelf, ledge, rack EXAMPLES:
棚 tana = shelf; 戸棚 todana = cupboard
DESCRIPTION: on the left, 木 ki (wood, # 118); on the right, two 月 tsuki (moons, # 148) CUES: a cowboy in Mon**Tana** who wears a ban**Dana** had a surplus of 月 (moons), so he used 木 (wood) to build a 棚 **tana** (shelf) on which to store them

743. 餅 PRONUNCIATIONS: **mochi, bei**
MEANING: mochi rice cake EXAMPLES: 餅 mochi = Japanese rice cake; 煎餅 senbei = rice cracker NOTE: the radical on the left is a simplified way of writing 食(べる) taberu (to eat, # 398) DESCRIPTION: on the left, 食 (to eat); on the right, Ken, the tall researcher from 研(究) kenkyuu (research, # 442), standing on his toes and wearing rabbit ears CUES: the tall researcher on the right is celebrating the New Year by wearing rabbit ears, and he wants to 食 (eat) **M**ore **Chee**se with his 餅 **mochi** (Japanese rice cake), so he asks a **Ba**ker to add some

744. 銭 PRONUNCIATIONS: **zeni, sen**
MEANINGS: small change, coins EXAMPLES:
小銭 kozeni = coin, small change; 金銭 kinsen = money; 一銭 issen = 0.01 yen
DESCRIPTION: on the left, 金 kin (gold, # 301); on the right, this resembles a halberd (combination axe and lance) with some additional horizontal lines at the top CUES: **Zen** is an **Ea**stern religion that places a low value on 金 (gold) and halberds like this, but its **Cen**ters still need 金銭 kin**sen** (money) to operate, and there was a time when its monks carried weapons like this
....

Chapter 18

745. 舎 PRONUNCIATIONS: *ka*, sha

MEANING: house **EXAMPLES:** 田舎 inaka = rural area, hometown; 校舎 kousha = school building **DESCRIPTION:** on the top, a roof; under the roof, 土 tsuchi (dirt, # 59); at the bottom, 口 kuchi (mouth, # 426), but this resembles a box **CUES:** **Ka**rl Marx came from the 田舎 ina**ka** (countryside), where he lived in this **Sha**ck with dirt and a box inside **COMPARE:** 古(い) furui = old, # 392; 捨(てる) suteru= to throw away, # 594

746. 叫 PRONUNCIATIONS: sake, kyou

MEANINGS: shout, exclaim **EXAMPLES:** 叫ぶ sakebu = to shout, yell, scream; 絶叫 zekkyou = a scream or shriek **DESCRIPTION:** on the left, 口 kuchi (mouth, # 426); on the right, this resembles the number 4 **CUES:** after drinking 4 bottles of **Sake** in **Kyou**to, I opened my 口 (mouth), and a 絶叫 zek**kyou** (scream) emerged **COMPARE:** 呼(ぶ) yobu = to call, # 428; 収(入) shuunyuu = income, # 1113

747. 血 PRONUNCIATIONS: ketsu, chi, ji

MEANING: blood **EXAMPLES:** 血圧 ketsuatsu = blood pressure; 血 chi = blood; 鼻血 hanaji = a nosebleed **DESCRIPTION:** 皿 sara (dish, # 567), with a line above it which may represent a drop of ketchup being added to this dish **CUES:** when I add **Ket**chup to my **Sou**p, or to my **Chee**rios, I'm reminded of the 皿 (dishes) of animal 血 **chi** (blood) that were formerly offered to the gods as part of religious rites, and I'm careful not to spill any ketchup on my **Jea**ns

748. 圧 PRONUNCIATION: atsu

MEANINGS: to press, pressure **EXAMPLES:** 血圧 ketsuatsu = blood pressure; 気圧 kiatsu = atmospheric pressure; 圧力 atsuryoku = pressure **DESCRIPTION:** at the upper left, a lean-to; at the lower right, 土 tsuchi (dirt, # 59)

CUE: this lean-to **At Su**perman's house is putting a lot of 圧力 **atsu**ryoku (pressure) on the pile of 土 (dirt) that is stored inside of it **COMPARE:** 厚(い) atsui = thick, # 185

749. 抜 PRONUNCIATIONS: ba, batsu, nu

MEANINGS: to extract, pull out, omit **EXAMPLES:** 抜てきする batteki suru = to select; 人気抜群 ninkibatsugun = very popular; 抜く nuku = to extract, omit, outrun, skip; 抜ける nukeru = to come off, fall out, escape, go through, lack; 抜きに nuki ni = without (omitting) **DESCRIPTION:** on the left, a kneeling guy; on the right, 友(達) tomodachi (friend, # 459) **CUES:** this kneeling guy and his 友 (friend) are both **Ba**tty and run around in **Ba**t **Su**its, threatening **Nu**clear war, so it might be best to 抜く **nu**ku (extract) our citizens from their vicinity

750. 焦 PRONUNCIATIONS: ase, ko, shou

MEANINGS: hurry, impatient, burn, scorch **EXAMPLES:** 焦る aseru = to be in a hurry, be impatient, anxious & eager; 焦げる kogeru = to be scorched or burned; 焦点 shouten = focus, central issue **DESCRIPTION:** at the top, a cage, as seen in 集(める) atsumeru = to collect, # 202; at the bottom, four vertical lines suggesting fire **CUES:** if **Asse**s (donkeys) in Colombia are put into this cage and suspended over this fire as part of a **Show**, you can be sure that they will 焦る **ase**ru (be eager) to escape before they 焦げる **ko**geru (get burned) **ALSO COMPARE:** 黒(い) kuroi = black, # 76; 無(理) muri = impossible, # 583, which features a net instead of a cage

751. 鳴 PRONUNCIATIONS: na, mei

MEANINGS: chirp, bark, honk **EXAMPLES:** 鳴る naru = to chime, ring, sound; 鳴く naku = to chirp, bark, cry (animal sounds); 悲鳴 himei = scream, shriek, cry of distress **DESCRIPTION:** on the left, 口 kuchi (mouth, # 426); on the right, 鳥

tori (bird, # 555) **CUES:** this 鳥 (bird) serves as a lookout for some **Na**rcos, and it uses its 口 (mouth) to 鳴く **na**ku (chirp) when their **Ma**il arrives **COMPARE:** 鶏 niwatori = chicken, # 754

752. 組 PRONUNCIATIONS: so, ku, kumi, gumi MEANINGS: group, to braid

EXAMPLES: 組織 soshiki = organization; 組む kumu = to assemble, unite, pair, fold (arms or legs), make (a plan); 組 kumi = group, team, school class; 番組 bangumi = TV or radio program **DESCRIPTION:** on the left, a 糸 skeet shooter (# 219); on the right, a solar panel, as seen in 祖(父) sofu (grandfather,# 272), which helps us to pronounce this **CUES:** this 糸 (skeet shooter) stands next to a **S**olar panel which will provide electricity to mix the **Koo**l-Aid for a **Coo**l **Mee**ting that has been organized by his 組 **kumi** (group), where **Gum**my snacks will be served **ALSO COMPARE:** 相(談) soudan = consultation, # 787

....

Chapter 19

753. 織 PRONUNCIATIONS: ori, o, shiki

MEANING: to weave **EXAMPLES:** 組織 soshiki = organization; 羽織 haori = short jacket worn over kimono; 織る oru = to weave **DESCRIPTION:** on the left, 糸 skeet shooter (# 219); in the middle, 音 oto (sound, # 266); on the right, a halberd (combination axe and lance) **CUES:** this 糸 (skeet shooter) is listening to a loud 音 (sound) created by a 組織 so**shiki** (organization) of **O**riental **O**rthodontists who buy **S**heep in **K**iev and work on their teeth with halberds **COMPARE:** 職(業) shokugyou = occupation, # 696, which features 耳 (ear) on the left instead of a skeet shooter

754. 鶏 PRONUNCIATIONS: niwatori, kei MEANING: chicken EXAMPLES: 鶏 niwatori = chicken; 鶏肉 keiniku = chicken meat

DESCRIPTION: at the upper left, a barbecue grate; at the lower left, 夫 otto (husband, # 614); on the right, 鳥 tori (bird, # 555) **CUES:** in the **Niwa** (garden), a 鳥 **To**ri (bird) was barbecued by my 夫 (husband) on a grate like this, and this was a 鶏 **niwatori** (chicken) that he kept in a **C**age **COMPARE:** 鳴(る) naru = to chime or ring, # 751

755. 羽 PRONUNCIATIONS: hane, ha, wa, u MEANINGS: feather, counter for birds & rabbits EXAMPLES: 羽 hane = feather, wing;

羽織 haori = short jacket worn over kimono; 一羽 ichiwa = one bird; 羽毛 umou = down, feathers **DESCRIPTION:** these two feathers are somewhat simpler than those seen in 弱(い) yowai (weak, # 471) **CUES:** at **Ha**neda airport, I saw these two **hane** 羽 (feathers) in the **H**at of a **W**arrior who was driving an **U**ber car **ALSO COMPARE:** 翼 tsubasa = wing, # 912

756. 演 PRONUNCIATION: en

MEANING: to perform **EXAMPLES:** 演奏 ensou = musical performance; 演じる enjiru = to perform or act **DESCRIPTION:** on the left, a water radical; at the upper right, a bad haircut; in the middle right, a 田 (rice paddy, # 68) connected to a handle, as seen in (映)画 eiga (movie, # 77); at the lower right, a pair of legs **CUE:** actors with bad haircuts like this one 演じる **en**jiru (perform) in 画 (movies) and **E**ntertain us on sets which include water like this and 田 (rice paddies) that are connected to handles and are attached to legs like the ones shown here

757. 奏 PRONUNCIATIONS: kana, sou

MEANINGS: to play music **EXAMPLES:** 奏でる kanaderu = to play a stringed instrument; 演奏 ensou = musical performance; 伴奏 bansou = musical accompaniment

DESCRIPTION: as seen in 春 haru (spring, # 506), the upper radical is 人 hito (person, # 13) with 三 san (three, # 3) inscribed across her body; in this kanji, 天 ten (sky, # 189) is seen under her skirts, instead of 日 (sun) **CUES:** this 人 (person) gave 三 (three) 演奏 en**sou** (musical performances) under the open 天 (sky) in Cana**da**, featuring **Soul** music **ALSO COMPARE:** 棒 bou = stick, # 820

758. 描 PRONUNCIATIONS: ega, byou, ka

MEANINGS: to draw or paint, to depict or describe **EXAMPLES:** 描く egaku = to draw, paint, depict, describe; 描写する byousha suru = to describe; 描く kaku = to draw, paint, depict, describe **DESCRIPTION:** on the left, a kneeling guy; at the upper right, a plant radical; at the lower right, 田 (rice paddy, # 68) **CUES:** this kneeling guy 描く **ka**ku (paints) plants like these in 田 (rice paddies) using a technique called **Egg Art**, since he uses egg yolk for paint, and he sells his work to **Bee**rhall **Ow**ners in **Ca**lifornia **COMPARE:** 書(く) kaku = to write, # 415

759. 完 PRONUNCIATION: kan

MEANINGS: perfect, completion, end **EXAMPLES:** 完了する kanryou suru = to finish; 完成する kansei suru = to complete, accomplish; 完全な kanzen na = perfect, entire **DESCRIPTION:** at the top, a bad haircut; at the bottom, 元 moto (base, # 421) **CUE:** in **Ca**nada, a man with a bad haircut like this one has a strong 元 (base) of operations like this and 完了する **kan**ryou suru (finishes) his projects

760. 了 PRONUNCIATION: ryou

MEANINGS: to complete, finish **EXAMPLES:** 終了 shuuryou = ending, termination; 完了する kanryou suru = to finish; 了解 ryoukai = agreement, consent, understanding; 了承 ryoushou = acknowledgement, understanding

DESCRIPTION: compared to 子 ko (child, # 182), this kanji lacks arms **CUE:** Pope **Leo** was born without arms, but his 了承 **ryou**shou (understanding) was profound from the beginning

....

Chapter 20

761. 純 PRONUNCIATION: jun

MEANING: pure **EXAMPLES:** 純粋な junsui na = pure, pure-blooded, genuine; 単純な tanjun na = simple **DESCRIPTION:** on the left, a skeet shooter (# 219); on the right, 七 nana (seven, # 20) with the letter U superimposed on it; this reminds us of the seven Universal laws of the Jungle **CUE:** this skeet shooter thinks that the 七 (seven) Universal laws of the **Jun**gle are 単純 tan**jun** (simple)

762. 格 PRONUNCIATIONS: kou, ka, kaku

MEANINGS: status, rank, capacity, character **EXAMPLES:** 格子 koushi = lattice work or grill; 格好 kakkou = form, appearance, suitability; 合格する goukaku suru = to pass an exam or be accepted to a school; 性格 seikaku = personality, disposition

NOTE: the related phrase "kakko ii" = stylish or attractive and is usually written かっこいい or カッコイイ **DESCRIPTION:** on the left, a cactus 木 ki (tree, # 118); on the right, a dancer jumping over a box, as seen in 客 kyaku (customer, # 524), without the bad haircut **CUES:** this 客 (customer) from **Co**lombia is expressing her 性格 sei**kaku** (personality) by leaping over this box, but she hears a **Car** coming, loses her balance and lands on this **Cactus** 木 (tree)

COMPARE: 各(自の) kakuji no = one's own, # 1033, which helps us to pronounce this

763. 姿 PRONUNCIATIONS: sugata, shi

MEANINGS: figure, form EXAMPLES: 姿 sugata = figure, shape, condition; 容姿 youshi = appearance, looks; 姿勢 shisei = posture, stance

DESCRIPTION: at the top, 次 tsugi (next, # 536); at the bottom, 女 onna (female, # 235)

CUES: this 女 (female) has diabetes and worries about what will happen 次 (next) if her blood sugar gets too low, so she keeps **S**ugar **T**ablets handy, runs with her **Sh**eep, and maintains a good body 姿 **sugata** (shape)

764. 派 PRONUNCIATIONS: ha, pa

MEANINGS: faction, to split, to stand out

EXAMPLES: 派遣する haken suru = to send (a person), to dispatch; 派手 hade = showy, gaudy, colorful; 立派な rippa na = splendid, impressive DESCRIPTION: on the left, a water radical; in the middle, a lean-to; on the right, the radical seen in 旅 tabi (trip, # 116), which appears to be a person stepping out on a journey

CUES: **Ha**nsel has been 派遣された **ha**ken sareta (sent) on a 旅 (trip) by his **Pa** (father), and he is waiting for a boat in this lean-to by the water

COMPARE: 脈 myaku = pulse, # 770, in which the water radical on the left is replaced by 月 (moon)

765. 遣 PRONUNCIATIONS: ken, tsuka, zuka[1] MEANINGS: dispatch, send, give, do

EXAMPLES: 派遣する haken suru = to send (a person), to dispatch; 遣わす tsukawasu = to dispatch; 気遣う kizukau = to care for, worry, pay attention DESCRIPTION: on the lower left, a snail; at the upper right, 中 naka (inside, # 8) on a platform; at the lower right, a bunk bed

CUES: **K**en 遣わす **tsuka**wasu (dispatches) Barbie on a trip aboard this snail, where she will

sleep 中 (inside) the bottom bunk and keep her **Tsui**tcase (suitcase) **C**arry-on in the top bunk

COMPARE: 追(いかける) oikakeru = to pursue or chase after, # 821, which omits 中 and the platform under it

766. 浜 PRONUNCIATIONS: hama, hin

MEANINGS: seacoast, beach EXAMPLES: 浜辺 hamabe = beach; 海浜 kaihin = seaside DESCRIPTION: on the left, a water radical; on the right, a pair of pliers on a stand, but this also resembles a lifeguard's chair on a stand, shielded from the sun by a cover CUES: a lifeguard bought some **Ham** at the **Ma**ll and ate it in this chair near water at the 海浜 kai**hin** (seaside), but seabird attacks **Hin**dered his enjoyment of the meal

COMPARE: 兵(隊) heitai = soldier, # 917

767. 凧 PRONUNCIATION: tako

MEANING: kite EXAMPLES: 凧 tako = kite DESCRIPTION: the continuous line extending from the lower left to the lower right suggests wind, as seen in 風 kaze (wind, # 479); under this line stands Bo Peep, the spinning lady seen in 帽(子) boushi (hat, # 243)

CUE: Bo Peep eats **Taco**s while she stands under this wind and flies her **tako** 凧 (kite)

768. 揚 PRONUNCIATIONS: a, you

MEANINGS: to hoist or to fry in deep fat

EXAMPLES: 揚げる ageru = to hoist, to fly a kite, to fry in deep fat; 抑揚 yokuyou = intonation, inflection DESCRIPTION: on the left side, a kneeling guy; on the right side, 易(しい) yasashii (easy, # 402) CUES: this guy has to kneel for his **A**gricultural research in **Yo**semite, but his work is 易 (easy), and he often finds time to 揚げる **a**geru (fly) kites COMPARE: 場(所) basho = place, # 403; (お)湯 oyu = honorable hot water, # 404; (太)陽 taiyou = sun, # 891, which helps us to pronounce this

....

Chapter 21

769. 壮 PRONUNCIATION: sou

MEANINGS: robust, manhood, prosperity
EXAMPLES: 壮大な soudai na = magnificent,
imposing; 壮観 soukan = magnificent view
DESCRIPTION: on the left, a bench with two legs,
standing on end; on the right, (紳)士 shinshi
(gentleman, # 66) CUE: this 士 (gentleman) sits
on this bench admiring a 壮観 soukan (magnificent view) while listening to Soul music

770. 脈 PRONUNCIATION: myaku

MEANINGS: vein, pulse EXAMPLES: 脈
myaku = pulse or vein; 山脈 sanmyaku =
mountain range; 動脈 doumyaku = artery
DESCRIPTION: compared to 派(手) hade
(showy, gaudy, # 764), the water radical on the left
has been replaced with 月 tsuki (moon, # 148); as
in 派, the radical on the right suggests a person
waiting in a lean-to before stepping out on a journey
CUE: this person is about to step out from a lean-to
under the light of the 月 (moon) on a journey to get
some Miami Kool-Aid, and he feels his 脈 myaku
(veins) throbbing in anticipation

771. 美 PRONUNCIATIONS: utsuku, bi,

mi, o MEANINGS: beautiful EXAMPLES:
美しい utsukushii = beautiful; 美術 bijutsu
= fine arts; 美人 bijin = beautiful woman;
夏美 Natsumi = a woman's given name;
美味しい oishii = delicious (usually written
おいしい) DESCRIPTION: at the top, 羊
hitsuji (sheep, not included in this Catalog); at the
bottom, 大(きい) ookii (big, # 188)
CUES: this 美しい utsukushii (beautiful) 羊
(sheep) has an Uruguayan Tsuitcase (suitcase) full of
Kool-Aid, and she admires her Beauty when she
looks into a 大 (big) Mirror although she is starting
to get Old COMPARE: (木の)実 kinomi = nut,
195, which helps us to pronounce this and has a
bad haircut at the top instead of sheep horns

772. 責 PRONUNCIATIONS: seki, se

MEANINGS: liability, to blame EXAMPLES:
責任 sekinin = responsibility; 責める semeru
= to accuse, reproach, torment DESCRIPTION: at
the top, an owl's perch as seen in 青(い) aoi (blue,
155); at the bottom, 貝 kai (shell, or money chest,
83) CUES: this 貝 (money chest) belongs to a
Selfish King who allows an owl sit on this perch;
the owl has sekinin 責任 (responsibility) for
Selling pardons and puts the proceeds in the money
chest COMPARE: 真 makoto = truth, # 101, in
which the chest rests on a table, and there is only a
simple antenna at the top; (面)積 menseki = area,
931, which helps us to pronounce this, in which a
selfish king allows an owl to conduct *grain* sales

773. 瞬 PRONUNCIATIONS: matata,

shun MEANINGS: wink, blink, twinkle
EXAMPLES: 瞬く matataku = to blink or
twinkle; 瞬く間に matataku ma ni = in an
instant; 瞬間 shunkan = moment; 瞬間的に
shunkanteki ni = momentarily DESCRIPTION: on
the left, 目 me (eye, # 51); at the upper right, a
tabletop with three exam booklets covered by a cloth,
as seen in 受(ける) ukeru (to take an exam,
577); at the bottom center, 夕 yuu (evening,
160); at the bottom right, a knee, as seen in 年
nen (year, # 177) CUES: on certain 夕 (evenings)
during the 年 (year), this 目 (eye) watches people
受 (take) exams to become Master Tatami makers;
if the eye looks away 瞬間的に shunkanteki ni
(momentarily), some people may cheat, but if they
are caught, they are Shunned

774. 染 PRONUNCIATIONS: sen, so, ji,

shi MEANINGS: dye, color, paint, stain
EXAMPLES: 感染 kansen = contagion,
infection; 汚染 osen = pollution; 染まる
somaru = to be dyed or stained, to be influenced;
馴染む najimu = to adapt or become accustomed
to; 染み込む shimikomu = to soak into or

penetrate **DESCRIPTION:** at the upper left, a water radical; at the upper right, 九 kyuu (nine, # 111); at the bottom 木 ki (tree, # 118) **CUES:** a **Sen**ator visited **Soma**lia in a **Jee**p, where he saw 九 (nine) bodies of water, many 木 (trees), and some **Sheep**, but 汚染 o**sen** (pollution) was a problem **COMPARE:** 雑(誌) zasshi = magazine, # 785

775. 胸 PRONUNCIATIONS: kyou,
mune, muna MEANINGS: chest **EXAMPLES:** 胸中 kyouchuu = heart, mind or intentions; 度胸 dokyou = courage or audacity; 胸 mune = chest; 胸毛 munage = chest hair **DESCRIPTION:** on the left, 月 tsuki (moon, # 148); on the upper right, the hook seen in 約(束) yakusoku (promise, # 225); under the hook, a box, which resembles the chest of a person, containing an X which may symbolize unknown dreams **CUES:** when the 月 moon shines in **Kyou**to, a hook sometimes snags people whose 胸 **mune** (chests) are filled with unknown dreams of **Moon** Encounters with **Moon Animals**

776. 駆 PRONUNCIATIONS: ka, ku
MEANING: to run **EXAMPLES:** 駆ける kakeru = to run; 先駆者 senkusha = originator, pioneer **DESCRIPTION:** on the left, 馬 uma (horse, # 958); on the right, 区 ku (ward, # 320), which helps us to pronounce this **CUES:** this 馬 (horse) 駆ける **ka**keru (runs) around our 区 (ward) **Ca**lling for **Kool**-Aid
....

Chapter 22
777. 垣 PRONUNCIATIONS: kaki, kai
MEANINGS: fence, hedge, wall **EXAMPLES:** 垣根 kakine = hedge, fence; 垣間見る kaimamiru = to take a peep at, to catch a glimpse of **DESCRIPTION:** on the left, 土 tsuchi (dirt, # 59); on the right, 日 hi (sun, # 32), framed by vertical lines above and below, resembling a framed double-

paned window in a fence **CUES:** my **Cocky** Neighbor put a window in our 垣根 **kaki**ne (fence) so that he could watch me fly my **Kite**, but I covered it up with 土 (dirt)

778. 巡 PRONUNCIATIONS: jun, megu,
mawa **MEANINGS:** patrol, go around, circumference **EXAMPLES:** 巡査 junsa = patrolman; 巡礼 junrei = Buddhist pilgrimage; 巡る meguru = to go or come around, to surround; お巡りさん omawarisan = a policeman **DESCRIPTION:** on the lower left, a snail; on the snail, a chevron as seen on the sleeves of police or military uniforms **CUES:** this snail is wearing a chevron to indicate its status as a **Jun**ior member of the fraternity of **Men** with **Goo**, and as it 巡る **megu**ru (goes around) the neighborhood carrying a grease gun, it behaves like a **Marine Warrior COMPARE:** 回(る) mawaru = to rotate, # 4; 周(り) mawari = surrounding, # 630

779. 芝 PRONUNCIATION: shiba
MEANINGS: turf, lawn **EXAMPLES:** 芝生 shibafu = lawn, turf **DESCRIPTION:** at the top, a plant radical which suggests a lawn; at the bottom, a somewhat irregular letter Z which reminds us of **Zebras CUE:** the Queen of **Sheba** used to Fool around on this 芝生 **shiba**fu (lawn) with **Zebras**

780. 弾 PRONUNCIATIONS: hi, dan,
hazu, tama MEANINGS: bullet, twang, snap **EXAMPLES:** 弾く hiku = to play a piano or guitar; 爆弾 bakudan = bomb; 弾圧する danatsu suru = to oppress or suppress; 弾む hazumu = to become lively, to accelerate; 弾 tama = bullet **DESCRIPTION:** on the left, the bow seen in 引(く) hiku (to pull, # 476), which helps us to pronounce this; on the right, (簡)単 kantan (easy, # 636) **CUES:** it's 単 (easy) for me to **Hear** the **Dan**ce music at the Hawaiian **Zoo**, where people 引 (pull) strings as they 弾く **hi**ku (play) guitars and eat **Tamal**es

781. 詰 PRONUNCIATIONS: tsu, kitsu
MEANINGS: packed, fill, stuff **EXAMPLES:**
詰める tsumeru = to stuff, fill or pack into;
詰まる tsumaru = to be packed, to be blocked;
に詰まる ni tsumaru = to be at a loss; 詰問
kitsumon = cross-examination, close questioning
DESCRIPTION: on the left, 言(う) iu (to speak,
430); at the upper right, 士 shi (man, # 66); at
the lower right, 口 kuchi (mouth, # 426), but this
could be a tsuitcase (suitcase) CUES: this 士
(man) 言 (says) that he has 詰めた **tsu**meta
(stuffed) this 口 (Tsuitcase) with **Ki**ttens from
Sudan, and he is offering them for adoption
COMPARE: 結(果) kekka = result, # 231;
話(す) hanasu = to talk, # 433

782. 砂 PRONUNCIATIONS: ja, sha, suna,
sa MEANING: sand EXAMPLES: 砂利道
jarimichi = gravel path; 土砂降り doshaburi =
pouring rain; 砂 suna = sand; 砂漠 sabaku =
desert; 砂糖 satou = sugar DESCRIPTION: on
the left, 石 ishi (stone, # 458); on the right,
少(し) sukoshi (a few, # 254); together these
suggest a few small stones, or sand CUES: Jack
Nicholson uses a **Sha**rp tool to turn 少 (a few) 石
(stones) like this into 砂 **suna** (sand), but his
Supervisor **Na**gs him, and his **Sa**lary is low

783. 頂 PRONUNCIATIONS: chou, itada,
itadaki MEANINGS: summit, to receive
EXAMPLES: 登頂する touchou suru = to
climb to the summit; 頂く itadaku = to humbly
receive (usually written いただく); 頂 itadaki
= peak, summit DESCRIPTION: on the left, a nail,
as seen in 丁(目) choume (city block, # 702),
which helps us to pronounce this; on the right, 貝
kai (shell, or money chest, # 83), with a platform
mounted at the top where a head could fit, as seen in
頭 atama (head, # 93) CUES: Margaret **Cho** used

this 丁 (nail) to fasten an **I**talian **D**ark **K**imono that
she wore when she climbed to an 頂 **itada**ki
(summit) to retrieve a 頭 (head) that a friend had
lost ALSO COMPARE: 貯(金) chokin =
savings, # 667

784. 徴 PRONUNCIATION: chou
MEANINGS: indications, sign, omen
EXAMPLES: 特徴 tokuchou = characteristic,
special feature DESCRIPTION: on the left, a man
with a double hat; in the upper center, 山 yama
(mountain, # 146); in the lower center, 王 ou (king,
1077); on the right, a dancer with a ponytail
CUE: this man with a double hat will join this 王
(king) on this 山 (mountain), where they will watch
this dancer named Margaret **Cho**, who has 特徴
toku**chou** (special features)
....

Chapter 23

785. 雑 PRONUNCIATIONS: zatsu, zou,
za MEANINGS: various, assorted EXAMPLES:
複雑な fukuzatsu na = complicated; 雑巾
zoukin = dust cloth, cleaning cloth; 雑誌 zasshi =
magazine DESCRIPTION: at the upper left, 九
kyuu (nine, # 111); at the lower left, 木 ki (tree,
118); on the right, a cage CUES: 九 (nine) 木
(trees) surround this cage where **Za**ch's **Tsu**itcase
(suitcase) was stored in a 複雑な fuku**zatsu** na
(complicated) **Z**one in **Z**ambia
COMPARE: 難(しい) muzukashii = difficult,
198; 誰 dare = who, # 440

786. 誌 PRONUNCIATION: shi
MEANINGS: magazine, journal EXAMPLES:
雑誌 zasshi = magazine; 週刊誌 shuukanshi
= weekly magazine DESCRIPTION: on the left,
言(葉) kotoba (words, # 430); on the upper right,
士 shi (man, # 66), which helps us to pronounce
this; on the lower right, 心 kokoro (heart, # 306)

CUE: this 士 (man) uses 言 (words) well, and he writes articles about 心 (heart) problems in **Sheep** for a 雑誌 zas**shi** (magazine)

787. 相 PRONUNCIATIONS: shou, sou, ai

MEANINGS: mutual, state, minister
EXAMPLES: 首相 shushou = prime minister; 相談 soudan = consultation, advice; 相手 aite = opponent or partner DESCRIPTION: on the left, 木 ki (tree, # 118); on the right, 目 me (eye, # 51) CUES: I have my 目 (eye) on this 木 (tree) by the **Sho**re, under which I plan to listen to **Soul** music and drink **I**ced tea while I 相談する **sou**dan suru (consult) with my friends COMPARE: 組(織) soshiki = organization, # 752

788. 炎 PRONUNCIATIONS: en, hono'o

MEANING: inflammation, flare, blaze
EXAMPLES: 肺炎 haien = pneumonia; 肝炎 kan'en = hepatitis; 火炎 kaen = fire; 炎 hono'o = blaze, flame DESCRIPTION: at the top, 火 hi (fire, # 443); at the bottom, 火 hi (fire) again CUES: an **E**ntertainer piled 火 (fire) upon 火 (fire) until a large 火炎 ka**en** (fire) was blazing at my **H**ome in **N**orthern **O**regon

789. 算 PRONUNCIATIONS: san, zan, *soro* MEANING: to count EXAMPLES:

計算 keisan = calculation; 算数 sansuu = arithmetic; 暗算 anzan = mental calculation; 算盤 soroban = abacus DESCRIPTION: at the top, 竹 take (bamboo, # 134); in the middle, 目 me (eye, # 51); at the bottom, legs with a welcoming stance, as seen in 開(く) aku (to open, # 413) CUES: **San**ta Claus holds a 竹 (bamboo) cane over his head when he teaches his 算数 **san**suu (arithmetic) class in **Zan**zibar, and his 目 (eyes) watch the students **Sorro**wfully as he assumes a 開 (welcoming) stance

790. 談 PRONUNCIATION: dan

MEANING: to talk EXAMPLES: 相談 soudan = consultation; 冗談 joudan = a joke DESCRIPTION: on the left, 言(う) iu (to speak, # 430); on the right, (火)炎 kaen (fire, # 788) CUE: a **Dan**cer 言 (talked) to her neighbors about 炎 (fire) prevention, and their conversation turned into a general 相談 sou**dan** (consultation)

791. 額 PRONUNCIATIONS: gaku, hitai

MEANING: forehead, sum of money, frame
EXAMPLES: 金額 kingaku = a sum of money; 額 hitai = forehead DESCRIPTION: on the left, 客 kyaku (customer, # 524); on the right, 貝 kai (shell, or money chest, # 83), with a platform mounted at the top where a head could fit, as seen in 頭 atama (head, # 93) CUES: this 客 (customer), who is trying to get her 頭 (head) back, offers to exchange a 金額 kin**gaku** (sum of money), a **Gal**lon of **Kool**-Aid, and some **H**ebrew **T**iles for it

792. 嘆 PRONUNCIATIONS: nage, tan

MEANING: sign, lament, moan, grieve
EXAMPLES: 嘆く nageku = to lament, grieve; 感嘆する kantan suru = to admire or be astonished at DESCRIPTION: compared to 漢(字) kanji (# 197), the water radical on the left has been replaced by 口 kuchi (mouth, # 426) CUES: I **Nag** my **Gu**ests to learn 漢 (kanji), but they use their 口 (mouths) to 嘆く **nage**ku (lament) the difficulty of the task and would rather work on their **Tan**s

....

Chapter 24

793. 敗 PRONUNCIATIONS: **hai, yabu, pai** MEANINGS: to lose, to fail EXAMPLES: 敗戦 haisen = a defeat or loss; 敗れる yabureru = to lose or be defeated; 失敗する shippai suru = to fail or make a mistake

DESCRIPTION: on the left, 貝 kai (shell or money chest, # 83); on the right, a dancer with a ponytail CUES: this dancer, whose name is **Hei**di and who wears **Ya**kskin **Boo**ts, got an idea to **Ship Pie**s to foreign countries, but the idea 失敗した ship**pai** shita (failed), and she had to empty this 貝 (money chest) COMPARE: 破(れる) yabureru = to be torn, # 837

794. 喉 PRONUNCIATIONS: **kou, nodo** MEANINGS: throat, voice EXAMPLES: 耳鼻咽喉科 jibiinkouka = ear, nose and throat specialty; 喉 nodo = throat DESCRIPTION: on the left, 口 kuchi (mouth, # 426); in the middle, a man with a slanted hat; at the upper right, the katakana ユ yu, which reminds us of Utah; at the lower right, an American Indian chief, as seen in 知(る) shiru (to know, # 323) CUES: this man with a slanted hat is an ear, nose & throat doctor who takes care of American Indian patients in ユ (Utah) and who 知 (knows) a lot about the 口 (mouth) and the 喉 **nodo** (throat), but his bedside manner is **Co**ld, and as a result on some days he earns **No Dough** (money)

795. 鼻 PRONUNCIATIONS: **hana, bi** MEANING: nose EXAMPLES: 鼻 hana = nose; 耳鼻科 jibika = ear, nose & throat specialty DESCRIPTION: at the top, 自(分) jibun (self, # 55), which has a projection at the top that resembles a nose or possibly a beak; in the middle, 田 (rice paddy, # 68); at the bottom, legs with a welcoming stance, as seen in 開(く) aku (to open, # 413) CUES: this **Ha**waiian **Na**nny has a tiny 鼻 **hana** (nose) resembling a **Bea**k on top of her head

which expresses her 自 (self), and she 開 (welcomes) us to her 田 (rice paddy)

796. 邪 PRONUNCIATIONS: **ze, ja** MEANINGS: wicked, injustice, wrong EXAMPLES: 風邪 kaze = upper respiratory infection; 無邪気 mujaki = innocence DESCRIPTION: on the left, a man with a forbidding stance, as seen in 閉(める) shimeru (to close, # 414), carrying a Jar on his left shoulder; on the right, ß beta from the Greek alphabet CUES: the figure on the left is a **Ze**n monk with a 閉 (forbidding stance) who is carrying a **Ja**r of a vaccine that can prevent 風邪 ka**ze** (upper respiratory infections) in ß (Greek) people COMPARE: 牙 kiba = fang, # 921

797. 浸 PRONUNCIATIONS: **shin, tsu, hita** MEANINGS: soak, dip, wet, dunk EXAMPLES: 浸かる tsukaru = to be soaked in; 浸水する shinsui suru = to be flooded; 浸す hitasu = to soak, dip or drench DESCRIPTION: on the left, a water radical; on the upper right, long hair flowing to the left; on the lower right, a simple table covered with a cloth CUES: this **Shin**to priest with long flowing hair saw this water and realized that his temple had 浸水した **shin**sui shita (flooded), but he was able to save a **Tsu**itcase (suitcase) and a **Hii**ta (heater) by placing them onto this table covered by a cloth

798. 爽 PRONUNCIATION: **sou** MEANINGS: refreshing, clear EXAMPLES: 爽快 soukai = refreshing, exhilarating DESCRIPTION: 大(きい) ookii (big, # 188), with two X's on each side which represent unknown songs CUE: this 大 (big) guy likes to listen to **Sou**l music, and these X's represent four songs that he finds especially 爽快 **sou**kai (refreshing)

799. 垂 PRONUNCIATIONS: sui, ta
MEANINGS: droop, suspend, hang, slouch
EXAMPLES: 垂直 suichoku = vertical, perpendicular; 垂れる tareru = to hang, droop, dangle, sag, lower DESCRIPTION: this resembles 重(い) omoi (heavy, # 284), which incorporates 車 kuruma (car, # 283) with extra hubcaps; this kanji retains the hubcaps at the ends of the axle, but it omits the wheels; it also adds three short projections on the front and back, which may be wings for streamlining CUES: this 車 (car), which has three wings on the front and back and is lying on its side with its hubcaps aligned 垂直に **sui**choku ni (vertically), is based on advanced **Sui**dish (Swedish) technology, allowing it to run on hubcaps without wheels, and it's being used as a **Ta**xi
ALSO COMPARE: 乗(る) noru = to board, # 509

800. 睡 PRONUNCIATION: sui
MEANING: drowsy, sleep, die EXAMPLE: 睡眠 suimin = sleep DESCRIPTION: on the left, 目 me (eye, # 51); on the right, 垂(直) suichoku (vertical, perpendicular, # 799), which helps us to pronounce this CUE: during 睡眠 **sui**min (sleep), I dreamed that my 目 (eyes) saw a **Sui**dish (Swedish) 車 (car) lying on its side with its hubcaps aligned 垂 (vertically)

....

Chapter 25

801. 移 PRONUNCIATIONS: utsu, i
MEANINGS: to transfer or move EXAMPLES: 移る utsuru = to move (one's lodging), to change or be infected with; 移動する idou suru = to move (an object) DESCRIPTION: on the left, 禾 (a ripe head of grain); on the right, 多(い) ooi (many, # 161) CUES: we **U**tilize **S**uperman to 移動する **i**dou suru (move) 多 (many) stalks of 禾 (grain) because it's **Ea**sy for him

802. 避 PRONUNCIATIONS: sa, hi
MEANINGS: to evade, avoid, avert, ward off, shun
EXAMPLES: 避ける sakeru = to avoid; 避難 hinan = taking refuge; 回避 kaihi = evasion, avoidance; 避妊 hinin = contraception
DESCRIPTION: on the lower left, a snail; in the middle, a P, which reminds us of Poison, above 口 kuchi (mouth, # 426); on the right, 辛(い) karai (spicy, # 384) CUE: **Sa**ruman was hailed as a **He**ro after he detected that the 辛 (spicy) substance above the 口 (mouth) of this snail was Poison, allowing the snail to 避ける **sa**keru (avoid) ingesting it

803. 暇 PRONUNCIATIONS: hima, ka
MEANINGS: spare time, rest, leisure
EXAMPLES: 暇 hima = free time; 休暇 kyuuka = vacation, day off DESCRIPTION: on the left, 日 hi (sun, # 32); in the middle, a ladder with a box at the top; at the upper right, the katana コ ko which reminds us of corn; at the lower right, 又 mata (again, # 24), but this resembles a simple table CUES: the 日 (sun) shines on this ladder in the **Hima**layas, which **Ka**rl Marx climbs while carrying boxes of コ (corn) to store on this 又 (table), since he has 暇 **hima** (free time)

804. 諦 PRONUNCIATION: akira
MEANINGS: to abandon, give up EXAMPLE: 諦める akirameru = to give up
DESCRIPTION: on the left, 言(う) iu (to say, # 430); on the upper right, 立(つ) tatsu (to stand, # 11), with downward-facing spikes on its base; at the lower right, Bo Peep, as seen in 帽(子) boushi (hat, # 243) CUE: people 言 (say) that a cook who 立 (stands) on slippery floors should wear spikes on her shoes, but **A**chilles' **Ra**Men (noodles) were Ruined because Bo Peep 諦めた **akira**meta (gave up) on that advice and switched to ordinary shoes COMPARE: 締(める) shimeru = to fasten, # 1173

805. 浪 PRONUNCIATION: rou

MEANINGS: wandering, waves **EXAMPLES:** 浪費 rouhi = waste, extravagance; 浪人 rounin = wandering samurai without a master, a person waiting for another chance to take a university exam **DESCRIPTION:** on the left, a water radical; on the right, 良(い) yoi (good, # 303)

CUE: a 浪人 rounin (masterless samurai) can find 良 (good) work on this water **Row**ing boats

806. 没 PRONUNCIATIONS: bo, botsu

MEANINGS: drown, sink, hide, fall into, disappear, die **EXAMPLES:** 没頭 bottou = immersing oneself; 没する bossuru = to sink, go down, to set, to pass away, to die, to disappear; 日没 nichibotsu = sunset **DESCRIPTION:** compared to 役 yaku (role, # 557), the man with a double hat on the left has been replaced by a water radical, but π (the Greek letter pi, also known as a pious yak) remains on the table to the right **CUES:** this π (yak) looks down at the water from his perch on a table and **Boa**sts that, if he jumps in, the people in some nearby **Boat**s will make sure that he doesn't 没する **bo**ssuru suru (sink)

807. 悶 PRONUNCIATIONS: moda, mon

MEANINGS: to be in agony, to worry **EXAMPLES:** 悶える modaeru = to be in agony, to worry; 悶々 monmon = worry, agony

DESCRIPTION: on the right and left, 門 mon (gate, # 409), which helps us to pronounce this; in the center, 心 kokoro (heart, # 306) **CUES:** Moses and his **Da**d have their 心 (hearts) set on a new 門 (gate), but they 悶える **moda**eru (worry) and **Moan** about the expense

808. 術 PRONUNCIATIONS: sube, jutsu

MEANINGS: methods, means, trick, skill, technique **EXAMPLES:** 為す術もない nasusubemonai = at one's wit's end; 手術 shujutsu = surgery; 美術 bijutsu = visual art **DESCRIPTION:** on the left and right, 行(く)

iku (to go, # 334); in the middle, a woman wearing a skirt, with something jutting out over her right shoulder **CUES:** this woman in the middle wants to 行 (go) out and serve **S**oup to **B**eggars, but she has a lump that **Jut**s out over her right shoulder, and it will require 手術 shu**jutsu** (surgery)

··········

Chapter 26

809. 居 PRONUNCIATIONS: kyo, i

MEANINGS: to exist or reside **EXAMPLES:** 住居 juukyo = dwelling; 居間 ima = living room **DESCRIPTION:** on the left, a lean-to with a double roof; inside the lean-to, 古(い) furui (old, # 392) **CUES:** I have an 古 (old) 住居 juu**kyo** (residence) in **Kyo**to, which is a lean-to with a double roof, and my life is E**a**sy

810. 求 PRONUNCIATIONS: kyuu, moto

MEANINGS: to seek, to request **EXAMPLES:** 追求する tsuikyuu suru = to pursue a goal, to chase; 要求 youkyuu = a request or demand; 求める motomeru = to ask, request or buy; 求む motomu = to seek or demand

DESCRIPTION: this radical is seen in (野)球 yakyuu (baseball, # 606), which helps us to pronounce this **CUES:** this reminds us of a 球 (baseball) player from **Cu**ba who 求む **moto**mu (seeks) a **Mo**torcycle **ALSO COMPARE:** (健)康 kenkou = health, # 831; 救(済) kyuusai = rescue, # 977, which also helps us to pronounce this

811. 健 PRONUNCIATIONS: ken, suko

MEANING: healthy **EXAMPLES:** 健康 kenkou = health; 健やか sukoyaka = vigorous, healthy, sound **DESCRIPTION:** on the left, a man with a slanted hat; on the right, 建(築) kenchiku (architecture, # 363), which helps us to pronounce this **CUES:** this man with a slanted hat is named **Ken**, he works as an 建 (architect) with Barbie, and they are **Su**ing **Co**ke over the effects of its beverage on their 健康 **ken**kou (health)

812. 冒 PRONUNCIATIONS: oka, bou

MEANINGS: to transfer or move **EXAMPLES:** 冒険 bouken = adventure, risk; 冒す okasu = to brave or risk, to face or venture **DESCRIPTION:** at the top 日 hi (sun, # 32) ; at the bottom, 目 me (eye, # 51) **CUES: Occa**sionally, when I go out in my **Boat**, I use my 目 (eyes) to look directly into this 日 (sun), but I know that I am taking a 冒険 **bou**ken (risk) in doing so

COMPARE: 畳 tatami = tatami mat, # 876

813. 論 PRONUNCIATION: ron

MEANINGS: logic, argument **EXAMPLES:** 口論 kouron = argument, quarrel

DESCRIPTION: on the left, 言(う) iu (to speak, # 430); on the upper right, a roof with a ceiling; on the lower right, 冊 satsu (counter for books, # 568); together, the two radicals on the right suggest a library **CUES: Ron**ald Reagan got into a 口論 kou**ron** (argument) at a 冊 (library) and 言 (said) some things that were **Wrong**

COMPARE: (車)輪 sharin = wheel, # 690

814. 氷 PRONUNCIATIONS: koori, koo, hyou

MEANING: ice **EXAMPLES:** 氷 koori = ice; 氷る kooru = to freeze; 氷山 hyouzan = iceberg **DESCRIPTION:** 水 mizu (water, # 251) with one extra line in the upper left corner, suggesting an ice crystal **CUES:** when the Lone Ranger visited **Cor**inth, they served him a **Cold** drink of 水 (water) containing silver crystals that turned out to be 氷 **koo**ri (ice), and he said "**Hi-Yo** Silver" **ALSO COMPARE:** 永(久) eikyuu = eternity, # 870, in which there are *two* small lines in the upper left corner

815. 溶 PRONUNCIATIONS: you, to

MEANINGS: melt, dissolve, thaw **EXAMPLES:** 溶岩 yougan = lava; 溶ける tokeru = to melt or dissolve, intransitive; 溶かす tokasu = to melt or dissolve, transitive **DESCRIPTION:** on the left, a water radical; on the right, (内)容 naiyou (content, # 296), which helps us to pronounce this

and which resembles a bird hovering over a roof that covers a box of yogurt **CUES:** the 容 (content) of this box is frozen **Yo**gurt, and if a **Torch** is lit under it, it will 溶ける **to**keru (melt) and turn into water like this

816. 岩 PRONUNCIATIONS: iwa, gan

MEANING: rock **EXAMPLES:** 岩 iwa = rock; 溶岩 yougan = lava **DESCRIPTION:** at the top, 山 yama (mountain, # 146); at the bottom, 石 ishi (stone, # 458)
CUES: while fighting in an **Ea**stern **War**, **Gan**dalf rolled 石 (stones) down a 山 (mountain), and the enemy was buried in 岩 **iwa** = rock

··········

Chapter 27

817. 嫌 PRONUNCIATIONS: gen, iya, kira, ken **MEANINGS:** to dislike or hate

EXAMPLES: 機嫌 kigen = mood feeling; 嫌な iya na = unpleasant, disgusting; 嫌い kirai = to hate; 嫌悪 ken'o = hatred, disgust

DESCRIPTION: on the left, 女 onna (female, # 235); at the top right, this resembles the head of 羊 hitsuji (sheep); at the bottom right, this appears to be a 木 ki (tree, # 118) whose trunk has been split down the middle but which is being held together by a trident piercing it from the right side **CUES:** this 女 (female) on the left is staring at this split 木 (tree) that has been patched together with a trident, and 嫌いです **kira**i desu (she doesn't like it), but her husband **Gen**ghis puts on some **Iya**hon (earphones), grabs a key from his **Key Ra**ck, and goes out to talk to **Ken** and Barbie about the 羊 (sheep) that is stuck at the top of the tree

COMPARE: 謙(虚) kenkyo = modesty, # 965

818. 匹 PRONUNCIATIONS: hiki, piki[1], biki[1], hi MEANINGS: to exist or reside EXAMPLES: 二匹 nihiki = two small animals or bolts of cloth; 一匹 ippiki = one small animal or bolt of cloth; 三匹 sanbiki = three small animals or bolts of cloth; 匹敵 hitteki suru = to equal or match DESCRIPTION: 四 yon (four, # 6), which resembles the floor diagram of a house, with a wall missing on the right CUES: I kicked a wall out of my house, 四匹 yon**hiki** (four) of my cats escaped, and now I have a **Hickey** on my **Heel**

819. 泥 PRONUNCIATIONS: doro, dei MEANINGS: mud or mire EXAMPLES: 泥棒 dorobou = thief; 泥水 deisui = muddy water, red-light district; 泥酔する deisui suru = to get dead drunk DESCRIPTION: on the left, a water radical; in the middle, a lean-to with a double roof; under the lean-to, the katakana ヒ hi, which reminds us of a heel (a contemptible person) CUES: **Doro**thy went on a **Da**te with the Scarecrow, and they sat together under this reinforced lean-to, but he turned out to be a ヒ (heel) who threw 泥水 **dei**sui (muddy water) on her and, on top of that, he was a 泥棒 **doro**bou (thief)

820. 棒 PRONUNCIATION: bou MEANINGS: club or pole EXAMPLES: 棒 bou = a stick; 相棒 aibou = a buddy or partner; 泥棒 dorobou = thief DESCRIPTION: on the left, 木 ki (wood, # 118); at the upper right, 人 hito (person, # 13), with the number 三 san (three) inscribed across it, as seen in 春 haru (spring, # 506); at the lower right, a telephone pole CUE: this 人 (person) used a **Bo**at to bring us 三 (three) telephone 棒 **bou** (poles) made out of 木 (wood) COMPARE: (演)奏 ensou = musical performance, # 757

821. 追 PRONUNCIATIONS: tsui, o MEANING: to chase, follow, pursue EXAMPLES: 追求する tsuikyuu suru = to pursue a goal, to chase; 追う ou = to chase; 追いかける oikakeru = to pursue or chase after DESCRIPTION: on the lower left, a snail; on the snail, bunk beds CUES: this snail is carrying these **Tsui**dish (Swedish) bunk beds to **O**saka and trying to 追いかける o**i**kakeru (chase) a rival snail, but progress is slow COMPARE: (旅)館 ryokan = Japanese inn, # 305; (気)遣(う) kizukau = to care for, worry, pay attention, # 765; (警)官 keikan = policeman, # 880

822. 照 PRONUNCIATIONS: te, shou, de MEANING: to shine or illuminate EXAMPLES: 照らす terasu = to illuminate or light; 照る teru = to shine; 照れる tereru = to be shy or feel embarrassment; 対照的に taishouteki ni = diametrically opposite; 照明 shoumei = lighting; 日照り hideri = dry weather, drought DESCRIPTION: on the left, 日 hi (sun, # 32); at the upper right, katana 刀 (sword, # 102); at the middle right, 口 kuchi (mouth, # 426), but this resembles a television set; at the bottom, a fire, as seen in 熱 netsu (fever, # 65) CUES: this **T**elevision set displays a **Show** featuring a **D**ebutante who fights with 刀 (swords), and this 日 (sun) and fire are being used to 照らす **te**rasu (illuminate) the stage

823. 振 PRONUNCIATIONS: shin, fu, furi MEANINGS: to shake, wave, swing EXAMPLES: 振動数 shindousuu = frequency; 振る furu = to shake or wave; 振り返る furikaeru = to turn the head, look back, think back; 振り向く furimuku = to turn around; 銀行振込み ginkou furikomi = bank transfer DESCRIPTION: on the left, a kneeling guy; on the right, a lean-to; under the lean-to, a horizontal arrow; below the arrow, L and Y holding up a roof, which remind us of friend**LY**

CUES: this kneeling guy is usually friend**LY**, but when he 振り返る <u>furi</u>kaeru (looks back) at this lean-to and sees a **Shin**to priest **Fool**ishly pointing this arrow at him, he gets **Fur**ious

824. 似 PRONUNCIATIONS: ni, *ne*, ji

MEANINGS: to resemble or take after

EXAMPLES: 似ている nite iru = resembling; 真似 mane = imitation, mimicry; 類似の ruiji no = similar; 類似品 ruijihin = imitation, or similar article **DESCRIPTION:** on the left, a man with a slanted hat; on the right, 以(前) izen (a long time ago, # 601), which resembles someone sliding off the neck of a giraffe **CUES:** my **Niece** 似ている <u>ni</u>te iru (is resembling) this man with a slanted hat, and they used to ride on giraffes' **Necks** 以 (a long time ago), but now she has a **Jeep**

....

Chapter 28

825. 釘 PRONUNCIATION: kugi

MEANINGS: nail, tack, peg **EXAMPLES:** 釘 kugi = nail or peg; 釘付けになる kugizuke ni naru = to be unable to take one's eyes from **DESCRIPTION:** on the left, 金(属) kinzoku (metal, # 301); on the right, 丁(目) choume (city block, # 702), which resembles a nail

CUE: I used 金 (metal) 釘 <u>kugi</u> (nails) to build a shed for my **Cool Gee**se

826. 騒 PRONUNCIATIONS: sawa, sou

MEANINGS: make noise, disturb, excite

EXAMPLES: 騒ぐ sawagu = to make noise, to make a fuss; 騒々しい souzoushii = noisy **DESCRIPTION:** on the left, 馬 uma (horse, # 958); at the upper right, 又 mata ("again," resembling a table, # 24); at the lower right, 虫 mushi (insect, # 9) **CUES:** this 馬 (horse) 騒いだ <u>sawa</u>ida (made a fuss) when it **Saw** a **W**arlord

listening to **Sou**l music at a 又 (table) with buzzing 虫 (insects) nearby

827. 尻 PRONUNCIATION: shiri

MEANINGS: buttocks, hips **EXAMPLES:** お尻 oshiri = buttocks **DESCRIPTION:** on the upper left, a lean-to with a double roof; under the lean-to, 九 kyuu (nine, # 111)

CUE: when these 九 (nine) **Sheep Rea**lized that it was raining, they all sheltered their 尻 <u>shiri</u> (buttocks) under this heavy-duty lean-to

828. 呆 PRONUNCIATIONS: aki, bo, ho, a MEANINGS: to be amazed, disgusted or shocked

EXAMPLES: 呆れる akireru = to be disgusted or astonished, usually written あきれる; 呆け boke = fool, usually written ボケ; 阿呆 aho = a fool or silly person, usually written アホ; 呆気にとられる akke ni torareru = to be taken aback, to be dumb-founded **DESCRIPTION:** at the top, 口 kuchi (mouth, # 426); at the bottom, 木 ki (tree, # 118) **CUES:** **Achi**lles saw a man with a big 口 (mouth) **Boa**sting from the top of this 木 (tree), and he 呆れた <u>aki</u>reta (got astonished) and went **Home** to tell his **Aunt**

829. 褒 PRONUNCIATIONS: ho, hou

MEANINGS: to praise or extol

EXAMPLES: 褒める homeru = to praise, admire or speak well of; 褒美 houbi = reward **DESCRIPTION:** at the top, a tire stop, as seen in 対(する) tai suru (to confront, # 674); at the center left, a man with a slanted hat; at the center right, 呆(れる) akireru (to be astonished, # 828); at the bottom the katana エ e and the letter Y **CUES:** this man with a slanted hat, whose name is **Homer** Simpson, has built this tire stop in order to stop cars from colliding with the **Home** of エ and Y, who are 呆 (astonished) and 褒める <u>ho</u>meru (praise) him highly

830. 飼 PRONUNCIATIONS: kai, shi, ka

MEANINGS: to domesticate, raise, keep, feed
EXAMPLES: 飼主 kainushi = shepherd, pet owner (also written 飼い主); 飼犬 kai'inu = a pet dog (also written 飼い犬); 飼育 shi'iku = breeding, raising, rearing; 飼育員 shi'ikuin = a caretaker at a zoo or aquarium; 飼う kau = to keep a pet or raise livestock **DESCRIPTION:** on the left, 食(べる) taberu (to eat, # 398); on the right, (寿)司 sushi (# 607), which helps us to pronounce this **CUES:** the 飼主 **kai**nushi (shepherd) that the **Kai**ser employs to watch his **Sheep** sits in his **Car** at lunchtime and 食 (eats) 司 (sushi)

831. 康 PRONUNCIATION: kou

MEANING: healthy, peaceful **EXAMPLES:**
健康 kenkou = health **DESCRIPTION:** on the upper left, a lean-to, with a small chimney; under the lean-to, 求(む) motomu (to demand, # 810), with a trident piercing its upper half, but the ball above its right shoulder is absent
CUE: after this man was stabbled with a trident, he crawled under this lean-to to get out of the **Cold**, but he 求 (demands) an ambulance, since this is affecting his 健康 ken**kou** (health)

832. 骨 PRONUNCIATIONS: ko, kotsu, hone

MEANING: bone **EXAMPLES:** 骨折する kossetsu suru = to break a bone; 骸骨 gaikotsu = skeleton; 骨 hone = bone
DESCRIPTION: at the top, the floor plan of a one-room apartment on a roof, with a bathroom in the right lower corner; at the bottom, 月 tsuki (moon, # 148) **CUES:** I rest my **hone** 骨 (bones) in this roof-top apartment on the 月 (moon), where I drink **Co**la, wear several **Co**ats to keep warm and use a **Ho**me **Ne**twork **COMPARE:** 滑(る) suberu = to slip, # 981

....

Chapter 29
833. 皮 PRONUNCIATIONS: kawa, gawa[1], hi MEANING: skin EXAMPLES: 皮 kawa = skin, peel; 毛皮 kegawa = fur; 皮膚 hifu = skin; 皮肉 hiniku = sarcasm, cynicism, irony DESCRIPTION: this is Straight Arrow, as seen in 彼 kare (he, # 371), who stands on springy legs and has a long cape that trails down to the floor CUES: Straight Arrow works at a Car Wash, he has thin 皮 kawa (skin), and he Hears everything that people say about him

834. 隠 PRONUNCIATIONS: kaku, in

MEANINGS: conceal, cover **EXAMPLES:**
隠す kakusu = to hide or cover up; 隠れる kakureru = to conceal oneself or disappear; 隠元豆 ingenmame = green bean, string bean
DESCRIPTION: on the left, ß beta, from the Greek alphabet; at the upper right, a barbecue grate, as seen in (野)菜 yasai (vegetable, # 121); at the middle right, long hair flowing to the left; at the lower right, 心 kokoro (heart, # 306)
CUES: this ß (Greek) guy was barbecuing some **Cactus** on this grate when his long hair caught fire, causing 心 (heart) ache, and now he will spend time on the **Internet** and 隠す **kaku**su (hide) until his hair grows back

835. 沈 PRONUNCIATIONS: shizu, chin

MEANINGS: sink, submerge, subside, be depressed
EXAMPLES: 沈める shizumeru = to sink or submerge; 沈む shizumu = to set (sun or moon), to sink, to feel depressed; 沈黙 chinmoku = silence **DESCRIPTION:** on the left, a water radical; at the upper right, Straight Arrow's head, as seen in 彼 kare (he, # 371); at the lower right, sturdy legs, as seen in 兄 ani (big brother, # 420)
CUES: 彼 (Straight Arrow), who has developed these sturdy legs, was wading in this water with some **Sheep** at the **Zoo** when one of them struck him on the **Chin,** and he 沈めた **shizu**meta (sank)

836. 黙 PRONUNCIATIONS: **dama, moku** MEANING: silence EXAMPLES: 黙る damaru = to keep silent; 沈黙 chinmoku = silence DESCRIPTION: at the upper left, a sincere guy wearing bifocals, as seen in 野(菜) yasai (vegetables, # 545); at the upper right, 犬 inu (dog, # 190); at the bottom, a fire, as seen in 熱 netsu (fever, # 65) CUES: when this sincere guy in **Dama**scus was sitting with his 犬 (dog) watching a fire, he wanted **More Kool**-Aid, but he 黙った **dama**tta (kept silent) COMPARE: (自)然 shizen (nature, # 611), in which the sincere guy is replaced by a three-legged bench

837. 破 PRONUNCIATIONS: **ha, yabu, pa** MEANINGS: to break or tear EXAMPLES: 読破する dokuha suru = to finish reading a book; 破る yaburu = to break, tear or violate; 破れる yabureru = to be torn, ripped or broken, or to fail; 突破する toppa suru = to break through DESCRIPTION: on the left, 石 ishi (stone, # 458); on the right, Straight Arrow, as seen in 皮 kawa (skin, # 833), who stands on springy legs and has a long cape that trails down to the floor CUES: Straight Arrow was in **Ha**waii when he tripped on this 石 (stone), and his **Y**a**k** skin **B**oo**t**s 破れた **yabu**reta (tore) apart, so that he couldn't go to the **P**arty COMPARE: 彼 kare = he, # 371; 敗(れる) yabureru = to lose or be defeated, # 793; 波(止場) hatoba = pier, # 878, which helps us to pronounce this

838. 殺 PRONUNCIATIONS: **satsu, sa, koro** MEANINGS: to kill or reduce EXAMPLES: 殺人 satsujin = murder; 殺到する sattou suru = to rush at or surge; 殺す korosu = to kill DESCRIPTION: at the upper left, an X, which may represent a drone; at the lower left, 木 ki (tree, # 118); on the right, π (the Greek letter pi, also known as a pious yak), standing on 又 mata ("again,"# 24), which resembles a simple table CUES: I read a **Sat**isfying **Su**perman novel about a **Sal**aryman who suffered a **Coro**nary when he saw this drone fly over this 木 (tree) and 殺す **koro**su (kill) this π (yak) on a table

839. 影 PRONUNCIATIONS: **ei, kage** MEANINGS: shadow, silhouette, phantom EXAMPLES: 影響 eikyou = influence, effect; 影 kage = shadow, silhouette DESCRIPTION: on the left, 景(色) keshiki (view, # 516); on the right, three lines, as seen in 形 katachi (shape, # 573) CUES: looking at this 景 (view), I saw a 形 (shape) which seemed to be the 影 **kage** (shadow or silhouette) of an **A**pe, and I **C**alled a **Gue**st to investigate

840. 響 PRONUNCIATIONS: **hibi, kyou** MEANINGS: echo, sound, resound, ring, vibrate EXAMPLES: 響く hibiku = to resound, to be heard far away; 響き hibiki = echo, repercussion, sound; 影響 eikyou = influence, effect DESCRIPTION: at the upper left, the top portion of 糸 skeet shooter (# 219); at the upper middle, 良(い) yoi (good, # 303), without its pointy hat; at the upper right, ß beta from the Greek alphabet; at the bottom, 音 oto (sound, # 266) CUES: whenever this 糸 (skeet shooter) **Hea**rs **Bee**s, he catches some for his ß (Greek) friend who lives in **Kyou**to, since their buzzing 音 (sound) has a 良 (good) 影響 ei**kyou** (effect) on him

Chapter 30

841. 添 PRONUNCIATIONS: ten, so, zo[1]
MEANINGS: annex, accompany, attach, append, garnish EXAMPLES: 添加物 tenkabutsu = an additive (e.g., to food); 添える soeru = to attach to, to garnish a dish, to help or support; 付き添う tsukisou = to accompany, chaperone, take care of; 力添え chikarazoe = assistance, support DESCRIPTION: on the left, a water radical; at the upper right, 天 ten (sky, # 189), which helps us to pronounce this; at the lower right, 小(さい) chiisai (small, # 253), with a piece of gum lying on the ground to the right CUES: as Ten people walk by, a 小 (small) piece of gum is Soaking in this water under this 天 (sky), until it finally 添える soeru (attaches) to someone's shoe

842. 延 PRONUNCIATIONS: en, no
MEANINGS: to extend or postpone EXAMPLES: 延期 enki = postponement; 引き延ばす hikinobasu = to delay; 延びる nobiru = to lengthen or stretch DESCRIPTION: at the lower left, a 3X snail, as seen in 建(てる) tateru (to build, # 363), which consists of a 3 intersected at the bottom to form an X; at the upper right, 正(しい) tadashii (correct, # 174)

CUES: an Engineer who is always 正 (correct) visited Norway, but he had to request an 延期 enki (postponement) of his appointments because the 3X snail on which he traveled was so slow COMPARE: 伸(びる) nobiru = to lengthen or stretch, # 697; 庭 niwa = garden, # 495

843. 餌 PRONUNCIATIONS: e, esa
MEANINGS: animal food, bait EXAMPLES: 餌食 ejiki = prey or victim; 餌 esa = animal food or bait DESCRIPTION: on the left, a modified version of 食(べる) taberu (to eat, # 398); on the right, 耳 mimi (ear, # 57) CUES: an Eskimo uses Eggs and Sardines as 餌 esa (animal food) for his

dog, and the dog's 耳 (ears) prick up before it 食 (eats) them

844. 視 PRONUNCIATION: shi
MEANINGS: inspection, regard as, see, look at EXAMPLES: 無視 mushi = disregarding, ignoring; 視力 shiryoku = eyesight DESCRIPTION: on the left, the Shah, as seen in (会)社 kaisha (company, # 271); on the right, 見(る) miru (to watch, # 53)
CUE: this Shah 見 (watches) his Sheep, using his good 視力 shiryoku (eyesight)

845. 肩 PRONUNCIATIONS: kata, ken
MEANING: shoulder EXAMPLES: 肩 kata = shoulder; 肩甲骨 kenkoukotsu = shoulder blade or scapula DESCRIPTION: on the upper left, a lean-to with a double roof and a cloth on top, but this resembles a shoulder under a shirt, with an arm extending down to the left; on the lower right, 月 tsuki (moon, # 148) CUES: there was a Catastrophe at the Kentucky Derby, and this man with a 月 (moon) tattoo on his chest sustained an injury to his 肩 kata (shoulder)

846. 撫 PRONUNCIATIONS: na, bu
MEANINGS: to stroke, pat, smooth down EXAMPLES: 撫でる naderu = to rub or stroke; 愛撫 aibu = a caress DESCRIPTION: on the left, a kneeling man; on the right, 無(くす) nakusu (to lose, # 583) or 無(事) buji (safety, # 583), both of which help us to pronounce this CUES: this kneeling man was once a Nazi and a Boozer, but he 無 (lost) everything that he owned, and now he 撫でる naderu (rubs) the heads of stray animals that he meets

847. 精 PRONUNCIATIONS: sei, shou
MEANINGS: pure, essence, details, energy, vitality EXAMPLES: 精一杯 seiippai = the best of one's ability, with all one's might; 精密な seimitsu na = detailed, precise, thorough;

精神 seishin = mind, soul, spirit; 精神的な seishinteki na = spiritual, mental; 精進料理 shoujin ryouri = vegetarian cuisine, as eaten by Buddhist monks **DESCRIPTION:** on the left, 米 kome (uncooked rice, # 326); on the right, 青(い) aoi (blue, # 155) or 青(年) seinen (young man, # 155), which helps us to pronounce this **CUES:** a **Sai**lor saw some 青 (blue) 米 (rice) at a food **Show**, and the color was so bizarre that it caused him to have 精神的な **sei**shinteki na (mental) problems

848. 杯 **PRONUNCIATIONS: hai, bai[1], pai[1], sakazuki MEANINGS:** wine glass, toast **EXAMPLES:** 二杯 nihai = two cups, glasses, spoons or bowls; 一杯 ippai = one cup, etc., or full of; 三杯 sanbai = three cups, etc.; 杯をする sakazuki wo suru = to share a cup of sake **DESCRIPTION:** on the left, 木 ki (tree, # 118); on the right, 不(便) fuben (inconvenient, # 176) **CUES: Hei**di saw that this 木 (tree) in the middle of a field made it 不 (inconvenient) to play **Sakkaa** (soccer) with the **Zoo Kee**per, so she decided to share 一杯 ip**pai** (one cup) of sake with him instead

....

Chapter 31

849. 兆 **PRONUNCIATIONS: kiza, chou MEANINGS:** sign, omen, trillion **EXAMPLES:** 兆し kizashi = sign, omen; 前兆 zenchou = premonition, omen; 一兆円 itchouen = one trillion yen **DESCRIPTION:** two benches stored vertically, with their legs projecting to the sides **CUES:** we were sitting on these two benches, looking at 一兆 it**chou** (one trillion) stars, and I was getting ready to **Ki**ss **Za**ch when he started talking about Margaret **Cho**, and I took that as a bad 兆し **kiza**shi (omen) **COMPARE:** 非(常) hijou = emergency, # 682; 逃(げる) nigeru = to run away, # 850

850. 逃 **PRONUNCIATIONS: ni, tou, noga MEANING:** to run away **EXAMPLES:** 逃げる nigeru = to escape or run away; 逃亡 toubou = escape, flight; 逃れる nogareru = to escape; 逃す nogasu = to let go, to allow to escape **DESCRIPTION:** on the lower left, a snail; on the upper right right, 兆 chou (trillion, # 849) **CUES:** my **Ni**ece was on a **Toll** road when she spotted this snail carrying 兆 (a trillion) bacteria that were trying to 逃げる **ni**geru (escape) from a hurricane, and she thought about escaping with them, but her car had **No Gas**

851. 悲 **PRONUNCIATIONS: hi, kana MEANINGS:** sad, sorrow **EXAMPLES:** 悲観する hikan suru = to be pessimistic, feel hopeless; 悲鳴 himei = scream, shriek, cry of distress; 悲しい kanashii = sad **DESCRIPTION:** at the top, 非(常) hijou (emergency, # 682), which reminds us of a hero with wings and helps us to pronounce this; at the bottom, 心 kokoro (heart, # 306) **CUES:** this **He**ro at the top puts his 心 (heart) into his work dealing with 非 (emergencies), but during the long **Cana**dian winters he sometimes feels 悲しい **kana**shii (sad)

852. 揺 **PRONUNCIATIONS: yu, you MEANINGS:** swing, sway, rock, tremble, vibrate **EXAMPLES:** 揺れる yureru = to sway or shake; 動揺 douyou = uneasiness, agitation **DESCRIPTION:** on the left, a kneeling guy; at the upper right, a barbecue grate, as seen in (野)菜 yasai (vegetable, # 121); at the lower right, 山 yama (mountain, # 146) with a forked tongue emerging from its center, as seen in 話(す) hanasu (to talk, # 433) **CUES:** this kneeling guy was 話 (talking) and barbecuing some **Yu**cca on a grill on a 山 (mountain) in **Yo**semite when the earth began to 揺れる **yu**reru (shake), driving him to his knees

853. 器 PRONUNCIATIONS: utsuwa, ki

MEANING: container EXAMPLES: 器 utsuwa = container or receptacle, ability; 食器 shokki = tableware; 便器 benki = toilet bowl, urinal DESCRIPTION: at the top, two 口 kuchi (mouths, # 426); in the middle, 大(きい) ookii (big, # 188); at the bottom, two more 口 (mouths) CUES: this 大 (big) family has four 口 (mouths) to feed, and they **U**tilize **S**upermarket **W**alnuts, as well as **Qu**iche, which they store in 器 **utsuwa** (containers)

854. 奇 PRONUNCIATION: ki

MEANINGS: strange, curiosity EXAMPLES: 奇妙な kimyou na= strange, unique; 好奇心 koukishin = curiosity DESCRIPTION: at the top 大(きい) ookii (big, # 188); at the bottom, 可(愛い) kawaii (cute, # 615) CUE: this reminds us of a 可 (cute) person wearing a **Ki**mono that is too 大 (big) for her, which is a 奇妙な **ki**myou na (strange) sight COMPARE: 寄(付) kifu = donation, # 604, which features a *bird* at the top and which helps us to pronounce this

855. 椅 PRONUNCIATION: i

MEANING: chair EXAMPLES: 椅子 isu = chair DESCRIPTION: on the left, 木 ki (wood, # 118); on the right, 奇(妙) kimyou (unique, # 854) CUE: this 木 (wood) on the left is **Ea**sy to work with, and I was able to make a 奇 (unique) 椅子 **i**su (chair) from it

856. 妙 PRONUNCIATIONS: tae, myou

MEANINGS: exquisite, excellent, strange, queer EXAMPLES: 妙なる taenaru = exquisite; 妙な myou na = strange, odd, unique; 奇妙な kimyou na = strange; 微妙な bimyou na = subtle, delicate, ticklish DESCRIPTION: on the left, 女 onna (female, # 235); on the right, 少(し) sukoshi (a little, # 254) CUES: this 女 (woman) is a **T**all **E**xpert on cats, but she was 少 (a little) surprised when she heard a **Meow** from a 奇妙な ki**myou** na (strange) animal

....

Chapter 32

857. 比 PRONUNCIATIONS: hi, kura

MEANING: to compare EXAMPLES: 比較 hikaku = comparison; 対比する taihi suru = to compare, contrast; 比べる kuraberu = to compare DESCRIPTION: two variations of the katakana ヒ hi, which remind us of heros and help us to pronounce this CUES: these two ヒ's (**H**eroes) both raise **C**ool **R**abbits, but they look different, prompting us to 比べる **kura**beru (compare) them

858. 鮮 PRONUNCIATIONS: sen, aza

MEANING: fresh EXAMPLES: 新鮮な shinsen na = fresh; 鮮明な senmei na = bright, clear, vivid; 鮮やかな azayaka na = colorful, bright, vivid, impressive, beautiful DESCRIPTION: on the left, 魚 sakana (fish, # 80); on the right, 羊 hitsuji (sheep, not included in this Catalogue) CUES: a **Sen**ator eats this 新鮮な shin**sen** na (fresh) 魚 (fish), while keeping an eye on this 羊 (sheep) to make sure that it doesn't eat his **Aza**leas

859. 検 PRONUNCIATION: ken

MEANING: to examine or inspect EXAMPLES: 検査 kensa = investigation, examination; 探検 tanken = exploration, expedition (this can also be written 探険 tanken, # 196) DESCRIPTION: compared to (危)険 kiken (danger, # 196), which features a horizontally placed keg stuck inside a 大 (big) washing machine on the right, and which helps us to pronounce this, the ß (Greek) guy on the left has been replaced by 木 ki (tree, # 118)

CUE: **Ken** climbs this 木 (tree) in order to 検査する **ken**sa suru (inspect) this stuck-keg problem for Barbie

860. 査 PRONUNCIATION: sa

MEANING: to examine closely EXAMPLES: 検査 kensa = investigation, examination; 調査 chousa = investigation, survey, analysis; 巡査 junsa = patrolman DESCRIPTION: at the top, 木 ki (tree, # 118); at the bottom, a solar panel, as seen in 祖(母) sobo (grandmother, # 272)

CUE: after a 木 (tree) was allowed to grow over a solar panel, blocking its sunlight, **Sa**msung conducted a 調査 chou**sa** (investigation)

COMPARE: 畳 tatami = tatami mat, # 876

861. 膝 PRONUNCIATION: hiza

MEANING: knee, lap EXAMPLES: 膝 hiza = knee, lap DESCRIPTION: on the left, 月 tsuki (moon, # 148); at the upper right, this resembles 夫 otto (husband, # 614), but the two arms on each side originate at the same point rather than separately; at the lower right, 求(む) motomu (to seek or demand, # 810), without its hat brim and the ball above its right shoulder CUE: my 夫 (husband), whose arms grow close together, got down on his 膝 **hiza** (knees) by the light of the 月 (moon) and 求 (demanded) more alcohol, and I said, "**He's A** little drunk"

862. 我 PRONUNCIATIONS: wa, ware, ga MEANINGS: I, my EXAMPLES: 我が国 wagakuni = one's country; 我がままな wagamama na = selfish, spoiled; 我 ware = self; 我々 wareware = we; 我ら warera = we; 我慢 gaman = patience, endurance, tolerance

DESCRIPTION: on the left, 手 te (hand, # 23); on the right, a halberd (combination lance and axe) CUES: this reminds us of General **Wa**shington, who always kept his 手 (hand) on his halberd; he was a **Wa**rrior **Re**bel who had the gift of **Ga**b, and

he used to say, "我が国 **wa**gakuni (our country) is going to win"

863. 腹 PRONUNCIATIONS: fuku, puku[1], *naka*, hara, para[1] MEANINGS: abdomen, belly EXAMPLES: 腹痛 fukutsuu = stomachache; 満腹 manpuku = full stomach; 空腹 kuufuku = hunger; お腹 onaka = stomach; 腹 hara = stomach, abdomen; 横つ腹 yokoppara = side of the body, flank

DESCRIPTION: compared to (回)復 kaifuku (recovery, # 527), which helps us to pronounce this, the man with a double hat on the left has been replaced by 月 tsuki (moon, # 148); on the right, we still see a crutch at the top, 日 hi (sun, # 32) in the middle, and a dancer with a ponytail at the bottom CUES: this dancer from **Fuku**oka, who uses a crutch and dances in both 月 (moon) and 日 (sun) light, has a **Na**sty **Ca**t that **Hara**sses her when it suffers from 空腹 kuu**fuku** (hunger)

864. 寂 PRONUNCIATIONS: jaku, sabi

MEANINGS: loneliness, quietly, mellow EXAMPLES: 静寂 seijaku = silence, stillness; 寂しい sabishii = lonely DESCRIPTION: at the top, a bad haircut; on the left, a portable cannon, as seen in 点 ten (points, score, # 29) on top of a spinning base; on the lower right, 又 mata (again, # 24), which resembles a simple table CUES: **Jack** Nicholson, who has a bad haircut like this, is seated at this 又 (table), eating **Salty Bean**s with only a spinning cannon for company, and he feels 寂しい **sabi**shii (lonely)

....

Chapter 33

865. 敷 PRONUNCIATIONS: shiki, shi

MEANINGS: spread, pave, sit **EXAMPLES:**
座敷 zashiki = Japanese-style room with tatami flooring; 屋敷 yashiki = estate, mansion, residence; 敷く shiku = to lay out, spread or enact **DESCRIPTION:** at the upper left, this resembles the top of a dog chasing a ball, as seen in 犬 inu (dog, # 190); at the middle left, 田 (rice paddy, # 68); at the lower left, 方 kata (honorable person, # 114), who seems to have the dog and the rice paddy on his mind; on the right, a dancer with a ponytail **CUES:** this 方 (honorable person) on the left has this 犬 (dog) and this 田 (rice paddy) on his mind, but this dancer on the right wants him to explain the use of the **Shift Key** to some **Shi**ites in the 座敷 za**shiki** (Japanese-style room)

866. 丸 PRONUNCIATIONS: gan, maru

MEANINGS: round, circle, completely, name of a ship **EXAMPLES:** 弾丸 dangan = bullet; 丸い marui = round; 丸 maru = circle **DESCRIPTION:** 九 kyuu (nine, # 111) with a slash drawn through it **CUES: Gan**dalf was **Maroo**ned on a 丸い **maru**i (round) island after 九 (nine) pirates slashed a hole in his boat

867. 局 PRONUNCIATION: kyoku

MEANINGS: section, circumstances, government agency **EXAMPLES:** 郵便局 yuubinkyoku = post office; 結局 kekkyoku = after all **DESCRIPTION:** on the upper left, a lean-to with a double roof; on the lower right, 可(愛い) kawaii (cute, # 615) **CUE:** the **Kyo**to **Kool**-Aid club is located in a sturdy lean-to next to the 郵便局 yuubin**kyoku** (post office), and this 可 (cute) person is inside it

868. 突 PRONUNCIATIONS: totsu, tsu, to

MEANINGS: to thrust or protrude **EXAMPLES:**
突然の totsuzen no = abrupt or sudden;

突入する totsunyuu suru = to enter or rush into;
突き当たり tsukiatari = dead end;
突破する toppa suru = to break through **DESCRIPTION:** at the top, a swooping bird; at the bottom, 大(きい) ookii (big, # 188) **CUES:** this 大 (big) swooping bird appeared 突然に **totsu**zen ni (suddenly) and offered to **Tote Su**perman's **Tsui**tcase (suitcase) to Tony Blair's house

869. 恐 PRONUNCIATIONS: oso, kyou

MEANING: to fear **EXAMPLES:** 恐れ osore = fear; 恐ろしい osoroshii = frightening, terrible; 恐れる osoreru = to fear or be apprehensive; 恐慌 kyoukou = panic **DESCRIPTION:** at the upper left, the katakana エ e, which stands for eggs; at the upper right, π (the Greek letter pi, which represents a pious yak), with a slash across it; at the bottom, 心 kokoro (heart, # 306) **CUES:** an **O**ld **S**oldier was buying エ (eggs) in **Kyo**uto when he saw a π (yak) which had been slashed, and he felt 恐れ **oso**re (fear) in his 心 (heart) **COMPARE:** 認(める) mitomeru = to admit, # 1036, which features a slashed 刀 (sword) instead of a slashed π (yak)

870. 永 PRONUNCIATIONS: ei, naga

MEANING: long time **EXAMPLES:** 永遠 eien = eternity; 永眠 eimin = death; 永久 eikyuu = eternity; 永田町 Nagatachou = a district in Tokyo **DESCRIPTION:** compared to 水 mizu (water, # 251), the central line in this kanji has two smaller lines on the left projecting from the top, representing a hat with a feather in it **CUES:** when **Honest A**be drank 水 (water), he would wear this hat with a feather in it and tell stories for what seemed like an 永遠 e**ien** (eternity) while **Naga**ina (a snake) lurked outside

ALSO COMPARE: 泳(ぐ) oyogu = to swim,

461

461 left column

461 page

#255; 氷 koori = ice, # 814, in which there is only one small line in the upper left corner

871. 戸 PRONUNCIATIONS: to, do, ko, be MEANINGS: door, household, counter for houses EXAMPLES: 戸 to = door; 戸締り する tojimari suru = to lock the doors and windows; 戸棚 todana = cupboard; 井戸 ido = well; 一戸 ikko = one house or household; 神戸 Koube = a city in Japan DESCRIPTION: a 門 mon (gate, # 409) gate consists of two doors, each of which resembles this kanji

CUES: when Tolstoy returned to this 戸 **to** (**Do**or) on **Co**ld nights, it always opened for him, and then he would go to **Be**d

872. 句 PRONUNCIATION: ku

MEANINGS: phrase, haiku EXAMPLES: 文句 monku = complaint, phrase, words; 俳句 haiku = poem; 句読点 kutouten = punctuation marks

DESCRIPTION: 可(愛い) kawaii (cute, # 615), with an added awning on the upper left

CUE: our 可 (cute) customer submitted a 文句 mon**ku** (complaint) to the effect that this awning we installed didn't keep her house **Coo**l enough

....

Chapter 34

873. 敬 PRONUNCIATIONS: kei, uyama

MEANINGS: to respect or revere EXAMPLES: 敬語 keigo = honorific language; 尊敬する sonkei suru = to respect; 敬う uyamau = to respect or venerate DESCRIPTION: at the upper left, a plant radical; at the lower left, (俳)句 haiku (poem, # 872), but this looks like the mouth of a cave; on the right, a dancer with a ponytail CUES: this dancer, who lives in a **Ca**ve in the Uruguayan **Ya**ma (mountains), wrote a 句 (poem) about the plants around her, which she 敬う **uyama**u (respects)

874. 警 PRONUNCIATION: kei

MEANINGS: to alarm or warn EXAMPLES: 警察 keisatsu = the police; 警戒する keikai suru = to be cautious or watch out

DESCRIPTION: at the top, (尊)敬 sonkei (respect, # 873), which helps us to pronounce this and includes a dancer with a ponytail near the mouth of a cave; at the bottom, 言(う) iu (to say, # 430)

CUE: this dancer with a ponytail 敬 (respects) the 警察 **kei**satsu (police), and she 言 (says) that she invites them to parties in her **Ca**ve COMPARE: 驚(く) odoroku = to be astonished, # 971

875. 戒 PRONUNCIATIONS: kai, imashi

MEANINGS: to alarm or warn EXAMPLES: 警戒する keikai suru = to be cautious or watch out; 戒める imashimeru = to admonish, warn, prohibit, be cautious DESCRIPTION: at the upper right, a halberd (combination axe and lance); at the lower left, handcuffs, as seen in (機)械 kikai (machine, # 138), which helps us to pronounce this CUES: since the **Kai**ser's men carry handcuffs and halberds, and talk to **I**maginary **Sh**eep, the public should 警戒する kei**kai** suru (be wary)

876. 畳 PRONUNCIATIONS: tatami, tata, jou

MEANINGS: tatami mat, to fold, counter for tatami mats EXAMPLES: 畳 tatami = tatami mat; 畳む tatamu = to fold; 六畳 rokujou = six tatami mats DESCRIPTION: at the top, 田 (rice paddy, # 68); in the middle, a roof; at the bottom, a solar panel CUES: a **Ta**ll **Ta**lented **M**ediator came to this 田 (rice paddy), sat on our 畳 **tatami** mats, complimented our **Ta**rnished **Ta**pestries, and **J**oked about the fact that we keep this solar panel under this roof

877. 津 PRONUNCIATIONS: shin, tsu, zu[1] MEANINGS: haven, port, harbor, ferry

EXAMPLES: 興味津々 kyoumi shinshin = very interesting; 津波 tsunami = tidal wave; 宮津 Miyazu = a town in Kyoto Prefecture DESCRIPTION: on the left, a water radical; on the right, compared to 書(く) kaku (to write, # 415), the two-drawer cabinet at the bottom is missing, but a three-fingered hand is still grasping what appears to be a brush CUES: a 津波 **tsu**nami of water struck a calligrapher as he was 書 (writing) a message with this brush at a **Shin**to shrine, soaking his **Tsu**it (suit)

878. 波 PRONUNCIATIONS: wa, nami, ha, pa MEANINGS: waves, billows

EXAMPLES: 阿波踊り Awa'odori= a type of Bon dance; 津波 tsunami = tidal wave; 波止場 hatoba = pier, wharf; 音波 onpa = sound wave; 突破する toppa suru = to break through DESCRIPTION: on the left, a water radical; on the right, 皮 kawa (skin, # 833), also known as Straight Arrow CUES: a 津波 tsu**nami** of **W**ater like this struck Straight Arrow, who had just eaten a **N**asty **M**eal with **H**ansel and Gretel, but a **Pa**dre rescued him COMPARE: (読)破(する) dokuha sura = to finish reading, # 837, which helps us to pronounce this

879. 隙 PRONUNCIATION: suki

MEANING: crevice, fissure, discord, opportunity, leisure EXAMPLES: 隙間 sukima = gap, hole; 隙 suki = gap, opening, carelessness, inattentiveness DESCRIPTION: on the left, ß beta from the Greek alphabet; on the right, 日 hi (sun, # 32) pierced by a central rod on which it spins and surrounded by four offshoots which could be flames CUE: **Su**perman bakes **Qui**che in an oven in ß (Greece) which is hot like the 日 (sun) and spins out flames through four 隙間 **suki**ma (openings) COMPARE: 原(因) gen'in = cause, # 888

880. 官 PRONUNCIATION: kan

MEANINGS: government official, sense EXAMPLES: 警官 keikan = policeman; 仕官 shikan = military officer; 総司令官 soushireikan = commander-in-chief DESCRIPTION: at the top, a bad haircut; at the bottom, a bunk bed CUE: this guy from **Can**ada, who is a 警官 kei**kan** (policeman), retreated to the top of this bunk bed after he got this bad haircut COMPARE: (旅)館 ryokan, # 305, which helps us to pronounce this; 追(う) ou = to chase, # 821

··········

Chapter 35

881. 敵 PRONUNCIATIONS: teki, kataki

MEANING: enemy EXAMPLES: 敵 teki = enemy, opponent; 素敵な suteki na = great, wonderful; 敵 kataki = enemy, rival

DESCRIPTION: at the upper left, the bell from 音 oto (sound, # 266); at the lower left, the box from 固(体) kotai (solid, # 731), but the bottom has fallen out; on the right, a dancer with a ponytail CUES: this dancer on the right is a **Techie** who deals with her 敵 **teki** (enemies) by directing loud 音 (sounds) at them and by building 固 (solid) fortifications, but the bottom has fallen out of her fortifications, and she **Calls** a **Talented King** for help COMPARE: (指)摘 shiteki = pointing out, # 1083, which helps us to pronounce this

882. 辿 PRONUNCIATION: tado

MEANINGS: to follow (a road) or pursue EXAMPLES: 辿る tadoru = to follow or trace; 辿り着く tadoritsuku = to find one's way to a place at last DESCRIPTION: on the lower left, a snail; at the upper right, 山 yama (mountain, # 146) CUE: a **Tan Doe** and this snail 辿った **tado**tta (followed) the same path up this 山 (mountain), but the doe arrived at the top first

883. 及 PRONUNCIATIONS: **kyuu, oyo**
MEANINGS: to reach, in addition   EXAMPLES:
普及する fukyuu suru = to become popular or
widespread; 及ぶ oyobu = to reach or extend to;
及び oyobi = and, in addition   DESCRIPTION:
compared to 吸(収する) kyuushuu suru (to
digest, # 427), which helps us to pronounce this, this
kanji is missing the cute baby's mouth and only
retains the graph of its breathing patterns
CUES: this graph of a **C**ute baby's breathing
patterns 及ぶ <u>oyo</u>bu (extends) to occasions when
she was fed **O**ld **Y**ogurt

884. 腰 PRONUNCIATIONS: **koshi,
goshi[1], you**   MEANINGS: loins, hip waist
EXAMPLES: 腰 koshi = low back, waist, hip;
及び腰 oyobigoshi = a bent back; 腰痛
youtsuu = low back pain   DESCRIPTION: on the
left, 月 tsuki (moon, # 148); on the right, (必)要
hitsuyou (necessary, # 238), which helps us to
pronounce this   CUES: after a **C**obra bit a **Shi**ite
under this 月 (moon), he found it 要 (necessary) to
practice **Y**oga for 腰 <u>koshi</u> (low back) pain

885. 平 PRONUNCIATIONS: **byou, hira,
hei, tai**   MEANINGS: flat, calm   EXAMPLES:
平等 byoudou = equality; 平たい hiratai = flat,
simple; 平屋 hiraya = one-story house; 平和
heiwa = peace, tranquility; 平気な heiki na =
unconcerned, nonchalant; 平らな taira na = flat,
level   DESCRIPTION: in the center, a telephone
pole; on both sides, flames shooting out
CUES: a **B**eerhall **Ow**ner said that a **H**ero **Ra**n to
fight the fire in this telephone pole, which was
disturbing the 平和 <u>hei</u>wa (peace) and creating a
Haze, but after awhile the hero got **Ti**red
COMPARE: 半 han = half, # 331; 評判
hyouban = reputation, # 1053 and # 1054

886. 観 PRONUNCIATIONS: **kan, mi**
MEANING: to look over   EXAMPLES: 観光
kankou = sightseeing; 楽観 rakkan = optimism;
花を観る hana wo miru = flower viewing (this
can also be written 花を見る)

DESCRIPTION: compared to 勧(告) kankoku
(recommendation, # 698), which features an
American Indian chief hugging a cage and helps us
to pronounce this, 力 chikara (force) has been
replaced by 見 mi (to look, # 53), which *also* helps
us to pronounce this   CUES: this Indian chief made
a 勧 (recommendation) that the **Can**adian people
Meet together, 見 (look) at the problems involving
animals in cages like this and face them with 楽観
rak<u>kan</u> (optimism)   ALSO COMPARE: 権(威)
ken'i = authority, # 916

887. 裏 PRONUNCIATIONS: **ura, ri**
MEANINGS: back, reverse   EXAMPLES: 裏 ura
= back, rear, hidden aspect; 裏切る uragiru = to
betray or deceive; 表裏 hyouri = two sides, inside
and out   DESCRIPTION: at the top, a tire stop, as
seen in 対(する) tai suru (to confront, # 674); in
the middle, a sincere guy wearing bifocals, as seen in
野(菜) yasai (vegetables, # 545); at the bottom,
the katakana エ plus y   CUES: this sincere guy,
エ, and y have a **U**ranium mine, and they've
installed this tire stop at the 裏 <u>ura</u> (back) of the
mine to keep cars from driving in from the **Rear**
ALSO COMPARE: 里 sato = village, # 1060

888. 原 PRONUNCIATIONS: **gen, hara,
bara[1]**   MEANINGS: field, meadow, original,
source   EXAMPLES: 原因 gen'in = cause;
原爆 genbaku = atomic bomb; 野原 nohara =
field; 海原 unabara = ocean   DESCRIPTION:
at the upper left, a lean-to; under the lean-to,
白(い) shiroi (white, # 44), above 小(さい)
chiisai (small, # 253)   CUES: **Gen**ghis built this
小 (small) 白 (white) lean-to in a 野原 no<u>hara</u>
(field), where No one would **Hara**ss him
COMPARE: 願(う) negau = to beg, # 94;
隙(間) sukima (gap, hole, # 879)

....

Chapter 36

889. 畑 PRONUNCIATIONS: hatake, hata MEANING: agricultural field

EXAMPLES: 畑 hatake = field for cultivation or field of expertise; 田畑 tahata = field (crops)

DESCRIPTION: on the left, 火 hi (fire, # 443); on the right, 田 (rice paddy, # 68); these images allude to the practice of periodically burning rice paddies, which was thought to increase nutrients in the soil CUES: in Hawaii, a Tall Kennedy sets 火 (fire) to his 畑 **hatake** (fields) after the harvest, and he pays a Harbor Tax when he ships his crops

890. 頬 PRONUNCIATIONS: hoo, hoho

MEANING: cheek EXAMPLES: 頬 hoo = cheek; 頬 hoho = cheek; 頬張る hoobaru = to stuff one's cheeks or fill one's mouth with food

DESCRIPTION: on the left, 大(きい) ookii (big, # 188) with four extra arms, suggesting something very big, as seen in 狭(い) semai (narrow, # 194); on the right, 貝 kai (shell, # 83), with a platform on top, where a head could fit, as seen in 頭 atama (head, # 93)

CUES: a very 大 (big) Hornet came flying toward Santa's 頭 (head) and stung him on the 頬 **hoo** (cheek), causing him to say "Ho ho"

891. 陽 PRONUNCIATION: you

MEANINGS: sunny, positive EXAMPLES: 太陽 taiyou = the sun; 陽性の yousei no = cheerful, positive; 陽気な youki na = merry, happy-go-lucky DESCRIPTION: on the left, ß beta from the Greek alphabet; on the right, 易(しい) yasashii (easy, # 402) CUE: if you live in ß (Greece), spend a lot of time in the 太陽 tai**you** (sun) and eat a lot of Yogurt, life seems 易 (easy) COMPARE: 場(所) basho = place, # 403; (お)湯 oyu = hot water, # 404; 揚(げる) ageru = to hoist a kite, # 768

892. 折 PRONUNCIATIONS: setsu, o, ori

MEANINGS: to break or fold, occasion EXAMPLES: 骨折する kossetsu suru = to break a bone; 折る oru = to break, transitive; 折れる oreru = to break, intransitive; 折り ori = occasion, opportunity, time; 折り紙 origami = Japanese paper folding; 時折 tokiori = once in awhile DESCRIPTION: on the left, a kneeling person; on the right, a pair of pliers

CUES: this kneeling person Set up a Super business selling Oreo cookies in the Orient, but she uses these pliers to hand them to her customers, and sometimes the cookies 折れる **o**reru (break)

COMPARE: 新(しい) atarashii = new, # 389; 所 tokoro = place, # 391; 断(る) kotowaru = to refuse, # 704; 祈(る) inoru = to pray, # 955

893. 覆 PRONUNCIATIONS: oo, fuku, puku[1], kutsugae MEANINGS: capsize, be ruined, cover, shade, mantle EXAMPLES: 覆う oou = to cover, conceal, wrap, disguise; 覆面 fukumen = mask; 転覆する tenpuku suru = to capsize or overturn; 覆す kutsugaesu = to overturn or overthrow DESCRIPTION: at the top, three eyes suspended from a platform, as seen in 要(る) iru (to need, # 238); at the bottom, (回)復 kaifuku (recovery, # 527), which helps us to pronounce this CUES: an Old surgeon in Fukuoka met this guy with three eyes who worked for Superman and 要 (needed) 復 (recovery) from an illness, and the doctor Cut Superman's Guy and 覆った **oo**tta (covered) the wound with a dressing

894. 逆 PRONUNCIATIONS: saka, gyaku

MEANINGS: inverted, reverse, opposite, wicked EXAMPLES: 逆らう sakarau = to oppose or disobey; 逆さまの sakasama no = reverse, upside-down, topsy-turvy; 逆説 gyakusetsu = paradox; 逆の gyaku no = contrary, opposite, antithetical DESCRIPTION: at the lower left, a snail; on the snail, a ghost floating in the air, with two antennae and two arms holding candlesticks

CUES: this antennae-wearing ghost floats and plays **Sakkaa** (soccer), which is a 逆説 **gyaku**setsu (paradox) since it has no feet, and the snail on which it rides can outrun **Geeky Yaku**za (gangsters)

895. 鹿 PRONUNCIATIONS: shika, jika[1], ka

MEANING: deer EXAMPLES: 鹿 shika = deer; 小鹿 kojika = fawn; 馬鹿 baka = fool, idiot, usually written バカ DESCRIPTION: at the upper left, a lean-to with a chimney; under the lean-to, at the upper right, three eyes suspended from the ceiling; at the lower right, 比(べる) kuraberu (to compare, # 857) CUES: a 鹿 **shika** (deer) with three eyes lives close to **Sheep** in **Ca**lifornia, and it 比 (compares) lean-to's, **Ca**lculates the available space and crowds in with them for the night

896. 察 PRONUNCIATION: satsu

MEANINGS: to conjecture, perceive, look thoroughly EXAMPLES: 警察 keisatsu = police; 観察 kansatsu = observation DESCRIPTION: at the top, a bad haircut; at the bottom, 祭(り) matsuri (festival, # 377)

CUE: a **Sa**tisfied **Su**perintendent from the 警察 kei**satsu** (police) visited a 祭 (festival) where he received this bad haircut, and then he was *dis*satisfied

....

Chapter 37

897. 宇 PRONUNCIATION: u

MEANINGS: roof, space EXAMPLES: 宇宙 uchuu = universe, cosmos, space DESCRIPTION: at the top, a bad haircut; at the bottom, a kneeling telephone pole CUE: in **U**ruguay they place what look like bad haircuts over kneeling telephone poles to conceal detectors that search the sky for 宇宙人 **u**chuujin (space aliens)

898. 宙 PRONUNCIATION: chuu

MEANINGS: space, sky EXAMPLES: 宇宙 uchuu = universe, cosmos, space; 宙返り chuugaeri = somersault; 宙に浮く chuu ni uku = to float in air DESCRIPTION: at the top, a bad haircut; at the bottom, (理)由 riyuu (reason, # 73)

CUE: the 由 (reason) that I got this bad haircut is to make myself less attractive to 宇宙人 u**chuu**jin (space aliens) who might want to **Chew** on me

899. 柵 PRONUNCIATION: saku

MEANINGS: fence, stockade EXAMPLES: 柵 saku = fence; 鉄柵 tessaku = iron fence DESCRIPTION: on the left, 木 ki (wood, # 118); on the right, 冊 satsu (counter for books, # 568), which reminds us of a bookstore

CUE: when I bought a **Sack** of books at the 冊 (bookstore), I noticed that they had built a 木 (wooden) 柵 **saku** (fence) around the store

900. 汁 PRONUNCIATIONS: juu, shiru, jiru

MEANINGS: soup, liquid, juice EXAMPLES: 果汁 kajuu = fruit juice; 肉汁 nikujuu = gravy; 汁 shiru = soup; 鼻汁 hanajiru = nasal discharge DESCRIPTION: on the left, a water radical; on the right, 十 juu (ten, # 18), which helps us to pronounce this CUES: we drank 十 (10) bottles of 果汁 ka**juu** (fruit **J**uice) with a **Shi**nto **Ru**ler who parks his **Jeep** under a **Roof**

901. 犯 PRONUNCIATIONS: han, oka

MEANINGS: crime, to violate EXAMPLES: 犯人 han'nin = criminal, culprit; 犯す okasu = to violate DESCRIPTION: on the left, a woman contorting her body, as seen in 狭(い) semai (narrow, # 194); on the right, a snake, as seen in 危(ない) abunai (danger, # 547) CUES: when **Han**sel walks with Gretel, he **Occa**sionally sees her contorting her body to avoid snakes like this one, and he attacks the 犯人 **han**'nin (culprits)

ALSO COMPARE: 狙(う) nerau = to aim, # 948

902. 厳 PRONUNCIATIONS: gen, kibi, gon

MEANINGS: strict, stern, rigid

EXAMPLES: 厳格な genkaku na = stern, strict; 厳しい kibishii = stern, rigid, strict; 荘厳な sougon na = solemn DESCRIPTION: at the top, three lines representing three bees rising from the top of a lean-to; on the lower left, a swivel chair attached to the top of 耳 mimi (ear, # 57); on the lower right, a dancer with a ponytail

CUES: Genghis, who has big 耳 (ears), lives with this dancer under this lean-to, where he swivels in this chair, and they Keep Bees like these up on the roof, which they frighten with a Gong, since they are 厳しい kibishii (strict) with them

903. 湧 PRONUNCIATION: wa

MEANINGS: to gush out EXAMPLES: 湧く waku = to gush out, well up, appear
DESCRIPTION: on the left, a water radical; at the upper right, the katakana マ ma, which reminds us of Ma (mother); at the lower right, 男 otoko (male, # 109) CUE: マ (Ma) and her 男 (male) friend open a valve, and Water 湧く waku (gushes out)

904. 徐 PRONUNCIATION: jo

MEANINGS: gradually, slowly, deliberately

EXAMPLES: 徐々に jojo ni = gradually, step by step; 徐行する jokou suru = to slow down
DESCRIPTION: on the left, a man with a double hat; on the right, 余(計) yokei (excessive, # 637) CUE: this man with a slanted hat criticized Joan of Arc for 余 (excessive) haste, and she learned to 徐行する jokou suru (slow down)

COMPARE: (削)除 sakujo = to delete, # 646, which helps us to pronounce this and in which the man with a slanted hat is replaced by a ß (Greek) guy

....

Chapter 38

905. 想 PRONUNCIATIONS: so, sou, omo MEANINGS: to contemplate or think

EXAMPLES: 愛想がいい aiso ga ii = sociable; 想像 souzou = imagination; 想う omou = to imagine or contemplate

DESCRIPTION: at the upper left, 木 ki (tree, # 118); at the upper right, 目 me (eye, # 51); at the bottom, 心 kokoro (heart, # 306) CUES: during the Soviet era, a Soldier with an Old Motorcycle who had some 想像 souzou (imagination) and 心 (heart) could climb this 木 (tree) and use his 目 (eyes) to find a way to escape COMPARE: 思(う) omou = to think/feel, # 308

906. 象 PRONUNCIATIONS: zou, shou

MEANINGS: elephant, pattern, shape

EXAMPLES: 象 zou = elephant; 対象 taishou = the object; 印象 inshou = impression
DESCRIPTION: at the top, the upper half of 色 iro (color, # 473); at the bottom, the lower half of 家 ie (house, # 405); taken together, these suggest a colorful house CUES: when you go to the circus to see the 象 zou (elephants), there is a Zone that you can visit before the Show, where you will find 家 (houses) painted in bright 色 (colors)

907. 像 PRONUNCIATION: zou

MEANINGS: image, shape EXAMPLES: 想像 souzou = imagination; 仏像 butsuzou = image or statue of Buddha DESCRIPTION: on the left, a man with a slanted hat; on the right, 象 zou (elephant, # 906), which helps us to pronounce this CUE: this man with a slanted hat is able to use his 想像 souzou (imagination) to think of a Zone where 象 (elephants) can be protected

908. 亀 PRONUNCIATIONS: **kame, game**[1]**, ki** MEANINGS: turtle, tortoise EXAMPLES: 亀 kame = turtle, tortoise; 海亀 umigame = sea turtle; 亀裂 kiretsu = crack, crevice, fissure DESCRIPTION: at the top, a fish head; under that, two 田 (rice paddies, # 68), linked by a long line that terminates in a tail CUES: this resembles a 亀 **kame** (turtle) that I photographed with my **Ca**mera in **Ki**ev, since it has a head like a fish, a shell that resembles two linked 田 (rice paddies) and a tail COMPARE: 縄 nawa = rope, # 1003

909. 草 PRONUNCIATIONS: **kusa, gusa**[1]**, sou, zou**[1] MEANINGS: grass, plant EXAMPLES: 草 kusa = grass; 仕草 shigusa = gesture, mannerism; 草原 sougen = grasslands, prairie; 草履 zouri = Japanese sandals DESCRIPTION: at the top, a plant radical, which could represent grass; under that, 早(い) hayai (early, # 34) CUES: some **Co**ol **Sa**xaphone players got up 早 (early) and were playing music in this 草 **kusa** (grass) when a **So**ldier joined them

910. 斜 PRONUNCIATIONS: **nana, sha** MEANINGS: diagonal, slanting, oblique EXAMPLES: 斜めの naname no = diagonal, oblique; 斜面 shamen = slope, slanting surface DESCRIPTION: on the left, 余(計) yokei (excessive, # 637); on the right, the slanted shelf seen in 料(理) ryouri (cuisine, # 512), holding two cans of food CUES: when **Na**ncy's **Na**nny **M**et the **Sh**ah, she asked him for these two cans of food from his 斜めの **nana**me no (slanted) shelf, but he said that her request was 余 (excessive)

911. 崖 PRONUNCIATIONS: **gake, gai** MEANINGS: precipice, cliff EXAMPLES: 崖 gake = precipice, cliff; 断崖 dangai = precipice, cliff DESCRIPTION: at the top, 山 yama (mountain, # 146), on top of a lean-to; under the lean-to, 土 tsuchi (dirt, # 59), piled on 土 (dirt) CUES: **Ga**llant **Ke**n was working as a **Gui**de on this 山 (mountain) when he saw this lean-to under a **gake** 崖 (cliff) which was full of 土 (dirt) due to a landslide

912. 翼 PRONUNCIATIONS: **tsubasa, yoku** MEANINGS: wing, plane, flank EXAMPLES: 翼 tsubasa = wing; 右翼 uyoku = right wing (politics); 左翼 sayoku = left wing (politics) DESCRIPTION: at the top, 羽 hane (feather, wing, # 755); in the middle, two 早(い) hayai's (early, # 34) next to each other; at the bottom, a stand for a lifeguard's chair, as seen in 浜(辺) hamabe (beach, # 766) CUES: I took my **Tsui**tcase (suitcase) to **B**arcelona's **S**andy beaches and arrived 早早 (very early) to sit on a lifeguard stand, where I found a **Yoku** (well)-formed 羽 (feather) from a bird with powerful 翼 **tsubasa** (wings)

....

Chapter 39

913. 旋 PRONUNCIATION: **sen** MEANINGS: rotation, go around EXAMPLES: 旋回 senkai = rotation, turning; 旋律 senritsu = melody DESCRIPTION: on the left, 方 kata (honorable person, # 114); on the upper right, a crutch; on the lower right, (予)定 yotei (plan, # 455), missing its bad haircut and with a modification to its top portion, which now resembles a spear CUE: the 方 (honorable person) on the left is a **Sen**ator who 旋回する **sen**kai suru (turns) to see a modified 定 (plan) under a crutch, suggesting that someone wants his support for a health care bill COMPARE: 疑(う) utagau = to doubt, # 978

914. 脅 PRONUNCIATIONS: odo, kyou, obiya MEANINGS: threaten, coerce

EXAMPLES: 脅かす odokasu = to threaten or startle; 脅す odosu = to threaten; 脅威 kyoui = a threat, peril, menace; 脅かす obiyakasu = to menace or threaten NOTE: both odokasu and obiyakasu are written 脅かす DESCRIPTION: at the top, 力 chikara (force, # 107), repeated three times; at the bottom, 月 tsuki (moon, # 148)

CUES: I looked up to see three men of 力 (force) dancing on the 月 (moon), and they 脅した odoshita (threatened) to send some foul Odors down to us in Kyouto, but I just kept on eating Oily Beans and Yak soup COMPARE: 協(力する) kyouryoku suru = to cooperate, # 940, which helps us to pronounce this

915. 威 PRONUNCIATION: i

MEANINGS: intimidate, dignity, majesty, threaten EXAMPLES: 脅威 kyoui = a threat, peril, menace; 権威 ken'i = authority; 威厳 igen = dignity; 威張る ibaru = to look down on, to brag about DESCRIPTION: on the upper left, a lean-to, supported on the right by a halberd (combination lance and axe); under the lean-to, 女 onna (female, # 235), wearing a flat hat CUE: this 女 (woman) with a flat hat enjoys tremendous 権威 ken'i (authority), and she finds it Easy to avoid 脅威 kyoui (threats) by hiding under this hat in this lean-to, with a big halberd by her side

916. 権 PRONUNCIATIONS: gon, ken

MEANINGS: authority, power, rights EXAMPLES: 権現 gongen = an incarnation of Buddha, an avatar; 権威 ken'i = authority; 権利 kenri = right, privilege DESCRIPTION: on the left, 木 ki (tree, # 118); on the right, an American Indian chief hugging a cage, as seen in 勧(告) kankoku (recommendation, # 698) CUES: this American Indian chief named Gonzalez used to work at the Kentucky Derby, where he pruned 木 (trees), but now he has 権威 ken'i

(authority) over a zoo and hugs a cage because he cares about the animals in it ALSO COMPARE: 観(光) kankou = sightseeing, # 886

917. 兵 PRONUNCIATIONS: hei, hyou

MEANINGS: soldier, army, warfare EXAMPLES: 兵隊 heitai = soldier; 兵庫県 hyougoken = Hyogo prefecture DESCRIPTION: at the top, a pair of pliers; at the bottom, a stand

CUES: a 兵隊 heitai (soldier), who was using these pliers to create defensive barriers using Haywire, put them on this stand, and the Lone Ranger said "Hi-yo Silver" when he saw them COMPARE: 浜(辺) hamabe = beach, # 766

918. 衛 PRONUNCIATION: ei

MEANINGS: defense, protection EXAMPLES: 衛生 eisei = hygiene, sanitation; 衛星 eisei = satellite; 防衛 bouei = defense

DESCRIPTION: on the left and the right, 行(く) iku (to go, # 334); in the middle, 違(う) chigau (to differ, # 355), without its snail

CUE: honest Abe liked to 行 (go) and check on the 防衛 bouei (defense) of his capital, but he took a 違 (different) route every time he went

919. 庫 PRONUNCIATIONS: ko, go

MEANINGS: warehouse, storage EXAMPLES: 車庫 shako = garage; 金庫 kinko = safe 冷蔵庫 reizouko = refrigerator; 兵庫県 hyougoken = Hyogo prefecture DESCRIPTION: at the upper left, a lean-to with a chimney, which could be a garage; under the lean-to, 車 kuruma (car, # 283) CUES: when it's Cold, I keep my 車 (car) in this 車庫 shako (garage), except when I take it to the Golf course

920. 防 PRONUNCIATIONS: fuse, bou
MEANINGS: ward off, defend, resist
EXAMPLES: 防ぐ fusegu = to prevent or defend; 防衛 bouei = defense; 予防 yobou = prevention; 消防士 shouboushi = firefighter
DESCRIPTION: on the left, ß beta from the Greek alphabet; on the right, 方 kata (honorable person)
CUES: this 方 (honorable person) is a **F**ood **Se**ller from ß (Greece) who **Boa**sts about his record in the 予防 yo**bou** (prevention) of food-borne illness

....

Chapter 40
921. 牙 PRONUNCIATIONS: ge, kiba, ga
MEANINGS: fang, tusk EXAMPLES: 象牙 zouge = ivory; 牙 kiba = fang, tusk; 牙城 gajou = stronghold DESCRIPTION: this is the man with a forbidding stance seen inside the gate in 閉(める) shimeru (to close, # 414); he is wearing a flat-topped helmet with a visor extending to the left
CUES: a **Gue**st of the **K**ing of **Ba**ghdad visited his hanging **Gar**dens, where he assumed a forbidding stance and wore this helmet with an impressive visor designed to hide his 牙 **kiba** (fangs) COMPARE: (風)邪 kaze = upper respiratory infection, # 796

922. 雅 PRONUNCIATIONS: ga, miya
MEANINGS: gracious, elegant, refined
EXAMPLES: 優雅な yuuga na = elegant; 温雅 onga = graceful, affable; 雅びた miyabita = gracious, elegant, refined
DESCRIPTION: on the left, 牙 kiba (fangs, # 921); on the right, a cage
CUES: when a **Ga**mbler went to **Me**et a **Ya**nkee, he noticed a vampire in this 誰 (cage), wearing 優雅な yu**ga** na (elegant) robes and sporting these large 牙 (fangs)

923. 狩 PRONUNCIATIONS: ga, ka, shu
MEANINGS: hunt, raid, gather EXAMPLES: キノコ狩り kinokogari = mushroom gathering; 狩る karu = to hunt (animals), to gather (mushrooms, etc.); 狩り kari = hunting, gathering; 狩猟 shuryou = hunting
DESCRIPTION: on the left, a woman contorting her body; on the right, 守(る) mamoru (to protect, # 214) CUES: this woman on the left is a **Ga**dfly who contorts her body in order to try to 守 (protect) animals threatened by 狩り **ka**ri (hunting), and she uses a **Ca**mera and **Shoo**ts photos of hunters COMPARE: 猫 neko = cat, # 72; 狭(い) semai = narrow, # 194; 独 doku = unmarried, # 724; 犯(人) han'nin = criminal, # 901; 狙う nerau = to aim, # 948

924. 飢 PRONUNCIATIONS: ki, u
MEANINGS: to starve, to be hungry or thirsty
EXAMPLES: 飢饉 kikin = famine; 飢える ueru = to starve, to be thirsty or hungry; 飢え死に uejini = death from starvation
DESCRIPTION: on the left, 食(べる) taberu (to eat, # 398); on the right, the tall desk seen in 机 tsukue (desk, # 140) CUES: the **K**ing of **U**ganda 食 (ate) too much and stored all of his left-over food in this very tall 机 (desk), so that some people 飢えた **u**eta (starved)

925. 傾 PRONUNCIATIONS: katamu, kei
MEANINGS: lean, incline, tilt, sink EXAMPLES: 傾く katamuku = to tilt or incline, to go down; 傾斜する keisha suru = to tilt or slant
DESCRIPTION: on the left, a man with a slanted hat; in the middle, the katakana ヒ hi, which reminds us of a hero; on the right, a headless platform on a money chest, as seen in 頭 atama (head, # 93)
CUES: this man on the left, who has a hat that 傾く **katamu**ku (tilts), wants to **Ca**tapult men to the **Moo**n, but first he plans to launch this ヒ (hero) to the top of this headless platform, where he will wave his **Ca**pe to try to attract attention to the plan

926. 退 **PRONUNCIATIONS: no, shirizo, tai** **MEANINGS:** retreat, withdraw, retire, resign **EXAMPLES:** 立ち退く tachinoku = to evacuate, vacate; 退く shirizoku = to retreat; 退屈 taikutsu = boredom; 退職 taishoku = retirement, resignation **DESCRIPTION:** on the lower left, a snail; riding on the snail, 良(い) yoi (good, # 303), without its pointy hat

CUES: a 良 (good) **N**orwegian rode up on this snail and said that, if **Sh**eep could **Rea**d the signs of the **Z**odiac, they might experience less 退屈 **tai**kutsu (boredom), but then a **Ti**ger ate him

927. 屈 **PRONUNCIATIONS: ku, kutsu** **MEANINGS:** to yield, submit, bend **EXAMPLES:** 屈服する kuppuku suru = to surrender; 退屈 taikutsu = boredom; 理屈 rikutsu = argument, theory, pretext **DESCRIPTION:** on the upper left, a lean-to with a double roof; under the lean-to, 出(る) dasu (to extract, # 147), which resembles 山 (mountains) stacked on each other; together these radicals look like a cooped-up human figure

CUES: these two stacked 山 (mountains) represent a **Coop**ed-up **Su**perman under this lean-to with a double roof; he is suffering from 退屈 tai**kutsu** (boredom), and we want to 出 (extract) him, but we must avoid **Cut**ting **Su**perman in the process

928. 懐 **PRONUNCIATIONS: futokoro, kai, natsu** **MEANINGS:** pocket, breast, feelings, heart **EXAMPLES:** 懐 futokoro = bosom, heart; 懐が広い futokoro ga hiroi = is kind-hearted; 懐中電灯 kaichuu dentou = flashlight; 懐かしい natsukashii = nostalgic, evocative of times past **DESCRIPTION:** on the left, an erect man; at the upper right, 十 too (ten, # 18); below that, 目 me (eye, # 51) turned horizontally, which could represent three eyes; below the eyes, the katakana エ and the letter y, supporting a platform

CUES: this erect man, who has 十 (ten) houses and three eyes and sleeps on a **Fu**ton in his **Coro**lla, feels 懐かしい **natsu**kashii (nostalgia) for エ

and y, two friends with whom he used to fly **Ki**tes in **Na**tsu (summer) but who are now trapped under this platform

....

Chapter 41
929. 群 **PRONUNCIATIONS: mu, mura, gun** **MEANINGS:** group, throng, herd **EXAMPLES:** 群れ mure = herd, crowd, group; 群がる muragaru = to flock or throng; 群集 gunshuu = group of living things, crowd, community; 群衆 gunshuu = group of people, crowd, mob **DESCRIPTION:** on the left, 君 kimi (you, # 419); on the right, 羊 hitsuji (sheep, not included in this Catalog) **CUES:** I saw 君 (you) in a **M**ovie, painting a **Mur**al of a 群れ **mu**re (herd) of 羊 (sheep), and waving a **Gun**

930. 衆 **PRONUNCIATION: shuu** **MEANINGS:** group, throng, herd **EXAMPLES:** 群衆 gunshuu = group of people, crowd, mob **DESCRIPTION:** at the top, 血 chi (blood, # 747); on the lower left, two swords; on the lower right, the letters T and y, which remind us of "thank you" **CUE:** when I saw this 血 (blood) and these two swords in a 群衆 gun**shuu** (crowd), I ducked into a **Sh**oe store and said T y (thank you) to the owner

931. 積 **PRONUNCIATIONS: seki, se, tsu** **MEANINGS:** volume, acreage, stack **EXAMPLES:** 面積 menseki = area; 積極 sekkyoku = positive, progressive; 積もる tsumoru = to pile up (intransitive); 積む tsumu = to heap up, accumulate, load (transitive) **DESCRIPTION:** on the left, 禾 (a grain plant with a ripe head); on the right, 責(任) sekinin (responsibility, # 772) or 責(める) semeru (to accuse, # 772), both of which help us to pronounce this, which feature an owl's perch on top of a money chest **CUES:** a **S**elfish **K**ing, who 積む **tsu**mu (accumulates) this 禾 (ripe grain) and wants to **S**ell it, sets up an owl's perch on this 貝 (money chest) overlooking the grain so that an owl can take 責 (responsibility) for **Tsu**pervising (supervising) the sales

932. 射 PRONUNCIATIONS: sha, i

MEANING: to shoot **EXAMPLES:** 反射 hansha = reflection; 注射 chuusha = injection; 射る iru = to hit or shoot (an arrow)

DESCRIPTION: on the left, 身 mi (body, person, # 651); on the right, the kneeling guy seen in 付(く) tsuku (to attach, # 132), with a stick of gum on the ground nearby **CUES:** the **Shah** of **I**ran tells this kneeling guy on the right to stop chewing gum for a moment and deliver a 注射 chuu**sha** (injection) to this 身 (person) on the left

933. 戦 PRONUNCIATIONS: sen, ikusa, tataka **MEANINGS:** war, to fight

EXAMPLES: 戦争 sensou = war; 戦 ikusa = battle; 戦う tatakau = to fight (this can also, less frequently, be written 闘う tatakau, # 728)

DESCRIPTION: on the left, (簡)単 kantan (easy, # 636), which includes three vertical lines at the top, suggesting ear cooties; on the right, a halberd (combination lance and axe)

CUES: our **Sen**ator says that it's 単 (easy) to fight a 戦争 **sen**sou (war), if you carry **Ear Coo**ties in a **Sack** to cast on your enemies and if a **Tall Taxi** driver with a **Car** carries this halberd for you

934. 聴 PRONUNCIATIONS: chou

MEANINGS: to listen **EXAMPLES:** 聴衆 choushuu = audience; 聴解力 choukairyoku = listening comprehension **DESCRIPTION:** on the left, 耳 mimi (ear, # 57); at the top right, 十 too (ten, # 18); at the middle right, 目 me (eye, # 51), turned on its side, resembling three eyes; at the lower right, 心 kokoro (heart, # 306) **CUES:** Margaret **Cho** likes to remind her 聴衆 **chou**shuu (audiences) that she has good 耳 (ears), 十 (ten) houses, three eyes and a 心 (heart) of gold **COMPARE:** (道)徳 doutoku = morality, # 1159

935. 競 PRONUNCIATIONS: kiso, se, kei, kyou **MEANINGS:** to compete or race, a contest, to sell at auction **EXAMPLES:** 競う kisou = to compete with; 競り seri = auction; 競馬 keiba = horse racing; 競争する kyousou suru = to compete; 競技 kyougi = competition **DESCRIPTION:** two nearly identical figures, each with the bell from 音 oto (sound, # 266) at the top, suggesting noise, and 兄 ani (older brother, # 420) at the bottom, but the 兄 on the left seems to have a broken leg **CUES:** these two noisy bell-topped 兄 (older brothers) are **Killer So**ldiers who ride **Seg**ways out of **Ca**ves near **Kyou**to in order to 競争する **kyou**sou suru (compete)

936. 争 PRONUNCIATIONS: araso, sou

MEANINGS: to compete or race, a contest, to sell at auction **EXAMPLES:** 争う arasou = to fight, dispute or compete; 競争する kyousou suru = to compete; 戦争 sensou = war **DESCRIPTION:** a monster with a fish head that someone has stabbed with a trident, as seen in 静 (か) shizuka (quiet, # 418) **CUES:** an **Ara**b **So**ldier from **So**malia 争う **araso**u (fights) this fish-headed monster and stabs it with a trident

....

Chapter 42

937. 眩 PRONUNCIATIONS: kura, mabu

MEANINGS: faint, dizzy EXAMPLES: 眩む kuramu = to be blinded or dazzled; 眩しい mabushii = dazzling, blinding DESCRIPTION: on the left, 目 me (eye, # 51); on the upper right, a tire stop as seen in 対(して) tai shite (against, # 674), from which a swinging pendulum is suspended; on the lower right, the katakana ム mu, the sound made by a cow CUES: this 目 (eye) belongs to a museum **Cura**tor who had been drinking **Ma**ssachusetts **B**ooze and should have seen that this swinging pendulum was about to strike this ム (cow), but a sudden 眩しい **mabu**shii (dazzling) light distracted him

938. 峰 PRONUNCIATIONS: hou, pou, mine MEANINGS: summit, peak EXAMPLES:

名峰 meihou = famous mountain; 連峰 renpou = mountain range; 峰 mine = mountain peak

DESCRIPTION: on the left, 山 yama (mountain, # 146); on the upper right, a dancer with a ponytail; on the lower right, a telephone pole CUES: this dancer, who is also a **H**ostess, dances on top of a telephone **P**ole next a 名峰 mei**hou** (famous mountain) in **Minne**sota

939. 富 PRONUNCIATIONS: fu, to, tomi

MEANINGS: wealth, enrich, abundant EXAMPLES: 富士山 fujisan = Mt. Fuji; 豊富な houfu na = abundant; 富む tomu = to be rich or prosper; 富 tomi = wealth DESCRIPTION: at the top, a bad haircut; under the haircut, 口 kuchi (mouth, # 426) with a line of tape above it; at the bottom, 田 (rice paddy, # 68) CUES: this **Foo**lish guy with a bad haircut has 豊富な hou**fu** na (abundant) 田 (rice paddies) and also **To**mato fields, but he tends to brag about them and has to keep a strip of tape over his 口 (mouth) and employ guards with **Tommy** guns to protect his 富 **tomi** (wealth) COMPARE: 福 fuku = happiness, # 661; 幅 haba = width, # 1185

940. 協 PRONUNCIATION: kyou

MEANINGS: to cooperate EXAMPLES: 協力する kyouryoku suru = to cooperate; 協同 kyoudou = cooperation DESCRIPTION: on the left, 十 juu (ten, # 18); on the right, three 力 chikara (force, # 107) CUE: in **Kyou**to, 十 (ten) policemen 協力する **kyou**ryoku suru (cooperate) with three men of 力 (force) to keep the peace COMPARE: 脅(威) kyoui = a threat, # 914, which helps us to pronounce this

941. 襲 PRONUNCIATIONS: oso, shuu

MEANINGS: to attack EXAMPLES: 襲う osou = to attack; 襲撃 shuugeki = an attack DESCRIPTION: on the upper left, 立(つ) tatsu (to stand, # 11) above 月 tsuki (moon, # 148); on the upper right, a complex structure resembling a comb; at the bottom, a platform supported by the katakana エ and the letter y CUES: this comb belongs to an **O**ld **S**oldier who once 立 (stood) on the 月 (moon) and used to **Sh**oot at the enemy and 襲う **oso**u (attack) them but is now content to rest on this platform supported by エ and y

942. 油 PRONUNCIATIONS: abura, yu

MEANING: oil EXAMPLES: 油 abura = oil; 油断 yudan = negligence, inattentiveness; 石油 sekiyu = petroleum DESCRIPTION: on the left, a water radical; on the right, (理)由 riyuu (reason, # 73), which helps us to pronounce this

CUES: the 由 (reason) that we can't dilute the fuel for our **Abu** Dhabi **L**amp with this water is that 油 **abura** (oil) doesn't mix with water, according to a **You**th whom we asked

943. 禁 PRONUNCIATION: kin

MEANING: to forbid EXAMPLES: 禁じる kinjiru = to prohibit; 禁物 kinmotsu = a forbidden thing; 禁煙 kin'en = no smoking

DESCRIPTION: at the top, two 木 ki (trees, # 118) on a platform; at the bottom, the lower part of a spinning pavilion, as seen in 余(計) yokei (excessive, # 637) CUE: our King 禁じる kinjiru (prohibits) 余 (excessive) spinning of trees like these, since it isn't good for them, even if they are stabilized on this pavilion's base

944. 吠 PRONUNCIATIONS: ho, bo

MEANINGS: to bark, howl, cry EXAMPLES: 吠える hoeru = to bark, howl, roar, cry; 遠吠え tooboe = howling DESCRIPTION: on the left, 口 kuchi (mouth, # 426); on the right, 犬 inu (dog, # 190) CUES: the 犬 (dog) on the right uses his 口 (mouth) to 吠える hoeru (bark), as he protects his master's Home and Boat

....

Chapter 43

945. 伏 PRONUNCIATIONS: fu, fuku, bu

MEANINGS: prostrated, bend down, bow EXAMPLES: 降伏する koufuku suru = to surrender; 伏せる fuseru = to lay an object upside down or face down, to lie down; うつ伏せに utsubuse ni = face down DESCRIPTION: on the left, a man with a slanted hat; on the right, 犬 inu (dog, # 190) CUES: this man with a slanted hat gives Food to this 犬 (dog) in Fukuoka, drinks some Booze and 伏せる fuseru (lies down)

946. 床 PRONUNCIATIONS: yuka, shou, toko MEANINGS: floor, bed EXAMPLES: 床 yuka = floor; 起床 kishou = rising, getting out of bed; 床 toko = bed, floor; 床屋 tokoya = barbershop DESCRIPTION: on the upper left, a lean-to with a chimney; under the lean-to, 木 ki (wood, # 118) CUES: a Youthful Carpenter works in this lean-to with a chimney, in which he Shows 木 (wooden) items that he has created, including a 床 yuka (floor) and a Toy Koala

947. 獲 PRONUNCIATIONS: kaku, e

MEANINGS: seize, get, find, acquire EXAMPLES: 獲得する kakutoku suru = to win or obtain; 獲物 emono = game (hunting) or catch (fishing) DESCRIPTION: on the left, a woman contorting her body; at the upper right, a plant radical, which reminds us of cactus; at the middle right, a cage; at the lower right, 又 mata (again, # 24) which resembles a table CUES: this woman on the left contorts her body as she views this Cactus tree towering over a cage on this 又 (table), which contains Eggs that she hopes to 獲得する kakutoku suru (obtain)

948. 狙 PRONUNCIATION: nera

MEANINGS: aim at, stalk EXAMPLES: 狙う nerau = to aim DESCRIPTION: on the left, a woman contorting her body; on the right, a solar panel, as seen in 祖(父) sofu (grandfather, # 272) CUE: this woman on the left contorts her body as she tries to hide behind this solar panel, since a Negative Rascal 狙っている neratte iru (is aiming) at her COMPARE: 猫 neko = cat, # 72; 狭(い) semai = narrow, # 194; 独 doku = unmarried, # 724; 犯(人) han'nin = criminal, # 901; 狩(る) karu = to hunt, # 923

949. 匂 PRONUNCIATION: nio

MEANINGS: fragrant, stink, glow, insinuate EXAMPLES: 匂う niou = to smell of; 匂い nioi = fragrance, scent NOTE: niou and nioi can also be written 臭う and 臭い, not included in this Catalogue DESCRIPTION: on the upper right, a giant hook, as seen in (目)的 mokuteki (purpose, # 45), which reminds us of fish hooks; on the lower left, the katakana ヒ hi, which reminds us of a hero CUE: on the lower left, this is a Neonatologist who is a ヒ (hero) and who likes to fish with fish hooks like this, but she has a fishy 匂い nioi (scent) COMPARE: (文)句 monku = complaint, # 872

950. 闇 PRONUNCIATION: yami

MEANINGS: get dark, gloom, disorder
EXAMPLES: 闇 yami = darkness; 暗闇
kurayami = darkness DESCRIPTION: on the left
and the right, 門 mon (gate, # 409); in the center,
音 oto (sound, # 266) CUE: when I'm out
shopping for **Yak Meat**, and the 暗闇 kura**yami**
(darkness) increases, my family makes 音 (sounds)
in this 門 (gate) to help me find my way home

951. 臓 PRONUNCIATION: zou

MEANINGS: organ, body part EXAMPLES:
心臓 shinzou = the heart (organ); 内臓 naizou =
internal organ, intestines DESCRIPTION: on the
left, 月 tsuki (moon, # 148); at the upper right, a
plant radical; on the lower right, a lean-to supported
by a halberd (combination axe and lance); under the
lean-to, a swing set lying on its left side, but the
swing ropes have been tied on both sides to make the
swing inoperable CUE: my 心臓 shin**zou** (heart)
rates fall into different **Z**ones associated with my
moods, which can be represented by the 月 (moon)
which is volatile, plants which are soothing,
inoperable swing sets which are frustrating, and
halberds which are scary COMPARE:
(冷)蔵(庫) reizouko = refrigerator, # 1190,
which helps us to pronounce this

952. 斉 PRONUNCIATION: sei

MEANINGS: adjusted, alike, equal EXAMPLES:
一斉に issei ni = all at once, at the same time, all
together DESCRIPTION: compared to 済(ま
せる) sumaseru (to end, transitive, # 259), which
we described as water near a scientist and a truncated
moon, the water is missing CUE: when the water
near this 済 (scientist with a truncated moon)
disappeared, the **Sai**lors all noticed it 一斉に
is**sei** ni (at the same time)

....

Chapter 44

953. 猛 PRONUNCIATION: mou

MEANINGS: fierce, rave, become furious, wildness,
strength EXAMPLES: 猛暑 mousho = fierce
heat, heat wave; 猛勉強 moubenkyou = studying
extra hard; 猛練習 mourenshuu = hard training;
猛犬 mouken = savage dog DESCRIPTION: on
the left, a woman contorting her body; on the upper
right, 子 ko (child, # 182); on the lower right, 皿
sara (dish, # 567) CUE: the woman on the left is
contorting her body and anxiously approaching this
子 (child) who is **Moa**ning while sitting in cold
water in this 皿 (dish), trying to cope with a 猛暑
mousho (heat wave)

954. 程 PRONUNCIATIONS: hodo, tei

MEANINGS: degree, moderation, a limit
EXAMPLES: 程 hodo = extent, degree, limits,
moderation, approximate time, about so much
(usually written ほど); 程度 teido = criterion,
standard, extent DESCRIPTION: on the left, 禾
(a grain plant with a ripe head); on the upper right,
口 kuchi (mouth, # 426); on the lower right, 王 ou
(king, # 1077) CUES: this 王 (king) is standing
next to this 禾 (ripe grain) on the left, and he says to
a servant, "**Hold** the **Do**or while I **Ta**ste this with my
口 (mouth) to determine the 程度 **tei**do (extent)
to which it meets my standards"

955. 祈 PRONUNCIATIONS: ki, ino

MEANINGS: to pray or wish EXAMPLES:
祈祷 kitou = a prayer; 祈る inoru = to pray
DESCRIPTION: on the left, the Shah; on the right,
a pair of pliers CUES: this Shah is a **K**ing who
carries these pliers when he 祈る **ino**ru (prays)
for **Inno**cent people around the world, since they
remind him to be practical in his requests
COMPARE: 新(しい) atarashii = new, # 389;
所 tokoro = place, # 391; 断(る) kotowaru = to
refuse, # 704; 折る oru = to break, # 892

956. 俺 PRONUNCIATION: ore

MEANINGS: I, myself **EXAMPLES:** 俺 ore = I, me; 俺たち oretachi = we, us; 俺ら orera = we, us **DESCRIPTION:** on the left, a man with a slanted hat; at the upper right, an extra-wide 大(きい) ookii (big, # 188); at the lower right, a transformer with a wire emerging from the bottom, as seen in 電(気) denki (electricity, # 263) **CUE:** this man with a slanted hat works for 俺たち <u>ore</u>tachi (us) in **Ore**gon, operating this 大 (big) 電 (electric) transformer

957. 苔 PRONUNCIATION: koke

MEANINGS: moss, lichen **EXAMPLES:** 苔 koke = moss, lichen **DESCRIPTION:** at the top, a plant radical; at the bottom, 台 dai (platform, # 538) **CUE:** this plant radical at the top resembles 苔 <u>koke</u> (moss) growing over a 台 (platform) which also holds **Coke** stored in **Kegs**

958. 馬 PRONUNCIATIONS: uma, ba, ma

MEANING: horse **EXAMPLES:** 馬 uma = horse; 絵馬 ema = a drawing or painting of a horse; 馬鹿 baka = stupid person, usually written バカ; 木馬 mokuba = a wooden horse; 競馬 keiba = horse racing **DESCRIPTION:** at the top, this is said to represent the horse's mane flowing to the rear; the projection at the lower right may be the horse's tail **CUES:** this 馬 <u>uma</u> (horse) with a flowing mane and a long tail belongs to an **U**ru**gua**yan **Ma**n who works in a **Bar** at a **Ma**ll **COMPARE:** 鳥 tori = bird, # 555

959. 嗅 PRONUNCIATIONS: kyuu, ka

MEANINGS: smell, sniff, scent **EXAMPLES:** 嗅覚 kyuukaku = sense of smell; 嗅ぐ kagu = to sniff or smell **DESCRIPTION:** on the left, kuchi 口 (mouth, # 426); on the upper right, 自(分) jibun (self, # 155); at the lower right, 犬 inu (dog, # 190) **CUES:** my 自 (self) has a **C**ute 犬 (dog) which always 嗅ぐ <u>ka</u>gu (sniffs) my **Car** for bombs and grabs any that it finds in its 口 (mouth)

960. 態 PRONUNCIATION: tai

MEANINGS: demeanor, appearance of intent or ability **EXAMPLES:** 態度 taido = attitude; 変態 hentai = pervert or perversion, metamorphosis (insect) **DESCRIPTION:** at the top, 能(力) nouryoku (ability, # 616); at the bottom, 心 kokoro (heart, # 306) **CUE:** my **Thai** friend has 能 (ability) and a good 心 (heart), as well as a good 態度 <u>tai</u>do (attitude)

....

Chapter 45

961. 命 PRONUNCIATIONS: inochi, mei, myou

MEANINGS: life, order **EXAMPLES:** 命 inochi = life, most precious possession or person; 命じる meijiru = to command or appoint; 命令 meirei = a command or order; 寿命 jumyou = life span **DESCRIPTION:** at the top, a roof with a ceiling; on the lower left, kuchi 口 (mouth, # 426), which resembles a box; on the lower right, a wobbly table with an extra-long leg **CUES:** **I**nnocent **Ch**ildren live with a **Mai**d in this house with a box on the left and a wobbly table on the right, and their 命 <u>inochi</u> (most precious possession) is a cat that lives in the box and **Meow**s too much **COMPARE:** 冷(たい) tsumetai = cold, # 299; (号)令 gourei = command, # 962

962. 令 PRONUNCIATION: rei

MEANINGS: orders, command, decree **EXAMPLES:** 命令 meirei = a command or order; 号令 gourei = a command or order **DESCRIPTION:** this looks like a person under a roof who is about to run a race **CUE:** the person under this roof is about to run a **Ra**ce and is just waiting for the 命令 mei<u>rei</u> (command) to start **COMPARE:** 冷(蔵庫) reizouko = refrigerator, # 299, which helps us to pronounce this; 命(じる) meijiru = to command, #961, which adds a box under the roof

963. 洞 PRONUNCIATIONS: dou, hora

MEANINGS: den, cave, excavation **EXAMPLES:** 洞窟 doukutsu = cave, grotto; 洞察 dousatsu = insight, discernment; 洞穴 hora'ana = cave, den **DESCRIPTION:** on the left, a water radical; on the right, 同(意) doui (the same opinion, # 339), which helps us to pronounce this; this represents a box in a cave with an old nasty doughnut above it (see # 339) and a stream nearby **CUES:** I found this box inside this symmetrical lean-to, with an old nasty **D**oughnut above it, next to this stream in a 洞穴 **hora**'ana (cave), but it was **H**ome to **R**ats

964. 穴 PRONUNCIATION: ana

MEANINGS: hole, aperture, cave den **EXAMPLES:** 穴 ana = hole; 洞穴 hora'ana = cave, den **DESCRIPTION:** at the top, a bad haircut; at the bottom, 八 hachi (eight, # 15) **CUE:** 八 (eight) students in an **Ana**tomy class all have bad haircuts, but they are busy studying the major 穴 **ana** (holes) in a dog's head and don't care

965. 謙 PRONUNCIATION: ken

MEANINGS: self-effacing, modest **EXAMPLE:** 謙虚 kenkyo = modesty **DESCRIPTION:** compared to 嫌(い) kirai (to dislike, # 817), the 女 (woman) on the left has been replaced by 言(う) iu (to speak, # 430); this retains the split tree trunk on the right, patched together with a trident **CUE:** although **Ken** and Barbie repaired this tree using a trident, they are aware that people 嫌 (dislike) the job they did, and their 謙虚 **ken**kyo (modesty) enables them to 言 (say) that their work wasn't perfect

966. 虚 PRONUNCIATION: kyo

MEANINGS: void, emptiness, unpreparedness, untruth **EXAMPLES:** 謙虚 kenkyo = modesty **DESCRIPTION:** at the upper left, a lean-to; at the top, a periscope for observing the outside world; under the roof, 七 shichi (seven, # 20); on the floor, four burners on a stove, as seen in 普(通) futsuu (ordinarily, # 576) **CUE:** 七 (seven) people who

are known for their 謙虚 kenkyo (modesty) live in this lean-to in **Kyo**to, cook on this four-burner stove and observe the outside world through this periscope **COMPARE:** 嘘 uso = lie, # 967; 虎 tora = tiger, # 1057; (捕)虜 horyo = captive, # 1107; (遠)慮 enryo = hesitation, # 1194

967. 嘘 PRONUNCIATION: uso

MEANINGS: lie, falsehood **EXAMPLES:** 嘘 uso = lie; 嘘をつく uso wo tsuku = to tell a lie **DESCRIPTION:** compared to (謙)虚 kenkyo (modesty, # 966), this adds 口 kuchi (mouth, # 426) on the left side **CUE:** the addition of this 口 (mouth) to 虚 (modesty) suggests that, although these 七 (seven) people may be modest, they used their 口 (mouths) to tell an 嘘 **uso** (lie) when they claimed to have **U**ber **S**olar panels

968. 荒 PRONUNCIATION: ara, a, kou

MEANINGS: laid waste, rough, wild, rude **EXAMPLES:** 荒い arai = violent, rough, rude; 荒らす arasu = to lay waste, damage, devastate; 荒れる areru = to be stormy or rough, to fall into ruin; 荒野 kouya = wilderness, the wild **DESCRIPTION:** compared to 慌(てる) awateru (to panic, # 710), this omits the erect man on the left, but it retains the three-legged Arab man with the plant material, suggesting agriculture, and the fish hook **CUES:** this three-legged **Ara**b man engages in **A**griculture and grows **C**orn, but when he threatens people with this fish hook, he is considered 荒い **ara**i (rude) **ALSO COMPARE:** 忘(れる) wasureru = to forget, # 310

....

Chapter 46

969. 共 PRONUNCIATIONS: tomo, kyou

MEANING: together **EXAMPLES:** 共に tomo ni = together; 共同の kyoudou no = cooperative, communal; 共感 kyoukan = sympathy; 共通の kyoutsuu no = common, mutual

DESCRIPTION: compared to (子)供 kodomo (child, # 486), this omits the man with a slanted hat, but it retains the bushes balanced on a dome in Kyouto **CUES:** these two bushes balanced on a dome are 共に **tomo** ni (together), and they are located outside of a **Tomo**graphy center in **Kyou**to **ALSO COMPARE:** 洪(水) kouzui = flood, # 1119

970. 異 PRONUNCIATIONS: koto, i
MEANINGS: uncommon, strangeness **EXAMPLES:** 異なる kotonaru = to differ; 驚異 kyoui = miracle, marvel; 異議 igi = objection **DESCRIPTION:** at the top, 田 (rice paddy, # 68); at the bottom, 共(に) tomo ni (together, # 969) **CUES:** I attended a **Koto** (Japanese harp) concert on **Ea**ster at this 田 (rice paddy) 共 (together) with some friends, and we found that it 異なった **koto**natta (differed) from the one we attended last year

971. 驚 PRONUNCIATIONS: kyou, odoro
MEANINGS: to wonder, be surprised, amazed, frightened **EXAMPLES:** 驚異 kyoui = miracle, marvel; 驚く odoroku = to be astonished **DESCRIPTION:** at the top, 敬(う) uyamau (to respect, # 873); at the bottom, 馬 uma (horse, # 958) **CUES:** when I go to **Kyou**to, I 敬 (respect) their 馬 (horses), but I 驚く **odoro**ku (get astonished) at the **Odoro**us Kool-Aid served at their riding academies **ALSO COMPARE:** 警(察) keisatsu = police, # 874; (推)薦(する) suisen suru = to recommend, # 1030

972. 巣 PRONUNCIATION: sou, su
MEANING: nest **EXAMPLES:** 卵巣 ransou = ovary; 精巣 seisou = testicle; 巣 su = nest, animal habitat, cobweb, honeycomb, den **DESCRIPTION:** at the top, the heads of three chicks sticking out of a nest; at the bottom, 果(物) kudamono (fruit, # 587), which incorporates 木 ki (tree, # 118) **CUES:** a **S**oldier asked **Su**perman to check on the three chicks in the 巣 **su** (nest) at the top of this 果 (fruit) 木 (tree)

973. 崩 PRONUNCIATIONS: hou, kuzu
MEANINGS: crumble, demolish, die **EXAMPLES:** 崩壊 houkai = collapse, crumbling, decay; 崩す kuzusu = to dismantle or destroy, to change money, to throw off balance; 崩れる kuzureru = to collapse, be destroyed **DESCRIPTION:** at the top, 山 yama (mountain, # 146); at the bottom, two 月 tsuki (moons, # 148) **CUES:** my **H**ome is on this 山 (mountain), where I grow **Cool Zu**cchinis, but it is supported by only these two 月 (moons), and if they drift apart, the mountain will 崩れる **kuzu**reru (collapse)

974. 就 PRONUNCIATIONS: shuu, tsu
MEANINGS: to take up a job, to be completed **EXAMPLES:** 就職する shuushoku suru = to find employment; 就く tsuku = to set out, obtain a position **DESCRIPTION:** on the left, 京 kyou (capital, # 514); on the right, 犬 inu (dog, # 190), but its right leg is swollen and kneeling **CUES:** I went to the 京 (capital) in order to 就職する **shuu**shoku suru (find employment) so that I could pay for a **Sho**e to put on my 犬 (dog)'s swollen right leg, and I carried my **Tsu**itcase (suitcase)

975. 蹴 PRONUNCIATION: ke
MEANING: to kick **EXAMPLES:** 蹴る keru = to kick; 蹴飛ばす ketobasu = to kick away, to refuse curtly **DESCRIPTION:** on the left, a simplified version of 足 ashi (foot, # 449); on the right, 就(職) shuushoku (finding employment, # 974), which includes the radical 京 kyou (capital) **CUE:** this reminds us of a salesman who has 就 (found employment) in the 京 (capital) selling **Ke**ds (a brand of shoes) to people with strong 足 (feet) who want to 蹴る **ke**ru (kick) balls

976. 黄 PRONUNCIATIONS: ou, kou, ki

MEANING: yellow EXAMPLES: 卵黄 ran'ou = egg yolk; 黄金 ougon = gold; 黄砂 kousa = yellow dust from the Yellow River region, which blows to Japan; 黄色 ki'iro = yellow; 黄身 kimi = egg yolk DESCRIPTION: this is the Cheshire cat belonging to Yoko Ono, as seen in 横(断する) oudan suru (to cross, # 135), which helps us to pronounce this and includes a plant radical at the top resembling prominent eye whiskers, two large yellow eyes, two large teeth, and extended front paws CUES: this Cheshire cat 横 (crossed) the Ocean on a Coal ship, carrying a 黄色 ki'iro (yellow) Key on a string around its neck

....

Chapter 47

977. 救 PRONUNCIATIONS: kyuu, suku

MEANINGS: salvation, help, rescue, reclaim EXAMPLES: 救急車 kyuukyuusha = ambulance; 救済 kyuusai = help, rescue, relief; 救う suku'u = to rescue; 救い sukui = help, hope DESCRIPTION: on the left, (要)求 youkyuu (a request or command, # 810), which helps us to pronounce this; on the right, a cute dancer with a ponytail CUES: the person on the right is a Cute dancer who gets energy from Superior Kool-Aid, and is able to 救う suku'u (rescue) other dancers who 求 (request) her help ALSO COMPARE: (野)球 yakyuu = baseball, # 606, which also helps us to pronounce this

978. 疑 PRONUNCIATIONS: utaga, gi

MEANING: to doubt EXAMPLES: 疑う utagau = to doubt or suspect; 疑問 gimon = a question or doubt; 疑惑 giwaku = a suspicion or doubt DESCRIPTION: at the upper left, the katakana ヒ hi, which reminds us of a hero; at the lower left, an American Indian chief, as seen in 知(る) shiru (to know, # 323); at the upper right, the katakana マ ma, which reminds us of Ma (mother); at the lower right, a taser on 足 ashi (foot,

449), incorporating a spear at the top, as seen in 旋(回) senkai (rotation, # 913) CUES: this ヒ (hero), his マ (Ma), and an American Indian chief are traveling to Utah wearing Gaudy jewelry, which some people 疑う utagau (doubt) is a good idea, and they plan to hunt Geese there with this taser that they have mounted on Ma's 足 (foot)

979. 輝 PRONUNCIATIONS: ki, kagaya

MEANINGS: radiance, shine, sparkle, gleam EXAMPLES: 光輝 kouki = brightness, splendor; 輝く kagayaku = to shine, glitter, sparkle DESCRIPTION: on the left, 光 hikari (light, # 448); on the right, 軍(人) gunjin (soldier, # 725) CUES: this 光 (light) on the left 輝く kagayaku (shines) brightly, and it is being used in a signal lamp in Kiev by the 軍 (soldier) on the right to Call a Gallant Yachtsman

980. 肌 PRONUNCIATION: hada

MEANING: texture, skin, body, grain EXAMPLES: 肌 hada = skin, personality; 肌着 hadagi = underwear; 木肌 kihada = bark of a tree DESCRIPTION: on the left, 月 tsuki (moon, # 148) ; on the right, a tall desk, as seen in 机 tsukue (desk, # 140) CUE: my Hawaiian Daughter hides under this 机 (desk) during the day and only exposes her 肌 hada (skin) to the sky when the 月 (moon) shines

981. 滑 PRONUNCIATIONS: sube, name, katsu MEANINGS: slippery, slide, slip, flunk

EXAMPLES: 滑る suberu = to slide or slip, to fail an exam; 滑りやすい suberiyasui = slippery; 滑らかな nameraka na = smooth, mellow (usually written なめらかな); 円滑 enkatsu = smooth, harmonious DESCRIPTION: on the left, a water radical; on the right, 骨 hone (bone, # 832), which depicts a roof-top apartment on the 月 (moon, # 148)

CUES: I rest my 骨 (bones) in this roof-top apartment, which I can afford thanks to my job as a **Sub-e**ditor, and I have a **N**anny from **Me**xico who helps to take care of my **C**ats, but we have a problem with this water leaking, and our floors are

滑りやすい **suber**iyasui (slippery)

982. 覗 PRONUNCIATION: nozo

MEANING: peek, peep, come in sight

EXAMPLES: 覗く nozoku = to snoop;

覗き込む nozokikomu = to peer into

DESCRIPTION: on the left, (上)司 joushi (one's superior in a company, # 608); on the right, 見(る) miru (to watch, # 53)

CUE: my 司 (supervisor) 見 (watches) me and 覗く **nozo**ku (snoops) to make sure that I don't park in the **No Z**one

983. 井 PRONUNCIATIONS: jou, i, ino

MEANINGS: well, community

EXAMPLES: 天井 tenjou = ceiling; 井戸 ido = water well; 井上 Inoue = a family name

DESCRIPTION: the pound sign

CUES: **Jo**an of Arc decided to try to lose some # (pounds) on **E**aster, so she walked down to the 井戸 **i**do (well) with some **Inno**cent children

COMPARE: (周)囲 shuui = surroundings, # 1202, which helps us to pronounce this

984. 桜 PRONUNCIATIONS: sakura, zakura¹ MEANING: cherry EXAMPLES:

桜の花 sakura no hana = cherry blossoms;

夜桜見物 yozakura kenbutsu = going out to look at cherry blossoms in the evening

DESCRIPTION: on the left, 木 ki (tree, # 118); on the upper right, three vertical lines representing flowers; on the lower right, 女 onna (female, # 235) **CUES:** when a 女 (woman) said that these three 桜 **sakura** (cherry) flowers were blooming on this 木 (tree), a **Sa**laryman turned off his **Kuuraa** (cooler, or air conditioner) and went out to see them

....

Chapter 48

985. 悠 PRONUNCIATION: yuu

MEANINGS: permanence, long time, leisure

EXAMPLES: 悠々 yuuyuu = quiet, calm, leisurely; 悠長 yuuchou = leisurely, slow, deliberate, easy-going; 悠久の yuukyuu no = eternal **DESCRIPTION:** at the upper left, a man with a slanted hat facing a vertical line, which is the horn of a unicorn; at the upper right, a dancer with a ponytail; at the bottom, 心 kokoro (heart, # 306) **CUE:** this man with a slanted hat on the left and this dancer on the right have big 心 (hearts), but they keep this **U**nicorn horn between them, for the sake of keeping things 悠々 **yuu**yuu (quiet or calm)

986. 抱 PRONUNCIATIONS: bou, da

MEANINGS: embrace, hug, hold in arms

EXAMPLES: 辛抱 shinbou = endurance, patience; 抱く daku = to embrace, hold or hug; 抱きしめる dakishimeru = to hug someone tightly **DESCRIPTION:** on the left, a kneeling guy; on the right, 包(む) tsutsumu (to wrap, # 548) **CUES:** this kneeling guy 包 (wraps) a **B**owling ball as a present for his **D**aughter and then 抱く **da**ku (embraces) her

987. 融 PRONUNCIATION: yuu

MEANINGS: dissolve, melt **EXAMPLES:** 金融 kinyuu = finance, loaning money; 融合 yuugou = fusion, adhesion, blending

DESCRIPTION: at the top left, 口 kuchi (mouth, # 426), with a piece of tape above it; at the lower left, 四 yon (four, # 6), which is the floor plan of a house, with a missing wall at the bottom and the letter T inside, which reminds us of **T**arantulas; on the right, 虫 mushi (insect, # 9) **CUE:** on the lower left, the floor plan of a house in the **Yu**kon, with a wall missing at the bottom, which promotes a sense of 融合 **yuu**gou (fusion) between the inside of the house and the outside but allows 虫 (insects) like this **T**arantula to get in, so that the occupants need to keep strips of tape like this over their 口 mouths to avoid screaming whenever they see them

988. 均 **PRONUNCIATION: kin**

MEANINGS: level, average **EXAMPLE:** 平均 heikin = average, mean **DESCRIPTION:** on the left, tsuchi 土 (dirt, # 59); on the right, a hook; inside the hook, two lines representing nearly horizontal plants which are not very healthy

CUE: at our **Kin**dergarten, we plow this 土 (dirt) with this hook and grow plants like these, but our results are only 平均 hei**kin** (average)

COMPARE: 匂(う) niou = to smell of, # 949

989. 齢 **PRONUNCIATION: rei**

MEANING: age **EXAMPLES:** 年齢 nenrei = age **DESCRIPTION:** on the left, 歯 ha (tooth, # 533); on the right, (命)令 meirei (command, # 962), which looks like a person who is preparing to run a race and which helps us to pronounce this

CUE: during the **Ra**ce of life, our 年齢 nen**rei** (age) increases, and we develop problems with our 歯 (teeth), but we also get to give more 令 (orders) to younger people

990. 刊 **PRONUNCIATION: kan**

MEANING: to publish **EXAMPLES:** 朝刊 choukan = morning paper; 週刊誌 shuukanshi = weekly magazine; 刊行する kankou suru = to publish **DESCRIPTION:** on the left, a telephone pole; on the right, the katakana リ ri, which reminds us of reading **CUE:** in **Can**ada, people stand next to telephone poles like this and リ (read) 刊行した **kan**kou shita (published) books

COMPARE: 軒 noki = eaves, # 1146

991. 賞 **PRONUNCIATION: shou**

MEANINGS: prize, reward, praise **EXAMPLES:** 受賞する jushou suru = to win an award or prize; 入賞する nyuushou suru = to win an award or prize **DESCRIPTION:** at the top, three old boys on a roof, as seen in 覚(える) oboeru (to memorize, # 54); at the bottom, 員 in (member, # 88) **CUE:** these three old boys on a roof, who are 員 (members) of a club, 覚 (memorize) scripts for **Show**s and 入賞する nyuu**shou** suru (win prizes) **ALSO COMPARE:** (優)勝 yuushou = championship, victory, # 149; (非)常 hijou = emergency, # 683; 営業 eigyou = business, # 684 and # 332; (苦)労 kurou = hardship, # 1075

992. 躍 **PRONUNCIATION: yaku**

MEANINGS: leap, dance, skip **EXAMPLES:** 躍進 yakushin = progress; 活躍する katsuyaku suru = to be active **DESCRIPTION:** compared to 曜 you (day of the week, # 200), the 日 (sun) on the left has been replaced by 足 ashi (leg, # 449) **CUE: Yaku**za (gangsters) 活躍する katsu**yaku** suru (are active) and exercise their 足 (legs) every 曜 (day of the week)

··········

Chapter 49

993. 佐 **PRONUNCIATION: sa**

MEANINGS: assistant, help **EXAMPLES:** 佐賀県 saga ken = Saga Prefecture; 大佐 taisa = colonel; 補佐 hosa = aid, help **DESCRIPTION:** on the left, a man with a slanted hat: on the right, 左 hidari (left, # 456) **CUE:** this man with a slanted hat had some **Sa**gging on the 左 (left) side of his face until he got 補佐 ho**sa** (help) from a plastic surgeon

994. 賀 **PRONUNCIATION: ga**

MEANINGS: congratulations, joy **EXAMPLES:** 祝賀会 shukugakai = celebration; 佐賀県 saga ken = Saga Prefecture; 年賀状 nengajou = New Year's card **DESCRIPTION:** at the upper left, 刀 katana (sword, # 102); at the upper right, 口 kuchi (mouth, # 426); at the bottom, 貝 kai (shell, or money chest, # 83) **CUE:** a **Ga**mbler uses a 刀 (sword) to protect the money in this 貝 (money chest), which he spends on 祝賀会 shuku**ga**kai (celebrations), where he puts food in his 口

(mouth) **COMPARE:** 資(金) shikin = capital, # 91; (家)賃 yachin = rent, # 707

995. 補 PRONUNCIATIONS: ho, ogina

MEANINGS: supplement, supply **EXAMPLES:** 補佐 hosa = aid, help; 補給する hokyuu suru = to supply or supplement; 候補 kouho = candidate; 補う oginau = to supplement or compensate for **DESCRIPTION:** on the left, happy Jimmy Carter, as seen in 初(めて) hajimete (for the first time, # 104); at the upper right, the top half of 犬 inu (dog, # 190) juggling a ball; at the lower right, 用 you (to use, # 364) **CUES:** happy Jimmy is a 候補 kou**ho** (candidate), and he 用 (uses) this 犬 (dog) at his **H**ome to impress the voters, while some of **O**prah's **G**eese take a **N**ap

COMPARE: 捕(虜) horyo = captive, # 670, which helps us to pronounce this

996. 候 PRONUNCIATION: kou

MEANINGS: supplement, supply

EXAMPLES: 気候 kikou = climate; 天候 tenkou = weather; 候補 kouho = candidate **DESCRIPTION:** on the left, a man with a slanted hat; at the upper right, the katakana ユ yu, which reminds us of the Yukon; at the lower right, an American Indian chief, holding a rod in his left hand **CUE:** this man with a slanted hat is telling this American Indian chief that he should move to the ユ (Yukon), where he can use this rod to make a living as a prison guard, but the chief says that the 気候 ki**kou** (climate) up there is too **C**old

997. 給 PRONUNCIATION: kyuu

MEANINGS: salary, wage, gift, bestow on **EXAMPLES:** 給料 kyuuryou = salary; 補給する hokyuu suru = to supply or supplement **DESCRIPTION:** on the left, 糸 (skeet shooter, # 219); on the right, 合(う) au (to come together or match, # 294)

CUE: this 糸 (skeet shooter) 合 (matched) up with a **C**ucumber company and now earns a high

給料 **kyuu**ryou (salary) shooting cucumbers

COMPARE: 絵(本) ehon = picture book, # 223; 紹(介) shoukai = introduction, # 658

998. 状 PRONUNCIATION: jou

MEANINGS: condition, letter **EXAMPLES:** 年賀状 nengajou = New Year's card; 状態 joutai = condition, circumstances, state; 紹介状 shoukaijou = letter of introduction **DESCRIPTION:** on the left, a two-legged bench standing on end; on the right, inu 犬 (dog, # 190) **CUE:** **Joa**n of Arc thought that the 状態 **jou**tai (circumstances) were right to bring her 犬 (dog) to a park, and she sat on this bench while the dog ran around

999. 録 PRONUNCIATION: roku

MEANING: to record **EXAMPLES:** 記録 kiroku = a record or document; 録音 rokuon = a sound recording; 登録 touroku = registration, enrollment **DESCRIPTION:** on the left, 金 kane (money, # 301); on the right, a green flag on a miniature dory in 水 (water), as seen in 緑 midori (green, # 227) **CUE:** if you pay this 緑 (green) 金 (money) to a **Ro**botic **Kool**-Aid dispenser, it will mix some Kool-Aid for you, and it will also make a 記録 ki**roku** (record) of the transaction

1000. 更 PRONUNCIATIONS: kou, sara

MEANINGS: again, further, night watch **EXAMPLES:** 変更 henkou = a change or alteration; 更新 koushin = renewal; 更に sara ni = again, furthermore **DESCRIPTION:** compared to 便(利) benri (convenient, # 481), this omits the man with a slanted hat; it retains the radical that resembles Benjamin Franklin wearing bifocals **CUES:** Benjamin Franklin, who invented these bifocals, made a 変更 hen**kou** (change) in his kitchen, stipulating that leftover food should be kept **C**old and covered with **Sara**n wrap

ALSO COMPARE: 丈 take = size, # 613

....

Chapter 50

1001. 挑 PRONUNCIATIONS: chou, ido

MEANINGS: challenge, contend for, to pressure someone for sex, to woo EXAMPLES: 挑戦する chousen suru = to challenge; 挑む idomu = to challenge DESCRIPTION: on the left, a kneeling man; on the right, 兆 chou = one trillion, # 849, which helps us to pronounce this

CUES: this kneeling guy has a 兆 (trillion) **Ch**ores that 挑む **ido**mu (challenge) him, but he has to wait until his **E**agle is **D**ozing to do them

COMPARE: 眺(望) choubou = a view, # 1136, which also helps us to pronounce this

1002. 沖 PRONUNCIATION: oki

MEANINGS: open sea, off the coast, rise high into sky EXAMPLES: 沖 oki = open sea, off the coast; 沖縄 Okinawa DESCRIPTION: on the left, a water radical; on the right, 中 chuu (inside, # 8) CUE: an **O**ld **K**ing who lived in 沖縄 **Oki**nawa used to get 中 (inside) this water

1003. 縄 PRONUNCIATIONS: nawa, jou

MEANINGS: straw rope, cord EXAMPLES: 縄 nawa = rope; 沖縄 Okinawa; 縄文時代 joumon jidai = the Jomon period (14,000 – 300 BC) DESCRIPTION: on the left, 糸 ito (thread, # 219); on the right, two 田 (rice paddies, # 68), linked by a rope CUES: **Na**rco **Wa**rlords make coarse 糸 (thread) out of the straw that they get from 田 (rice paddies) and weave it together to make 縄 **nawa** (rope), after which they tie the paddies together like this as a **Jo**ke

COMPARE: 亀 kame = turtle, # 908

1004. 府 PRONUNCIATION: fu

MEANINGS: borough, government office, urban prefecture, storehouse EXAMPLES: 都道府県 todoufuken = administrative division of Japan; 政府 seifu = government; 京都府 kyoutofu = Kyouto prefecture DESCRIPTION: at the upper left, a lean-to with a chimney; under the lean-to, 付(く) tsuku (to adhere, # 132)

CUE: the 政府 sei**fu** (government) stores **Food** under lean-to's like this, but the food tends to 付 (adhere) together when it rains

1005. 阪 PRONUNCIATIONS: saka, han

MEANINGS: slope, heights EXAMPLES: 大阪 oosaka = Osaka, large hill; 阪神 hanshin = Osaka and Kobe DESCRIPTION: on the left, ß from the Greek alphabet; on the right, an F over an X CUES: we play **Sakkaa** (soccer) against ß (Greek) opponents in 大阪 oo**saka** (Osaka), but our skill level is poor, and **Han**sel says that our play deserves an F, or possibly an X

COMPARE: 坂 saka = slope, hill, # 1130, which helps us to pronounce this

1006. 奈 PRONUNCIATION: na

MEANINGS: Nara EXAMPLES: 奈良 Nara = ancient capital of Japan; 神奈川 Kanagawa = a prefecture in Japan DESCRIPTION: at the top, an extra-wide 大(きい) ookii (big, # 188); at the bottom, a spinning pavilion, as seen in 余(り) amari (surplus, rest, # 637)

CUE: in 奈良 **Na**ra, 大 (big) **N**annies ride on spinning 余 (pavilions) like this one

1007. 茨 PRONUNCIATION: ibara

MEANINGS: briar, thorn EXAMPLES: 茨城 Ibaraki = a prefecture in Japan DESCRIPTION: at the top, a plant radical; at the bottom, 次 tsugi (next, # 536) CUE: when these plants overgrew his hair salon and he had to find something to do 次 (next), an **I**talian **B**arber opened a **R**amen shop in 茨城 **Ibara**ki (Prefecture) COMPARE: 羨(ましい) urayamashii = envious, # 662

1008. 城 PRONUNCIATIONS: shiro, *ki,* jou MEANING: castle EXAMPLES: 城 shiro = castle; 茨城 Ibaraki = a prefecture in Japan; 荒城 koujou = ruined castle; 名城 meijou = famous castle DESCRIPTION: on the left, 土 tsuchi (dirt, # 59); on the right, 成(功) seikou (success, # 633) CUES: after I had a lot of 成 (success), I decided to build a **Shiro** (white) 城 **shiro** (castle) on this big patch of 土 (dirt) in **Kiev**, in order to impress **Joan** of Arc

··········

Chapter 51

1009. 挟 PRONUNCIATION: hasa MEANINGS: pinch, between EXAMPLES: 挟む hasamu = to hold or place between, to pinch; 挟まる hasamaru = to get between, to get caught in DESCRIPTION: on the left, a kneeling man; on the right, 夫 otto (husband, # 614), with flames shooting out from both sides CUE: this kneeling man, who is a **H**andsome **S**alaryman, watches this 夫 (husband) 挟まれる **hasa**mareru (get caught between) two walls of flame COMPARE: 鋏 hasami = scissors, not included in this Catalogue; 狭(い) semai = narrow, # 194

1010. 省 PRONUNCIATIONS: shou, habu, sei MEANINGS: focus, conserve, government ministry EXAMPLES: 省略 shouryaku = abbreviation, omission; 省く habuku = to omit, to cut down (cost); 反省 hansei = scrutiny, self-scrutiny, regret DESCRIPTION: at the top, 少(し) sukoshi (a little, # 254), which seems to be pushing down on 目 me (eye, # 51) CUES: a **Sho**gun drank 少 (a little) **Ha**waiian **Boo**ze and felt that it was pushing down on his 目 (eyes), causing him to worry about his **S**afety, so he did some 反省 han**sei** (self-scrutiny) and decided to 省く **habu**ku (cut down) on his drinking

1011. 携 PRONUNCIATIONS: tazusa, kei MEANINGS: portable, carry in hand EXAMPLES: 携わる tazusawaru = to engage (in); 携える tazusaeru = to carry with; 携帯する keitai suru = to carry; 携帯電話 keitai denwa = cellular phone; 提携する teikei suru = to form a partnership or cooperate DESCRIPTION: on the left, a kneeling guy; at the upper right, a cage; at the lower right, a graph similar to the one seen in 及(ぶ) oyobu (to reach, # 883) but missing the horizontal slash CUES: this kneeling guy is a **T**all **Z**ookeeper from **Sa**skatchewan, and he 携帯する **kei**tai suru (carries) this graph diagramming escape attempts by animals from this **C**age at the zoo COMPARE: 訪ねる tazuneru = to visit, # 713

1012. 帯 PRONUNCIATIONS: obi, tai MEANINGS: belt, sash, to carry on the body EXAMPLES: 帯 obi = a kimono sash; 携帯電話 keitai denwa = cellular phone; 所帯 shotai = household, family DESCRIPTION: at the top, 山 yama (mountain, # 146), with a horizontal line drawn through it which resembles cloud cover; on the lower right, 市 shi (city, # 242), but the 十 (ten) at the top has been replaced by a lid, suggesting that this city needs to be protected from rain CUES: **O**prah drank **B**eer in a protected 市 (city) under a cloud-covered 山 (mountain) in **Thai**land, and afterwards her 帯 **obi** (sash) no longer reached around her

1013. 滞 PRONUNCIATION: tai MEANINGS: stagnate, be delayed or overdue EXAMPLES: 滞在する taizai suru = to stay (at a hotel, etc.); 渋滞 juutai = congestion (e.g., traffic), delay, stagnation DESCRIPTION: on the left, a water radical; on the right, (携)帯(電話) keitai denwa (cellular phone, # 1012), which helps us to pronounce this CUE: when I'm **T**ired, I 滞在する **tai**zai suru (stay) at a hot springs inn, and sometimes I accidentally drop this 帯 (phone) into this water

1014. 在 **PRONUNCIATIONS: zai, a**
MEANINGS: exist, outskirts, located in
EXAMPLES: 滞在する taizai suru = to stay
(at a hotel, etc.); 現在 genzai = nowadays, present
time; 在る aru = to exist, usually written ある;
cf. 有る aru = to exist, # 460 **DESCRIPTION:**
on the left, a hugging person, plus an additional
vertical line, as seen in 存(じる) zonjiru (to
humbly know, # 462); on the right 土 tsuchi (dirt,
59) **CUES:** this person hugging 土 (dirt) may be
expressing the **Z**eitgeist (spirit of the Age) of certain
people at the 現在 gen**zai** (present time), who are
embracing **A**griculture

1015. 陸 **PRONUNCIATION: riku**
MEANINGS: land EXAMPLES: 大陸 tairiku =
continent, mainland (China); 離陸する ririku
suru = to take off (flight); 陸軍 rikugun = army
DESCRIPTION: on the left, ß beta from the Greek
alphabet; at the upper right, 土 tsuchi (dirt, # 59),
with a pair of sturdy legs; at the lower right, 土
(dirt) again
CUE: this ß (Greek) guy lives on an island of 土
(dirt) piled on 土 (dirt), and he will have to use
these sturdy legs to swim to the 大陸 tai**riku**
(mainland) in order to get some **Real Kool**-Aid

1016. 湾 **PRONUNCIATION: wan**
MEANINGS: gulf, bay, inlet **EXAMPLES:**
湾 wan = gulf, bay; 台湾 taiwan = Taiwan
DESCRIPTION: on the left, a water radical; at the
upper right, a swooping hen, as seen in (大)変
taihen (terrible, # 553); at the lower right, a radical
suggesting "twisted," as seen in 弟 otouto (little
brother, # 529)
CUE: when I visited 台湾 Tai**wan** and
Wandered over to this water, I saw this 変
(swooping hen) flying over some 弟 (twisted) ruins
....

Chapter 52
1017. 旧 **PRONUNCIATION: kyuu**
MEANINGS: old times, former **EXAMPLES:**
旧正月 kyuu shougatsu = lunar New Year, or
Chinese New Year; 旧年 kyuunen = last year
DESCRIPTION: on the left, a vertical line which
resembles a 1; on the right, 日 hi (day, # 32)
CUE: the # 1 日 (day) of the year is 旧正月
kyuu shougatsu (lunar New Year), and it's a good
time to eat a **C**ucumber salad

1018. 盛 **PRONUNCIATIONS: mo, saka,
jou, sei** MEANINGS: to thrive, prosperous
EXAMPLES: 盛る moru = to fill or pile up;
盛んな sakan na = active, enthusiastic, energetic,
thriving; 繁盛 hanjou = success or prosperity (in
business); 全盛 zensei = culmination, heyday,
peak; 盛大な seidai na = grandiose, pompous,
thriving, successful **DESCRIPTION:** at the top,
成(功) seikou (success, # 633), which helps us to
pronounce this; at the bottom, 皿 sara (dish, # 567)
CUES: **Mo**ses was a **Sakkaa** (soccer) player who
had a lot of 成 (success) with a 皿 (dish) factory
that he started with **Joa**n of Arc, which 盛んだ
sakan da (is thriving) and is selling its products at
Safeway

1019. 災 **PRONUNCIATIONS: sai,
wazawa** MEANINGS: serious trouble, calamity
EXAMPLES: 震災 shinsai = great earthquake;
火災 kasai = fire; 災難 sainan = misfortune,
disaster; 災い wazawai = calamity, disaster
DESCRIPTION: at the top, a chevron like those
sewn onto uniforms, as seen in 巡(る) meguru (to
go around, # 778); at the bottom, 火 hi (fire, # 443)
CUES: this chevron is a **S**ign that a 災難 **sai**nan
(disaster) is likely, since it suggests that **W**acky
Zambian **W**arriors are 巡 (going around) in
uniforms decorated with chevrons like this and
starting 火 (fires)

1020. 乱 PRONUNCIATIONS: **mida, ran** MEANING: to be out of order EXAMPLES: 乱れる midareru = to become chaotic or windblown (hair); 乱暴な ranbou na = violent, disorderly DESCRIPTION: on the left, a forked tongue emerging from 口 kuchi (mouth, # 426); on the right, a breast, as seen in 乳 nyuu (milk, # 186) CUES: during a **Mea**l with **Dar**win, when we 話 (talked) about the evolution of 乳 (breast) feeding, he became 乱暴 **ran**bo (violent) and **Ran**sacked the place ALSO COMPARE: (生)活 seikatsu = livelihood, # 260

1021. 暴 PRONUNCIATIONS: **bou, aba** MEANINGS: to expose, violent EXAMPLES: 暴れる abareru = to become violent; 乱暴な ranbou na = violent or disorderly DESCRIPTION: at the top, 日 hi (sun, # 32); below that, 共 tomo (together, # 969); at the bottom, 求(む) motomu (to seek or demand, # 810), without its hat brim and the ball above its right shoulder CUES: when **Bo**ys are **Ab**andoned, they sit 共 (together) under this 日 (sun), 求 (demand) care and threaten to become 乱暴 ran**bou** (violent)

1022. 爆 PRONUNCIATION: **baku** MEANINGS: bomb, burst open, pop, split EXAMPLES: 爆弾 bakudan = bomb; 原爆 genbaku = atomic bomb DESCRIPTION: on the left, 火 hi (fire, # 443); on the right, (乱)暴 ranbou (violent, # 1021) CUE: I was sitting in a **Bar** drinking **Kool**-Aid when a 暴 (violent) person set off a 爆弾 **baku**dan (bomb) and started this 火 (fire)

1023. 縁 PRONUNCIATION: **en** MEANINGS: chance, fate, destiny EXAMPLES: 縁 en = relation, bond, kinship, fate; 縁起 engi = omen, sign of luck, origin, causation DESCRIPTION: on the left, 糸 (skeet shooter, # 219); on the upper right, the green flag seen in 緑 midori (green, # 227); on the lower right, a radical seen in 家 ie (house, # 405) CUE: this 糸 (skeet shooter) thinks that the 緑 (green) flag flying from this 家 (house) is a good 縁起 **en**gi (omen), suggesting that **E**ntertainers are inside

1024. 怪 PRONUNCIATIONS: **aya, ke, kai** MEANINGS: suspicious, mystery, apparition EXAMPLES: 怪しい ayashii = suspicious, doubtful; 大怪我 ookega = serious injury; 怪物 kaibutsu = monster DESCRIPTION: on the left, an erect man; on the right, an athlete leaping over 土 tsuchi (dirt) CUES: this erect man, who is an **Aya**tollah, is 怪しい **aya**shii (doubtful) that this athlete, who just drank a **Ke**g of beer and is carrying a **Ki**te, can leap over this patch of 土 (dirt) COMPARE: 軽(い) karui = light weight, # 289

....

Chapter 53

1025. 松 PRONUNCIATIONS: **matsu, shou** MEANINGS: pine tree EXAMPLES: 松 matsu = pine tree; 老松 roushou = old pine tree DESCRIPTION: on the left, 木 ki (tree, # 118); on the right, 公 kou (public, # 16) CUES: this 木 (tree) in a 公 (public) park is a 松 **matsu** (pine tree), and people sit under it on **Mats** and **Sho**w off their legs

1026. 江 PRONUNCIATIONS: **e, kou** MEANINGS: creek, inlet, bay EXAMPLES: 江戸 edo = old name for Tokyo; 長江 choukou = Yangtze River in China DESCRIPTION: on the left, a water radical; on the right, 工 kou (crafted object, # 246), which helps us to pronounce this CUES: **E**xcellent craftsmen carved precious 工 (crafted objects) from **Co**ral, found in water like this, during the 江戸 **e**do (ancient Tokyo) period COMPARE: 紅(茶) koucha = black tea, # 247, which helps us to pronounce this

1027. 講 PRONUNCIATION: kou

MEANING: to lecture   EXAMPLES: 講義 kougi = lecture; 講堂 koudou = auditorium   DESCRIPTION: compared to (結)構 kekkou (fine, # 141), which helps us to pronounce this, the 木 (wood) on the left has been replaced by 言(う) iu (to speak, # 430); this retains the radicals on the right which resemble bushes on the roof of a strong building   CUE: when a woman 言 (spoke) and gave a 講義 kougi (lecture) about Korean Geese in this strong building with plants on the roof, her explanations seemed 構 (fine) to me

1028. 義 PRONUNCIATION: gi

MEANINGS: justice, morality   EXAMPLES: 義理 giri = moral debt, limited duty to the outside world; 義務 gimu = unlimited duty to the emperor, ancestors and descendants; 講義 kougi = lecture   DESCRIPTION: compared to (会)議 kaigi (meeting, # 438), which helps us to pronounce this, 言 (to speak) is absent

CUE: I went to a 議 (meeting) to hear a 講義 kougi (lecture) about Korean Geese

1029. 推 PRONUNCIATIONS: sui, o

MEANINGS: to push forward, recommend, guess   EXAMPLES: 推薦する suisen suru = to recommend; 推測 suisoku = an assumption or guess; 推す osu = to recommend   DESCRIPTION: on the left, a kneeling guy; on the right, a cage   CUES: this Swedish kneeling guy approaches the cage in which I am confined and 推薦する suisen suru (recommends) that the jailor Open the door

1030. 薦 PRONUNCIATIONS: susu, sen

MEANINGS: recommend, advise   EXAMPLES: 薦める susumeru = to advise (this is usually written 勧める susumeru, # 698); 推薦する suisen suru = to recommend   DESCRIPTION: at the top, a plant radical; below that, a lean-to with a chimney; suspended from the ceiling of the lean-to, three eyes; below the eyes, the lower half of 鳥 tori (bird, # 555)   CUES: when a Superman found a Super 鳥 (bird) with three eyes in this lean-to with plants on the roof, he 推薦した suisen shita (recommended) that it be protected and given to a Senator   COMPARE: 驚(く) odoroku = to be astonished, # 971

1031. 測 PRONUNCIATIONS: haka, soku   MEANINGS: fathom, plan, scheme, measure   EXAMPLES: 測る hakaru = to measure or gauge (usually written 計る hakaru); 推測 suisoku = an assumption or guess; 予測 yosoku = a prediction or supposition; 測定する sokutei suru = to measure   DESCRIPTION: compared to 側 gawa (side, # 490), the man with a slanted hat on the left has been replaced by a water radical   CUES: リ Ri made a 推測 suisoku (assumption) that the man with a slanted hat was still standing on the opposite 側 (side) of this 貝 (money chest), but the man had left to attend a Hackathon, and that allowed this water to pour in, so that the 貝 (chest) and リ Ri got Soaked

1032. 再 PRONUNCIATIONS: sai, futata, sa   MEANING: again   EXAMPLES: 再会する saikai suru = to meet again; 再開する saikai suru = to reopen or resume; 再三 saisan = many times, again and again; 再び futatabi = again; 再来年 sarainen = the year after next   DESCRIPTION: at the top, a model of a 田 (rice paddy) with a handle, as seen in (映)画 eiga (movie, # 77); at the bottom, the legs of 円 en (yen, # 39), with an added projection on each side   CUES: a Scientist made this model of a rice paddy with a handle and was hoping to get some 円 (yen) for it, but a guy who was eating Food on a Tatami mat wouldn't buy it, even though he asked him 再び futatabi (again), and he felt Sad

....

Chapter 54

1033. 各 PRONUNCIATIONS: kaku, ka
MEANINGS: each one, individual **EXAMPLES:**
各自の kakuji no = each, one's own; 各駅
kakueki = each station; 各国 kakkoku = each
country **DESCRIPTION:** this is the dancer who
leaps over a box in 客 kyaku (customer, # 524),
without her bad haircut **CUES:** after this dancer
jumps over this box and gets rid of her bad haircut,
she decides to break up with **K**arl the **Kool**-Aid
vendor (see # 524), and they both drive away in
各自の **kaku**ji no (their own) **C**ars

ALSO COMPARE: (性)格 seikaku = personality,
762, which helps us to pronounce this

1034. 繰 PRONUNCIATION: ku
MEANINGS: winding, spin, refer to
EXAMPLES: 繰り返す kurikaesu = to repeat,
to do something over again **DESCRIPTION:** on
the left, 糸 skeet shooter (# 219); at the upper right,
品(物) shinamono (merchandise, # 5); at the lower
right, 木 ki (tree, # 118) **CUE:** this 糸 (skeet
shooter) sees this 品 (merchandise) which is three
packages of **Kool**-Aid stuck at the top of this 木
(tree), tries to shoot it down and then 繰り返す
kurikaesu (does it again) **COMPARE:** 操(作)
sousa = operation (machine), # 1192

1035. 是 PRONUNCIATIONS: ze, kore
MEANINGS: just so, this **EXAMPLES:**
是非とも zehitomo = by all means; 是認
zenin = approval; 是等 korera = these (usually
written これら); 是程 kore hodo = so much,
this much (usually written これほど)

DESCRIPTION: at the top, 日 hi (sun, # 32); at
the bottom, a foot radical with a taser mounted on it,
as seen in (予)定 yotei (plan, # 455) **CUES:** a
Zen monk who has a taser mounted on his foot sits in
the 日 (sun) and says that 是非とも **ze**hitomo
(by all means) he will use this taser **C**orrectly

ALSO COMPARE: 提(出する) teishutsu suru
= to hand in, # 1156

1036. 認 PRONUNCIATIONS: nin, mito
MEANING: to recognize **EXAMPLES:** 是認
zenin = approval; 確認 kakunin = confirmation;
認める mitomeru = to recognize or admit
DESCRIPTION: on the left, 言(う) iu (to speak,
430); at the upper right, 刀 katana (sword, # 102),
with a slash across the handle; at the lower right,
kokoro 心 (heart, # 306) **CUES:** when a **N**inja
Meets Tony Blair and gets 是認 ze**nin** (approval)
for an undercover project, he 言 (speaks) from his
心 (heart) and shows Tony this 刀 (sword), which
was damaged during one of his missions

COMPARE: 恐(れ) osore = fear, # 869, which
includes a slashed yak instead of a slashed sword,
among other differences

1037. 遺 PRONUNCIATIONS: i, yui
MEANINGS: bequeathe, leave behind, reserve
EXAMPLES: 遺産 isan = inheritance, legacy,
heritage; 遺言 yuigon = will, deathbed
instructions **DESCRIPTION:** on the lower left, a
snail; at the upper right, 中 chuu (inside, # 8),
resting on a platform; at the lower right, 貝 kai
(shell, or money chest, # 83) **CUES:** my father
keeps only dried **E**els 中 (inside) this 貝 (money
chest), and his only 遺産 **i**san (legacy) to me will
be a **Y**ukon **E**agle and this snail

1038. 総 PRONUNCIATION: sou
MEANINGS: all, whole **EXAMPLES:** 総じて
soujite = in general, on the whole; 総理大臣
souridaijin = prime minister; 総会 soukai =
general meeting **DESCRIPTION:** on the left, 糸
(skeet shooter, # 219); at the upper right, 公 kou
(public, # 16); at the lower right, 心 kokoro (heart,
306) **CUE:** this 糸 (skeet shooter), who has a
good 心 (heart), is employed in the 公 (public)
sector as a **S**oldier, 総じて **sou**jite (in general)

1039. 臣 PRONUNCIATIONS: shin, jin
MEANINGS: subject, minister EXAMPLES: 臣民 shinmin = royal subject; 総理大臣 souridaijin = prime minister DESCRIPTION: this resembles a child's swing set turned on its side, but the swing ropes have been tied on both sides to make the swing inoperable CUES: a **Shin**to priest, who is a 臣民 **shin**min (royal subject), puts on his **Jeans**, turns this swing set on its side, and ties the swing ropes in order to prevent harm to royal children COMPARE: 巨 kyo = huge, # 689

1040. 姫 PRONUNCIATION: hime
MEANINGS: princess EXAMPLES: 姫 hime = princess DESCRIPTION: on the left, 女 (female); on the right, 臣(民) shinmin (royal subject, # 1039), which resembles an inoperable swing set on its side CUE: the emperor's daughter is a 女 (female) and a 姫 **hime** (princess) who is attracted to **He-Men**, but she is too young to use this swing set safely, so it has been made inoperable

....

Chapter 55

1041. 塗 PRONUNCIATIONS: nu, to
MEANINGS: paint, plaster, smear, coating EXAMPLES: 塗る nuru = to paint, plaster, spread, smear; 塗り替える nurikaeru = to repaint, rewrite; 塗装 tosou = a coat of paint DESCRIPTION: at the upper left, a water radical; at the upper right, 余(り) amari (surplus, # 637), which resembles a spinning pavilion; at the lower right, 土 tsuchi (dirt, # 59) CUES: I have a 余 (spinning pavilion) that is sitting on a pile of 土 (dirt) and is exposed to a lot of water, and I want to 塗る **nu**ru (paint) it so that it will look like **New** and then use it to store **To**matoes

1042. 衣 PRONUNCIATIONS: kata, i, koromo
MEANINGS: clothes, garment, dressing EXAMPLES: 浴衣 yukata = informal summer kimono; 衣服 ifuku = clothing; 衣類 irui = clothing; 衣 koromo = coating or breading (food), clothes DESCRIPTION: at the top, a tire stop as seen in 対(して) tai shite (against, # 674); at the bottom, エ and y CUES: エ and y are two **Kata** (honorable people) who stand near this tire stop as they manufacture 衣服 **i**fuku (clothing) for **E**aster, and they use their **Co**rolla's **Mo**tor for warmth during their break periods

1043. 装 PRONUNCIATIONS: sou, yoso, shou
MEANINGS: to wear or equip EXAMPLES: 服装 fukusou = outfit, dress style, attire; 装置 souchi = equipment, device; 装備 soubi = equipment; 装う yosou = to serve or dish up; 衣装 ishou = clothing, costume DESCRIPTION: at the upper left, a bench placed on its end; at the upper right, 士 shi (man, # 66); at the bottom, 衣(服) ifuku (clothing, # 1042) CUES: this 士 (man) is a **So**ldier who can **Yo**del when he's **So**ber, and he leans this bench up against a wall in order to clear a space for a military **Show** and examines this 衣 (clothing) which will be his 服装 fuku**sou** (outfit) during the show COMPARE: 製(品) seihin = finished product, # 580

1044. 弓 PRONUNCIATIONS: yumi, kyuu
MEANING: bow EXAMPLES: 弓 yumi = bow; 弓矢 yumiya = bow and arrow; 弓道 kyuudou = archery DESCRIPTION: this is the bow seen in 引(く) hiku (to pull, # 476) CUES: I 引 (pulled) the string on this 弓 **yumi** (bow) at a **You**th **Mee**ting when I visited **Cu**ba

1045. 矢 PRONUNCIATION: ya
MEANING: arrow EXAMPLES: 矢 ya = arrow; 矢印 yajirushi = arrow (on a map or sign); 弓矢 yumiya = bow and arrow DESCRIPTION: this is an American Indian chief, as seen in 知(る) shiru (to know, # 323) CUE: this American Indian chief guards his **Ya**rd with 弓矢 yumi**ya** (a bow and arrows) COMPARE: 失(敗する) shippai suru = to lose, # 206

1046. 印 PRONUNCIATIONS: shirushi, jirushi[1], in MEANINGS: sign, seal, symbol

EXAMPLES: 印 shirushi = sign, symbol, indication; 矢印 yajirushi = arrow (on a map or sign); 印鑑 inkan = signature seal; 印象的 inshouteki = impressive DESCRIPTION: on the left, a ladder, as seen in (階)段 kaidan (stairs, # 559); on the right, this radical reportedly represents a signature seal used to stamp documents; the seal is located at the lower tip of the vertical line on the left, and the rest is a handle
CUES: a Shiite is Rushing up this ladder to an Internet cafe in order to look up the unusual 印 shirushi (symbol) that is used in this seal

1047. 季 PRONUNCIATION: ki

MEANINGS: season, a quarter of a year
EXAMPLES: 季節 kisetsu = season; 四季 shiki = the four seasons DESCRIPTION: at the top, 禾 (a grain plant with a ripe head); at the bottom, 子 ko (child, # 182)
CUE: the Key to remembering the 季節 kisetsu (seasons), is to associate 禾 (ripe grain) with autumn and 子 (children) with spring

1048. 節 PRONUNCIATIONS: setsu, sechi, fushi MEANINGS: section, holiday, occasion, joint, tune EXAMPLES: 季節 kisetsu = season; 関節 kansetsu = joint (e.g., knee); 節約する setsuyaku suru = to economize; お節料理 osechi ryouri = food served during the New Year's holidays; 節 fushi = knot (wood), joint (body), melody DESCRIPTION: at the top, 竹 take (bamboo, # 134); at the lower left, 良(い) yoi (good, # 303), without its pointy hat; at the lower right, this is the "seal" radical seen in 印 shirushi (sign, # 1046) CUES: we Set up a Super farm during the spring 季節 kisetsu (season) in order to grow 竹 (bamboo) like this to make 良 (good) seals like this one, and we also Sell Cheese so that we can buy Food for our Sheep
....

Chapter 56

1049. 修 PRONUNCIATIONS: osa, shuu, shu MEANINGS: to learn or master

EXAMPLES: 修める osameru = to learn or master; 修理 shuuri = repairs; 修行 shugyou = training, apprenticeship DESCRIPTION: on the left, a man with a slanted hat, with a fence post to his right; at the upper right, a dancer with a ponytail; at the lower right, a rocker-bottom shoe as seen in 参(る) mairu (to humbly come or go, # 406) CUES: Osama bin Laden wore this slanted hat, and he tried to recruit this dancer with 参 (rocker-bottom) Shoes for 修行 shugyou (training), but the dancer always kept this fence post between them and was prepared to Shoot him ALSO COMPARE: 悠(長) yuuchou = leisurely, # 985; 治(める) osameru = to govern or reign, # 539; 納(める) osameru = to put away or conclude, # 705; 収(める) osameru = to put away or conclude, # 1113

1050. 般 PRONUNCIATIONS: han, pan

MEANINGS: carrier, carry, all EXAMPLES: 般若 han'nya = prajna, wisdom, insight into the nature of reality (Buddhism); 一般的に ippanteki ni = commonly, generally, usually
DESCRIPTION: on the left, a boat, as seen in 船 fune (boat, # 602); on the right, π (the Greek letter pi, also known as a pious yak) on a table, as seen in 役 yaku (service, # 557)
CUES: Hansel 般的に ippanteki ni (usually) stores Pan (bread) on the top of the table in this leaky 船 (boat), but sometimes he keeps π (yaks) on it as well COMPARE: 投(げる) nageru = to throw, # 558; 没(頭) bottou = immersing oneself, # 806; 殺(す) korosu = to kill, # 838

1051. 壁 PRONUNCIATIONS: kabe, heki, peki[1] MEANINGS: wall, fence

EXAMPLES: 壁 kabe = wall; 壁画 hekiga = mural painting; 絶壁 zeppeki = cliff

DESCRIPTION: on the upper left, a lean-to with a double roof; inside the lean-to, 口 kuchi (mouth, # 426), which resembles a box; at the upper right, 辛(い) karai (spicy, # 384), which resembles a needle; at the bottom, 土 tsuchi (dirt, # 59)

CUES: I Called Ben Franklin and asked him to Help the King by inventing a 壁 kabe (wall) for the castle, and he came up with this design combining double-roofed lean-to's, 口 (boxes), 辛 (needles) and 土 (dirt)

1052. 編 PRONUNCIATIONS: hen, pen, a MEANINGS: to arrange, edit or knit

EXAMPLES: 編集 henshuu = editing; 短編 tanpen = short story or film; 編む amu = to knit

DESCRIPTION: on the left, 糸 (skeet shooter, # 219); at the upper right, a lean-to with a double roof, covered with a layer of snow; at the lower right, 冊 satsu (counter for books, # 568) CUES: this 糸 (skeet shooter) lives in this double-roofed lean-to on which there is often a layer of snow and works on 編集 henshuu (editing) a 冊 (book) about Hens that use Pens to make Art

1053. 評 PRONUNCIATION: hyou

MEANINGS: to comment EXAMPLES: 評判 hyouban = reputation, popularity, rumor; 評価 hyouka = assessment, evaluation; 不評 fu'hyou = bad reputation or review, unpopularity; 定評 teihyou = reputation, notoriety DESCRIPTION: on the left, 言(う) iu (to speak, # 430); on the right, 平(和) heiwa (peace, tranquility, # 885), which resembles a telephone pole that is on fire

CUE: the Lone Ranger has a good 評判 hyouban (reputation) in these parts, and when he heard that our telephone pole was on fire, he stopped by to 言 (say) "Hi-Yo Silver"

1054. 判 PRONUNCIATIONS: han, ban MEANINGS: to judge EXAMPLES:

判断する handan suru = to judge; 評判 hyouban = reputation, popularity, rumor

DESCRIPTION: on the left, 半 han (half, # 331), which helps us to pronounce this; on the right, the katakana リ ri CUES: Hansel says that when he went to a Banquet, he only received 半 (half) a serving, and he 判断した handan shita (judged) that リ Ri was responsible

1055. 猿 PRONUNCIATIONS: saru, zaru[1], en MEANINGS: monkey EXAMPLES:

猿 saru = monkey; 日本猿 nihonzaru = Japanese macaque; 類人猿 ruijin'en = ape

DESCRIPTION: on the left, a person contorting her body, as seen in 狭(い) semai (narrow, # 194); at the upper right, 土 tsuchi (dirt, # 59); at the middle right, 口 kuchi (mouth, # 426); at the lower right, エ and y CUES: this woman is contorting herself to support Saruman's scheme to train 猿 saru (monkeys) to work as Entertainers in Middle Earth, taking them out of the 土 (dirt) where they live, teaching them to do tricks with their 口 (mouths), and giving them names that start with エ and y, like Eric and Yolanda

1056. 芸 PRONUNCIATION: gei

MEANINGS: art, skill; artistic skill or technique

EXAMPLES: 芸 gei = art or craft, animal trick; 芸術 geijutsu = art; 芸術館 geijutsukan = art museum; 芸者 geisha = female entertainer DESCRIPTION: at the top, a plant radical; at the bottom, a bicycle with a basket, as seen in 伝(える) tsutaeru (to convey, # 345)

CUE: I'm playing a computer Game in which I try to fill the basket of this bike with plants like these and then 伝 (convey) them to as many 芸者 geisha (female entertainers) as possible
....

Chapter 57

1057. 虎 PRONUNCIATION: tora

MEANINGS: tiger EXAMPLES: 虎 tora = tiger
DESCRIPTION: at the upper left, a lean-to; at the top, a periscope for observing the outside world; under the roof, 七 shichi (seven, # 20); on the floor, two sturdy legs CUE: 七 (seven) people who live in a lean-to and observe the outside world through a periscope are holding **Tony Blair** for **Ra**nsom, and they sometimes dangle his sturdy legs out through a window to entice passing 虎 **tora** (tigers)

COMPARE: (謙)虚 kenkyo = modesty, # 966; 劇 geki = a play, # 1058; (捕)虜 horyo = captive, # 1107; (遠)慮 enryo = modesty, # 1194

1058. 劇 PRONUNCIATION: geki

MEANINGS: a drama, intensely EXAMPLES: 劇 geki = a play; 劇場 gekijou = a theater; 歌劇 kageki = opera DESCRIPTION: at the upper left, a lean-to; at the top, a periscope for observing the outside world; under the roof, 七 shichi (seven, # 20); on the floor, a radical seen in 家 ie (house, # 405), which is said to represent a pig CUE: 刂 Ri has a **Gue**st **Key** for this lean-to in which 七 (seven) people observe the world through a periscope, keep a 家 (pig) and enjoy going to the 劇場 **geki**jou (theater) COMPARE: 虎 tora = tiger, # 1057; (捕)虜 horyo = captive, # 1107; (遠)慮 enryo = modesty, # 1194

1059. 郷 PRONUNCIATIONS: sato, kyou, gou MEANINGS: hometown, village

EXAMPLES: 故郷 furusato = hometown, often written ふるさと, or ふる里, # 1060; 故郷 can also be pronounced kokyou; 郷里 kyouri = hometown; 水郷 suigou = riverside or lakeside location DESCRIPTION: on the left, a jagged lightning strike; in the middle, 良(い) yoi (good, # 303), without its pointy hat; on the right, ß beta from the Greek alphabet CUES: when my 良 (good) ß (Greek) friend saw this lightning hit a **S**atellite **T**ower in **Kyou**to, which is my 郷里 **kyou**ri (hometown), he was afraid to play **G**olf

1060. 里 PRONUNCIATIONS: sato, zato[1], ri MEANINGS: village, ri (approx 4 km)

EXAMPLES: 里 sato = hometown, village; ふる里 furusato = hometown, often written ふるさと or 故郷, # 1059; 人里 hitozato = human habitation; 郷里 kyouri = hometown DESCRIPTION: this is a sincere guy wearing bifocals, as seen in 野(菜) yasai (vegetable, # 545) CUES: this sincere guy admires a **S**atellite **T**ower in a 里 **sato** (village), which is covered in Christmas **W**reaths COMPARE: (児)童 jidou = child, # 1094; 甲(羅) koura = shell, # 1157

1061. 量 PRONUNCIATIONS: ryou, haka MEANINGS: mass, amount EXAMPLES:

量 ryou = quantity; 大量 tairyou = large amount; 量る hakaru = to weigh DESCRIPTION: at the top, 日 hi (sun, # 32); in the middle, a rug; at the bottom, 里 sato (hometown, # 1060), which reminds us of a sincere guy

CUES: **P**ope **Leo** is a sincere guy who visits his 里 (hometown) to **H**arvest **C**arnations, and when he has 大量 tai**ryou** (a large amount) he arranges them on this rug in the 日 (sun)

1062. 幹 PRONUNCIATIONS: miki, kan MEANINGS: trunk of a tree, main EXAMPLES:

幹 miki = tree trunk; 幹部 kanbu = an executive; 新幹線 shinkansen = bullet train

DESCRIPTION: on the left, the wagon seen in 朝 asa (morning, # 291); on the right, a telephone pole which is sheltered by a peaked roof CUES: **M**ickey Mouse lives in this wagon in **Can**ada next to a sheltered telephone pole, which was made from a 幹 **miki** (tree trunk)

1063. 央 PRONUNCIATION: ou
MEANINGS: center, middle EXAMPLES: 中央 chuu'ou = center, middle DESCRIPTION: this is a movie screen, as seen in 映(画) eiga (movie, # 36) CUE: I like to watch movies starring Oprah on this movie screen, and I sit in the 中央 chuuou (middle) of the theater

1064. 請 PRONUNCIATIONS: sei, ko
MEANINGS: solicit, invite, ask EXAMPLES: 請求 seikyuu = demand, request; 申請する shinsei suru = to apply for or request; 請う kou = to beg or ask; 請い求める koimotomeru = to beg or request DESCRIPTION: on the left, 言 (う) iu (to speak, # 430); on the right, 青(い) aoi (blue, # 155) CUES: a Sailor 言 (speaks) about his love for 青 (blue) skies, and he 請求する seikyuu suru (demands) an end to air pollution caused by Coal COMPARE: 精(神) seishin = mind, # 847, which helps us to pronounce this; 清(掃) seisou = cleaning, # 1112, which also helps us to pronounce this
··········

Chapter 58
1065. 老 PRONUNCIATIONS: o, rou, fu
MEANING: old EXAMPLES: 老いる o'iru = to grow old; 老人 roujin = elderly person; 老ける fukeru = to age or lose one's youthful appearance DESCRIPTION: compared to 者 mono (person, # 276), the 日 (sun) at the bottom has been replaced by the katakana ヒ hi, which reminds us of hearing loss CUES: this Old 者 (person) is a 老人 roujin (elderly person) who has ヒ (hearing loss) and employs Robots to prepare her Food

1066. 祉 PRONUNCIATION: shi
MEANINGS: welfare, happiness EXAMPLES: 福祉 fukushi = welfare DESCRIPTION: on the

left, the Shah, as seen in (会)社 kaisha (company, # 271); on the right, 止(める) tomeru (to stop, # 173) CUE: this Shah tried to 止 (stop) rustling activity in order to ensure the 福祉 fukushi (welfare) of his Sheep farmers

1067. 施 PRONUNCIATIONS: se, hodoko, shi
MEANINGS: give alms, apply bandages or first aid EXAMPLES: お布施 ofuse = alms or offerings (e.g., given to monks); 施す hodokosu = to donate, perform, give time; 施設 shisetsu = facility, institution, equipment; 実施する jisshi suru = to carry out or effect DESCRIPTION: on the left, 方 kata (honorable person, # 114); at the upper right, a crutch; at the lower right, a scorpion, as seen in 池 ike (pond, # 504) CUES: this 方 (honorable person) uses this crutch and has to use a Segway to get around, but she can Hold the Door for a Co-worker while he carries a Sheepdog that has been stung by this scorpion into a treatment 施設 shisetsu (facility)

1068. 設 PRONUNCIATIONS: se, mou, setsu
MEANINGS: to set up EXAMPLES: 設計 sekkei = design or plan; 設定する settei suru = to set up; 設ける moukeru = to set up; 設備 setsubi = equipment, facility; 施設 shisetsu = facility, institution, equipment DESCRIPTION: on the left, 言(う) iu (to speak, # 430); on the right, π (the Greek letter pi, also known as a pious yak), standing on 又 mata ("again,"# 24), which resembles a simple table CUES: a Settler named Moses 言 (says) that he will 設定する settei suru (set up) this 又 (table) and Set this Super π (yak) on it COMPARE: 役 yaku = role, service, # 557; 投(げる) nageru = to throw, # 558

1069. 療 PRONUNCIATION: ryou
MEANINGS: heal, cure EXAMPLE: 治療 chiryou = medical treatment DESCRIPTION: at

the upper left, a vertical bed as seen in 病(気) byouki (illness, # 369), with legs pointing to the left and a headboard at the top; just below the headboard, a wide 大(きい) ookii (big, # 188); at the lower right, the spinning 日 (sun) seen in 隙 suki (gap, # 879), emitting a somewhat different pattern of flames **CUE:** when Pope **Leo** is 病 (sick), he lies in this 大 (big) bed and undergoes chi**ryou** 治療 (medical treatment), consisting of heat therapy that is produced by this spinning 日 sun

ALSO COMPARE: 症(状) shoujou = symptoms, # 1085

1070. 与 PRONUNCIATIONS: ata, yo
MEANINGS: bestow, participate in, give, provide **EXAMPLES:** 与える ataeru = to give, award, cause; 賞与 shouyo = reward, bonus **DESCRIPTION:** this is a kangaroo, up to its calves in yogurt, as seen in 写(真) shashin (photograph, # 468), without its roof **CUES:** when I worked at the **At**ari company, I got a 賞与 shou**yo** (bonus) for taking a 写 (photograph) of this kangaroo standing in a pool of **Yo**gurt

1071. 州 PRONUNCIATIONS: su, shuu
MEANINGS: sandbank, large area, state (in the U.S.) **EXAMPLES:** 三角州 sankakusu = a delta; 九州 kyuushuu = Kyushu island; 本州 honshuu = Honshu island **DESCRIPTION:** three toboggans lined up **CUES:** Superman rode these three toboggans down a **Ch**ute in 本州 Hon**shuu**

1072. 孫 PRONUNCIATIONS: son, mago
MEANINGS: grandchild, offspring **EXAMPLES:** 孫 mago = grandchild; 孫娘 magomusume = granddaughter; 子孫 shison = descendant **DESCRIPTION:** on the left, 子 ko (child, # 182); on the right, a 糸 (skeet shooter, # 219) with a cape over his head, as seen in (関)係 kankei (relationship, # 492) **CUES:** this 子 (child) is the 孫 **mago** (grandchild) of this 糸 (skeet-shooter), with whom he has a good 係 (relationship),

and the skeetshooter waves this cape and sings a **S**ong when the child scores a **M**agnificent **G**oal
....

Chapter 59
1073. 遭 PRONUNCIATIONS: sou, a
MEANINGS: encounter, meet, association **EXAMPLES:** 遭難 sounan = accident, disaster; 遭う au = to be involved (in an accident, etc.), to get caught in **DESCRIPTION:** on the lower left, a snail; riding on the snail, 曲 kyoku (tunes, # 82) at the top and 日 hi (sun, # 32) at the bottom **CUES:** this snail uses 日 (**S**olar) power to listen to 曲 (tunes) as it travels, but sometimes it 遭う **a**u (gets involved) in **A**ccidents

1074. 昏 PRONUNCIATION: kon
MEANINGS: dark, evening **EXAMPLES:** 昏睡 konsui = coma, stupor **DESCRIPTION:** compared to (結)婚 kekkon (marriage, # 240), which helps us to pronounce this, the 女 (female) radical is missing, leaving a 紙 (paper) pavilion and the 日 (sun) **CUE:** after a 女 (female) from the **Con**go completed her 婚 (marriage), she fell into a 昏睡 **kon**sui (stupor) and disappeared, leaving an empty 紙 (paper) pavilion in this 日 (sun)

1075. 労 PRONUNCIATION: rou
MEANINGS: labor, reward for, toil, trouble **EXAMPLE:** 苦労 kurou = hardship **DESCRIPTION:** at the top, three old boys on a roof, as seen in 覚(える) oboeru (to memorize, # 54); at the bottom, 力 chikara (power, # 107) **CUE:** these three old boys go through a lot of 苦労 ku**rou** (hardship) as they train 力 (powerful) **R**obots on this roof

ALSO COMPARE: (非)常 hijou = emergency, # 683; 営業 eigyou = business, # 684 and # 332; (受)賞 jushou = winning (a prize), # 991

1076. 叶 PRONUNCIATION: kana

MEANINGS: grant, answer EXAMPLES: 叶える kanaeru = to grant or answer a request, to meet requirements; 叶う kanau = to come true or be fulfilled (referring to a wish or dream) DESCRIPTION: on the left, 口 kuchi (mouth, # 426); on the right, 十 juu (ten, # 18) CUE: I had to open my 口 (mouth) 十 (ten) times and beg before they 叶えた **kana**eta (granted) me **Cana**dian citizenship COMPARE: 計(る) hakaru = to measure, # 434

1077. 王 PRONUNCIATION: ou

MEANINGS: king, rule, jade EXAMPLES: 王様 ousama = king; 女王 jo'ou = queen; 王子 ouji = prince DESCRIPTION: compared to 主(人) shujin (master, # 166), this is missing its tiny cap CUE: when my **O**ld 主 (master) met the 王様 **ou**sama (king), he removed his tiny cap

1078. 妃 PRONUNCIATION: hi

MEANINGS: queen, princess EXAMPLES: 王妃 ouhi = queen DESCRIPTION: on the left, 女 onna (female, # 235); on the right, a snake CUE: a **He**ro saved an 王妃 ou**hi** (queen), who was a 女 (female), from this snake COMPARE: 姫 hime = princess, # 1040

1079. 宮 PRONUNCIATIONS: guu, kyuu, miya

MEANINGS: palace, prince EXAMPLES: 神宮 jinguu = high-status Shinto shrine, e.g., 平安神宮 Heian Jinguu, a shrine in Kyoto; 宮殿 kyuuden = palace; 子宮 shikyuu = uterus; お宮参り omiyamairi = shrine visit DESCRIPTION: at the top, a bad haircut; at the bottom, (風)呂 furo (bath, # 7) CUES: a **G**oofy **C**uban dictator with a bad haircut like this built a 宮殿 **kyuu**den (palace) with a 呂 (bath), where he planned to **M**eet **Y**ankees COMPARE: 営(業) eigyou = business, # 684

1080. 殿 PRONUNCIATIONS: den, tono

MEANINGS: lord, hall, mansion, temple EXAMPLES: 宮殿 kyuuden = palace; 殿様 tonosama = daimyo, feudal lord DESCRIPTION: on the upper left, a lean-to with a double roof; under the lean-to, 共(に) tomo ni (together, # 969); on the right, π (the Greek letter pi, also known as a pious yak), standing on 又 mata ("again,"# 24), which resembles a simple table CUES: a **Den**tist plans to enlarge this lean-to with a double roof until it's a 宮殿 kyuu**den** (palace) where she can live 共 (together) with her π (yak) on a 又 (table), and she says that this is all **T**otally **N**ormal
....

Chapter 60

1081. 崎 PRONUNCIATION: saki

MEANINGS: cape, promontory EXAMPLES: 川崎 Kawasaki = city in Japan; 長崎 Nagasaki = city in Japan DESCRIPTION: on the left, 山 yama (mountain, # 146; on the right, 奇(妙) kimyou (strange, # 854) CUE: I ate some **S**alty **Q**uiche on this 山 (mountain) overlooking 長崎 Naga**saki**, and then I felt 奇 (strange)

1082. 批 PRONUNCIATION: hi

MEANINGS: to disparage EXAMPLES: 批判 hihan = criticism; 批評 hihyou = review, remark, criticism DESCRIPTION: on the left, a kneeling guy; on the right, 比(べる) kuraberu (to compare, # 857) CUE: the kneeling guy on the left 比 (compares) **H**eroes and directs 批判 **hi**han (criticism) at the ones he finds lacking

1083. 摘 PRONUNCIATIONS: teki, tsu

MEANINGS: pinch, pick, pluck, clip EXAMPLES: 指摘 shiteki = pointing out, identification; 摘む tsumu = to pick tea, cotton, etc. DESCRIPTION: on the left, a kneeling person; on the right, a radical seen in 敵 teki (enemy, # 881), which helps us to pronounce this

CUES: this kneeling person 指摘する shi**teki** suru (points out) that her 敵 (enemy) is selling Terrible **Qui**che at his **Tsu**permarket (supermarket) **ALSO COMPARE:** 積(む) tsumu = to heap up, # 931

1084. 跳 PRONUNCIATIONS: ha, to

MEANINGS: hop, leap up, spring **EXAMPLES:** 跳ねる haneru = to jump or hop, to splash; 跳ぶ tobu = to jump or leap; 跳び箱 tobibako = a vaulting box **DESCRIPTION:** on the left, a square head on 正(しい) tadashii (correct, # 174), suggesting a correct gentleman, as seen in 踊(る) odoru (to dance, # 366); on the right, 兆 chou (trillion, # 849) **CUES:** this correct gentleman has 踊 (danced) with a 兆 (trillion) partners, including Prince **Harry** and **Tony** Blair, but he only knows how to 跳ねる **ha**neru (hop)

COMPARE: 飛(ぶ) tobu = to fly or skip, # 574

1085. 症 PRONUNCIATION: shou

MEANINGS: symptoms, illness **EXAMPLES:** 症状 shoujou = symptoms, condition of a patient; 感染症 kansenshou = infectious disease **DESCRIPTION:** at the upper left, a vertical bed as seen in 病(気) byouki (illness, # 369), with legs pointing to the left and a headboard at the top; below the headboard, 正(しい) tadashii (correct, # 174)

CUE: if you are in a 病 (sick) bed like this, the 正 (correct) thing to do is to **Show** a doctor a list of your 症状 **shou**jou (symptoms) **COMPARE:** (治)療 chiryou = medical treatment, # 1069

1086. 版 PRONUNCIATIONS: han, pan[1]

MEANINGS: printing block, edition **EXAMPLES:** 版画 hanga = woodblock print; 出版 shuppan = publication **DESCRIPTION:** on the left, 片(方) katahou (one side, # 181), which resembles a person kneeling and holding a tray with something on it; on the right, a large F over a smaller X, as seen in (ご)飯 gohan (cooked rice, # 400), which helps us to pronounce this

CUE: **Han**sel is kneeling on the left, showing Gretel a 版画 **han**ga (woodblock print) on this tray, but she gives it an F and marks it with an X

1087. 翻 PRONUNCIATION: hon

MEANINGS: flip, turn over, flutter, change (mind) **EXAMPLES:** 翻訳 hon'yaku = translation **DESCRIPTION:** on the left, 番 ban (number, # 328); on the right, 羽 hane (feather, # 755) **CUE:** a guy from **Hon**duras wrote a book saying that their birds' 羽 (feathers) are 番 (number) one, and he 翻訳した **hon**'yaku shita (translated) his book into English

1088. 著 PRONUNCIATIONS: cho, arawa, ichijiru MEANINGS: to write,
conspicuous, remarkable **EXAMPLES:** 著者 chosha = author; 著名 chomei = famous; 著す arawasu = to write or publish; 著しい ichijirushii = remarkable, conspicuous **DESCRIPTION:** at the top, a plant radical which could represent poison ivy; at the bottom, 者 mono (person, # 276)

CUES: Margaret **Cho** is a 者 (person) who is the 著者 **cho**sha (author) of a book which she was scheduled to discuss on TV, but her pants came into contact with this poison ivy plant and, although her **Ara**b friend **Wa**shed them, the **Itchy Jea**ns **Ru**ined her TV appearance

··········

Chapter 61

1089. 樹 PRONUNCIATIONS: ju, ki

MEANINGS: tree, to establish **EXAMPLES:** 樹木 jumoku = trees; 直樹 naoki = a man's given name **DESCRIPTION:** on the far left and the far right, 村 mura (village, # 131); inserted into this village are 士 shi (man, # 66) at the top and 豆 mame (bean, # 721), without the cloth over its head, at the bottom **CUES:** this 士 (man) is a **Ju**nior baker who makes **Qui**che with 豆 (beans) like this under 樹木 **ju**moku (trees) like these, and he has inserted himself into this 村 (village)

1090. 訓 PRONUNCIATION: **kun**
MEANINGS: lesson, Japanese (as opposed to Chinese) reading of kanji EXAMPLES: 訓練 kunren = training; 教訓 kyoukun = moral, teaching, lesson DESCRIPTION: on the left, 言(う) iu (to speak, # 430); on the right, 川 kawa (river, # 250) CUE: a **Cun**ning **Rent** collector was 言 (speaking) about the 訓練 **kun**ren (training) that he received when he worked along this 川 (river)

1091. 筆 PRONUNCIATIONS: **fude, hitsu, pitsu[1], hi** MEANING: writing brush EXAMPLES: 筆 fude = writing brush; 毛筆 mouhitsu = writing (painting) brush; 鉛筆 enpitsu = pencil; 筆者 hissha = writer
DESCRIPTION: at the top, 竹 take (bamboo, # 134); at the bottom, a vertical line with a three-fingered hand grasping it near the top, resembling the brush seen in 書(く) kaku (to write, # 415)
CUES: a **Fool**ish **D**ebutante grasps the 竹 (bamboo) handle at the top of this 筆 **fude** (brush), **Hits U** (you) with it and bruises your **Heel**

1092. 鉛 PRONUNCIATIONS: **namari, en** MEANING: lead (the element) EXAMPLES: 鉛 namari = lead; 鉛筆 enpitsu = lead pencil
DESCRIPTION: compared to 船 fune (boat, # 602), the leaky boat on the left has been replaced by 金 kane (money, # 301); on the right, this retains 八 hachi (eight, # 15) above 口 kuchi (mouth, # 426) which could represent eight guys working on a dock CUES: a **Na**rco named **Mari**o uses this 金 (money) to buy 鉛 **namari** (lead) for the bullets that he uses to **En**force discipline on the 八 (eight) guys who are working on this dock

1093. 児 PRONUNCIATIONS: **ni, go, ji** MEANING: very young child EXAMPLES: 小児科 shounika = pediatrics; 鹿児島 Kagoshima = a city in Kyushu; 児童 jidou = child;

孤児 koji = orphan DESCRIPTION: at the top, 旧(正月) kyuushougatsu (lunar New Year, # 1017), but the vertical line at the upper left may represent a golf club; at the bottom, a pair of sturdy legs, with a bad knee seen on the right CUES: this is a guy with a bad right **Knee** holding up a club on 旧 (lunar New Year) to salute a 児童 **ji**dou (child) who plays **G**olf like a **G**enius

1094. 童 PRONUNCIATION: **dou**
MEANING: child EXAMPLES: 児童 jidou = child; 童話 douwa = fairy tale
DESCRIPTION: at the top, 立(つ) tatsu (to stand, # 11); at the bottom, 里 sato (village, # 1060) CUE: a 児童 **ji**dou (child) 立 (stands) in this 里 (village), eating a **Dou**ghnut

1095. 奄 PRONUNCIATION: **ama**
MEANINGS: cover, obstruct EXAMPLE: 奄美大島 Amami Ooshima = an island between Kyushu and Okinawa DESCRIPTION: at the top, a wide 大(きい) ookii (big, # 188); at the bottom, the transformer seen in 電(気) denki (electricity, # 263) CUE: an **Ama**teur scientist makes 電 (electricity) using a 大 (big) kite during a storm on 奄美大島 **Ama**mi Ooshima (an island)

1096. 底 PRONUNCIATIONS: **soko, zoko[1], tei** MEANING: bottom EXAMPLES: 底 soko = bottom; 靴底 kutsuzoko = shoe sole; 海底 kaitei = bottom of the sea
DESCRIPTION: on the upper left, a lean-to with a chimney; inside the lean-to, a radical seen in (最)低 saitei (the worst, # 222), which helps us to pronounce this and resembles a 紙 (paper) pavilion taped to a rock CUES: after I **S**old my **C**oal for 低 (the worst) price, I hit 底 **soko** (bottom), and now I live in this paper pavilion **Ta**ped to a rock inside a lean-to

....

Chapter 62

1097. 径 PRONUNCIATION: kei

MEANING: narrow straight path EXAMPLES: 直径 chokkei = diameter; 半径 hankei = radius DESCRIPTION: on the left, a man with a double hat; on the right, 又 mata ("again," # 24), which resembles a dog groomer's table, above 土 tsuchi (dirt, # 59) CUE: this man with a double hat is a dog groomer who keeps dogs in Cages with narrow 直径 chokkei (diameters) when he isn't grooming them on this 又 (table) on 土 (dirt)

COMPARE: 経(験) keiken = experience, # 224, which helps us to pronounce this

1098. 種 PRONUNCIATIONS: tane, shu

MEANINGS: seed, kind EXAMPLES: 種 tane = seed; 種類 shurui = kind, type; 人種 jinshu = race of people; 一種の isshu no = a kind of, a type of DESCRIPTION: on the left, 禾 (a grain plant with a ripe head); on the right, 重(い) omoi (heavy, # 284) CUES: in order to grow 重 (heavy) 禾 (ripe grain) like this, I store 種 tane (seeds) in Tan Eggshells and Shoot them over my fields

1099. 酎 PRONUNCIATION: chuu

MEANING: sake EXAMPLES: 焼酎 shouchuu = a Japanese spirit distilled from sweet potatoes, rice, etc. DESCRIPTION: on the left, the radical seen in 酒 sake (# 465); on the right, the kneeling guy seen in 付(く) tsuku (to adhere, # 132), who has dropped a piece of gum on the ground CUE: this kneeling guy on the right was drinking this 酒 (sake) while Chewing this gum, but after he started drinking 焼酎 shouchuu (Japanese liquor) as well, he dropped the gum on the ground

1100. 沢 PRONUNCIATIONS: sawa, zawa[1], taku MEANING: swamp EXAMPLES:

沢村 Sawamura = a family name; 金沢 Kanazawa = a city in Honshu; 光沢 koutaku = luster; 沢山 takusan = many or much (usually written たくさん) DESCRIPTION: on the left, a water radical; on the right, the wakeful eye seen in 訳 wake (reason, # 437) CUES: this wakeful eye Saw this Water, and it reminded him of the 沢山 takusan (many) 訳 (reasons) that he likes to use Tap water to make Kool-Aid

1101. 蒸 PRONUNCIATIONS: jou, mu

MEANING: steam EXAMPLES: 蒸気 jouki = vapor, steam; 蒸発 jouhatsu = evaporation; 蒸す musu = to steam, to be hot and humid; 蒸し暑い mushiatsui = hot and humid DESCRIPTION: in the top row, a plant radical; in the middle row, on the left, the katakana フ fu, which reminds us of Food; in the center, 子 ko (child, # 182); on the right, the letter y which reminds us of yams; at the bottom, a fire CUES: when Joan of Arc was in the Mood to eat yams, which are a plant Food, she would ask this 子 (child) to help her 蒸す musu (steam) them over this fire

1102. 芋 PRONUNCIATION: imo

MEANING: potato EXAMPLES: 芋 imo = potato; じゃが芋 jagaimo = Irish potato (usually written ジャガイモ) DESCRIPTION: at the top, a plant radical; at the bottom, the axis seen in the center of 余(り) amari (surplus, # 637), which resembles a barbed nail, without its peaked roof and skirts

CUE: 芋 imo (potatoes) come from plants like this, and when I pierce them with nails like this before baking them, I experience positive Emotions

1103. 麦 PRONUNCIATIONS: **baku,** *ba,* **mugi** MEANING: barley plant EXAMPLES: 麦芽 bakuga = malt; 蕎麦屋 sobaya = a soba restaurant; 麦 mugi = barley, wheat; 小麦 komugi = wheat; 小麦粉 komugiko = wheat flour DESCRIPTION: at the top, an owl's perch, as seen in 青(い) aoi (blue, # 155); at the bottom, a dancer with a ponytail CUES: this dancer is a **B**armaid who drinks **K**ool-Aid, as well as beer made from 麦 **mugi** (barley), and when she carries this owl's perch into the **B**ar, we have to **M**ove our **G**ear

1104. 粉 PRONUNCIATIONS: **kona, ko, fun** MEANING: flour EXAMPLES: 粉 kona = flour, powder; 小麦粉 komugiko = wheat flour; 花粉 kafun = pollen DESCRIPTION: on the left, 米 kome (uncooked rice, # 326); on the right, 分(ける) wakeru (to split or divide, # 105) CUES: **Con**an O'Brien takes this 米 (uncooked rice) and 分 (divides) it into 粉 **kona** (flour), which he spills onto his **Co**at while trying to be **Fun**ny

....

Chapter 63

1105. 農 PRONUNCIATION: **nou** MEANINGS: agricultural, farming EXAMPLES: 農業 nougyou = agriculture; 農家 nouka = farmer, farmhouse; 農夫 noufu = farmer DESCRIPTION: at the top, 曲 kyoku (song, # 82); below that, a lean-to; at the lower right, the katakana エ e and the letter y are supporting a pencil on a platform CUE: エ and y are 農家 **nou**ka (farmers) who work in this lean-to, and they sing 曲 (songs) as they use pencils to take **N**otes about their crops

1106. 濃 PRONUNCIATIONS: **ko, nou** MEANINGS: dark, strong EXAMPLES: 濃い koi = dark, thick, strong, dense; 濃度 noudo = concentration DESCRIPTION: on the left, a water radical; on the right, 農(家) nouka (farmer, # 1105), which helps us to pronounce this CUES: this 農 (farmer) is growing **Co**rn, and when he adds water like this to his crops, he **N**otices that the dirt in the fields becomes 濃い **ko**i (dark)

1107. 虜 PRONUNCIATIONS: **toriko, ryo** MEANINGS: captive, barbarian EXAMPLES: 虜 toriko = captive, prisoner; 捕虜 horyo = prisoner of war, captive DESCRIPTION: at the upper left, a lean-to; at the top, a periscope for observing the outside world; under the roof, 七 shichi (seven, # 20); on the floor, 男 otoko (male, # 109)

CUES: the 七 (seven) **T**ory **Co**rporals who live in this lean-to with a periscope have captured this 男 (male) 虜 **toriko** (prisoner of war) named Pope **Leo** ALSO COMPARE: (謙)虚 kenkyo = modesty, # 966; 虎 tora = tiger, # 1057; 劇 geki = a play, # 1058; (遠)慮 enryo = modesty or reserve, # 1194, which helps us to pronounce this

1108. 造 PRONUNCIATIONS: **tsuku, zou** MEANINGS: to create EXAMPLES: 造り tsukuri = structure (usually written 作り); 造り酒屋 tsukurizakaya = a sake brewery; 造る tsukuru = to create or make (usually written 作る); 製造 seizou = manufacture, production; 改造 kaizou = remodeling DESCRIPTION: on the lower left, a snail; on the snail, (報)告 houkoku (report, # 429), which resembles a person holding out a shield to the left while standing on a 口 (box) CUES: this person is standing on a 口 (box) which represents a **Tsu**itcase (suitcase) of **K**ool-Aid and holding out a shield as he travels on this snail to the Canal **Z**one, where he plans to file a 告 (report) about his plans to 製造する sei**zou** suru (manufacture) shields like this one

1109. 募 PRONUNCIATIONS: tsuno, bo

MEANINGS: recruit, campaign, gather (contributions), grow violent **EXAMPLES:**
募る tsunoru = to advertise, recruit, intensify;
応募 oubo = application, subscription
DESCRIPTION: at the top, a plant radical; below that, 日 hi (sun, # 32); below that, a wide 大(きい) ookii (big, # 188); at the bottom, 力 chikara (force, # 107) **CUES:** this is a poster designed to 募る **tsuno**ru (recruit) **Ts**uperior (superior) **N**orwegians for a **Bo**at trip to a land where the plants are 大 (big), 日 (sun) light is abundant, and the 力 (force) is strong **COMPARE:**
暮(らす) kurasu = to make a living, # 641, in which 力 (force) is replaced by a second 日 (sun); 幕 maku = theater curtain, # 653, in which 力 (force) is replaced by Bo Peep

1110. 催 PRONUNCIATIONS: moyo'o, sai

MEANINGS: sponsor, hold (a meeting or dinner) **EXAMPLES:** 催す moyo'osu = to hold an event; 催し moyo'oshi = an event or meeting; 開催する kaisai suru = to hold a meeting or open an exhibition **DESCRIPTION:** on the left, a man with a slanted hat; at the upper right, 山 yama (mountain, # 146); at the lower right, a cage, suggesting a zoo **CUES:** this man with a slanted hat will 催す **moyo'o**su (hold) a convention of zookeepers under this 山 (mountain), and he will ask a **Mo**tormouth **Y**ogi to **O**pen the ceremonies and demonstrate **Sci**entifically designed cages like this one

1111. 跡 PRONUNCIATIONS: seki, ato

MEANINGS: tracks, mark, impression
EXAMPLES: 奇跡 kiseki = miracle, wonder, marvel; 跡 ato = trace, track, ruin
DESCRIPTION: on the left, a square head on 正(しい) tadashii (correct, # 174) which suggests a correct gentleman, as seen in 踊(る) odoru (to dance, # 366); on the right, this resembles 赤(い) akai (red, # 447), but 土 (dirt) at the top has been replaced by a tire stop, as seen in (絶)対 zettai (absolutely, # 674)
CUES: this correct gentleman on the left is trying to **Sell Qui**che near this tire stop, but he uses **A**rtificial **T**omatoes in his recipe, and their 赤 (red) color leaves an 跡 **ato** (trace) in the food
COMPARE: 跳(ぶ) tobu = to jump, # 1084

1112. 清 PRONUNCIATIONS: sei, kiyo

MEANINGS: pure, clean **EXAMPLES:** 清掃 seisou = cleaning; 清算 seisan = adjustment (financial); 清い kiyoi = clear, pure; 清らかな kiyoraka na = clean, pure, chaste; 清める kiyomeru = to purify or cleanse; 清水 kiyomizu = spring water, pure water **DESCRIPTION:** on the left, a water radical; on the right, 青(い) aoi (blue, # 155) **CUES:** this 清い **kiyo**i (pure) water, which we bought at a **Saf**eway store, comes in a 青 (blue) bottle, and we will use it to make the **King's Y**ogurt **COMPARE:** 精(神) seishin = mind, # 847, which helps us to pronounce this; 請(求) seikyuu = demand, # 1064, which also helps us to pronounce this

....

Chapter 64

1113. 収 PRONUNCIATIONS: osa, shuu

MEANINGS: to collect or store **EXAMPLES:**
収める osameru = to put away in a closet, conclude, pay a bill (this can also be written 納める, # 705); 回収する kaishuu suru = to recover, recall, collect (bills or garbage); 収入 shuunyuu = income **DESCRIPTION:** on the left, this resembles the number 4; on the right, 又 mata (again, # 24), which resembles a simple table
CUES: because his 収入 **shuu**nyuu (income) was high, **Osa**ma bought 4 又 (tables) on which to store his **Sho**es
ALSO COMPARE: 治(める) osameru = to govern, # 539; 修(める) osameru = to learn or master, # 1049; 叫(ぶ) sakebu = to shout, # 746

1114. 拭 PRONUNCIATIONS: nugu, fu

MEANINGS: to wipe, mop, swab **EXAMPLES:**
拭う nuguu = to wipe; 拭く fuku = to wipe or
mop **DESCRIPTION:** on the left, a kneeling guy;
on the right, 式 shiki (ceremony, # 249)
CUES: a **Neu**tered **Goo**se scattered **F**ood on the
floor just before a 式 (ceremony), and this kneeling
guy had to 拭く **fu**ku (wipe) it up

1115. 賛 PRONUNCIATION: san

MEANINGS: to assist or praise **EXAMPLES:**
賛成 sansei = agreement; 絶賛する zessan
suru = to praise highly **DESCRIPTION:** compared
to 替(える) kaeru (to exchange money, # 551),
the two 夫 otto (husbands, # 614) remain at the top,
but the 日 (sun) at the bottom has been replaced by
貝 kai (shell, or three-drawer money chest, # 83)
CUE: these two 夫 (husbands) 賛成する
sansei suru (agree) to use the money from this 貝
(money chest) to buy **Sand**wiches

1116. 型 PRONUNCIATIONS: kata,

gata[1], kei **MEANINGS:** mold, pattern
EXAMPLES: 型 kata = form (e.g., dance), posture,
style; 髪型 kamigata = hair style (this can also be
written 髪形); 典型的な tenkeiteki na =
typical **DESCRIPTION:** at the upper left, a tower
representing a catapult, as seen in 形 katachi (shape,
573); at the upper right, the katakana リ ri; at the
bottom, 土 tsuchi (dirt, # 59)
CUES: リ Ri uses this **C**atapult on the upper left to
send **C**ake to prisoners who are being held in this
土 (dirt), and she always insists on using proper 型
kata (form) when doing so

1117. 典 PRONUNCIATION: ten

MEANINGS: law, code **EXAMPLES:**
百科事典 hyakkajiten = encyclopedia; 典型
的な tenkeiteki na = typical; 古典 koten =
classical work, classic **DESCRIPTION:** 曲 kyoku
(tune, # 82) on a two-legged table

CUE: we keep CD's of 古典の ko**ten** no
(classical) 曲 (tunes) on this two-legged table and
listen to them while we play **Ten**nis

1118. 侍 PRONUNCIATION: samurai

MEANINGS: samurai, waiter, to serve
EXAMPLES: 侍 samurai = Japanese warrior
DESCRIPTION: compared to 待(つ) matsu (to
wait, # 217), the man with two slanted hats waiting
outside a temple has been replaced by a man with
only a single slanted hat
CUE: this man with a single slanted hat is **S**ad
because a **M**oonie took his **R**ice and one of his hats
and gave them to a 侍 **samurai** (Japanese warrior)

1119. 洪 PRONUNCIATION: kou

MEANINGS: deluge, flood **EXAMPLES:** 洪水
kouzui = flood **DESCRIPTION:** on the left, a
water radical, which suggests a flood; on the right,
共(に) tomo ni (together, # 969), which represents
two bushes balanced on a dome **CUE:** due to a
洪水 **kou**zui (flood) in **C**olombia, we had to climb
up onto this dome 共 (together) and find shelter in
these bushes **ALSO COMPARE:** (子)供
kodomo = child, # 486

1120. 遇 PRONUNCIATION: guu

MEANINGS: treat, entertain, encounter (e.g., an
accident) **EXAMPLES:** 遭遇する souguu
suru = to encounter; 待遇 taiguu = treatment (of
customer), salary and benefits **DESCRIPTION:** at
the lower left, a snail; at the upper right, a radical
seen in 隅 sumi (inside corner, # 79) which depicts
the roots of a 田 (rice paddy) growing more
vigorously on the right side of its pot
CUE: a **Goo**se 遭遇した sou**guu** shita
(encountered) this 田 (rice paddy) in a pot on a
snail, and it ate the snail
....

Chapter 65

1121. 妓 PRONUNCIATION: ko

MEANINGS: singing girl, geisha **EXAMPLES:**
舞妓 maiko = an apprentice geisha, a dancing girl;

芸妓 geiko = 芸者 geisha **DESCRIPTION:** on the left, 女 onna (female, # 235); on the right, 支(社) shisha (branch office, # 26) **CUE:** the 女 (female) who was drinking **C**ola at the 支 (branch office) was a 舞妓 mai**ko** (apprentice geisha) **ALSO COMPARE:** 技(術) gijutsu = skill, # 1133

1122. 誕 PRONUNCIATION: tan

MEANINGS: to be born **EXAMPLES:** 誕生 する tanjou suru = to be born; 誕生日 tanjoubi = birthday **DESCRIPTION:** on the left, 言(う) iu (to speak, # 430); on the right, 延(期) enki (postponement, # 842) **CUE:** a soldier was scheduled to 言 (speak) at my 誕生日 **tan**joubi (birthday) party, but we had to 延 (postpone) the speech because his **Tan**k broke down

1123. 称 PRONUNCIATION: shou

MEANINGS: name, title, admire, fame **EXAMPLES:** 対称 taishou = symmetry; 対称的な taishouteki na = symmetrical; 通称 tsuushou = a nickname or alias **DESCRIPTION:** on the left, 禾 (a grain plant with a ripe head); on the right, a crutch above 小(さい) chiisai (small, # 253) suggesting a handicapped guy who is small **CUE:** the handicapped guy on the right, who is 小 (small) and whose 通称 tsuu**shou** (alias) is **Sho**rty, is celebrating the harvest of this 禾 (ripe grain)

1124. 列 PRONUNCIATIONS: retsu, re

MEANINGS: line, row **EXAMPLES:** 列 retsu = line; 配列 hairetsu = arrangement, disposition; 列車 ressha = train **DESCRIPTION:** on the left, 夕 yuu (evening, # 160), wearing a flat hat; on the right, the katakana リ ri **CUES:** wearing a **Re**tro **Su**it and a flat hat, リ **R**i went out one 夕 (evening)

and stood in 列 **retsu** (line) at a **R**estaurant **COMPARE:** 死(ぬ) shinu = to die, # 164

1125. 統 PRONUNCIATION: tou

MEANINGS: to unify, ruling **EXAMPLES:** 統一 tou'itsu = standardization, unification; 統計 toukei = statistics; 大統領 daitouryou = president of a country **DESCRIPTION:** on the left, 糸 skeet shooter (# 219); at the upper right, a pedaling leg, as seen in 流(す) nagasu (to flush, # 654); at the lower right, a pair of sturdy legs **CUE:** our 大統領 dai**tou**ryou (president) was pedaling a bike with these sturdy legs when this 糸 (skeet shooter) started shooting **T**omatoes at him

1126. 領 PRONUNCIATION: ryou

MEANINGS: head, chief, domain **EXAMPLES:** 領土 ryoudo = territory; 領収書 ryoushuusho = receipt; 大統領 daitouryou = president of a country **DESCRIPTION:** on the left, a house with a peaked roof containing a shaky table with an extra-long leg, as seen in 冷(たい) tsumetai (cold, # 299); on the right, 貝 kai (shell, money chest, # 83) with a platform at the top where a head could fit, as seen in 頭 atama (head, # 93) **CUE:** Pope **Le**o is missing his 頭 (head), and he is living in this 冷 (cold) house with a shaky table while he waits for the 大統領 daitou**ryou** (president) to find it

1127. 慢 PRONUNCIATION: man

MEANINGS: ridicule, laziness **EXAMPLES:** 自慢 jiman = pride, boast; 我慢 gaman = patience, endurance **DESCRIPTION:** on the left, an erect man; at the upper right, 日 hi (sun, # 32); at the middle right, 目 me (eye, # 51), turned on its side, resembling three eyes; at the lower right, 又 mata ("again," # 24), which resembles a simple table **CUE:** this erect man on the left stands near this 又 (table) in **Man**hattan and 自慢する ji**man** suru (boasts) about his three 目 (eyes) which are never bothered by this 日 (sun)

1128. 嵐 PRONUNCIATION: **arashi**

MEANINGS: storm, tempest EXAMPLES: 嵐 arashi = storm DESCRIPTION: at the top, 山 yama (mountain, # 146); at the bottom, 風 kaze (wind, # 479) CUE: an **Ar**ab who is a **Shi**ite visited this 山 (mountain), and was caught in an 嵐 **arashi** (storm) with strong 風 (winds)

....

Chapter 66

1129. 幻 PRONUNCIATIONS: **gen, maboroshi** MEANINGS: apparition, vision, dream EXAMPLES: 幻想 gensou = fantasy, illusion; 幻覚 genkaku = hallucination; 幻 maboroshi = illusion, vision DESCRIPTION: on the left, this is a 糸 (skeet shooter, # 219) without its legs; on the right, the katakana フ fu, which looks like an oar CUE: **Gen**ghis Khan told a **Mar**iner to get into a **Bo**at and **Row** a **Sheep** across a lake, using this フ (oar), and while he was doing so, the mariner saw this 幻想 **gen**sou (illusion) of a 糸 (skeetshooter) without legs

1130. 坂 PRONUNCIATIONS: **saka, zaka**[1] MEANINGS: slope, incline EXAMPLES: 坂 saka = slope, hill; 下り坂 kudarizaka = downward slope DESCRIPTION: on the left, 土 tsuchi (dirt, # 59); on the right, an F over an X CUE: making us play **Sakkaa** (soccer) on 土 (dirt) like this is OK, but you get an **F** and an **X** for making us play on a steep 坂 **saka** (slope)

COMPARE: (大)阪 oosaka = city in Japan, large hill, # 1005, which helps us to pronounce this

1131. 級 PRONUNCIATION: **kyuu**

MEANINGS: order, class EXAMPLES: 高級 koukyuu = high class or quality; 同級生 doukyuusei = classmate; 等級 toukyuu = grade, ranking DESCRIPTION: on the left, 糸 skeet shooter (# 219); on the right, a graph of breathing patterns, as seen in 吸(収する) kyuushuu suru (to digest, # 427), which helps us to pronounce this CUE: this 糸 (skeet shooter) is examining the breathing patterns of a **Cute** baby, which it thinks will grow up to be a 高級 kou**kyuu** (high class) person ALSO COMPARE: (普)及(する) fukyuu suru = to become popular, # 883, which also helps us to pronounce this

1132. 等 PRONUNCIATIONS: **tou, dou, hito, nado** MEANINGS: equal, equivalent, etcetera EXAMPLES: 上等 joutou = excellent, very good; 平等 byoudou = equal; 等しい hitoshii = same, equal; 等々 nadonado = etcetera DESCRIPTION: at the top, 竹 take (bamboo, # 134); at the bottom, 寺 tera (temple, # 213) CUES: the two 竹 (bamboo) clamps at the top of this 寺 (temple) indicate that it has earned a ranking of 二等 ni**tou** (2nd place) for the bamboo **Toys** it sells, including small statues of **Do**es and **Hito** (people), but it also sells **Na**sty **Dou**ghnuts, and overall it is about 等しい **hito**shii (equal) to other temples

1133. 技 PRONUNCIATIONS: **waza, gi**

MEANINGS: skill, work, deed EXAMPLES: 技 waza = skill, technique; 技術 gijutsu = technology, technique, skill; 競技 kyougi = competition DESCRIPTION: on the left, a kneeling guy; on the right, 支(社) shisha (branch office, # 26) CUES: when a **Wa**tercooler got **Za**pped by a power surge at our 支 (branch office) we asked this **Geek** to get down on his knees and fix it, since he has 技術 **gi**jutsu (skill) in repairing things

ALSO COMPARE: 枝 eda = branch, # 128; (舞)妓 maiko = apprentice geisha, # 1121

1134. 房 PRONUNCIATIONS: **bou, fusa** MEANINGS: bunch, house, room EXAMPLES: 暖房 danbou = heating, heater; 冷房 reibou = air conditioning; 女房 nyoubou = one's wife; 房 fusa = a bunch, cluster, tassel DESCRIPTION: on the upper left, a lean-to with a double roof and a layer of snow on top, as seen in 戻(る) modoru (to return, # 75); inside the lean-to, 方 kata (honorable person, # 114) **CUES:** in winter, this 方 (honorable person) lives a **Bo**ring life in this lean-to with a double roof and a layer of snow on top, heated by a single 暖房 dan**bou** (heater), and his only **Foo**d is **S**ardines

1135. 粒 PRONUNCIATIONS: tsubu, ryuu MEANINGS: a grain or drop EXAMPLES:

粒 tsubu = grains, drops, counter for tiny particles; 雨粒 amatsubu = raindrop; 粒子 ryuushi = a particle or grain **DESCRIPTION:** on the left, 米 kome (uncooked rice, # 326); on the right, 立(つ) tatsu (to stand, # 11)
CUES: we were 立 (standing) in a 米 (rice) field when I noticed 雨粒 ama**tsubu** (rain drops) collecting on my **Tsu**pervisor's (supervisor's) **Boo**ts, and I realized that we could **Reu**se that water

1136. 眺 PRONUNCIATIONS: naga, chou MEANINGS: watch, look at, see

EXAMPLES: 眺める nagameru = to gaze or look at; 眺め nagame = a view; 眺望 choubou = a view **DESCRIPTION:** on the left, 目 me (eye, # 51); on the right, 兆 chou (trillion, # 849), which helps us to pronounce this **CUES: Naga**ina (a snake from a Kipling story) uses her 目 (eyes) to survey the 眺め **naga**me (view) in front of her, as she ima-gines that there are a 兆 (trillion) mice out there and that her primary **Cho**re is to catch them **ALSO COMPARE:** 逃(げる) nigeru = to run away, # 850; 挑(戦する) chousen suru = to challenge, # 1001, which also helps us to pronounce this

....

Chapter 67
1137. 秒 PRONUNCIATION: byou

MEANINGS: tiny, second **EXAMPLES:** 一秒 ichibyou = a second (1/60 minute); 秒針

byoushin = the second hand on a clock **DESCRIPTION:** on the left, 禾 (a grain plant with a ripe head); on the right, 少(し) sukoshi (a little, # 254) **CUE:** a **B**ee **O**wner gets 少 (a little) pleasure from watching his bees fly among heads of 禾 (ripe grain) like this one, and he sees a bee fly past every 秒 **byou** (second)

1138. 針 PRONUNCIATIONS: hari, shin

MEANINGS: needle **EXAMPLES:** 針 hari = needle; 方針 houshin = policy, principle, direction; 秒針 byoushin = the second hand on a clock
DESCRIPTION: on the left, (黄)金 ougon (gold, # 301); on the right, 十 too (ten, # 18)
CUE: Prince **Har**ry received 十 (ten) 金 (golden) 針 **hari** (needles) from a **Shin**to priest

1139. 効 PRONUNCIATIONS: ki, kou
MEANINGS: having an effect **EXAMPLES:** 効く kiku = to be effective; 効果 kouka = effect; 効力 kouryoku = an effect
DESCRIPTION: on the left, 交(通) koutsuu (traffic, # 144), which helps us to pronounce this; on the right, 力 chikara (force, # 107)
CUES: the threat of 力 (force) is the **K**ey to 交 (traffic) code enforcement in **Ko**rea, and it 良く 効く yoku **ki**ku (has a good effect)

1140. 免 PRONUNCIATIONS: men, manuga MEANINGS: excuse, dismissal
EXAMPLES: 免許 menkyo = license; 免除 menjo = exemption; 免状 menjou = diploma, license; 免疫 men'eki = immunity; 免れる manugareru = to be exempted from, to avoid
DESCRIPTION: this is the octopus seen in 勉(強) benkyou (study, # 474), with a fish head at the top and two tentacles at the bottom
CUES: this octopus knows that 勉 (studying) is all **Men**tal, and after receiving his 免状 **men**jou (diploma), he will **Ma**nage a **N**ew **Ga**s station

1141. 許 PRONUNCIATIONS: yuru, kyo
MEANINGS: excuse, dismissal **EXAMPLES:**
許す yurusu = to forgive, accept, permit; 免許
menkyo = license; 許可 kyoka = permission,
approval **DESCRIPTION:** on the left, 言(う) iu
(to speak, # 430); on the right, 午 go (noon, # 207)
CUES: You Ruined the class at **Kyo**to University
when you 言 (said) that everyone had 許可
kyoka (permission) to show up at 午 (noon)

1142. 疫 PRONUNCIATION: eki
MEANINGS: epidemic **EXAMPLES:** 疫病
ekibyou = plague, epidemic; 免疫 men'eki =
immunity **DESCRIPTION:** on the upper left, a bed
with a headboard, as seen in 病(気) byouki (sick,
369); in the bed, π (the Greek letter pi, also known
as a pious yak) on 又 mata ("again,"# 24, which
resembles a simple table) **CUE:** this π (yak) on a
table was 病 (sick) in this bed during an
疫病 **eki**byou (epidemic), but he was healed by an
Excellent **K**ing **ALSO COMPARE:** 役(に立
つ) yaku ni tatsu = to make use of, # 557

1143. 樋 PRONUNCIATIONS: hi, doi
MEANINGS: water pipe, gutter **EXAMPLES:**
樋口 Higuchi = family name; 雨樋 amadoi =
rain gutter **DESCRIPTION:** on the left, 木 ki
(tree, # 118); on the right, 通(る) tooru (to pass
through, # 365), which resembles a マ (mammoth)
on a fence on top of a snail **CUES:** this snail is 通
(passing through) an 雨樋 ama**doi** (gutter) as it
carries this マ (mammoth) on a 用 (fence) past this
木 (tree), and the reason that it can't **H**ear us is that
it has **Doi**lies stuffed into its ears

1144. 箸 PRONUNCIATIONS: hashi,
bashi[1] MEANINGS: chopsticks **EXAMPLES:**
箸 hashi = chopsticks; 割り箸 waribashi =
splittable (disposable) chopsticks

DESCRIPTION: at the top, 竹 take (bamboo,
134); at the bottom, 者 mono (person, # 276)
CUE: this 者 (person) eats **Hash** made with **E**els
using 竹 (bamboo) 箸 **hashi** (chopsticks)
··········

Chapter 68

1145. 志 PRONUNCIATIONS: kokoroza,
kokorozashi, shi MEANINGS: will, aspiration
EXAMPLES: 志 kokoroza = kokorozashi =
ambition, wish, goal; 志望 shibou = ambition,
wish, goal **DESCRIPTION:** at the top, 士 shi
(gentleman, # 66), which helps us to pronounce this;
at the bottom, 心 kokoro (heart, # 306), which also
helps us to pronounce this
CUE: this 士 (man) has his 心 **Kokoro** (heart) set
on **Za**mbia, and in particular he has his **Kokoro** set
on **Za**mbian **Sh**eep, since his 志望 **shi**bou
(ambition) is to sell **Sh**eets made from Zambian wool

1146. 軒 PRONUNCIATIONS: ken, noki
MEANINGS: flats, eaves, counter for houses
EXAMPLES: 一軒 ikken = one house; 軒 noki
= eaves **DESCRIPTION:** on the left, 車 kuruma
(car, # 283); on the right, a telephone pole
CUES: Senator **Ken**nedy parked this 車 (car) next
to this telephone pole while he was visiting 一軒
ik**ken** (one house), but he had **No Key**

1147. 激 PRONUNCIATIONS: hage,
geki MEANINGS: intense, agitated, violent
EXAMPLES: 激しい hageshii = fierce,
tempestuous, crowded (traffic), frequent (change);
激減 gekigen = sharp decrease; 過激な kageki
na = aggressive, radical; 激戦 gekisen = fierce
competition or battle **DESCRIPTION:** on the left,
a water radical; at the upper middle, 白(い) shiroi
(white, # 44); at the lower middle, 方 kata
(honorable person, # 114); on the right, a dancer with
a ponytail **CUES:** when we lived in a 白 (white)
house by this water, we had a 過激 ka**geki**
(aggressive) **Ha**waiian **Gue**st who was a dancer and

who we thought was an 方 (honorable person), but the **Gue**st stole our **Key**s

1148. 減 PRONUNCIATIONS: gen, he

MEANINGS: to reduce **EXAMPLES:** 激減 gekigen = sharp decrease; 減少 genshou = a decrease; 加減する kagen suru = to moderate, downgrade; 半減する hangen suru = to reduce by half; 減る heru = to reduce, lose (weight) **DESCRIPTION:** compared to 感(じる) kanjiru (to feel, # 640), this adds a water radical on the left, and it subtracts 心 (heart) from the bottom; it retains the lean-to, the 口 (mouth) with a piece of tape over it, and the halberd on the right **CUES: Gen**ghis imagined **Hell** as a lean-to like this by the water, with tape covering his mouth which would force him to 減る **he**ru (lose) weight while being guarded by halberds **ALSO COMPARE:** (絶)滅 zetsumetsu = extinction, # 1193, which replaces 口 (mouth) with 火 (fire)

1149. 処 PRONUNCIATIONS: dokoro, sho MEANINGS: deal with EXAMPLES:

お食事処 oshokujidokoro = restaurant (Japanese style); 処理する shori suru= to deal with, handle, eliminate; 対処する taisho suru = to deal with; 処分 shobun = disposal, expulsion, punishment **DESCRIPTION:** on the left, a dancer with a ponytail and a long right leg; on the dancer's right leg, a tall desk, as seen in 机 tsukue (desk, # 140 **CUES:** a **D**oorman's **Coro**lla hit this desk causing it to land on this dancer's right leg, but he 処理した **sho**ri shita (dealt with) the situation and later attended her **Show**

1150. 証 PRONUNCIATION: shou

MEANINGS: to certify, proof **EXAMPLES:** 証拠 shouko = evidence, proof, testimony; 証明 shoumei = proof, identification **DESCRIPTION:** on the left, 言(う) iu (to speak, # 430); on the right, 正(直) shoujiki (honest, # 174), which helps us to pronounce this **CUE:** if you have 証拠

shouko (evidence) of a crime, it is 正 (honest) to 言 (speak) up and **Show** your support for the law

1151. 拠 PRONUNCIATIONS: kyo, ko

MEANINGS: foothold, based on **EXAMPLES:** 拠点 kyoten = position, location, base, point; 根拠 konkyo = basis or foundation (of a belief, etc.); 証拠 shouko = evidence, proof, testimony **DESCRIPTION:** on the left, a kneeling guy; on the right, 処(理する) shori suru (to deal with, # 1149), which shows a 机 (desk) resting on the right leg of a dancer with a ponytail **CUES:** this kneeling guy went to **Kyo**to and also to **Ko**be to give 証拠 shou**ko** (testimony) to support this dancer whose leg had been injured by this 机(desk)

1152. 唱 PRONUNCIATIONS: shou, tona MEANINGS: to recite or sing energetically

EXAMPLES: 合唱 gasshou = chorus, singing in a chorus; 独唱 dokushou = solo singing; 唱える tonaeru = to advocate or recite **DESCRIPTION:** on the left, 口 kuchi (mouth, # 426); on the right, two 日 hi (suns, # 32) **CUES:** a 合唱 gas**shou** (chorus) of singers opened their 口 (mouths) for a **Show** on a planet with two 日 (suns), and their **Ton**al quality was excellent

··········

Chapter 69

1153. 満 PRONUNCIATIONS: mi, man

MEANINGS: full, to be filled **EXAMPLES:** 満ちる michiru = to become full; 満員 man'nin = full house, no vacancy; 満腹 manpuku = full stomach; 満足 manzoku = satisfaction; 不満 fuman = dissatisfaction **DESCRIPTION:** on the left, a water radical; at the upper right, a plant radical; at the lower right, 両(方) ryouhou (both, # 579) **CUES:** since I consumed 両 (both) this water and this plant material at a **Meal** in **Man**hattan, I had 満腹 **man**puku (a full stomach)

1154. 杉 PRONUNCIATION: sugi

MEANINGS: Japanese cedar tree EXAMPLES: 杉 sugi = Japanese cedar tree DESCRIPTION: on the left, 木 ki (tree, # 118); on the right, 三 san (three) CUE: Superman's Geese gathered under 三 (three) 木 (trees) which turned out to be 杉 **sugi** (Japanese cedar trees)

1155. 制 PRONUNCIATION: sei

MEANINGS: to put in order, to control EXAMPLES: 制度 seido = system or regime; 制服 seifuku = a uniform DESCRIPTION: on the left, ushi 牛 (cow, # 205) sitting on a revolving chair; on the right, the katakana リ ri; compared to 製(品) seihin (finished product, # 580), which helps us to pronounce this, this omits 工 and Y at the bottom CUE: this 牛 (cow) on a spinning chair and リ Ri work for Safeway, where they have set up 制度 **sei**do (systems) to control the workers

1156. 提 PRONUNCIATION: tei

MEANINGS: to carry, hold hands, commander EXAMPLES: 提出する teishutsu suru = to hand in or submit; 前提 zentei = premise, prerequisite DESCRIPTION: compared to 是(非) zehi (by all means, # 1035), this adds a kneeling guy on the left; on the right, it retains 日 hi (sun, # 32) and a foot radical with a taser mounted on it CUE: this guy kneeling in the 日 (sun) has this taser mounted on his foot, but he is planning to 提出する **tei**shutsu suru (hand in) his resignation to the police department 是 (by all means) ALSO COMPARE: (予)定 yotei = plan, # 455, which helps us to pronounce this

1157. 甲 PRONUNCIATION: kou

MEANINGS: armor, high (voice), first class EXAMPLES: 甲羅 koura = shell; 足の甲 ashi no kou = top of the foot DESCRIPTION: 田 (rice paddy, # 68) balanced on a stick, but this resembles a person wearing bifocals

CUE: these bifocals allow me to Cope with my nearsightedness, and they help to bring me out of my 甲羅 **kou**ra (shell) COMPARE: 申(す) mousu = to humbly speak, # 10; (理)由 riyuu = reason, # 73; 押(す) osu = to push, # 592; 里 sato = village, # 1060

1158. 羅 PRONUNCIATION: ra

MEANINGS: to carry, gauze, thin silk EXAMPLES: 甲羅 koura = shell DESCRIPTION: at the top, 目 me (eye, # 51), turned on its side, resembling three eyes; at the lower left, 糸 skeet shooter (# 219); at the lower right, a cage CUE: this 糸 (skeet shooter) is a Rascal with three eyes who is shooting at the 甲羅 kou**ra** (shell) of a turtle that is being held in this cage

1159. 徳 PRONUNCIATION: toku

MEANINGS: virtue EXAMPLES: 道徳 doutoku = morality, moral, ethics; 美徳 bitoku = virtue DESCRIPTION: compared to 聴(衆) choushuu (audience, # 934), 耳 mimi (ear) on the left has been replced by a man with two slanted hats; on the right, this retains 十 too (ten, # 18), which helps us to pronounce this, 目 me (eye, # 51) turned on its side, resembling three eyes, and 心 kokoro (heart, # 306) CUES: this guy has two slanted hats, 十 (ten) houses, three eyes, and a 心 (heart) full of 美徳 bi**toku** (virtue), he is Totally Cool, and he consumes a lot of Tofu and Kool-Aid

1160. 祥 PRONUNCIATION: shou

MEANINGS: happiness, good fortune EXAMPLES: 発祥 hasshou = origin; 不祥事 fushouji = scandal DESCRIPTION: on the left, a Shah, as seen in (会)社 kaisha (company, # 271); on the right, 羊 hitsuji (sheep, not included in this Catalogue) CUE: this Shah traces the 発祥 has**shou** (origin) of his wool business to a 羊 (sheep) Show that he watched in his youth

Chapter 70

1161. 勘 PRONUNCIATION: kan

MEANINGS: intuition, perception EXAMPLES: 勘弁 kanben = pardon, forgiveness; 勘違い kanchigai = misunderstanding, wrong guess; 勘定 kanjou = bill, check, calculation DESCRIPTION: at the upper left, a bucket with three compartments; at the lower left, 匹 hiki (small animal, # 818); on the right, 力 chikara (strength, # 107) CUE: when I visited **Can**ada, my lunch was served in this bucket with three compartments carried by a 匹 (small animal) who had a lot of 力 (strength), and I was happy until I saw the 勘定 **kan**jou (check) COMPARE: (時)期 jiki = season, # 711

1162. 弁 PRONUNCIATION: ben

MEANINGS: speech, flower, petal, valve EXAMPLES: 弁護士 bengoshi = lawyer; 弁当 bentou = box lunch; 弁 ben = dialect, e.g., 名古屋弁 nagoyaben = Nagoya dialect; 弁解 benkai = excuse, justification DESCRIPTION: at the top, the katakana ム mu, which reminds us of the sound made by a cow; at the bottom, a tower representing a catapult, as seen in 形 katachi (shape, # 573), without its roof CUE: this ム (cow) is working at the top of this tower, but it isn't happy with the **Ben**efits the job provides and plans to contact its 弁護士 **ben**goshi (lawyer)

1163. 護 PRONUNCIATION: go

MEANINGS: to protect EXAMPLES: 弁護士 bengoshi = lawyer; 看護婦 kangofu = female nurse DESCRIPTION: on the left, 言(う) iu (to speak, # 430); at the upper right, a plant radical; at the middle right, a cage; at the lower right, 又 mata (again, # 24) which resembles a simple table CUE: a 看護婦 kan**go**fu (nurse) had just placed this cage on this 又 (table) under some hanging plants when she heard a **Gho**st 言 (speak) from the branches

1164. 看 PRONUNCIATION: kan

MEANINGS: watch over, see EXAMPLES: 看板 kanban = signboard; 看護婦 kangofu = female nurse DESCRIPTION: at the top, 三 san (three, # 3) superimposed on the katakana ノ no; at the bottom 目 me (eye, # 51) CUE: this 目 (eye) belongs to a watchful 看護婦 **kan**gofu (nurse) from **Can**ada who repeated the Nightingale pledge 三 (three) times and is a ノ (no) nonsense person COMPARE: 春 haru = spring, # 506

1165. 婦 PRONUNCIATION: fu

MEANINGS: woman EXAMPLES: 婦人 fujin = woman; 主婦 shufu = housewife; 夫婦 fuufu = married couple; 看護婦 kangofu = female nurse DESCRIPTION: compared to 帰(る) kaeru (to return, # 566), リ Ri has been replaced on the left by a female radical; on the right, this retains the long hair streaming to the left and the face of an elephant, with low-hanging ears and a long trunk CUE: when this 婦人 **fu**jin (woman) with long hair 帰 (returns), she will give **Fo**od to this elephant ALSO COMPARE: 掃(除する) souji suru = to clean, # 645

1166. 板 PRONUNCIATIONS: ban, ita, pan

MEANINGS: plank, board, plate EXAMPLES: 看板 kanban = signboard; 鉄板焼き teppanyaki = food grilled on an iron griddle; 板 ita = wooden board, metal plate DESCRIPTION: on the left, 木 ki (tree, # 118); on the right, an F over an X CUES: I cut down this **Ban**ana 木 (tree) to make an 板 **ita** (wooden board) to cut Italian **Pan** (bread) on, but my teacher graded my work with an F and marked it with an X COMPARE: 反(対) hantai = opposition, # 680; (大)阪 oosaka = Osaka, # 1005; (出)版 shuppan = publication, # 1086; 販(売) hanbai = sales, # 1199

1167. 盆 PRONUNCIATION: bon

MEANINGS: basin, lantern festival, tray
EXAMPLES: お盆 Obon = a Buddhist festival devoted to ancestor worship; 盆踊り bonodori = a dance performed at Obon **DESCRIPTION:** at the top, 分(かる) wakaru (to understand, #105); at the bottom, 皿 sara (dish, # 567) **CUE:** I bought some nice 皿 (dishes) at お盆 O**bon** (a Buddhist festival), and as a **Bon**us the seller helped me to 分 (understand) how they were made

1168. 鬼 PRONUNCIATIONS: oni, ki

MEANINGS: ghost, devil **EXAMPLES:** 鬼 oni = devil, cruel person; 殺人鬼 satsujinki = killer, cutthroat **DESCRIPTION:** at the top, 田 (rice paddy, # 68) wearing a pointy hat, but this resembles a person wearing bifocals; at the bottom, two sturdy tentacles, as seen in 勉(強) benkyou (study, # 474); above the tentacle on the right, the katakana ム mu, which reminds us of the sound a cow makes
CUES: this 鬼 **oni** (devil) wears a pointy hat and bifocals, stands on sturdy tentacles, and is **Own**ing this ム (cow) which he plans to **K**eep

....

Chapter 71
1169. 魅 PRONUNCIATION: mi

MEANINGS: charm, fascination, glamour
EXAMPLES: 魅力 miryoku = attractiveness, charm; 魅力的な miryokuteki na = fascinating, charming **DESCRIPTION:** on the left, 鬼 oni (devil, # 1168); on the right, 未(来) mirai (future, # 672), which helps us to pronounce this
CUE: this 鬼 (devil) is looking into the 未 (future) to try to figure out the **Mea**ning of life, and if he does, he may acquire some 魅力 **mi**ryoku (charm)

1170. 倉 PRONUNCIATIONS: sou, kura

MEANING: storage, warehouse **EXAMPLES:** 倉庫 souko = warehouse; 倉 kura = storehouse; 穀倉 kokusou = granary **DESCRIPTION:** at the top, a peaked roof, with a ceiling; below that, a lean-to with a double roof; below that, 口 kuchi (mouth, # 426), which resembles a kuuraa (air conditioner)
CUES: since **S**oldiers value their 口 **Kuuraa** (coolers) highly, they store them in secure 倉庫 **sou**ko (warehouses) like this, with several layers of roofing above them

1171. 創 PRONUNCIATION: sou

MEANINGS: to start, create, hurt **EXAMPLES:** 創造 souzou = creation; 創立する souritsu suru = to establish; 創設する sousetsu suru = to found, establish; 独創性 dokusousei = originality, creativity **DESCRIPTION:** on the left, 倉(庫) souko (storehouse, # 1170), which helps us to pronounce this; on the right, the katakana リ ri, which reminds us of "retreat"
CUE: some **S**oldiers 創立した **sou**ritsu shita (established) this 倉 (warehouse) in a forward area, but now they have to リ (retreat)

1172. 穀 PRONUNCIATION: koku

MEANINGS: grain **EXAMPLES:** 穀倉 kokusou = granary; 穀物 kokumotsu = grain, cereal **DESCRIPTION:** at the upper left, 士 shi (man, # 66); at the middle left, a roof; at the lower left, 禾 (a grain plant with a ripe head); at the upper right, π (the Greek letter pi, also known as a pious yak); at the lower right, 又 (a simple table)
CUE: this 士 (man) stands high on this roof and drinks **Coke** as he surveys this 禾 (grain plant with a ripe head), and he wonders how much of the 穀物 **koku**motsu (grain) he will be able to stack on this 又 (table), from where he plans to feed it to this π (yak)

1173. 締 **PRONUNCIATIONS: shimari, ji, shi** **MEANINGS:** tighten, tie, shut, lock, fasten **EXAMPLES:** 取締役 torishimariyaku = a representative director (a director chosen by a board to represent it); 戸締まり tojimari = door fastening; 締める shimeru = to fasten (seatbelt), tie (necktie), strangle, tighten (transitive); 締まる shimaru = to tighten (intransitive); 締め切り shimekiri = closing, deadline **DESCRIPTION:** compared to 諦(める) akirameru (to give up, # 804), this replaces 言 (to say) on the left with 糸 (skeet shooter, # 219); on the right, it retains the cook named Bo Peep, who 立 (stands) on slippery floors, wearing spikes on her shoes **CUES:** Bo Peep and this 糸 (skeet shooter) are in a relationship, and **She** plans to **Marry** him, but sometimes she slides around while cooking, so he consulted a **Ge**nius who sold him a harness made out of **Shee**ts to 締める **shi**meru (fasten) her to the ceiling

1174. 偉 **PRONUNCIATIONS: i, era** **MEANINGS:** admirable, greatness, famous **EXAMPLES:** 偉人 ijin = an exceptional person; 偉大 idai = great, grand; 偉い erai = great, excellent, eminent, distinguished **DESCRIPTION:** on the left, a man with a slanted hat; on the right, compared to 違(う) chigau (to differ, # 355), the snail is missing, but the two feet still face in opposite directions **CUES:** this man with a slanted hat had feet facing in opposite directions, and his life wasn't **Ea**sy during an **Era** when everyone had to walk everywhere, but he was an 偉人 **i**jin (exceptional person)

1175. 載 **PRONUNCIATION: no** **MEANINGS:** to publish in, load with **EXAMPLES:** 載る noru = to be printed or placed on; 載せる noseru = to put on top of, to publish **DESCRIPTION:** at the upper left, 十 too (ten, # 18); at the lower left, 車 kuruma (car, # 283); on the right, a halberd (combination axe and lance) **CUE:** a **No**rwegian is guarding this 車 (car) with this halberd, and he has 載せた **no**seta (placed)

the number 十 (ten) on top of the car to indicate the hours remaining in his shift

1176. 阿 **PRONUNCIATION: a** **MEANINGS:** to flatter, fawn upon **EXAMPLE:** 阿波踊り Awa Odori = a dance festival held in Tokushima City during Obon **DESCRIPTION:** on the left, ß beta from the Greek alphabet; on the right, 可(愛い) kawaii (cute, # 615) **CUE:** this ß (Greek) **A**rtist looked 可 (cute) when she danced in the 阿波踊り **a**wa'odori (an Obon dance festival)

....

Chapter 72

1177. 援 **PRONUNCIATION: en** **MEANINGS:** aid, help, cheering **EXAMPLES:** 応援 ouen = support; 援助 enjo = assistance, support; 救援 kyuuen = rescue; 声援 seien = support, cheering **DESCRIPTION:** on the left, a kneeling guy; at the upper right, a barbecue grate, as seen in (野)菜 yasai (vegetables, # 121); at the lower right, an F above 又 ("again," # 24, which resembles a simple table) **CUE:** this crawling guy was barbecuing on this grate, and at first he got 応援 ou**en** (support) and **En**couragement from his family, but when he put the food on this 又 (table), they gave it an F

1178. 箕 **PRONUNCIATION: mi** **MEANING:** winnowing **EXAMPLE:** 箕面市 Minooshi = a city north of Osaka **DESCRIPTION:** at the top, 竹 take (bamboo, # 134); at the bottom, a woman with a wide skirt **CUE:** I had a **Mea**l in 箕面市 **Mi**nooshi with this woman with a wide skirt, and we ate these 竹 (bamboo) shoots **COMPARE:** (時)期 jiki = season, # 711

1179. 滝 PRONUNCIATION: taki

MEANINGS: waterfall, rapids **EXAMPLES:** 滝 taki = waterfall, cascade **DESCRIPTION:** on the left, a water radical; at the upper right, 立(つ) tatsu (to stand, # 11); at the lower right, a transformer with a wire protruding from it, as seen in 電(気) denki (electricity, # 263)

CUE: we were 立 (standing) and **T**alking about a scheme to make 電 (electricity) using hydropower from this water that flows over a 滝 **taki** (waterfall)

1180. 脂 PRONUNCIATIONS: abura, shi

MEANINGS: fat, grease, tallow, lard
EXAMPLES: 脂 abura = fat; 脂肪 shibou = fat
DESCRIPTION: compared to 指 yubi = finger, # 691, the kneeling guy on the left has been replaced by 月 tsuki (moon, # 148) **CUES:** I pressed my 指 (finger) into the side of an **Ab**u Dhabi **R**am in the 月 (moon) light in order to assess its 脂 **abura** (fat) content, as compared to that of other **Sheep**
ALSO COMPARE: 油 abura = oil, # 942

1181. 悩 PRONUNCIATIONS: naya, nou

MEANINGS: trouble, worry, in pain, distress
EXAMPLES: 悩む nayamu = to be troubled or worried; 悩み nayami = distress, worry; 苦悩 kunou = agony, anguish **DESCRIPTION:** on the left, an erect man; at the upper right, three lines which represent buzzing bees; at the lower right, an open box with an X inside, which represents an unknown number of bees inside a hive
CUES: when this erect man on the left took a **N**ap in the **Y**ard, these three buzzing bees from this hive stung him on the **N**ose, causing him 悩み **naya**mi (distress)

1182. 河 PRONUNCIATIONS: ka, ga, kawa MEANINGS: large river EXAMPLES:

河口 kakou = mouth of a river; 運河 unga = canal; 河 kawa = river (usually written 川)
DESCRIPTION: compared to 何 nani (what, # 338), the man with a slanted hat on the left has

been replaced with a water radical **CUES:** when I took my **C**ar to buy **G**as, I decided to get a **C**ar **W**ash, but a 河 **kawa** (river) had flooded the town, and I said, 何 (what) is this water doing here?
ALSO COMPARE: 可(愛い) kawaii = cute, # 615, which helps us to pronounce this

1183. 焚 PRONUNCIATION: ta

MEANINGS: burn, build a fire, cook
EXAMPLES: 焚き火 takibi = bonfire; 焚く taku = to burn (wood) **DESCRIPTION:** at the top, 林 hayashi (grove, # 125); at the bottom, 火(事) kaji (fire, # 443) **CUE:** **T**arzan started this 火 (fire) in this 林 (grove) in order to make a 焚き火 **ta**kibi (bonfire)

1184. 梨 PRONUNCIATION: nashi

MEANINGS: pear tree **EXAMPLES:** 梨 nashi = pear tree, or a pear **DESCRIPTION:** at the upper left, 禾 (a grain plant with a ripe head); at the upper right, the katakana リ ri; at the bottom, 木 ki (tree, # 118) **CUE:** リ **R**i looked at this 木 (tree), saw that the 梨 **nashi** (pears) were 禾 (ripe), and started **Gnashi**ng his teeth

....

Chapter 73

1185. 幅 PRONUNCIATION: haba

MEANINGS: hanging scroll, width **EXAMPLES:** 幅 haba = width **DESCRIPTION:** compared to 福 fuku (good luck, # 661), the Shah on the left has been replaced by Bo Peep, as seen in 帽(子) boushi (hat, # 243); on the right, this retains 口 kuchi (mouth, # 426) with a piece of tape over it, suggesting that this person is being inhibited from talking, plus 田 (rice paddy, # 68) **CUE:** Bo Peep is a **Ha**waiian **Ba**rber with tape over her 口 (mouth) which prevents her from talking about the 幅 **haba** (width) of this 田 (rice paddy) which, like the Shah (see # 661), she acquired through 福 (good luck)

ALSO COMPARE: 富(士山) fujisan = Mt. Fuji, # 939; 副(産物) fukusanbutsu = a byproduct, # 1206

1186. 茂 PRONUNCIATION: shige

MEANINGS: to grow thickly, be rampant
EXAMPLES: 茂る shigeru = to grow thickly
DESCRIPTION: at the top, a plant radical; at the bottom, a lean-to containing an X, which represents an unknown fertilizer
CUE: the **Sheep** at **Ge**ttysburg feed on these plants which 茂る **shige**ru (grow thickly), thanks to the X (unknown fertilizer) stored in this lean-to

1187. 秘 PRONUNCIATIONS: pi, hi

MEANING: to keep secret **EXAMPLES:** 神秘 shinpi = a mystery; 秘密 himitsu = a secret; 秘書 hisho = a secretary **DESCRIPTION:** on the left, 禾 (a grain plant with a ripe head); on the right, 必(要) hitsuyou (necessary, # 307), or 必(死に) hisshi ni (desperately, # 307), which helps us to pronounce this
CUES: when our 秘書 **hi**sho (secretary) **Pee**ks out the window and sees that this 禾 (grain) is ripe, it's 必 (necessary) that she take off her **Hee**ls and trample it to separate the wheat from the chaff

1188. 密 PRONUNCIATIONS: mitsu, mi,

hiso **MEANINGS:** secrecy, density, carefulness
EXAMPLES: 秘密 himitsu = a secret; 綿密な menmitsu na = detailed, meticulous; 密会 mikkai = secret meeting; 密かに hisoka ni = secretly, behind the scenes
DESCRIPTION: at the top, a bad haircut; in the middle, 必(要) hitsuyou (necessary, # 307); at the bottom, 山 yama (mountain, # 146)
CUES: it's 必 (necessary) that you **Meet Su**perman at the top of this 山 (mountain), sympathize with his bad haircut, share his **Mea**l, and see if he knows any 秘密 hi**mitsu** (secrets) that might help to **Hea**l our **So**ldiers

1189. 綿 PRONUNCIATIONS: wata,

men **MEANING:** cotton **EXAMPLES:** 綿 wata = cotton; 綿 men = cotton; 木綿 momen = cotton; 綿密な menmitsu na = detailed, meticulous **DESCRIPTION:** on the left, 糸 skeetshooter (# 219); at the upper right, 白(い) shiroi (white, # 44); at the lower right, Bo Peep, as seen in 帽(子) boushi (hat, # 243)
CUES: this 糸 (skeetshooter) and Bo Peep **Walk Ta**ll, and all of the **Men** admire their 白 (white) 綿 **men** (cotton) shirts

1190. 蔵 PRONUNCIATIONS: kura, zou

MEANINGS: vault, treasure, storage
EXAMPLES: 冷蔵庫 reizouko = refrigerator; 蔵書 zousho = a book collection or library; 蔵 kura = a storehouse (this can also be written 倉, # 1170) **DESCRIPTION:** compared to (心)臓 shinzou (heart, # 951), which reminds us of different heart rate zones and helps us to pronounce this, the 月 (moon) on the left is missing
CUES: after the 月 (moon) disappears (compared to # 951), I open my 冷蔵庫 rei**zou**ko (refrigerator) and turn on my **Kuu**ra (air conditioner), and my 臓 (heart) rate goes into a lower **Z**one

1191. 胴 PRONUNCIATION: dou

MEANINGS: trunk, torso **EXAMPLES:** 胴体 doutai = body, torso **DESCRIPTION:** on the left, 月 tsuki (moon, # 148); on the right, 同(情) doujou (sympathy, # 339), which helps us to pronounce this **CUE:** when I watch this 月 (moon), I feel 同 (sympathy) for hungry people and eat a lot of **Dough**nuts, and that's why my 胴体 **dou**tai (torso) is so large

1192. 操 PRONUNCIATIONS: ayatsu, sou MEANINGS: to operate, fidelity

EXAMPLES: 操る ayatsuru = to control, manipulate, handle; 操作 sousa = operation (of a machine); 体操 taisou = gymnastics, exercise DESCRIPTION: compared to 繰(り返す) kurikaesu (to repeat, # 1034), the 糸 (skeetshooter) on the left has been replaced by a kneeling guy; on the right, there are still three packages of Kool-Aid stuck in a tree CUES: an Ayatollah Tsued (sued) the 糸 (skeet shooter) who was 繰 (repeatedly) unable to dislodge these Kool-Aid 品 (packages) from this 木 (tree) and then told this kneeling guy, who is a Soldier, to 胴体する sousa suru (operate) a machine to do the job

....

Chapter 74

1193. 滅 PRONUNCIATIONS: metsu, me, horo MEANINGS: destroy, ruin, overthrow, perish

EXAMPLES: 絶滅 zetsumetsu = extinction; 破滅 hametsu = devastation, ruin; 不滅の fumetsu no = immortal, eternal; 滅入る meiru = to feel depressed; 滅ぼす horobosu = to ruin or destroy DESCRIPTION: compared to 減(る) heru (to reduce weight, # 1148), the 口 (mouth) below the piece of tape inside this lean-to has been replaced by 火 hi (fire, # 443) CUE: when I Met Superman in this lean-to in Mexico, he told me that, according to his Horoscope, we were threatened with 絶滅 zetsumetsu (extinction) from a combination of this water, this 火 (fire) and halberds like this one, and I began to 滅 (lose) weight

1194. 慮 PRONUNCIATION: ryo MEANINGS: prudence, thought, concern

EXAMPLES: 配慮 hairyo = consideration, concern; 考慮 kouryo = consideration; 遠慮 enryo = hesitation, reserve, restraint, modesty

DESCRIPTION: compared to (捕)虜 horyo (captive, # 1107), which helps us to pronounce this, the 男 (male) prisoner named Leo at the lower right has been replaced by 思(う) omou (to think/feel, # 308) CUE: when Pope Leo was a prisoner in this lean-to with a periscope at the top, he often 思 (thought) about the 配慮 hairyo (consideration) that his captors failed to give him ALSO COMPARE: (謙)虚 kenkyo = modesty, # 966; 虎 tora = tiger, # 1057; 劇 geki = a play, # 1058

1195. 抵 PRONUNCIATION: tei MEANINGS: resist, reach, touch EXAMPLES:

抵抗 teikou = resistance, opposition; 抵当 teitou = mortgage DESCRIPTION: compared to (最)低 saitei (the worst, # 222), which shows a 紙 (paper, # 221) pavilion taped to a flat rock and helps us to pronounce this, the guy with a slanted hat on the left has been replaced by a kneeling guy CUE: this guy is kneeling in order to try to move this 紙 (paper) pavilion, but the Tape that was used to attach it to this flat rock produces too much 抵抗 teikou (resistance)

1196. 抗 PRONUNCIATION: kou MEANINGS: prudence, thought, concern

EXAMPLES: 抵抗 teikou = resistance, opposition; 抗議 kougi = protest; 反抗 hankou = rebellion, defiance, resistance; 対抗する taikou suru = to oppose or fight DESCRIPTION: on the left, a kneeling guy; at the upper right, a tire stop, as seen in 対(して) taishite (against, # 674); at the lower right, π (the Greek letter pi, also known as a pious yak) CUE: this kneeling guy and this π (yak) don't like the tire stop at the upper right, which was installed by a Corporation, and they are organizing a 抗議 kougi (protest) against it

1197. 盤 PRONUNCIATION: ban MEANINGS: tray, shallow bowl EXAMPLES:

吸盤 kyuuban = suction cup, sucker; 基盤 kiban = foundation, basis DESCRIPTION: at the top, (一)般(的に) ippanteki ni (commonly, usually, # 1050) which includes a 船 (boat), a 兀 (pious yak) and a 又 (table); at the bottom, 皿 sara (bowl, # 567) **CUE:** **Ban**anas are shipped on this 船 (boat), and 般 (usually) I mash them in this 皿 (bowl) before eating them with my 兀 (yak) at this 又 (table), since they are the 基盤 ki**ban** (foundation) of our diet

1198. 基 PRONUNCIATIONS: moto, ki

MEANINGS: foundation, base **EXAMPLES:** 基ずく motozuku = to be based on; に基づいて ni motozuite = based on, according to; 基準 kijun = criterion, standard; 基盤 kiban = foundation, basis; 基金 kikin = fund; 基地 kichi = base **DESCRIPTION:** at the top, a bucket with three compartments above a wide skirt, but this could be a rocket; at the bottom, 土 tsuchi (dirt, # 59), but this resembles a propeller on a motor **CUES:** this rocket is powered by this **Motor** at the bottom, and our space program in **Ki**ev will 基ずく **moto**zuku (be based on) it

1199. 販 PRONUNCIATION: han

MEANINGS: marketing, sell, trade **EXAMPLES:** 販売 hanbai = sales, marketing; 自働販売機 jidouhanbaiki = vending machine **DESCRIPTION:** on the left, 貝 kai (shell, or a three-drawer money chest, # 83); on the right, an F over an X **CUE: Han**sel wanted a career in 販売 **han**bai (marketing) so that he could fill up this 貝 (money chest), but he got an F on his final exam, and the teacher also marked it with an X **COMPARE:** (ご)飯 gohan = cooked rice, # 400, which helps us to pronounce this; 反(対) hantai = opposition, # 680, which also helps us to pronounce this; (大)阪 oosaka = Osaka, # 1005

1200. 綱 PRONUNCIATION: tsuna

MEANINGS: rope, cord, cable **EXAMPLES:** 綱 tsuna = a rope, cord, cable; 綱引き tsunahiki = tug of war **DESCRIPTION:** on the left, 糸 ito

(thread, # 219); on the right, this resembles 両(方) ryouhou (both, # 579) which we described as a chairlift seat, but the seats have slipped down and appear to be hanging by mere threads on both sides **CUE:** due to a **Tsuna**mi, the 綱 **tsuna** (cables) that support this chairlift seat (see # 579) were damaged, and the seats are hanging by mere 糸 (threads)

....

Chapter 75

1201. 雰 PRONUNCIATIONS: fun, *fu*

MEANINGS: atmosphere **EXAMPLES:** 雰囲気 fun'iki (usually pronounced fu'inki) = atmosphere, ambience, mood **DESCRIPTION:** at the top, 雨 ame (rain, # 261); at the bottom, 分 fun (minute, # 105), which would help us to pronounce this if the pronunciation were as expected **CUES:** 雨 (rain) is going to fall any 分 (minute) now, but we are having **Fun,** and the rain won't spoil the 雰囲気 **fun**'iki (pronounced **fu**'inki) (ambience) of our party, where already some **Foo**ls are **Win**king at me

1202. 囲 PRONUNCIATIONS: kako, i, *in*

MEANINGS: atmosphere **EXAMPLES:** 囲む kakomu = to surround or circle; 周囲 shuu'i = surroundings; 雰囲気 fun'iki (usually pronounced fu'inki) = atmosphere, ambience, mood **DESCRIPTION:** a fence surrounding 井(戸) ido (water well, # 983), which helps us to pronounce this **CUES:** a **C**arpentry **C**orporation built this fence to 囲む **kako**mu (surround) this 井 (well), and now it's **E**asy for them to keep **In**truders out

1203. 飾 PRONUNCIATIONS: kaza, shoku MEANINGS: decorate, ornament

EXAMPLES: 飾る kazaru = to decorate; 装飾 soushoku = decoration **DESCRIPTION:** on the left, 食(事) shokuji (meal, # 398), which helps us to pronounce this; on the right side, Bo Peep, as seen in 帽(子) boushi (hat, # 767), who is balancing a crutch on her head **CUES:** Bo Peep, who uses this crutch, just got back from **Kaza**khstan, and if you invite her to a 食 (meal) she will **Shock** you by offering to 囲む **kaza**ru (decorate) your house

1204. 詣 PRONUNCIATIONS: mou, moude, kei MEANINGS: visit a temple

EXAMPLES: 詣でる mouderu = to make a pilgrimage or visit a temple; 詣で moude = a temple or shrine visit; 初詣 hatsumoude = first shrine visit of the year (this can also be written 初詣で); 造詣 zoukei = knowledge, mastery DESCRIPTION: compared to 指 yubi (finger, # 691), this replaces the kneeling guy on the left with 言(う) iu (to speak, # 430); it retains the ヒ (hero) and the 日 (sun) on the right

CUES: this ヒ (hero) is sitting in this 日 (sun), thinking about **Mow**ing the lawn, but he puts his 指 (finger) in the air and 言 (says) "This isn't a **Mow Day**. Let's do a 詣で **mou**de (temple visit) instead and then get some **Cake**."

1205. 寛 PRONUNCIATION: kan

MEANINGS: tolerance, leniency, be at ease, generosity EXAMPLES: 寛大 kandai = understanding, lenient, tolerant, generous, broad-minded; 寛容 kanyou = tolerance, open-mindedness, forbearance, generosity

DESCRIPTION: at the top, a bad haircut; under the haircut, a plant radical; at the bottom, 見(る) miru (to look, # 53) CUE: this guy from **Ca**nada wears these plants on his head to try to hide his bad haircut, and he 見 (looks) out for people, since he is 寛大 **kan**dai (generous)

1206. 副 PRONUNCIATION: fuku

MEANINGS: duplicate, copy, deputy

EXAMPLES: 副作用 fukusayou = a side-effect; 副産物 fukusanbutsu = a byproduct; 副住職 fukujuushoku = vice-priest DESCRIPTION: compared to 福 fuku (good luck, # 661), which helps us to pronounce this, this subtracts the Shah on the left and adds リ ri on the right; it retains the 口

(mouth) with a piece of tape over it, and the 田 (rice paddy) CUE: リ Ri might buy this 田 (rice paddy) in **Fuku**oka, but he has put tape over his 口 (mouth), since he's not allowed to talk about it yet, and a 副産物 **fuku**sanbutsu (byproduct) of his silence is that he seems more shy than usual

ALSO COMPARE: 富(士山) fujisan = Mt. Fuji, # 939; 幅 haba = width, # 1185

1207. 互 PRONUNCIATIONS: go, taga

MEANINGS: mutually, reciprocally, together EXAMPLES: 相互 sougo = each other, one another, mutuality; 互い tagai = each other, one another; 互いに tagai ni = with each other, mutually, reciprocally DESCRIPTION: this resembles two katakana ユ yu characters, one upside down and the other right side up, touching in the center, which remind us of Youths

CUES: these two ユ (Youths) have discovered a **Gold** mine, and they speak **Taga**log 互いに **taga**i ni (with each other) COMPARE: 五 go = five, # 179, which helps us to pronounce this

1208. 尊 PRONUNCIATIONS: son, touto MEANINGS: to revere or respect

EXAMPLES: 尊重する sonchou suru = to respect or value; 尊敬する sonkei suru = to respect; 尊い toutoi = sacred, important, valuable

DESCRIPTION: at the top, 酒 sake, without its water radical, and with two added antennae at the top; at the bottom, an asymmetrical structure that appears to be built into the side of a hill, as seen in 寺 tera (temple, # 213) CUES: the **Son**y Corporation has constructed this 酒 (sake) factory on the side of a hill, where they eat a lot of **To**fu and **To**matoes, and they have placed antennae at the top to help broadcast the message that they 尊敬する **son**kei suru (respect) everyone

515

Hiragana Review

わ wa	ら ra	や ya	ま ma	は ha	な na	た ta	さ sa	か ka	あ a
	り ri		み mi	ひ hi	に ni	ち chi	し shi	き ki	い i
を wo	る ru	ゆ yu	む mu	ふ fu	ぬ nu	つ tsu	す su	く ku	う u
	れ re		め me	へ he	ね ne	て te	せ se	け ke	え e
ん n	ろ ro	よ yo	も mo	ほ ho	の no	と to	そ so	こ ko	お o

Katakana Review

ワ wa	ラ ra	ヤ ya	マ ma	ハ ha	ナ na	タ ta	サ sa	カ ka	ア a
	リ ri		ミ mi	ヒ hi	ニ ni	チ chi	シ shi	キ ki	イ i
ヲ wo	ル ru	ユ yu	ム mu	フ fu	ヌ nu	ツ tsu	ス su	ク ku	ウ u
	レ re		メ me	ヘ he	ネ ne	テ te	セ se	ケ ke	エ e
ン n	ロ ro	ヨ yo	モ mo	ホ ho	ノ no	ト to	ソ so	コ ko	オ o

Rendaku

Rendaku is a phenomenon that can affect the pronunciations of kanji in compound words, when kanji appear in the middle or at the end of a word. Kanji pronunciations that contain the consonants in the following table can change as shown below.

ch → j (e.g., chi → ji)	k → g (e.g., koto → goto)
f → b (e.g., fun → bun)	s → z (e.g., sushi → zushi
f → p (e.g., fuku → puku)	sh → j (e.g., sha → ja)
h → b (e.g., hito → bito)	t → d (e.g., toki → doki)
h → p (e.g., hai → pai)	ts → z (e.g., tsukai → zukai

If you cannot find a kanji pronunciation that you are seeking in the Pronunciation Index starting on page 517, it may have been affected by rendaku. If so, you may be able to use the table above to help find it.

In the Kanji Catalogue starting on page 321, we are unable to provide retrieval cues for all of the alternative pronunciations associated with the rendaku phenomenon. For this reason, you will sometimes see a kanji pronunciation without an accompanying cue in the Catalogue. For example, 人 hito, reference # 13, can also be pronounced "bito," but only a retrieval cue for "hito" is provided. [The cue is "Hiro**Hito** was a 人 **hito** (person)..."] In this reference, and in some other kanji references, we use a superscripted "1" to identify pronunciations like bito[1], for which no retrieval cues are provided. The footnote to which this superscript refers appears only on page 322.

In some words, two Japanese kanji are repeated, one after the other, and the second kanji is replaced by the repetition symbol 々. If this repetition occurs with kanji pronunciations that are affected by rendaku, the second kanji may be pronounced differently from the first one, in accordance with the rules of rendaku. For example, 木々 kigi = many trees, 人々 hitobito = people, 口々 kuchiguchi = every mouth, 久々 hisabisa = a long time ago, 日々 hibi = every day, 国々 kuniguni = countries, 時々 tokidoki = sometimes, 様々 samazama = various and 花々 hanabana = flowers.

For some words containing the repetition symbol 々, like 少々 shoushou (a little) and 次々 tsugitsugi (one after the other), the rules of rendaku are not applied, and both kanji are pronounced in the same way. Words like 色々 iroiro (various), which don't contain any of the consonants listed in the table above, are obviously not affected by rendaku.

Kanji Pronunciation Index

Some kanji pronunciations are non-standard, i.e., they are neither "on'yomi" (Chinese readings) nor "kun'yomi" (Japanese readings) nor "nanori" (readings associated primarily with Japanese names), and they only appear in a single word. We call these pronunciations **exceptional** because they are unique exceptions to the standard ways in which the kanji are pronounced, and we mark them with **italics** in the Kanji Catalogue and in the Index.

For example, consider the word 海女 *ama* (female pearl diver), which we italicize in romaji in the Kanji Catalogue and the Index. The **italics** tell us that the "a" pronunciation is exceptional, meaning that when "a" is used as a pronunciation for 海, it is neither on'yomi nor kun'yomi nor nanori, and it is used in only one word. The same thing is true for the "ma" pronunciation in this word.

Japanese people use kanji combinations for some words without breaking the words into separate pronunciations for each kanji. In spite of that, we have chosen to break such words into separate pronunciations whenever it seemed practical to do so, so that students would be able to look them up easily.

For example, 足袋 *tabi* (Japanese socks) is recognized as a single word by Japanese people, not as a combination of two kanji with different pronunciations that can be combined. The same thing is true for 今日 *kyou* (today), 一日 *tsuitachi* (the first of the month), 昨日 *kinou* (yesterday), 大人 *otona* (adult), and so forth. The pronunciations that we assign to the individual kanji in these words are only intended to help people who are looking up pronunciations in this book, and they have no other significance.

There are two words used in this book that contain kanji with exceptional pronunciations which cannot be practically divided into separate sounds for each kanji: *obaasan* お祖母さん (grandmother) and お祖父さん *ojiisan* (grandfather). These two pronunciations, "*baa* 祖母" and "*jii* 祖父," are the only ones listed in this Index as **combinations** of kanji.

Finally, please note that sometimes **stem forms** of verbs, i.e., pre-masu forms, are used as pronunciations for kanji. For example, hanashi, derived from 話します hanashimasu (to speak), is a possible pronunciation of 話. Also, 読 yomi, derived from 読みます yomimasu (to read), is a possible pronunciation of 読. In this Index, we include a number of pronunciations based on stem forms, but there are may be others that we omit.

Ki 黄 – 976
Ki 輝 – 979
Ki 城 – 1008
Ki 季 – 1047
Ki 樹 – 1089
Ki 効 – 1139
Ki 鬼 – 1168
Ki 基 – 1198
Kiba 牙 – 921
Kibi 厳 – 902
Kimi 君 – 419
Kin 金 – 301
Kin 近 – 390
Kin 勤 – 517
Kin 緊 – 732
Kin 禁 – 943
Kin 均 – 988
Kira 嫌 – 817
Kishi 岸 – 500
Kiso 競 – 935
Kita 北 – 373
Kitana 汚 – 467
Kitsu 喫 – 192
Kitsu 詰 – 781
Kiwa 際 – 379
Kiwa 極 – 610
Kiyo 清 – 1112
Kiza 刻 – 565
Kiza 兆 – 849
Ko 木 – 118
Ko 国 – 170
Ko 子 – 182
Ko 小 – 253
Ko 今 – 292
Ko 来 – 327
Ko 去 – 343

Ko 込 – 357
Ko 古 – 392
Ko 故 – 394
Ko 個 – 395
Ko 呼 – 428
Ko 越 – 453
Ko 己 – 652
Ko 湖 – 716
Ko 孤 – 723
Ko 固 – 731
Ko 焦 – 750
Ko 骨 – 832
Ko 戸 – 871
Ko 庫 – 919
Ko 請 – 1064
Ko 粉 – 1104
Ko 濃 – 1106
Ko 妓 – 1121
Ko 拠 – 1151
Koe 声 – 40
Koi 恋 – 695
Koke 苔 – 957
Koko 心 – 306
Kokono 九 – 111
Kokoro 心 – 306
Kokoro 試 – 436
Kokoroyo 快 - 734
Kokoroza 志 -1145
Kokorozashi 志 - 1145
Koku 黒 – 76
Koku 国 – 170
Koku 告 – 429
Koku 石 – 458
Koku 刻 – 565
Koku 穀 – 1172
Koma 細 – 220

Koma 困 – 280
Kome 米 – 326
Komi 込 – 357
Kon 婚 – 240
Kon 困 – 280
Kon 今 – 292
Kon 金 – 301
Kon 建 – 363
Kon 根 – 741
Kon 昏 – 1074
Kona 粉 – 1104
Kono 好 – 239
Koo 氷 – 814
Koori 氷 – 814
Kore 是 – 1035
Koro 頃 – 96
Koro 転 – 285
Koro 殺 – 838
Koromo 衣 – 1042
Koshi 越 – 453
Koshi 腰 – 884
Kota 答 – 295
Kota 応 – 677
Koto 事 – 416
Koto 言 – 430
Koto 異 – 970
Kotobuki 寿 – 607
Kotowa 断 – 704
Kotsu 骨 – 832
Kou 公 – 16
Kou 高 – 19
Kou 校 – 130
Kou 構 – 141
Kou 交 – 144
Kou 郊 – 145
Kou 降 – 178

Kou 厚 – 185
Kou 好 – 239
Kou 工 – 246
Kou 紅 – 247
Kou 神 – 273
Kou 行 – 334
Kou 後 – 335
Kou 向 – 340
Kou 幸 – 385
Kou 口 – 426
Kou 光 – 448
Kou 考 – 469
Kou 広 – 494
Kou 港 – 549
Kou 功 – 634
Kou 垢 – 665
Kou 香 – 681
Kou 興 – 693
Kou 慌 – 710
Kou 格 – 762
Kou 喉 – 794
Kou 康 – 831
Kou 荒 – 968
Kou 黄 – 976
Kou 候 – 996
Kou 更 – 1000
Kou 江 – 1026
Kou 講 – 1027
Kou 洪 – 1119
Kou 効 – 1139
Kou 甲 – 1157
Kou 抗 – 1196
Kowa 怖 – 463
Ku 公 – 16
Ku 久 – 30
Ku 九 – 111

Na 亡 – 585	Nara 習 – 472	*Nii* 兄 – 420	Nu 塗 – 1041
Na 成 – 633	Nara 並 – 575	Niku 難 – 198	Nugu 拭 – 1114
Na 那 – 669	Nari 成 – 633	Niku 肉 – 397	Nuno 布 – 687
Na 納 – 705	Nasa 情 – 156	Nin 人 – 13	Nushi 主 – 166
Na 鳴 – 751	Nashi 梨 – 1184	Nin 任 – 483	Nya 若 – 461
Na 撫 – 846	*Nata* 向 – 340	Nin 認 – 1036	Nyou 女 – 235
Na 奈 – 1006	Natsu 夏 – 522	Nina 担 – 729	Nyuu 入 – 14
Nabe 辺 – 362	Natsu 懐 – 928	Nio 匂 – 949	Nyuu 乳 – 186
Nado 等 – 1132	Nawa 縄 – 1003	Nishi 西 – 464	Nyuu 柔 – 546
Naga 長 – 502	Naya 悩 – 1181	Niwa 庭 – 495	O 百 – 47
Naga 流 – 654	Ne 熱 – 65	Niwatori 鶏 – 754	O 負 – 87
Naga 永 – 870	Ne 練 – 229	No 飲 – 399	O 男 – 109
Naga 眺 – 1136	Ne 音 – 266	No 乗 – 509	O 下 – 172
Nage 嘆 – 792	Ne 寝 – 372	No 野 – 545	O 降 – 178
Nago 和 – 513	Ne 値 – 571	No 伸 – 697	O 生 – 208
Nai 内 – 396	Ne 廻 – 692	No 延 – 842	O 緒 – 232
Naka 中 – 8	Ne 根 – 741	No 退 – 926	O 終 – 233
Naka 半 – 331	*Ne* 似 – 824	No 載 – 1175	*O* 女 – 235
Naka 仲 – 657	*Nee* 姉 – 241	Nobo 上 – 171	O 小 – 253
Naka 腹 – 863	Nega 願 – 94	Nobo 登 – 297	O 悪 – 313
Nama 生 – 208	Nei 寧 – 703	Nochi 後 – 335	O 起 – 452
Namari 鉛 – 1092	Neko 猫 – 72	Nodo 喉 – 794	O 汚 – 467
Name 滑 – 981	Nemu 眠 – 376	Noga 逃 – 850	O 和 – 513
Nami 並 – 575	Nen 年 – 177	Noki 軒 – 1146	O 落 – 526
Nami 波 – 878	Nen 念 – 314	Noko 残 – 605	O 置 – 569
Namida 涙 – 649	Nen 然 – 611	*Noo* 面 – 282	O 押 – 592
Nan 男 – 109	Nera 狙 – 948	*Nou* 日 – 32	O 織 – 753
Nan 難 – 198	Netsu 熱 – 65	Nou 能 – 616	*O* 美 – 771
Nan 何 – 338	Ni 二 – 2	Nou 納 – 705	O 追 – 821
Nan 南 – 388	Ni 日 – 32	Nou 農 – 1105	O 折 – 892
Nana 七 – 20	Ni 荷 – 342	Nou 濃 – 1106	O 推 – 1029
Nana 斜 – 910	Ni 似 – 824	Nou 悩 – 1181	O 老 – 1065
Nani 何 – 338	Ni 逃 – 850	Nozo 除 – 646	Obi 帯 – 1012
Nano 七 – 20	Ni 児 – 1093	Nozo 望 – 664	Obiya 脅 – 914
Nao 治 – 539	Nichi 日 – 32	Nozo 覗 – 982	Obo 覚 – 54
Nao 直 – 570	Niga 苦 – 393	Nu 抜 – 749	Odo 踊 – 366

Sho 処 – 1149	Shu 出 – 147	Soba 側 – 490	Sou 争 – 936
Shoku 食 – 398	Shu 主 – 166	Soda 育 – 151	Sou 巣 – 972
Shoku 色 – 473	Shu 守 – 214	Soko 底 – 1096	Sou 総 – 1038
Shoku 触 – 475	Shu 酒 – 465	Soku 束 – 99	Sou 装 – 1043
Shoku 職 – 696	Shu 趣 – 715	Soku 息 – 315	Sou 遭 – 1073
Shoku 飾 – 1203	Shu 狩 – 923	Soku 速 – 359	Sou 倉 – 1170
Shou 勝 – 149	Shu 修 – 1049	Soku 足 – 449	Sou 創 – 1171
Shou 消 – 158	Shu 種 – 1098	Soku 側 – 490	Sou 操 – 1192
Shou 正 – 174	Shuku 祝 – 274	Soku 測 – 1031	*Su* 日 – 32
Shou 笑 – 199	Shuku 宿 – 491	Somu 背 – 152	Su 磨 – 126
Shou 生 – 208	Shun 春 – 506	Son 村 – 131	Su 住 – 167
Shou 性 – 209	Shun 瞬 – 773	Son 存 – 462	Su 子 – 182
Shou 小 – 253	Shutsu 出 – 147	Son 孫 – 1072	Su 守 – 214
Shou 少 – 254	Shuu 集 – 202	Son 尊 – 1208	Su 好 – 239
Shou 将 – 374	Shuu 終 – 233	Sona 備 – 367	Su 空 – 248
Shou 焼 – 446	Shuu 祝 – 274	Sona 供 – 486	Su 済 – 259
Shou 招 – 560	Shuu 週 – 346	Sono 園 – 279	Su 過 – 361
Shou 紹 – 658	Shuu 秋 – 445	Sora 空 – 248	Su 吸 – 427
Shou 焦 – 750	Shuu 習 – 472	Soro 揃 – 644	Su 直 – 570
Shou 相 – 787	Shuu 拾 – 595	*Soro* 算 – 789	Su 捨 – 594
Shou 照 – 822	Shuu 周 – 630	Soso 注 – 168	Su 寿 – 607
Shou 精 – 847	Shuu 宗 – 676	Soto 外 – 163	Su 素 – 712
Shou 象 – 906	Shuu 衆 – 930	Sotsu 卒 – 27	Su 巣 – 972
Shou 床 – 946	Shuu 襲 – 941	Sou 早 – 34	Su 州 – 1071
Shou 賞 – 991	Shuu 就 – 974	Sou 窓 – 311	Sube 全 – 300
Shou 省 – 1010	Shuu 修 – 1049	Sou 送 – 348	Sube 術 – 808
Shou 松 – 1025	Shuu 州 – 1071	Sou 走 – 450	Sube 滑 – 981
Shou 装 – 1043	Shuu 収 – 1113	Sou 掃 – 645	Sue 末 – 119
Shou 症 – 1085	So 卒 – 27	Sou 宗 – 676	Sugata 姿 – 763
Shou 称 – 1123	So 祖 – 272	Sou 奏 – 757	Sugi 杉 – 1154
Shou 証 – 1150	So 反 – 680	Sou 壮 – 769	Sugu 優 – 528
Shou 唱 – 1152	So 素 – 712	Sou 相 – 787	Sui 出 – 147
Shou 祥 – 1160	So 組 – 752	Sou 爽 – 798	Sui 水 – 251
Shu 手 – 23	So 染 – 774	Sou 騒 – 826	*Sui* 西 – 464
Shu 首 – 56	So 添 – 841	Sou 想 – 905	Sui 吹 – 537
Shu 取 – 58	So 想 – 905	Sou 草 – 909	Sui 垂 – 799

Uchi 家 – 405	Wa 割 – 562	Yado 宿 – 491	Yon 四 – 6
Ue 上 – 171	Wa 輪 – 690	*Yage* 産 – 210	Yone 米 – 326
Ugo 動 – 286	Wa 羽 – 755	Yakata 館 – 305	*Yori* 和 – 513
Uji 氏 – 709	Wa 我 – 862	Yaku 約 – 225	Yoroko 喜 – 599
Ukaga 伺 – 341	*Wa* 波 – 878	Yaku 訳 – 437	Yoru 夜 – 489
Uke 受 – 577	Wa 湧 – 903	Yaku 薬 – 521	Yoso 装 – 1043
Uki 浮 – 671	Waka 若 – 461	Yaku 役 – 557	You 八 – 15
Uma 馬 – 958	Waka 別 – 561	Yaku 躍 – 992	*You* 日 – 32
Umi 海 – 337	Wake 訳 – 437	Yama 山 – 146	You 様 – 136
Un 雲 – 264	Waku 惑 – 624	*Yama* 大 – 188	You 曜 – 200
Un 運 – 354	Wan 湾 – 1016	Yamai 病 – 369	You 要 – 238
Una 海 – 337	Wara 笑 – 199	Yami 闇 – 950	You 容 – 296
Uo 魚 – 80	Ware 我 – 862	Yasa 易 – 402	You 洋 – 330
Ura 裏 – 887	Wari 割 – 562	Yasa 優 – 528	You 用 – 364
Uraya 羨 – 662	Waru 悪 – 313	Yashiro 社 – 271	You 踊 – 366
Ure 嬉 – 600	Wasu 忘 – 310	Yasu 休 – 122	You 葉 – 543
Uri 売 – 425	Wata 渡 – 499	Yasu 安 – 236	You 揚 – 768
Ushi 牛 – 205	Wata 綿 – 1189	Yawa 和 – 513	You 溶 – 815
Ushi 後 – 335	Watakushi 私 - 510	Yawa 柔 – 546	You 揺 – 852
Ushina 失 – 206	Watashi 私 – 510	Yo 四 – 6	You 腰 – 884
Uso 嘘 – 967	Waza 業 – 332	Yo 良 – 303	You 陽 – 891
Usu 薄 – 258	Waza 技 – 1133	Yo 呼 – 428	Yowa 弱 – 471
Uta 歌 – 534	Wazawa 災 - 1019	Yo 読 – 432	Yu 由 – 73
Utaga 疑 – 978	Ya 八 – 15	Yo 夜 – 489	Yu 結 – 231
Utsu 映 – 36	Ya 屋 – 63	Yo 世 – 542	*Yu* 浴 – 256
Utsu 写 – 468	Ya 止 – 173	Yo 予 – 544	*Yu* 雨 – 261
Utsu 移 – 801	Ya 病 – 369	Yo 代 – 552	Yu 輸 – 288
Utsuku 美 – 771	Ya 辞 – 387	Yo 寄 – 604	Yu 行 – 334
Utsuwa 器 – 853	Ya 家 – 405	Yo 余 – 637	Yu 湯 – 404
Uwa 上 – 171	Ya 焼 – 446	Yo 与 – 1070	Yu 愉 – 733
Uwa 浮 – 671	Ya 夜 – 489	Yogo 汚 – 467	Yu 揺 – 852
Uyama 敬 – 873	Ya 薬 – 521	Yoko 横 – 135	Yu 油 – 942
Wa 分 – 105	Ya 野 – 545	Yoku 浴 – 256	Yubi 指 – 691
Wa 話 – 433	Ya 矢 – 1045	Yoku 欲 – 535	Yue 故 – 394
Wa 和 – 513	Yabu 敗 – 793	Yoku 翼 – 912	Yui 由 – 73
Wa 沸 – 531	Yabu 破 – 837	Yomi 読 – 432	Yui 遺 – 1037

Kanji Groups

(Note: Kanji Groups only apply to Kanji numbers 1-608.)

Above & Below (171-176)
American Indian Chief (323-325)
Bench Hats (297-298)
Bicycle (343-345)
Big (188-199)
Bird (555-556)
Cage (200-204)
Capital (514-516)
Car (283-291)
Child (182-187)
Citizen (375-376)
Complicated Boxes (279-282)
Cow (205-210)
Crafted Object (246-249)
Crossing (143-145)
Dancer (522-528)
Deep Inside (532-533)
Dirt (59-65)
East (508-509)
Eat (398-400)
Evening (160-165)
Every (336-337)
Everyone (597-598)
Eye (51-58)
Feathers (471-472)
Female (235-245)
Fence (364-367)
Festival (377-379)
Fire (443-448)
Fish Head (473-475)
Foot (449-455)
Fruit (587-560)
Gate (409-414)
Grain Plants (510-513)
Hair (501-502)
Hanging Bucket (541-543)

Heart (306-319)
Horse (380-382)
Hugging (456-463)
Inside (396-397)
Kaeru & Kawaru (551-554)
Kangaroo (467-470)
Knee (177-181)
Kneeling Person (590-596)
Lean-to (493-500)
Man with a Double Hat (334-335)
Man with a Slanted Hat (480-492)
Master (166-170)
Miscellaneous (601-608)
Money Chest (83-99)
Moon (148-159)
Mountain (146-147)
Mouth (426-442)
Needle (383-388)
Net (583-584)
Now (292-296)
Nurse (599-600)
Oil Derrick (534-537)
Old (392-395)
Peaked Roof (299-305)
Person (276-278)
Plants (211-212)
Platform (538-50)
Pleasant (520-521)
Pliers (389-390)
Pull (476-479)
Rain (261-265)
Ri (561-566)
Rice Paddy (68-82)
Rocker-Bottom (406-408)
Rotated M (544-546)

Scorpion (503-505)
Shah (271-275)
Shaky Table (585-589)
Sheep (330-333)
Shelf Storage (569-572)
Simple Shapes (1-31)
Skeet Shooter (219-234)
Skirts (506-507)
Snail (346-363)
Snake (547-550)
Sound (266-270)
Sturdy Legs (420-425)
Sun (32-50)
Sword (102-117)
Table Cabinet (100-101)
Temple (213-218)
Tower (573-574)
Tree (118-142)
Trident (415-419)
Tsutomeru (517-519)
Twisted (529-531)
Uncooked Rice (326-329)
Various (401-405)
Vertical Bed (368-374)
Vertical Lines (575-579)
Vertical Storage (567-568)
Warrior (66-67)
Water (250-260)
West (464-466)
What (338-342)
X's (320-322)
Yak or Sword on a Table (557-560)
エ & Y (580-582)

28203080R00309

Printed in Poland
by Amazon Fulfillment
Poland Sp. z o.o., Wrocław